To
the folly of Man
and
the mercy of God

# Praise for David Pietrusza's *1920*

"A colorful, nonacademic account . . . Most of all, there are the characters. Pietrusza draws them sharply: the imperious Wilson, the obliging Harding, the dour and honest Coolidge and the ambitious and dissembling Franklin Roosevelt. Fans of political history will enjoy this book."

—*Seattle Times*

"Fascinating and compelling . . . Highly recommended."

—*Library Journal*

"An ably popular treatment that fans of campaign histories will enjoy."

—*Booklist*

"More than just a story of six men who either already had been president or would be, this is the story of America as it moved into the modern age."

—*Denver Post*

"A very vivid portrait of each of these presidents."

—Ann Compton, ABC News

"Through a lens trained on a long-ago election, David Pietrusza's *1920: The Year of Six Presidents*, delivers a rich and compelling narrative of American politics. Exploring a year when giant figures of American history were waxing and waning, he deftly explains how we ended up with a presidential showdown between two largely unknown—yet surprisingly randy—editors of small-town Ohio newspapers, which Warren Harding won principally by being 'nice.'"

—David O. Stewart, author of *The Summer of 1787: The Men Who Invented the Constitution*

"Sweeping and original." —The History Book Club

"In *1920: The Year of the Six Presidents*, writer David Pietrusza shows the right way to pull together disparate characters into a coherent narrative . . . this book portrays an America that has stopped looking backward and has begun to craft a new country and a new world role."

—*The Washington Times*

# 1920

## The Year of the
## Six Presidents

# 1920

## The Year of the Six Presidents

DAVID PIETRUSZA

A MEMBER OF THE PERSEUS BOOKS GROUP
NEW YORK

# Contents

⁓

# The Players in Our Drama

**Nan Britton**—A small-town girl with a big crush; she's taken a shine to the next president of the United States, United States Senator Warren G. Harding—and she will bear his child.

**Heywood Broun**—The Republican *New York Tribune*'s in-house radical. Trenchantly brilliant observer of the 1920 Democratic and Republican conventions.

**William Jennings Bryan**—The "Silver-Tongued Orator of the Platte." Legendary voice of the old agrarian-based populism. Three-time Democratic presidential nominee. Woodrow Wilson's disgruntled pacifist Secretary of State. Waiting in the wings in 1920, but the times have passed him by.

**Carrie Chapman Catt**—Prohibitionist. President of the National American Woman Suffrage Association. In August 1920, her battle for women's votes races to its conclusion.

**Professor William Estabrook Chancellor**—The obsessively racist Ohio college professor whose accusations that Warren Harding is part black tosses the election into last-minute turmoil.

1

**Calvin Coolidge**—Silent Cal. The taciturn Vermonter who became Massachusetts's coldly efficient governor. His words following the September 1919 Boston police strike ("There is no right to strike against the public safety by anybody, anywhere, anytime") transform him into presidential timber. In Chicago, the GOP convention stampedes to anoint him its vice-presidential candidate.

**Grace Goodhue Coolidge**—Calvin's charming and ever-patient wife. Her husband writes: "She has borne with my infirmities, and I have rejoiced in her graces." No one disagreed with the assessment.

**Governor James Middleton Cox**—Warren Harding's feisty Democratic twin, a small-town Ohio newspaper editor who dabbles in state politics, has his own marital troubles, and, when no other candidate proves suitable, wins a presidential nomination of dubious value.

**Josephus Daniels**—The North Carolina segregationist and prohibitionist newspaper baron. Woodrow Wilson's Secretary of the Navy and FDR's long-suffering boss.

**Harry Micajah Daugherty**—The unsavory Ohio politico and lobbyist who attaches himself to Warren Harding and rides him all the way to the Attorney Generalship—and ultimately to disgrace.

**Eugene Victor Debs**—Imprisoned anti-war Socialist Party ideologue and editor. "Federal Prisoner 9653" campaigns for the presidency from his Atlanta Penitentiary jail cell—and garners nearly a million votes.

**Henry Ford**—Hero of the American industrial revolution, father of the burgeoning auto industry, pacifist, politician, and, as publisher of the *Dearborn Independent*, the nation's premier anti-Semite.

**Marcus Garvey**—Jamaican-born founder of the mass-movement Universal Negro Improvement Association. Self-proclaimed Provisional President of Africa. Garvey launches a black-owned steamship company, numerous other black businesses—and the back-to-Africa movement.

**Admiral Cary Grayson**—Woodrow Wilson's personal physician. With Edith Wilson, Grayson hides President Wilson's crippling infirmities from the American people.

**Florence Kling DeWolfe Harding**—"The Duchess." Warren Harding's strong-willed older wife. The brains behind his modest newspaper empire. The Duchess prophesizes: "I can see but one word written above his head if they make [Warren] President, and that word is Tragedy."

**Senator Warren Gamaliel Harding**—Ohio small-town newspaper editor, Republican politician, and serial adulterer. His strengths: He looks like a president, sounds like a president (if you don't listen too carefully), and is sufficiently vague on most issues to be nominated. "America's present need," he intones, "is not heroics, but healing; not nostrums, but normalcy." America agrees.

**Colonel George B. Harvey**—Publisher of *Harper's Weekly* and *The North American Review*. Wilson's earliest political backer. Wilson openly repays Harvey with ingratitude and scorn. At the 1920 Republican convention, Harvey will demand to know if Harding's record contains anything to disqualify him from the presidency. Harding will lie.

**Will Hays**—Indiana-born chairman of the Republican national committee. The nation's savviest political operative. Presidential timber.

**William Randolph Hearst**—America's most controversial press baron. Still a radical Democrat, he opposes the League of Nations and toys with third-party presidential schemes.

**Herbert Hoover**—The Great Engineer. International gold-mining adventurer. Multimillionaire. Savior of war-ravaged Europe's starving masses. Political progressive. A key member of the Wilson administration. A national hero. In 1920, Hoover covets the presidency but has one big problem: He can't decide if he's a Republican or a Democrat.

**J. Edgar Hoover**—The ambitious young Justice Department lawyer who orchestrates Attorney General A. Mitchell Palmer's anti-radical crusade.

**Colonel Edward Mandell House**—The brilliant, manipulative little Texan who flatters his way into Woodrow Wilson's heart. Wilson loved him—until he dumped him.

**Senator Hiram W. Johnson**—Theodore Roosevelt's 1912 running mate hopes to inherit TR's progressive mantle. Johnson's liberalism alienates the right. His "irreconcilable" isolationism alienates the left. His personality alienates everybody. Johnson looked, said one historian, "like a bad-tempered baby."

**John T. King**—Bridgeport, Connecticut's Republican boss. He manages TR's campaign, then Leonard Wood's. "John supplies the efficiency," says TR, "and I supply the morals."

**Albert D. Lasker**—The Texas-born Chicago advertising genius who—despite isolationist misgivings—helps fuel Warren Harding's 1920 campaign steamroller.

**Senator Henry Cabot Lodge**—The quintessential Boston Brahmin. Author. Classical scholar. Intellectual. Chairman of the Senate Foreign Relations Committee. Lodge's loathing of Woodrow Wilson ("I never expected to hate anyone in politics with the hatred I feel toward Wilson") helps fuel his vendetta against Wilson's League of Nations.

**Alice Roosevelt Longworth**—TR's daughter, wife of House Speaker Nicholas Longworth, lover of progressive Idaho Senator William E. Borah. The most deliciously acerbic observer of Washington's social scene—and of Warren Harding.

**Governor Frank O. Lowden**—Illinois's capable, middle-of-the-road Republican reform governor. A prime contender for the nomination. His presidential ambitions founder on charges of campaign irregularities.

**Dudley Field Malone**—The trusted Wilson crony who quits his lucrative patronage position to protest the imprisonment of suffragettes. Later, he seeks the presidency on a radical third-party ticket.

**William Gibbs McAdoo**—Wall Street lawyer and financier. Secretary of the Treasury. Woodrow Wilson's son-in-law. McAdoo plans to succeed his father-in-law in the White House. His problem: Wilson has no intention of leaving.

**H. L. Mencken**—The Baltimore *Sun*'s dyspeptic observer of both major conventions, nearly laid low during the Democratic convention by San Francisco's creature comforts. The "creator of a new and distinct style of journalism . . . 'big-city smartass.'"

**Lucy Mercer**—Eleanor Roosevelt's social secretary. In 1917, Eleanor discovers that Lucy has become too social with Franklin. The affair permanently damages the Roosevelt marriage, but some excuse it. "He deserved a good time," TR's sharp-tongued daughter Alice observes; "he was married to Eleanor."

**A. Mitchell Palmer**—Wilson's ambitious Attorney General. After an anarchist bomb destroys Palmer's home, Palmer transforms himself from Quaker progressive to fierce Red-hunter, jailing 10,000 radicals, deporting 556, and warning of a Red uprising—all while gearing up for a presidential run. His chances evaporate when the uprising never occurs.

**Alice Stokes Paul**—Anti-war activist. Hunger-striker. Suffragette leader. Founder of the National Women's Party. Vengeful forces bar her from enjoying suffrage's triumph.

**Mary Allen Hulbert Peck**—Engaging, artistically inclined New England widow. Was she Woodrow Wilson's correspondent, friend, and Bermuda-vacation chum? Or his lover?

**Senator Boies Penrose**—Boss of the Pennsylvania Republican Party and unofficial leader of the national GOP's stand-pat wing. Is he manipulating the Republican National Convention from his Philadelphia sickbed?

**Carrie Fulton Phillips**—Marion, Ohio, housewife and friend of Warren and Florence Harding who became Warren's most dangerous mistress. German sympathizer. She successfully blackmails her lover during the 1920 presidential campaign.

**William Cooper Procter**—Millionaire Ivory Soap manufacturer. Early adversary of Woodrow Wilson. In 1920, Procter manages Leonard Wood's campaign. His soap floats. His candidate sinks.

**John R. Rathom**—The controversial, rotund, Australian-born *Providence Journal* publisher who exposes FDR's scandalously inept handling of an explosive homosexual scandal at the Newport Navy base.

**Eleanor Roosevelt**—TR's niece. FDR's fifth cousin and wife. By 1920, their marriage is already seriously frayed from his infidelities. A sheltered child of privilege, her social conscience is just beginning to emerge.

**Franklin D. Roosevelt**—The handsome, jaunty, Harvard-educated dilettante who hopes to parlay his Roosevelt pedigree and charm into the presidency. He's already retraced TR's steps as Assistant Secretary of the Navy. Is he mature enough to go farther?

**Theodore Roosevelt**—The Rough Rider himself. President. Historian. Cowboy. Police commissioner. Trust-buster. Explorer. Naturalist. Big-game hunter. Nobel Prize-winner. He has been president once—and wants the job again. Only the hand of God can keep him from the White House in 1920.

**Nicola Sacco and Bartolomeo Vanzetti**—Italian immigrant anarchists accused of murder and robbery. Their case explodes into an international cause célèbre.

**Colonel William J. Simmons**—Inspired by D. W. Griffith's *The Birth* *of a Nation*, this failed ex-preacher creates "The World's Greatest Secret, Social, Patriotic, Fraternal, Beneficiary Order" of them all—the infamous Ku Klux Klan.

**Mark Sullivan**—America's foremost political journalist. Republican.

**William Howard Taft**—The seventh president on the scene for the election of 1920. Taft has learned his lesson and wants no part of the White House. Once derided as a hide-bound conservative, Big Bill Taft now personifies moderation: pro–League of Nations and anti-Wilson.

**Joseph P. Tumulty**—The savvy New Jersey Irish Catholic politico who serves as Wilson's loyal and efficient personal secretary.

**Wayne B. Wheeler**—Wily boss of the Anti-Saloon League. He bestows prohibition upon a thirsty nation.

**Edith Bolling Galt Wilson**—"America's First Female President." The Washington, D.C., jeweler's widow who became Woodrow Wilson's second wife. Their whirlwind courtship provokes scandalous Washington whispers. With her husband incapacitated, she rules the nation.

**Woodrow Wilson**—Brilliant, eloquent, progressive, and self-confident. But also bigoted, self-centered, stubborn, and messianic. He grandly envisions a League of Nations to prevent future wars, but can't sell the idea, either at home or abroad. Compromising article after article of his Fourteen Points, he sows the seeds of another war. "Woodrow Wilson is an exile from the hearts of his people," says Gene Debs. "The betrayal of his ideals makes him the most pathetic figure in the world." An October 1919 stroke leaves him too crippled to lead the nation, but the nation is never told. Fantastically, he hopes for an unprecedented third term.

**General Leonard Wood**—A law-and-order Man on Horseback. Heir to TR's "Rough Rider" traditions. Early favorite for the 1920 Republican nomination.

# Chapter 1

## "Discover a Common Hate"

The President of the United States lay bleeding on the bathroom floor.

He could not move.

He could not speak.

He lay abed for weeks, an unshaven, listless old man, never to recover.

Less than a year before, the world was his, the nation he led victorious in war, the world's peoples begging him to fashion the peace, create a new world order, end the killing.

Their cheers had been loud. They had not been long. Plans lay ruined, dreams shattered.

Woodrow Wilson lay bleeding on the bathroom floor—thirteen months to the day before the 1920 presidential election.

Woodrow Wilson thought thirteen his lucky number.

His very name contained thirteen letters.

He taught at Princeton for thirteen years.

As the thirteenth president of Princeton, he presided over thirteen hundred students.

When an influential backer first boomed him for president, the man listed thirteen of Wilson's qualifications.

Thirteen miles measured the distance from his home to his first campaign office.

The Electoral College formally elected him on January 13, 1913.

Thirteen governors and thirteen state militias marched in his inaugural parade. Princeton students marched thirteen abreast.

When he landed in Europe to make peace, it was on Friday, the 13th—by design.

When he returned to Europe to finalize that peace, it was the 13th—again by design.

Woodrow Wilson lay bleeding on the bathroom floor—thirteen months to the day before the 1920 presidential election.

꒰

Six presidents—Wilson, Theodore Roosevelt, Warren Harding, Calvin Coolidge, Herbert Hoover, Franklin Roosevelt—would compete in that election, men whose rule spanned five defining decades of American history, whose eras and personas ranged from Normalcy to New Deal, from Trust-Buster to Silent Cal, from Great War to Great Depression, all six vying in a single contest.

Never before, and never again, had so many presidents jostled so closely, in a battle marked by tradition and by innovation, influenced by old bosses and by new voters, by high principle and low scandal, by fear and by hope.

1920—the year of the six presidents, the election that witnessed the birth of modern America.

꒰

But of all the six presidents in our drama, merely one *actually* was president in 1920—and he lay bleeding on the bathroom floor on October 2, 1919, exactly thirteen months before election day, 1920.

꒰

And so we start with him.

Three accidents of birth had fashioned Woodrow Wilson. His Scotch blood made him "canny, tenacious, cold, and perhaps a little exclusive"—

as he himself confessed. His Southern roots bestowed fierce loyalty to the Democratic Party and a deep, powerful dose of Anglo-Saxon racism. His religious background provided a profoundly moral outlook, and though there is no evil in righteousness, there is in self-righteousness, which Wilson possessed in abundance. As his press secretary, Ray Stannard Baker, once phrased it, "He is a good hater."

Born in Staunton, Virginia, on December 28, 1856, Thomas Woodrow Wilson grew up in Augusta, Georgia. His parents, Presbyterian minister Dr. Joseph Ruggles Wilson and Janet "Jessie" Woodrow, came from clerical families. Thoroughly Southern in sympathy, they bequeathed their loyalties to a son who never forgot hearing with dread the news of Lincoln's election and later of seeing a defeated Jefferson Davis paraded in handcuffs.

Dyslexic, Woodrow initially displayed little brilliance. But he persisted, taught himself shorthand, and attended Charlotte, North Carolina's Davidson College before graduating from Princeton in 1879. He studied law at the University of Virginia, then enrolled at Johns Hopkins where, in 1886, he obtained a doctorate in political science. His dissertation, "Congressional Government," earned him a publishing contract and a reputation as a rising author and scholar.

He taught at Bryn Mawr and Wesleyan before returning to Princeton in 1890 as a professor of jurisprudence and political science, establishing himself as the university's most popular and influential lecturer. If academicians can be stars, Professor Wilson was a star.

He was a charismatic instructor and great orator. To look at him, you would think his voice thin, reedy, prissy. It was not. It was a rich baritone, manly and forceful. Its very sound convinced audiences as much as his high-flown ideas and ideals. It convinced them and made them say: *This* was a leader. *This* was the sound of the future.

In June 1902, university trustees unanimously elected him university president, Princeton's first without formal theological training. Wilson modernized and reformed the once-sleepy campus, improving its academic standing and democratizing its aristocratic institutions. Yet he remained a political conservative, as his biographer Arthur Link noted, "a foe of Bryanism, governmental regulation, and the restrictive practices of labor unions."

He had already established a solid imperious streak, so focused on the importance of his ideals (and of their guardian—himself) that he ignored the feelings of even his closest supporters. Once, he summoned his staunchest admirers—from New York, from Philadelphia, from Baltimore, from Chicago—and, for two full hours, proceeded to lecture them on his plans for the university. No conversation. No questions. No answers. And no thanks for interrupting their schedules and traveling to Princeton. Finished, he bade them a terse good morning and showed them the door. It was the same when he was president. To a group of senators and congressmen, he delivered an hour-long lecture. Again, there was no dialogue. They were there to hear, admire, and obey. Even Mississippi Senator John Sharp Williams, an ardent Wilson loyalist, snorted "And he calls that a conference."

At Princeton, Wilson lost two bitter battles. The first involved his plan to integrate undergraduates and resident faculty on an English "quad" model. Opposed by faculty and alumni, compromise was in order. Wilson didn't and wouldn't. When his best friend among the faculty, John Grier Hibben, urged negotiation, Wilson cut him finally and irretrievably dead, a pattern he repeated ceaselessly—a stubborn refusal to compromise followed by the jettisoning of old disciples who failed to blindly obey their master.

Wilson's second major altercation involved Graduate School Dean Andrew F. West. West wanted a new residential graduate campus built somewhat distant from the main campus. Wilson wanted it at Princeton's center and somehow managed to transform this petty academic squabble into a national moral concern. "Will America tolerate the seclusion of graduate students?" he thundered. "Will America tolerate the idea of having graduate students set apart?"

One doubts if America cared then—or ever—about such issues, but the controversy accelerated Wilson's transition from hidebound conservative to idealistic progressive. Wilson won the war of high-flown rhetoric, but West trumped him in the donation department. First, he secured $500,000 from Procter and Gamble's William Cooper Procter (Procter's wife had been West's student at a Cincinnati high school), the offer hinging on *not* using Wilson's site. Then, West received an $800,000 bequest from the estate of alumnus Isaac C. Wyman, whose will stipulated that the money be used to build the school near where his father fought in the Revolutionary War Battle of Princeton. These massive cash infusions tipped the scales. "We have beaten the living," Wilson admitted, "but we cannot fight the dead. The game is up."

Enter Colonel George Harvey, the conservative Democratic publisher of both the *North American Review* and *Harper's Weekly*. Harvey had grown rich under the tutelage of Wall Street financiers William Whitney and Thomas Fortune Ryan. Present at Wilson's inaugural as university president, he departed Princeton, convinced that Wilson was a great man, the embodiment of the leadership Democrats needed to recapture the White House. He ordered that each front page of *Harper's Weekly* run the banner headline FOR PRESIDENT—WOODROW WILSON, helping elevate the only hitherto moderately well-known academic to a position as a reasonably viable presidential possibility. On January 18, 1908, the *New York World* front-paged that same message. Anonymously, Harvey had written that too.

But first, Wilson needed to win some other elective office, and the New Jersey governorship would do just fine. In 1910, Harvey persuaded James Smith Jr., the state's most powerful Democratic boss (he controlled Newark's Essex County), to nominate Wilson.

Both Harvey and Smith thought Wilson still to be conservative, and Smith thought Wilson could be trusted not to attack his machine. Wilson vowed that he would not, providing he remained "absolutely free in the matters of measures of men."

Wilson won comfortably. Democrats captured the traditionally Republican state legislature. Here lay great opportunities and pitfalls. Would Wilson prove conservative or progressive? How strong would he push for a reform agenda against the Machine Democrats in the legislature? Wilson, however, faced an even more dangerous dilemma. State legislators still elected United States senators at that time—the Sixteenth Amendment, providing for their direct popular election, was not yet in force—but New Jersey had just held its first advisory primary on the subject. No one—particularly Democrats, who thought the legislature would remain Republican—took the vote seriously. Accordingly, few people voted, and the "people's choice" was Democrat James E. Martine, a long-time political joke alternately known as "Farmer Jim," "The Sage of

Cedar Brook," and "The Farmer Orator." Smith, who had served in the United States Senate in the 1890s, now saw an opportunity to return to Washington. He asked Wilson for support. Wilson said no, writing Colonel Harvey:

> I have learned to have a very high opinion of Senator Smith. But his election would be intolerable to the very people who elected me and gave us a majority in the legislature. It was no Democratic victory. It was a victory of the "Progressives" of both parties, who are determined to live no longer under either of the political organizations that have controlled the two parties of the State. . . .

The bewhiskered, bespectacled Martine became a United States Senator, but the bigger winner was Wilson. His high-profile break with the bosses made progressives forget (or at least forgive) his conservative, boss-ridden origins. Next came a flurry of progressive reforms—the initiative and referendum (both derided in Wilson's academic days), a corrupt-practices act, regulation of public utilities, and direct primaries. Wilson earned even more antipathy from the state's Democratic machines. On July 25, 1911, State Democratic Chairman James R. Nugent—Jim Smith's nephew—publicly raised a toast: "To the Governor of New Jersey, the commander-in-chief of the Militia, an ingrate and a liar. I mean Woodrow Wilson. I repeat, he's an ingrate and a liar." Wilson got Nugent fired, but Nugent and Smith soon had their revenge, sandbagging their own candidates to hand the legislature back to the GOP. Better the Republicans, they thought, than the Honorable Woodrow Wilson.

Wilson had now established (albeit rather late) solid progressive credentials and an image as the bookish but manly professor valiantly combating the bosses. He also had some problems. Losing his legislative majority was one. The impending end of his gubernatorial career was another: New Jersey law limited him to a single three-year term. He now focused on the biggest prize of all: the White House.

Moving leftward, Wilson quickly distanced himself from Colonel Harvey, whose conservative politics now embarrassed him. Wilson—as he had cast off Senator Smith and Jim Nugent—now jettisoned not only Harvey but also another conservative Democratic press baron and ally,

*Louisville Courier-Journal* publisher Colonel Henry "Marse Henry" Watterson. As Wilson's brother-in-law, Stockton Axson, later observed:

> Those who have loved Mr. Wilson without cessation have often wished, for his own sake as well as for the sake of former friends, that he could extend the olive branch or accept [one]. They have seen him torn, bleeding, and writhing under a severed friendship, and have wished, and sometimes even advised, that he go to the estranged friend with open hands and say: never mind the past; never mind how we have differed; let's forget all that; let's be friends again and happy. But Woodrow Wilson would never do that. Perhaps he could not. In time the pain would pass and it would be as if the former friend were dead. He did not hate him; he simply ignored him in his mind and consciousness. Occasionally he might refer to him, seldom with bitterness, but with what was worse—that impersonality of fate, like the thunder cloud from which the bolt of lightning has stricken a man dead and then passed on, with neither anger nor remorse.

As Harvey and Watterson exited, the shadowy but talented Colonel Edward Mandell House entered. House had money, brains, breeding, an English education, and a talent for politics, having helped elect four separate Texas governors. Recognizing his own limitations of personality and health, he never ran for office himself. Still, House possessed a powerful ego and lofty objections. "My ambition," he once explained, "has been so great that it has never seemed to me worthwhile to strive to satisfy it."

He grew bored with electing Texas governors. Longing to elect a Democratic president, he reasoned that the ideal candidate would be of Southern birth, yet sufficiently progressive to suit the rest of the nation. Wilson fit the bill. In November 1911, House arranged a meeting, thus beginning, in his overblown description, "the strangest and most fruitful personal alliance in human history."

They seemed more like friends than political allies, more like brothers than friends. House could offer excellent advice, arrange meetings, forge alliances, and clear any path for his new front man. But more important,

House generated enough trust (almost unlimited at first) in the normally aloof Wilson for the schoolmaster–politician to take the little colonel's counsel, to let House work his magic: to make him president.

House capitalized on Wilson's vanity, but also on his more sinister traits, his pettiness, his vindictiveness, his ability to hold a grudge and never let go. "Never begin by arguing [with Wilson]," House once explained. "Discover a common hate, exploit it, get the president warmed up, and then start your business."

President-maker was a great ambition. But in 1912, House hinted at even higher, darker—or at least more bizarre—dreams. Anonymously, he published a rather badly written novel, *Philip Dru: Administrator*. House's character Dru, a West Point graduate-turned-social-worker, busted trusts, reformed the tariff, overhauled the national banking system, and enacted a federal income tax (still not yet constitutional in 1912). There was nothing particularly remarkable about any of these things (they, in fact, matched Wilson's New Freedom very nicely) except that Philip Dru was not merely the president, he was a military dictator. "He comes," wrote House, "panoplied in justice and with the light of reason in his eyes. He comes as the advocate of equal opportunity, and he comes with the power to enforce his will." And after enforcing that will domestically, Dru turned to foreign affairs to work his weal there as well.

Pretty heady stuff, and even headier in November 1912, when vacationing President-elect Wilson brought *Philip Dru* along for light reading. In the interim, however, Wilson's presidential path was by no means assured. The 1896, 1900, 1904, and 1908 elections had proven uniformly disastrous for Democrats. They had tried and failed with William Jennings Bryan's prairie populism. They stumbled even more miserably with Judge Alton Parker's Eastern conservatism. The year 1912, however, promised success. The bitter personal rift between William Howard Taft and Theodore Roosevelt had split the Republican Party. Whoever the Democrats nominated would have an excellent shot at the White House.

There was nothing inevitable about its being Wilson, however. Speaker of the House Champ Clark of Missouri enjoyed the support of many old Bryanites. Also running were two relative conservatives, sixty-six-year-old Ohio Governor Judson Harmon (formerly Grover Cleveland's Attorney General) and pudgy, greasy-haired House Majority

Leader Oscar W. Underwood of Alabama, a tenacious low-tariff man, along with dark horse Indiana Governor Thomas R. Marshall ("Bitterness may induce the Democrats to nominate a dark horse, and my enemies will tell you I am the blackest one you ever saw"). None seemed particularly inspiring, which only encouraged Bryan to hope that the party might yet turn to him again.

Wilson had begun running almost immediately upon becoming governor, undertaking a well-received three-week Western speaking tour in May 1911. Newspaper magnate William Randolph Hearst offered support, but Hearst was too controversial and too radical. "Tell Mr. Hearst to go to hell," sneered Wilson. Hearst threw his support to Clark ("a man's man"), spewing editorial venom on Wilson, dismissing him as an overrated intellect and a pro-English snob. Clark crushed Wilson nearly three to one in Illinois's key primary and entered the July 1912 Baltimore convention with a formidable delegate lead: Clark 413, Wilson 274, Underwood 91, Harmon 57, Marshall 30.

But two thirds of the delegates—724—were needed to nominate. A simple majority of the 1,085 delegates (which Clark reached only on the tenth ballot) wasn't enough. Eventually Clark peaked, and on the thirtieth ballot Wilson passed him. On the forty-sixth, he won. For vice-president, the convention selected Thomas Marshall, who proved as realistic regarding the vice-presidency as he did about the presidential nomination. "Once there were two brothers," he observed. "One ran away to sea, the other was elected vice president. Neither one of them was heard of again."

Wilson was less modest. During the campaign, he curtly informed an aide, "I wish it to be clearly understood that I owe you nothing. Remember that God ordained that I should be the next president of the United States. Neither you nor any other mortal could have prevented that."

The general election proved far easier than the nomination, though Theodore Roosevelt still overshadowed Wilson. "I do not [excite the public imagination]," Wilson explained. "He [TR] is a real, vivid person . . . I am a vague, conjectural personality, more made up of opinions and academic prepossessions than of human traits and red corpuscles." Wilson received just 41.8 percent of the popular vote, less than Bryan's lowest total; but with Roosevelt and Taft ripping each other to pieces, Wilson garnered 435 electoral votes to TR's 88 and Taft's pathetic 8.

As president, erstwhile conservative Wilson now implemented much of the progressive agenda: the Underwood Tariff and the Federal Farm Loan Act, a Federal Reserve System, the Federal Trade Commission, a workmen's compensation system, the banning of child labor, and improved conditions and wages for railroad workers.

In August 1914 his life came crashing to the ground. On the first day of the month, Germany declared war on Imperial Russia . . . and World War I began. On August 6, Woodrow Wilson's wife, Ellen Axson Wilson, died of Bright's disease. But there was more to it than that. As she lay dying, White House physician Dr. Cary Grayson wrote: "The chief cause of Mrs. Wilson's present critical condition is a chronic kidney disease . . . developed as one of the results of a nervous breakdown."

The Axsons had a history of mental illness. Ellen's father had undergone a similar breakdown. Her brother, Stockton, suffered from depression. The White House had proven too much for this gentle Southern lady. By May 1914, she was a wreck. By June, she no longer retained food. Ellen Wilson was just 50 years old; she and her husband had been married for 29 years.

Her death crushed him. "Oh my God," he cried, "what am I going to do? What am I going to do?" Many of his associates feared a collapse. Wilson survived. His Scotch–Irish sense of duty pulled him through. The Progressive agenda remained unfulfilled. Europe, engulfed in war, threatened to drag America into the morass. Wilson *had* to get through it.

He would not be alone for long. In March 1915—through Dr. Grayson and through Wilson's cousin, Helen Bones—he met a local widow, a Mrs. Edith Bolling Galt. Edith and Helen were at the White House one day, when Dr. Grayson and the president returned, muddy and disheveled, from golf. After they tidied up, everyone took tea in the Oval Room. "I can't say I foresaw in the first minute what was going to happen," Helen Bones recalled. "It may have taken ten minutes."

A whirlwind courtship followed—as whirlwind as possible when the suitor is virtually a prisoner of the White House and his office. The couple met when they could. Two months later, he told Edith he loved her. She professed shock. "Oh, you can't love me," she protested; "you don't really know me. And it is less than a year since your wife died."

"I know you feel that," he replied. "But, little girl, in this place time is not measured by weeks, or months, or years, but by deep human experience; and since her death I have lived a lifetime of loneliness and heartache. I was afraid, knowing you, I would shock you; but I would be less than a gentleman if I continued to make opportunities to see you without telling you what I have told my daughters and Helen: that I want you to be my wife."

The relationship intensified. Presidential depression shifted to schoolboy giddiness. The general public remained ignorant of it all. Wilson's closest advisers did not. They were not pleased. White House Chief Usher Irwin "Ike" Hoover wrote in his memoirs:

> The President was simply obsessed. He put aside practically everything, dealing only with the most important matters of state. Requests for appointments were put off with the explanation that he had important business to attend to. Cabinet officers, Senators, officials generally were all treated the same. It had always been difficult to get appointments with him; it was now harder than ever, and important state matters were held in abeyance while he wrote to the lady of his choice. When one realizes that at this time there was a war raging in Europe, not to mention a Presidential campaign approaching, one can imagine how preoccupied he must have been. There was much anxiety among his political friends, who just had to accept the inevitable, but who began to look about for a way to postpone it until after the election, for fear lest the people would not approve.

Many did *not* approve—or, at least, they scoffed. "What did the new Mrs. Wilson do when the President proposed?" joked British Embassy attaché Major Charles Crauford-Stuart.

The ribald answer: "She fell out of bed with surprise."

Colonel House and Treasury Secretary William Gibbs McAdoo had not reached the pinnacles of power only to tumble downward because of a president acting like a lovesick swain. McAdoo, a wealthy railroad executive, was not only a member of Wilson's cabinet; he was his son-in-law, having married the president's youngest daughter Eleanor in May 1914. McAdoo, along with House, plotted to prevent any Wilson remarriage—and went about it as irresponsibly as possible.

Woodrow and Ellen Wilson had been a devoted couple—some might say a passionate couple—as witnessed by this letter from Wilson in 1902 to his wife of 17 years:

> How do you expect me to keep *my* head, you dear thing . . . when you lavish upon me such delicious praise? Surely there was never such a lover before, and even after all these years it seems almost too good to be true that you are my lover. All I can say in return is that I love you as you deserve to be loved—as much as you can possibly *want* to be loved.

Then, in 1906, a period of "marked depression" debilitated Ellen. The following January, her husband, vacationing—alone—in Bermuda, made the acquaintance of forty-four-year-old Mary Allen Hulbert Peck, wife of a Pittsfield, Massachusetts, woolen manufacturer. Mrs. Peck was artistic and intellectual enough to fascinate Wilson and enough of a good listener to provide the support and comfort he needed. "She was," wrote Wilson's daughter Eleanor, "a charming woman, with great intelligence and humor." She was also a woman whose own marriage was unraveling.

Whether Wilson and Mary Peck became lovers remains unknown. Some say yes; some say no. For years, they exchanged correspondence (227 letters survive). And considering that he lived either in New Jersey or Washington and she in New England or New York, they met in person a significant number of times—ninety times. Ellen Wilson knew of their relationship, or, at least, knew what Woodrow told her of it. She did not particularly care for it—or for Mary Peck, whom she met on several occasions—and termed the episode the one unhappiness in her marriage.

Ellen was not the only one in the know. In 1912, the Wilson–Peck friendship threatened to derail Wilson's presidential effort. Supposedly, during Mary's recent divorce proceedings, a judge had seen one of Wilson's letters to her and had not liked what he read. In Chicago, in April 1912, unknown persons broke into Wilson's Hotel Sherman suite and stole his valise, allegedly to purloin incriminating correspondence from Mrs. Peck. Theodore Roosevelt, always the nineteenth-century gentleman, refused to profit from the issue. "What's more," he rationalized, "it won't work. You can't cast a man as Romeo who looks and acts like the apothecary's clerk."

To frighten his father-in-law into abandoning his burgeoning love affair with Edith Galt, McAdoo fabricated a story that he had received anonymous correspondence from Los Angeles alleging that Mrs. Peck was circulating Wilson's letters to her. The news *frightened the hell* out of Wilson. On Saturday morning, September 18, 1915, he wrote Edith begging to see her at her Twentieth Street home that night at eight—an unprecedented request, since they always met at the White House. Wilson arrived. They talked. Correspondence flew back and forth for the next twenty-four hours. Edith pledged to stand by her skittish president, "not for duty, not for pity, not for honor—but for love—trusting protecting, comprehending love."

Edith provided Wilson with the courage he desperately needed, and cemented his love for her. McAdoo's strategy had backfired miserably. On Sunday, September 19, 1915, Wilson wrote:

My noble, incomparable Edith,

I do not know how to express or analyze the conflicting emotions that have surged like a storm through my heart all night long. I only know that first and foremost in all my thoughts has been the glorious confirmation you gave me last night—without effort, unconsciously, as of course—of all I have ever thought of your mind and heart.

You have the greatest soul, the noblest nature, the sweetest, most loving heart I have ever known, and my love, my reverence, my admiration for you, have increased in one evening as I should have thought only a lifetime of intimate, loving association could have increased them.

You are more wonderful and lovely in my eyes than you ever were before; and my pride and joy and gratitude that you should love me with such a perfect love are beyond all expression, except in some great poem which I cannot write.

Your own,
Woodrow

Yet Wilson's spirit remained troubled. On Monday, September 20, he composed a partly enigmatic, partly damning document—a series of notes or talking points—that he, no doubt, hoped would never be made public, but that he must have feared very likely would be if the Peck letters were made public:

## Analysis of the Statement
### *Admission*

Even while it lasted I knew and made explicit what it *did not* mean.

It did not last, but friendship and genuine admiration ensued. . . .

These letters disclose a passage of folly and gross impertinence in my life. I am deeply ashamed and repentant. Neither in act nor even in thought was the purity or honor of the lady concerned touched or sullied, and my offense she has generously forgiven. Neither was my utter allegiance to my incomparable wife in anyway by the least jot abated. She, too, knew and understood and has forgiven, little as I deserved the generous indulgence. But none of this lessens the blame or the deep humiliating grief and shame I suffer, that I should have so erred and forgotten the standards of honorable behavior by which I should have been bound.

These letters are genuine, and I am now ashamed of them—not because the lady to whom they are addressed was not worthy of the most sincere admiration and affection, but because I did not have the moral right to offer her ardent affection which they express. I am happy to remember that the only thing that at all relieves the pain and shame with which this correspondence could ever in the least degree affect is the honor of the noble lady to whom I then had the distinction and happiness to be married.

His letters to Peck were *not* made public. Wilson announced his engagement to Edith on October 6, 1915. They wed at the bride's home at 8:30 P.M., Saturday, December 18, 1915. The public did not seem to care.

Of course, they might have been concerned with bigger events—say, world wars.

"It would be an irony of fate," Wilson had remarked, "if my administration had to deal chiefly with foreign affairs." In fact, it did. In 1916,

Wilson ran for re-election on a platform of peace, uniting his normally fractious party about him. "I agree with the American people," said William Jennings Bryan, who had quit as Wilson's Secretary of State when Wilson seemed too aggressive toward Germany, "in thanking God we have a President who has *kept—who will keep—us* out of war."

Democrats knew where they stood. Republicans did not. Roosevelt and the Progressives had returned to the Republican Party, but only grudgingly. The Rough Rider wanted war. Many in his party did not. The Republican candidate in 1916 was Charles Evans Hughes, former Associate Justice of the United States Supreme Court and previously a reform governor of New York. Sometimes he echoed Roosevelt. Other times (particularly before German audiences), he advocated peace and neutrality. Critics dubbed him "Charles Evasive Hughes."

Hughes looked like a winner. On Sunday, November 5, two days before the election, Wilson sent Secretary of State Robert Lansing a fantastic proposal for a quick abdication of the Oval Office, allowing Hughes four extra months in office. If Hughes won, Lansing should resign; Wilson would then appoint Hughes as Lansing's successor. Then, Vice President Marshall would resign, placing Hughes next in line for the White House (the secretary of state was next in the order of succession at the time). Finally, Wilson would quit, giving Hughes the four months. It was wartime. The country could ill afford a powerless lame-duck president and a lengthy transition period. But, Wilson being Wilson, he would not have concocted such a stratagem without inviting another inescapable conclusion: the Lord of Princeton was picking up his marbles and going home.

On Election Night, Hughes seized the lead, even carrying New Jersey. The West, however, remained solidly Democratic. Whoever won Republican stronghold California would be president, and early returns favored Hughes. The *New York Times* headlined "THE PRESIDENT-ELECT— CHARLES EVANS HUGHES." Instead, Hughes, who had alienated California's progressive Republican Senator Hiram Johnson, lost the Golden State by 3,800 votes.

"'Tis not so deep as a well, nor so wide as a church door," twanged Vice President Marshall, "but 'tis enough. 'Twill serve."

Marshall and Wilson were safe, but a key member of Wilson's inner circle wasn't: his secretary, Joseph P. Tumulty. At Jim Nugent's request, Tumulty, a Jersey City attorney, had joined Wilson's 1910 gubernatorial campaign. An academician like Wilson needed someone like Tumulty to guide him through New Jersey's often-fractious politics. Tumulty performed so skillfully that Wilson retained him as his private secretary (i.e., his chief of staff) both as governor and as president. Educated, mildly progressive, and intensely loyal, Tumulty possessed one major problem: he was Catholic.

At first, this was an advantage. When Wilson knifed New Jersey's urban Catholic bosses, he needed a Papist at his side to defuse suspicions of anti-Catholicism. And Wilson, perhaps from sheer orneriness, seemed to relish having a close Catholic adviser, boasting in 1910 that he would "ram" Tumulty's appointment down opponents' throats. By 1916, however, national anti-Catholic sentiment was on the rise. Tumulty had become a political liability. Additionally, the new Mrs. Wilson, jealous of her husband's old guard, wanted Tumulty banished. Wilson turned on Tumulty, as he had on Smith and Harvey and Watterson, planning to mothball him to the obscure Board of General Appraisers. You "could not know what this means to me and to mine," Tumulty begged. "I am grateful for having been associated so closely with so great a man. I am heart-sick that the end should be like this." Wilson, for once repaying loyalty with loyalty, let Tumulty stay.

Edith Wilson failed to engineer Tumulty's exile, but her influence remained in the ascent. Wilson shared the most secret conversations and documents with this jeweler's widow, a woman completely inexperienced and uneducated in affairs of state and politics, soliciting and valuing her advice on the most sensitive and complex issues. Even Colonel House was being shunted aside. To his diary in November 1915, House complained: "No one can see him to explain matters or get his advice. Therefore they come to me and I have to do it at long-range which is difficult and unsatisfactory. The President lacks executive ability and does not get the best results from his Cabinet or those around him."

"Wilson," journalist William Allen White once explained, "in his gayest hours, in his times of greatest happiness, stood always aloof, distrusting men instinctively. It was this suspicion of men, founded upon ignorance of men, which led Wilson always to question the strong, to fraternize with the meek, and to break ruthlessly and irrevocably, without defense or explanation, any friendship which threatened his own prestige."

Or, as White phrased it most succinctly, "Wilson trusted only errand boys."

War was fast approaching. November 1916 had seen Wilson re-elected on the slogan "He kept us out of war." In January 1917, Berlin resumed unrestricted submarine warfare. In February, the British released the "Zimmermann Note," revealing Germany's plan to incite Mexican and Japanese attacks on the United States. Inaugurated again in March, the next month Wilson asked for a declaration of war on Germany, "to make the world safe for democracy."

The nation was not particularly prepared for war. Not until June did the first American troops land on French soil; not until November (i.e., not until after the Bolsheviks seized power in Russia and pulled out of the war) did doughboys see combat.

Nevertheless, the Central Powers were being bled white, and the hundreds of thousands of fresh American troops tipped the balance. So did Wilson's rhetoric, his idealism, his vision of a post-war democratic world—his Fourteen Points, a heady stew of self-determination, disarmament, and international cooperation that helped bring Germany to the peace table. On November 9, 1918, the Kaiser abdicated. At 11:11 A.M. on November 11, 1918, the killing stopped.

Woodrow Wilson's crusade was just beginning.

## Chapter 2

≈

# "Something Queer Was Happening"

Woodrow Wilson wanted to go to Europe, to negotiate a just peace, to remake the world, to outlaw war.

Nobody—save Mrs. Wilson—liked the idea. Presidents did not go to Europe. Presidents *never* crossed the nation's borders (try telling Teddy Roosevelt the Canal Zone *wasn't* American). But in the days following the Armistice, Wilson's obsession grew.

At Hoboken, New Jersey, just before noon on Wednesday, December 4, 1918, he boarded the 700-foot-long *George Washington*, the former German liner *Kaiser Wilhelm*. The battleship *Pennsylvania* escorted it across the Atlantic, as did a flotilla of ten destroyers. Although the war was over, this remained a dangerous voyage, the waters still filled with mines and possibly harboring German U-boat commanders ignorant of the Armistice.

Aboard were Woodrow and Edith Wilson, eight Secret Service men, Secretary of State Robert Lansing, and retired diplomat Henry White, the only Republican on Wilson's peace commission. White, as Secret Service agent Colonel Robert Starling put it, was "one of the most engaging men I have ever met," but he had no standing with either the Republicans, who now controlled the Congress, or the general public. Merely a nice old man, he would not resist anything Woodrow Wilson might say or propose. Already in Europe were such key administrative figures as Colonel House, George Creel, financier Bernard Baruch, and Food Administrator Herbert Hoover.

Just before dawn on Friday, December 13, Wilson's flotilla neared the French coast and caught the faint sparkling of lights onshore. A few hours later, nine more immense American battleships came into view—the *New York*, the *Texas*, the *Arizona*, the *Arkansas*, the *Florida*, the *Nevada*, the *Wyoming*, the *Utah*, and the *Oklahoma*. Each thundered a 21-gun salute. Twenty-one destroyers (twelve American, nine French) and two cruisers (both French) joined them. "The ocean," Ike Hoover wrote home, had become "one moving mass of ships as far as the eye can see."

Woodrow Wilson was about to land in Europe.

A tumultuous crowd greeted him at Brest. A bigger crowd cried *Vive l'Amérique! Vive le Président!* in Paris. London cheered. As did Rome and Turin and Milan. "It was a reception," Secretary of State Lansing wrote, "which might have turned the head of a man far less responsive than the President was to public applause, and have given him an exalted opinion of his own power of accomplishment and of his individual responsibility to mankind. It is fair, I think, to assume that this was the effect on the President. It was the natural one."

At Buckingham Palace, Wilson moralistically lectured King George V on how only a "community of ideals and interests," rather than ancestry or language, bound their two nations together. "I could not bear him," the monarch complained. "An entirely cold academic professor—an odious man."

Or, as French Premier Georges Clemenceau phrased it, "I never knew anyone to talk more like Jesus Christ, and act more like Lloyd George."

The United States' peace commission included not just Wilson and Henry White, but also Colonel House, Secretary of State Lansing, and General Tasker H. Bliss, a member of the Supreme War Council in Paris. But it didn't really matter who was along for the ride, for Woodrow Wilson *was* the American delegation—and, more than that, or at least so he thought, the conscience of the world.

Even Colonel House didn't count. Of anyone, he might have helped Wilson the most. But Wilson was not about to share this grand stage with lesser actors. Ike Hoover recalled how the situation deteriorated:

Colonel House would seek out the President . . . as had always been his custom and his privilege. But now . . . the President seemed to have lost patience. Once when the Colonel called him on the telephone and asked for an appointment, I heard him say, "I wish he would leave me alone!" at the same time granting the request. Lost confidence was followed by a suspicion of treachery, the President feeling that House was trying to make himself too conspicuous and important. How foreign this was to the truth! Colonel House saw the situation coming on, but he was helpless. There was nothing that he had done for which amends could be made. I am sure [that] if there were[,] he would have gone to the very limit of his endurance in his loyalty and his faithfulness to the President. No one was more loyal than he.

It was House who should have negotiated the treaty. No sitting president should have sat day after day, week after week, in Paris, listening to minute details of European boundaries, harangued by diplomats settling scores of centuries-old grudges at a single conference. He should have been above the fray, an ocean away, not its center.

Wilson's Fourteen Points, compelling and inspiring as abstractions, proved difficult, if not impossible, to apply in reality. Their most powerful promise, the self-determination of nations, was particularly incendiary. "The phrase is simply loaded with dynamite," mused Robert Lansing en route to Paris. "What a pity it was ever uttered! What misery it will cause!" He was right. Europe's multitude of nationalities had not settled in neat little areas. They overlapped, creating minorities within minorities within minorities. Poland and Germany feuded over Silesia; Italy and the new Kingdom of Jugo-Slavia battled over the Adriatic port city of Fiume. Greece and Turkey and Italy presented competing claims in the Aegean.

The Fourteen Points also targeted secret diplomacy. "Open covenants of peace, openly arrived at" were all well and good—for the future. But what of the secret agreements that had brought Italy and Japan into the just-concluded war? Italy loudly demanded territory all over the eastern Mediterranean. Japan, having seized China's Shantung Province from Germany, was determined to keep it, no matter how many Chinese lived there.

"Freedom of navigation upon the seas"? Britain had starved Berlin into submission with a vise-like naval blockade that remained in force even after the war. London wasn't about to surrender so powerful a weapon. Nor did it relish taking orders from any international organization regarding Ireland and India, or, indeed, any portion of its huge empire. France, having lost a million men and fearing a war of revenge, demanded a Germany crippled by reparations, annexations, and armament restrictions. "Please do not misunderstand me," the aged Clemenceau informed Wilson; "we too came into the world with the noble instincts and the lofty inspirations which you express so eloquently. We have become what we are because we have been shaped by the rough hand of the world in which we have to live[,] and we have survived only because we are a tough bunch."

There was the colonial question. France, Britain, Japan, Italy, South Africa, Belgium, Australia, and even the United States all coveted chunks of the defunct German and Ottoman empires. If the self-determination of nations had any validity, those territories' inhabitants should determine their own destinies. But they would not.

And reparations. Who would pay for the war—or, more realistically, *how much would defeated Germany pay*? Allied diplomats, reflecting the will of their respective electorates, wanted Germany, irrespective of its ability to do so, to pay. On the very day Wilson landed at Brest, Britain re-elected its prime minister, David Lloyd George. His platform: Squeeze Germany "until the pips squeak."

Wilson ultimately fell into the same trap. South Africa's Jan Christiaan Smuts proposed adding Allied veterans' pensions to the reparation bill, and Wilson thought it a fine idea. When an economist called the idea illogical, he screamed: "Logic! Logic! I don't give a damn for logic. I am going to include pensions." The cost of reparations doubled.

As Clemenceau observed, it is "much easier to make war than peace."

Harder still, if one arrived at the peace table carrying one grotesquely heavy piece of baggage: Point XIV, "a general association of nations . . . for the purpose of affording mutual guarantees of political independence and territorial integrity to great and small states alike."

This "general association" became the League of Nations, the lodestone of the peace as far as Woodrow Wilson was concerned. Wilson would abandon principle after principle to implement his League. After all, it made sense: If the treaty possessed flaws, the League could repair them. This naïve delusion drove his actions. If Japan threatened to boycott the League if it didn't get Shantung, it got Shantung. If Britain wanted Iraq and France wanted Togoland, what was the harm?

Still, the negotiations were ugly. On February 7, Wilson threatened to sail home. "I am disgusted," fumed Clemenceau; "Wilson acts like a cook who keeps her trunk ready in the hallway. Every day[,] he threatens to leave."

Aside from territorial issues, Japan exhibited a remarkable indifference to conference affairs. That changed on February 13, 1919, when Baron Nobuaki Makino lobbed a grenade into the proceedings: "The equality of nations being a basic principle of the League of Nations, the High Contracting Parties agree to accord, as soon as possible, to all alien nationals of States [who are] members of the League equal and just treatment in every respect, making no distinction, either in law or in fact, on account of their race or nationality." Britain, ruling over various discontented races and making all sorts of distinctions between them, wanted no part of that. Arch-racist Australian Premier Billy Hughes vowed to head home. Makino's proposal threatened not only American exclusion of Oriental immigrants but its entire Jim Crow system. Colonel House warned Wilson: "If this . . . should pass . . . , it would surely raise the race issue throughout the world." The proposition died in April.

On February 14, 1919, Wilson finally did leave, to confer with—and alienate—Congress. He then returned to France, meeting House at Brest on March 13. House detailed his own actions in Wilson's absence, working with the British and French to resolve sticking points that Wilson had been unable to untangle. Wilson felt betrayed. "House has given away everything I had won before we left Paris," he confided to Edith. "He has compromised on every side, and so I have to start all over again. . . ." House had done no such thing. Though relishing his presence at the conference and now less circumspect about speaking to the press, House's crime was not disloyalty, but honesty. Seeing the great stakes and tremendous risks involved, House shifted from flattery to frankness, increasingly tendering Wilson advice that he did not want to hear. It was a dangerous game.

Wilson also faced another major foreign policy conundrum: Russia. After seizing power (with German help) in November 1917, Lenin's Bolsheviks had pulled the country out of the Great War. Wilson and the Allies reacted by launching a half-hearted intervention in support of the confused, often mutually hostile patchwork of White armies, hoping to return Russia to the Allied fold. The effort accomplished nearly nothing, but continued after the Armistice (fifteen thousand American troops eventually served in Siberia and the Russian far north), alienating not only America's pro-Soviet radicals but large numbers of progressives, liberals, and isolationists.

In March 1919, Wilson secretly dispatched Assistant Secretary of State William C. Bullitt, a twenty-eight-year-old Philadelphia socialite and a protégé of Colonel House, to Russia to confer with Lenin's government. The Bolsheviks charmed the left-leaning Bullitt and offered him a deal: If the Allies would recognize their legitimacy, lift their blockade, withdraw their troops, and halt funding for the White armies, Lenin would allow the Whites to retain what territory they had (fairly sizable chunks in 1919), declare an amnesty, and even honor a portion of Russia's foreign debts. The terms were decent. That the Bolsheviks said they would not propose this deal publicly, but would only react to it if proposed by the Allies, should have made Bullitt suspicious. It did not. Bullitt sped back to Paris with the proposal. Wilson said he had a headache and was too busy to see him. Even House had little interest. American intervention continued to stumble along. Bullitt resigned in May.

By now, the important work of the conference lay in the hands of the Big Four—Wilson, Lloyd George, Clemenceau, and Italian Prime Minister Vittorio Orlando. Wilson, alone of the Four, attended sessions without a single staff member to assist him. Worse, he forbade his delegation to even see transcripts of the sessions. So much for "open covenants of peace, openly arrived at."

On April 3, 1919, Wilson took ill: very, very ill. His fever reached 103 degrees. His body was racked with pain. A horrid cough kept him fitfully awake. Finally came violent diarrhea. Dr. Grayson thought Wilson had influenza—or, at least, that is what he said. Rumors flew of poison.

The truth may have been even worse. Woodrow Wilson was acting very strangely. Ike Hoover wrote:

Even while lying in bed he manifested peculiarities, one of which was to limit the use of all the automobiles to strictly official purposes, when previously he had been so liberal . . . in view of the long hours we were working. When he got back on the job, his peculiar ideas were even more pronounced. He now became obsessed with the idea that every French employee about the place was a spy for the French Government. Nothing we could say could disabuse his mind of this thought. He insisted [that] they all understood English, when, as a matter of fact, there was just one of them among the two dozen or more who understood a single word of English. About this time[,] he also acquired the peculiar notion that he was personally responsible for all the property in the furnished palace he was occupying. He raised quite a fuss on two occasions when he noticed [that] articles of furniture had been removed. Upon investigation— for no one else noticed the change—it was learned that the custodian of the property for the French owner had seen fit to do a little rearranging. Coming from the President, whom we all knew so well, these were very funny things, and we could but surmise that something queer was happening in his mind.

One thing is certain: He was never the same after this little spell of sickness.

Wilson had suffered a stroke—not his first. In actuality, his health had been unsteady for years, so fragile that he probably should have retired from Princeton, let alone ever run for governor or president. An 1896 stroke had temporarily hampered his control of his right hand. A 1906 stroke had briefly blinded his left eye and permanently robbed him of everything but its peripheral vision.

His health never fully recovered—and his judgment may have similarly suffered. In 1906, his personal ophthalmologist, Dr. George E. Schweinitz, diagnosed him with arteriosclerosis. From the very beginning of Wilson's White House tenure, Admiral Grayson had carefully husbanded Wilson's strength, as if he might wear down, or even collapse, at any moment. Working just three or four hours a day, Wilson enjoyed long automobile rides, golfed, whiled away time at theaters, took it very easy each summer—and rested completely on the Sabbath.

32

In Paris, Wilson's peculiarities continued. After lunch on May 1, something was bothering him. In his quarters, he finally informed Admiral Grayson what it was:

> I don't like the way the colors of this furniture fight each other. The greens and the reds are all mixed up here and there is no harmony. Here is a big purple high-backed covered chair, which is like the Purple Cow, strayed off to itself, and it is placed where the light shines on it too brightly. If you will give me a lift, we will move this next to the wall where the light from the window will give it a subdued effect. And here are two chairs, one green and the other red. This will never do. Over in the right-hand corner at our meetings are the British together; in the left-hand corner the Americans; in the middle the French are seated. When we meet every day[,] it would amuse you to see us walk to our respective corners just as if we were school children occupying our regular seats. Now, we will put all the reds over here in the American corner, next to the red sofa; the greens we will put over here for the Britishers; the odds and ends we will put here in the center for the French, and we will harmonize them as much as possible. The other chairs that do not harmonize we will put on the edge where the experts can occupy them when they are called in before the Big Three.

Dr. Grayson recorded that Wilson seemed much more relaxed once the furniture had been moved.

Such incidents subsided, but so did Wilson's mental vigor, his flexibility, his physical energy. "When he returned [to the negotiations]," recalled Herbert Hoover:

> . . . he was drawn, exhausted, and haggard. He sometimes groped for ideas. His mind constantly strove for previous decisions and precedents in even minor matters. He clung to them.
>
> Prior to that time in all matters with which I had to deal, he was incisive, quick to grasp essentials, unhesitating in conclusions, and most willing to take advice. After the time I mention, . . . I found that we had to push against an unwilling mind. And at

times, when I just had to get decisions, our constant resort was to find a "precedent."

While the president's staff hunted for precedents, everything on the negotiating table revolved around the League. If France wanted to demilitarize the Rhineland (or even create a separate puppet Rhenish state) or annex the coal-rich Saarland, it held the League over Wilson's head. When, for domestic political purposes, the president wanted concessions to recognize American prerogatives under the Monroe Doctrine, France and Britain dragged their heels. They had no territorial interests in the Western Hemisphere, but realized that the League was the best bargaining chip they could have.

The Italians somehow never realized that; and because they never threatened to sabotage the League, Wilson held to principle, rejecting Italian demands for Fiume. Wilson even went over Orlando's head, issuing "An Appeal to the Italian People," grandly asking their support against their own government. The ploy backfired, transforming Wilson into the most-hated man in Italy. Orlando stalked home in protest. Noticing a week later that he wasn't missed, he slunk back.

Also slinking out was Colonel House. Edith Wilson confronted House with a newspaper article praising him as "the brains of the commission" and accused him of planting such stories through his son-in-law and secretary, Gordon Auchincloss. It was another plunge downward in the deteriorating House–Wilson relationship. House never again visited Wilson's Paris quarters.

Lloyd George had second thoughts about the harshness of the peace treaty's terms, but Clemenceau wouldn't budge. Wilson listlessly ignored the debate. The Germans couldn't sabotage his League—they couldn't even join it until 1926—and were, thus, of no consequence.

Finally, on June 28, 1919, the convening powers solemnly affixed signatures to the 15-part, 214-page, 440-article treaty. Germany expected to negotiate terms, to ameliorate its conditions. It couldn't. There would be no bargaining. It was a *Diktat*, take it or else.

Germany forfeited its colonial empire, 10 percent of its population, 13 percent of its territory and economic output, 25 percent of its coal production, 75 percent of its iron-ore production, the great bulk of its army and navy, and all of its deadly submarine fleet. The Rhineland, to be occupied for fifteen years, would then be permanently demilitarized. France obtained the Saarland's coal deposits for fifteen years. Article 231—the "war guilt clause"—branded upon Germany the total blame for the Great War. Germany would pay an unknown amount of reparations— a sum fixed in 1921 at $33 billion.

Wilson now had his treaty. He did not necessarily have his League. House urged conciliation with the Senate, which would have to confirm Wilson's treaty and, thus, his international association of nations. "House," Wilson lectured, "I have found [that] one can never get anything in this life worthwhile without fighting for it." House reminded him that Anglo-Saxon civilization had been constructed on compromise.

And so they parted, not agreeing on that or much else anymore.

## Chapter 3

⁓

# "I Seem to Have Gone to Pieces"

Woodrow Wilson returned home.

It was a rough voyage. For half the passage, the *George Washington*'s passengers were confined to quarters. Influenza broke out, though the Wilsons themselves remained unaffected. Assistant Secretary of the Navy Franklin Roosevelt and his wife Eleanor were aboard, and while Edith Wilson found them to be "delightful companions," the Roosevelts found the president off-putting, ignoring invitations to shipboard events, keeping to himself.

Roosevelt hoped to learn about the treaty firsthand from his president. Wilson ignored him for the most part, only occasionally sharing some thoughts. He revealed to FDR that he never read the newspapers, only excerpts from them compiled by Tumulty. He contended that "the United States must go in [the League] or it will break the heart of the world, for she is the only nation that all feel is disinterested and all trust"; but that was mere podium rhetoric. As usual, he refused to discuss substantive matters with anyone outside his tight little circle. Wilson, Eleanor later wrote, "seemed to have very little interest in making himself popular with groups of people whom he touched." The trip's most amusing moment came when a troupe of sailors adorned in chorus-girl drag performed for the presidential party, and one rouged dancer boldly chucked Wilson on the chin. Roosevelt never forgot Wilson's shocked expression.

Just off Cape Ann, on Monday, February 24, fog shrouded the coast. The *George Washington* and its destroyer escort, the *Harding*, risked running aground. Roosevelt, taking the bridge with the *George Washington*'s captain, drew upon his local yachting experiences and guessed they were off Marblehead. Actually, they were off Thacher Island, near Rockport to the north, but press reports generously contended that FDR was "nearly accurate." Within an hour, the fog lifted completely, and the ships steamed south to Boston.

The party received a tumultuous, unprecedented welcome, nearly akin to the adulation Wilson had witnessed in Rome and Paris. Shops were closed. A half million flag-waving, cheering souls lined Boston streets. But the atmosphere was edgy, nervous. Sharpshooters manned fishing boats near Commonwealth Pier, where the presidential party arrived aboard the Coast Guard cutter *Ossipee*. Police searched docks for explosives. They arrested twenty-two members of the National Women's Party who planned to burn copies of Wilson's speeches at the Boston Commons. While the president lunched, police noticed a suspicious character nearby. They searched thirty-one-year-old Andrew J. Rogosky of Worcester, found a blackjack and a .32-caliber revolver, and promptly arrested him.

At Mechanics Hall, tenor John McCormack sang for the overflow crowd and Governor Calvin Coolidge twanged a brief presidential introduction, fitting neatly on three notecards. Realizing that more was needed, he turned to Wilson, flashed a rare smiled, and said:

> We welcome him as the representative of a great people, as a great statesman, as one to whom we have entrusted our destinies and one whom we are sure we will support in the future in the working out of those destinies, as Massachusetts has supported him in the past.

It was all downhill from there.

By landing in Boston, Wilson had purposely flung a pointed barb at Massachusetts Senator Henry Cabot Lodge, Chairman of the Foreign Relations Committee and the Senate's de facto majority leader. Colonel House had urged Wilson to present his first exposition of the treaty to members of Lodge's committee. Instead, acting upon Tumulty's counsel, he delivered it publicly, in Lodge's own back yard, and in belligerent "I-have-fighting-blood-in-me-and-it-is-sometimes-a-delight-to-let-it-have-scope" fashion.

"Any man," thundered Wilson, "who resists the present tides that run in the world will find himself thrown upon a shore so high and barren that it will seem as if he had been separated from his human kind forever."

Wilson meant that for Lodge. Lodge meant that for Wilson. Lodge was, in fact, the Republican Wilson—a distinguished academic, a successful politician. Yet there were differences. Wilson had evolved from conservative to progressive, Lodge had moved from good-government independent to party regular. Lodge hated Wilson. In February 1915, Teddy Roosevelt wrote Lodge: "Lord, I am feeling warlike with this administration." Lodge responded: "I do not wonder that you feel warlike . . . I never expected to hate anyone in politics with the hatred I feel toward Wilson."

His animus merely intensified when Wilson drafted his treaty without consulting him or any other Republican of note. Had Teddy lived, he and Lodge would have attacked the League in tandem. "When Theodore Roosevelt was ill in Roosevelt Hospital," his sister Corinne recalled, "Senator Lodge wrote, asking if he could see him. . . . So Senator Lodge made a night trip to New York and every one of the Lodge reservations . . . was arranged in this conference and approved by Theodore Roosevelt."

Two days after landing in Boston, Wilson (at House's urging) invited members of the House and Senate Foreign Relations committees to dinner to discuss the treaty. It did not go well. Edith Wilson exacerbated matters by gushing over her husband's wonderful reception in Boston. Woodrow lectured all. "I feel," Connecticut Republican Senator Frank Brandegee confessed to the *New York Sun*, "as if I had been wandering with Alice in Wonderland and had tea with the Mad Hatter. When I awakened this morning[,] I expected the White Rabbit to go to breakfast with me."

Two days later, Wilson lunched at the White House with members of the Democratic National Committee, hinting that he would not pursue a third term and lambasting League opponents as "blind and little provincial people" with "pygmy minds" who should be "hanged on gibbets as high as heaven, but pointing in the opposite direction." His intemperate remarks quickly became public, fueling Lodge and Brandegee's already raging animosity.

On Monday, March 3, 1919, Lodge checkmated Wilson, announcing a round-robin of thirty-seven Republican senators (two more would shortly join) who pledged to vote against the League in the "form now proposed"—i.e., without formal reservations. Lodge had the votes, and Wilson did not.

"Senator," Indiana Republican Senator James Watson asked Lodge, "suppose that the President accepts the Treaty with your reservations. Then we are in the League, and once in, our reservations become pure fiction."

Lodge wasn't worried. He had seriously studied Wilson. "But, my dear James," he answered, "you do not take into consideration the hatred that Woodrow Wilson has for me personally. Never under any set of circumstances in this world could he be induced to accept a treaty with Lodge reservations appended to it."

"But," Watson retorted, "that seems to me to be a slender thread on which to hang so great a cause."

"A slender thread!" Lodge exclaimed. "Why, it is as strong as any cable with strands wired and twisted together."

Even Wilson's allies questioned his judgment. As the debate accelerated, Franklin Roosevelt wrote Eleanor:

This business of the President and the Secretary of State negotiating and signing a treaty, and then handing it cold to the Senate is all wrong. . . . If I were doing it, I'd take the Senate, and maybe the House, into my confidence as far as I could. I'd get them committed to a principle and then work out the details in negotiations. In that way the thing could be secured.

On Tuesday evening, March 4, 1919, Wilson delivered an incendiary speech at New York's Metropolitan Opera House (compounding his gaffes by snubbing a waiting contingent of influential Irish Americans). He sailed for Europe an hour later, eventually signing the Treaty of Versailles on June 28.

When he returned stateside on July 8, it was to a different nation. Public and congressional support for the League, once overwhelming, was dwindling rapidly. Only a sparse throng greeted his arrival in Washington. As he passed by, TR's daughter, Alice Roosevelt Longworth, crossed her fingers and chanted: "A murrain [plague] on him, a murrain on him, a murrain on him!" Her companion thought they'd both be arrested.

Two days later, Wilson traveled to the Senate to personally present his treaty for ratification, the first time a president had done so since 1789. His speech illustrated his decline, emboldening enemies and disappointing allies. "His audience," thought Arizona Democrat Henry Fountain Ashurst, "wanted raw meat, he fed them cold turnips." The *Chicago Tribune* dismissed his words as mere "blah."

Still another Wilson stratagem boomeranged on Tuesday, August 19. Having invited members of the Senate Foreign Relations Committee for lunch and conversation at the East Room, he stayed in character by lecturing rather than conversing, swaying no one.

Attending was Ohio Republican Warren G. Harding. Despite Wilson's intellectual reputation and the Senator's lack of one (Harding even referred to his own "slow mind" in one exchange), Harding held his own.

Contention swirled around Article X of the League Covenant:

The members of the League undertake to respect and preserve as against external aggression the territorial integrity and existing political independence of all Members of the League.

Wilson contended that American obligations under Article X were more moral than legal. Then why, Harding asked, was Article X necessary at all? Why indeed was a League necessary? Would a League sway America's view of "morality," bending it "to the prejudices or necessities of the nations of the Old World"? Wilson responded that had America stood morally with the Allies in 1914, Germany would never have started a war—an egregious oversimplification of events.

Wilson had once admitted that though he had trouble speaking one-on-one with anyone, he could convince virtually any crowd, and, indeed, had accomplished that throughout his career—as a teacher, university president, governor, and president. When he could not spellbind an audience—as he could not at Versailles and with small groups of senators—failure beckoned.

Wilson decided to orate the League of Nations into existence, circumventing opposing senators, embarking on a grand whistle-stop tour designed to directly sway tens of thousands of their constituents. He would avoid the South; he already enjoyed substantial support there. He would avoid the East; even his oratory was no match for that region's conservative Republicanism. But the middle and far West were up for grabs; and so, on a steamy Wednesday evening, September 3, 1919, he commenced a grueling 22-day, 9,981-mile speaking tour designed to save his League.

He was not up to it. His crusade would have taxed a healthy man, and Wilson was anything but. He had not been well entering the presidency, and he had certainly not been well since his stroke in Paris that April. Admiral Grayson advised against the trip. Other aides suggested building a week's vacation at the Grand Canyon into the itinerary. Wilson refused: "The people would never forgive me if I took a rest on a trip such as the one I contemplate taking. This is a business trip, pure and simple, and the itinerary must not include rest of any kind."

Aggravating matters, Wilson had not done his homework. Unprepared for day-after-day, night-after-night stump speaking, aboard his private car he toiled until 11 P.M. each evening refining his thoughts. Not having worked more than three or four hours a day when reasonably healthy, he was now severely overtaxing his limits.

Beyond that, Wilson had no mechanical amplification, no microphones, no loudspeakers, at his disposal. He had to shout out his words, day after day, speech after speech. Finally, on Friday, September 19, at San Diego Stadium, they gave him a newfangled "voice phone" to address the 50,000 enthusiasts crowding the 25,000-seat stadium. It was a crude system, and he had to stand in a glass enclosure, very carefully speaking into two large loudspeaker-like horns suspended overhead. He hated the experience.

But technology was the least of Wilson's problems. Irish Nationals, incensed by his antipathy to Irish freedom, shadowed him, presenting speakers before and after he hit each town. On Wednesday, September 10, irreconcilable senators William Borah of Idaho and Hiram Johnson of California initiated an aggressive, well-received counter-tour of their own.

From San Diego, Wilson traveled to Los Angeles—and an awkward meeting. At 1:30 P.M. on Sunday, September 21, Woodrow and Edith took lunch at the city's Alexandria Hotel. Their guests: Mrs. Mary Peck and her chronically ill adult son, Allen Schoolcraft Hulbert. Both now lived in genteel poverty in Hollywood. Twice, Mary worked as an extra in films, on D. W. Griffith's *The Great Love* and Harry Garson's *The Forbidden Woman*. Mary claimed not to remember the latter title.

Peck thought Edith "Junoesque." Edith was less impressed, dismissing the now-fifty-seven-year-old Mary (nine years her senior) as "a faded, sweet-looking woman . . . absorbed in an only son." Secret Service man Colonel Edmund Starling concurred, characterizing Mary as "drab . . . how anyone could have cast her in a romantic role was more than I could imagine."

Mrs. Peck complained of being hounded during the 1916 campaign by a "representative of the Republican Party" to release her correspondence with Wilson. Edith blurted out, regarding the Wilson–Peck rumors, "Where there's so much smoke, there must be some fire." It was a very stressful day of rest from the campaign trail.

On Friday, September 12, news arrived from Washington. Former American Peace Commission staff member William C. Bullitt (of the failed peace mission to Russia) had testified before the Senate Foreign Relations Committee. He disclosed not only his own disappointments with the treaty, the League, and Woodrow Wilson, but he also alleged that Secretary of State Lansing shared many of his concerns. Wilson was incensed. On Tuesday, September 16, Lansing telegraphed Wilson that Bullitt had resigned. "I told [Bullitt]," Lansing wired Wilson, "that I would say nothing against his resigning since he put it on conscientious grounds, and that I recognized that certain features of the Treaty were bad, as I presumed most everyone did, but that was probably unavoidable in view of conflicting claims and that nothing ought to be done to prevent the speedy restoration of peace by signing the Treaty."

*Certain features of the Treaty were bad?*

Lansing's heresy only compounded Wilson's fury. "The testimony of Bullitt is a confirmation of the suspicions I have had with reference to this individual [Lansing]," he exploded to Tumulty. "I found the same attitude of mind . . . on the other side. I could find his trail everywhere I went, but they were only suspicions and it would not be fair for me to act upon them. But here in his own statement is a verification at last of everything I have suspected. Think of it! This from a man whom I raised from the level of a subordinate to the great office of Secretary of State of the United States. My God!" Had Wilson not been aboard a train, half a continent from Lansing, he probably would have fired him on the spot.

The Bullitt–Lansing incident only further endangered the president's already fragile health. Wilson had begun his trip ill. Then, in San Francisco on Wednesday, September 17, his mood fouled by the Lansing–Bullitt episode, his headaches worsened, blinding, dizzying, throbbing. Ray Stannard Baker, Wilson's press secretary, recorded Edith Wilson's account of her husband's ordeal:

> The President . . . went against the express and urgent advice of his physician. . . . From the first[,] he had no appetite and could not digest what he did eat because he was under such nervous strain. The Doctor had to feed him liquid and pre-digested foods during the day and night. Soon he could not sleep. The western altitudes affected him: but he would not give up. In Montana the hot dry weather and the dust caused an affection [infection] of the throat & he developed a kind of asthma. The Doctor repeatedly sprayed out his nose and throat: often having to do it in the middle of the night. In Washington he began to have terrible headaches—so blinding, that when he got up to speak he would see double. Yet he would not give in. At several functions in California—one a dinner in which those present smoked inordinately, he suffered frightfully—but made a wonderful speech. He never complained, he never scorned his condition—and he refused the beseeching requests of Dr. Grayson to stop and rest.

Relying on diminishing reserves of energy and will, Wilson soldiered on. After a sluggish beginning, his oratory had peaked in California, where, invigorated by fighting on Hiram Johnson's home turf, he delivered some of the better speeches of his career. Huge crowds greeted him in

San Francisco. He packed the 12,000-seat Auditorium. Third-term rumors began percolating.

It was all for naught. His personal bravery may have been inspiring, but only those close to him—Edith, Tumulty, Grayson, Colonel Starling—knew about it. The millions reading his words remained largely unimpressed. George Creel termed the trip a "fatal blunder." Secretary of State Lansing expressed concern about the president's "undignified expressions about the opposition in the Senate" (in one case, Wilson derided his opponents as "quitters") and soon came to feel that the whole operation had been counterproductive:

> I am sure the performance lost rather than gained support for the Treaty. It came to me from various sources that the public began to consider that the objections had some merit[,] otherwise the President would not have taken so much trouble to answer them. Prior to his western trip[,] the public were disposed to brush the objections aside on the supposition that they were only put forward to discredit the President rather than the Treaty. Thus, the President's speeches, while they may have won over a few, lost, in my opinion, a great deal of public support, especially as the whole proceeding took on the character of a party issue.

There was some good news. On Thursday, September 25, Arizona Senator Henry Ashurst, leader of a group of eight Democratic reservationists, wired Wilson, pledging support. Similar messages arrived from Senators Robinson of Arkansas and Simmons and Overman of North Carolina. Perhaps, thought Wilson, the tide was finally turning.

That morning, he reached Denver. Seventy-year-old former governor Alva Adams introduced him to the crowd of fifteen thousand as "a twentieth century Paul . . . the greatest prophet of peace." In late afternoon, at Pueblo's new City Hall Auditorium, his audience included six thousand striking steel miners. Adams again likened him to the Apostle Paul, adding that Paul had "shattered the heathen idols of ancient Rome."

At Pueblo, Wilson summoned what strength remained in his worn body, allowing for no compromise, no olive branch toward opponents:

I find . . . that there is an organized propaganda against the League of Nations . . . proceeding from exactly the same sources that the organized propaganda proceeded from which threatened this country here and there with disloyalty, and I want to say—I cannot say too often—any man who carries a hyphen about with him carries a dagger that he is ready to plunge into the vitals of this Republic whenever he gets ready. If I can catch any man with a hyphen in this great contest I will know that I have got an enemy of the Republic. . . .

There is no middle course. You cannot go in on a special-privilege basis of your own[,] . . . exempted from responsibilities which the other members of the league will carry. We go in upon equal terms or we do not go in at all; and if we do not go in, my fellow citizens, think of the tragedy of that result—the only sufficient guaranty to the peace of the world withheld! Ourselves drawn apart with that dangerous pride which means that we shall be ready to take care of ourselves and that means that we shall maintain great standing armies and an irresistible navy. It always seems to make it difficult for me to say anything, my fellow citizens, when I think of my clients in this case. My clients are the children. My clients are the next generation. They do not know what promises and bonds I undertook when I ordered the armies of the United States to the soil of France, but I know and I intend to redress my pledges to the children; they shall not be sent upon a similar errand.

There is one thing that the American people always rise to and extend their hand to, and that is the truth of justice and of liberty and of peace. We have accepted that truth and we are going to be led by it, and it is going to lead us, and through us the world, out into pastures of quietness and peace such as the world never dreamed of before.

Then as Wilson continued in Pueblo, uttering the words "Germany must never again he allowed . . . ," he faltered. The words simply did not come. It wasn't his voice; it was his brain. His finely tuned mind was failing him. He started again: "A lesson must be taught to Germany." Again, he stumbled. And then again.

Colonel Starling shuddered at the sight:

> I stood close behind him, afraid he might collapse at any moment.
> Much of his speech was mumbled; he mouthed certain words as if
> he had never spoken them before. There were long pauses. He
> had difficulty following the trend of his thought. It was a travesty
> of his usual brilliant delivery and fine logic. His voice was weak,
> and every phrase was an effort for his whole body. Once he wept.
> We left at five o'clock, bound for Wichita. In the cool of the
> evening[,] the train stopped, and I was called to go with him and
> Mrs. Wilson for a walk. Doctor Grayson thought the exercise in the
> open country would do him good.
>
> I followed the two down a dusty country road, until they
> reached a wooden bridge over a stream. There they paused,
> staring at the water. Then they returned, the President walking
> slowly, lifting his feet that were once so light, as if they were
> weighted and shackled.
>
> Back on the train[,] I crawled into my bunk and slept until
> early next morning. In the corridor I met [Wilson's black servant
> Arthur] Brooks. He told me that during the night the President
> had suffered what appeared to be a stroke. He was in a state of
> collapse.
>
> "It's all over now," the faithful valet said gloomily.

Wilson begged to continue. He didn't want to be branded a "quitter." His
body overruled him. His five remaining speeches were canceled.
Grayson informed reporters that the president was suffering from
"nervous exhaustion," which was "not alarming"—as if a president suffering from "nervous exhaustion" was not "alarming." Wilson's private
car, blinds drawn to shut out a curious world, raced toward Washington.
"I seem to have gone to pieces," Wilson told Grayson. But the worst was
yet to come.

Secluded at the White House, he rested and hoped for the best. He
had always recovered; he might do so once more. On Monday night,
October 1, he went to bed, but there was no rest for his worried wife. "I
had been sleeping fitfully," Edith would write:

. . . getting up every hour or so to see how my husband was. It was so on this night. At five or six in the morning[,] I found him still sleeping normally, as it appeared. Relieved, I dozed off again until after eight. This time I found him sitting on the side of the bed trying to reach a water bottle. As I handed it to him[,] I noticed that his left hand hung loosely. "I have no feeling in that hand," he said. "Will you rub it? But first help me to the bathroom."

He moved with great difficulty, and every move brought spasms of pain; but with my help he gained the bathroom. This so alarmed me that I asked if I could leave him long enough to telephone the Doctor. He said yes, and hurrying into my room I reached Dr. Grayson at his home. While at the 'phone[,] I heard a slight noise, and[,] rushing into my husband's apartment, found him on the bathroom floor unconscious.

He had suffered a massive stroke, falling against the bathtub, cutting his nose and temple. Worse, he had forfeited control of his left side and much of the remaining sight in his left eye. "My God," cried Admiral Grayson, "the president is paralyzed!"

Grayson summoned a team of prominent specialists. At 10 P.M., he issued a bulletin, admitting that his patient was a "very sick man."

But the time for truth passed quickly. Soon Grayson was issuing only encouraging statements, downplaying the gravity of the situation.

Secretary of State Lansing reminded Joe Tumulty that the Constitution provided for such a situation: "In case of the removal of the President from office, or his death, resignation, or inability to discharge the powers and duties of the said office, the same shall devolve upon the Vice-President." Lansing's suggestion outraged the fearsomely loyal Tumulty. He and Grayson refused to certify the president as incapacitated. Also uncooperative was Vice President Marshall, who feared both Edith Wilson and the very thought of assuming presidential powers. He would do nothing during the entire crisis.

While Wilson lay abed and Marshall hid under his, others maneuvered.

On Tuesday, October 28, 1919, Henry Cabot Lodge received a visitor. Colonel House had dispatched Lieutenant Colonel Stephen Bonsal to Lodge's Washington home. Bonsal, a noted journalist who had attended

St. Paul's School with Lodge's late son-in-law, Representative Augustus Peabody Gardiner, had served as House and Wilson's interpreter at Versailles. Bonsal and Lodge examined the League Covenant. Lodge penciled in necessary changes. They amounted to barely fifty words. Bonsal, amazed at their reasonableness (particularly compared to Lodge's previous statements), phoned House, who instructed Bonsal to send the changes to Wilson. Neither House nor Bonsal received the courtesy of a reply. Lodge dug in his heels.

Of course, Wilson may not have been able to reply. As White House Chief Usher Ike Hoover noted:

> For at least a month or more[,] not one word, I believe, was mentioned to him about the business of the office[,] and he was so sick [that] he did not take the initiative to inquire. No secretary, no official, no stenographer, no one with business had even seen him. He was lifted out of bed and placed in a comfortable chair for a short while each day. He gradually seemed to get used to his helpless condition. At times Mrs. Wilson would read to him. Finally, when it could no longer be delayed, some matters of importance requiring his signature were read to him and with a pencil, his hand steadied and pointed, he would sign where the hand had been placed. I saw many of these signatures[,] and they were but mere scribbles compared to his normal signature. Even this mechanical process seemed to exhaust him.

Lansing remained alarmed. "If he has only progressed thus far toward recovery during the last month," he observed on Saturday, November 1, 1919, "I cannot see how he can really conduct the Government for months to come."

One need not have possessed any inside knowledge to realize that; reading the papers would have done. "I saw a snapshot photograph of him the night he landed in Washington . . . ," Warren Harding wrote to his wife's physician; "it was about the most pathetic picture I have ever seen. He really looked like a perfectly helpless imbecile."

In late September 1919, with Wilson still in the West, a new British Ambassador, Sir Edward Grey, had arrived in Washington. When Wilson returned, he was, of course, incapable of receiving visitors. But even when he was, Edith refused to allow Grey entrance unless he dismissed embassy attaché Major Charles Crauford-Stuart, guilty of having circulated the "fell out of bed" version of Woodrow's marriage proposal. Crauford-Stuart had also gossiped that Edith had accompanied her husband to Paris simply to obtain the social status she, the jeweler's widow, had never quite attained in Washington. Grey wouldn't dismiss Crauford-Stuart, and when Eleanor and Franklin Roosevelt entertained Grey, they, too, earned places on Edith's growing blacklist. Spurning Grey, however, was a major blunder. Dispatched to Washington—on Colonel House's urgings—to help ratify the League, he could not move Wilson toward compromise if he could not even see him. That December, the frustrated Grey returned to London, the first British ambassador not to be received by a U.S. president.

On Thursday, November 6, 1919, the Foreign Relations Committee approved fourteen reservations proposed by Senator Lodge. They centered on Article X, which, Lodge contended, committed the United States to employ economic or military force to maintain the security and, indeed, the very boundaries of member nations. Was America obliged to fight over Trieste, the Aegean Islands, Shantung Province, or over a hundred other flashpoints? Or to maintain British imperial control of India or—God forbid, to a large chunk of the Massachusetts electorate—of Ireland?

Lodge thus proposed: "The United States assumes no obligation to preserve the territorial integrity of any other country or to interfere in controversies between nations . . . or to employ the military or naval forces of the United States . . . unless in any particular case the Congress shall by act or joint resolution so provide."

To Wilson, this was a "knife thrust at the heart of the treaty." The debate was about far more than what reasonable men could reasonably disagree on: It was about Woodrow Wilson having his way.

Senate Democratic Leader Gilbert Hitchcock of Nebraska had his own doubts about the League, and Wilson had his doubts about Hitchcock (he had undercut him for years), but now Hitchcock gingerly sought to salvage Wilson's dream. On November 13, 1919, he proposed five relatively harmless alternatives to Lodge's reservations. Lodge's Foreign Relations Committee rejected each one.

On Monday, November 17, 1919, Hitchcock and Wilson conferred, their first meeting since the stroke. Wilson was much improved but still pitiably weak. "As he lay in bed," Hitchcock remembered, "slightly propped up by pillows with the useless left arm concealed beneath the covers[,] I beheld an emaciated old man with a thin white beard which had been permitted to grow."

He was, nonetheless, feisty and combative, comparing Lodge's reservations to John C. Calhoun's antebellum doctrine of nullification. "I could not stand for those changes for a moment," he fumed, "because it would humiliate the United States before all of the Allied countries. . . . The United States would suffer the contempt of the world."

Wilson reserved his contempt for any senator daring to oppose his League. "I want the vote of each, Republican and Democrat, recorded," he ordered, "because they will have to answer to the country. . . . They must answer to the people. I am a sick man, lying in this bed, but I am going to debate this issue with these gentlemen in their respective states whenever they come up for re-election if I have breath enough in my body to carry on the fight. I shall do this even if I have to give my life to it. And I will get their political scalps when the truth is known to the people. They have got to account to their constituents for their actions in this matter. I have no doubt as to what the verdict of the people will be when they know the facts. Mind you, Senator, I have no hostility towards these gentlemen but an utter contempt."

On Tuesday, November 18, 1919, Wilson wrote to Hitchcock's fellow Senate Democrats, urging defeat of the Lodge reservations. That day, the cabinet met—without Wilson. Instead, he had been wheeled out to the White House lawn. There he sat, absorbing the afternoon sun.

The next day, Wednesday, November 19, 1919, the full Senate voted. By a solid 39–55 vote (35 Republicans and 4 Democrats voted aye; 13 Republicans and 42 Democrats nay), it rejected the treaty as amended by Lodge's reservations. By a 38–53 vote (1 Republican and 37 Democrats aye; 46 Republicans and 7 Democrats nay), it rejected the original treaty. Wilson had defeated Lodge's reservations. He had also defeated his own treaty.

The opposition celebrated at an informal gathering at Nick and Alice Longworth's Massachusetts Avenue home. Irreconcilables like Frank

Brandegee, James A. Reed, William E. Borah, George Moses, and Medill McCormick mingled with reservationists like Lodge, Harding, James Wadsworth, Thomas P. Gore, and Joseph Frelinghuysen. Florence Harding, Alice remembered, "cooked the eggs."

"We were jubilant," said Alice, "—too elated to mind the reservationists—now that it was over, they seemed quite as happy as we were."

On November 24, 1919, Colonel House had former Attorney General Gregory hand-carry a message to Wilson. He advised acquiescing in the reservations and then allowing the Allies to determine if they were acceptable. Wilson never responded, acknowledged receipt, or saw House again. House never again offered him advice.

Having slain Wilson's League, Congress now focused on Wilson himself, pondering if the sick, grizzled old man on the White House lawn actually ran the country—or had any hope of doing so. "We have petticoat Government!" New Mexico Senator Albert B. Fall exclaimed, "Mrs. Wilson is President!"

Fall had articulated what many senators thought. Edith Wilson virtually ran the country, controlling access to her debilitated husband, filtering information to him, hiding his condition from the public. To ascertain the truth, on Friday, December 5, 1919, Fall and Senator Hitchcock visited the White House, staying for forty-five minutes. Wilson, in bed and wearing a brown sweater, shook hands with both men, showing that his right arm was not paralyzed as rumored. It was as fine a day as Wilson would enjoy for months. "His color was good," Fall observed. "He was clean-shaven. I understand he now shaves himself. He seemed to me to be in excellent trim, both mentally and physically."

"Well, Mr. President," Fall supposedly told Wilson, "we have all been praying for you."

"Which way, Senator?" Wilson retorted acerbically.

Wilson had passed the test. He would remain in office—sick, ineffectual, bitter, but he would remain in office.

His staff loyally continued to bolster his spirits. Taking him for rides, they organized little knots of people to stand and cheer on his return. Wilson's eyes filled with tears. "You see," he murmured, "they still love me."

The Socialist *New York Call* saw it differently. In March 1920, with perhaps more accuracy than sympathy, it recorded this morbid little scene:

No sign of applause or greeting came from the citizens, who gazed with frightened eyes upon the haggard, yellow countenance of the Chief Executive of the Nation. The President sat low among the cushions of his car. Suffering carried to the verge of dull apathy shone through the dry, drawn skin of his face. He did not smile. His car rolled through the iron gate, and the people drew deep breaths of pained astonishment when it had passed.

Wilson remained "irascible." His thought processes remained disordered. Though his car traveled at only fifteen to twenty miles per hour, he was convinced that anyone passing him was speeding, and he ordered Secret Service agents to arrest "speeders" and "bring them back for questioning." They concocted reasons why they couldn't, invariably arguing that the offending vehicles were going far too fast to apprehend. Eventually, Wilson, again quite seriously, decided that "he wanted to be a justice of the peace so that he could arrest these drivers and try their cases." He wrote Attorney General Palmer requesting an opinion.

In 1916 Wilson had threatened to resign before the end of his term if rejected by the voters. He now trotted out a similar stratagem. After having Postmaster General Albert S. Burleson list the Senate's thirty-five most anti-League senators, Wilson drafted this message for delivery at the Democrats' January 8, 1920, Jackson Day Dinner: "I challenge the following named gentlemen, members of the Senate of the United States, to resign their seats in that body and take immediate steps to seek re-election to it on the basis of their several records with regards to the ratification of the treaty. For myself, I promise if all of them or a majority of them are re-elected, I [and Vice-President Marshall] will resign. . . ." It took great difficulty to prevent him from sending it.

What he finally did send was nearly as inflammatory, a repetition of his disastrous 1918 election strategy, excoriating the Republicans. "The clear and single way out," he wrote, "is to submit it for determination at the next election to the voters of the nation, to give the next election the form of a great and solemn referendum."

William Jennings Bryan did speak that night, and his long-standing resentment shredded the president's leadership. "Our nation," Bryan chided, "has spent a hundred thousand precious lives and more than twenty billion dollars to make the world safe for democracy, and the one fundamental principle of democracy is the right of the majority to rule. It applies to the Senate and to the House as well as to the people. A majority of Congress can declare war. Shall we make it more difficult to conclude a treaty than to enter war?"

Wilson's disgruntled former Secretary of State had "thrust his knife home," observed the *Baltimore News*, "and turned it round in the heart of the single great issue on which Mr. Wilson sought to prove the control of his party."

Wilson physically regressed, in late January contracting severe influenza. Admiral Grayson now finally dared to recommend that he quit. Wilson nearly did go "before the Senate in a wheeled chair for the purpose of resigning." Edith Wilson talked him out of it.

Had Wilson resigned, he might have saved the treaty. At any rate, other parties made valiant efforts. On Tuesday, January 27, 1920, Senator Hitchcock submitted his own version of an Article X reservation. Republicans rejected it.

On Sunday, February 1, 1920, England and France declared that they would accept the Lodge reservations. When the French ambassador so informed Wilson, he spat back: "No, Ambassador. I shall consent to nothing. The Senate must take its medicine." On February 9, the Senate, nonetheless, voted to reconsider the treaty and to refer it back to committee.

While Wilson fitfully recuperated (or, rather, failed to recuperate), Secretary of State Lansing, with Tumulty and Grayson's concurrence, had summoned the cabinet twenty-five times. At least twice, Lansing informed Wilson of his actions. However, on Saturday, February 7, Wilson wrote to Lansing, suddenly expressing shock that cabinet meetings were being called in his absence, citing "constitutional" issues. His tone was petulant and hostile. Even Edith Wilson found her husband's actions impossible to defend ("the letter as written made him look small"). Wilson laughed and wouldn't be swayed. On Thursday, February 12, Lansing, angered by Wilson's "brutal and offensive" message, resigned. The public sympathized with the Secretary of State. Some questioned Wilson's sanity. Some questioned his judgment in appointing a New York attorney with no foreign-policy experience, Bainbridge Colby,

53

as Lansing's replacement. Even Admiral Grayson thought Colby's appointment odd at best.

The White House attempted damage control. On Tuesday, February 10, Dr. Hugh H. Young of Johns Hopkins, one of the president's physicians, announced that Wilson was:

> . . . organically sound, able-minded and able-bodied. . . . The President walks sturdily now without assistance and without fatigue. And he uses the still slightly impaired arm more and more every day. As to his mental vigor, it is simply prodigious. Indeed, I think in many ways the President is in better shape than before the illness came.

The treaty, with the fifteen Lodge reservations attached, returned to the Senate floor on Friday, March 19, 1920. Wilson ordered Senate Democrats to vote no. Defeated 49–35, it was finally, irretrievably dead. "We can always depend on Mr. Wilson," Frank Brandegee congratulated Lodge. "He never has failed us."

# Chapter 4

## "HE IS THE ONLY CANDIDATE"

Theodore Roosevelt would have relished Woodrow Wilson's defeat, for if Woodrow Wilson was "a good hater," so was TR, and the man Colonel Roosevelt hated most of anyone was Professor Wilson.

Teddy Roosevelt. Energetic. Brilliant. Opinionated. Charismatic. Fearless. Independent. Intellectual. Heroic. Enthusiastic. Or, as one British observer once phrased it, more in truth than delicacy, "You must always remember that the president is about six."

Americans had never known an ex-president like Teddy.

Former chief executives tended to fade into the woodwork. Occasionally, one might return to Congress like John Quincy Adams or Andrew Johnson, make an abortive comeback like Millard Fillmore, or even actually return to the White House like Grover Cleveland; but no ex-president had ever *dominated* the country, dominated the *world*, like TR.

*Ex*-president Theodore Roosevelt wrote books, gave lectures, explored Africa and the Amazon—and now traversed the hardest, most treacherous route of all: the one back to the White House.

Theodore the boy hadn't started out dominating anything. Weak, myopic, and asthmatic, he transformed himself by work and will. By the time this scion of a patrician old Dutch New York family entered Harvard in 1876, he was an exponent of "the strenuous life," a creed trumpeting public service, and a spirited, frenzied physical and mental toughness.

At age twenty-three, in 1881, he won election from Manhattan's "Silk Stocking" 21st District to the State Assembly. He was a reformer, supporting clean government and slum clearance and making a name for himself doing it. Within three years—and just twenty-six—he became Assembly Minority Leader. On Valentine's Day 1884, tragedy struck. His twenty-two-year-old wife Alice died of Bright's disease, just two days after giving birth to their daughter Alice (causing TR to never actually be able to bear hearing the name "Alice"). Just hours previously, TR's mother had died of typhoid fever. "The light," he confided to his diary, "has gone out of my life."

Roosevelt abandoned politics, abandoned Manhattan, fleeing to his working ranch in North Dakota. He was a frontiersman, albeit one whose Bowie knife came from Tiffany's and who startled ranch hands with the command "Hasten forward quickly there." Roosevelt rode the range, fought saloon brawls, shot a grizzly bear, captured outlaws, learned the ways of people not of his own social class, and, above all, healed his broken heart.

He published a book about his experiences (not his first—that was in law school) and returned to politics. In 1886, he ran for mayor of New York and lost. A month later, he married again, a childhood friend, twenty-five-year-old Edith Kermit Carow, in London. Ten months later, son Theodore Jr. was born.

Theodore Roosevelt never believed in wasting time.

He wrote prolifically and well, and served as a U.S. Civil Service Commissioner, resigning in 1895 to become New York City Police Commissioner, where he continued his reforming ways, disciplining and toughening a force not always New York's finest.

Appointed Assistant Secretary of the Navy by William McKinley, he labored to modernize the fleet. When war with Spain arrived in April 1898, Roosevelt leaped to enlist, raising a regiment of "Rough Riders" composed of his former North Dakota ranch hands, various other flotsam and jetsam from the rapidly disappearing American frontier, and Easterners of his own elevated social class. His pace, previously frenetic, was now cyclonic. He stormed San Juan Hill in July 1898 and captured not only a Spanish battlement but the public imagination. That November, he ran for governor. New York's Republican boss, the wily Tom Platt, wasn't crazy about having a reformer of TR's stripe in the executive mansion, but he was less enamored of having a Democrat there. Boss Platt needed a winner, and TR won.

Platt's fears proved warranted. Roosevelt wouldn't be bossed, wouldn't be bought. In November 1899, Vice President Garret Hobart died, and Platt shoved Roosevelt into the vacancy in the 1900 election—and far from Albany. Not everyone approved. Ohio Senator Mark Hanna had engineered McKinley's ascent to the presidency, but he couldn't derail Platt's machinations. "Don't any of you realize," he shouted, "that there's only one life between that madman and the White House?"

In the vice-presidency, even TR might have faded into inertia and oblivion. But as the hand of death made him vice-president, it now made him president. In September 1901, twenty-eight-year-old immigrant anarchist Leon Czolgosz shot McKinley as he was touring Buffalo's Pan-American Exposition. "Now," Mark Hanna cursed, "that damn cowboy is president."

He was right to curse. Teddy Roosevelt would soon overturn the staid conservatism that McKinley and Hanna had represented. Roosevelt battled for railroad regulation, and for pure food and drug acts; forcibly acquired the land for the Panama Canal (from what he termed "a bunch of dagoes" in Colombia); sent the Great White Fleet to circle the globe; won the Nobel Peace Prize for ending the Russo–Japanese War; arbitrated international disputes in Morocco and Venezuela; designated 150 national forests and eighteen national monuments; and, for good measure, reduced the national debt by over $90 million.

Hanna and party conservatives—and they were still powerful—conspired to deny Roosevelt the nomination in 1904; and, as party conventions and not primaries controlled the great majority of delegates, they might well have given TR a tussle. But once again fate intervened: in February 1904, Mark Hanna died of typhoid. And amazingly, that same month, the Democrats' potentially strongest challenger, financier and former Navy Secretary William C. Whitney, died of appendicitis. Roosevelt won a second term in a walk.

Teddy departed on his own steam in 1908. Still only fifty, he handpicked an heir, his fifty-one-year-old Secretary of War, William Howard Taft, threatening his remaining adversaries in the party: "They'll take Taft or they'll get me."

Taft was a good man, but no Roosevelt. He wasn't even close. Conservative, self-effacing, judicial in temperament (he wanted to be Chief

Justice of the Supreme Court; his ambitious and demanding wife Helen demanded he be president)—and cartoonishly overweight—that was Big Bill Taft. Taft, who during his presidency weighed three hundred pounds, once reported back from the Philippines, where he was then Governor-General: "Stood trip well. Rode horseback twenty-five miles."

Secretary of War Elihu Root wired back: "How is the horse?"

Not surprisingly, Roosevelt tired of his idea of Taft as his replacement—actually, of the idea of *anyone* as his replacement—almost faster than the above-referenced equine must have wearied of Taft. On March 2, 1909—two days before Taft's inaugural—*Collier's Weekly* correspondent Mark Sullivan asked TR, "How do you really think Taft will make out?"

"He's all right. He means well and he'll do his best," TR grudgingly admitted, and then stuck the knife in. "But he's weak."

Egos aside, policy divided the two men—personnel, the tariff, anti-trust strategy, and conservation. Despite the fact that Taft, in little more than half the time, had initiated eighty anti-trust actions to Roosevelt's twenty-five and dedicated more land to conservation than had TR, party progressives rebelled against Taft.

Initially, TR remained uncharacteristically circumspect. Old personal feelings played a part. Calculation might have, too. If TR waited, he might return to the presidency in 1916. But if Roosevelt didn't challenge Taft, Wisconsin Senator Robert La Follette might. "Fighting Bob" had long enjoyed a reputation as, perhaps, the nation's orneriest progressive, first as a governor, then in the Senate. He announced a challenge to Taft in June 1911, assuming TR's support. He didn't have it; and when he suffered a mental breakdown delivering a speech in Philadelphia in February 1912, the die was cast: La Follette was out. Roosevelt would run.

And so would Taft. He had never wanted the presidency, and he wanted it less since Helen Taft had suffered a stroke in May 1909. More hurt than angered by TR's actions and attitudes, Taft nonetheless refused to be driven from office. "Even a rat in a corner," Taft sputtered to a Maryland audience, "will fight."

In primary states, Roosevelt captured 281 delegates to Taft's 71. It did Roosevelt little good. Most delegates were selected in party conventions, by Taft-appointed postmasters and judges and customs-house flunkies. The Rough Rider never stood a chance. Yet, what TR lacked in votes, he had in the volume of his voice, screaming bloody murder that Taft had pilfered delegates in the back rooms.

When the Republicans convened at Chicago's cavernous Coliseum in June 1912, the fighting escalated. Seventy-four delegates were contested. Taft won virtually all of them, and Roosevelt's supporters cried foul once again. And loudly. Columbia University president Nicholas Murray Butler commented to Pennsylvania United States Senator Boies Penrose, on the Roosevelt camp's riotous behavior. "Oh," Penrose, a Taft man, calmly responded, "those are the corks, bottles, and banana peels washed up by the Roosevelt tide!"

Butler never forgot Penrose's words: "To anyone who had ever seen a ferry-slip on the Hudson River at high tide with a west wind blowing," he would write, "this was a perfect description."

Finally, the Roosevelt forces could take no more and could remain in the Republican Party no longer. As Roosevelt biographer William Roscoe Thayer described it:

> There was one dramatic moment which . . . has had no counterpart in a National Convention. When the Machine had succeeded, in spite of protests and evidence, in stealing the two delegates from California, the friends of Mr. Taft gave triumphant cheers. Then the Roosevelt men rose up as one man and sent forth a mighty cheer which astonished their opponents. It was a cheer in which were mingled indignation and scorn, and, above all, relief. Strictly interpreted, it meant that those men who had sat for four days and seen their wishes thwarted, by what they regarded as fraud, and had held on in the belief that this fraud could not continue to the end, that a sense of fairness would return and rule the Regulars, now realized that Fraud would concede nothing and that their Cause was lost. And they felt a great load lifted. No obligation bound them any longer to the Republican Party which had renounced honesty in its principles and fair play in its practice. Henceforth they could go out and take any step they chose to promote their Progressive doctrines.

Two California votes didn't make much difference. The final vote was Taft 561, Roosevelt 107, La Follette 41, Senator Albert B. Cummins of

Iowa 17, Charles Evans Hughes 2, Absent 7—and 348 present and not voting. Roosevelt's crowd was so disgusted that it had not even placed his name in nomination.

At least not there, not then. Two thousand delegates and alternates representing a new party—the Progressives, the "Bull Moose Party" (named after TR exclaimed to a newsman: "I'm feeling like a bull moose!")—reassembled at Chicago's Orchestra Hall on August 6, nominating Roosevelt for president and fiery California Governor Hiram W. Johnson for vice president. Their platform demanded women's suffrage, an income tax, an inheritance tax, the direct election of United States senators, the recall of judicial decisions, an end to child labor, a minimum wage for women, tariff reform, and—rather pointedly—a ban on federal officeholders as national convention delegates.

Conservatives, and even moderates, expressed alarm. The *New York Times* categorized the Progressive conclave as "a convention of fanatics," then thought better of it: "It was not a convention at all. It was an assemblage of religious enthusiasts. It was such a convention as Peter the Hermit held. It was a Methodist camp following[,] done over into political terms."

Nor did the *Times* think much of Roosevelt himself. TR, it fumed:

. . . preaches contempt for law, defiance of law, Government without Law. . . . He would set up despotism and tyranny, the unlimited despotism of the majority which is more dangerous than the despotism of one monarch, and they call it emancipation. He writes whole pages of socialistic doctrine into his address and his platform. . . . His followers and his worshippers are quite without perception of the moral defects and delinquencies of the dangerous temperamental aberrations of THEODORE ROOSEVELT.

But for others, it was hard *not* to worship TR. He was bigger than life, a force of nature, maybe even bulletproof. On Monday evening, October 14, 1912, Roosevelt paused at Milwaukee's Hotel Gilpatrick en route to address followers at that city's Coliseum. Shadowing him, from Charlestown to Atlanta to Chattanooga to Evansville to Indianapolis to Chicago and finally to Milwaukee, was a thirty-six-year-old Bavarian immigrant, former saloonkeeper John Flammang Schrank of 370 East Tenth Street, New York City. Fanatically opposed to a third presidential term, Schrank fancied himself McKinley's "avenger."

Roosevelt entered a waiting limousine. Schrank drew a .38-caliber revolver from his coat, aiming at Roosevelt's head. Schrank squeezed the trigger. Roosevelt's secretary, Albert H. Marti, noticed a "flash of metal" and grabbed Schrank about the neck, deflecting the shot into TR's chest. The bullet tore through the fifty-page speech Roosevelt had nestled inside his jacket pocket, and through the metal spectacle case TR also kept jammed there. The slug ripped three inches into TR—just short of vital organs.

Roosevelt, being TR, didn't even realize he was hit until a bodyguard noticed the bullet hole in his jacket. The Rough Rider reached inside and felt warm, fresh blood.

At the Coliseum, he told the crowd: "I'm going to ask you to be very quiet. And please excuse me from making you a very long speech. I'll do the best I can, but you see, there's a bullet in my body. But it's nothing. I'm not hurt badly." He unbuttoned his coat and vest, displaying to the crowd his blood-soaked white shirt. For over an hour he spoke. Only then did he consent to enter a hospital.

By the time he returned to the campaign, everyone knew that the election was over. Said one Vermont Republican newspaper editor: "Vote for Taft, pray for Roosevelt, and bet on Wilson." Former United States Senator Chauncey Depew phrased it less delicately, regarding Taft and Teddy: "The only question now is which corpse gets the most flowers."

Democrat Woodrow Wilson won just 41.8 percent of the vote, more than sufficient in the great Republican train wreck of 1912. And Wilson in the White House was enough to channel TR's vitriol away from Taft and the conservatives to a new target.

By 1916, Roosevelt was again a Republican, blasting Wilson as a "damned Presbyterian hypocrite" and a "Byzantine logothete." He weighed another run ("The country ought not to take me unless it is in an heroic mood"), but intra-party wounds were still too fresh. Former New York governor Charles Evans Hughes, a moderate progressive, got the nod—and Roosevelt's public support. Privately, Roosevelt dismissed Hughes as a "bearded iceberg" and the "whiskered Wilson," once remarking that the only difference between Wilson and Hughes was "a shave."

Wilson narrowly defeated Hughes but could not overcome TR's antipathy. The Wilson–Hughes election had hinged on the ongoing European war. Should America fight? Wilson's argument that "a nation may be too proud to fight" disgusted the increasingly belligerent Roosevelt ("The man . . . too proud to fight is in practice always treated as just proud enough to be kicked"). Were we prepared for combat if war came? Roosevelt argued that Wilson had been derelict in his duty.

"These are the shadows . . . of deeds that were never done"; he fumed at Cooper Union in November 1916, "the shadows of lofty words that were followed by no action; the shadows of the tortured dead."

War arrived in April 1917. As in 1898, TR longed for combat, volunteering to fight in France. His cousin, Assistant Secretary of the Navy Franklin Roosevelt, helped arrange a meeting with Secretary of War Newton D. Baker. Baker said no. Theodore Roosevelt appealed to Wilson. They met at the White House. Wilson found Teddy to be "a great big boy [with] a sweetness about him that is very compelling"—but not compelling enough for Wilson, fearful of granting TR too big a spotlight, to relent. Not surprisingly, TR was incensed. That August, he wrote his friend and supporter, the progressive editor of the *Emporia* (Kansas) *Gazette*, forty-nine-year-old William Allen White:

What is perfectly impossible, what represents really nauseous hypocrisy, is to say that we have gone to war to make the world safe for democracy, in April, when sixty days previously we had been announcing that we wished a "Peace without victory," and had no concern with the "cause or object" of the war. I do not regard any speech as a great speech when it is obviously hypocritical and in bad faith; nor do I regard the making of such a speech of service to the world. I regard it as a damage to the cause of morality and decency. So far as concerns what Wilson has done in the past few months, I think on the whole it has been badly done; and, what is more, that it has been badly done because of very evil traits on his part. He was emphatically right about the draft. He was emphatically wrong about the militia and about turning down the volunteer system as a vitally necessary stopgap. He took these attitudes because he was much more anxious to spite [General] Leonard Wood and myself than he was to save the country. . . . To have appointed [pacifists like Secretary of the Navy Josephus] Daniels and [Secretary of War Newton] Baker originally was evil enough; to have kept them on during a great war was a criminal thing. The greatest damage that can be done to the cause of decency in this country is to stand by Wilson in such a way as to imply that we approve or condone his utterly cynical disregard of considerations of patriotism and national efficiency and his eagerness to sacrifice anything if to do so will advance his own political interests. He has just one kind of ability; a most sinister and adroit power of appealing in his own interest to all that is foolish and base in our people. He not only appeals to base and foolish men; he appeals also to the Mr. Hyde who, even in many good and honorable men, lurks behind the Dr. Jekyll in their souls.

His public statements were barely more restrained. While Socialists and radicals were being jailed for opposing the war and the administration, Roosevelt, being Roosevelt, was beyond prosecution, an irony not missed by the administration itself. In October 1917, Navy Secretary Josephus Daniels recorded in his diary:

T. R. at large, writing and speaking in disparagement of America's preparation for war, is helping Germany more than the little fellows who are being arrested for giving aid and comfort to the enemy. Can *Kansas City Star*, containing his allusions to soldiers training with broom-sticks, be excluded from the mails along with other papers spreading what is construed as seditious? B—— [probably Postmaster General Burleson] said he was having paper read carefully and would not hesitate to act.

In May 1918, TR, en route to a speech in Des Moines, stopped off at Chicago's Blackstone Hotel. By chance, so had Taft, who learned in the elevator that Roosevelt was not only a fellow guest but also currently in the hotel dining room. He could stand their separation no longer.

Ordering the elevator operator to reverse course, he headed for the dining room. Heads turned. A murmur turned into a cheer, growing louder and louder as Taft shoehorned himself between tables to reach Roosevelt. Teddy, ignorant of what was transpiring, thought that, amid the din, he heard: "Theodore."

As Roosevelt remembered it, he:

> . . . looked up just as Taft reached the table with his hand stuck out. There was so much noise being made by the people in the room[,] I am not quite sure what he said. I think it was "Theodore, I am glad to see you." I grabbed his hand and told him how glad I was to see him. By Godfrey, I never was so surprised in my life. . . . But, wasn't it a gracious thing for him to do. . . . I never felt happier over anything in my life. . . . It was splendid of Taft. . . . I've seen old Taft and we're in perfect harmony on everything.

The war had revived and largely re-united the Republican Party, as well as rejuvenating TR's presidential chances. Republicans could taste the White House, and their ambitions made them ignore old wounds and grudges. Even hard-shell conservatives now flocked to the Roosevelt banner.

Some wanted him to run for governor of New York in 1918, but New York already had a Republican governor, and TR refused the honor. There was, of course, another reason: his health. In December 1913, he and his son Kermit had embarked on a Rooseveltian expedition to explore the wild Amazon basin, a rash, ill-planned adventure—well beyond the physical capacity of a fifty-six-year-old man. Roosevelt contracted malaria. Lucky to return alive, he was never the same again.

Still, he now was not only the "leader" of the Republicans; he was their presumptive candidate. At the March 1918 Maine Republican Convention, delegates hailed him as "the next President of the United States." The *New York Herald* stated flat-out that he would be "the Republican candidate for President in 1920."

While TR himself was not allowed to wear a military uniform, his four sons—Theodore Jr., Kermit, Archie, and Quentin (TR's favorite)—did, and he cared deeply about them. "All that is near to me in the male line, is in France," he wrote. "If they do not come back[,] what is the Presidency to me?"

It was soon more than a theoretical question. On July 10, 1918, Quentin, serving in the Army Air Corps near Chateau-Thierry, downed his first enemy aircraft. Three days later, his plane disappeared. Faint and desperate hope initially existed, but those who saw TR in the twilight world of uncertainty, not knowing if his son lived or not, saw a man as racked by pain and hurt as they had ever seen. Soon, it was official: his hope was false. The young lion was gone.

Words had never failed TR. They did not now. Eulogizing his dead son, he said:

> Only those are fit to live who do not fear to die; and none are fit to die who have shrunk from the joy of life. Both life and death are parts of the same Great Adventure. Never yet was worthy adventure worthily carried through by the man who put his personal safety first. Pride is the portion only of those who know bitter sorrow or the foreboding of bitter sorrow. But all of us who give service, and stand ready for sacrifice, are the torch-bearers. We run with the torches until we fall, content if we can then pass them to the hands of the other runners. The torches whose flame is brightest are borne by the gallant men at the front, by the gallant women whose husbands and lovers[,] whose sons and brothers are at the front. These men are high of soul, as they face their fate on the shell-shattered earth, or in the skies above or in the waters beneath; and no less high of soul are the women with torn hearts and shining eyes; the girls whose boy-lovers have been struck down in their golden morning, and the mothers and wives to whom word has been brought that henceforth they must walk in the shadow.
>
> These are the torch-bearers; these are they who have dared the Great Adventure.

Theodore's heart was broken, but he had one last race to run. "There was only one way to give Quentin's death meaning," wrote historian Thomas Fleming: "Woodrow Wilson had to die an equivalent political death. His presidency must be—and would be—destroyed."

Yet Roosevelt hesitated. His time for great adventures was running short. Tired and sick, he carried with him strains of Amazonian malaria, and, worse, the hurt and despair of a grieving father. In late 1918, *New York Evening Mail* editor Henry L. Stoddard urged him to run and received an unambiguous *No.* "I shall never make another campaign tour," TR vowed, "nor shall I be the candidate. . . . Let 1920 take care of itself when it comes—but I shall not be the candidate. . . . I shall make no public announcement now, but I will do so long enough before 1920 to get out of the way of anyone who wants the nomination."

But to others, he admitted that old bonds of duty were too strong to break. Author and political associate Joseph Bucklin Bishop also spoke with him in late 1918. Roosevelt repeated his earlier weary disquiet but, nonetheless, left the door open:

I am indifferent to the subject. I would not lift a finger to get the nomination. Since Quentin's death[,] the world seems to have shut down upon me. . . . If they [Roosevelt's other sons] do not come back, what would the Presidency mean to me? . . . I have only a few remaining years, and nothing could give me greater joy than to spend them with my family. I have been President for seven years and I am not eager to be President again. But if the leaders of the party come to me and say that they are convinced that I am the man the people want and the only man who can be elected, and that they are all for me, I don't see how I could refuse to run.

All the while, he hammered away at Wilson, shifting to Wilson's plans for the victorious peace now in sight. Roosevelt wished to be as fierce in peace as at war. He fumed:

The trouble with Mr. Wilson's utterances . . . and the utterances of acquiescence in them by European statesmen, is that they are still absolutely in the stage of rhetoric, like the Fourteen Points. Would it not be well to begin with the League which we actually have in existence, the League of the Allies who have fought through this great war? Let us at the peace table see that real justice is done as among these allies and that while the sternest reparation is demanded from our foes . . . yet should anything be done in the spirit of mere vengeance? Then let us agree to extend the privileges of the League as rapidly as their conduct warrants it to other nations. Let each nation reserve to itself and for its own decision to clearly set forth questions which are non-justiciable.

On November 2, 1918, at Carnegie Hall, Roosevelt addressed the Circle for Negro War Relief at Carnegie Hall on the topic "The American Negro and the War." Introduced by the NAACP's W. E. B. Du Bois, he took a veiled shot at Wilson's segregationist racial policies:

I don't ask for any man that he shall, because of his race, be given any privilege. All I ask is that in his ordinary civil and political rights, in his right to work, to enjoy life and liberty and the pursuit of happiness, that as regards these rights he be given the treatment that we would give him if he was an equally good man of another color.

Three days later, America went to the polls, delivering a solid Republican Congressional electoral victory—a stinging rebuke to its president. "Our allies and our enemies and Mr. Wilson himself," Roosevelt fairly chortled, "should all understand that Mr. Wilson has no authority whatever to speak for the American people at this time. His leadership has been emphatically repudiated by them . . . and all his utterances every which way have ceased to have any shadow of right to be accepted as expressive of the will of the American people."

That election day, TR was not well, suffering from what the press called "a slight degree of sciatica." His doctor ordered him to stay home. He walked a mile to the polls, but then missed a speech in Pittsburgh. By Monday afternoon, November 11, he was transported to Roosevelt Hospital in New York—with what was now termed "an attack of lumbago."

As November turned into December, Roosevelt remained hospitalized with his "lumbago," in actuality, a severe "inflammatory rheumatism" effecting virtually his every joint. William Allen White, en route to Europe, visited and found his hero "propped up in a bed, sweet as a cherub." The talk quickly turned political; White revealed that Roosevelt's old associate, General Leonard Wood, was preparing a run for the presidency. "Well," TR responded, "probably I shall get in this thing in June [1919]." He revealed that he had secured the support of his old conservative foes, but still intended to pursue a progressive, if not radical, GOP platform in 1920, including such measures as old-age pensions and the eight-hour workday.

"I am satisfied," White recalled, "that, if the Colonel had lived, he would have been the Republican nominee and the country would have had, in workable terms, from a Republican administration, much of the social program that came a dozen years later under the second Roosevelt. It would have been adopted in normal times. . . . It would not have disturbed economic and industrial traffic, and a great cataclysm might have been avoided."

Teddy's younger sister, Corinne Roosevelt Robinson, also visited. "Well," he confided to her, "anyway, no matter what comes, I have kept the promise that I made to myself when I was twenty-one."

"What promise, Theodore? You made many promises to yourself, and I am sure you have kept them all."

"I promised myself that I would work *up to the hilt* until I was sixty, and I have done it. I have kept my promise, and now, even if I should be an invalid—I should not like to be an invalid—but even if I should be an invalid, or if I should die [and here he snapped his fingers], what difference would it make?"

"Theodore," Corrine asked, "do you remember what you said to me nearly a year ago when you thought you were dying in this same hospital? You said that you were glad it was not one of your boys that was dying at that time in this place, for they could die for their country. Do you feel the same way now?"

"Yes, just the same way. I wish that I might, like Quentin, have died for my country."

In the fall of 1918, before TR's hospitalization, his campaign manager, John T. King, had asked him to receive a pair of visitors. The request revealed just how much the Old Guard had reconciled itself to the Rough Rider. Pennsylvania's Boies Penrose and Indiana's James Watson were among the Senate's most conservative members. Penrose officially commanded the Pennsylvania Republican Party and unofficially led the national party's conservative faction. Before meeting with TR, he conferred with his fellow stand-patters at his apartment at Washington's Hotel Willard. "There is but one candidate for president," he said matter-of-factly. "He is the only candidate. I mean Theodore Roosevelt."

Someone queried Penrose if he now personally supported TR. Penrose shot back: "No, I don't like him. I once despised him. But that doesn't alter the fact that Theodore Roosevelt is now the one and only possible Republican candidate in 1920. He will surely receive the nomination."

Penrose and Watson's visit was friendly, indeed jocular. To Watson, Roosevelt seemed fine, possessing his usual "buoyancy and . . . vitality."

Back in his car, Penrose remarked: "Jim, the Colonel won't be with us very long."

"What do you mean by that?" Watson asked edgily.

"Why," Penrose responded, "didn't you see that he is a marked man?"

"I certainly did not," Watson protested nervously. "He seemed to me just as vigorous and as explosive and as full of life as ever, and I don't know what you discovered to lead you to believe that he is anywhere near dissolution."

Penrose continued: "My father was as great a doctor as ever lived in Pennsylvania, my brother is a natural diagnostician of great ability, and I have a sort of intuition or instinct in sizing up a man physically. I tell you now that Colonel Roosevelt will not be alive in three months and that your promise to support him will prove of no avail."

Roosevelt left the hospital on Christmas Eve 1918, contending that he "felt bully." Reaching the elevator, he faltered but refused help. "I am not sick," he protested, "and it will give the wrong impression." His doctor warned that it would take six to eight weeks for a full recovery. He did not disclose to his patient that three weeks previously, TR had suffered a pulmonary embolism.

On Sunday, January 5, 1919, TR, though bedridden, worked an eleven-hour day and planned to meet with the Republican National Committee to discuss party matters. He leafed through a book on pheasants. He dictated a statement to the American Defense Society ("We have room for but one flag . . . we have room for but one language"). That night, he seemed at peace, or, at least, as much as a man of his tempera-ment might be—though, at 10:30, he felt odd, as if both his breathing and his heart had stopped. "I am perfectly all right," he told his wife, explaining how he, of course, knew that neither was the case, "but I have a curious feeling." He went to bed, instructing his black servant, James Otis, "Put out the light, please."

At 4 A.M., Otis, sleeping in the next room, heard odd sounds coming from TR's room. TR was having trouble breathing. Alarmed, Otis rushed in.

Someone handed a telegram to Woodrow Wilson in Modena, Italy. He unfolded it, read it, exhibited a brief moment of shock, then smiled a smile of "transcendent triumph." Theodore Roosevelt was dead. David Lloyd George also witnessed Wilson's reaction. Tough, cynical, worldly, Lloyd George was shocked by "the outburst of acrid detestation which flowed from Wilson's lips."

Others displayed more heart. Vice President Thomas Marshall responded with eloquence: "Death had to take him sleeping. For if Roo-sevelt had been awake, there would have been a fight."

Franklin and Eleanor Roosevelt, aboard the *George Washington* heading for the Paris Peace Conference, heard the news via wireless. FDR seemed unaware of the real state of Teddy's health. "My cousin's death was in every way a great shock[,] for we heard just before leaving that he was better—and he was after all not old," he wrote to Josephus Daniels. "But I cannot help think that he himself would have had it this way and that he has been spared a lingering illness of perhaps years."

Eleanor—whom TR had given away at her wedding—responded in an oddly impersonal way, more in the nature of an editorial writer than a favored niece. "Another big figure gone from our nation," said Eleanor, "the loss of his influence and example."

Admirers treasured his memory. On the day TR died, William Lawrence, Episcopal Bishop of Massachusetts, underwent surgery in his office. He paused to glance upward to a framed photograph of Teddy on the office wall. "No one can wince while Theodore is looking on," he remarked, and went ahead without anesthesia.

After Roosevelt and Taft had reconciled, TR had invited his old friend to visit Oyster Bay. The two often met, corresponded, and strategized in the interim, but Taft had never followed up on that invitation. Now he did.

Taft trudged from the train station to Oyster Bay's Christ Episcopal Church, pushing his bulk gently through the throngs of neighbors surrounding the little red-gabled building. Roosevelt's former secretary, William Loeb, noticed him at the door and maneuvered him through the crowd to a pew full of the family servants. Roosevelt's son, Archie, still healing from wounds suffered in France, took Taft's hand, commanding: "You're a dear personal friend and you must come up farther."

The service was spare and solemn. The church's great organ remained silent. Roosevelt's favorite hymn, "How Firm a Foundation," was recited, not sung. Taft went by car to the cemetery, forcing himself up the steep hill to the grave, standing in the melting snows and matted-down grass of midwinter Long Island. He felt uncomfortable, perhaps wondering what others thought of his presence. So he stood apart, though not so far away that the others could not hear him joining in the Lord's Prayer.

And he wept. They could hear that, too. No one there, not widow, nor son nor daughter, cried more or longer than TR's friend, William Howard Taft.

## Chapter 5

~

## "A Turtle on a Log"

Warren Harding was a dark horse—but not all that dark.

As 1920 opened—and with TR dead—the aging but still handsome Ohio senator found himself numbered among the party's top three presidential possibilities, nestled just below war hero General Leonard Wood and Illinois's capable governor, Frank O. Lowden.

America, becoming a land of cities and bright lights and jazz, grew more nostalgic regarding its small-town and rural roots. If anyone epitomized small-town boosterism, it was Senator Warren Gamaliel Harding.

Born near Corsica (now Blooming Grove), Ohio, on November 2, 1865, Harding was the oldest of eight children born to Dr. George Harding and his wife Phoebe Dickerson Harding—who ultimately would obtain her own homeopathic medical license. The Hardings later moved to Caledonia, in nearby Marion County, where Dr. Harding acquired a modest weekly paper, *The Argus*, providing Warren with an introduction to life in the newspaper business.

Harding never strayed much from his roots. Following graduation from the rather unimpressive Ohio Central College (it even unimpressed Warren), the family moved to the Marion County seat, the small but growing city of Marion. In 1884, with two friends and $300, nineteen-year-old Warren acquired the worst of Marion's three papers, the insolvent *Marion Daily Pebble*. He renamed it the *Star*.

His partners soon departed: the first after a matter of weeks; the second when Harding spent good money to install an office telephone.

Harding leaned the *Star* toward the Republicans and made it a success, in the process antagonizing Marion's richest and most irascible citizen, merchant Amos H. Kling.

Mr. Kling had a daughter named Florence. In 1880, a pregnant Florence had married—perhaps only by the common law—a local drunk named Henry Athenton DeWolfe. The marriage failed. Florence supported herself by giving piano lessons. Her father refused to provide her support, took her son away, and raised him as his own.

Eventually, Florence set her sights on Marion's most eligible bachelor, and her father's bête noir, Warren Harding. Amos Kling objected. Florence didn't care. The couple married on July 8, 1891. Mr. and Mrs. Amos Kling didn't attend the ceremony. Though the bride claimed to be twenty-nine, she was actually just shy of thirty-one. The groom was twenty-six.

Amos Kling *literally* regarded his new son-in-law as his bête noir. Long-standing local rumors claimed that the Hardings were part black. Kling muttered—and sometimes shouted—that his new son-in-law was a "nigger." In response, Dr. Harding once beat Kling up on the streets.

Florence had her revenge served cold, helping her husband make the *Star* the county's premier paper, managing its office and overseeing its newsboys. Together, Warren and Florence grew rich—not as rich as Amos Kling, but rich enough for revenge.

Along the way, Warren Harding made himself a community leader, Marion's great booster. He participated in the town's events, subscribed to new businesses, and ran his paper to give value but not offense. He composed a code for the *Marion Star*. It was not heroic, but it was decent, and he tried to keep to it:

> If it can be avoided, never bring ignominy on a man or child, in telling of the misdeeds or misfortunes of a relative. Don't wait to be asked, but do it without the asking. . . .
>
> Never needlessly hurt the feelings of anybody.
>
> Be decent; be fair; be generous.
>
> I want this paper to be so conducted that it can go into homes without destroying the innocence of any child. . . .

In 1895, he eyed a political career, seeking the post of county auditor. Marion County, however, was solidly Democratic. Harding, not unexpectedly, lost. He returned to the campaign trail the following year—not as a candidate, but as a surrogate speaker for Ohio's own presidential candidate, William McKinley. Three years later, the thirty-three-year-old Harding fought an uphill race for the state senate. His four-county 13th District was as staunchly Democrat as Marion County. Harding won anyway, garnering four times the votes of the GOP's previous nominee.

In the state senate, his easy manner won friends. Soon he was the Republican floor leader. Harding eyed the governorship in 1904, but party bosses shunted him into the lieutenant-governorship. Lieutenant Governor Harding used the position to stump the state, honing his oratorical skills, and politicking among the Republican faithful. His political prospects seemed bright; but with Florence sick with the kidney disease nephritis, he declined re-election, returning to Marion to care for both her and the *Star*.

He also cared for his neighbor's wife, the neighbor being local department store owner James E. Phillips. The wife, Carrie Fulton Phillips, was one of Marion's more beautiful and charming young women. The Hardings and the Phillipses were close friends, Warren and strawberry blond Carrie closer still.

Logistically, it was all quite easy. Florence was hospitalized in nearby Columbus. Jim Phillips, suffering from exhaustion (and depression from the death of his only son in 1904) was at Michigan's Battle Creek Sanitarium. Carrie Phillips was drop-dead gorgeous, fun-loving, and, evidently, sexually compatible with Warren—everything Florence was not. Carrie and Warren consummated their affair. They continued it in numerous out-of-town assignations. They continued it for years.

It was, however, not Harding's first dalliance. In 1894, he had impregnated Florence's childhood friend, Susan Hodder. She delivered their child in Nebraska. It would not be his last affair—or child.

As Harding could not resist female temptation, he could not resist political temptation. In 1908, he eyed Joseph B. Foraker's United States Senate seat. The state legislature appointed not Harding, but Congressman Theodore Elijah Burton.

The year Harding chose for his political return could not have much worse—1910, the beginning of the great Republican schism. Drafted by the party for governor, he was assigned a suicide mission. Theodore Roosevelt stumped Ohio on his behalf, but an estimated quarter-million Republican progressives stayed home, and incumbent Judson Harmon won by 100,377 votes, the largest plurality ever provided an Ohio Democratic governor.

More significant, however, than Harding's lackluster showing was the identity of his new campaign manager, Harry Micajah Daugherty, a pillar of the Ohio party's stand-pat wing, wheeler-dealer par excellence, and a very successful and wealthy state lobbyist. Daugherty had served in the Ohio legislature and as state Republican chairman—a long time ago. He still fancied himself electable, but no one else did. He sought the governorship (twice), the attorney-generalship, a house seat, and the U.S. Senate—all fruitlessly. There was just something about him. Even professional politicians found him too obviously shady. His unseemly reputation ignited a minor national scandal in January 1912, when he helped secure a presidential pardon for Charles W. Morse—serving a fifteen-year sentence for misappropriating Bank of North America funds—on the grounds of "incurable and progressive" conditions of health. Morse was fine, went back into business, outlived Warren Harding, outlived his second wife, was again indicted, outlived Taft, and died at seventy-seven in 1933.

But before Daugherty's scandal unfolded, Harding dealt with a more personal one. In the summer of 1911, Florence opened a letter—and found out about her husband and her neighbor. She contemplated divorce, but stayed. In an odd way, they drew closer.

But as Harding's relationships with Daugherty—and even, strangely, with Florence—deepened, his less-than-sturdy ties to party progressives frayed even further. With the Roosevelt–Taft rift widening, Harding, the ultimate party regular, predictably followed Taft, flaying TR in the *Star* as "utterly without conscience and regard for truth, the greatest fakir of all times." He meant it.

Usually cautious (save, of course, for sexual matters), Harding now abandoned caution. He compared TR to Aaron Burr. Roosevelt, posited Harding, possessed "the same overbearing disposition and ungovernable temper [as Burr], the same ruthlessness . . . the same tendency to bully and browbeat. . . ." The words would return to haunt him.

But that was in the future. Harding's loyalty, his oratorical skills, and perhaps his sheer availability when few others wanted the job, led Taft to select Harding to nominate him at the 1912 Republican National Convention. Harding's speech may not have been a masterpiece of oratory, but it was of pro-Taft party regularity.

Even in such fractious times, Harding could not help trying to mollify opponents. Cincinnati Republican Congressman Nicholas Longworth had higher ambitions. At the convention, Harding offered to aid Longworth in securing the gubernatorial nomination—not that it was worth much that year. In 1906, Longworth had married TR's only daughter, Alice Roosevelt. Formerly a precocious child, she had grown into a spectacularly precocious adult. Still smarting from Harding's attacks on her father, she snapped at Warren: "One should not accept favors from crooks."

"I must say it was a little obtuse and raw of Harding to make that offer to Nick in my presence," Alice would later muse. "Insight and taste, however, were not his strong points."

When the dust settled on the "War of 1912," the Republican Party had fallen to its lowest ebb. Harding's *Marion Star* continued the intra-party fight, bitterly commenting:

> Well, the mad Roosevelt has a new achievement to his credit. He succeeded in defeating the party that furnished him a job for nearly all of his manhood days after leaving the ranch, and showed his gratitude for the presidency, at that party's hands. The eminent fakir can now turn to raising hell, his specialty, along other lines.

Party politics may have grown unpleasant, but Harding could enjoy other distractions, most notably Carrie Phillips. Their affair continued—and torridly—as evidenced by this letter he wrote her in 1912:

> I love your mouth, I love your fire
> I love the way you stir desire
> I love your size and daintiness
> Love every thread in which you dress
> I love you garb'd, but naked MORE!
> Love your beauty to thus adore.

Luck plays its part, a very large part, in politics, and luck's favorite companion is timing. In 1910 and 1912, Harding's timing had been atrocious. In 1914, it was very good. In the first year that Ohioans voted directly for their United States senators, Theodore Burton had pretty much botched his chances for re-election and knew it. His withdrawal created a slot for Harding—a marvelous opportunity in a year when Republican chances were excellent for retaining the seat.

Harding, however, still carried wounds from his 1908 and 1910 setbacks. And besides, life was good in Marion. He was not sure he should enter the race. Harry Daugherty thought otherwise. "I found him [Harding] sunning himself like a turtle on a log," Daugherty later boasted, "and I pushed him into the water."

Popular history depicts the Harding–Daugherty relationship as of the master-and-puppet variety, with the wily Daugherty pulling the strings. But their partnership was really far more complex than that. Warren Harding may not have been monogamous, nor intellectual, may never have been as cunning as Daugherty, but he was also no dolt. Nor was he a political neophyte. In his own way, he was a very smooth and successful political operator—and he knew it. If Daugherty acted a tad uppity, the almost invariably gentle Harding was fully capable of slapping him down, as witnessed by this December 20, 1918 correspondence:

> The trouble with you, my dear Daugherty, in your political relations with me, is that you appraise my political sense so far below par that you have no confidence in me or my judgement. Pray do not think[,] because I can and do listen in politeness to much that is said to me, that I am always being "strung." I cannot and will not suspect everyone of wanting to use me. I must and will believe in professed political friendship until I find myself imposed upon. It is the only way that I know of to political happiness.

Unfortunately, in some of those cases, he should have listened to Daugherty—and he should have listened to what others said *about* Daugherty.

By now—with a senatorial race in view—Harding had switched gears, regarding TR's Progressives as long-lost brothers. The Republican Party was healing, and Warren Harding was a healer. "Our action," he wrote, "is to assure those who got off the reservation in 1912 . . . that they are welcome to continue with the old party."

It was sound strategy. He won the primary comfortably, if not handily, receiving 88,540 votes to 76,817 votes for former Senator Foraker, and 52,237 for a political unknown, businessman Ralph Cole—but still far less than a majority of votes cast.

The general election proved far simpler, with Harding facing weak opposition, Ohio Attorney General Timothy S. Hogan. In 1912, Hogan had barely won election, though securing far fewer votes than any other Democrat in that landslide year. The reason: Hogan's Catholicism—Ohio would not elect a Roman Catholic governor or senator until 1944. Bigots flooded Ohio with anti-Catholic material. "Read the *Menace* and get the dope," read one piece of doggerel; "Go to the polls and beat the Pope."

Harding won by 102,000 votes, 73,000 votes more than that year's next most popular Republican, largely because 70,000 anti-Catholic Democrats and Socialists didn't bother to mark their ballots.

By now, Amos Kling had long since made his peace with his son-in-law. "My daughter married a nigger," Kling still admitted, but magnanimously added, "but he's a smart nigger."

Harding settled into the United States Senate with ease—perhaps a little too much ease, missing two-thirds of all roll-call votes. Though hardly a leader, or identified with any particular issue, he again proved popular with colleagues. People thought of him as a possible dark horse—even for 1916's presidential race. New York Senator James W. Wadsworth Jr. pointed out Harding to his wife and said, "That's presidential timber."

Yet Progressives—TR among them—remembered his role in the acrimony of 1912. To the Rough Rider, Warren Harding remained "utterly unacceptable."

Nonetheless, the party selected Warren as temporary president of its 1916 convention and its keynote speaker. The *New York Times* mocked him: "His full name is Warren G. Harding and he is Senator from Ohio; but it is not necessary to burden one's memory with these statistics if one is merely trying to remember the names of persons likely to be president." Columnist Irvin S. Cobb dismissed Harding's speech as having "keyed nothing and was without note," but it did what it was meant to do—impress the party faithful. Warren Harding, just two years a Senator, was already a modest national figure.

In 1917, Warren Harding's complicated love life grew more complicated still. In Marion, there had been a girl, a schoolgirl really, named Nan Britton. In high school, she had developed a classic adolescent crush on Marion's most prominent citizen, mooning over Harding from afar, scribbling his name in her copybooks. In May 1917, now eighteen years old, Nan wrote to Harding from New York City, asking help in obtaining employment when she completed a secretarial course in three weeks' time. He secured for her a $16-per-week stenographic position at United States Steel. He was very friendly.

In mid-July 1917, the Senator traveled from Washington to New York. They registered at a "moderate-priced" Seventh Avenue hotel, but did not yet consummate their relationship, as Nan was still holding back. On Monday, July 30, they rendezvoused again, this time at the Hotel Imperial at Thirty-second and Broadway. "I became," she wrote primly, "Mr. Harding's bride—as he called me—on that day."

It was not the most romantic of experiences. Shortly after Nan became a "bride," the phone rang. "You've got the wrong number," Harding barked into the receiver. There was a hard knock at the door. Two men stormed in, demanding Nan's name. "Tell them the truth," Harding balefully advised; "they've got us."

He sat on the bed, pleading with the intruders: "I'll answer for both, won't I? Let this poor little girl go!" They curtly informed him he should have considered her safety before registering for a room. They asked her age. Harding lied. She was twenty-two, he said. Nan interrupted to say she was really twenty—another lie.

Every time Harding raised an objection, the men snapped, "Tell that to the judge." They were about to call the police, when one of them picked up the Senator's hat. Inside, he read the gold inscription, "W. G. Harding." Nan thought the two men became instantly "calm," even "respectful."

The embarrassed couple "finished dressing" and was escorted to a side entrance. Harding slipped one man twenty dollars. Safely inside a taxi, he turned to his paramour, confiding, "Gee, Nan, I never thought I would get out of that under a thousand dollars."

In February 1919, Nan Britton began suffering bouts of nausea. By month's end, she "knew for a certainty" that she was pregnant. She wrote Harding. He wrote back. She thought he wanted to keep the child, though another option was clearly crossing his worried mind. They met once or twice in New York, then at Washington's New Willard Hotel. "I do not fear for the future, after the child comes," he repeatedly told her, "but only for the now." His words gave Nan even more hope that he wanted to keep the child.

He sighed, "You know, Nan, I have never been a father"—but then purchased for her a bottle of Dr. Humphrey's No. 11 tablets, which Florence had used for birth control. Nan thought the idea was ridiculous. She was too far gone to be helped by *that*. "No faith, no works," her lover joked.

Now he tried a new tack:

> He sat in the big chair by the window and took me on his lap. He told me how I had filled him with the first *real* longing he had known to have children. He said he had wanted them, yes, but Mrs. Harding had been a mother when he married her, and she had not wanted any more children, and, he reminded me, "You know Mrs. Harding is older than I." I think very probably the glory and wonder of having a child or children could not be aroused within him to the fullest by Mrs. Harding because she had already shared the initial glory of that experience with another man. Mr. Harding always spoke disparagingly to me of Mrs. Harding, and in loving as well as in disposition and everything else he certainly failed to picture her as his ideal. Rather did I seem to be his ideal woman. This never failed to fill me with wonderment.

Harding trembled. He took her hand and stared out the window. He spoke to her as "his bride," "the perfect sweetheart and the perfect mother," of how they would go away together to some distant farm when he was finally freed from politics. Even Nan had trouble believing this story. She had heard it before. But now, his eyes welling with tears, she could almost believe.

Harding forced himself to continue: "and I would take you there,

Nan darling, as—my—wife." He grabbed her arms with real force. "Look at me, dearie! You would be my wife, wouldn't you? You would marry me, Nan? Oh, dearie, dearie . . . if only I could . . . if we could have our child—together!"

He never actually told her to keep the baby. Letters followed that made repeated, ominous references to medicine and "the knife." In one, he advised the latter: an abortion would be his choice. The thought repulsed Nan. She wrote back that she would have the child. Harding immediately responded. He was "strong for her." Motherhood was "the greatest experience a woman ever has." Harding had no real choice now but fatherhood, unless he considered divorce and disgrace as options. He moved Nan into an apartment at New York's Hotel La Salle, and later to a small house in Asbury Park, New Jersey. He bought her a sapphire-and-diamond ring. "We performed a sweet little ceremony with that ring," she recalled, "and he declared that I could not belong to him more utterly had we been joined together by fifty ministers." On October 22, 1919, Senator Warren Harding became a father. They named the baby Elizabeth Ann Christian.

But we are ahead of the story. The Republican healing process advanced, and even TR was in a forgiving mood (particularly after Harding introduced legislation to allow TR into the army), inviting Harding to Oyster Bay, realizing that in politics the support of old enemies may count for far more than that of old friends. Some even mentioned a possible Roosevelt–Harding ticket in 1920.

A scattered few believed Harding could head the ticket. Frank E. "Ed" Scobey, a Harding crony relocated to Texas, wrote him in November 1918: "Heretofore you have always told me you did not want . . . the Presidency—but no man is too big for the job if he can get it."

When Roosevelt died, Harding's chances immeasurably improved. In late January 1919, Harry Daugherty, not waiting for Harding's authorization, began rounding up delegates. That same month, Harding received an unlikely and prescient boost. Kansas City businessman E. Mont Reily, a member of the Missouri State Republican Committee, had never met Harding, but from afar he surveyed possible nominees and determined that the Ohioan was the party's best bet. He wrote to dozens of his "Fellow Republicans" explaining why:

1. Harding was relatively young, just fifty-three.
2. The Democrats would most likely nominate Ohio Governor James M. Cox; Republicans needed Harding to carry this usually swing state.
3. Harding was "not too far West to upset the traditions of the effete East; neither is he too far East to be unsatisfactory to the sturdy West."
4. Harding hailed from the state that was "the mother of Republican presidents."
5. He would "make a greater campaign than even McKinley could [since] he is a more attractive orator."
6. He was a loyal party man who "remained 'regular' and supported Taft" in 1912.
7. Most prophetically, Reily pointed out that Harding stood for "normal things, normal thinking and normal legislation." "Our motto for 1920," Reily proposed, "should be, 'Harding and Back to Normal.'"

Others, far more powerful than Reily, were seriously eying Harding. One day in the summer of 1919, Pennsylvania's Boies Penrose summoned Harding to his home. Indiana's James Watson remembered the scene:

> Penrose said: "Take off your coat, Senator, and sit down." The next thing from Penrose was: "Harding, how would you like to be President?" I don't think anyone could have registered more surprise than Harding. He said: "Why, Penrose, I haven't any money and I have my own troubles in Ohio. In fact, I will be mighty glad if I can come back to the Senate." Penrose said: "You don't need any money. I'll look out after that. You will make the McKinley type of candidate. You look the part. You can make a front-porch campaign like McKinley's and we'll do the rest."

Penrose didn't do much of anything, actually, but the incident helped crystallize the reluctant Harding's thinking. At one point, unsure of his own credentials, Harding asked Daugherty, "Am I a big enough man for the race?"

"Don't make me laugh," Harry responded. "The days of giants in the Presidential chair is passed. Our so-called Great Presidents were all made by the conditions of war under which they administered the office. Greatness in the presidential chair is largely an illusion of the people."

Harding remained unconvinced. Even among his fellow congressional Republicans, his support remained negligible. A November 1919 *Chicago Tribune* poll of House and Senate Republicans gave Wood 136, Lowden 44, and Jim Watson (who wasn't even running) and Harding 26 each. Neither Calvin Coolidge nor Herbert Hoover garnered a single vote.

There was the matter of his health. His heart was not good—"doubtful to begin with," as Harry Daugherty later put it. There was blood in his urine. His blood pressure was a dangerous 185. He didn't want to end up like Wilson.

There was Carrie. The war had made her unstable, dangerous. Sympathizing with Germany, she periodically threatened to expose her lover if he supported the war. He supported it anyway.

There was Nan, and Nan's baby.

And there were other women: a violent affair with a Senate staffer named Grace Cross, and pregnancies by a maid named Rosa Cecilia Hoyle (a son) and a woman named Augusta Cole (an abortion). Warren Harding's personal life was a mess.

So, quite often, was his oratory. His speeches were good enough to elect Harding in Ohio and even to earn him a paycheck on the summer Chautauqua Circuit, but they lacked elegance and precision. Harding himself called his style "bloviating." When Harding was dead, William Gibbs McAdoo skewered him thusly: "His speeches left the impression of an army of pompous phrases moving over the mindscape in search of an idea. Sometimes these meandering words would actually capture a straggling thought and bear it triumphantly, a prisoner in their midst, until it died of servitude and overwork."

So in the end, why *did* Harding run?

Survival.

Ohio politics did not foster job security. Harding had replaced one-term Theodore Burton. James M. Cox and Frank Willis had played musical chairs in the governor's office. Harding wasn't sure he would be returned to the Senate. A modest presidential run, if properly conducted, might enhance his chances. He gave Harry Daugherty the go-ahead.

And so, despite all his agonizing, Harding announced for the presidency relatively early in the game, on December 16, 1919. Technically not a favorite son, he nonetheless made his announcement in a letter to the Republican Chairman of largely rural Miami County, Ohio. The news barely dented page four of the *New York Times*—or page *seven* of the *Indianapolis Star*.

Harding's skepticism remained. "The only thing I really worry about," he wrote Frank Scobey on December 30, "is that I am sometimes very much afraid I am going to be nominated and elected. That's an awful thing to contemplate."

He was not the only one with doubts. In January, Harry Daugherty visited New York, revealing his plans to Senator Wadsworth and to state Republican powerhouse Billy Barnes. Wadsworth, once so impressed by his colleague, was now aghast. He and Barnes simply stared back at Daugherty in stunned disbelief.

Yet, while Harding enjoyed none of the support flowing to Leonard Wood or Governor Lowden, nor even to California progressive Hiram Johnson, his chances were by no means negligible, his reputation by no means insubstantial. In January 1920, William Howard Taft wrote: "My natural affiliations are with Harding of Ohio, who is a good man and to whom I am indebted for very effective support in 1912"—a good man with "many elements that made McKinley successful."

To modern ears, that may seem shorthand for "Harding's an Old Guard Republican from Ohio." But it meant something deeper. People loved McKinley not so much for high tariffs or the gold standard, but for his innate and palpable graciousness. Harding had the same quality.

"Kindliness and kindness . . . fairly radiate from him," observed the often-acerbic Washington journalist Edward G. Lowry, "He positively gives out even to the least sensitive a sense of brotherhood and innate good-will toward his fellow man. With it he imparts a certain sense of simpleness and trustfulness, an easy friendliness, an acceptance of people he meets as good fellows. It is in his eyes, in his voice, in his manners."

Irvin S. Cobb felt that way. "Following his election[,] I came to know

President Harding fairly well," Cobb wrote, "and with all my heart to like him and before very long with all my heart to pity him. I think I never met a kindlier man or a man of better impulses or one with more generous and gracious opinions of his fellow men."

Or as Harry Daugherty said as he cajoled Harding into running, "The truest greatness lies in being kind."

Harding picked his spots in the primaries, avoiding challenges to favorite sons like Calvin Coolidge, Nicholas Murray Butler, and Senators Howard Sutherland and Miles Poindexter. Daugherty didn't want to anger anyone. He wasn't trying to create a big splash right away. He knew that that strategy would never work—at least not for Harding. No, Warren would not be a front-runner. He would not even stand within striking distance of front-runner status as convention balloting commenced, but he would be everyone's third, or fourth, or even fifth choice, rising to the top on the eighth, ninth, or tenth ballot when his competition had evaporated. In most years, such a strategy would be mere delusion, but 1920 was not "most years."

Nonetheless, Harding's very limited forays into the primaries proved disastrous and very nearly terminal. In Montana on April 23, Harding received just 723 votes of the more than 40,000 cast, trailing not just Johnson, Wood, and Lowden, but also Hoover.

Hoping to enter not only the Ohio contest on April 27 but also New Jersey's that same day, lack of cash kept him out of the Garden State. Even in Ohio, the going proved far rougher than either Harding or Daugherty imagined. Wood poured $128,300 into Ohio, hoping to defeat or seriously weaken Harding. Harding won, but so unimpressively (by just 15,000 votes) that Daugherty did not even obtain an at-large seat to the national convention. The *Chicago Tribune* ominously headlined: HARDING FLASH IN PAN.

Harding couldn't even flash in May 5's Indiana primary. He should have. The state lay next door, and its two U.S. Senators, Jim Watson and Harry S. New, supported him. But Harding still limped in an exceedingly poor last (Wood 85,776, Johnson 79,829, Lowden 31,118, Harding 20,819), garnering nary a single delegate. Receiving the results at Harry New's Indianapolis home, Harding wanted to withdraw. New advised him to do so and save his Senate seat. Harding called Daugherty. The

Duchess, never enthusiastic about the race, suddenly and inexplicably stopped him. "Warren Harding," she shouted, "what are you doing? Give up? Think of your friends in Ohio!" She grabbed the phone and bellowed, "Hello! This is Mrs. Harding. Yes, Mrs. Harding. You tell Harry Daugherty we're in this fight till hell freezes over!" Warren Harding was still in the race.

Not that he wanted to be. On May 14, he spoke on the same bill as Governor Coolidge and Wisconsin Senator Irvine Lenroot at Boston's Home Market Club. On the train to Massachusetts, Harding had confided to Lenroot that he was just about finished and ready to quit. But in Boston, he delivered the speech that would set the tone of his campaign—"Normalcy":

> America's present need is not heroics, but healing; not nostrums, but normalcy; not revolution, but restoration; not agitation, but adjustment; not revolution, but restoration; not surgery, but serenity; not the dramatic, but the dispassionate; not experiment, but equipoise; not submergence in nationality, but sustainment in triumphant nationality.

"Harding," biographer John Dean would write decades later, "was reading the nation's pulse correctly."

Harding may have been reading the nation's pulse, but the nation was not aware that he had any. His popularity sank with each passing month. At this pace, by November he would be lucky to be elected mayor of Marion. The June 6 *Literary Digest* poll ranked him dead last behind two gentlemen who weren't even running:

Wood 186,946
Johnson 161,670
Lowden 129,992
Hoover 120,430
Hughes 88,787
Coolidge 67,047
Taft 62,871
Harding 42,212

Even Boies Penrose skulked away. After Harding spoke to the Manufacturers' Association in Philadelphia, Penrose lamented: "Harding isn't as big a man as I thought he was. He should have talked more about the tariff and not so much about playing cymbals in the Marion brass band." Herbert Hoover privately said Harding had a "bungalow mind."

There were dissenters. Not many, but a few. Just before the convention was to open, New Mexico Senator Albert Fall remained aboard the lonely Harding bandwagon:

> They say Warren Harding is not getting newspaper publicity. Well, I'm glad he isn't, but you haven't heard anyone say that Warren Harding is making any enemies anywhere[,] have you? That's the answer. Harding will be nominated.

Fall wasn't alone in that prediction. In January 1920, Florence Harding and the wives of fellow dark-horse senators Poindexter and Sutherland visited the R Street townhouse of Washington's most prominent astrologer, Brooklyn-born Madame Marcia Champney. In 1909, so had Edith Galt. Madame Marcia predicted that Edith would be First Lady; five years—and one president—later, she was.

Now, three women asked who would succeed Edith Wilson. The Madame settled on the Duchess. "If this man [Harding] runs for the presidency," Madame Marcia revealed, "no power on earth can defeat him."

"He is in the running."

"But you must know. . . ," Marcia warned, "he will die a sudden death, perhaps of poison. The stars say that he will give his life for a cause. Or that he will sacrifice himself for his friends. . . . This person will be the next president of the United States, but he will not live out his term. He will die in a sudden if not violent death. The end, when it comes[,] will be sudden, after an illness of short duration. . . . Poison or its effects is indicated. . . . It is written in the stars. . . . Following the splendid climax in the House of Preferment, I see the Sun and Mars in conjunction in the eighth house of the zodiac. And this is the House of Death—sudden, violent, or peculiar death. Tragedy. . . . The stars, Jupiter, never lie."

Tragedy—or, at least, disaster—already beckoned. Carrie Phillips, tired of Harding's treatment of her, told her husband everything. Jim

Phillips did not seem that angry, but Carrie was. Angry that her lover had remained with Florence. Angry in his seeking the White House (which would keep the Hardings formally together). Angry over his "affairs with other women." She would not only wreck his presidential chances, she would drive him from his beloved Senate—unless he ponied up substantial cash. In April 1920, she wrote to Harding, threatening blackmail.

Harding responded in a lengthy, occasionally guarded, occasionally very open, letter. Mixing firmness with conciliation and diplomacy, he fought for his political life. "We both understood. We were married," he wrote:

No lies were told. We felt the same sense of family obligations. Happily there have been no irreparable damages [*sic*]. There have been disappointments, irritations, the one break, and all the regrets you utter and no incurable revealment. It is my philosophy of life that mistakes can not be wholly cured[,] but their injuries can be minimized. I would make every reparation I can. It is all we can do.

I have oftened [*sic*] wishes [*sic*] the final out for myself. In remorse, worry and distress I would welcome the great sleep. But normal beings cannot command it. We must live to make the best amends we can. Self destruction will add to the injuries done.

We have obligations, we owe to ourselves and those we have injured to meet these obligations. Your proposal to destroy me, and yourself in doing so, will only add to the ill we have already done. It doesn't seem like you to think of such a fatal course. . . .

Now to specific things—I can't secure you the larger competence you have frequently mentioned. No use to talk about it. I can pay with life or reputation but I can't command such a sum! To avoid disgrace in the public eye[,] to escape ruin in the eyes of those who have trusted me in public life—whom I have never betrayed—I will if you demand it as the PRICE—retire at the end of my term, and never come back to M[arion] to reside. I will also avoid any elevation[,] but retire completely to obscurity. You must let me choose the process, but I will be retired fully, utterly, finally after next March 1. I can't instantly get out of the present entanglement, I can't get out until June, but I write you the solemn pledge to retire wholly and finally next March. I'll pay this price to save my own disgrace and your own self destruction to destroy me. That is one proposal, complete, final and covers all.

Here is another. If you think I can be more helpful by having a public position and influence, probably a situation to do some things, worthwhile for myself and you and yours, I will pay you $5000 per year, in March each year, so long as I am in that public service. It is not big, it is not what you have asked, but it will add to your comfort and make you independent to a reasonable degree. It is the most within my capacity. I wish it might be more, but one can only do that which is in his power. Destroy me and I have no capacity, while the object of your dislike [Florence] is capable of going on on her own account.

I write these [words] in good faith. I will, I must abide your decision. I am helpless to hinder. I beg of you to ponder it all and I beg of you to chose [sic] the way that will admit us to do the most and best we can to make it [sic ] reparation to those we injured, and still make the most of life which is only a possibility if we make it so. So much depends on your decision. I am nearly ill with the worry involved, but still hope, and still believe in your deliberate good sense. . . .

## Chapter 6

~

# "I Am Governor of Massachusetts"

What Warren Harding was, Calvin Coolidge was not. What Warren Harding was not, Calvin Coolidge was.

Calvin Coolidge, Governor of Massachusetts, was no glad-hander, no charmer. He was not genial. He had no use for small talk. Certainly he was not a philanderer. He could—and usually did—strike people as inhospitable, unfriendly, uncommunicative, even hostile.

But he was upright, personally and professionally. One could not imagine him cheating on his beautiful, charming—and patient—wife, or wasting time playing poker with cronies, trading votes, or making promises he could not keep. His appeal emanated from not promising anyone *anything*—in fact, of not even appearing interested in someone's problem—and then quietly, almost furtively, proceeding, gathering all the facts, and doing his job.

Calvin hailed not from industrial Massachusetts, but from tiny, rural, isolated Plymouth Notch, Vermont. Born on the Fourth of July, 1872, silent and circumspect, canny and practical, he was a throwback to old New England values that even then, even there, seemed oddly archaic.

Family meant everything to him. Of his mother, Victoria Moor Coolidge, this coldly reserved man could write poetically:

Whatever was grand and beautiful in form and color attracted her. It seemed as though the rich green tints of the foliage and the blossoms of the flowers came for her in the springtime, and in the autumn, it was for her that the mountain sides were struck with crimson and gold.

She died in March 1885, when Calvin was just twelve, and the sadness of her passing never left him.

Calvin, physically weak and painfully shy, admired his strong and quietly self-assured father, Colonel John Coolidge, as greatly as a son could esteem a father. Of his father, Coolidge wrote:

> My father had qualities that were greater than any I possess. He was a man of untiring industry and great tenacity of purpose. . . . He always stuck to the truth. It always seemed possible for him to form an unerring judgment of men and things. He would be classed as decidedly a man of character. I have no doubt he is representative of a great mass of Americans who are known only to their neighbors; nevertheless, they are really great. It would be difficult to say that he had a happy life. He never seemed to be seeking happiness. He was a firm believer in hard work. Death visited the family often, but I have no doubt he took a satisfaction in accomplishment and always stood ready to meet any duty that came to him. He did not fear the end of life, but looked forward to it as a reunion with all he had loved and lost.

"The lines he laid out were true and straight," Coolidge concluded, speaking both literally and metaphorically, "and the curves regular. The work he did endured."

Plymouth Notch was a mere hamlet, fewer than a dozen homes, nestled upon a fog-shrouded Vermont mountainside, barely accessible once snows fell. Yet it provided the quiet little redheaded boy with a permanent frame of reference—a world inhabited by hardworking, frugal, basically decent, God-fearing people. They worked for their money, didn't waste it, couldn't afford to waste it, and deserved to keep as much of it as possible. He wrote in his *Autobiography*:

> They drew no class distinctions except towards those who assumed superior airs. Those they held in contempt. . . .

It was all a fine atmosphere in which to raise a boy. As I look back on it[,] I constantly think how clean it was. There was little about it that was artificial. It was all close to nature and in accordance with the ways of nature. The streams ran clear. The roads, the woods, the fields, the people—all were clean. Even when I try to divest it of the halo which I know always surrounds the past, I am unable to create any other impression than that it was fresh and clean.

He loved Plymouth Notch, yet was afraid of it—or, at least, afraid of facing its handful of inhabitants. For a politician, Coolidge was unusually reticent, and the habit stole over him very early:

When I was a little fellow, as long as I can remember, I would go into a panic if I heard strange voices in the house. I felt I just couldn't meet people, and shake hands with them. Most of the visitors would sit with Mother and Father in the kitchen, and it was the hardest thing in the world to have to go through the kitchen door and give them a greeting. I was almost ten before I realized I couldn't go on that way. And by fighting hard[,] I used to manage to get through that door. I'm all right with old friends, but every time I meet a stranger, I've got to go through the old kitchen door, back home, and it's not easy.

He wanted to remain at the Notch, minding his father's general store, but Colonel Coolidge had bigger plans for his boy. Calvin departed for Amherst in September 1894 to earn a degree and a reputation as a taciturn, rural eccentric. "A drabber, more colorless boy I never knew than Calvin Coolidge when he came to Amherst," one classmate recalled. "He was a perfect enigma to us all."

He was a puzzle even to himself, undecided as to his future: Return home? Relocate to Boston or New York? Study law? But he had one clear idea: public service. In January 1895, he wrote Colonel John: "I . . . am not in any hurry to get rich. I should like to live where I can be of some use to the world and not simply where I should get a few dollars together."

At Northampton, Massachusetts, just south of Amherst, he studied law, passed the bar in July 1897, and, in February 1898, opened his own practice. There was no great reason for anyone to notice.

Nonetheless, Calvin Coolidge had settled down and would need a bride. He met her in most unlikely fashion. Grace Goodhue, a fellow Vermonter, taught at Northampton's Clarke School for the Deaf. Walking through the neighborhood, she looked up to spy a man shaving—in long johns and wearing a derby hat: Coolidge. She laughed. He heard her through his open bathroom window and, instead of taking offense, was intrigued. He sought her out, courted her, and slowly won her heart—much to amazement of all observers—for she was everything he was not.

Journalist Alfred Pearce Dennis knew them both, and wondered along with the rest:

> I remember Grace Goodhue vividly . . . [a] creature of spirit, fire, and dew, given to blithe spontaneous laughter, with eager birdlike movements, as natural and unaffected as sunlight or the sea, a soul that renders the common air sweet.
>
> What did she see in him?—everybody asked. Certainly no Prince Charming or knight in shining armor. She saw, let us believe, as by swift divination that unseen thing which we call, for want of a better name, character. As by revelation, she apprehended what had to be beaten into the heads of the rest of us.

In the summer of 1905, Calvin—uninvited—traveled to Burlington, Vermont, to Grace's parents' home. Andrew Goodhue, startled to find Calvin sitting in the family parlor reading a magazine, asked what the young man was doing there. Coolidge had come to ask for Grace's hand in marriage. "Does she know it?" Goodhue asked.

"No," Coolidge responded, "but she soon will."

His proposal consisted of ten blunt syllables, "I am going to be married to you."

Soon, he was. In that same parlor, on October 4, 1905, they wed. "We thought we were made for each other," Coolidge wrote in his autobiography, choosing his words with greater care than those he employed for

93

his proposal. "For almost a quarter of a century she has borne with my infirmities and I have rejoiced in her graces."

In August 1906, the couple moved into one half of a two-family address: 21 Massasoit Street, Northampton. It was not fancy. The family china came on the cheap from a bankrupt local hotel. Rent was $27 a month. "Of course, my expenses increased," he would later explain, "and I had to plan very carefully for a time to live within my income. I know very well what it means to awake in the night and realize that the rent is coming due, wondering where the money is coming from with which to pay it. The only way I know of to escape from that constant tragedy is to keep running expenses low enough so that something may be saved to meet the day when earnings may be small."

But there was more to his frugality than fear. There was calculation. If his expenses were large, he would be in thrall to a deeper apprehension—of losing whatever elective office he held and thus his livelihood, a fear handicapping him from doing the right thing—or what he felt like doing. His little duplex bestowed freedom. "We liked the house where our children came to us," he wrote, "and the neighbors who were so kind. When we could have had a more pretentious home[,] we still clung to it. So long as I lived there, I could be independent and serve the public without ever thinking that I could not maintain my position if I lost my office. . . . We lived where we did that I might better serve the people."

In 1898, Coolidge initiated his political career, as a Northampton city councilman, beginning the steadiest political rise in American history, holding more different offices than any other president—perhaps more than any other American, period, advancing step by step to Northampton city solicitor, city Republican chairman, and Clerk of the Courts of Hampshire County. Elected to the Massachusetts general assembly in 1906, he traveled to Boston, carrying with him a reference from a former state senator:

This will introduce to you the new member-elect from my town, Calvin Coolidge. Like the singed cat, he is better than he looks.

He did, and he was. But he didn't remain in the legislature long, returning home after just two one-year terms, taking a brief sabbatical from public office (his last stint as a private citizen until vacating the White House in March 1929). Then, in 1909, Northampton's Democratic mayor retired. It looked as if the post would remain Democratic, and no Republican filed save Coolidge. He won by 187 votes. "At least 400 Democrats voted for me," he wrote his father. "Their leaders can't see why they did it. I know why. They knew I had done things for them, bless their honest Irish hearts."

Coolidge won the mayoralty by 256 votes in 1910, and, in 1911, earned promotion again, now to the state senate, for the first of four one-year terms. In 1913, when suffragettes helped defeat the incumbent senate president, Coolidge, in two days, collected votes from not only every Republican state senator—but from ten of seventeen Democrats. A year later, they re-elected Senate President Coolidge unanimously.

Coolidge assumed the state senate presidency for his first term on January 7, 1914. With his father watching from the gallery, in his terse, clipped style, he delivered a speech that helped shape his career. "Have Faith in Massachusetts" enunciated his philosophy—conservative, straightforward yet non-confrontational, pro-business yet oddly spiritual:

> Government cannot relieve from toil. It can provide no substitute for the rewards of service. It can, of course, care for the defective and recognize distinguished merit. The normal must care for themselves. Self-government means self-support. Man is born into the universe with a personality that is his own. He has a right that is founded upon the constitution of the universe to have property that is his own. Ultimately, property rights and personal rights are the same thing. The one cannot be preserved if the other be violated. Each man is entitled to his rights and the rewards of his service[,] be they never so large or never so small.
>
> The Commonwealth [of Massachusetts] is one. We are all members of one body. The welfare of the weakest and the welfare of the most powerful are inseparably bound together. Industry cannot flourish if labor languish. Transportation cannot prosper if manufactures decline. The general welfare cannot be provided for in any one act, but it is well to remember that the benefit of one is the benefit of all, and the neglect of one is the neglect of all. . . .

Do the day's work. If it be to protect the rights of the weak, whoever objects, do it. If it be to help a powerful corporation better to serve the people, whatever the opposition, do that. Expect to be called a stand-patter, but don't be a stand-patter. Expect to be called a demagogue, but don't be a demagogue. Don't hesitate to be as revolutionary as science. Don't hesitate to be as reactionary as the multiplication table. Don't expect to build up the weak by pulling down the strong. Don't hurry to legislate. Give administration a chance to catch up with legislation.

We need a broader, firmer, deeper faith in the people—a faith that men desire to do right, that the Commonwealth is founded upon a righteousness which will endure, a reconstructed faith that the final approval of the people is given not to demagogues, slavishly pandering to their selfishness, merchandising with the clamor of the hour, but to statesmen, ministering to their welfare, and representing their deep, silent, [and] abiding convictions.

The speech caught the tenor of the times. The progressive groundswell was fast receding. Theodore Roosevelt and Taft and Wilson had implemented anti-trust suits, labor legislation, constitutional amendments, reforms of all shapes and colors. The people now wanted consolidation, not innovation. The speech made Coolidge gubernatorial timber.

First, though, came a stop in the lieutenant governorship. In the 1915 primary, Coolidge faced one of the party's most brilliant young speakers, and observers expected Cal's demolition. He won easily. In the general election, he ran forty thousand votes ahead of the party's successful gubernatorial candidate, Samuel W. McCall—and won re-election in 1916 and 1917. There wasn't much to being lieutenant governor; he had wielded more power as senate president. But Coolidge eyed a higher prize. "Under the custom of promotion in Massachusetts," he would write, "a man who did not expect to be advanced would scarcely be willing to be lieutenant-governor."

Assisting Coolidge was a round, older little man named Frank Waterman Stearns, proprietor of R. H. Stearns & Co., one of Boston's premier dry goods stores. "Lord Lingerie," as Stearns was sometimes called, was, like Coolidge, an Amherst man (class of 1878), and he believed Amherst men should stick together.

His initial impression of Calvin was not good. Coolidge had responded curtly to other alumni regarding a bill expanding Amherst's sewer system. Coolidge got the job done, but Stearns didn't appreciate Coolidge's ice-cold style. Then Stearns witnessed Coolidge in action at the state capitol. Coolidge was even more curt to fellow senators, communicating only by blunt monosyllables. Stearns, however, was now completely charmed: "This entire absence of effort to impress me was different from the action of any politician that I had ever met, and it finally interested me so much that I began to look him up."

There remained in Coolidge a touch of the progressive—or, putting it another way, of the Christian. During his 1916 re-election campaign, he dared inform voters: "Our party will have no part in a scheme of economy which adds to the misery of the wards of the Commonwealth—the sick, the insane and the unfortunate—those who are too weak even to protest. Because I know these conditions, I know a Republican administration would face an increasing state tax rather than not see them remedied."

Said one Massachusetts labor leader: "In all my years of work in the Legislature I have never met a man [in] whose sense of justice and courage I had more trust."

In 1918, Governor McCall, having completed the customary gubernatorial limit of three terms, decided to run for the Senate seat of Republican John W. Weeks, a not particularly strong incumbent. McCall changed his mind about the Senate, but not about leaving the governorship. Coolidge faced no opposition for the Republican nomination. On October 7, 1918, Henry Cabot Lodge wrote to Theodore Roosevelt, dutifully soliciting an endorsement for his party's standard-bearer:

> Calvin Coolidge . . . is a graduate of Amherst, a very able, sagacious man of pure New England type. He is not only wise and tolerant, but he also has an excellent capacity for firmness when firmness is needed. He has been ardently for the war from the beginning. He has been in thorough sympathy with your views and mine, and in his campaign he has not been talking for himself at all but just making war speeches.

Roosevelt provided a ringing endorsement:

Mr. Coolidge is a high-minded public servant of the type which Massachusetts has always been honorably anxious to see at the head of the state government; a man who has the forward look and who is anxious to secure genuine social and industrial justice in the only way it can effectively be secured, that is, by basing a jealous insistence upon the rights of all, on the foundation of legislation that will guarantee the welfare of all.

Under normal conditions, Coolidge should have won easily. But tens of thousands of Massachusetts men were at war. A deadly influenza epidemic raged. The party organization proved unusually weak. Voter turnout—particularly Republican turnout—declined. Coolidge squeaked in, by just 16,773 votes. Yet he finished twenty-five thousand votes ahead of Weeks's total for the Senate. Weeks lost his seat.

As governor, Coolidge retained his laconic ways. Once, three fairly prominent civic leaders desired that a specific appropriation be increased by fifty thousand dollars. One advocated passionately for his cause. Coolidge eyed him, then asked: "Anybody else got anything to say?" Another repeated essentially the same points but in wordier fashion. When he finished, Coolidge commented: "I understand you all agree on what you want." The trio cheerily confirmed that, anticipating his assent.

"Can't be done," Coolidge twanged. "Good-bye."

What could be done, however, was the seemingly impossible: reorganizing state government. Massachusetts's legislature had mandated consolidating 118 different state departments into 20. Coolidge did it, making enemies, of course, but also making friends, primarily by appointing a number of capable Democrats and Boston Irish to the newly consolidated positions.

By now, Frank Stearns's opinion of Coolidge was adulatory. He *knew* this shy little governor was meant for great things. Just two days after TR's death, Stearns wrote Coolidge's Amherst classmate, banker Dwight W. Morrow: "I had a talk with Norton yesterday in New York. He said, 'Roosevelt is gone. Now there is Coolidge.'"

The year 1919 was a year of strikes, and the fever of unrest spared few occupations. In Boston, it hit the police department particularly hard. Police had their grievances. Their minimum pay was just $1,100 per annum—even for the times, pitifully small. They worked twelve-hour shifts, had to supply and maintain their own uniforms, even had to buy their own bullets. Station houses were deplorable—overcrowded, dirty, vermin-infested.

Though state law prohibited their unionization, they organized. Authorities tolerated their quasi-union, the Boston Social Club, until it affiliated with the American Federation of Labor. For that act, Police Commissioner Edwin U. Curtis—a gubernatorial, not a mayoral, appointee—disciplined nineteen union leaders, ultimately removing them from the force on Monday, September 8, 1919.

The next day, the union voted 1,134 to 2 to strike. At 5:45 that evening, 1,117 of the force's 1,544 men walked out. Those remaining were largely older men, fearful of jeopardizing pensions. Curtis boasted he was "ready for anything"; but with Boston left virtually unprotected, chaos erupted. Gamblers shot dice openly on Boston Common. Vandals smashed store windows and looted goods. Thugs assaulted and robbed passersby. On Wednesday, September 10, patrician Democrat Mayor Andrew J. Peters summoned 5,000 Boston-based National Guardsmen to restore order. By the next morning, the situation was largely under control.

Thursday night, Woodrow Wilson, speaking in Helena, Montana, articulated the mood of a frightened, angry nation, denouncing "a crime against civilization" that had left Boston "at the mercy of an army of thugs."

"In my judgment," said Wilson, "the obligation of a policeman is as sacred and direct as the obligation of a soldier. He is a public servant, not a private employee, and the whole honor of the community is in his hands."

The threat of a citywide general strike remained, but union leaders quickly grasped that local and national sentiment ran overwhelmingly against the police and overwhelmingly disapproved of any action in their behalf. That night, their strike vote lost.

In the process, however, Mayor Peters had usurped Commissioner Curtis's authority. Worse, he seemed ready to allow strikers back on the job. The next day, Coolidge, who had refrained from interfering with Curtis's authority, now dispatched the entire state's National Guard into the streets, a powerful message in support of Curtis.

On Friday, September 12, American Federation of Labor president

Samuel L. Gompers telegraphed both Coolidge and Peters, urging that strikers be allowed to return. Coolidge and Curtis considered the men deserters in time of crisis, who should never be allowed back. Coolidge wired Gompers that he supported Curtis's decision. Business supporters warned Coolidge that his stand might offend labor and cost him his office. "It is not necessary for me to hold another office," he snapped.

The next day, Gompers telegraphed Coolidge again, reiterating his points and deriding Curtis as "autocratic" and wrong in his decisions. Coolidge responded that any action by Curtis did not "justify the wrong of leaving the city unguarded." Then he tersely wrote the fifteen words that ultimately made him president: "There is no right to strike against the public safety by anybody, any time, anywhere."

His statement electrified the country. Coolidge had reduced to an epigram what the nation thought. His terseness also served another purpose, saving him from the rhetorical excesses sinking so many law-and-order candidates, Leonard Wood and A. Mitchell Palmer being the most recent examples. Coolidge didn't blast the strikers as Reds, didn't invent anarchist plots or predict the end of American civilization. He just wanted safe streets and men to do their duty. He didn't want men who wouldn't.

Coolidge, nonetheless, fretted that he had miscued politically. He was nearly sure of that. Having squeaked into the governorship, he had now alienated organized labor. That November, his Democratic opponent pledged to reinstate the police. The public disagreed. Coolidge captured 62 percent of the vote, and Woodrow Wilson broke precedent to cross party lines and wire him:

> I congratulate you upon your election as a victory for law and order. When that is the issue, all Americans must stand together.

Others besides Frank Stearns now viewed Coolidge as presidential timber. His Bay State record might bridge the gap between party progressives and conservatives. The *Chicago Tribune* wrote in November 1919 that "among the liberal measures he worked for while in the legislature were":

> Appropriation for pure food bill.
> New housing laws for Boston.

Fee employment bureau.

Old age pension commission.

Bill against overtime for women and children.

Pensions for widows and children of policemen and firemen.

Eight-hour day for state and city employees.

Workmen's compensation act.

Pensions for school teachers.

Shorter hours for women and children.

Better medical inspection for schools.

Limit to assumption of risk by rail employees.

Half fare for schoolchildren.

Modification of injunction processes.

On January 4, 1920, James B. Reynolds, secretary of the Republican national committee since 1912, quit his post to run the Coolidge campaign, opening an office in Washington's Hotel Raleigh. Two days later, Reynolds opened a second office in Chicago. The next day, however, Coolidge declared that he would not actively seek the presidency. Usually this meant nothing. Candidates always started out by denying they were candidates. It was the American way. The unusual dimension of Coolidge's statement was that he never consulted Frank Stearns about it.

Stearns and Reynolds chugged along. Few viewed Coolidge as a front-runner, but many regarded him as vice-presidential material. Stearns and Reynolds supplied prospective delegates with hardbound copies of *Have Faith in Massachusetts*, a ploy that proved remarkably effective. In *The Outlook*, popular author Bruce Barton highlighted Silent Cal's homely virtues. Law-and-order remained a big issue, and Coolidge had possibilities.

Then Coolidge struck again.

Ever the realist, he knew that he was a long shot. He lacked the support, the organization, and the financial backing to field an aggressive national campaign. And, besides, grasping for office simply wasn't his style. He never forced himself on voters. He just presented himself at the right time after the right amount of preparation, and the party and the public invariably responded: "Coolidge? Yes, why not?"

On January 25, 1920, he issued a typically brief statement, deriding the "curse" of "the almost universal grasping for power" and unequivocally stating that he would not seek the nomination. "I am not a candidate for the presidency," he said. "I am Governor of Massachusetts, and am content to do my only duty, the day's work as such." Again, he didn't consult with Stearns.

Normally, such statements were considered mere coyness and bosh, but this seemed different. The *New York Times* editorialized that while Coolidge had never "conspicuously" sought an office, he had, nonetheless, successfully grasped each rung of the political ladder. To change his *modus operandi* now would "probably lose the prize he coveted."

In any case, noted the normally Democratic *Times*, there was nothing in Calvin Coolidge's career "to show that he is a politician in any sense. . . . A proper description of Mr. Coolidge would be that of public servant."

On January 8, Coolidge began his second term, delivering an inaugural address that became known as his "Law and Order" speech, balancing, in Coolidgian clipped tones, humanitarian and anti-radical sentiments:

> Healthful housing, wholesome food, sanitary working conditions, reasonable hours, a fair wage for a fair day's work, opportunity full and free, justice speedy and impartial and at a cost within the reach of all, are among the objects not only to be sought but made absolutely certain and secure. Government is not, must not be, a cold, impersonal machine, but a human and more humane agency, appealing to the reason, satisfying the heart, full of mercy, assisting the good, resisting the wrong, delivering the weak from the impositions of the strong.
>
> There are strident voices urging resistance to law in the name of freedom. They are not seeking freedom for themselves—they have it; they are seeking to enslave others. Their works are evil. They know it. They must be resisted. The evil they represent must be overcome by the good others represent. These ideas, which are wrong, for the most part imported, must be supplemented by ideas that are right. This can be done. The meaning of America is a power which cannot be overcome. Prosecution of the criminal and education of the ignorant are the remedies.

It is fundamental that freedom is not to be secured by disobedience to law. Government must govern. To obey is life. To disobey is death. Organized government is the expression of the life of the commonwealth. . . .

Such talk normally preceded a presidential campaign. But twenty-one days later, the month's lease up, Coolidge shuttered his Washington headquarters.

Coolidge had his reasons. One was former United States Senator Winthrop Murray Crane. If Coolidge was anyone's protégé, he was Crane's. If anyone was more laconic than Calvin Coolidge, it was Murray Crane. It was Crane who would have to carry the Coolidge gospel to Washington. But Crane's health was fading fast. He lacked the necessary strength to organize a Coolidge boom.

Another factor involved the Massachusetts delegation. Warren Harding had the sense to avoid a direct challenge, but former Massachusetts resident Leonard Wood did not. In the April 27 state primary, voters selected 29 unpledged electors, presumably for Coolidge, and 6 for Wood. But Coolidge's Massachusetts base was already seriously weakened, wounded by the maneuverings of Senator Lodge, who had no real enthusiasm for Coolidge for president—or, now, for anybody at all, really.

Coolidge continued to spurn popular support—and then gain it anyway. On May 6, 1920, he vetoed legislation legalizing beer containing 2.75 percent alcohol. Overwhelmingly approved by the legislature just after the enactment of National Prohibition, this 2.75 percent beer legislation nonetheless enjoyed broad support. A veto seemed like political suicide and ripe for an override. Coolidge vetoed it anyway, blasting the measure as unconstitutional and a fraud upon the public. "No one would dare act under it, or, if anyone should do so, he would certainly be charged with [a] crime," said Coolidge, who condemned the bill as an example of "the practice of a legislative deception."

The *New York Times* considered his action a work of rare and refreshing statesmanship.

Refreshing though it was, fewer and fewer people could conceive of Coolidge going anywhere. His train had never been a long one, and he had jumped off before it left the station. In May, Senator Harding visited the state—to deliver his "Normalcy" address—and said that if he lived in Massachusetts, he'd support Coolidge for president. He was probably being nice. Mr. Harding had a habit of being nice.

Meanwhile, by early May, though neither politicians nor press noticed, *Have Faith in Massachusetts* had aroused enough public interest to generate four printings, and Frank Stearns had printed up another little book titled *Law and Order* for distribution at the upcoming convention.

Frank Stearns knew how to sell.

## Chapter 7

∽

# "HE IS CERTAINLY A WONDER"

Politicians were a dime a dozen in 1920. Some good. Some bad. Some indifferent. Some Democrat. Some Republican. Some even Socialist.

There was only one Herbert Clark Hoover.

Hoover wasn't a politician. He was a humanitarian, savior of a million lives, a genuine hero in an era of villains. Horatio Alger incarnate. The orphan boy who *made good*, and *did good* in the bargain.

Herbert Hoover wasn't a politician. That was his strength—and his weakness.

He had made a fortune before the war, and he made a name for himself during it. He fed millions of starving Europeans on both sides of the trenches. He galvanized the home front. Tens of millions admired this utterly colorless engineer, a man whose cold efficiency saved more lives than all the eloquence and passion of a thousand politicians and statesmen. Ambassador to France Walter Hines Page would later call him this "simple, modest, energetic little man who began his career in California and will end it in Heaven."

By 1920, Herbert Hoover was rich, his fortune made in the gold fields of California, Australia, and China. Born on August 10, 1874, in tiny West Branch, Iowa, his family was not quite dirt-poor, but close to it. The Hoovers, and most of West Branch, were Quakers: frugal, modest, temperate, patient—and Republican. As Hoover remembered:

There was only one Democrat in the village. He occasionally fell under the influence of liquor; therefore in the opinion of our village he represented all the forces of evil. At times he relapsed to goodness in the form of a ration of a single gumdrop to the small boys who did errands at his store. He also bought the old iron from which added financial resources were provided for firecrackers on the Fourth of July. He was, therefore, tolerated and he served well and efficiently for a moral and political example.

Herbert's father, Jesse, made a tolerable living blacksmithing—but died at thirty-four in December 1880. Hulda Minthorn Hoover, forced to earn a living for herself and her three children as a seamstress, died not long afterward, in February 1884. Eleven-year-old Herbert was sent to his uncle Dr. John Minthorn in Newberg, Oregon—with two dimes sewn into his clothing. At Uncle John's land company, he learned bookkeeping and typing.

The Hoovers valued education (Hulda had somehow squirreled away $2,000 for the education of Herbert and his brother and sister), and Herbert enrolled at Stanford University when it opened in October 1891. The family preferred a Quaker school, but Stanford possessed the charm of being tuition-free. There, Herbert won class office (on the "Barbarian" ticket), operated a laundry and a newspaper route, managed the varsity baseball and football teams, sold theater tickets—and met his future wife, fellow geology student Lou Henry. Geology Department chairman Dr. John Branner found the young man invaluable. "I can tell Hoover to do a thing and never think of it again," Branner marveled. "If I told him to start to Kamchatka tomorrow to bring me back a walrus tooth, I'd never hear of it again until he came back with the tooth. And then I'd ask him how he had done it." A rare Hoover failure occurred when he booked an eloquent young Nebraska congressman—William Jennings Bryan—to speak at Stanford. Gate receipts were disappointing. Both Hoover and Bryan were merely ahead of their time.

Graduating in May 1895, his economic chances seemed less than glittering and he accepted ("because I had to eat") a job in a Nevada City, California mine working deep under the earth in twelve-hour shifts, seven days a week, for between $1.50 and $2.50 a day. Another underground job followed before he won a promotion to a mining-office typist position, where his diligence and energy soon advanced him to assistant manager at a New Mexico mine. From there, he moved to a British gold-mining firm, Bewick, Moreing & Co., in western Australia. Again, he made good, solving technical mining problems, placing a veneer of efficiency on a land of uncivilized chaos, inspiring the loyalty of subordinates (who called the youngster "the Chief," as, henceforth, would all his subordinates), and the admiration of his superiors. In 1898, Bewick, Moreing transferred Hoover to Tientsin to organize their hitherto unprofitable Chinese holdings. Before leaving for the Middle Kingdom, he detoured Stateside where, in Monterey, California, on February 11, 1899, he married Lou Henry. The bride and groom both wore brown.

China, angered by decades of European imperialism, soon erupted in convulsive anti-Western hostility, culminating in June 1900's bloody Boxer Rebellion. Tientsin's small garrison safeguarded three hundred Westerners and a larger number of mostly Christian natives ("collaborationists"). Hoover supervised city defenses, organized the food supply and work force, and labored on the fire brigade. Lou Hoover coordinated Tientsin's hospitals. Boxers lobbed an estimated sixty thousand shells into Hoover's defenses, but they held. The Hoovers evacuated the city in August 1900; but when calm returned, so did Hoover, who performed his usual magic with ailing Bewick, Moreing properties. Offered a partnership, he relocated once more, this time not to wild gold fields, but to the London home office. Hoover was rich. He was also just twenty-seven years old.

He could not stand still. Five times he circled the world, overseeing Bewick, Moreing's far-flung interests (five-week-old Herbert Jr. came along, packed neatly in a little basket). In 1908, Hoover founded his own engineering company. Along the way, he wrote extensively. His 1909 collection of lectures, *Principles of Mining*, would remain in print until 1967. In 1912, he and Lou undertook a more ambitious task, translating Georgius Agricola's classic Latin mining text, *De Re Metallica*, published posthumously in 1556. They toured ancient Alpine mining sites, verified Agricola's experiments, issued a 637-page, vellum-bound translation—and won the Mining and Metallurgy Association's first gold medal for achievement.

"The Great Engineer" was famous, at least in his field, rich, and, if he minded his own business, sure to grow richer still.

World War I changed everything. A hundred and twenty thousand American citizens found themselves trapped on the European continent. Hoover assumed leadership of the newly formed Committee of American Residents in London for Assistance to American Travelers. He got his fellow Americans home in six weeks, extending them over $1 million in loans. They repaid all but $300.

He now became the logical choice to organize relief for occupied Belgium. Before 1914, Belgium had imported much of its food. The Allied naval blockade made that impossible, and Germany, with its own blockade-created supply problems, wasn't eager to divert foodstuffs to a nation with (justifiably) little sympathy for its war aims. Encouraged by Walter Hines Page and Belgian banker Emile Franqui, Hoover took the reins of the newly-formed Committee for Relief of Belgium, overcoming massive logistical problems and the even more daunting suspicions of combatant nations to feed not only Belgium (including 2.5 million children) but also German-occupied northern France.

Some believed that Hoover aided the Germans by enabling them to retain food supplies for their own use, particularly their army's. Hoover thought little of such arguments and less of Britain's blockade. He later wrote:

> To lower the morale of the enemy by reducing his food supply was one of the major strategies of the war. I did not myself believe in the food blockade. I did not believe that it was the effective weapon of which the Allies were so confident. I did not believe in starving women and children. And above all, I did not believe that stunted bodies and deformed minds in the next generation were secure foundations upon which to rebuild civilization.
>
> The facts were that soldiers, government officials, munitions workers and farmers in enemy countries would always be fed; that the impact of blockade was upon the weak and the women and children.

Hoover's mission soon increased yet again, as he provided badly needed winter clothing to his charges. Overall, Hoover raised more than a billion dollars, largely from private American sources, history's largest relief effort, unprecedented in every way. With typical Hoover efficiency, only one half of one percent of the funds went for administrative expenses. The "Great Engineer" was now the "Great Humanitarian."

Hoover, of course, had help, assembling a team of able young assistants, "Hoover Men," who worshipped their leader. "His least word meant everything," one recalled. "He just charged us like a dynamo with enthusiasm and devotion and willingness to go through any experience to please him as well as to do our job."

Some remained un-mesmerized. Winston Churchill said that Berlin was responsible for feeding occupied Belgium and called Hoover "a positive son of a bitch." Hoover reminded Wilson's propaganda chief, George Creel, of a cockroach. Henry Cabot Lodge viewed Hoover as pro-German and demanded that he be prosecuted for trading with the enemy. Hoover returned home to quiet such criticism, even visiting Teddy Roosevelt at Oyster Bay. Roosevelt promised to help. "I will hold his [Lodge's] hand," he assured the Great Humanitarian.

Woodrow Wilson was not among the critics. After meeting Hoover, he wrote his future wife: "He is a real man . . . one of the very ablest men we have sent over there . . . a great international figure. Such men stir me deeply and make me in love with duty!"

When America entered the war in April 1917, Wilson provided Hoover with a new responsibility: to mobilize America's food supplies, to free up enough foodstuffs at home to support two million men abroad. Hoover cajoled, exhorted, conserved, eliminated waste, published cookbooks, and instituted such gimmicks as wheatless Wednesdays and meatless Mondays. He reduced domestic food consumption by 15 percent—without rationing. Most remarkably, he increased his popularity. Americans, swept up in patriotic fervor, loved Hoover. If he was a hero for his work in distant Belgium and France, he was now a demigod, a part of the popular culture, a topic of everyday conversation, the stuff of songs and vaudeville reviews, and all of it favorable. "I can hooverize on dinner," read a wartime Valentine card, "and on lights and fuel too, but I'll never learn to hooverize, when it comes to loving you."

Hoover remained a dynamo of efficiency but was awkward socially. Colonel House begged Washington hostesses: "Be nice to Hoover because he's not happy. He doesn't understand how to work with Congress or politicians."

He *did* understand that most people in Congress wanted something, something from *him*—a contract, an appointment, a favor. The steady stream of official visitors exhausted him. One day, yet another member of Congress arrived, sufficiently important to be ushered in immediately. Sensing Hoover's wariness, he explained: "I haven't come to get anything. I just want you to know that if you wish the help of a friend, telephone me what you want. I am here to serve and to help." And so an amazed Herbert Hoover made the acquaintance of Senator Warren Harding.

In November 1918, the war ended; the specter of mass starvation didn't. Peace existed on corpse-strewn battlefields but not in men's hearts. Italians obstructed food shipments to their new rival Jugo-Slavia. Britain's continuing blockade of Germany left civilians to fortify their diet with flour made from clover, with just about everything made from turnips, to brew coffee from crushed acorns, to fight over scraps of garbage—and to starve and watch their children starve. All that Hoover had previously accomplished was mere prologue to this. He now fed three hundred million persons across Europe and the Middle East.

In Warsaw in 1919, Poland's grateful children organized a rag-tag parade in his honor. Hour after hour, they marched. By sunset, fifty thousand children had trooped past Hoover. General Paul-Prosper Henrys, head of the French military mission, exclaimed: "There has never been a review of honor in all history that I would prefer for myself to that which you received today."

At one point, the children caught sight of a rabbit, broke ranks, and chased and caught it. With tattered honor, they presented it to their benefactor. "[T]hey were," Hoover biographer Vernon Kellogg noted, "astonished to see, as they gave him their gift, that this great strong man did just what you or I or any other sort of human being could not have helped doing under the circumstances. They saw him cry."

Hoover might also have cried at the Paris Peace Conference. As an economic adviser to the American delegation, he viewed Wilson's decline at close range, witnessing him jettisoning ideals one by one. Particularly unnerving was the news that the Allies would re-impose their blockade if

Berlin refused to sign the Treaty of Versailles. Hoover wrote Wilson. He confronted him in protest. Wilson wouldn't budge.

The great shock came on seeing the complete treaty, delivered at four in the morning to his hotel. He pored over it, not believing what he saw. Unable to sleep, he ventured out to the streets of Paris. At daybreak, he stumbled upon South Africa's General Jan Christiaan Smuts and Britain's John Maynard Keynes. "It all flashed into our minds why each was walking about at that time of the morning . . . ," Hoover later wrote. "We agreed that the consequences of many parts of the proposed Treaty would ultimately bring destruction."

Nonetheless, he refused to publicly distance himself from Wilson and his League. "With all my forebodings about the Treaty," he later noted, "I decided for myself to support its ratification . . . as a lesser evil."

"Mr. Hoover," Keynes wrote in his 1919 best-seller *The Economic Consequences of the Peace*, "was the only man who emerged from the ordeal of Paris with an enhanced reputation. This complex personality, with his habitual air of weary Titan (or, as others might put it, of exhausted prize fighter), his eyes steadily fixed on the true and essential facts of the European situation, imported into the Councils of Paris, when he took part in them, precisely that atmosphere of reality, knowledge, magnanimity and disinterestedness which, if they had been found in other quarters, also, would have given us the Good Peace."

The opinion molders and the masses agreed with Keynes. "I now found myself in a burst of popularity," Hoover would recall. "The newspapers dubbed me, falsely, a 'leading American.'" In a world of pygmies, Hoover was a giant, but a giant untested in any political sense. The Great Engineer had faced every other challenge and succeeded. Why not in politics—and at the highest level?

As early as 1915, Hoover's associates had viewed him as a future president. By spring 1917, British stockbroker Francis A. Govett openly predicted that Hoover would eventually hold "the Presidential Chair." Hoover denied such ambitions, but more cynical observers accused him of constructing a publicity machine for just that purpose.

The question remained: What *was* Hoover? A Wilson Democrat? A Teddy Roosevelt Progressive? A mainstream or moderate Republican? The *Saturday Evening Post*'s Will Irwin, Hoover's Stanford roommate, revealed that Hoover had cast his 1896 ballot for McKinley. Since then, he had not lived long enough anywhere to vote at all. In 1912, Hoover supported Theodore Roosevelt's third-party crusade. He had served faithfully—and, at least publicly, uncritically—at Wilson's side. He had socialized with administration officials. The Franklin Roosevelts had dined at the Herbert Hoovers'—and, said Hoover, he and the Navy assistant secretary had become "good friends."

He even joined in Wilson's political jibes. Following Wilson's 1918 call for a Democratic congress in 1918, Hoover released his own ill-conceived missive:

> We must have united support to the President. . . . I am for President Wilson's leadership not only in the conduct of the war but also in the negotiation of the peace, and afterwards in the direction of America's burden in the rehabilitation of the world. . . . The President has spoken throughout this war the aspirations of the vast majority of the American people. There is no other leadership possible now if we are to succeed in these great issues.

The letter didn't *say* vote Democratic, but outraged Republicans knew it *meant* vote Democratic.

Since then, however, Hoover seemed measurably less Democratic. "I am not a party man," he explained in early 1920. "There are about forty live issues in the country today in which I am interested and before I can answer whether I am a Democrat or a Republican I shall have to know how each party stands on those issues."

Nobody else knew his affiliation either, though they knew that Herbert Hoover was highly popular—and highly electable—in any party. In a year of Mitchell Palmers and James M. Coxes and Warren Hardings, that was not such a bad thing.

"I had some nice talks with Herbert Hoover before he went west for Christmas," Franklin Roosevelt wrote to their mutual friend, diplomat Hugh Gibson, on January 2, 1920. "He is certainly a wonder, and I wish we could make him President of the United States. There could not be a better one."

Secretary of the Interior Franklin K. Lane felt similarly, writing a friend that same month:

> There is talk among the business people of setting up a third party and nominating Hoover. Two things the next President must know— . . . European conditions and American conditions. The President . . . must be his own Secretary of State. We need administration of our internal affairs and wise guidance economically. Hoover can give these. He has the knowledge and he has the faculty. He has the confidence of Europe and the confidence of America. He is not a Democrat, nor is he a Republican. . . . But he is sane, progressive, competent. The women are strong for him and there are fifteen million of them who will vote this year. It would not surprise me to see him nominated on either ticket, and I believe I will vote for him now as against anybody else.

By now, Hoover had closed out his office in Europe and returned stateside. Presidential speculation accelerated, a rumor here, a newspaper article there. The *New York Times* noted that Hoover "comes into the presidential gossip more prominently than that of any man other than Mr. Bryan and Mr. Palmer," though serious questions remained as to his Democratic credentials.

The "best people" all seemed to favor Hoover: William Allen White in the Republican Party, reformer Jane Addams among the Democrats—and, according to polls, the majority of the faculty at Cornell, and the majority of faculty *and* students at Harvard. The *New Republic* classified him as "a Providential gift to the American people." The *Review of Reviews* went further: Hoover, it gushed, was the "savior of society."

Republicans maintained an interested, but wary, eye. Their chances in the coming election remained excellent, with Wilson ill and the country falling apart; but if the Great Engineer ran as a Democrat, he could upset the applecart. William Howard Taft optimistically theorized how to use the Hoover-as-Democrat boomlet to keep Senate Republican isolationists in line. On January 21, Taft wrote to his younger brother Horace:

If Lodge and Johnson et al. were to break up the treaty and Hoover were nominated on the Democratic ticket[,] it would be easy to get up an Independent Republican party to support Hoover and it would carry most of the Republicans in favor of the treaty which . . . would probably be enough to beat the Republican candidate. Fear of this may be most useful to bring pressure to bear on Lodge to lose his truculent attitude.

A month later, Taft was issuing the same warning in his syndicated newspaper column.

Not all Republicans approved of the "Great Humanitarian." The Old Guard certainly did not. Party regulars did not. And, surprisingly, neither did many progressives. Hoover, grumbled *Wallace's Farmer* editor Henry C. Wallace, was "more responsible than any other for starting the dissatisfaction which exists among the farmers of the country," and "of all the men suggested as a possible presidential candidate of either the Democratic or Republican party, is the most objectionable to the farmers of this country, and the most vulnerable." Gifford Pinchot snapped: Hoover was "neither a real Republican nor a real American."

To a close acquaintance, he was certainly *not* a Democrat. Julius H. Barnes, his former aide at the Federal Food Administration and Hoover's "Colonel House," addressed the National Wholesale Dry Goods Association, dismissing the idea:

. . . only one conceivable development could place him on the Democratic ticket. I believe that would come about only if overconfidence . . . blinds the Republican Party to adopt a non-progressive platform and to nominate candidates of reaction. Herbert Hoover is instinctively a liberal and a progressive. His political affiliations have been with the Progressive-Republicans.

Minority Leader Gilbert Hitchcock and California's James D. Phelan remained open to Hoover, but most Senate Democrats didn't, often violently. South Carolina's "Cotton Ed" Smith fussed, "Republicans are welcome to him." Georgia's Hoke Smith jeered, "I won't vote for Hoover no matter what party nominates him. I wouldn't vote for any Englishman."

Anti-League Missouri Democrat James A. Reed delivered a fiery Senate speech, connecting Hoover to Colonel House, and charging that he had "served a tutelage all his adult life" to British interests. "I think," Reed charged, "Mr. Hoover's nomination would put the finishing touch to the League of Nations and that the League would surrender the sovereignty of the world to the British Empire."

The Bryan wing of the party, isolationist and wary of the rich and the foreign-connected, proved particularly hostile. Rumors of a Hoover–House connection only magnified their alarm. They were right to be worried; House and Hoover *were* communicating. That February, Hoover confided to House that he might well succeed where TR had failed in 1912—to remake the GOP into a true progressive force.

Nor did the Wilson cabinet support Hoover. In January 1920, Secretary of the Navy Josephus Daniels recorded in his diary:

[Postmaster General] Burleson wanted no Hoover. Said Democrats had tried [Horace] Greely [*sic*] & it would be another case of leaving party principle for expediency & defeat. [Attorney General] Palmer thought it would be to throw up our hands and say the Democratic party was a bankrupt."

And former Treasury Secretary McAdoo, himself coveting the presidency, derided Hoover not only as a "cast-off Republican," but a "sexless one" besides.

But Hoover's public backing only grew. A late January 1920 poll showed that 74 percent of California voters (including 69 percent of union members and 74 percent of women) supported his candidacy.

In February, Hoover spoke out, in a statement widely interpreted as predicating his choice of party on which party supported the League. Actually, he hedged so much (i.e., by recognizing the need for reservations) that he said virtually nothing. "Until it more definitely appears what the party managers stand for," he concluded, "I must exercise a prerogative of American citizenship and decline to pledge my vote blindfolded."

115

He seemed more tractable two days later, when he conferred with Democratic national chairman Homer Cummings. "I did not gather," Cummings recorded, "that there was anything in the Democratic attitude with regard to either foreign or domestic problems which was distasteful to him."

The cabinet, however, remained unconvinced. Josephus Daniels's diary entry for March 2, 1920, read:

McAdoo thinks H's nom & election, if possible[,] would wreck the Dem. party. Thinks H— really wants to force Reps to nominate him & is not looking for Dems nomination. If nominated he thinks Dems. would not vote for Hoover. He says he will not enter in any primary—does not want nomination unless people want him enough to say so without contest.

Hoover, it turned out, possessed a diminishing affection for the Democratic Party. In his memoirs, he wrote:

By spring 1917[,] work in Washington had given me intimate opportunity to observe the Democratic party in its political aspects, all of which re-enforced my Republicanism. It was obvious that the Democratic party at that time was composed of three widely divergent elements: First, an ultraconservative Southern group whose actions were often dominated by the black specter of the Reconstruction period . . . ; second, a set of plundering political machines in many of the large cities; third, in the North generally the party embraced the whole lunatic fringe of greenback, "free silver" agrarian fanatics and near-Socialists. These latter elements had grown into a large voice in the party through Bryanesque demagoguery. In order to maintain "white ascendancy" and political office, the Southern Democrats were prepared to cater to these Northern groups.

There were in the Democratic party men of the highest purpose and ideals. Woodrow Wilson had been a beneficent accident due to a last-minute compromise in the Democratic Convention and a split in the Republican party. With fine exceptions, such as

[Secretary of Agriculture David F.] Houston, [Secretary of War Newton D.] Baker, [Interior Secretary Franklin K.] Lane, [financier Bernard] Baruch, and [Chairman of the War Trade Board Vance C.] McCormick, the leaders in Washington expressed this chaotic combination.

I also disliked such Republican phenomena as Senators [Boies] Penrose, [James] Watson, [Philander] Knox, Lodge, and their followers. But the rank and file membership of the Republican party in the North and West comprised the majority of skilled workmen, farmers, professional and small-business men. They gave it cohesion in ideas whose American aspirations I greatly preferred.

But such niceties aside, Hoover possessed a far simpler reason for his Republicanism. "I knew no Democrat could win in 1920," Hoover said years later, "and I did not see myself as a sacrifice."

There remained another flaw in Hoover. He was a Great Humanitarian, but not a great human. The public could not warm up to him, or he to it. He could rescue the starving masses of Europe, but he could not do it with the noble words of a Woodrow Wilson, the energy of a Theodore Roosevelt, the amiability of a Warren Harding, or the grinning charm of a Franklin Roosevelt. He merely did it.

Warren Harding knew that competence wasn't enough. In February 1920, he wrote an associate: "In its deliberate moments, the country does not want a dictatorial and autocratic personality like that we know our friend, Hoover, to possess. There is no doubt about his ability."

Or, as one political commentator wrote:

All his advertising has made him appeal to the American imagination, but not to the American heart. He is a sort of efficiency engineer, installing his charts and his systems into public life—and who loves an efficiency engineer? There are no stories about him which give him a place in the popular breast. It is impossible to interest yourself in Hoover as Hoover; in Hoover as the man who did this, or the man who did that, or the man who will do this or that, yes—but not in Hoover, the person.

The reason is that he has little personality. On close contact, he is disappointing, without charm, given to silence, as if he had nothing for ordinary human relations which had no profitable bearing on the task in hand. His conversation is applied efficiency engineering; there is no lost motion, though it is lost motion which is the delight of life. At dinner, he inclines to bury his face in his plate until the talk reaches some subject important to him, when he explodes a few facts, and is once more silent.

Not the stuff of presidents.

Still, his supporters had hope. On March 15, 1920, FDR wrote a former classmate:

People are more and more seeming to get away from the old political stuff, and to be insisting upon a practical business admin-istration of their governmental affairs. Of course, Hoover, of all the candidates[,] is more ideally fitted for this particular line of administrative work than any other, and I am especially gratified to see the apparent interest in Hoover's candidacy in the solid South.

It still made sense for Hoover to run Democratic. He was progressive. He had served the Wilson administration. He supported the League of Nations. And he certainly did not enjoy the confidence of the Republican leadership.

But Hoover continued slouching toward the GOP. In March 1920—just as FDR expressed his continued support—Hoover released an April 1919 letter to Wilson supporting Lodge's reservations. Then he began scotching rumors of any third-party effort.

All of which did not prevent Hoover from winning March's New Hampshire *Democratic* primary.

Then came an even more confusing message. Lou Hoover didn't want her Herbert to be president. Speaking at Bryn Mawr College that April, she confided that she was "not in favor of Hoover clubs since I do not approve of my husband running for the Presidency."

As Hoover agonized over party affiliation, he also agonized over what sort of campaign to run. Teddy Roosevelt demonstrated in 1912 that winning primaries didn't guarantee nomination; but it didn't hurt either, particularly for a newcomer to electoral office, let alone the highest office. Hoover, nonetheless, pursued a coy, half-hearted strategy, alternately running and not running, authorizing and not-authorizing activity, entering and not-entering primaries. Somehow, Hoover counted on winning in the back rooms, in the state conventions, or on the national convention floor. It was a foolhardy strategy, not helped by results from the few primaries he finally did enter.

Counting on a strong showing in the March 15 Minnesota primary, he finished a disappointing third, behind Wood and Harding.

He finished a distant fourth in April 7's Michigan Republican primary, though he surprised everyone by coasting to victory in the state's *Democratic* contest. "It was explained," noted the flummoxed *New York Times*, "that the Democrats of Michigan are not aware that Mr. Hoover has declared himself only a candidate for the Republican Presidential nomination."

When Montanans voted on April 23, few voters provided support. In the GOP primary, he limped in fourth, besting only Harding. Among Democrats, he fared worse, swamped by both Bryan and Wilson, barely apace with McAdoo.

In California, Hoover—who considered himself a native—removed his name from the May 4 Democratic ballot. He should have left it there. Instead, he competed directly in the GOP contest with isolationist Senator Hiram Johnson. The campaign began inauspiciously when Herbert and Lou, so long absent from the state, failed to even qualify to vote there. It lurched downward with extravagant spending and vituperative charges and countercharges. It thumped to an end with Johnson crushing Hoover, 369,853 to 209,009. Johnson cackled that the vote was a referendum on the League.

The *New York World*, originally a Hoover supporter, now distanced itself:

When Hoover ceased to be an "independent progressive" and entered the California primaries as an active Republican candidate[,] he practically threw away the Presidency. Up to that time[,] his position was impregnable. . . . If the Republicans rejected him at Chicago, the Democrats were certain to nominate him, and his nomination spelled the election. The moment Hoover entered the Republican primaries in California[,] the situation instantly changed. . . . He was not only a Republican of dubious partisan antecedents, an outsider trying to break into a game to which he had not been invited. . . . Hoover's mistake was in entering the primaries at all. The advice he took was bad advice. . . . The "sniping" of the professional politicians might have been annoying, but it was not serious. The country recognized in Hoover a man who was fully equipped and qualified for the Presidency, who was not seeking it and was making no concession to any political group, and the trend of public opinion was all his way. Had he maintained that position[,] he would have acquired by this time a leadership too formidable to be ignored or flouted.

More trouble lay ahead. In May 1920, the Senate investigated campaign expenditures—including Hoover's. The "Hoover National Republican Club" reported spending $62,185, exclusive of another $83,000 expended in the ill-fated California effort—which, it claimed, had been launched by local Hoover Clubs against the organization's orders. Captain John F. Lucey, Hoover Club president, explained to the Senate that his club was unlike any other campaign—purely educational and "organized without the knowledge or sanction of Mr. Hoover. He was not and is not an active candidate."

Committee members expressed skepticism. Senator James Reed asked: "How long did you succeed in keeping from [Hoover] the knowledge of your activities?"

"Oh, we didn't keep it a secret," Lucey, an Irish-born California oil millionaire, who had helped coordinate Hoover's war-relief measures, answered.

"What do you do?"

"We stimulate Hoover organizations."

"How?"

"By means of literature, mostly."

New Jersey Senator Walter Edge: "Any stimulating done with cash?"

"No."

Reed followed up: "Did Mr. Hoover ever tell you to stop stimulating these organizations?"

"No, and we would not have stopped even if he had."

"You're just going to force him to take it[,] whether or no."

"Yes, if we have to."

They might have been able to force Hoover, but they weren't about to force Hoover on the Republican Party.

## Chapter 8

≈

# "A Twentieth-Century Apollo"

Assistant Secretary.

Not a particularly impressive title. Certainly lackluster compared to Mr. President. Or Rough Rider. Or Senator. Or Governor. Or Great Humanitarian.

But Assistant Secretary Franklin Delano Roosevelt. *There* was a string of words with potential.

*Real* potential.

Or, at least, Assistant Secretary of the Navy Franklin Delano Roosevelt thought so.

He was Teddy's fifth cousin, a Roosevelt—rich, progressive but not too progressive, and, above all, self-confident and ambitious.

He was handsome too, the type of hale fellow who commands attention by merely striding into a room, before speaking a single jaunty word. At 6'2" and 188 pounds, he was, as his boss at the Navy Department, Josephus Daniels, said admiringly, "a twentieth-century Apollo."

"Roosevelt," observed the *New York Tribune*, "has a bearing that even [matinee idol] William Faversham might envy. His face is long, firmly shaped and set with marks of confidence. . . . Intensely blue eyes rest in light shadow. A firm, thin mouth breaks quickly to laugh, openly and freely. His voice is pitched well, goes forward without tripping. . . . He is a young man, a young man with energy and definite ideas, as well as a definite objective. . . ."

His objective—yes, even then—was the presidency.

Born in Hyde Park, New York on January 30, 1882, Franklin was the only child of wealthy James and Sara Delano Roosevelt. The Roosevelt family had arrived in New Amsterdam around 1650. By the early 1800s, the Roosevelts didn't need to worry about such mundane things as money—which suited FDR's father just fine. James Roosevelt's first wife died in August 1876. In October 1880, the fifty-two-year-old widower married twenty-six-year-old Sara Ann Delano. Her new stepson, James Roosevelt "Rosy" Roosevelt, FDR's half-brother, was twenty-five.

James died in December 1900, but not before Sara had become the guiding force in her only son's life, a life of privilege and snobbery. "The Roosevelts," observed one biographer, "were not as rich as the . . . Vanderbilts, but they were snootier."

Educated by private tutors and at exclusive Groton (1896–1900), FDR earned his BA in history from Harvard in only three years (1900–03), edited the *Harvard Crimson*—and almost married. In 1902, twenty-year-old Franklin courted seventeen-year-old Alice Sohier. "In a day and age," recalled Alice, "when well brought-up young men were expected to keep their hands off the persons of young ladies from respectable families, Franklin had to be slapped—hard."

They soon parted. The reason remains unknown, and adding to the mystery are three short coded passages in FDR's diary relating to Alice—the *only* coded entries in the entire journal:

July 8, 1902: "Alice confides in her doctor."
July 9, 1902: "Worried over Alice all night."
October 8, 1902: "See Alice Sohier off on the Commonwealth for Europe."

Was Alice Sohier pregnant? Packed off to Europe for an abortion? Diagnosed as having difficulty conceiving? (Franklin had told her he wanted six children, and she later sniffed that she "did not wish to be a cow.") Was she just avoiding an unwanted suitor?

Whatever happened—and perhaps nothing happened—Franklin proposed. Alice said no. Franklin, never one to admit a setback, later rationalized that he "was saved but it was an awfully narrow escape."

Five weeks later, in late November 1902, the rebounding FDR ran into a distant cousin at the Madison Square Garden Horse Show—nineteen-year-old Anna Eleanor Roosevelt, the daughter of President Theodore Roosevelt's hopelessly alcoholic and dissolute late younger brother Elliott.

By November 1903, Franklin had confided to his mother that he wanted to marry Eleanor. Sara warned her son about the perils of early marriages—but even she could hardly say no to her son marrying a Roosevelt.

They wed under a canopy of a thousand pink roses on Friday, March 17, 1905—Eleanor's mother's birthday—at 8 East Seventy-sixth Street, Eleanor's grandmother's home. Uncle Theodore gave the bride away—just thirteen days after his first formal inauguration. His daughter Alice acted as one of the two bridesmaids. The couple received three hundred wedding gifts.

Roosevelt studied law at New York's Columbia University so he could be near Eleanor. His grades were unexceptional, ranging from B to F. Passing the bar in the spring of 1907, he left Columbia without a degree, for the next three years practicing law with Carter, Ledyard and Milburn, a Wall Street firm prominent in corporate and admiralty matters.

The newlyweds took a West Forty-fifth Street apartment, but then Sara rented a four-story brownstone for them at 125 East Thirty-fifth Street, not two blocks from her own home. At Christmas 1908, she presented them with a grand five-story townhouse at 49 East Sixty-fifth Street. Sara now lived at No. 47.

Not at ease sexually, Eleanor nonetheless produced six children ("I knew my obligations as a wife and did my duty"). Five survived infancy: Anna (1906), James (1907), Elliott (1910), Franklin Delano Jr. (1914) and John (1916). The first Franklin Roosevelt Jr., born in March 1907, died that November.

In 1910, after their first choice declined, Dutchess County Democrats asked FDR to accept their normally worthless nomination for the state senate. Franklin approached TR for advice. Teddy said run. FDR did. He was not, however, a polished stump performer—far from it. The first time Eleanor saw her husband speak, she thought him "high-strung, and at times, nervous."

"He spoke slowly," she recalled, "and every now and then, there would be a long pause, and I would be worried for fear that he would never go on."

He compensated by punctuating his remarks with such TR-like phrases as "bully" and "de-lighted"—and by advocating such popular local measures as state-regulated uniform apple barrels.

One day, the candidate's rented red Maxwell, "The Red Peril," ran over a dog. There were no witnesses, but FDR paid the owner $5.00—creating a local "Honest Franklin" persona. On another occasion, stopping at a remote tavern, he treated locals to drinks. Discreetly inquiring what town he was in, he learned that he was in Connecticut. Despite such lapses, he won the state senate seat, 15,798 to 14,568.

In Albany, neither regulars nor reformers seemed enamored of the twenty-eight-year-old freshman. "Tall and slender, very active and alert," is how New York Consumers' League President Frances Perkins remembered FDR, "moving around the floor, going in and out of committee rooms, rarely talking with the members, not particularly charming (that came later), rarely smiling, with an unfortunate habit—so natural he was unaware of it—of throwing his head up. This, combined with his pince-nez and great height, gave him the appearance of looking down his nose at most people."

One person just about everybody looked down on was diminutive *New York Herald* reporter Louis McHenry Howe. Howe considered FDR to be a "spoiled silk-pants sort of guy." FDR, as did everybody else, regarded Howe as dwarfish, unwashed, reeking of smoke and booze, asthmatic, and just plain unattractive (some called him simian). Howe's second impression of Roosevelt was that he was damn near like God. Roosevelt's second impression was that Howe was smart as a whip, hard-working, and, given his dog-like loyalty, an invaluable asset.

Roosevelt arrived in the Senate already detesting Manhattan's powerful Tammany Hall. Much of his hostility stemmed from a natural revulsion at these machine Democrats' grafting peccadilloes. Part was pure snobbery, though some observers suspected something more sinister: anti-Catholicism.

The landslide of 1910 not only carried Roosevelt to Albany; it provided Democrats with the opportunity to choose a United States senator—still elected not by popular vote, but by state legislatures. Veteran Republican Chauncey Depew's term was expiring, and, with Democrats controlling both houses of the legislature, they would crown his successor, a situation analogous to Farmer Jim Martine's election in New Jersey.

All they had to do was agree on who.

Ex-saloonkeeper Charles Francis Murphy, Tammany Hall's taciturn but wily boss, had settled on William F. "Blue Eyed Billy" Sheehan, a wealthy Manhattan corporate and utility attorney. Sheehan, though not a Tammany man, was formerly chieftain of Buffalo's Democrats, Speaker of the Assembly, and lieutenant governor. As Speaker, Sheehan had opposed most reforms and grabbed whatever he could, most notably when the Assembly chamber's ceiling literally collapsed due to shoddy, graft-ridden construction. One could only ask: What was erstwhile savvy Mr. Murphy thinking?

Most Democrat legislators didn't ask that question. In the Assembly, Greenwich Village's Jimmy Walker certainly didn't. He'd vote as he had to. The same went for his fellow Manhattan assemblymen Al Smith and Bob Wagner. But Franklin Roosevelt cared, and he soon emerged as spokesman for a coterie of 21 reform-minded Democrats who for three months and 64 ballots valiantly blocked Sheehan. Murphy proposed a compromise: his able chief adviser, Daniel Florence Cohalan. FDR said no. Facing pressure from national Democrats to elect *somebody*, Murphy then proposed a reasonably respectable State Supreme Court Justice named James Aloysius O'Gorman. FDR said yes. Everybody won. In O'Gorman (a Tammany committeeman since law school), Murphy obtained an organization loyalist as Senator and even slid Cohalan into O'Gorman's old judgeship. Franklin Roosevelt got to claim victory and establish himself as a reformer to be reckoned with.

It was the episode that cemented Louis McHenry Howe's fealty. "I was so impressed with Franklin Roosevelt," he would recall, "his serious-ness, his earnestness, his firm dedication to his cause, that from that moment we became friends—and almost at that very first meeting I made up my mind that he was Presidential timber and that nothing but an accident could keep him from becoming President of the United States."

FDR, however, exhibited interest only in causes that he might lead. Unconcerned with the labor and safety laws emanating from the Triangle Shirtwaist Fire tragedy, he pointedly ignored Frances Perkins's entreaties on the matter, and wasn't even in the Senate Chamber for the final votes—none of which kept him from later taking credit for the bills.

He sought re-election in 1912—not an easy task. The district remained Republican, and, Franklin had been laid low by typhoid. Louis Howe rode to the rescue, skillfully managing a narrow victory.

Roosevelt had been an early Woodrow Wilson supporter, helping to found the New York State Wilson Conference (Howe did most of the heavy lifting), securing state convention votes, and leading pro-Wilson demonstrations at the fractious Baltimore convention. The politicking paid off: On Monday, March 17, 1913, his eighth wedding anniversary, the Senate confirmed the thirty-one-year-old FDR as Wilson's Assistant Secretary of the Navy.

He would serve under an unlikely Secretary: *Raleigh News & Observer* publisher Josephus Daniels. Daniels possessed no naval or military experience. Some considered him a pacifist. He possessed, however, solid connections to Wilson's new secretary of state, William Jennings Bryan. Daniels looked like a hick, with a flowing black tie, white socks, and invariably rumpled ("like an accordion") suits. FDR thought him "the funniest-looking hillbilly" he had ever seen. Daniels's initial Navy Department actions did little to inspire confidence, as he attempted to ban the terms "starboard" and "port" and substitute "right" and "left." An ardent prohibitionist, he also abolished officers' wine messes.

But Daniels was not a clown. An able administrator, a promoter of efficiency, and a man of measured judgment, the *Chicago Tribune* sized him up as "an even minded man [who] does not worry, and sleeps well at night." Most importantly, he possessed almost infinite patience.

Daniels needed patience. "In the 604 densely printed pages of Josephus Daniels's published diaries," writes FDR biographer Geoff Ward, "his Assistant Secretary's name appears just 113 times, and then as often as not only when he was making trouble."

Daniels had been warned about Franklin Roosevelt. New York Senator Elihu Root had cautioned Daniels of his under-secretary's ambitions, saying: "Whenever a Roosevelt rides, he rides in front." Daniels brushed aside Root's advice.

He had also been warned—though obliquely—by FDR himself. As Daniels wrote in his diary:

> Mr. R told me on the night before the inauguration that if he served in any place in the administration, he preferred to be in the Navy Department. His distinguished cousin TR went from that place to the presidency. May history repeat itself?

Roosevelt brought with him Louis McHenry Howe, who would assist him in building up not only the Navy but also FDR's efficient little political machine, cementing contacts in Washington and, almost as importantly, overseeing postal and other patronage appointments back home in New York.

In 1914, rumors circulated (FDR started them) of a gubernatorial race. In actuality, he had his sights on another office. Encouraged by Treasury Secretary McAdoo, FDR—hero of New York's last legislatively elected United States Senate race—now sought victory in its first popularly elected one (replacing Elihu Root). It was a disaster. FDR hoped to secure Wilson's endorsement. He couldn't. He counted on his Democratic opponent being the controversial William Randolph Hearst. It wasn't. Tammany—in those days never to be underestimated—fielded a respectable candidate of its own, Ambassador to Berlin James W. Gerard. Gerard humiliated Roosevelt, 210,765 to 85,203.

Occasionally FDR took a respite from political intrigue, to deal with a far larger issue: World War I. Regarding American neutrality and preparedness, FDR was far closer to cousin Theodore than to boss Josephus or boss Woodrow. The Wilson–Daniels policies frustrated him. He wanted action. He wanted preparedness. He wanted war.

Franklin also wanted Daniels's job and did what he could to undermine him. He conspired against him with Massachusetts Republican Senator John Weeks. He publicly criticized his Department's early lack of preparedness for war. At one point, he cajoled novelist Winston Churchill (an American) to compile a critical report on Daniels and to send it to Churchill's personal friend, President Wilson. Churchill did his job. Wilson didn't respond. Louis Howe spread anti-Daniels rumors in the press, planting articles favoring his firing and his replacement by his "virile-minded, hard-fisted" assistant. Word of Howe's treachery reached Daniels's friend, Wilson's propaganda chief, George Creel, who confronted Howe and threatened to reveal his machinations to Wilson, "who had a very precise idea of what constituted loyalty."

On Sunday, March 11, 1917, Franklin conferred secretly in New York with cousin Teddy, Teddy's friend General Leonard Wood, Elihu Root, J. P. Morgan, and Republican New York Mayor John Purroy Mitchell to plot preparedness strategy. Returning to Washington, he found Daniels still reluctant to allow U.S. merchantmen to fire at sight on German U-boats—despite Berlin's resumption of unrestricted submarine warfare. On March 18, 1917, however, Germany sank three American ships, the *City of Memphis*, the *Vigilante*, and the *Illinois*, without warning. America entered the war. The Navy implemented two high-profile FDR initiatives—110-foot wooden submarine chasers, and anti-submarine mine barriers—but they had only marginal effect. FDR's influence clearly had its limits. When Daniels left—say to Europe—and left FDR in charge, he left detailed instructions on what to do.

FDR pondered his gubernatorial possibilities in 1918. While soliciting Wilson for his approval, he snidely commented on rival Al Smith's Catholicism. Wilson countered to FDR that nobody was asked their religion on the front lines. By the time Wilson warmed to FDR's candidacy, FDR had decided to remain in the Navy Department. Swimming against the year's Republican tide, Smith became governor.

Eleanor Roosevelt made news in 1917. The July 17 *New York Times* reported on her attempts to Hooverize her humble Washington household: "Mrs. Roosevelt does the buying, the cooks see that there is no food wasted, the laundress is sparing in her use of soap, each servant has a watchful eye for evidence of shortcomings on the part of the others." It ended by quoting her: "Making ten servants help me do my saving has not only been possible but highly profitable."

The Franklin Roosevelts of New York City, Hyde Park, Campobello, and Washington, D.C., looked like rich twits, hopelessly, cluelessly removed from the problems of everyday folk—and FDR knew it. Unable to restrain his sarcastic bent, he wrote Eleanor:

All I can say is that your latest newspaper campaign is a corker and I am proud to be the husband of the Originator, Discoverer and Inventor of the New Household Economy for Millionaires! Please have a photo taken showing the family, the ten cooperating servants, the scraps saved from the table. . . . Honestly[,]

you have leaped into public fame, all Washington is talking of
the Roosevelt plan.

The Roosevelt marriage was indeed unhappy. Franklin loved the social
life, the parties, the clubs, the attention of Washington's most powerful
men—and its most beautiful women. Eleanor often remained home. She
and her husband grew apart. Words were said. Tempers flared. "It was
impossible not to feel resentful when left alone by the 'gay cavalier,'"
noted Eleanor's biographer Blanche Wiesen Cook, "whose every word
was filled with mirth and seemed mired in falsehood."

Much of the falsehood revolved around Lucy Mercer. In 1914, Eleanor
engaged the twenty-two-year-old Lucy to assist in social duties and caring
for the Roosevelt children. Miss Mercer came from good, but down-on-its-
luck, Maryland stock, her alcoholic father having been cashiered from the
Marines and having squandered the family wealth. Lucy had youth, good
looks, charm, a sense of fun. She was everything Eleanor was not—and
everything, it turned out, Franklin wanted. The two became lovers. Matters came to a boil in the summer of 1917. The Roosevelts should have
summered together at Campobello Island off New Brunswick's Atlantic
coast, but Franklin tarried in Washington, delaying his departure,
pleading the press of official business. Still, he had time for numerous
excursions with Lucy (by now dumped as Eleanor's social secretary
and working in—of all places—the Navy Department) and her supposed
boyfriend, British diplomat Nigel Law, outings FDR casually mentioned in correspondence to Eleanor. There were other rendezvous he
neglected to mention. Franklin's adultery was soon common knowledge
in Washington. Alice Roosevelt Longworth once spied the two of them out
driving together and complimented FDR on the "perfectly lovely lady" he
was with—and clearly transfixed by. "Isn't she perfectly lovely," Franklin
replied. Alice invited the couple over for dinner. "He deserved a good
time," TR's daughter remarked, "he was married to Eleanor."

Eleanor had once liked Lucy. Everyone liked Lucy. She was like a
member of the family. The children loved her. Even Franklin's mother
was fond of her. Eleanor was by now, however, properly suspicious and
wrote repeatedly and, increasingly, nervously, asking her husband when
he would join the family. In mid-August, a severe throat infection hospi-

talized him. Eleanor traveled home to care for him. She wanted him to return to Campobello with her. He refused. She wrote from Campobello: "I *count* on seeing you the 26th [of August]. My threat was no idle one." He obeyed, but not before spending still more time with Lucy.

In October 1917, Lucy Mercer lost her job. It might have been Eleanor's doing. It might have been Josephus Daniels's. Franklin, however, continued seeing her, continued touring the Maryland and Virginia countryside with her, continued exchanging love letters with her.

In September 1918, FDR visited Europe. Returning, he contracted double pneumonia and influenza. Eleanor met the ship and, while she was unpacking his luggage, something fell out, a packet of letters, letters from Lucy Mercer. How much Eleanor read of them we do not know, but she read enough. She offered Franklin his "freedom." He didn't take it, for divorce from Eleanor meant ruin. Voters would shun him. Bible-believing Josephus Daniels, who had fired his own brother-in-law when he divorced, would finally have fired him. And, worst of all, Sara Roosevelt would have disowned him, casting her son off without a cent. Franklin Delano Roosevelt would have to work for a living.

And he might not have been able to keep Lucy Mercer either. Lucy was Catholic. She might rationalize being a married Franklin Roosevelt's mistress, but she could never have been a divorced Franklin Roosevelt's wife.

Franklin did the only sensible thing: he stayed with Eleanor.

The decision did not bring her peace, but it may have brought her wisdom. Later, Eleanor wrote of those years:

I think I learned then that practically no one in the world is entirely bad or entirely good, and that motives are often more important than actions. I had spent most of my life in an atmosphere where everyone was sure of what was right and what was wrong, and as life progressed I have gradually come to believe that human beings who try to judge other human beings are undertaking a somewhat difficult job.

During the war I became a more tolerant person, far less sure of my own beliefs and methods of action, but I think more determined to try for certain ultimate objectives. . . . I knew more about the human heart, which had been somewhat veiled in mystery.

131

Some say that Eleanor never again slept with Franklin. Certainly, their children grew to believe that. No one knows for sure. We do know that the relationship, however damaged it now was—and it was seriously damaged—was, curiously, also stabilized. The whole episode gave Franklin a start. He no longer took his wife for granted. He took greater care to avoid tendering her insults and no longer tolerated those who did. She developed her own opinions on politics and events, and he in turn developed a respect for them.

A marriage—in conjugal terms—may have ended, but a political partnership was being born.

Other wars continued. In September 1918, TR's sixty-three-year-old brother-in-law, Douglas Robinson, died of a heart attack. At Robinson's funeral, TR took Eleanor aside, urging that Franklin swap his desk job for a uniform. Eleanor protested that Franklin had offered to do just that, but President Wilson would not allow it. Teddy persisted. Eleanor normally deferred to Uncle Theodore. This time she didn't. Her face flushed. She stood her ground. She never saw him again.

In truth, FDR attempted to enlist only very late in the game. On October 31, 1918—a dozen days before the Armistice—he petitioned Wilson in that regard. Wilson said no.

In his own mind, though, he served. Following the war, a Groton classmate wrote to him, raising funds for a plaque honoring Groton boys who wore the uniform. "I believe that my name should go in the first division of those who were 'in the service,'" he responded, claiming that his sightseeing inspections to France somehow qualified him, "especially as I saw service on the other side, and was missed by torpedoes and shells." In July 1915, after a Haitian mob had literally ripped its latest president to pieces, Woodrow Wilson had ordered Marines (which are part of the U.S. Navy) to pacify that unfortunate and chaotic country. Technically, FDR oversaw that occupation, though the nation's actual rule fell largely to Marine Corps General Smedley Darlington Butler, and Butler's methods were none too humane. As Butler wrote to FDR in December 1917 on how his road-building program was doing (forced labor): "It would not do to ask too many questions as to how we accomplish this work."

In January 1917, FDR undertook an official inspection of Haiti, observing the diplomatic niceties of the situation, though when Haiti's puppet mulatto president Sudre Dartiguenave attempted to enter a limousine ahead of Roosevelt, Butler forcibly grabbed Dartiguenave by the collar like a common field hand. Roosevelt himself couldn't resist being amused by a traveling companion's remark regarding the Haitian minister of agriculture, "I couldn't help saying to myself that that man would have brought $1,500 at auction in New Orleans in 1860 for stud purposes."

Such incidents reflected the racial attitudes of occupation forces. "Haiti has been regarded and has been treated as conquered territory," wrote NAACP secretary Herbert J. Seligman in the July 10, 1920 *Nation*. "Military camps have been built throughout the island. The property of natives has been taken for military use. Haitians carrying a gun were for a time shot at sight. Many Haitians not carrying guns were also shot at sight. Machine guns have been turned into [*sic*] crowds of unarmed natives, and United States marines have, by accounts which several of them gave me in casual conversation, not troubled to investigate how many were killed or wounded."

The Haitian people rebelled. In late 1918, nearly 40,000 Haitians took up arms, and between two and three thousand Haitians died—against thirteen American fatalities. "This," contended *Nation* editor Oswald Garrison Villard, "was the completest proof that it was not war that was waged in Haiti."

Franklin Roosevelt also involved himself in operating naval prisons. In 1912, on the New York State Wilson Conference (the state group supporting Wilson's nomination), Franklin had collaborated with upstate millionaire Thomas Mott Osborne. An ardent prison-reform advocate, Osborne once had himself incarcerated in Auburn Penitentiary as "Tom Brown," prisoner 33,333X, recording his experiences in the bestseller *Within Prison Walls*. In 1914, Osborne became warden of Sing Sing prison. Conditions at the Portsmouth Naval Prison at that time were crying out for reform, with disproportionate punishments regularly meted out for minor infractions. In January 1917, Daniels and Roosevelt chose Osborne to investigate, making him the commandant of the prison.

Superficially, their selection made perfect sense. Actually, it was unconscionable. Osborne had resigned under fire from Sing Sing, indicted in December 1915 for perjury, absenteeism, general incompetence, and, most ominously, "unlawful and unnatural acts."

In the guarded language of the day, that meant homosexuality. Osborne had often roamed through rough neighborhoods in a variety of exotic disguises (his Auburn prison adventure was just another aspect of that predilection), and "ostensibly" employed (in one historian's circumspect terminology) "a handsome, muscular young" ex-reform school inmate as his handyman.

At Portsmouth, Osborne returned brig inmates to active duty rather than cashiering them to civilian life. He once proposed staffing an entire ship with former Portsmouth inmates. Two thousand offenders eventually returned to active duty from there during the time he was commandant. Regular Navy officers questioned Osborne's approach, discerning a direct correlation between ex-convicts aboard and personal property disappearing ("Nobody could own a watch. They'd steal you blind"). Years later, Admiral Richard L. Conolly recalled: "Only two or three [of the twenty-three Portsmouth Prison inmates on his ship] were any good at all. Maybe only one that was rehabilitated. [Osborne's program] had been highly unsuccessful. And they blamed Franklin D. for that."

Sailors were even warier having shipmates who had been incarcerated for "unlawful and unnatural acts." Countering such hostility, an unsigned article in the January 3, 1920 *Army and Navy Journal* contended that Osborne's policy had the full support of the service's commanding officers. Its author was Franklin D. Roosevelt.

Captain Joseph K. Taussig, senior commander of the first U.S. destroyer division to reach Europe, knew it didn't. "The good men of the ships," Taussig wrote in rebuttal, "must, of necessity, owing to the intimate way of living on board and the requirements of working in the same confined places, associate to a more or less extent with these moral perverts, and thereby be exposed to contamination. . . . In the redemption of an individual we should not permit the degradation of the Navy."

On January 24, Roosevelt fired back, warning Taussig that a mere two sodomites had been returned to active service—both under special conditions. He further scolded that "Anyone who, like Captain Taussig, attempts to give the wrong impression, deliberately or otherwise, can only harm the service itself."

Taussig, backed by Rear Admiral William S. Sims, former commander of U. S. Naval Forces in Europe, wouldn't recant. He demanded that Daniels conduct a formal inquiry. He also took his complaints to Navy Department critic *Providence Journal* publisher John R. Rathom, dredging up some unpleasant facts: the number of returned perverts wasn't two, it was over a hundred; and that Roosevelt himself had signed an order returning ten in a single instance.

Roosevelt, hoping to charm Taussig into submission, summoned him for a two-hour private meeting. Taussig departed unconvinced, but that didn't prevent Franklin from drafting a memorandum of understanding between the two men that he sent to be published in the *Army and Navy Journal*. Taussig disowned it and reiterated his demand for a court of inquiry.

Roosevelt imperiously told Taussig that he had two choices: "Either [the request] be withdrawn by you, or [it will be] pro forma refused by the Secretary on the ground that the matter was one of misunderstanding and has been satisfactorily ended. Will you let me know which you think is the best thing to do?"

Taussig again refused. In February 1920, Daniels rode to FDR's rescue, not only rejecting Taussig's request for a court of inquiry but reminding him that he had violated Article 1535 of Navy regulations stating that no sailor could serve as a newspaper correspondent—which Taussig technically did by writing for the *Army and Navy Journal*. Taussig finally backed down.

Taussig wasn't the only officer creating controversy for Roosevelt— and Josephus Daniels. Admiral Sims had long feuded with Daniels over policy and personnel, and their relationship only deteriorated when Daniels refused to allow Sims to accept the title of honorary sea lord from the British Admiralty. In December 1918, when Daniels published the official list of those to be awarded medals for heroism and meritorious service, he ignored many of Sims's recommendations. Infuriated, Sims refused to accept his own Distinguished Service Medal, triggering a flurry of similar refusals and a congressional investigation. Privately, Franklin didn't mind the fuss. "Strictly between ourselves," he wrote Eleanor, "I should like to shake the Admiral warmly by the hand."

In January 1920, Sims struck again. In a scathing *Washington Post* article, he charged that Daniels's stewardship had cost the Navy $15 billion, 2.5 million tons of shipping, and 500,000 lives. Now FDR backed away from Sims. Writing to Livingston "Livy" Davis, an old Harvard friend and his former Navy Department assistant now working for Herbert Hoover, FDR complained that it wasn't just Daniels and Roosevelt being harmed by Sims, but the very institution of the Navy itself.

Then FDR shifted gears yet again, now siding with the maverick admiral against his own administration. In a February 1, 1920 speech at the Brooklyn Academy of Music, Franklin boasted that to advance naval preparedness, he himself had acted without administration approval and "committed enough illegal acts to put him in jail for 999 years." He even bragged that he had selected Sims to head the fleet. "I was opposed by the president," he continued, "who said that he did not want to commit any overt act of war. . . . Two months after war was declared, I saw that the Navy was still unprepared, and I spent 40 million for guns before Congress gave me or anyone any permission to spend any money."

This exceeded even FDR's standards of bravado and self-aggrandizement. "What in the world is the matter with you?" Livy Davis demanded. The betrayal outraged Daniels, who had, in fact, cleared all the "illegal" acts his subordinate brazenly claimed as his own. Hastily retreating, FDR claimed misquotation, then issued a "clarification."

Congressional Republicans, thinking that FDR might prove a willing witness regarding administration nonfeasance, requested his testimony before a Senate Naval Affairs Subcommittee. This was more than Franklin had bargained for. You might boast in Brooklyn; that was risky enough. But you didn't publicly sandbag your superior and your president on Capitol Hill. Such behavior might easily prove career-ending. Franklin fought his way out, threatening Republicans with testimony that would flay their own lack of funding for defense measures. They withdrew their request.

In February 1920, Daniels and Wilson conferred at the White House. Some of Daniels's anger over Franklin's backstabbing had passed. Some hadn't, and he wanted to discuss FDR's disloyalty. Wilson, however, had his own reasons for displeasure with Franklin. He had learned of British ambassador Lord Grey's Christmas visit to the Roosevelts and was not amused—primarily because of Grey's failure to sack gossipy Major

Crauford-Stewart from the embassy staff. Daniels suddenly realized that if he brought up FDR's Brooklyn antics, Wilson might fire Franklin on the spot, and no matter how angry Daniels became at his subordinate, he was never *that* angry. "F D R persona non grata with W.," Daniels confided to his diary. "Better let [Brooklyn] speech pass."

Franklin Roosevelt had survived again.

⁓

Despite such controversies, FDR was already being mentioned for president. The conservative Republican *New York Sun* boosted him for the job. A Boston paper noted: "Some of Massachusetts' most clever Democratic politicians have been whispering around the name of Franklin D. Roosevelt as possibly, quite possibly if you will, the most available man the Democrats will have to put forward for the great prize next summer."

Roosevelt sensed that such talk was premature. He dismissed the *Sun*'s endorsement as "one of the best jokes on record." In November 1919, he wrote an admirer, New York City Judge Henry M. Heymann: "Thanks for your action in nipping my Presidential boom in the bud. Being early on the job is sometimes wise and sometimes not; I sometimes think we consider too much the good luck of the early bird, and not the bad luck of the early worm."

In January 1920, an extraordinary opportunity materialized. With Democratic prospects so dismal, and party leaders desperately seeking new strategies, Kentucky attorney Louis B. Wehle, a nephew of Supreme Court Justice Louis Brandeis, conceived a brainstorm: Herbert Hoover for president, Franklin Roosevelt for vice president.

Wehle, a member of the War Industries Board and FDR's fellow former *Harvard Crimson* editor, first developed the idea on Thursday, January 8, as he and Democratic national committee executive committee member Angus McLean pondered their party's slim chances, and Wehle suggested such a ticket as a way to carry both California and New York. The following day, at Washington's Shoreham Hotel, they lunched with A. Mitchell Palmer and former Democratic national chairman Vance McCormick. Even Palmer, harboring his own presidential ambitions, admitted that this was about the only Democratic ticket that could win.

On Saturday, January 10, Wehle visited FDR's office. Roosevelt disliked neither Hoover nor the idea of being vice president, but predictably countered that the Democratic Party was about to sink like a rock that November. "Frank," Wehle argued, "you have everything to gain and nothing to lose. . . . Whether you win or lose, you would suffer the stigma of mediocrity that seems to attach to the Vice-Presidency or to one who tries for it. But you are young and you could live it down for several reasons: first, you bear the name Roosevelt; second, you have a first-rate record of public service . . . ; and third, in your campaign tours you would make a great number of key acquaintances in every state." And then came the clincher—"if you would methodically build on them . . . would come to have such a personal following in the Democratic Party that it would probably lead you eventually to the Presidency."

That sealed it. "You can go to it so far as I am concerned," responded FDR; "Good luck! And it will certainly be interesting to hear what the Colonel says about it."

Wehle met Colonel House on Thursday, January 15. "It is a wonderful idea," House confided, adding less enthusiastically, "and the only chance the Democrats have in November." Wehle wanted House to approach Hoover and convince him that his best interests lay with the Democrats. Direct action was not House's style. He preferred circuity and deniability. He wanted *Wehle* to approach Hoover, and Hoover to approach *him*.

The very next day, January 16, 1920, Wehle journeyed to Hoover's lower Manhattan offices, outlining his scheme. Hoover avoided eye contact, doodling away with a pencil. Head bowed, he informed Wehle: "I don't believe that I want to get into a situation where I have to deal with a lot of political bosses."

Wehle slapped Hoover's desk, startling Hoover and capturing his attention. "I caught his eye and held it," Wehle recalled, and then informed "The Great Engineer": "Let me tell you[,] if you expect ever to get into American political life, you'll have to take it as you find it. You can't make it over first from the outside."

The conversation petered out; but before Wehle departed, he had secured a promise from Hoover that he "would phone House and try to make an engagement with him for that evening."

Hoover did call House, and House, behind the scenes and as mysterious as ever, did commence working toward a Hoover–FDR ticket, even dispatching Wehle to meet with Hoover's very own "Colonel House," Julius H. Barnes, in New York; but nothing could be done to persuade Hoover to cast his lot with a sinking ship.

If Franklin Roosevelt was going to be vice-presidential nominee, it wouldn't be on a Hoover–Roosevelt ticket.

# Chapter 9

~

# "CRIMINAL INTRIGUES EVERYWHERE"

It was a time of personalities—TR's, Wilson's, Harding's, FDR's, Hoover's, even Coolidge's—but it was also a time of issues, and among the gravest was that of loyalty—and of suspicion.

Woodrow Wilson had set the tone. In his war message of April 6, 1917, he informed Congress and the nation:

> One of the things that has served to convince us that the Prussian autocracy was not and could never be our friend is that from the very outset . . . it has filled our unsuspecting communities and even our offices of government with spies and set criminal intrigues everywhere afoot against our national unity of council, our peace within and without, our industries and our commerce.

What was German was now suspect. Sauerkraut became "Liberty Cabbage," hamburgers "Liberty Sandwiches." Passersby kicked dachshunds (the Kaiser's favorite breed). Concert halls prohibited German music. Schools banned the language ("Dropped! Hun language barred," the *Cincinnati Enquirer* headlined *after* the Armistice). A Collinsville, Illinois, mob lynched German American Robert Prager. In Marion, Ohio, Florence Kling DeWolf Harding tried to convince people that she was "Pennsylvania Dutch" rather than German. "If you turn hell upside down," thundered evangelist Billy Sunday, "you will find 'Made in Germany' stamped on the bottom."

Anti-war activity was more than suspect, it was illegal. In May 1918, Congress passed the Sedition Act, authorizing the Postmaster General to deny mail delivery to radicals and dissenting publications and prohibiting "uttering, printing, writing or publishing any disloyal, profane, scurrilous, or abusive language" about the government or military. Federal authorities launched widespread raids on International Workers of the World (the IWW, known by their nickname "the Wobblies") and Socialist Party offices, arresting hundreds of offenders, up to and including IWW leader Big Bill Haywood, perennial Socialist Party presidential candidate Eugene V. Debs, Socialist editor Rose Pastor Stokes, and Wisconsin Socialist Congressman Victor Berger.

Not satisfied with merely silencing dissent, the Wilson administration had on April 14, 1917, moved to mold public opinion so as to prevent it, creating the Committee on Public Information. The CPI had four co-chairs: Missouri-born newspaperman George Creel, Secretary of State Lansing, Navy Secretary Daniels, and Secretary of War Newton D. Baker. Lansing advocated outright censorship on the British model. Baker wasn't interested, and Creel, with Daniels's support, took charge, instituting a fearsome and unprecedented propaganda machine. Millions of copies of Wilson's speeches circulated at home and abroad. Government-produced war films inspired—and perhaps even entertained—movie audiences. "I WANT YOU!" posters glared down on the populace. Seventy-five thousand "Four-Minute Men" delivered over 7.5 million patriotic speeches to over 314 million listeners. Each speech, Creel boasted, "had the projectile force of a French .75 [artillery piece]."

Radicals and pacifistic-minded progressives objected to wartime censorship, but, by and large, criticism operated on the lines of the *New York Times*'s questioning of Creel's particular qualifications. One Associated Press assistant managing editor theorized that censorship ought to be "administered by trained newspapermen, and not by retired Army and Navy officers, who may suffer from physical or mental gout and antagonize the press at every turn. . . . Newspapermen cannot command battleships, and military staff officers cannot conduct newspapers."

"People generally, and the press particularly," Creel recalled, "were keyed up to a high pitch, an excited distrust of our foreign population, and a percentage of editors and politicians were eager for a campaign of 'hate' at home."

A remarkable admission from the man who stirred up the hate.

When war ended, whisperings of "criminal intrigues everywhere" continued, as the Armistice brought battlefield peace but domestic turmoil. Millions of servicemen returned home, and unemployment and inflation skyrocketed. War contracts vanished. Farm surpluses grew. Government economic agencies went out of business. The jobless rate reached 12 percent. Inflation averaged 14.55 percent for 1919 and remained at 8.9 percent for the first six months of 1920.

Nationally, men formed "Overall Clubs," pledging to wear denim to protest high clothing costs (women wore gingham). Five thousand joined in Birmingham; 4,500 in Atlanta; 2,000 in Chattanooga; 1,500 in Richmond; 1,400 in Roanoke. In Boston, pastors of Methodist congregations in Medford Hillside and Orient Heights preached in white denim overalls. In Concord, New Hampshire, newly ordained Baptist minister Percy A. Kilmeister donned similar attire to exhort his flock to frugality. Reverend J. C. Brogan of Emporia, Kansas (another Methodist) wore overalls to his inauguration as mayor. Newly elected Atlanta Congressman William D. Upshaw sported them on the House floor. The movement sputtered when the craze forced the price of overalls from $3.10 to $8.00 a pair.

The administration, obsessed with the League of Nations and later hamstrung by a president who was an invalid, did nothing about the economy and didn't even seem to notice. The humor magazine *Life* printed a series of cablegrams addressed to "Wilson, Paris," and signed "The American People."

"Please hurry home and look after the labor situation," read one. Others followed in similar vein: "Please hurry home and look after the railroads." "Please hurry home and fire Burleson." "Please hurry home. Let someone else do it."

They were joking, but twenty-six Democratic members of the Massachusetts legislature weren't, when they cabled him with the same advice—come home and deal with the high cost of living, "which we consider *far more important than the League of Nations*."

Wilson wouldn't listen to them or to *Life*—or to Joe Tumulty. In May

1919, Tumulty cabled him: "YOU CANNOT UNDERSTAND HOW ACUTE SITUA-
TION IS BROUGHT ABOUT BY RISING PRICES OF EVERY NECESSITY OF LIFE." He
couldn't have been more blunt—or more ignored.

Massive labor unrest swept America. The year 1919 witnessed 2,665
strikes, involving 4,160,348 workers, fully a fifth of the workforce,
including 450,000 coal miners and 365,000 steelworkers. Longshoremen
struck. Garment workers struck. Cigar-makers struck. Pressmen struck.
Workers on New York's Interborough Rapid Transit subway line struck.
Eight thousand New England telephone operators struck. Entertainers
struck, shuttering theaters in New York and Chicago.

Abroad, it was a time of revolution. With German assistance, Bolsheviks had seized power in Russia. Journalist Lincoln Steffens visited there
in 1919 and pronounced "I have seen the future, and it works." Hun-
gary, Bavaria, and the Ruhr witnessed Bolshevik insurrections. Trotsky's
Red Army invaded Poland and Latvia and Lithuania. Civil war kept
erupting in Mexico. A general strike racked Winnipeg, Canada. People
wondered it if all might happen here.

It almost happened in Seattle. On January 21, 1919, seeking higher
wages and a 44-hour workweek, and angered by management's hard-line
negotiating position, 35,000 shipyard workers walked off the job. On
February 6, Seattle's 110 other unions, representing 25,000 workers,
joined in, triggering the nation's first general strike. Stores and businesses and schools closed. Streetcars and milk wagons and garbage trucks
halted. Anna Louise Strong, editor of the Labor Council's newspaper, the
*Union Record*, trumpeted "We are undertaking the most tremendous
move ever made by LABOR in this country. . . . We are starting on a road
that leads—NO ONE KNOWS WHERE!"

That destination was exactly what the rest of Seattle and the rest of
the country feared. They also feared Strong's follow-up call to action:
"Labor will not only SHUT DOWN the industries, but Labor will
REOPEN, under the management of the appropriate trades, such activities
as are needed to preserve public health and public peace. Under its OWN
MANAGEMENT." It all *sounded* like the workers' soviets now ruling Moscow
and St. Petersburg. Seattle Mayor Ole Hanson, once a friend to labor but
now an enemy of radical, IWW-style unionism ("the anarchists of this
community shall not rule its affairs"), dispatched 1,500 troops from

nearby Fort Lewis and deputized 2,400 college students to maintain order (actually, order wasn't in bad shape). Seattle's AFL-affiliated unions, wanting no part of general strikes, successfully pressured the Labor Council to back down. By Saturday morning, February 8, street-cars ran once more. Step by step, business resumed. By February 10, the strike was over; but, by then, it had scared the hell out of most of the nation and helped set back the labor movement by ten years.

Ole Hanson won headlines for his actions during the strike. He didn't mind headlines, but he did mind explosives. On April 28, 1919, his office received a package. It lay there unopened (he was in Colorado on a Victory Loan tour), and began leaking acid. It was a bomb. And more were in the mail, all over the country.

The next day, one arrived at the Atlanta home of former Georgia Senator Thomas W. Hardwick, injuring his wife Maude and blowing the hands off his black maid, Ethel Williams. Two days later, during his subway ride home to the Bronx, twenty-nine-year-old New York City post office clerk Charles Kaplan read about the Hanson and Hardwick incidents. The Hanson bomb had been packed in a very distinctive way, out of New York, a Gimbel Brothers department store label upon it, and marked "NOVELTY—A SAMPLE." Three days previously, the Russian-born Kaplan had noticed a stack of such packages, waiting to be returned to Gimbel's for insufficient postage. Kaplan rushed back to work and found sixteen of the suspect packages. Thanks to the incompetence (and cheapness) of the bombers—and the historic inefficiency of the post office—the plot had been foiled.

Thirty bombs were tracked down en route to their destinations. Recipients included Attorney General Palmer, Postmaster General Burleson, Supreme Court Justice Oliver Wendell Holmes, Secretary of Labor William B. Wilson, Commissioner of Immigration Anthony Caminetti, United States Senators Lee Overman (D-North Carolina) and Reed Smoot (R-Utah), Representatives John L. Burnett (D-Alabama) and Albert Johnson (R-Washington), federal appeals court judge Kenesaw Mountain Landis, Mayor John F. Hylan of New York, New York Police Commissioner Richard Enright, capitalists John D. Rockefeller and J. Pierpont Morgan, and governors Theodore Bilbo (D-Mississippi) and William C. Sproul (R-Pennsylvania).

The conspirators seemed unaware that most of these men did not open their own mail.

On Monday, June 2, the bombers struck again. Since mailing bombs didn't work, they delivered the devices themselves. Explosions rocked Boston; New York; Paterson, New Jersey; Philadelphia; Pittsburgh; Cleveland; and Washington. In Boston, they bombed the homes of a judge and a state representative, spraying the face of the latter's four-year-old daughter with flying glass. In Paterson, the victim owned a silk mill. In New York, bombers hit Judge Charles C. Nott's East Sixty-first Street brownstone with twenty pounds of dynamite and blew seventy-year-old night watchman William Boehner to pieces. In Philadelphia, a Catholic church was targeted; in Pittsburgh, a judge and an immigration official. In Cleveland, a bomb tore apart Mayor Harry C. Davis's home.

In Washington, at 11:15 P.M., a man with dark, curly hair, carrying a .32-caliber Smith & Wesson revolver, a .32-caliber Colt automatic pistol, and a black grip containing twenty pounds of dynamite approached the 2132 R Street N.W. home of Attorney General Palmer. On the second of its three front steps, he paused to light the bomb's fuse. It malfunctioned, blowing him to bits. Upstairs, Palmer had just moved away from the front window. In doing so, he escaped death. He raced downstairs, into the street, past the rubble and the scattered blood and flesh.

Franklin and Eleanor Roosevelt lived across R Street from the Palmers and were just arriving home. As FDR parked their car, the explosion ripped the night air, shattering their first-floor windows, tearing apart their sun parlor. The bomber's scalp was later found to have landed on the Roosevelts' roof. FDR rushed to check his children's safety, bounding upstairs, two at a time. "I'll never forget how uncommonly unnerved Father was when he dashed upstairs and found me standing at the window in my pajamas," James Roosevelt recalled. "He grabbed me in an embrace that almost cracked my ribs."

Eleanor displayed less emotion. Seemingly oblivious to the carnage wrought outside, she demanded of her eleven-year-old: "What are you doing out of bed at this hour, James? Get yourself straight to bed!"

Franklin phoned police. Returning outside, he found Palmer, who had regressed into childhood Quaker speech patterns. "He was 'theeing' and 'thouing' me all over the place," FDR recalled, "'thank thee,

Franklin!' and all that." That night, Palmer's family took shelter with the Roosevelts.

Nicholas and Alice Roosevelt Longworth were also returning home. They got the news from black police officer John B. Loftus. With the forty-eight-year-old Loftus "on the box of the motor," they raced to Palmer's. "As we walked across R Street[,] it was difficult to avoid stepping on bloody hunks of human being," Alice recalled. "The man had been torn apart, fairly blown to butcher's meat. It was curiously without horror . . . a large number of pieces had been assembled on a piece of newspaper, and seemed no more than so much carrion."

The carnage was incredible. The next morning, Eleanor wrote to her mother-in-law: "Now we are roped off, and the police haven't yet allowed the gore to be wiped up on our steps and James glories in every bone found! I only hope the victim was not a poor passerby instead of the anarchist!"

Palmer wanted revenge. "We could not take a step without seeing or feeling the grinding of a piece of flesh," Palmer later told a Senate investigating committee:

> I remember . . . , the morning after my house was blown up, I stood in the middle of the wreckage of my library with Congressmen and Senators, and without a dissenting voice they called upon me in strong terms to exercise all the power that was possible . . . to run to earth the criminals who were behind that kind of outrage.

Palmer, lacking resources, moved very cautiously at first, earning the scorn of those demanding a crackdown. But after receiving a $500,000 appropriation, on August 1, 1919 he established within the Justice Department's Bureau of Investigation an anti-radical General Intelligence Division, headed by twenty-four-year-old Washington-born Justice Department attorney J. Edgar Hoover. Hoover, a former Library of Congress staffer, quickly established an elaborate card-catalog system on the nation's 200,000 radicals.

Two weeks before, Palmer had raided a Buffalo, New York, Spanish anarchist group, El Ariete, accusing it of advocating a violent overthrow of the government ("Let the revolution come! Hail to the

146

immaculate and redeeming anarchy!"). A federal judge threw Palmer's case out of court.

Palmer tried a new tack. Most of the nation's radicals were foreign-born. Many, never having bothered to become citizens, could be deported. Secretary of Labor William B. Wilson had ruled that membership in the radical Federation of the Union of Russian Workers was grounds for deportation, but his department lacked the resources (and largely the interest) for such work. Palmer took it on.

The first series of Palmer Raids commenced on November 7, 1919. At dawn on December 21, 1919, he presided over the deportation of 249 resident aliens, most prominently the anarchists Emma Goldman (jailed for two weeks in 1901 but then released for her alleged role in the assassination of President McKinley) and her former lover Alexander "Sasha" Berkman (jailed for fourteen years for his 1892 attempt on the life of Carnegie Steel executive Henry Clay Frick). The radicals were shipped out for Mother Russia on the *Buford*, nicknamed the "Soviet Ark."

A more ambitious series of Palmer raids swept the nation from January 2 through January 6, 1920. Authorities arrested six thousand more radicals, four thousand on a single night, mostly anarchists and IWW members. Palmer respected few legal niceties. In Detroit, the accused were tossed into a particularly inhospitable prison dubbed the "Black Hole." In Boston, it wasn't much better. "The five hundred arrested," wrote former Bronx Assemblyman Benjamin Gitlow, "were shackled and chained hand and foot and marched through the streets. The conditions . . . where the prisoners were confined and held incommunicado were chaotic and brutal. One of the captives, unable to stand the strain, plunged headlong from the fifth floor to the corridor below and dashed his brains out. . . ." In Philadelphia, those arrested were subjected to a third degree employing "the worst physical force methods and torture known to the police."

Radical and liberal protests were soon joined by establishment criticism. In May 1920, twelve prominent attorneys and law-school professors, led by Harvard's Dean Roscoe Pound and Felix Frankfurter, issued a report blasting Palmer.

Palmer predicted a massive Red uprising on May Day, 1920. New York City placed its entire 11,000-man force on twenty-four-hour alert.

Machine guns ringed key positions in Boston. But nothing happened. Socialists dismissed "Mr. Palmer's dime novel plot," and other observers widely ridiculed the "Fighting Quaker" as the "quaking fighter" and the "faking fighter."

Palmer wasn't the only one reacting—or overreacting. In a Chicago theater on May 6, 1919, fifty-five-year-old tinsmith and IWW member George Goddard refused to stand and remove his hat during the "Star Spangled Banner." Apprentice seaman Samuel A. Hagerman shot three times. The audience cheered.

At 2 P.M. on November 11, 1919—the first anniversary of Armistice Day—the Centralia, Washington American Legion organized a parade. Legionnaires, Boy Scouts, the Red Cross, and the Elks all participated in what should have been a fairly humdrum event. Centralia, however, contained a sizable IWW contingent and simmered on the edge of violence. Fearing an attack on their Roderick Hotel headquarters, Wobblies stationed armed men atop a nearby hotel and a nearby hill. The parade filed once past and nothing happened. It came again. Then *it* happened. The IWW claimed that Legionnaires made a threatening move toward their headquarters. Most parade participants denied that claim. Wobblies opened fire, killing three Legionnaires (one just back from anti-Bolshevik service in Siberia) and wounding four more.

Angry townspeople arrested nearly two dozen Wobblies, but former serviceman Wesley Everest, who had killed two Legionnaires, escaped. A hastily formed posse found him just outside Centralia, wading across the swollen Skookumchuck River. Everest fired his revolver at his pursuers, killing Legionnaire John Haney. The mob beat Everest mercilessly, knocking out his teeth with a rifle butt, then dragging him back to jail. At 8 P.M., Centralia's power went dark. A mob hauled Everest from his cell, beat him further, and drove him to the Chehalis River Bridge. Along the route, he was allegedly castrated. On arrival, he pled: "Shoot me, for God's sake shoot me!" The mob hung him from the bridge, eventually strangling him. His tormenters riddled his dead body with bullets before cutting it down and returning it to town, so his former comrades might learn from his fate.

National outrage focused on the four dead Legionnaires, not on the savagery inflicted on Everest. His murderers were never punished, and nobody seemed to care much that they weren't.

In January 1920, a judge sentenced Waterbury, Connecticut, clothing salesman and Socialist Party member Joseph Yenowsky to six months in jail for allegedly remarking that Lenin was the smartest man in the world and that Yenowsky wanted a Soviet-style government here.

That same month, evangelist Billy Sunday informed an audience, "I would stand every one of the ornery, wild-eyed IWW's, anarchists, crazy Socialists, and other types of Reds up before a firing squad and save space on our ships."

In February 1920 in Hammond, Indiana, Italian-born Frank Petroni, a naturalized immigrant, argued with Austrian-born laborer Frank Petrich, an unnaturalized radical, over Italian claims to former Austrian territory. The twenty-five-year-old Petrich finally yelled, "To hell with the United States." Petroni shot him dead. Petroni pled not guilty by reason of patriotism. The jury deliberated two minutes before setting Petroni free.

New York State, with its large foreign-born population, grew particularly jittery. In March 1919, Joint Legislative Committee Investigating Seditious Activities chairman Clayton R. Lusk authorized a series of raids on New York radicals, swooping down on the Soviet Bureau (the de facto Soviet embassy), netting two tons of radical publications; the local IWW offices; and the socialist Rand School of Social Science. Senator Lusk's staff displayed an unusual regard for legalities in raiding the Rand School, but his committee became unhinged on the subject, believing the school was the linchpin of a vast radical conspiracy. It wasn't. The Lusk Committee's report recommended outlawing the hitherto legal Socialist Party, heavily regulating nonreligious private schools, and instituting a teacher loyalty oath. Governor Al Smith vetoed the measures, but his Republican successor signed them the following year.

New York legislators proved active on another front, voting to expel three of five elected Socialist Party New York City assemblymen. None of the five had yet been convicted, or even charged, with any crime. They were merely Socialists. The Assembly voted 116–28 to expel three of the members and 104–40 against expelling the two others. "It was an American vote altogether," observed the *New York Times*, "a patriotic and conservative vote. An immense majority of the American people will approve and sanction the Assembly's action."

Not everyone concurred. Theodore Roosevelt Jr. (now in his father's footsteps as an Assemblyman) voted no in all five cases. From Washington, Warren Harding and Hiram Johnson decried the situation, and Charles Evans Hughes denounced the action as "a serious blow to the standards of true Americanism and nothing short of a calamity."

In a September 16 special election, voters re-elected the three expelled Socialists. The Assembly again barred them. The other two refused to take their seats.

Congress witnessed a similar—but not entirely analogous—expulsion. In March 1918, federal authorities had indicted Milwaukee Socialist newspaper editor Victor Berger, party national executive secretary Adolf Germer, party director of publications J. Louis Engdahl, and two other prominent Socialists for Espionage Act violations. Under indictment, Berger finished a weak third when he ran in a special election for the United States Senate, behind pro-war Republican Congressman Irvine L. Lenroot and Democrat Joseph E. Davies, Wilson's 1912 Western campaign manager.

That November, Berger won election to Congress, winning in a normally Republican district. On January 8, 1919, after just three ballots, a jury found Berger and company guilty. The following month, Judge Kenesaw Mountain Landis sentenced each to twenty years in jail. In November 1919, the House, with only one dissenting vote, refused to seat Berger. Appealing his sentence (he never did serve time), he ran again in a special election the following month, this time triumphing 25,802 to 19,200 against a fusion Republican–Democrat candidate. In January 1920, the House voted once more, this time 330–6, against seating him. Wisconsin Governor Emanuel L. Philipp, fearing that Berger would win yet again, refused to call another special election, and the seat remained vacant.

"It was my great disappointment to give Berger only twenty years in Leavenworth," Judge Landis fumed. "I believe the law should have enabled me to have him lined up against the wall and shot. . . . The districts that voted to re-elect Berger ought to get out of this democracy and back in their monarchy. Berger's platform was that he was 100 percent German, and on that basis he was re-elected."

But not everyone was losing his head like Landis. When Rear Admiral

S. S. Robinson cashiered three Newport Naval Base machinists because of Socialist Party membership, Franklin Roosevelt chided: "Now, my dear Admiral, neither you nor I can fire a man because he happens to be a Socialist. It so happens that the Socialist party has a place on the official ballot in almost every state in the union . . . there was . . . no real justification for discharging them on that ground."

Admirals weren't the only ones confused regarding the differences between Communists and Socialists, who for a while still shared a home in the Socialist Party. In May 1920, the Socialist Party voted to align itself with Lenin's Third International, although drawing the line at a domestic "dictatorship of the proletariat." In any case, Socialist Party leader Morris Hillquit, a relative moderate, contended that there was no cause for concern. "Lenin is not a dictator," Hillquit informed delegates to the 1920 Socialist Party convention. "Trotsky is not a dictator. They have not proclaimed themselves such and can be recalled by the soviets or by the people at any time. They and the other officials of the soviet government were all elected."

A group of mostly Western native-born radicals wanted to remain in the Socialist Party and fight for its control. Eventually, they abandoned that hope, but during an August 31, 1919 Party gathering in the billiard room of Chicago's Machinists Hall, Benjamin Gitlow and journalists John Reed and Charles E. Ruthenberg helped found the Communist Labor Party. "The Bolsheviki believe in democracy of the working class," crowed Reed, "and no democracy for anybody else." Reed thought that was a good idea.

Within days, however, a second communist party, the Communist Party of America (CPA), had formed, with Ruthenberg jumping to it and becoming its national secretary. The almost entirely foreign-born CPA (only 7 percent of whose members spoke or read English) announced short-term plans to launch a national general strike on October 8 to free imprisoned San Francisco labor leader Tom Mooney. Presumably, they had longer-term plans to establish a government on soviet principles.

Some men hoped to bring about the revolution by political conventions and general strikes; others employed more direct approaches. Within a very short period of time, the radicals who met at Machinists Hall would be forgotten, but two other activists half a continent away would start on the path to becoming legends.

On Thursday afternoon, April 15, 1920, three men robbed two South Braintree, Massachusetts shoe factories—Slater & Morrill and Walker and Kneeland—of $15,766.51 in combined payrolls. No one in the general public noticed. Unless, of course, you were next of kin to paymaster Frederick A. Parmenter or guard Alessandro Berardelli. Berardelli lay dead in the street. Parmenter expired fourteen hours later.

Coincidentally, on the same day, Italian immigrant Feruchio Coacci failed to appear for a deportation hearing. Immigration officials surveilling Coacci's residence in nearby Bridgewater took notice of a visitor, another immigrant, dapper little Michael Buda, suspecting him of a connection to the recent robberies. On Wednesday night, May 5, 1920, authorities sprung a trap for Buda on a local streetcar. Missing Buda by minutes, they detained three of his associates, including thirty-year-old South Stoughton shoe-trimmer Nicola Sacco and thirty-three-year-old Plymouth fish-peddler Bartolomeo Vanzetti. Officials found a handwritten piece of anarchist literature on the men. Written in Italian, it announced a talk by Vanzetti in nearby Brockton:

> Proletarians, you have fought all the wars. You have worked for all the owners. You have wandered over all the countries. Have you harvested the fruits of your labors, the price of your victories? Does the past comfort you? Does the present smile on you? Does the future promise you anything? Have you found a piece of land where you can live like a human being and die like a human being? On these questions, on this argument, and on this theme, the struggle for existence, Bartolomeo Vanzetti will speak. Hour _____ Day _____ Hall _____ Admission free. Freedom of discussion to all. Take the ladies with you.

More significant were the firearms.

Vanzetti possessed a fully loaded five-shot, nickel-plated, .38-caliber

James M. Cox and Franklin Roosevelt in Cox's hometown of Dayton, Ohio, Notification Day, 1920.

California Senator Hiram Johnson's campaign button summed up his anti-League of Nations, isolationist platform.

The Big Four – Britain's Lloyd George, Italy's Orlando, France's Clemenceau, and America's Wilson. They dictated the Peace of Versailles.

Joseph Tumulty, Admiral Cary Grayson, Woodrow Wilson, and Brigadier General George R. Dyer in a Columbus Day Parade in New York City.

Florence Harding, Dr. George Harding, and Warren G. Harding.

Governor Calvin Coolidge of Massachusetts. His actions during the Boston Police Strike made him a potential presidential candidate. A delegate stampede made him the GOP vice-presidential nominee.

William Gibbs McAdoo—Wilson's son-in-law, his Secretary of the Treasury, and a front-runner for the Democratic nomination in 1920.

General Leonard Wood, the Republican front-runner, and Senator Warren G. Harding, the dark horse of all dark horses. (*Library of Congress*)

New York's Charles Evans Hughes, the 1916 Republican Presidential nominee, and Indiana's Will Hays, the 1920 Republican National Chairman.

Theodore Roosevelt—the Republican candidate in 1920—save for the hand of death.

Ohio's Harry M. Daugherty—Warren Harding's deft, but somewhat suspect, campaign manager.

Herbert Clark Hoover—the Great Humanitarian. A Hoover–FDR ticket was not out of the question in 1920.

Colonel Edward M. House—Woodrow
Wilson's Texas-born eminence grise. By 1920
House and Wilson were on the outs.

William Jennings Bryan—three times
the Democratic presidential candidate.
"The Great Commoner" hoped vainly
for another chance in 1920.

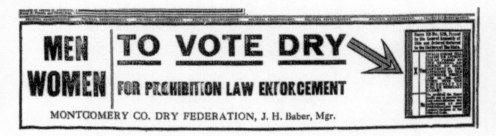

Newspaper advertisement for a Montgomery County, Ohio, prohibition referendum.

Ohio Governor James Middleton Cox.
Like Harding and Harry Daugherty, Cox
played the dark horse card perfectly.

Harding's public relations guru Albert Lasker (standing,
left) at a family wedding. (*Courtesy of Alan Schwarz*)

Wisconsin Senator Robert M. LaFollette—a radical Progressive threat to run third-party in 1920.

Woodrow and his second wife, Edith Galt Wilson, at the March 1917 Inaugural. (*Library of Congress*)

Harrington & Richardson revolver and four 12-gauge shotgun shells. Police assumed the revolver—the same type as normally carried by the slain South Braintree guard Alessandro Berardelli—to be the dead man's missing piece.

The shotgun shells (and eyewitness testimony) helped connect Vanzetti to a three-man Wednesday, December 24, 1919, Bridgewater payroll robbery.

Sacco, despite telling captors "I ain't got no gun," possessed a fully loaded nine-shot .32-caliber Colt pistol and twenty-three additional live rounds fitting that weapon. No other American-made weapon could have fired the slug that murdered Berardelli. Police arrested both Sacco and Vanzetti.

On July 1, 1920, a jury found Vanzetti guilty of the Bridgewater robbery. Judge Webster Thayer sentenced him to twelve to fifteen years at Charleston State Prison. That September, authorities indicted Sacco and Vanzetti for the South Braintree robbery and murders.

Sacco and Vanzetti may have been poor immigrants, but they were not alone or friendless. They were active anarchists (both had fled to Monterrey, Mexico, during the war to avoid the draft), part of a particularly radical wing of the movement, the Galleanists, and possessed widespread anarchist community connections.

Michael Buda was, indeed, a very dangerous man. When authorities indicted Sacco and Vanzetti ("the best friends I had in America," said Buda), he swore revenge on the capitalist system and headed for New York. After obtaining a horse and wagon—and a hundred pounds of dynamite—Buda, at noon on Monday, September 16, parked at Wall and Broad Streets, in front of the House of Morgan. Then Buda moved away very, very quickly. He would keep moving until he got back to Italy.

A minute later, 12:01 P.M.—lunchtime, with the streets packed with workers—hell broke loose. Five hundred pounds of shrapnel perforated the sky. Windows shattered. Awnings burst into flame. Fire charred the first twenty floors of the nearby Equitable Building. Over two hundred persons lay injured, burned, and bleeding on the streets. Inside J. P. Morgan's office, Morgan's secretary, Thomas Joyce, lay dead. The blast would eventually claim thirty-three lives.

The *New York World* editorialized on September 22, 1920: "Attorney

General Palmer is convinced that the Wall Street explosion was the result of a bomb plot. In spite of the Attorney General's opinion, it probably *was* the result of a bomb plot."

Sacco, Vanzetti, and Buda were not mere theoretical anarchists. They had helped plot the bombings that had rocked the nation in 1919, part of a group of fifty to sixty hardcore Galleanists, who had mailed the May Day bombs to Palmer, Ole Hanson, and the others. It was Sacco and Vanzetti's friend, Carlo Valdinoci, who had trudged to Palmer's doorstep and been blown literally to a thousand pieces for his efforts. Wrote Paul Avrich, the foremost expert on Sacco and Vanzetti's anarchist connections: "That Sacco and Vanzetti were involved in the 1919 bombings is, indeed, a virtual certainty. . . ."

Investigating the bombings, the Justice Department had arrested two Brooklyn anarchist printers, Andrea Salsedo and Roberto Elia. Department agents worked Salsedo over pretty good. He talked. So did Elia. After that, both men remained in a sort of protective custody. Salcedo grew increasingly agitated. Having breached the anarchist code of conduct, his conscience bothered him. More importantly, he feared revenge. Twice he smuggled letters to Vanzetti, asking for help. He knew that Vanzetti (just about a month before his arrest) was in New York, asking questions about the case. All this preyed upon Salcedo's mind. At 4:20 on the morning of May 2, 1920, he leaped from his fourteenth-story bedroom to the pavement below.

No wonder neither Sacco nor Vanzetti wanted to talk to the police.

Assisting in their defense was former IWW official Carlo Tresca, one of the nation's more prominent anarchists. Tresca viewed the evidence against Vanzetti in his Bridgewater robbery trial as weak. He thought it unusual for the state to try a lesser charge first, and that, for a first-time offender, Vanzetti's sentence was unusually harsh. Tresca believed Vanzetti had been railroaded, and that he and Sacco would receive similar treatment in their upcoming trial. With the death penalty in play, Tresca recruited Fred H. Moore, a colorful, if noticeably erratic, California radical, as Sacco's counsel. Moore would transform the case into a political case—but *that* would not happen until after the 1920 election.

## Chapter 10

# "SUPERIOR BIOLOGIC VALUES"

Modernity, or what passed for it, was in full force in 1920.

The automobile had replaced the horse. The number of cars owned by Americans had jumped dramatically in just ten years, from 500,000 in 1910 to 2.5 million in 1915, to 9 million in 1920. By now, one in every three families owned an automobile. And, for the first time, the majority of cars were enclosed, facilitating all sorts of activities that had previously required hotel rooms.

The boys were back from the war. The girls—"flappers"—were liberated. Their hair was short, "bobbed," and so were skirts, inching dangerously toward the knee. Not surprisingly, the divorce rate had nearly tripled since 1900—to 1.1 percent.

Popular culture also seemed to be going straight to hell as the Roaring Twenties began. There was, of course, the devil's music, jazz—until recently known as "jass." In July 1920, evangelist Melvin G. Morris berated jazz, modern music, and popular dance. "The modern dance," he declaimed, "was conceived by the devil, born in the darkest and vilest corners of hell, reared in savagery and places unspeakably vile. . . .

"When the Bible said 'there is a time to dance,' it does not mean there is a time to fox-trot, tango, jazz or shimmy." Even in 1920, he seemed hopelessly retrograde.

The motion picture remained silent but suggestive, with such lurid offerings as director Fred Niblo's *Sex*, Erich von Stroheim's *The Devil's Passkey*, and Cecil B. DeMille's *Why Change Your Wife?*, along with such lesser artistic efforts as *A He-Male Vamp* and *The Amateur Wife*. Broadway trafficked not only in Eugene O'Neill's respectable but depressing offerings, but also in skimpily unclad damsels in such mindless efforts as *George White's Scandals* and *The Ziegfeld Follies*.

Tabloid journalism ushered itself in without bothering to knock on the door, determined to outdo its immediate, somewhat stodgier, ancestor, "yellow journalism," with the first American tabloid, *The New York Daily News* (then the *Illustrated Daily News*), debuting in June 1919. Gossip, too, was in transition, making the jump from over-the-back-fence whispers to mass-circulation journalism. In November 1920, a twenty-three-year-old ex-song-and-dance man named Walter Winchell initiated his first column in *The Vaudeville News*.

The stock market boom was yet to be born, but greed and gullibility—always first cousins—grew particularly chummy in Boston in 1920, as immigrant swindler Charles Ponzi fleeced thousands of investors, promising to pay 50 percent interest in just ninety (later forty-five) days. At his peak, he took in a million dollars a week. A crowd of admirers once gathered around the 5'2" Ponzi, and a man shouted: "You're the greatest Italian of them all."

"No, no," the forty-three-year-old Ponzi protested, "Columbus and Marconi. Columbus discovered America. Marconi discovered the wireless."

"Yes," the man shouted back, "but you discovered money!"

Big business was getting bigger, with chain stores and installment buying on the rise, but sports, too, was becoming big business—with Babe Ruth, Jack Dempsey, Jim Thorpe, Man O' War, Big Bill Tilden, and even a woman, tennis champion Suzanne Lenglen, as its premier commodities, though suddenly it was all no longer quite so innocent: In September 1920, America learned that the 1919 World Series had been fixed—"Say, it ain't so, Joe."

And, last but not least, America was urban.

The Fourteenth Census of the United States had certified that fact, made it official, in Anno Domini 1920. The American Republic had officially turned from a rural to an urban society. The margin was narrow—just 51.4 percent urban—and the standard was, if possible, finer still: "urban" defined as any incorporated place with at least 2,500 residents—meaning that such entities as Osage, Iowa (pop. 2,876), Buford, Georgia (pop. exactly 2,500), and Sauk Centre, Minnesota (pop. 2,699) could count themselves citified.

Some regions were more metropolitan than others. The Middle Atlantic States and southern New England certainly were. The South and the upper Midwest remained stubbornly rural. Just 13.6 percent of North Dakota and 13.4 percent of Mississippi met even the government definition of urban.

And, of course, the census counted as urban those persons merely *currently* residing in an "urban area," even if they had lived their entire previous existence in a village in Poland or Sicily or sharecropping on a North Carolina tobacco farm. Merely by stuffing their few possessions into a valise for a move to America, or to Chicago, or to Sauk Centre, they now officially qualified as Jazz Age sophisticates.

In 1920, 13,920,692 of America's 105,273,049 souls were foreign-born—13.2 percent of the total white population—preponderantly in the Northeast: 29 percent of Rhode Island; 28.3 percent of Calvin Coolidge's Massachusetts; and 27.2 percent of Al Smith's New York. The cities were even worse. Only 17.9 percent of Manhattan, 24.9 percent of Boston, and 24.8 percent of Chicago was native-born, with two native-born parents. Even heartland cities like San Antonio (52 percent), Salt Lake City (48 percent), and Omaha (47.8 percent) featured low percentages of that category.

Of course, not all foreigners were menacing, swarthy types, hook-nosed peddlers, or heavyset, befuddled women in babushkas. A fair amount originated in "nice" countries—1,135,489 from England, Scotland, and Wales; 1,686,108 from Germany (Germany having been reasonably "nice" before 1914); Scandinavia (1,178,602); the Netherlands (131,766); and non-Quebec Canada (830,388). Even the ghastly Irish (1,037,234 souls) spoke a form of English and counted a fair number of Protestants among them.

Yes, America was changing, and Americans who hadn't done the same didn't like it a bit. The cities were not only filled with foreigners, they were polluted with saloons and brothels and all sorts of immorality, with corrupt political machines, with dangerous, often violent, ideologies.

It wasn't just the changing numbers that made native, rural Americans skittish; so did the changing mores and realities. The world war set people's teeth on edge. The Red scare sent shivers down their spines. People were afraid, afraid of demon rum, of Jews and blacks and Catholics.

They fought back.

Prohibition was their most powerful weapon.

The Temperance crowd had warned of demon rum for decades. "The saloon," thundered evangelist Billy Sunday, "will take off the shirt from the back of a shivering man. It will take the coffin from under the dead. It will take the milk from the breast of the poor mother who is the wife of a drinking man. It will take the crust of bread from the hand of the hungry child. It cares for nothing but itself—for its dirty profits. It will keep your boy out of college. It will make your daughter a prostitute. It will bury your wife in the potter's field. It will send you to hell." He spoke for millions, who knew that while there was hyperbole in his words, there was also too much truth.

Prohibitionists included not merely reactionaries like Sunday, but large numbers of political progressives. Prohibition had long been linked to reform—to abolition or women's suffrage or the fight for municipal good government. Progressives demanded not only trust-busting, better working conditions, safer food and drugs, and direct democracy; they also wanted moral uplift. Racetracks, prize fights, casinos, and brothels were shuttered, narcotics regulated. Booze was next. Temperance forces flooded the nation with anti-alcohol pamphlets, songs, plays, posters, and books. In 1905, only three states had enacted prohibition; by 1912, nine; by 1916, twenty-six. By 1919, thirty-three states plus Alaska, Puerto Rico, and the District of Columbia were dry.

On December 10, 1913, prohibitionists, led by the Anti-Saloon League's savvy counsel Wayne B. Wheeler, launched a drive for a national ban. Five thousand members of the Anti-Saloon League and the Women's Christian Temperance Union invaded D.C.'s Pennsylvania Avenue, prophetically singing "A Saloonless Nation by 1920." That same day, Texas Senator Morris Sheppard and Alabama Congressman Rich-mond Hobson introduced a prohibition constitutional amendment.

Drys didn't yet have anywhere near enough votes, but the 1916 election gave them a solid congressional majority, and the war provided a patriotic rationale for sobriety and grain conservation ("Shall the many have food, or the few have drink?"). In August 1917, Congress adopted the Food Control Law, banning the manufacture of distilled spirits from any form of foodstuff and closing distilleries. In September 1918, it shuttered the breweries and approved wartime prohibition—which, oddly enough, took effect only after the war was over, in July 1919.

Some politicians quickly chose up sides. Others remained unsure of the temper of the times—or, more importantly, of their constituents. Among the wavering was Warren Harding. "I am not a prohibitionist . . . ," he explained, "and never have pretended to be. I do claim to be a temperance man. I do not approach this question from a moral viewpoint, because I am unable to see it as a great moral question."

Harding wasn't the only wobbler. Wilson had supported the middle ground of local option (leaving the decision up to local governments) as governor, vacillated a little more in running for president in 1912, and unenthusiastically signed into law various wartime prohibition measures. In May 1919, however, he asked Congress to lift the ban on wine and liquor until full prohibition went into effect. It refused.

In 1907, Teddy Roosevelt had written: "Everybody ought to believe in temperance [and peace]; but the professional advocates of both tend towards a peculiarly annoying form of egoistic lunacy." His Progressive Party was chockablock with Prohibitionists. Roosevelt wasn't one of them—until 1918, that is, when he finally joined the now seemingly irresistible dry cause.

Franklin Roosevelt (for local option as a state senator) never quite made that jump, but Eleanor had. Her father, Theodore's younger brother Elliott, had been a pathetic alcoholic, and she supported prohibition. She refused to serve liquor at home—much to the chagrin of her husband, who had squirreled away four cases of "Old Reserve" at $1.90 per bottle just before prohibition kicked in—"47 East Sixty-fifth Street," Franklin chortled, "is for the time being at least on the 'wet' list!" As late as 1924, Eleanor attended a conference urging more efficient prohibition enforcement.

Eventually, every presidential candidate had to declare his sentiments. Harding, Hiram Johnson, Robert La Follette, and dark horses Howard Sutherland and Miles Poindexter all voted for prohibition in the Senate. Harding, once he was settled in the dry camp, even supported a proviso to the proposed amendment, banning even ownership and consumption of alcohol. Among Democrats, Bryan and McAdoo stood foursquare in favor. Governors Edward I. Edwards of New Jersey and Al Smith of New York were opposed. James Cox was mildly opposed, and Mitchell Palmer wobbled all over the place.

Harding further proposed a scheme to garner additional wavering votes, a time limit on state ratification. Following his lead, Congress established a six-year limit—a move that cost the Drys virtually nothing. Wayne Wheeler, a shrewd strategist as well as a shrewd tactician, realized that the nation was changing. Once the 1920 census figures triggered another round of legislative re-districting, the immigrant-dominated cities would again increase in power, substantially reducing any national amendment's chances. Because time was fast running out on him anyway, Wheeler acquiesced to Harding's limit. It was now or never.

On August 1, 1917, the Senate approved the Prohibition Amendment, the Eighteenth Amendment, 65–20 (Democrats voting 36–12; Republicans 29–8). On December 18, 1917, the House voted 282–128 (Democrats 141–64, Republicans 137–62, Others 4–2) to send the following Prohibition Amendment, six-year time limit and all, to the states for ratification:

After one year from the ratification of this article the manufacture, sale, or transportation of intoxicating liquors within, the importation thereof into, or the exportation thereof from the United States and all territory subject to the jurisdiction thereof for beverage purposes is hereby prohibited.

On January 6, 1919, only one year and eight days later, Nebraska became the requisite 36th state to ratify. On October 28, 1919, Congress enacted enabling legislation, the National Prohibition Act (better known as the Volstead Act). Wilson vetoed it, citing a narrow technicality regarding wartime prohibition. The House took two hours to override. The Senate followed the next day. Prohibition would commence on January 17, 1920.

It arrived, accompanied by the wailing of Wets and the hosannas of Drys. In Washington, temperance forces, led by Bryan, Wheeler, Methodist Bishop James Cannon, and Josephus Daniels gathered at the city's First Congregationalist Church. As midnight struck and Prohibition became official, Bryan shattered the silence, quoting Matthew 2:20: "They are dead that sought the child's life. They are dead! They are dead!"

John F. ("Honest John") Kramer, the nation's first Prohibition Commissioner, was less scriptural but equally optimistic. "This law," Kramer, a fifty-year-old Ohio Democrat, vowed, "will be obeyed in cities, large and small, and where it is not obeyed it will be enforced. . . . The law says that liquor to be used as a beverage must not be manufactured. We shall see that it is not manufactured. Nor sold, nor given away, nor hauled in anything on the surface of the earth, or in the air."

Within the year, in exchange for bribes ranging as high as $100,000, Kramer's office had allowed rumrunners to loot government stocks of a hundred million dollars' worth of high-quality liquor.

Perhaps anticipating such developments, no one seemed to think the issue was resolved—certainly not bootleggers or flask-carrying sheiks, tipsy flappers, or free-spending speakeasy patrons. Nor did Drys. Convening in Omaha in July 1920, the Prohibition Party remained open for business, scanning the horizon for signs of backsliding. Delegates determined to field not only a presidential ticket, but the strongest in party history, their veritable dream ticket: William Jennings Bryan for president and Billy Sunday for vice-president. Unfortunately, neither wanted the honor. Having lost three times on a major party ticket, Bryan didn't relish a fourth loss on a very minor party ticket. Sunday was a Republican. He liked Prohibition, but he liked Harding more, and that was that.

Prohibitionists turned to an even more accomplished loser than Bryan: Ohio party activist Dr. Aaron Sherman Watkins. Watkins had lost for vice president twice, for governor twice, for attorney general, and for secretary of state. He won the Prohibition Party nomination on the second ballot.

Miss Marie C. Brehm, permanent chairman of the convention, generated considerable early support for vice president, but the party ultimately selected New York author Dr. D. Leigh Colvin, a former United States Senate and New York mayoral candidate.

In 1905, another author had done very well for himself. North Carolina-born novelist Reverend Thomas Dixon Jr. issued *The Clansman: An Historical Romance of the Ku Klux Klan*. That same year, he combined *The Clansman* with an earlier Reconstruction-era novel, *The Leopard's Spots* (which had sold 100,000 copies in its first three months), to mount a stage play called *The Clansman*. New York critics dismissed *The Clansman* as "crude melodrama." Provincial audiences lapped it up.

Two years earlier, Dixon had produced an anti-Socialist novel entitled *The One Woman*. Its stage version starred (before Dixon fired him) one Lawrence Griffith, better known to history by his real name, D. W. Griffith. Lawrence Griffith had reason to employ a pseudonym: Largely a failure, he had barely survived as an itinerant (and bad) stage actor. Reluctantly, he moved to film, then an unproven medium derided by most actors. Fancying himself a playwright, Griffith soon began writing and directing for New York-based Biograph Studios. Possessing an uncanny grasp of what worked—and didn't—in the infant medium, Griffith essentially invented the role of director—and invented film as an American art form.

Like Dixon, the Kentucky-born Griffith possessed strong Southern sympathies and foresaw *The Clansman*'s huge possibilities, using it to create the infant industry's first true epic. No other Griffith film exceeded seven reels. *The Birth of a Nation* (the picture's ultimate title) ran twelve—a full two hours and forty-five minutes. The film featured unprecedented action, huge battle scenes, and blood-stirring Klan charges. It also possessed pathos, warmth, human interest—and a powerful dose of Southern racism. Promptly denounced as a slur on blacks, it nonetheless ran seven months at Los Angeles's 2,500-seat Clune's Auditorium.

Anticipating hostility (and outright censorship) in more liberal New York, Dixon approached an old friend from his days at Johns Hopkins University, asking President Woodrow Wilson if he cared for a private White House screening. Wilson saw it, loved it, and commented: "It is like writing history with Lightning. And my only regret is that it is terribly true."

"I didn't dare allow the president to know the real big purpose of my film," Dixon confided to Joe Tumulty, "—which was to revolutionize Northern sentiments by a presentation that would transform every man in the audience into a good Democrat! And make no mistake about it . . . we are doing just that thing."

*Birth of a Nation* didn't *quite* do that, but it did run eleven months at New York's Liberty Theater—twice a day, all seats reserved with a two-dollar top—and made millions.

Its unprecedented success inspired a thirty-four-year-old failed Methodist minister named William J. Simmons. In the dead of Thanksgiving night, 1915, Simmons, an inveterate joiner of fraternal organizations, gathered thirty-four men about him (including three members of the original Klan), drove them to the granite summit of Stone Mountain, Georgia, and there founded a new fraternal order based on the old Klan. Lighting a match to a kerosene-drenched cross, Simmons pronounced: "Under a blazing, fiery torch the Invisible Empire was called from its slumber of half a century to take up a new task and fulfill a new mission for humanity's good and to call back to mortal habitation the good angel of practical fraternity among men."

Most basically, the Klan was yet another fraternal society, in an age of fraternal societies, touched up with the usual trappings of secret ceremonies and laughable jargon. Klan gatherings ("Klonkaves") convened in "Klaverns," following the organizational manual, the "Kloran," and communicated in acronymic shorthand. "AYAK?" ("**A**re **Y**ou **A K**lansman?"), a member might ask. The desired response: "AKIA" ("**A K**lansman **I A**m"). Just about everyone had a nifty title: "Great Titans" and "Grand Dragons" and "Kludds" (chaplains), "Kligrapps" (secretaries), and "Klabees" (treasurers). Simmons was "King Kleagle."

The new Klan began with modest success and a smidgen of respectability. It might have been bigoted, but—initially, at least—not particularly so for its time and place, and not yet violent. It assumed an air of wartime vigilance, reporting on strikers, seditionists, camp followers, and the like. "[I]t is well to remember," noted one early study, "that men joined the Klan because it appealed to their patriotism and their moral idealism more than to their hates and prejudices. . . . [Often] the Klan secures a foothold in the community and makes itself felt, . . . in the role of moral reformer, unearthing the bootlegger or chastising criminals and disreputable characters that have escaped the law."

Its first few years witnessed only very modest growth. Then, in June

1920, Simmons engaged two professional fund-raisers: Edward Young Clarke of the Southern Publicity Association and his pudgy assistant, Mrs. Elizabeth Tyler. Their credentials included promoting harvest festivals and "Better Baby" parades and such organizations as the Anti-Saloon League and the Roosevelt Memorial Association. Nonetheless, they didn't come cheap, retaining $8 of each new recruit's $10 initiation fee (the "Klectoken"). With Clarke and Tyler emphasizing patriotic and racial motifs and trumpeting the group as white Protestant America's last bulwark against alien hordes, in just a few months membership jumped from a few thousand to a hundred thousand.

Violence surged too. By October 1920, the Klan was conducting wide-spread night-rider raids on black-owned cotton gins in Georgia and Alabama. In Jacksonville, five hundred Klansmen marched through the streets. Two hooded men rode on ahead, one sounding a bugle, the other announcing ominously: "We are a band of determined men and will brook no interference."

Still the Klan disavowed violence. "One of [our] aims," King Kleagle Simmons blandly explained, "is to prevent mob violence and lynchings—not to conduct such offenses against the law."

But soon he had changed his tune. "Now," Simmons roared, "let the Niggers, Catholics, Jews, and all others who disdain my imperial wizardry, come on."

The Klan wasn't the only one worrying about Jews.

Detroit auto magnate Henry Ford had his own ideologies and ambitions. In December 1915, he had funded an ill-fated peace mission to Europe, derisively dubbed the "Peace Ship." In 1916, he won the Michigan Republican presidential primary and very nearly won Nebraska's. Two years later, he barely lost for the United States Senate—as a Democrat. On January 11, 1919, the first issue of Ford's weekly newspaper, the *Dearborn Independent*, rolled off the presses. A year later, it had yet to cause a stir. It supported the League of Nations and women's suffrage, but was actually quite dull. One wit snidely termed it "the best weekly ever turned out by a tractor plant." When losses hit the $284,000 mark, Ford demanded a change. On May 22, 1920, the *Independent* ran the first installment, "The Jew in Character and Business," of a ninety-one-part series, "The International Jew: The World's Problem."

People—particularly Jews—noticed. On June 3, 1920, the American Jewish Committee's Louis Marshall telegraphed Ford, protesting "palpable fabrications" in the still-infant series. Ford's office responded: "Your rhetoric is that of a Bolshevik orator. You mistake our intention. You misrepresent the tone of our articles. . . . These articles shall continue[,] and we hope you will continue to read them[;] and when you have attained a more tolerable state of mind[,] we shall be glad to discuss them with you."

Later that month, one of Ford's few Jewish friends, Detroit Reform Rabbi Leo Franklin, returned the custom-built Model T that Ford had given him. Ford asked: "What's wrong, Dr. Franklin? Has anything come between us?" Ford didn't understand, and he didn't stop.

On June 26, 1920, the *Independent* began serializing *The Protocols of the Learned Elders of Zion*, purported proof of a Jewish conspiracy working toward world domination, the actual transcripts of a secret Zionist Congress held at Basel, Switzerland, in 1897. A new *Independent* employee, White Russian émigré Lieutenant Boris Brasol, had delivered a translation of the *Protocols* to the weekly. Some said Brasol had been brought to Ford by the *Independent*'s attorney, Charles C. Daniels—Josephus's fifty-five-year-old younger brother. He denied it.

The *Protocols* was a complete fake. Originally crafted by Tsarist agent Serge Nilius in 1903, it was nonetheless a bad idea whose time had come, published simultaneously in Germany, in London, in newspapers in Paris and Warsaw, and even in Tokyo.

In October, anti-Semites struck on two more fronts. G. H. Putnam & Son announced plans to publish Nesta H. Webster's *The Cause of World Unrest*, a series of essays treating the *Protocols* as genuine. Louis Marshall now excoriated Major George Haven Putnam for publishing "these outpourings of malice, intolerance and hatred, this witches' broth of violent poison . . . this stupid drivel . . . seeking to make the Jew, as he has been in all the centuries, the scapegoat of autocracy. . . . Mr. Putnam, whoever touches pitch is defiled. . . . [You are] sheltering yourself behind the bulwarks of an infamous pasquinade of the guttersnipe variety." Putnam first protested, then withdrew the book.

Ford was not so easily cowed. That same month, his Dearborn Publishing Company issued a 250-page paperback collection of the *Independent*'s series "The International Jew: The World's Problem." Costing a mere quarter, it sold like Model Ts.

Not just Southerners and Midwesterners and Russians were entering the hate market. In March 1920, Charles Scribner's Sons published Boston attorney Dr. Lothrop Stoddard's *The Rising Tide of Color Against White Supremacy*. Stoddard argued that Russia's humiliation in the Russo-Japanese War and then the ceaseless bloodletting of the Great War had shattered global white racial hegemony. "There is no immediate danger of the world being swamped by black blood," the Harvard-educated Stoddard concluded, "but there is a very imminent danger that the white stocks may be swamped by Asiatic blood."

Stoddard's racist tract achieved not only bestseller status but actual respectability. Author F. Scott Fitzgerald provided a thinly veiled reference ("*The Rise of the Colored Empires* by this man Goddard") in *The Great Gatsby*. The *New York Times* editorialized that the book was "as sane and measured as it is dramatically effective" and explained that "To the Bolshevik[,] the very existence of superior biologic values is a crime. Bolshevism has vowed the proletarianization of the world, beginning with the white race."

"Above all," the *Times* concluded, tying Stoddard's idée fixe to Woodrow Wilson's, melding high purpose and high prejudice, "[*The Rising Tide of Color*] throws new light upon the need of a league or association which will unite the nations in defense of what is precious in the Nordic inheritance."

Such was 1920.

## Chapter 11

~

## "THE FUNERAL BAKE MEATS"

The year 1920 opened with two favorites for the Republican presidential nomination—closely trailed by a rabble-rousing, vote-getting outsider. None was named Harding or Coolidge or Hoover.

The front-runner was an ambitious physician, Medal of Honor winner, general, and politician. Close on his heels was an honest, capable, middle-of-the road Midwestern governor whose campaign would founder on reports of campaign irregularities. The outsider defied such easy descriptions.

~

Leonard Wood was more than a general. He was a genuine hero—and the anointed heir to Teddy Roosevelt's political fortunes. He would be tough to beat, unless he beat himself.

Son of a Civil War army doctor, Wood was born on October 9, 1860, in Winchester, New Hampshire. Failing to obtain appointment to either West Point or Annapolis, he attended Harvard, graduating from its medical school in 1883 and serving as Boston's City Hospital's house surgeon. His strong-headedness soon collided with the institution's bureaucratic structures. Peremptorily dismissed in September 1884, Wood turned to practicing among Boston's poor. "You can't imagine the misery, crime, and suffering in the great city," he later wrote. "Dickens' wildest flights are but too true."

In June 1885, Wood secured a position as a United States Army assistant contract surgeon, assigned to the Fourth Cavalry at the Arizona Territory's Fort Huachuca. The following May, on Captain Henry Lawton's expedition to capture the renegade Apache Geronimo, Wood suffered a poisonous tarantula bite. Lawton, fearing the worst, wrote his wife: "I am almost broken up at this misfortune. It not only leaves the command without a medical officer, but no one to look after him, and he has always been my warmest friend and supporter. I don't know what I shall do without him."

Wood overcame immense pain, delirium, and a high fever to continue the 3,041-mile march. Beyond that, he carried dispatches a hundred miles through hostile territory and assumed command of an infantry detachment whose officers had been lost. Wood won the Congressional Medal of Honor—the only member of the expedition so honored.

In November 1890, he married Louise Condit Smith, niece and ward of Supreme Court Justice Stephen J. Field, a Democrat actually more conservative than archconservative Grover Cleveland. In 1895, Cleveland appointed Wood his personal physician, and William McKinley retained his services. At a June 1897 dinner party, Wood met McKinley's Assistant Secretary of the Navy, Theodore Roosevelt. The two became fast friends. "You will be pleased to hear," TR wrote Henry Cabot Lodge, "that I have developed at Washington a playmate who fairly walked me off my legs; a Massachusetts man moreover, an army surgeon named Wood." They played football, boxed, wrestled, and fenced.

"He combined in a very high degree," TR said of his friend, "the qualities of entire manliness with entire uprightness and cleanliness of character. It was a pleasure to deal with a man of high ideals, who scorned everything mean and base, and who also possessed those robust and hardy qualities of body and mind for the lack of which no merely negative virtue can ever atone."

They were warriors, too. When America declared war with Spain, Wood received command of the 1st Volunteer Cavalry Brigade—the "Rough Riders"—with Roosevelt second-in-command. Following San Juan Hill, Wood assumed command of the 2nd Cavalry Brigade.

In August 1898, Wood became military governor of the city of Santiago, Cuba, with his old comrade, Henry Lawton, commanding the surrounding province. The two soon clashed ("Lawton is simply an obstructionist," said Wood). In late September, Lawton embarked on a six-day drinking binge that saw him physically attack Santiago's chief of police, wreck a local bar, and destroy his own career. Wood's ambitions were, by now, well known, and many suspected him of leaking Lawton's indiscretions to President McKinley. Lawton was transferred to the Philippines, killed in action near Manila in December 1899.

Wood assumed Lawton's duties, then became military governor of all Cuba, improving sanitary conditions and instituting badly needed reforms. In October 1900, he authorized experiments by Major Walter Reed that ultimately eradicated malaria on the island. By now a national figure, Leonard Wood personified America's new imperial status.

In 1902, Wood assumed command of the Philippines Division. In the Philippines, Wood used rough tactics—many said too rough. Only TR's friendship prevented his recall. In December 1909, William Howard Taft, hoping to please TR, appointed Wood Army Chief of Staff—the only medical officer to hold the position. His rapid ascent incensed fellow officers.

Yet Wood was undoubtedly imaginative and competent, streamlining the hidebound army, reorganizing its officer corps, and increasing opportunities for civilian training and preparedness. His "Plattsburgh Idea," forerunner of the ROTC program, fired the imagination of a generation of patriotic young men, even causing Franklin Roosevelt to create a naval version.

Woodrow Wilson appointed a new chief of staff in April 1914, but Wood continued urging preparedness, his public criticisms of the administration often breaching the bounds of insubordination. During a December 1914 appearance with Henry L. Stimson, Taft's Secretary of War, Wood quoted Revolutionary War general Henry Lee, who said: "A government is a murderer of its people which sends them to the field uninformed and untaught." That was bad enough, but Wood continued: "These words are absolutely true and those fake humanitarians who recommend that we shall turn the youth of this country into the battlefield unprepared are the unconscious slayers of their people to an extent far greater than ordinary demands of war would render necessary." Secretary of War Lindley M. Garrison actually sympathized with Wood, but nonetheless formally rebuked him. Wood ignored him.

A similar incident occurred in August 1915, when TR himself visited the Plattsburgh camp and thundered:

I wish to make one comment on the statement so frequently made that we must stand by the President. I heartily subscribe to this on condition, and only on condition, that it is followed by the statement "so long as the President stands by the country."

Presidents differ just like other folks. No man could effectively stand by President Lincoln unless he had stood against President Buchanan. If after the firing on Fort Sumter President Lincoln had in a public speech announced that the believers in the Union were too proud to fight; and if, instead of action, there had been three months of admirable elocutionary correspondence with Jefferson Davis, by midsummer the friends of the Union would have followed Horace Greeley's advice to let the erring sisters go in peace, for peace at any rate was put above righteousness by some mistaken soul, just as it is at the present day.

TR's remarks earned Plattsburgh commandant Wood another reprimand.

In 1916, Wood sought the GOP presidential nomination, hoping for Roosevelt's support if TR did not himself run. It was not to be. Roosevelt, smarting from the Taft disaster, hesitated to anoint another crown prince. The Wood boomlet fizzled. On the second ballot, Wood and Warren Harding received a single vote each.

When war came, Wilson anointed John J. Pershing to command the American Expeditionary Force, exiling Wood to Camp Funston, Kansas, to train the 89th Infantry Division for service in France—a calculated humiliation. When the 89th shipped out for action, another indignity arrived: orders to remain in Kansas and train the 10th Infantry Division.

Wood finally reached France, but not the front lines. In January 1918, Wood reviewed a trench mortar demonstration at Fère-en-Tardennois. The mortar exploded, ripping through Wood's raincoat, leaving six holes in it and tearing open his arm. Said Wood:

The explosion was so violent that it stunned us all for a time. My right sleeve was torn by the piece which killed the man on my right. One was disemboweled and another had an ugly wound from which he later died. I found the front of my coat covered with the brains of the man on my left.

Wood escaped serious injury. Released after three weeks in Paris's Ritz Carlton Hospital, he remained barred from even the lowest combat command.

Had TR lived—and won in 1920—he most likely would have appointed Wood Secretary of War. Instead, Wood ran as the fallen chief's anointed successor. "It was taken for granted that Father's family would be for General Wood," TR's daughter, Alice Roosevelt Longworth, would write in her memoirs. "It was quite natural we should be."

"It would seem," sighed William Howard Taft, "as if the funeral bake meats had furnished forth the feast for the heir."

While Major General Wood never commanded troops in France, the post-war wave of labor and racial unrest supplied him with opportunities at home. In September 1919, a race riot swept Omaha. A mob broke into the city jail, seized a black man accused of raping a white woman, and lynched him from a light pole. Omaha's mayor ("Hang the mayor; he won't give us the nigger!" cried the mob) nearly met the same fate. Wood's troops restored order within twenty-four hours. On October 6, 1919, Indiana Governor James P. Goodrich requested Wood's assistance when thirty-five thousand steelworkers walked off the job in Gary. Wood maintained order, refrained from interfering with the strike itself, and bragged that he was:

. . . now, in addition to routine military duties, practically Mayor of Omaha and Gary, with prospects of additions to the crop. So far, although we have ruled with a heavy hand, not a shot has been fired or a life lost.

Wood had handled delicate situations with skill (and did the same in late October, commanding troops in West Virginia's coal-mining regions), but was soon employing a heated rhetoric regarding the national situation, becoming not so much the heir to Roosevelt as the proverbial man on horseback, threatening to settle every labor dispute at bayonet-point, to restore law-and-order at gunpoint. He even advocated vigilantism, calling for "platoons from the American Legion" to "meet any demands that civil authorities may find necessary in the maintenance of law and order."

America, never having seen a leader of this stripe, wasn't sure if it wanted one. Journalist Walter Lippmann warned that the General's supporters "have the mood, if not the courage[,] of a coup d'état."

Walter Lippman and Warren Harding rarely agreed on anything but agreed on Wood. Harding wrote to a friend in February 1920:

> We made presidents out of military men for more than thirty years after the Civil War but there doesn't seem to be any sentiment for a military candidate at the present time. I think General Wood is very much of a fellow himself but I do think his military connection and his militaristic ideas are going to put an end to his candidacy.

Yet Wood had supporters, millions of them. Not all were law-and-order types. Gifford Pinchot, catalyst of the TR–Taft feud, spoke for many old Roosevelt Progressives in April 1919, when he sputtered:

> I shall stand for a platform in harmony with the policies of Theodore Roosevelt and for the nomination of such a man as [Kansas Governor] Henry Allen, Hiram Johnson, Irvine Lenroot or Leonard Wood.
>
> I shall oppose the nomination of a reactionary like Senator Harding or Jim Watson, or any other supporter of special privilege. Such men cannot be trusted. . . .

Wood inherited not only the support of the Roosevelt family and legions of mourning TR devotees, but also the Rough Rider's campaign manager, a realistic Connecticut politician named John T. King. Of King, Wood's most prominent biographer recorded:

> King was a politician out of the story book, a bland, curly-haired Irishman who had achieved affluence as garbage contractor of

Bridgeport; and, as boss of its unsavory ruling class, was service-able to the owners of the city's industrial plants, organizing committees of bruisers who met labor agitators at the railroad station and turned them back with expressive words. He had self-assurance, suavity, and even charm of a sort; but his brown beady eyes did not seduce the wary. He dressed faultlessly and was always almost aggressively barbered and manicured.

Roosevelt had met King at a political rally in Bridgeport in 1916, and, having had his fill of political idealists in the preceding five or six years, had given him a gusty welcome as a kind of ambassador extraordinary from the courts of the unregenerate. He used him on political errands. He knew King's past, and recognized his limitations. "I like John King," he had a way of saying. "We have a perfect working arrangement. John supplies the efficiency, and I supply the morals."

The fact that King had been close to Roosevelt carried weight with Wood. Roosevelt's sister, Mrs. Douglas Robinson, gave him a word of warning. Roosevelt could handle King because, in the great game, King was a child compared with Roosevelt, and knew it. But with Wood, King would attempt to be the mentor and, in that situation, would Wood be able to exercise the necessary control? Wood, who in his own field could control men with his little finger, was certain that he could keep King in leash.

Wood didn't just keep King on a leash—he sent him to the pound. As Wood broke from the starting gate, he looked like an unstoppable winner. In horse races and politics, sure winners attract money. Wood attracted supporters, and he attracted money. One supporter with money, real money, was Woodrow Wilson's old Princeton nemesis, William Cooper Procter.

Procter, unaccustomed to taking orders from Bridgeport garbage contractors, soon clashed with King. Money talks, garbage walks. By January 1920, the unqualified Procter emerged as Wood's campaign manager. Two days later, the savvy King jumped ship.

Procter transformed a sure thing into a closely run, badly run thing. Experienced politicians know when not to fight, when not to anger people one will ultimately need on one's side. Procter and Wood compre-hended none of these things. Their idea of a campaign was charging San Juan Hill. Their method of securing delegates was akin to capturing Geronimo.

That might have worked for Teddy Roosevelt—who was, after all, Teddy Roosevelt. Wood was unproven, the new kid on the block. He could not afford enemies. He needed to unite a party, achieve consensus, and march to victory in November, not only *taking* minimal casualties, but *inflicting* minimal enemy Republican casualties.

*Instead, Procter chose the exact opposite of Harry Daugherty's strategy for Warren Harding.*

Procter launched largely futile forays into favorite-son states like Ohio, Massachusetts, and West Virginia, angering potential allies like Warren Harding, Calvin Coolidge, and Howard Sutherland. He wasted money and resources by invading Illinois to challenge Frank Lowden in his home state—infuriating the normally placid Lowden in the process, turning a rivalry into a death feud. He spurned regular party organiza-tions, creating committees filled with amateurs and malcontents.

While Procter's tactics alienated Republican regulars, Wood's over-heated law-and-order rhetoric disheartened progressives. William Allen White wrote to Wood:

> I cannot help but feel that you are getting yourself into a too con-servative attitude. This crazy notion to hunt 'em down and shoot 'em and see Red, and all that sort of thing is going to pass during the Spring, and leave you high and dry unless you definitely appeal to the Progressives. They are militant and they aren't going to he satisfied with the kind of speeches you are making.

People wondered not only about Wood's ambitions and ideology, they worried about his health—and his *mind*. Wood had long walked with a limp, one not connected with any injury to his foot or leg. It dated from 1899 in Santiago. As he recalled:

> My desk was in a particular room of the house there, and I got accustomed to this location. One very warm day[,] my secretary

moved the desk to another room where there was a chance of getting more air. Some one called me and I got up suddenly. Directly behind me there was a hanging chandelier. It must have been hanging extremely low[,] for when I arose[,] my head came in violent contact with it. The blow must have broken my skull.

Years later, doctors removed a benign cyst from right base of Wood's brain, leaving him with that pronounced limp in his left foot. As Wood eyed the presidency, his opponents eyed him. In March 1920, his campaign adamantly denied that he suffered from any "brainstroke."

"His mentality," TR's physician, Dr. Alexander Lambert, announced, "is not affected."

Just the sort of reassuring public statement a campaign can easily do without.

⁀

Frank Orren Lowden, the Republicans' other favorite in 1920, was a very different sort of fellow from Leonard Wood, but not necessarily a better politician.

Minnesota-born Lowden could actually boast of being born in a log cabin. His family had migrated, via prairie schooner, to Iowa, and, in 1885, he graduated as valedictorian from the University of Iowa. Clerking law in Chicago, he lived in an attic, but within a few years he had accumulated fortunes in both business and agriculture. In 1896, he became richer still, marrying Florence Pullman, daughter of George Mortimer Pullman, founder of the Pullman Sleeping Car Company and one of the nation's wealthiest men.

That same year, Lowden entered politics, assisting William McKinley's Illinois campaign. The victorious McKinley offered Lowden the position of Assistant Postmaster General, but Lowden turned it down. In 1904, he ran for governor with the backing of Chicago Republican chieftain William J. "The Blond Boss" Lorimer, but met defeat at the state GOP convention at Springfield on the 79th ballot. After a stint in the House, Lowden tried again for governor in 1916, again enjoying machine support, this time the machine being that of Chicago's buffoonish mayor, William "Big Bill" Thompson.

Lowden easily won that year's primary and defeated Democratic incumbent Edward Dunne in November. An unusually able administrator, he built five thousand miles of roads, consolidated departments, instituted a formal budget process, artfully settled a potentially troublesome Chicago streetcar strike, and cut taxes. He also distanced himself from Thompson. He endorsed women's suffrage early on, Illinois being first to ratify the Nineteenth Amendment. Supporting the war, he resisted its more pernicious forms of anti-German bigotry. Above all, he steered a middle path between organization men and reformers, between the Old Guard and progressives. Warren Harding said that if he couldn't win, he'd prefer Frank Lowden. He probably meant it.

"In mind, [Lowden] was able; in temperament hearty and forceful; in personality agreeable," recorded journalist Mark Sullivan. "He was of the best of the type from which the United States had been accustomed to choose its Presidents."

Yet he had problems. Big Bill Thompson now hated him and labored to undermine his home-state strength. Irreconcilables regarded him as insufficiently anti-League ("I do not see how permanent harm can come from it, and I do see the possibility of good"). Organized labor suspected his connections to the hated Pullman family. Those jealous and fearful of great wealth feared and dreaded his great wealth.

He lacked real national strength, his campaign relying too heavily on Illinois talent, some of which proved very thin indeed. Key Lowden backer East St. Louis Congressman William A. Rodenberg committed an amateurish blunder in November 1919 when, in praising Calvin Coolidge's record, he mentioned that the Massachusetts governor would fit well on a Lowden ticket.

The suggestion, calculated to curry Massachusetts support, destroyed it. "In no sense of the word," complained the *Boston Evening Transcript*, "can it be claimed that Governor Lowden of Illinois is a national figure, yet it is characteristic of the central western bumptiousness that this worthy governor's boom should be coupled with the gracious offer of second position to the Governor of Massachusetts."

"Why not the other way around?" inquired the *New Bedford Standard*. "A day coach is a better vehicle to the Presidency than a Pullman."

Beyond that, the rules had changed since McKinley's era, and Frank

Lowden wasn't paying attention. He despised modern campaign stratagems such as billboards and newspaper advertising. "I like to think that
the Presidency is still as dignified a place as a position at the bar," he
wrote to former New York Congressman J. Sloat Fassett. "I would rather
lose any primary state, including *my* own, than to put the Presidency on
the plane of a patent medicine."

He also hated primaries themselves, dismissing them as the "most
demoralizing departure we have ever made from the principle of representative government."

And so, of course, on December 17, 1919, Frank Lowden declared his
candidacy—by entering the South Dakota primary.

Far more colorful—and infinitely more controversial—was California
Senator Hiram Warren Johnson, described by one historian as looking
"like a bad-tempered baby" and by a contemporary as a man who "would
have enjoyed the French Revolution."

Neither assessment was necessarily incorrect.

Of all Republican hopefuls—and perhaps of *all* hopefuls—Hiram
Johnson was the most progressive, indeed the most radical, not only in
politics but in temperament. "The difference between Johnson and me is
that I regard questions from the point of view of principles," noted Idaho
Senator William E. Borah, "while he regards them from the point of view
of personalities. When a man opposes me[,] I do not become angry at
him. On the next issue[,] he may agree with me. When a man opposes
Johnson[,] he hates him. He feels that the opposition is directed personally against him, not against the policy that separates them."

And Borah was *Johnson's closest ally*.

Born in Sacramento on September 2, 1866, Johnson claimed descent
from nobility, Count Albert de Montfredy. Hiram's father, corporate
attorney Grove L. Johnson, however, was less noble, having fled a New
York indictment for forging promissory notes. Grove Johnson eventually
honored the notes, entered politics, and won election to both the California Assembly and Senate and the U.S. House.

Hiram spent two years at Berkeley, studied law in his father's firm, passed the bar, practiced law with his father, and served as Sacramento Corporation Counsel. He broke, however, with his father over Grove's support for the powerful Southern Pacific Railroad, withdrawing from the firm, relocating to San Francisco, and becoming an assistant district attorney.

In 1908, the district attorney's office prosecuted local political boss Abe Ruef. Johnson had begged off the case, deferring to special prosecutor Francis J. Heney. On November 13, 1908, ex-convict Morris Haas, who seven months earlier Heney had refused for jury duty, shot Heney point-blank in the head. Johnson assumed command of the case. His fiery summation implied that if jurymen freed Ruef, they would be suspected of accepting bribes. The judge rebuked Johnson, but Ruef went to jail, and Johnson ran for governor in 1910.

Running on a platform of "Kick the Southern Pacific out of Politics," he garnered 101,666 votes in the August Republican primary, only 12,273 fewer than his four opponents combined. In the same primary, voters denied his pro–Southern Pacific father renomination to the Assembly.

As governor, he advocated initiative, referendum, and recall; and supported the popular election of United States senators; the appointment, rather than the election, of minor state officers (such as clerk of the Supreme Court, State Printer, Superintendent of Public Instruction, and Surveyor General); an eight-hour day for women; county home rule; free textbooks for public-school students; a workers' compensation system; pure food and drug laws; teacher pensions; and greater railroad and utility regulation.

He also stood foursquare against Japanese immigration—a sentiment inherited from his father, whose anti-Japanese virulence had already attracted national attention.

In 1912, Johnson ran for vice president on the Progressive ticket, helping TR narrowly carry California. Two years later, he won re-election to the governor's mansion as a Progressive, even as the new party was disintegrating. In 1916, Johnson won election to the United States Senate, but otherwise the campaign was a disaster. His very public feuding with Republican presidential candidate Charles Evans Hughes helped cost Hughes California by 3,713 votes, with Johnson winning the state by

296,815 votes. Losing California cost Hughes the election. It also cost Johnson what little support he ever enjoyed from regular Republicans.

Considering Johnson's radical agenda and his immense popularity with voters, he might easily be classified as a demagogue and, by further inference, a fiery and powerful orator—a veritable San Francisco, Republican Huey Long. But while he may have been a demagogue, he was decidedly not an orator.

"He seemed to us utterly sincere, to the point of being inarticulate, although long winded," puzzled *New York Tribune* columnist Heywood Broun. "There is in him . . . a dogged persistence which is appealing, but he is utterly lacking in charm. Nothing blazes in him at the sight of a crowd. On the contrary, there is every evidence that the senator finds public speaking a duty and not a pleasure.

"There is no contact between him and an audience, even a huge and a friendly audience . . . he does not talk at his crowd but through them. There is always the feeling that he is talking for the record and not [to] the sea of faces in front of him."

While Johnson may not have supported civil—or any—liberties for Japanese Americans, he supported liberties for virtually everyone else. Measures like the Sedition Act, Johnson charged, "do not unite a people. They cause suspicion to stalk all through the land; . . . they take a great, virile, brave people and make that people timid and fearful."

Nor did Johnson support the expulsion of Socialist members from the New York State Assembly. "Socialists," said Johnson, "acting within the Constitution, have the right to preach their doctrine. When they are elected by their constituents they must be protected."

Hiram Johnson hated many things, but, above all, he despised the League of Nations. To him, it was pure evil, not only a betrayal of American independence but also a guarantee of American acquiescence in injustice abroad. The League, he maintained, "[forces] the chains of tyranny upon millions of people and cements for all times unjust and wicked annexations."

Not all the progressive isolationists supported Johnson. Some thought he couldn't win. Chicago's Harold Ickes was progressive, anti-League, and irascible as hell—a veritable Johnson clone. He supported Lowden: "Much to my surprise, Lowden had made a first-rate Governor

179

and . . . I could see nothing in the offing remotely resembling Illinois delegates for Hiram Johnson. So I adhered to Lowden with the distinct understanding that if he failed of nomination, he would make no attempt to deliver me to another. I told him frankly that Johnson was my first choice. Lowden, in turn, assured me that he would rather throw his strength to Johnson than to any of the reactionary candidates. So I went along."

And so the campaign began.

The Progressive movement had given the nation primaries, but primaries didn't anoint presidential candidates. Much to his chagrin, Theodore Roosevelt had proven that in 1912. There were too few primaries—twenty-one for the Republicans in 1920—with too few delegates at stake. Favorite sons dominated some key contests, further diminishing the process. Political machines dominated others, delivering uncommitted lists—slates—of delegates. The majority of delegates—in both parties—were still selected in statewide conventions, and, again, favorite sons might complicate that situation. Even winning a presidential primary had its limits. Some were purely advisory. And after a few ballots, delegates might vote for whomever they wished—and, being faithful local party people, they often had no love for the candidates they supposedly represented.

And yet one needed to perform respectably in primaries. Being embarrassed could prove not just deleterious, but fatal, to a candidacy.

It was a very complex process, requiring skill and nerve and, even, just a little grace.

Wood drew first blood, besting Lowden 2–1 in the December 2, 1919 South Dakota Republican convention.

He won again, defeating an unpledged slate and aided by his own native-son status and the active assistance of *Manchester Union* publisher Frank Knox, a former Rough Rider, in the first primary, March 9's New Hampshire contest.

A week later, Wood captured the March 15 Minnesota primary, but publicity for it was light, snows heavy, and turnout sparse. The results: Wood 12,627, Johnson 8,517, Hoover 4,486, and Lowden 3,510.

The next day saw Hiram Johnson snap Wood's modest victory streak, winning the North Dakota primary. It wasn't really much of a victory, though: Johnson ran unopposed.

On March 17, Lowden's organization showed what it could do in the back rooms, taking eight delegates in Virginia's Republican convention.

Bad road conditions depressed turnout in South Dakota's March 23 primary, though not nearly as much as in Minnesota the previous week. The atmosphere was now decidedly ugly. Wood accused Lowden of unfairly lowering Pullman Company taxes. Johnson whined that he was being outspent. The results: Wood 27,666, Lowden 23,385, Johnson 21,735, and Washington Senator Miles Poindexter, a junior-grade Hiram Johnson, 850.

April witnessed the main events. Women voted for the first time in a presidential primary in April 5's crucial Michigan contest, where Wood, Lowden, Johnson, and Hoover battled head to head. Lowden committed considerable resources to the effort, and Johnson was thought to have decent support within the city of Detroit from auto-workers, the Irish, and the Germans, but observers nonetheless forecast a Wood triumph. Johnson won easily, by 45,000 votes, demonstrating appeal beyond the underpopulated Far West and Upper Midwest. Hoover and Lowden ran neck-and-neck—and badly. Poindexter again finished last, trailing even perennial joke candidate New York attorney William Grant Webster, who had magically won the 1916 Oregon primary. In 1920, Webster entered six state vice-presidential primaries. Running against nobody in particular, he won five of them.

April 6 saw two primaries with slim possibilities for the front-runners: Wisconsin and New York. Wisconsin maverick Robert La Follette swept his home state, defeating an uninstructed slate headed by Governor Emanuel Philipp.

New York's regular organization defeated isolated Hoover (in the Upper East Side's "silk stocking" district) and Johnson efforts (in twelve Brooklyn and Manhattan districts). Hoover's lone slate lost 3–1. Every Johnson slate lost. New York's convention votes went for favorite son Columbia University President Nicholas Murray Butler. Butler harbored no illusions about his chances and personally favored Frank Lowden.

Georgia's April 7 convention illustrated the fractious nature of Southern Republican politics. Wood supporters literally bolted state

House of Representatives chamber doors shut to bar the "uninstructed" "black-and-tan" Lowden faction led by forty-nine-year-old black attorney Henry Lincoln ("Link") Johnson. Johnson, a former Taft appointee, had not lived in Georgia since 1910. Police quelled the resultant "riot."

April 13 saw Wood invade Illinois. With Mayor Thompson's help, the General carried Cook County, 84,946–48,293, but Lowden took 97 of 101 counties, swamping Wood, 197,073–132,522. Hiram Johnson ran strong in Cook County (48,293 votes) but weak downstate (7,949 votes). Virtually nobody—2,274 votes—went for Herbert Hoover.

April 20's Nebraska primary featured a new twist, a serious bid by native son General John J. Pershing. Johnson, now gaining momentum, crushed his nearest challenger Wood, 61,161–42,385. Pershing's hopes vanished, as he collected just 27,699 votes.

April 23's Montana primary saw another Johnson victory: Johnson 21,081, Wood 6,792, Lowden 6,402, and Hoover 5,073. Warren Harding received only 722 votes.

In New Jersey on April 27, Johnson stunned Wood—and just about everyone else—by nearly beating the General in the supposedly pro-Wood East. Harding had withdrawn because of lack of funds. Johnson scored a major moral victory, capping it by charging that he had lost only by fraud. Perhaps he had.

The same day saw primaries in Ohio and Massachusetts and a state convention in Washington. Wood, pouring money into Ohio, nearly defeated Harding and did defeat Harry Daugherty for delegate-at-large. Herbert Hoover, running as a write-in candidate, finished ahead of Johnson.

In Massachusetts, in light voting, an "Unpledged Group" (actually for Coolidge) headed by Lodge (actually leaning to Wood) defeated a group leaning to Wood and/or Hoover.

In Washington, favorite son Miles Poindexter secured that state's delegation—at least until it became opportune for it to vote for somebody else.

The May 3 Maryland primary witnessed the East's return to normal, with Wood defeating Johnson 2–1 (14,663–7,113).

The following day saw Hiram Johnson crush Herbert Hoover in the California primary, 369,853–209,009. He enjoyed doing it.

May 5's Indiana primary had a lot riding on it. Neither Harding nor Lowden, both next-door neighbors, could afford to lose the state, particularly Harding, who enjoyed the support of Indiana's two United States Senators, James E. Watson and Harry New. He finished an atrociously weak fourth—and was nearly driven out of the race. Lowden finished a poor third. Neither Lowden nor Harding carried a single county. The results: Wood 85,776, Johnson 79,829, Lowden 31,118, Harding 20,819. Wood had clearly verified his front-runner status.

The May 18 Pennsylvania primary saw big boss Boies Penrose repeat the New York model of keeping delegates out of the hands of the favorites—none of whom now enjoyed his confidence. Pennsylvania's votes would go to Governor William Cameron Sproul, a fairly decent governor, who, had he not been from too-solidly Republican Pennsylvania, might have been decent presidential timber.

General Wood won Vermont's May 19 non-binding primary, though his only formal competition was William Grant Webster. Wood captured 70 percent of the vote, with Johnson and Hoover jostling for second via write-ins. Grant and native son Calvin Coolidge (whose stepmother had died the day before) battled for fourth. Frank Lowden barely finished in triple digits. Only 5,659 of Vermont's 115,938 registered voters participated.

Hiram Johnson won the May 21 Oregon primary with 45,412 votes to 43,380 for Wood, and 15,581 for Lowden. Herbert Hoover, who asked supporters to do whatever was best to defeat Johnson, still received 14,557 votes.

The season's last contest arrived mercifully, if anticlimactically, on May 24, in West Virginia, where United States Senator Howard Sutherland fended off a strong effort by Wood and a not-unexpectedly weak effort from the mysterious William Grant Webster.

Hiram Johnson had performed spectacularly in the popular vote, collecting over a hundred delegates. But his victory proved hollow. He had alienated everyone else in the party. Virtually no other delegates would consider voting for him under any circumstances. And, beyond that, even his own delegates hated him, for they were largely local party people, not Johnson partisans, and were ready to jump ship at the earliest legal moment.

Lowden fared reasonably well. Unsuccessful in primaries, he secured his delegates from state conventions. To the casual observer, Harding had self-destructed, performing poorly in the handful of primaries he entered and garnering few first-ballot delegates. But Harry Daugherty had never counted on an initial splash for Harding. He would alienate no one and count on victory following a protracted Lowden–Wood stalemate. Hoover and Coolidge, meanwhile, *had* crashed and burned.

Wood entered the process as front-runner—and that is how he ended it. He had not, however, delivered anything approximating a knockout blow. Like Napoleon at Moscow, he had come a long way, but it was getting cold, and where would he go from here?

The answer was downward. Hiram Johnson was very good at two things: winning votes, and yelling about corruption. In North Dakota, he had complained about excessive Wood campaign spending. Since Wood looked like the ultimate GOP nominee, Democrats eagerly amplified Johnson's allegations. On March 26, the Democratic *New York World* repeated Johnson's charges that Wood was buying the nomination ("Millionaires Back Wood Boom"), listing such millionaires as California oilman Edward L. Doheny, Ohio banker Dan Hanna, and Chicago grocery store magnate A. A. Sprague, as major Wood contributors.

Johnson's ally, Senator Borah, brought these charges before the Senate. On May 20, it authorized an investigation of both parties' campaign expenditures—though everyone knew the inquiry was really aimed at Wood. The committee found what it was looking for: Wood had indeed outspent everybody in sight. No candidate had *ever* spent more *before* a national convention: over $2 million. Procter had contributed $521,000. Two banks had donated $100,000 each. Evangelist Billy Sunday's wastrel son George had persuaded John D. Rockefeller Jr. to pony up $25,000.

Reported campaign spending totaled: Wood $2,120,793, Lowden $414,984, Johnson $194,293, Hoover $173,542, Harding $113,109, Coolidge $68,375, Butler $40,550.

The committee damaged Wood. But it also severely crippled Lowden and Johnson. Lowden's total of $414,984 seemed modest in comparison to Wood's $2,120,793—and all but $35,000 of it had come from the candidate's own deep pockets. The committee, however, discovered that while securing Missouri delegates, Lowden forces had cut two $2,500 checks that went directly into the accounts of St. Louis circuit court clerk Nat Goldstein and his deputy, Robert F. Moore, both eventual Lowden delegates. The obvious implication: Lowden had bought their votes.

Lowden was innocent. The checks were the work of a local underling. Still, the charges stung, and Lowden's reputation suffered—at the worst possible time.

Hurt too was Johnson. His finances were fine, but the fact was that his camp had triggered an investigation that embarrassed everyone else, *infuriated* everyone else. Republicans who had entered the 1920 campaign thinking that they couldn't possibly hate Hiram Johnson more, admitted that they had been wrong. They *despised* Hiram Johnson.

Political polling had not yet advanced to its current scientific, unbiased (ahem!) status. Instead, the public relied upon *The Literary Digest*, which mailed out 11 million postcard ballots to addresses found in phone directories and city registers, waited for recipients to mail them back, and periodically printed the results. The final Republican tally, published on June 5, was:

| Candidate | Republican | Democrat | Other | Total |
|---|---|---|---|---|
| Wood | 245,994 | 25,096 | 36,396 | 307,486 |
| Johnson | 168,009 | 56,153 | 38,925 | 263,087 |
| Hoover | 105,356 | 94,081 | 41,031 | 240,468 |
| Lowden | 92,767 | 13,709 | 13,915 | 120,391 |
| Hughes | 42,056 | 4,834 | 7,829 | 54,719 |
| Harding | 29,042 | 3,478 | 4,275 | 36,795 |
| Coolidge | 23,095 | 5,364 | 5,162 | 33,621 |
| Taft | 21,363 | 6,519 | 4,858 | 32,740 |

Superficially, Wood possessed a commanding lead, but the poll actually revealed deadlock. Wood led with a mere 34 percent. Herbert Hoover stood much stronger with poll respondents than with Republican delegates—and led among Democratic respondents, besting Democrat McAdoo 94,081–86,025. Lowden, Harding, and Coolidge had hardly captured anyone's imagination, even for a second choice:

## Literary Digest Second Choice Results
Wood 186,946, Johnson 161,670, Lowden 129,992, Hoover 120,430, Hughes 88,787, Coolidge 67,047, Taft 62,871, Harding 42,212.

As the convention neared, some observers pondered the coming logjam and how to break it. Senators Henry Cabot Lodge, James W. Wadsworth Jr., and William M. Calder met in Washington, finally settling on the party's unsuccessful 1916 candidate, Charles Evans Hughes. Calder asked Meier Steinbrink, a young New York attorney, to sound out Hughes.

Hughes had officially withdrawn from the race when his twenty-eight-year-old daughter, Helen, died of tuberculosis in April 1920, even refusing Republican national committee chairman Will Hays's request to keynote the 1920 convention, for fear that if he were to deliver a sufficiently inspiring speech, he might face an unwanted draft.

Over lunch, Steinbrink began, "I'm going to ask you to do me a favor, don't interrupt me until I have finished what is on my mind."

"Steinbrink," Hughes responded, "there is no subject that you can't talk about with me."

"These Senators," Steinbrink eventually concluded, "want to be able to vote for you as their presidential candidate."

Hughes's eyes clouded. "I beg of you to believe me," the usually stolid politician said, "Since our daughter died, Mrs. Hughes and I are heartbroken. I don't want to be President of the United States. I request that my name be not even mentioned in the convention."

Steinbrink relayed Hughes's message back to Lodge, Wadsworth, and Calder. He did not convey the eerie prophecy Hughes made before parting: "Whoever is nominated will be elected, but in my opinion he will not fill out the term."

# Chapter 12

## "A 'SAFE' KIND OF LIBERAL"

Republicans faced an unprecedented problem in 1920: Their logical candidate was dead.

The Democrats' difficulty was even worse: A living president who would not get out of the way.

Theodore Roosevelt's passing allowed others to emerge. It was a crowded, confused path to the nomination, heavily rutted and choked with dust. Some of the candidates were good, some not. But the process proceeded. It would sort itself out. It *was* sorting itself out.

Woodrow Wilson remained alive, in the presidency. Healthy in 1920, he would have sought a third term, a vindication of his policies, a mandate for the League.

He was not well, not functioning, and refused to relinquish the presidency or his hold on the Democratic Party. Nor would he provide any indication that he was not running. None of the handful of people enjoying even limited access to him dared to ask.

This posed grievous risks for any potential candidate. Would announcing be perceived as disloyalty to a wounded leader? Would Wilson lash out at anyone daring to seek the office he would not yield?

Painfully awkward for any potential successor, it was an unbearable situation for the most likely heir: Wilson's own son-in-law, Treasury Secretary William Gibbs McAdoo.

McAdoo may have been the Wilson administration's most able member, even more capable than Hoover, with, of course, the added advantage of actually being a loyal Democrat. Tall and lanky, sharply angular in features, he reminded some observers of Lincoln. A Southerner by birth, he now lived in the North. A successful capitalist, he made all the right progressive noises.

He was a man of energy and ambition, a doer of great deeds, a candidate who couldn't miss.

He never got started.

Born near Marietta, Georgia, on Halloween, 1863, McAdoo left the University of Tennessee to husband his family's meager financial resources but later gained admission to the bar. Failing in his first business venture, an 1892 attempt to build the Knoxville trolley system, he moved, virtually penniless, to New York, elongating his name from the rather plebian William McAdoo to the more patrician William Gibbs McAdoo. There, he succeeded on a grand scale, creating the Hudson Tubes, the underwater rail tunnels linking Manhattan and New Jersey, a major engineering feat and one that made him comfortably rich.

McAdoo was not merely rich; he was progressive. While other magnates might mutter (or, more prudently, think) "the public be damned," McAdoo provided equal compensation to female workers and loudly trumpeted his slogan: "The public be pleased." In 1908, he took up the cudgel for equal pay for female teachers in the New York City school system.

McAdoo first met Woodrow Wilson in February 1909, when McAdoo's son Francis was attending Princeton. McAdoo was, to say the least, impressed. Wilson "had a way," McAdoo would write in his memoirs, "of lifting the most commonplace topic, spontaneously and without effort, to a height where it would catch the rays of the sun."

By spring 1911, McAdoo had raised $200,000 for Wilson's fledgling presidential campaign. By early 1912, he was vice chairman of the effort and being mentioned for governor of New York. By campaign's end, he had replaced Wilson's campaign manager, the brilliant but psychologically unstable New York attorney William F. McCombs, taking control of the operation. When Wilson won, McAdoo outmaneuvered McCombs for a far greater prize: Secretary of the Treasury.

It cannot, however, be said that McAdoo occupied the administration's center stage, since Wilson never allowed anyone near the spotlight.

But McAdoo came reasonably close. As Treasury Secretary, he oversaw creation of the twelve-district Federal Reserve System, a move that he modestly described as having delivered a "a blow in the solar plexus of the money monopoly."

When war came, McAdoo shifted gears, adding more responsibilities to his portfolio, serving as chairman of the Federal Reserve Board and the Federal Farm Loan Board. As director general of the country's nationalized railroads, he resuscitated a system whose collapse had threatened the delivery of war supplies to Eastern ports. McAdoo untangled the mess and made political points in the process. One million, eight hundred thousand people worked on the railroads. McAdoo granted them a 40 percent raise, allowed women and blacks equal pay, and protected union members from discrimination. As chairman of the War Finance Corporation, he oversaw the raising of over $17 billion through the Liberty Loan program.

"He was a strange paradox," remembered Louis Wehle. "In personal conversation he could sometimes seem petty; but in public affairs he was a titan. Probably no one else in Washington made difficult decisions as fast and as soundly or with a more statesmanlike regard for public policy. There was about McAdoo something of the cool, gambling adventurer, and he had a boundless self-confidence and courage, amply justified by his seeming power to put through anything he undertook."

"Indeed," wrote historian Paul Johnson, "it is probably right to see him [McAdoo] as a key figure in 20th century American history, who never quite got his deserts in the political arena at the time, or has received the historic accolades he deserved."

It is also probably right to see McAdoo as egotistical, boastful, and covetous of power, a Wall Street banker who pretended to be just-folks from Georgia. Secretary of War Newton Baker observed that McAdoo had "the greatest lust for power I ever saw." Wilson's friend Charles Hamlins went further, categorizing him as "the most selfish man I ever met."

Or as one little anti-McAdoo ditty went:

I don't believe he ever hid
A single thing he ever did.

McAdoo's downfall began when he married the boss's daughter. McAdoo, forty-nine, met Wilson's youngest offspring, Eleanor Randolph ("Nell") Wilson ("She was neither argumentative nor angular, but entirely womanly"), twenty-three, on inauguration day, March 4, 1913. For months, the smitten McAdoo hid his ardor, fearing censure over the age difference. He finally opened up and proposed in December 1913. He also offered to vacate his cabinet post. Wilson refused, saying McAdoo had obtained the job "solely on . . . merit" before becoming a member of the family, and he could keep it. The couple married in the White House on May 7, 1914.

Before November 1918 had ended and Wilson had set sail for France, McAdoo, pleading health and financial reasons, resigned all official duties. Not coincidentally, the first "McAdoo for President Club" formed. With Republicans now ruling Congress and arduous peace negotiations ahead, McAdoo's departure left his father-in-law in the lurch, and struck the rest of the cabinet as ill-timed at best. "Mac," George Creel fumed to Josephus Daniels, "has never been largely concerned in anybody but himself."

McAdoo improved his finances, in part, by taking the position of first counsel of the newly formed United Artists, the film company founded by Charlie Chaplin, Mary Pickford, Douglas Fairbanks, and D. W. Griffith, for $50,000 annually (some said $100,000) and a thousand shares of stock.

His health also seemed to improve enough that he was increasingly mentioned for the presidency. By October 1919, the McAdoo boom was in full swing. By January 1920, he had left United Artists.

McAdoo did not, however, recover his nerve. So long as his father-in-law stood in the way, he could not run. When, in January 1920, Democrats held their annual Jefferson–Jackson Day Dinner, McAdoo declined to speak. Nell didn't want him campaigning. He countered that her father could never win, but her husband could—if only Wilson would let him run.

In January and February 1920, McAdoo informed supporters that he was not actively seeking delegates—although he wouldn't refuse a draft. Muttered one exasperated supporter, "I never saw a man before take the position that he did. It was different from any politics I have ever seen."

Momentarily, McAdoo grew bold. When Mitchell Palmer entered the Georgia primary, McAdoo said he would, too. Then he wrote Dr.

Grayson asking for "suggestions." Dr. Grayson wrote back, and McAdoo withdrew.

Not helping was Edith Wilson. She never forgot McAdoo's hostility to her romance with Wilson. His name was not to be *mentioned* in her presence. His presidential candidacy was not to be *thought of* in her presence.

Meanwhile, Wilson's plans for a third term—so seriously interrupted by his stroke—were clearly, if unrealistically, reviving. As early as January 1920, reports appeared of Wilson coveting four more years in the White House. On March 25, 1920, he confided to Grayson:

> The Democratic Convention in San Francisco may get into a hopeless tie-up, and it may, by the time of the Convention, become imperative that the League of Nations . . . be made the dominant issue. The Convention may come to a deadlock . . . , and there may be practically a universal demand for the selection of someone to lead them out of the wilderness. The members of the Convention may feel that I am the logical one to lead—perhaps the only one to champion this cause. In such circumstances I would feel obliged to accept the nomination even if I thought it would cost me my life.

McAdoo *formally* withdrew. Still maintaining his coyness and his non-candidacy, he skillfully cobbled together the finest of non-campaigns. He made all the right contacts, won slate after slate of "uncommitted" delegates. As the national convention neared, McAdoo—the *non*-candidate—seemed *the* candidate.

Then Wilson barged in. On June 17, 1920, the staunchly Democratic *New York World* published an extensive interview between Wilson and its reporter, Louis Seibold, Wilson's first interview since his stroke. It was a fraud. Seibold and Joe Tumulty had cooked up the questions and answers between them. Their only problem was clearing the script with Edith Wilson. Their version had Wilson clearly rejecting a third term. Hers didn't.

"I saw [Wilson]," Seibold ("a trusted friend," as Tumulty delicately phrased it) lied to his readers, "transact the most important functions of his office with his old[-]time decisiveness, method and keenness of intellectual appraisement." The *New York Times* theorized that the President

191

had "thrown his hat into the ring of the San Francisco convention, not necessarily as a candidate but as the titular leader of the Democratic Party." Seibold won the Pulitzer Prize for this total fabrication.

The interview once more froze McAdoo in place. On June 18, he announced his "irrevocable" decision against having his name presented before the convention. His campaign began shutting down, some supporters drifting off to his replacement as Treasury Secretary, Carter Glass.

But the Seibold charade couldn't obscure the truth for long. On June 21, Third Assistant Secretary of the Treasury Jouett Shouse publicly stated the stark reality that Wilson was too sick to run: "No real friend of the president regards his nomination as a possibility."

Luckily, McAdoo had again left the door slightly ajar—and people soon noticed. Wilson asked Carter Glass's opinion of McAdoo's "irrevocable" decision. "He nowhere says he would not accept a nomination," Glass responded. Wilson shot back, "No, he does not, as I read it!"

If false rumors of Wilson being well weren't bad enough for McAdoo, false rumors of McAdoo *not* being well surfaced, as a New York City paper reported that he had tuberculosis. To some, the report made sense: How else could one explain the once-resolute McAdoo's halting behavior? McAdoo quickly denied all.

The White House continued projecting an image of Wilsonian vitality. On Tuesday, June 22, it released a photo, taken the previous Saturday, purportedly showing him at work. "The President looks fine," contended photographer George W. Harris, "better than I expected."

Finally, on Sunday, June 27, the convention just a day away, McAdoo shifted gears yet again. Because of "increased demand," he would accept the nomination if it were forced upon him.

⁀

While one cabinet member hesitated, another jumped right in.

Attorney General A. Mitchell Palmer, like Leonard Wood, was hoping to ride a law-and-order wave to the White House. Like Wood, he was finding it a short ride.

Born near White Haven, Pennsylvania, on May 4, 1872, Palmer worked as a court stenographer upon graduating from Swarthmore in

1891 and before gaining admission to the bar. He prospered, becoming a member of the Democratic state committee, and winning election to Congress in 1908, there establishing a progressive reputation. Wilson, upon taking office, offered him Secretary of War, but Palmer, because he was a Quaker, declined on religious grounds. At the 1912 Democratic convention, he had played a key role in swinging Pennsylvania's votes to Wilson. In 1914, he planned to run for governor. Instead, Wilson cajoled him into challenging Boies Penrose for Penrose's Senate seat. Palmer lost by 150,000 votes. In October 1917, Wilson appointed Palmer Alien Property Custodian. There, he seized $700 million in alien property, including key German chemical and dye patents, his moves triggering a blizzard of litigation. In February 1919, Wilson named him Attorney General, replacing Thomas W. Gregory, but controversy over Palmer's sale of seized German properties (without bid and largely to his cronies) delayed his confirmation until that August.

Palmer possessed a nasty, long-standing streak of Anglo-Saxon nativism. At Swarthmore, his commencement address defended the recent lynching of eleven Italians in New Orleans. In 1912, describing the accidental death of hundreds of quarry workers, he expounded: "They are a high class of workman—not cheap foreign labor." He described the Bolshevik Revolution as "a small clique of outcasts from the East Side of New York," explaining that "because a disreputable alien—Leon Bronstein, the man who now calls himself Trotsky—can inaugurate a reign of terror from his throne room in the Kremlin; because this lowest of all types known to New York can sleep in the Czar's bed . . . should America be swayed by such doctrines?"

Nonetheless, Palmer's Justice Department tenure commenced with moderation and restraint. The nation didn't quibble about how to crack down on radicals, but Palmer did. He released ten thousand enemy aliens from government parole. He ended the Department's reliance on intelligence from the amateur 250,000-member American Protective League (APL). When Ohio Governor James M. Cox requested information from the Justice Department's APL files on German wartime propaganda activities, Palmer refused, saying the material consisted of "gossip, hearsay information, conclusions, and inferences." He informed Cox that "information of this character could not be used without danger of doing serious wrong to individuals who were probably innocent."

On June 2, 1920, an anarchist bomb demolished A. Mitchell Palmer's home, as described above. The one-time progressive Quaker immediately morphed into a tough-talking law-and-order man, raiding the radicals' headquarters, seizing their propaganda and files, and deporting as many as possible. When 400,000 coal miners struck in the fall of 1920, Palmer secured a federal injunction, hamstringing their progress.

By February 1920, Palmer's crusade—and rhetoric—had reached fever pitch. In that month's *The Forum*, he wrote:

> Like a prairie fire, the blaze of revolution was sweeping over every American institution of law and order. . . . It was eating into the homes of the American workman, its sharp tongues of revolutionary heat were licking the altars of the churches, leaping into the belfry of the school bell, crawling into the sacred corners of American homes, seeking to replace the marriage laws with libertine laws, burning up the foundations of society.

Palmer announced on March 1, 1920. By now, his name was anathema to every progressive and liberal (and many a conservative) in the country.

Palmer thrived in the back room. "His critics called him a party hack," noted one historian, "but to Palmer that was a compliment." His popularity with party functionaries far exceeded his public favor. Where conventions selected delegates, he gathered steam. In primaries, he tanked. In April 7's Michigan primary, he finished last, with Hoover, McAdoo, Bryan, and New Jersey Governor Edwards all easily outpacing him. The Georgia primary proved little better. In February, former Congressman Thomas E. Watson, a populist and an anti-administration Democrat, entered the field, casting doubt on Palmer's ability to win the state. When United States Senator Hoke Smith also entered, it appeared that with the local vote split, Palmer's chances had improved considerably. They hadn't. Watson received 54,000 votes to Palmer's 47,000 and Smith's 46,000. Palmer was lucky to receive a bare plurality of delegates. His campaign was basically finished.

James M. Cox was the Democratic Harding—an Ohio-born-and-bred newspaper editor of middling political accomplishments, whose primary assets seemed to be an Ohio address, a frenzied feistiness, and his facile willingness to be the second choice of a brokered convention. Cox, observed historian Geoffrey Perrett, was "mildly liberal, mildly wet, mildly able."

Born on a farm near the hamlet of Jacksonburg, Ohio on March 31, 1870, Cox, again like Harding, came from a large family—Cox the youngest of seven children, Harding the oldest of eight. Like Harding, he began as a schoolteacher, then drifted into newspaper reporting, first on the *Middletown Signal*, later for the *Cincinnati Enquirer*.

He had his strengths and his weaknesses. Said one contemporary:

Jimmy Cox was about the best reporter and the worst writer in southern Ohio. There was not a week that he did not turn in a sensational scoop, and seldom were his facts wrong. He never spared himself in any effort to get firsthand, exhaustive information; his only vanity was in being first, his only pride in beating all rivals. But when it came to writing, his copy usually had to be done over in the office.

In 1895, the twenty-five-year-old Cox became secretary to Middletown, Ohio Congressman industrialist Paul J. Sorg. Three years later, he returned home to purchase the *Dayton Times* (renaming it the *News*) for $26,000. Like Harding, he made money in the newspaper game, served in the Ohio legislature, played golf, and had woman troubles, though they were nowhere near as lurid as Harding's. In 1908, he won his old boss's congressional seat, defeating an incumbent named Harding, J. Eugene Harding, in the bargain.

The following July, Cox's wife, Mayme (Mary), filed for divorce, charging him with cruelty and gross neglect. The break-up dragged on for two years. Mayme moved to Cleveland, establishing sufficient residency for her action. As the case wound its way through the courts, Cox tried preventing it from becoming public, including giving his profession as "traveling salesman" to mask his prominent, true identity.

It was no use. Noted the *Mansfield* (Ohio) *News*:

The marital troubles of Mr. and Mrs. Cox have been no secret. The separation came just about the time Cox was elected to congress. Mrs. Cox charges that for a year preceding the separation in April 1909, Cox scarcely spoke to her, almost completely ignoring her for a month at a time. This humiliation was brought to an end, Mrs. Cox charges, by her husband sending her to another state to visit with a friend. Immediately after Mrs. Cox had left Dayton, the petition says, Cox rented another house and moved into it with the three children, then wrote her telling her she could not re-enter his home.

On June 22, 1911, Cuyahoga County Common Pleas Judge Martin A. Foran granted the divorce after a fifteen-minute hearing, awarding Mrs. Cox alimony plus $350 per month child care. Each parent received custody of the children for half of each year. Mary Cox married her divorce lawyer.

In 1910, Cox easily won re-election. In 1912, divorced or not, he won the governorship by 156,823 votes, taking seventy-eight out of eighty-eight counties, as Republicans and Progressives split their vote. Cox's tenure was progressive, focusing on lobbying, rural schools, initiative and referendum, a unified state budget system, workers' compensation, prison and property tax reform, and a mother's pension law. Opposed to prohibition, he nonetheless instituted a saloon licensing system, limiting the number of saloons in each town and mandating midnight closings.

"The fact that I had achieved some measure of success in the business conduct of newspapers inspired conservative Ohioans with a certain confidence in me," Cox would later write. "They regarded me as a 'safe' kind of liberal."

But not that safe. The Democratic wave receded in November 1914, leaving upon the shore all sorts of Democratic beached whales, Cox's carcass among them. While Warren Harding was beating Timothy Hogan for the Senate, Cox met defeat at the hands of forty-three-year-old Congressman Frank B. Willis, 523,074 votes to 493,804 (Progressive James R. Garfield garnered 60,904 votes). Cox bounced back, defeating Willis in 1916 (568,218 to 561,602) and again (486,403 to 474,459) in 1918, becoming the state's first three-term Democratic governor, and Ohio's only three-term governor besides Rutherford B. Hayes.

On September 15, 1917, the forty-seven-year-old Cox remarried, taking as his bride twenty-seven-year-old Miss Margaretta P. Blair of Chicago. The new Mrs. Cox delivered an eight-and-a-half-pound daughter, Anne, at their opulent Dayton home, "Trails End," on the early morning of December 1, 1919.

When Cox had returned to office in 1915, however, times had changed, and so had Cox's style of government. His progressive agenda was largely fulfilled, and though he had opposed entering the war, he had become primarily a war governor, cracking down on labor violence and signing an anti-German-language measure into law.

Cox announced for the presidency on February 1, 1920. With McAdoo and Palmer being administration candidates, and the administration far from popular, Cox realized the value of sufficient distance from Washington. Beyond that, he was properly vague on the League. His campaign manager advised that the League should be ratified if necessary with Lodge's reservations. Cox, himself, suggested his own reservations.

But Cox's main strength came on the prohibition issue. Always a Wet, he had long battled the Ohio Anti-Saloon League. Such behavior generated substantial enthusiasm among Democratic big-city bosses, particularly Tammany's Charles Francis Murphy and Chicago's George E. Brennan. They didn't know if a man like Cox could win the presidency, but, under the circumstances, didn't much care. They did care about their local tickets. If a Dry like McAdoo—or, God forbid, Bryan—were nominated, that could prove disastrous. Cox was the bosses' candidate.

Though an uninspiring politician, Cox was a shrewd businessman. In the presidential contest, his product—himself—had very limited consumer appeal. Cox wasn't kidding himself, and he tailored his very circumscribed effort accordingly. "My friends are urging me to open up a vigorous campaign," he revealed. "But I prefer to wait. If, when the convention opens, they finally turn to Ohio, all right. We either have an ace in the hole, or we haven't. If we have an ace concealed, we win; if we haven't, no amount of bluffing and advertising can do much good."

Unlike Republicans, who enjoyed (if that is the word) a vigorous primary season, the Democratic version was an uninteresting joke. It's a wonder that anyone bothered to campaign, to run, or even to vote. In Illinois, 389,966 voters participated in the Republican primary, 19,088 in the Democratic. Woodrow Wilson received a grand total of 879 votes—*six* outside Cook County. Primaries in New Hampshire, North Dakota, South Dakota, New York, Wisconsin, Illinois, Montana, Massachusetts, and California resulted in uninstructed (i.e., uncommitted) delegate slates. Favorite sons won in Ohio (Cox), Nebraska (Senator Hitchcock), Pennsylvania (Palmer), and New Jersey (where Governor Edwards won with just 4,163 votes cast in his behalf; Wilson drew only 149 votes). Only former ambassador to Germany James J. Gerard in South Dakota, A. Mitchell Palmer in Georgia, and Edwards and McAdoo in the farcical, non-binding Illinois and Vermont primaries respectively breached the logjam, and Palmer's Georgia victory was so weak that it permanently damaged his campaign.

The convention process wasn't much better. Favorite sons were selected in Pennsylvania (Palmer), Iowa (Secretary of Agriculture Edwin T. Meredith), Oklahoma (Senator Robert L. Owen), Connecticut (Democratic national chairman Homer Cummings), Virginia (Senator Carter Glass), West Virginia (Ambassador to the Court of St. James John W. Davis), and North Carolina (Senator Furnifold Simmons), while Arizona, Nevada, Maine, the Philippines, Puerto Rico, Kansas, and Maryland selected uncommitted delegations. Cox won delegates in next-door Kentucky.

In 1920, the *Literary Digest* polled five million voters. Among Democrats, McAdoo placed first, then Wilson, Governor Edwards, and Bryan—and, only then, James Middleton Cox.

But one man forsook primaries and conventions, relying only on his own will to force a nomination.

Woodrow Wilson had never abandoned hope. He needed a third term to vindicate himself and to rescue his League. He never stepped aside, never cleared the field for a successor. He meant there to be no successor. His inaction fostered chaos, created a deadlock, stymied candidacies. Now he would take advantage of the situation.

Few could tell him not to. Few could tell him anything. He remained isolated, accessible only to a shrinking circle of trusted individuals—Edith,

Grayson, Tumulty—and they never dared say anything he didn't want to hear. The shock might injure his slim chances for recovery. His temper might cause you to be cut off. It had happened to others—John Grier Hibben, Dean Andrew West, Jim Smith, George Harvey, Colonel House, Henry Watterson. It could happen to you.

So nobody told him anything.

"Ike" Hoover recalled:

With spring came the prospect of the Democratic Convention and at the so-called cabinet meetings the nomination was discussed from time to time. . . . It became evident that the President was in a receptive mood for the nomination. The truth is he was not only receptive, but anxious and expectant. There was not a member of the cabinet present who did not know that it would be an impossibility, physically, mentally, and morally, even to harbor such a thought, and yet there were some who did encourage it. Whether they did it for sentiment, charity, or really expected to put such a thing over on the Convention, only they can answer. It was really sad how they deceived him. The disappointment they caused him could have been avoided if they had just kept silent.

On May 31, 1920, Wilson conferred with Democratic National Chairman Homer Cummings and proceeded to dismiss the entire roster of prospective Democratic candidates. McAdoo, he sniffed, was "not fit for it." Neither were Cox, Hoover, Carter Glass, Vice President Marshall, or Ambassador Davis. Picking Cox, Wilson jibed, "would be a fake."

As the convention neared, however, Grayson became increasingly alarmed at the possibility of a Wilson nomination. At one point, Interstate Commerce Commissioner Robert W. Woolley, Wilson's 1916 publicity director (and a McAdoo backer), asked the Admiral, "It is true that Mr. Wilson desires a third term?"

"Correct," Grayson answered. "He fervently believes it is still possible to have the United States join the League of Nations. But it is out of the question—he just must not be nominated. No matter what others may tell you, no matter what you may read about the President being on the road to recovery, I tell you that he is permanently ill physically, is gradually weakening mentally and can't recover. He couldn't possibly survive the campaign. Only the urgency of the situation justifies me in coming to you and making such a statement even in confidence. At times the President, whose grit and determination are marvelous, seems to show a slight improvement, is in good spirits for several days, even a week or ten days, transacts business with Tumulty—and then suffers a relapse, or I should say, becomes very morose. At such times it is distressing to be in the same room with him. I repeat, he is definitely becoming more feeble."

"Cary," Woolley tried to reassure him, "the name of the President will receive many an ovation, his desires as to the platform will prevail, in other ways will he be honored, but his ambition to succeed himself is definitely hopeless."

Grayson remained uneasy. He knew just how sick the president was: "We must not take any chances."

On June 10, 1920, Carter Glass confided to his diary that Grayson had told him that Wilson "seriously contemplates permitting himself to be named for [a] 3rd term and said it would kill him." Later that day, Postmaster General Burleson told Glass basically the same thing.

Just before the convention, Wilson again derided Cox's possibilities. "Oh!" he told Carter Glass, "you know Cox's nomination would be a joke."

In late June, Democrats headed west for the Democratic convention in far-off San Francisco, Glass among them. Tumulty and Grayson accompanied him to Washington's Union Station. In Glass's sleeper car, the president's physician had a last message for the Senator: "If anything comes up, save the life and fame of this man from the juggling of false friends."

# Chapter 13

~

# "RED FEATHERS, TIN BEARS, AND CARDBOARD ORANGES"

Republicans were in a rut.

On Tuesday, June 8, 1920, they convened—hoping to nominate the next president—in solemn and national convention at the Chicago Coliseum. Nine times previously, they had met in the Windy City, selecting Lincoln and Grant in Chicago, Hayes and Garfield and Blaine, Harrison, Roosevelt, and Taft. Since 1904, they had met in Chicago every four years. But if Republicans trudged a well-worn path regarding their convention site, they had lost their way regarding whom to nominate. Editorial writers and party outsiders might routinely decry "bossed" conventions, but while such gatherings lacked the proper quotient of suspense, they, at least, featured a veneer of coherence. This year's Republican event promised neither. True, each candidate boasted his admirers, and these admirers—whether idealistic or purely mercenary—supplied a certain enthusiasm, but there was no mania, no love, for any candidate, as there had been for a Lincoln or Roosevelt or even a Grant or McKinley.

There were just *too damned many* candidates—and not enough reasons to nominate any one of them. The *Chicago Tribune* handicapped the field like a horse race—a very crowded horse race—listing thirteen "actual starters" (all save one were eventually placed in nomination), two "probable starters" (neither actually started), sixteen "prominently mentioned" dark horses (ranging from General Pershing and William Howard Taft to Senators Lodge, Philander Knox, and Irvine Lenroot), and a category of "less prominently mentioned" dark horses who it defined, with only slight exaggeration, as "practically every Republican United States senator, member of congress, governor, prominent business [leader], mayor, and military hero."

The *Tribune* didn't even include International Anti-Cigarette League Superintendent Miss Lucy Page Gaston, who had filed unsuccessfully for South Dakota's Republican primary, pledging support for "clean morals, clean food, and fearless law enforcement" and, quite naturally, antipathy toward cigarettes. Gaston had dropped out on June 7 but promised to back anyone supporting her program. Presumably, cigarette smoker Warren Harding was not on her list.

Even without Miss Gaston, the convention's 984 voting delegates faced hard choices and arrived without a hint of consensus. Wood controlled 125 pledged delegates, Johnson 112, Lowden 72, and Harding 39. Favorite sons such as Coolidge, Sproul, Poindexter, and Butler held a combined total of 72 delegates. Five hundred and eight delegates—52 percent—remained unpledged and up for grabs.

Wall Street gamblers tried their best to make sense—and money—out of the uneasy, unsettling situation. By Monday, June 7, betting broke down this way:

> Hiram Johnson: even money
> Leonard Wood: 7–5
> Frank Lowden: 8–5
> Herbert Hoover: 4–1
> Charles Evans Hughes: 4–1 (up from 5–1)
> Nicholas Murray Butler: 5–1 (up from 10–1)
> Warren Harding: 5–1 (up from 8–1)
> Governor William C. Sproul: 5–1 (a new entry)
> Senator Philander Knox: 4–1 (up from 10–1)
> Governor Henry J. Allen: 6–1
> Calvin Coolidge: 8–1

Adding to the mess, precious few delegates had any experience at a national convention. Of the 1,031 persons holding delegate status, only 232 had been delegates or alternates in 1916. Of those, only 102 had participated in 1912's train wreck.

In the days before the convention opened, candidates, campaign workers, party operatives, reporters, columnists, and newsreel cameramen trickled into town. Also trickling was Warren Harding, who on June 7 visited a local friend—his mistress, Nan Britton, now residing at her sister's cramped 6103 Woodlawn Avenue apartment. It was a tense little tryst. Harding warned Nan that she might very well be shadowed if he were nominated. She wanted him to see their baby, Elizabeth Ann, who was quite nearby, on Michigan Avenue, living with Belle Woodlock, a twenty-eight-year-old nurse paid $20 per week to care for the infant. Harding claimed that he was as "crazy to do it [see his child]," just as enthusiastic to see the baby as Nan was. But he didn't, and he never would see Elizabeth Ann.

Hiram Johnson had no time for mistresses. He was a serious candidate: serious, and energetic, and far too angry. That night, before eight thousand serious, and energetic, and far too angry supporters at Chicago's Auditorium, Johnson, and his irreconcilable ally, William Borah, lambasted not only Woodrow Wilson and his damnable League but also their fellow Republicans Lowden and Wood and, in fact, any Republican who dared oppose them—those who would "dehumanize the Republican Party."

Two days later, on Wednesday, June 9, *Los Angeles Times* correspondent Robert B. Armstrong filed a prescient dispatch, noting that Johnson's tirade against front-runners Lowden and Wood had disgusted even his own supporters. That opinion wasn't surprising. The *Times* hated Johnson and had spent years writing him off. But Armstrong also dismissed Lowden and Wood, theorizing, rather remarkably, that the battle "has narrowed down tonight" to Harding and to Pennsylvania's Senator Philander Knox and Governor William Cameron Sproul. "The eastern leaders would like Knox best of all," Armstrong wrote, "but they fear he would be hard to elect. Harding comes from a pivotal state [Pennsylvania was solidly Republican]. He has antagonized none of the other candidates, is a good vote-getter, and would be supported by all elements of the party."

Cameron was writing it just as patient, careful Harry Daugherty would have wanted it.

At 11:30 on Tuesday morning, June 8, Republican national chairman

Will H. Hays gaveled the convention to order. Indiana-born Hays was the Republicans' no-longer-very-secret weapon. He didn't look like much, like a punier, Midwest version of Calvin Coolidge, but he was savvy, articulate, personable, diplomatic, and efficient. Hays worked his way up—from precinct committeeman and city attorney to Indiana state chairman and to national chairman in June 1918. If you were hiring a man to run a political party, you'd hire William Harrison Hays. Some people, in fact, considered hiring him for president.

As efficient as Will Hays might be, the convention started a half hour behind schedule, which may have been fine with everyone. Not many delegates relished time spent in the not-too-old, but not-too-clean, Coliseum at Fifteenth and South Wabash, as H. L. Mencken described it, "an old armory . . . used lately for prize fights, dog shows and a third-rate circus, [that] still smelled of pugs, kennels and elephants. To police this foul pen there was a mob of ward heelers armed with clubs, and bent on packing both the gallery and the floor with their simian friends."

"The dirtiest man that I have ever seen in my life," he later remembered, "was in charge of the sandwich counter in Chicago."

A powerful heat exacerbated the situation. Only early June, it was nonetheless damned *hot*. Inside, temperatures regularly exceeded 100 degrees for a good three hours each day.

"It isn't the humidity," observed *New York Tribune* columnist Heywood Broun, "it's the heat."

The *Tribune* was Republican. Big, burly, exceedingly rumpled, quite radical Heywood Broun was not. But he wrote with such wit and verve that the *Tribune* not only printed his stuff but often showcased it on the front page. In the run-up to the convention, Broun found himself accosted by an earnest Hiram Johnson worker, frantically attempting to convince one and all that, every appearance to the contrary, the California progressive was *not*, in fact, a dangerous radical.

"It distressed us," Broun wrote in the nation's foremost Republican paper, "to find that our favorite candidate [Johnson] wasn't a radical at all, but much more than that we were disturbed and puzzled at being taken so readily for a representative of big business. Evidently the spats were a mistake."

Broun's associate from New York's famed Algonquin Round Table,

Edna Ferber (her stories were short and so, come to think of it, was she), was also present, part of a United Press Association team including William Allen White and cartoonist Ding Darling. Ferber submitted her reports as though written by her popular fictional character "Emma McChesney." Miss McChesney seemed to lean toward Hoover. So did Miss Ferber.

"The sun beat down on the bald heads and heat-suffused faces of the delegates . . . ," Ferber would recall. " I idly wondered why we were known as the white race when we really were pink. The men sat in their shirt sleeves and as the sweltering week wore on[,] they shed collars, ties, even shoes in some cases. It was the American male politician reduced to the most common denominator."

Some folks, Calvin Coolidge and Herbert Hoover among them, preserved their shirt collars and their dignity. Coolidge had meant what he said—he invariably did—when he said he wasn't going to actively pursue the presidency. That meant staying home and governing Massachusetts.

Staying home—and maintaining a stolid sense of Yankee realism. On Sunday, June 6, he wrote his father:

> You know there is no chance for me except when it may appear none of the leaders can get it. Then if at all my chance will come.
> It may be Thursday. The situation is very chaotic. No one knows.

Like Coolidge, Hoover had avoided any personal campaigning prior to the convention. Now, again like Coolidge, the Great Engineer excused himself, attending commencement ceremonies at Swarthmore, vowing that there would be no Hoover third party.

Yet, absent or not, third party or not, governing or not, campaigning continued apace. Hoover's surrogates and supporters maintained convention offices and distributed their share of campaign materials. Like the man himself, his campaign contained no gimmicks, just a business-like exposition of actual issues. "Hoover is the only candidate whose campaign on the ground offers a definite choice of issues rather than souvenirs," Heywood Broun observed approvingly. "Elsewhere the voter is asked to choose between red feathers [the Wood emblem], tin bears and cardboard oranges [the Johnson emblem]."

Frank W. Stearns and James Reynolds established a modest Coolidge headquarters at the Congress Hotel. Dwight Morrow buttonholed delegates, informing them what a great man his Amherst classmate was. Nobody seemed to notice or care. What delegates did notice, however, was a trim little black-leather sixty-page book, bearing the title *Law and Order*. Containing yet another collection of Coolidge speeches, it had been, with typical Stearns efficiency, conceived, compiled, printed, and bound within an eighteen-hour span. Placed in the hands of every delegate, unlike most souvenirs, it would not be thrown away, for upon its cover Stearns had printed in handsome gilt each recipient's name. Thin enough to fit inside a breast pocket (or purse, in the case of female delegates), delegates and alternates could carry it with them, and when things got slow, or just plain boring (as Stearns knew they would), they could enjoy the terse rhetoric of Stearns's candidate. "It was," noted the head of Massachusetts's delegation, "as neat and effective a piece of political publicity as I have ever seen."

Coolidge had books. He didn't have votes. Beyond Massachusetts, he held few delegates, and even his home-state support was precarious at best. Murray Crane might back him all the way, but Crane was ill and unable to maneuver as necessary. Senator Lodge, who actually leaned toward Wood, now displayed open contempt for Coolidge. "Nominate a man who lives in a two-family house!" Lodge fumed at the Chicago Club. "Never! Massachusetts is not for him!"

Lodge was just getting started. "The rest of what he said," the *New York Evening Mail*'s Henry L. Stoddard informed Frank Stearns, "was so bad I did not have the courage to repeat it."

Like Coolidge, most candidates had their headquarters at the Congress. Hoover rented the huge eighth-floor ballroom with its magnificent view of Lake Michigan. Wood bivouacked in the Elizabethan Room, Lowden the Gold Room. Harding had the Florentine Room (ironically, TR's 1912 headquarters), and wondered if he could afford to pay for it. He also had a presence in the Morrison. As the convention started, Texas national committeeman Rentfro B. ("Gus") Kreager, leader of the Texas GOP's "lily-white" faction, loaned Harding his two-room suite at the nearby Auditorium Hotel.

There was even a headquarters of sorts for a vice-presidential candidate, rail-thin Samuel Adams, a Virginia apple farmer and agricultural magazine editor, a relative of some sort to all the famous Adamses. He handed out apples to whoever came by. As the convention opened, Rhode Island Governor R. Livingston Beekman also announced for the vice-presidency. His fellow state delegates confessed this was the first they had heard of his ambition, and they didn't know what to make of it.

The *New York Times* eagerly reported the scenery at Hiram Johnson's crowded Auditorium Hotel headquarters. "A big poster," it wrote, "shows the Senator with a little boy in his lap and a big collie dog leaning against the Senatorial knee. The boy is the Senator's son, Hiram Johnson Jr., and a handsome fellow he is. The little fellow has grown a bit since that picture was taken—grown enough to raise a moustache and be a Major in the war; and as for the collie, he has probably passed on to the happy hunting ground. Still, it is a good picture. . . ."

Heywood Broun took scrupulous note of Senator Harding's printed materials. "We also have a slight leaning toward Warren Harding," he confessed, using the royal "we" as was his (or was it "their"?) habit, "because in one of his campaign leaflets he is described as having been 'a toiler, earning his bread by the sweat of his face.' We can't believe that any man who sanctions such a departure from the traditional form can be entirely reactionary."

Harding had scraped bottom in the disastrous Indiana primary. Since then, he had been plagued by doubt. Should he withdraw? Was he wasting his time? Fooling himself—and precious few others? Jeopardizing his beloved Senate seat? Harding wavered. Harry Daugherty didn't. Somehow, this man who had failed repeatedly in Ohio politics instinctively grasped how to achieve victory in presidential politics. He would stay the course, never panic, nor anger any member of the opposition . . . and wait until the nomination would, by process of elimination, fall into his lap.

Daugherty's plan was *that* basic, a plodding strategy founded on patience, faith, and unfailing courtesy. But others feared that Harry was banking on classic inside politics. General Wood's forces reported a conversation that Daugherty had with two reporters on February 21, 1920 at Manhattan's old Waldorf-Astoria hotel. They quoted Daugherty as saying:

At the proper time after the Republican National Convention meets, some fifteen men, bleary[-]eyed with loss of sleep and perspiring profusely with the excessive heat, will sit down in seclusion around a big table. I will be with them and will present the name of Senator Harding to them, and before we get through they will put him over.

I don't expect Senator Harding to be nominated on the first, second or third ballot. But I think we can well afford to take chances that about eleven minutes after two o'clock on Friday morning at the convention, when fifteen or twenty men, somewhat weary, are sitting around a table, some one of them will say, "Who will we nominate?" At that decisive time the friends of Senator Harding can suggest him and afford to abide by the result.

Daugherty's words have become among the most quoted in political history.

He never said them.

In fact, reporters had accosted Daugherty as he hurriedly packed to catch a train, demanding to know how he could possibly believe that Warren Harding would be nominated. What commitments did he possess? What states harbored these phantom armies of Harding delegates? Daugherty wouldn't bite, so the reporter laid out the above smoke-filled room, 2 A.M. scenario. "Make it two eleven," Daugherty sarcastically snapped back, as he hopped into the elevator and into history.

New York reporters seemed to be planting words in other people's mouths with surprising frequency, and sometimes with remarkably similar words. A month earlier, the *Times* had quoted New Hampshire Senator George H. Moses, a staunch Wood supporter. "I know just what will happen at Chicago," Moses had said. "Wood will have a long lead on the first ballot, and then the favorite son managers will steal up dark stairways, and in the seclusion of a room at the Congress Hotel will draw lots to see which favorite is to receive the combined support. They will still be discussing it at breakfast time, and having reached no agreement thereon, will march meekly into the Convention Hall in time to take part in the Leonard Wood stampede."

Harry Daugherty's scheming didn't depend quite so much on hotel rooms but on hotel *lobbies*. Explained Daugherty:

We put loyal Harding lookouts in *every hotel in town* and got one or more of our representatives into the headquarters of every rival.

Our staff grew finally to two thousand men and women. They met every train, shook hands with the incoming delegates and made engagements to see them. . . . We gave out no claims. Made no statements to the press and carefully concealed every move from the reporters.

Daugherty did have cause to conceal some items from reporters. His use of the famed (at least in Ohio) seventy-five-man-strong Columbus Men's Glee Club, all in full evening dress, to serenade delegates was harmless enough. That could be reported on. But there were characters at the convention even oilier than Harry Daugherty—characters Daugherty *did* contact. Chicago's violently isolationist (and exuberantly corrupt) mayor, Big Bill Thompson, for example, now hated Frank Lowden. He offered Daugherty a working alliance. Daugherty gently declined.

Oklahoma railroad magnate and wildcat oilman Jake L. Hamon had married a remote cousin of Florence Harding. *New York Evening Post* columnist Mark Sullivan sized up Hamon as "an unusual combination of fat and force, gross as a pig and vain as a peacock." Jake had expended a fortune (including $50,000 in bribes, said the *Chicago Daily Journal*) to gain control of his delegation, holding it unenthusiastically for Lowden. At one point, Hamon promised to switch to Wood—whom he didn't particularly like, but business was business—in exchange for Wood's appointments to Interior Secretary and Ambassador to Mexico. Wood, as honest as he was stubborn, refused. Daugherty, however, aggressively wooed Hamon. Wary of Harding's chances, the oilman remained for Lowden but promised to keep Harding in mind. Hamon wasn't just talk. He sent Daugherty away with a $25,000 donation.

Daugherty also did business with Lowden. Harry knew that Leonard Wood might yet end the whole game. To derail him, Harry propped up Lowden—advancing him delegates from Harding's meager storehouse. "We can't allow Harding's vote to be too small, but we'll loan you every vote we can until you pass Wood . . . ," Daugherty assured Lowden campaign manager Louis L. Emerson. "The minute you pass Wood, the minute Wood is out of the race, all friendship between us on the floor of this convention ceases—you understand that?"

Harry Daugherty was certainly Harding's key backer, but Warren possessed another seasoned operative: his wife. Warren Harding regularly cheated on the Duchess but possessed a certain genuine respect—even a genuine, if deeply flawed, love—for her, and he relied on her for sound advice—at least politically. "In the days preceding and during the convention," recalled Ohio Congressman Simeon Fess, "she was by his [Harding's] side to counsel and advise him. . . . At Chicago, Mrs. Harding might be said to have been his manager. No step was taken without consulting her, and her advice was rarely, if ever, ignored."

Daugherty recognized political talent when he saw it, allowing Florence "a free hand in talking to anybody she pleased. I could trust absolutely her keen intuitions and her straightforward, honest thinking. She was a trained newspaper woman. She made friends with every reporter. . . . She disarmed criticism by her frank declaration that she only wished Harding's success because he wanted it. . . . We knew she would say this and she did. . . . She could talk indefinitely and never say a sharp or offensive word about a human being."

On Tuesday, June 8, the convention's keynote address was given by Henry Cabot Lodge, a striking figure in white whiskers and waistcoat, black cutaway and blacker mood regarding the current occupant of the White House. This was Henry Cabot Lodge's moment (actually, more than a moment: an hour and twenty minutes) to skewer the hated Wilson, using every arrow of wit and sarcasm and logic in his quiver. "In 1916," Lodge reminded his audience and the nation, "Mr. Wilson won on the cry that 'he had kept us out of war.' He now demands the approval of the American people for his party and his administration on the ground that he has kept us out of peace."

"Mr. Wilson," Lodge concluded, "and his dynasty, his heirs and assigns, or anybody that is his, must be driven from all control of the government and all influence in it."

All—even Heywood Broun—agreed. Wilson had been a disaster. They could not agree on his replacement, or about that damned League of Nations. It wasn't acceptable as Wilson proposed it. But was it fixable? Hiram Johnson said no and would likely bolt the party if its platform failed to appease his irreconcilable views. "I am not compromising," he vowed. "I have no compromise to make. I am against this league. There are no reservations that can cure its wickedness. I'm opposed to it with or without reservations." Otherwise, railed Johnson, the Republican Party would be "the tail of Mr. Wilson's kite."

Platforms are, most normally, written and quickly forgotten. That is certainly the case today. Rarely do they have impact. Then, Johnson's irreconcilables were warning that the wording of that year's document would possess real significance. If they did not like the wording on the League, they would bolt. If they did, a sure-thing Republican year would quickly slide into a disaster. It would be 1912 all over again.

A seven-man subcommittee including five current or former U. S. Senators—Murray Crane and North Dakota's Porter J. McCumber (both strong League men) and Minnesota's Frank B. Kellogg, Wisconsin's Irvine L. Lenroot, and Maine's Frederick Hale (all mild reservationists)— was appointed to draft a plank on the League. It fell, however, to TR's former Secretary of State Elihu Root to craft wording to prevent a party bloodbath. Root's supposedly gargantuan task proved to be an easy one, as he cribbed language from Indiana's Republican platform, a document drafted by Lodge, Philander Knox, and Iowa Senator Albert Cummins.

Root wrote:

The Republican party stands for agreement among the nations to preserve the peace of the world. We believe that such an international association must be based upon international justice, and must provide methods which shall maintain the rule of public right by the development of law and the decision of impartial courts, and which shall secure instant and general international conference whenever peace shall be threatened by political action, so that the nations pledged to do and insist upon what is just and fair may exercise their influence and power for the prevention of war.

We believe that all this can be done without the compromise of national independence, without depriving the people of the United States in advance of the right to determine for themselves what is just and fair when the occasion arises, and without

211

involving them as participants and not as peacemakers in a multitude of quarrels, the merits of which they are unable to judge.

No one, not even Root, knew what that actually meant. In any case, it
proved inoffensive to all factions and kept Hiram Johnson on the reservation. If the Republican Party was going to split once again, it would not
be over the platform. The convention adopted it unanimously.

Root's plank baffled editorial writers. The Democratic *New York World*
slammed it as a "surrender" to Johnson. The *Springfield Republican* concurred, finding that "a minority of desperadoes" had blackjacked the
majority of the party into subservience. The Republican *New York Tribune*
thought it didn't "preclude ratification." The *New York Sun* found it
"deplorable."

The *Washington Post*, however, termed it a "remarkably able composite
statement of the majority of the party as thrashed out in the Senate" that
dispelled the sense of doom that had been hanging over the convention—and, in fact, over the whole campaign. It had kept its eye on the
goal: election of a Republican president. The *Post* got it right.

Though everyone seemed to forget, the platform contained more
topics than just the League. The GOP endorsed revising the tariff,
restricting Asian immigration, the annual registration of aliens, ratification of the Nineteenth Amendment, and the Americanization of Hawaii;
and it opposed government ownership of railroads, an American mandate
in Armenia, and public employee strikes. It didn't mention Prohibition or
Irish independence. It also called on Congress "to consider the most effective means to end lynching," a stand maddeningly vague to modern ears
but exactly the language advocated by the NAACP—and much more than
what they got from Democrats.

The entire document reminded H. L. Mencken of "words scrawled on
a wall by feeble-minded children."

Meanwhile, Florence Harding gave a very odd interview. "I am content to bask in my husband's limelight, but I cannot see why anyone
should want to be President in the next four years," she began quite
unremarkably, before veering into unusually macabre territory. "I can
see but one word written over the head of my husband if he is elected,
and that word is 'Tragedy.'" She continued:

As a matter of fact[,] I would rather have him Senator than President. Being Senator and being a Senator's wife is really a wonderful life. Of course, now that he is in the race and wants to win[,] I must want him to, but down in my heart I am sorry.

He is the most wonderful man in the world. He can differ with people without offending them. His smile, so his friends in Washington tell him, should get him anything he wants.

I've lived with my husband for twenty-six years, and I know him. I'm not talking for effect; he is all the things that I say he is and more. The only reason I want to go to the White House is because it is his wish.

At ten minutes to ten, Friday morning, June 9, Henry Cabot Lodge gaveled the already listless and wilted proceedings back to order. First came the obligatory prayer and the seemingly even more obligatory hosannas to Theodore Roosevelt (presented this time by Pennsylvania delegate Alexander Moore, former Bull Mooser and current husband of Gay '90s icon Lillian Russell). Only then came the nominating speeches—an interminable string of nominating speeches.

Kansas's Governor Henry J. Allen, yet another publisher-politician, balding, Roman-nosed, and looking very much like a Republican William Jennings Bryan, led off, presenting Leonard Wood's name to a convention awash in red and green feathers, Wood's symbol. Allen's talk, punctuated by waves of sweat pouring down his pudgy face, proved lackluster. Corinne Roosevelt Robinson's seconding speech was not. Alice Roosevelt Longworth loved it, jumping up and down in the aisles in appreciation. So did just about everybody else. Proclaimed Mrs. Robinson:

People often say to me in these last days, "You wish to have Leonard Wood as President because he was a friend of your brother, Theodore Roosevelt. . . ." I want Leonard Wood for President, not because he was my brother's friend—although he was my brother's devoted friend, as was my brother his devoted friend; I want Leonard Wood for President not because he was his friend, but because he is his type. . . . There are three kinds of men: The man who uses only words; the man who uses the brawn and blood of another man by saying, "Go!" and the man, the kind of man we want who says, "Come!" and I want Leonard Wood.

It was said that "her splendid clear voice rang like the echo of a Gatling gun against a stone wall." Others claimed that if she had been a man, she would have been catapulted into instant dark-horse status.

Frank Lowden's nomination came next, to the tune of mustachioed Representative William A. Rodenberg's "soaring elephant oratory." Big-city writers unanimously derided this small-town congressman's embarrassingly small-town efforts. "One knows how Mr. Rodenberg spends the long winter evenings," sniped columnist Irwin S. Cobb; "he spends them memorizing all the platitudes that have been employed in political oratory since Demosthenes."

Heywood Broun concurred:

[Rodenberg] began with a long simile about a ship of state and it seemed it would never leave port. Finally, however, he switched to a long comparison of Lowden and Lincoln, but for all the time he took he neglected to point out the striking fact that the name of each began with an "L."

Defying the odds, the oratory worsened, progressing beyond just putridly bad to dangerously, counter-productively, offensively bad. After Rodenberg, San Francisco attorney Charles S. Wheeler nominated Hiram Johnson, and Cobb damned Wheeler's effort as "the worst speech that ever was." Broun marveled that Wheeler had "made every mistake known to public speaking except that of falling off the platform." Delegates jeered not only Wheeler's miserable efforts but also whom he represented. When Wheeler asked, "Who is the best candidate?" they screamed "Lowden!" and "Wood!" When he asked, "What will California do?" delegates angrily shouted: "What did California do in 1916?" harkening back to Johnson's knifing of Charles Evans Hughes.

Many puzzled over why Johnson, with William Borah—one of the country's great orators, at his disposal—had selected Wheeler. Johnson, Alice Roosevelt Longworth explained, feared Borah "might steal the show" and "turned the omission into an insult by asking him to make a seconding speech." Slighted, Borah refused.

So Johnson tapped Minnesota Congressman Thomas D. Schall. Schall, legally blind, needed to be guided to the podium by his young son, who wore a sailor suit for the occasion. Delegates gave Schall, actually a fine speaker in his own right, an appropriately appreciative hand.

Speaker of the House Frederick H. Gillett, Coolidge's own congressman, nominated Calvin Coolidge and did quite well. ("His speech," noted an early Coolidge biographer, "was in good taste.") Looking more than a bit like a balding Henry Cabot Lodge (or a Republican Lenin), the white-goateed Gillett said of Coolidge:

He is not showy or spectacular, but he never disappoints. The limelight attracts him less than the midnight oil. He never crooks the pregnant hinges of the knee before pretentious power nor stiffens his neck in pride before lowly weakness but follows the pole star to duty.

Would it not be a restful change to see such a man in the White House today? He is silent as Grant, diplomatic as McKinley, patient as Lincoln, with the political instincts of Roosevelt.

The demonstration that followed lasted but a minute, but those listening for omens could detect waves of genuine enthusiasm.

Wood may have had a Gatling gun in his corner, but it was left to sedate little Calvin Coolidge to be seconded by an English-born professional actress. Thirty-four years old, "plump but pleasant," Mrs. Alexandra Carlisle Pfeiffer had acted in such Broadway productions as *If I Were King* and *The Tragedy of Nan* and was fresh from directing *Barnum Was Right* for Harvard's Hasty Pudding Club. En route to Chicago, Frank Stearns had asked her to second Coolidge.

Hastily, they scribbled out a four-minute speech. From a Chicago department store, Mrs. Pfeiffer purchased several white nursemaid's uniforms, with all the necessary accessories—black patent-leather belts and black tie sailor hats. The rest of the Republican Party might look bedraggled. Mrs. Pfeiffer would not.

She was a hit. Heywood Broun thought her effort "second only to the

215

speech of Corinne Roosevelt." Columnist Frank Sullivan was blunter: Mrs. Pfeiffer had been "a refreshing oasis in the desert of turgid nominating speeches."

Hour after hour, speeches, bands, marching and cheering kept coming. Former North Carolina Senator Marion Butler ("a gent with whiskers and endurance," the term "endurance" not being complimentary) wordily nominated his state's favorite son, federal Appeals Court Judge (also a former United States Senator) Jeter C. Pritchard. Pritchard, realistic enough to know that he hadn't a prayer, was angling for vice president.

Thirty-five-year-old Manhattan socialite Ogden Livingston Mills (who had earlier lost a vote on chairing the platform committee, 41–3) nominated New York favorite son Nicholas Murray Butler. Delegates drifted in and out of the hall as Mills hammered away at the administration.

New York's delegation was an interesting microcosm of the entire fractured convention. Officially for Butler, it also cast votes for Lowden and Wood, for Coolidge and Hoover, and—from vociferously radical New York City Board of Aldermen president Fiorello LaGuardia—for Irvine Lenroot.

New York Court of Appeals Judge Nathan L. Miller of Syracuse (formerly a Wood supporter) nominated Herbert Hoover—"the man possessing the qualities, the equipment, and the ability to deal with the problems which are confronting us." Hoover drew loud, spontaneous cheers from the galleries (including some from William Howard Taft's son, Robert), but only hostility from the floor.

Former Ohio governor Frank B. Willis nominated Warren Harding. Harding and Willis, never particularly close, were now united in common cause: If Harding captured the nomination, Willis could take his Senate seat. Willis was from the old school of politics, big, hearty, booming, and bluff. He made Harding seem like Coolidge. "To hear him get every last bit of vocal value," marveled Frank Sullivan, "out of the 'R's and 'O's in 'four years ago' is to know the last word in oratory . . . the combined enjoyments of oratory, grand opera, and hog-calling."

Willis gave it all he had. His basic message: Harding wasn't dazzling, but he was sound, exactly what the country needed:

What we want is not brilliant maneuvers but safe and sane seaman-ship by a captain who knows the way, by a captain who as he walks the deck working with the officers and men in these troubling times can say, "Steady, boys, steady." That is the type of man Ohio is presenting today. McKinley was a great President because he understood Congress, and could cooperate with it. This man understands the viewpoint of Congress and can cooperate with it.

My friends, in the name of the Republicans of Ohio I present for your deliberate consideration this great stalwart American-thinking Republican; not a professing progressive but a per-forming progressive. He delivers the goods. He is a man of sane statesmanship with eyes fixed on the future, a great typical Amer-ican citizen. Ladies and gentlemen of the Convention, I name for the office of President of the United States that stalwart son of Ohio, Senator Warren G. Harding.

Not too far from the end of his peroration, Willis leaned down and remarked, in mock conspiratorial tones, "Say, boys—and girls—why not give your votes to nominate Senator Harding." The place went wild. Even Senator Lodge allowed himself a wan smile.

By now, delegates were exhausted, sick from heat, sick of speeches, sick of pretending to cheer. But they cheered Willis and lustily cheered for Harding. Will Hays found it all "quite spontaneous." Mark Sullivan thought it "unmistakably spontaneous." It was, and it meant something.

Among those cheering so enthusiastically was Nan Britton. Harding had obtained a convention pass for Nan, boldly presenting it to her in the Auditorium Hotel lobby. Nan had seen Willis once previously, in 1914, while she attended Kent Normal School. Then, she thought Willis an "illy-groomed, small-stage politician." Now, she thought he was just great.

The tail end of the parade finally came into sight. Philadelphia Mayor J. Hampton Moore nominated William C. Sproul ("a candidate who is in good health . . . the father of good roads . . . a modern McKinley"). George H. Walker of Seattle did likewise for Senator Miles Poindexter ("no clanging militarist"), while former West Virginia Supreme Court Justice Joseph M. Sanders nominated the eleventh candidate, United

States Senator Howard Sutherland. "The delegates were so fed up with seven hours of oratory," observed Will Hays, "that [Sanders's] fifteen-minute speech could not be heard ten feet from the speakers' platform over the hubbub of protesting delegates."

A twelfth candidate was to have been placed in nomination: Wisconsin's Robert La Follette, but when that time came, his state's delegation—much to an exhausted convention's relief—passed.

If delegates were restive, so was Warren Harding. He still didn't believe he had a chance and questioned the financial cost of the charade. Maybe Frank Lowden or Herbert Hoover had the resources to run for president, but a small-town publisher didn't. Somewhere between 11:00 and noon that Friday morning, he confided to Nicholas Murray Butler: "I cannot afford to keep these rooms any longer and I have sent word downstairs to say that I am giving them up this evening. This convention will never nominate me. I do not propose to go back to the Senate. I am going to quit politics and devote myself to my newspaper."

Balloting began at 4:58 P.M. The first ballot provided little excitement. Wood, Lowden (sidelined by a severe cold), and Johnson led. Harding remained poised to advance if the deadlock persisted. Coolidge couldn't even present a united Massachusetts delegation. La Follette, nominated or not, drew votes from the Wisconsin delegation—and hisses from other delegations.

When Lodge polled Missouri, its delegates whispered and fumbled. "Not ready?" Lodge inquired.

"Still counting the cash?" came a cry from the gallery—obviously not from a Lowden supporter.

The other excitement came when Lodge queried the Oregon delegation. Hiram Johnson won the state primary, but Portland delegate Judge Wallace McCamant (who had led the fight against adopting an Irish independence plank) refused to support the California maverick. Lodge let McCamant vote for Wood.

The wiry McCamant wasn't the only one voting for Wood. On the first ballot, he garnered fifty votes more than expected, leading Lowden 287–211. Harding remained viable—low-key, but viable. Coolidge garnered only six votes outside Massachusetts. Hoover was a god to those in the galleries, a joke to delegates. The first ballot went like this:

Wood 287
Lowden 211
Johnson 133
Sproul 83½
Butler 69
Harding 65
Coolidge 34
La Follette 24
Pritchard 21
Poindexter 20
Sutherland 17
Coleman du Pont 7
Hoover 5½
Borah 2
Charles B. Warren 1

The result scared the anti-Wood forces. Lowden needed propping up—and quickly. Harry Daugherty loaned him a few more of Harding's precious delegates. The second ballot showed significant Lowden movement, and not enough by Johnson:

Wood 289½
Lowden 249½
Johnson 146
Sproul 78½
Harding 59
Butler 41
Coolidge 32
La Follette 24
Poindexter 15
Sutherland 15
Pritchard 10
du Pont 7
Hoover 5½
Knox 1
Borah 1

The third ballot saw both Wood and Lowden gain (Wood now had two thirds of the votes needed for nomination), while Johnson, Harding, and Coolidge all stalled:

Wood 303
Lowden 282½
Johnson 148
Sproul 79½
Harding 58½
Coolidge 27
Butler 25
La Follette 24
Poindexter 15
Sutherland 9
Hoover 5½
du Pont 2
Knox 2
Watson 2
Borah 1

A motion to adjourn failed, 701½ to 275½. A fourth ballot witnessed the convention equivalent of trench warfare. Nobody moved much at all, though Johnson began losing delegates even from states where he had won primaries:

Wood 314½
Lowden 289
Johnson 140½
Sproul 79½
Harding 61½
Coolidge 25
La Follette 22
Butler 20
Poindexter 15
Hoover 5½
Watson 4

Sutherland 3
du Pont 2
Knox 2
Borah 1

Nothing would be settled by continued balloting. Backstage horse-trading was necessary to reach agreement on anything. Just after 7 P.M., Utah Senator Reed Smoot moved to adjourn. Lodge called for a voice vote. The Convention roared back "No!" The Wood and Lowden forces wanted to keep going. Adjournments don't help front-runners. Lodge ignored them: "The 'Ayes' have it and the convention is adjourned to tomorrow morning at ten o'clock."

"Oh, there's going to be a deadlock," Smoot blandly assured a reporter, "and we'll have to work out some solution; we wanted the night to think it over."

Hiram Johnson again threatened to bolt the party. "If [Wood or Lowden] is nominated," he fumed, "the issue before the American people will not be on the platform of the party—it will be on the issue of the corruption of the American people."

The *New York Times* opined that Harding had made a "poor showing" in the first day's balloting. Harding wasn't impressed either, unsure of his chances and afraid of losing not only the presidency but also his Senate seat.

Mysteriously, as the night progressed, he regained confidence. Suddenly he was no longer unsure. In fact, he was *very* sure. By 11 P.M., he jauntily informed a reporter, "I am the most likely candidate for President tonight."

He had finally convinced himself that Daugherty's plan had been right all along. If he bided his time and alienated no faction, the nomination would, at the proper time, be his prize.

The time was now.

"With Wood, Johnson, and Lowden out of the way," Harding later explained, "I knew I could count on friends in every one of their delegations, because I had followed . . . the rule that has guided me throughout my political career, which is not to hurt anyone's feelings or to step on anybody's toes if I could find foot room elsewhere. I figured that if politeness and an honest desire not to humiliate any rival just for the sake of winning a few votes were ever going to produce anything, this was the time. Other fellows, just as competent as I, or more so, had made enemies, and it looked to me that there was no one in sight that the convention could unite on except myself."

Everybody in the Harding camp was working hard: low-key, but hard. Harry Daugherty kept the Columbus Glee Club serenading the rival camps, and while most politicians would have annoyed the opposition with pro-Harding fight songs, the Hardingites never mentioned their favorite son. They merely added a pleasant, friendly, nonconfrontational touch to the scene. *Nothing* would be done to alienate *any* potential supporter.

Friday night was a night of myths, and William Allen White created the first of them, claiming that he had seen Harding, and the sight wasn't pretty:

> Harding wore, on the day I saw him, a two days' beard and was disheveled. His eyes were bloodshot. He evidently had been drinking. He looked little like the fine statuesque figure, all tailored, pressed, the "oiled and curled Assyrian bull," who had stood with a red boutonniere in his lapel, four years before, and abused Theodore Roosevelt to the yipping delight of the Republican convention when they were trying fusion in 1916. There was the front-window model for President. But the model I saw there at the elevator door looked like the wreck of the *Hesperus*. He was discouraged.

White's tale achieved wide circulation and embellishment, eventually taking such transmuted shapes as this: "The senator was stiff. . . . *Many* [emphasis added] were shocked to detect more than just a whiff of whiskey on his unshaven face."

In reality, William Allen White was the only person, out of the thousands attending the convention, claiming to have seen Harding soused. Warren Harding may not have been very careful *behind* closed doors, but he was generally circumspect and careful in public. Beyond that, no other known accounts of Harding's activities that night provide any hint that White was telling the truth. Harding was at the top of his game that evening. It was his moment. He made decisions—and made them right. He cajoled. He negotiated. He maneuvered.

He was not beaten. He was not drunk. He probably wasn't even unshaven.

Nor was he reckless. He carefully hedged his bets. At precisely two minutes before midnight, two minutes before the final deadline, he re-filed for the United States Senate.

But dangers remained, particularly regarding the restive, always-fractious Ohio delegation. The Buckeye State's nine Wood delegates had all but convinced four Harding men to join them. If they did, the whole delegation might jump ship. Harding pleaded and coaxed. The Ohio delegation had been shaken but remained largely in his camp.

Meanwhile, everybody was courting Hiram Johnson. Wood and Lowden offered him the vice-presidency. He turned them down. At 1 A.M., Harding, feeling increasingly confident, also approached Johnson, predicting point-blank that he would be nominated the next day on the tenth ballot. He also offered Johnson second place. Johnson, perhaps questioning how anyone with 61½ votes could be so positive, turned him down.

He underestimated him.

## Chapter 14

~

# "WARREN HARDING IS THE BEST OF THE SECOND-RATERS"

Meetings and conferences materialized everywhere. History might remember *a* smoke-filled room, but there were *dozens* of meetings—in rooms, in hallways, in back corners.

There was one room *everybody* remembered: Colonel George Harvey's quarters at the Blackstone Hotel—Room 404.

Harvey now hated Wilson. His magazines, *The North American Review* and *Harvey's Weekly* (his new magazine after his retirement from *Harper's Weekly*) maintained a loud, steady drumbeat against the League, and now prodigal Democrat Harvey appeared at a Republican convention to help scuttle his ungrateful protégé's legacy.

Through well past Friday midnight, a raft of Republican senators trooped through Room 404—Lodge, Watson, Brandegee, Smoot, Moses, Borah, Illinois's Medill McCormick, Kansas's Charles Curtis, New York's James W. Wadsworth and William M. Calder, Missouri's Selden Spencer, Colorado's Lawrence C. Phipps, New Jersey's Joseph S. Frelinghuysen, Massachusetts's two former senators, Crane and Weeks, and even Lowden campaign manager Alvin Tobias ("Tobe") Hert.

The gathering, or rather series of gatherings—for the participants came and went at will, with no one really presiding (though Lodge was its guiding spirit)—focused not so much on selecting a candidate but on eliminating them one by one. Lowden and Wood had killed each other off. Johnson and La Follette were simply impossible. Borah wasn't any better. Lodge and Philander Knox were too old. Lodge couldn't stand

Coolidge. Hoover wasn't even a Republican; Johnson *and* the Old Guard would bolt if Hoover were nominated. Watson was too conservative. Pritchard, Sutherland, and Poindexter were jokes. The unions hated Governor Allen. Sproul, Knox, and Coolidge hailed from states that were going Republican anyway. Colonel Harvey wanted National Chairman Will Hays, but Hays had never held public office, and, unless you were a general, the presidency usually wasn't an entry-level position.

That, Lodge pointed out, left you with Warren Harding. And who could disagree? "There ain't any first[-]raters this year," Connecticut's normally grammatical Frank Brandegee observed; "this ain't any 1880 or any 1904. We haven't any John Shermans or Theodore Roosevelts. We've got a lot of second[-]raters[,] and Warren Harding is the best of the second[-]raters."

A vote of sorts was taken. Everybody agreed to Harding, whether they meant it or not. At that hour, most just wanted to leave and go to sleep.

Harding could not sleep. In the hall, he accosted Senator Wadsworth and began pumping him about the New York delegation. Wadsworth did little to buoy his hopes—and didn't want to. "Do you think I will gain?" Harding bore on. "I haven't the slightest idea," Wadsworth coldly responded.

By 3 A.M., everyone had left Harvey's suite save for Harvey, Smoot, and Brandegee. Harvey asked Smoot to retrieve Harding. Miraculously, the Utah senator quickly found him out in the hall.

"We think you may be nominated tomorrow," Harvey bluntly told Harding (or, at least, that is what he claimed); "before acting, we think you should tell us, on your conscience and before God, whether there is anything that might be brought up against you that would embarrass the party, any impediment that might disqualify you or make you inexpedient, either as a candidate or as President."

There was a question. Harding took ten minutes to think it over. He wasn't a grafter. He was safe there. But there was Carrie Phillips—and Nan—and all those other women—and his health. His heart and his blood pressure could be better, much better. But, after all, if the crippled Wilson could be president . . .

No, said Harding, there was no reason he couldn't be president.

Popular history records the event as a clear-cut sequence: Senators

225

meet, senators decide on nominee, nominee dodges a question or two, senators ram nominee down convention's throat.

Except that there was no real agreement. Harvey, if he spoke to Harding at all in the manner he later related, spoke only for himself. James Wadsworth thought the whole affair was "like a lot of chickens with their heads off. If they came to any decision at all, it was a decision to let the Harding suggestion go through, the fact being that they did not have anyone else to propose." Each senator departed from Room 404 to do as he damned well pleased. Smoot, for Harding all along, stayed with Harding, with Curtis now along for the ride. Brandegee, like most every-body else, kept his options open.

A myth had been created, in large part by Harvey himself as he puffed himself up to any reporter who would listen: Harvey as Republican king-maker, senators of every temperament and ideological stripe now marching in lockstep.

It was a fantasy.

Senator Smoot didn't help, either. If anyone in the room was a Harding man, it was Smoot. He might have been the only genuine Harding booster present, and he soon gave this story to a *New York Telegram* reporter: "We decided on Harding and he will be nominated this afternoon, after we have balloted long enough to give Lowden a run for his money."

"Harding of Ohio," the Associated Press reported, "emerged this morning from an all[-]night conference of Republican chieftains as the man with whom they hoped to break the imminent deadlock. Delicate relationships were involved . . . but most of the leaders . . . appeared agreeable to trying Harding first among the large field of dark horses."

"Conventions, as all know, are subject to many strange influences," Henry Stoddard later wrote, "but a great stretch of imagination is needed to believe that many delegates to a Republican convention, while choosing a leader, would listen attentively to a dyed-in-the-wool Jersey Democrat whom no Jersey Republican district would send as a delegate and who had apologized to Wilson for the only Republican vote he had ever cast."

Morning came. At 6 A.M. Saturday, *Franklin Sentinel* publisher (and former Massachusetts state senator) Joe Martin walked along Michigan

Avenue. There, he met former Senator John W. Weeks. Martin, already having heard about Colonel Harvey's little conference, began pumping Weeks for information. Finally, Weeks, in nearly conspiratorial tones, confided, "I think it will be Harding."

Returning to the Congress Hotel, Martin wandered into Harding's Florentine Room headquarters, empty save for a janitor already hauling down the candidate's portraits. Martin, taking Weeks's prediction on faith, inquired, "Can I have a button of the next President of the United States?"

"Anyone who thinks this man is going to be President," the workman responded, "can have all that's left," presenting Martin with a handful.8

Harding, meanwhile, remained optimistic. At the LaSalle Hotel, he and Florence breakfasted with his forty-one-year-old brother, Dr. George T. ("Deac") Harding, and his two sons. "Do you really think you have any chance of getting the nomination?" the skeptical George Harding asked.

"Deac," Harding revealed, his confidence growing by the minute, "it looks like I might get the nomination on the seventh or eighth ballot."

The Duchess exploded: "It's utter nonsense. Warren hasn't a chance to get the presidential nomination, and he knows it as well as I do. He's happy in the Senate. He can stay there as long as he wishes to remain. If he hadn't filed for the Senate last night, he'd have lost that too. It's a waste of time and money for him to be here as a presidential candidate."

Senator Lodge gaveled the convention back to order at 10:23 A.M. on Saturday, June 12. Even then, the heat was stifling, and if any agreement had been reached in Colonel Harvey's suite, it wasn't apparent by fifth-ballot voting. Harding's total rose, but only by 16½ votes, to a sparse total of 78, still lagging behind even Governor Sproul. The big news was Frank Lowden. While both Wood and Johnson sank slightly, the Illinois governor finally seized the lead:

Lowden 303
Wood 299
Johnson 133½
Sproul 82½
Harding 78
Coolidge 29

La Follette 24
Poindexter 15
du Pont 6
Hoover 6
Butler 4
Sutherland 1
Kellogg 1
Watson L. Ward 1
Knox 1

On the sixth ballot, Wood and Lowden tied at 311½. Hiram Johnson's balloon continued leaking, while Harding advanced steadily if unspectacularly. Nonetheless, his path was not smooth. On that ballot, four Ohio Harding delegates prepared to defect to Wood. Daugherty alerted his forces, "watch now for the attempted betrayal." A round of boos and hisses greeted the switch. Again, there remained no evidence of a senatorial deal:

Wood 311½
Lowden 311½
Johnson 110
Harding 89
Sproul 77
Coolidge 28
La Follette 24
Poindexter 15
Hoover 5
du Pont 4
Butler 4
Ward 2
Knox 1
Kellogg 1
Lenroot 1

The seventh ballot saw the temperature reach 102 degrees and Harding press slowly forward, gaining between one and three additional votes apiece from nine different states. Wood and Lowden dropped slightly. Lowden regained a microscopic lead. The big news, however, was Hiram Johnson, sinking and never to rise again:

Wood 312
Lowden 311½
Harding 105
Johnson 99½
Sproul 76
Coolidge 28
La Follette 24
Poindexter 15
Hoover 4
du Pont 3
Butler 2
Ward 1
Knox 1
Kellogg 1
Lenroot 1

On the eighth ballot, the totals barely budged, but Harding continued gaining ground (even the four Ohio "deserters" returned). With Lowden and Wood proving incapable of advance, careful observers now saw that Harding's candidacy was real:

Lowden 307
Wood 299
Harding 133½
Johnson 87
Sproul 75½
Coolidge 30
Poindexter 15
Hoover 5
du Pont 3
Butler 2
Knox 1

Kellogg 1
Lenroot 1

Lowden leader "Tobe" Hert, hoping to blunt Harding's momentum, moved to recess until 4 P.M. Daugherty had to keep the pressure on. Frank Willis shouted for a roll call. A solid wall of "Nos" greeted Lodge. Once again, he pronounced that the "Ayes" had it and stalked off the podium. "You can't beat this man by any such tactics!" Daugherty shouted. "You ought to be ashamed of yourself! This is an outrage!"

Hert employed the recess for grand strategizing. Wood and Lowden were killing each other. Joining forces, they could still dominate the convention and prevent a turn toward Harding. At 1:30 Saturday afternoon, an extraordinary secret meeting occurred. Lowden recalled:

> While the balloting was proceeding on Saturday morning, Col. Theodore Roosevelt [Jr.] [a Wood backer] called at my rooms and said that he had suggested to [Michigan national committeeman] Charles B. Warren [a key Lowden supporter] that morning the desirability of Gen. Wood and me getting together. I told Col. Roosevelt that I would be very glad to meet Gen. Wood and a meeting was arranged over the telephone.
>
> It was arranged that Gen. Wood, in a closed car, should drive to the Michigan Avenue entrance of the Blackstone and that I should get into his car at that point. This was done, and we had a conference of perhaps three quarters of an hour, I should say. It was evident to both of us that the Senate combination was making great headway with Senator Harding. Gen. Wood suggested that we ought to get together, and that our managers should meet at once. I concurred in this.

The idea was hatched for a Wood–Lowden ticket. Lowden soon had second thoughts. He wasn't sure that his people would willingly vote for Wood. He didn't really want the vice-presidency. He thought that if the adjournment could be extended to Monday morning, he could somehow regroup and move forward again.

He was wrong. The wheels were falling off both the Wood and

Lowden wagons. Tobe Hert, despairing of Lowden's vanishing chances, now itched to conclude a deal with Harding.

Meanwhile, Kansas's solidly pro-Wood delegation was about to break toward Harding. Senator Charles Curtis informed delegates that the party leadership had decided to go with Harding, and, if Kansas went along, Governor Henry Allen could be vice president. "If you nominate Harding," William Allen White sputtered, "you will disgrace the Republican Party. You will bring shame to your country."

"Ah, White," Wichita delegate James Stewart chided, "you are a dreamer. Try to be practical once." White brokered a deal: Kansas for Harding on the ninth and tenth ballots, then for Hoover.

Connecticut—another formerly staunch Wood state—switched to Harding. But as Connecticut changed sides, Harvey and Brandegee urged its delegation to join a Will Hays boom that they—and Lodge—had concocted, lying that they had 600 Hays delegates ready to go. State Republican chairman J. Henry Roraback wouldn't budge: Connecticut was for Harding. Harvey warned Roraback that that might create a Harding stampede. "Nothing would please me more," Roraback replied. The Hays candidacy was over.

One last myth involved Pennsylvania's Old Guard political boss, Senator Boies Penrose. Penrose, originally for Harding, had soured on him, then returned—but still delivered Pennsylvania's votes to Governor Sproul. Seriously ill at his Spruce Street, Philadelphia home, Penrose remained a man of such power (and the bête noir of so many liberals) that it seemed impossible that he *wouldn't* be the force behind a sudden mysterious lurch to a mediocre stand-patter like Harding. The legend grew that on Saturday, June 13, Penrose awoke from a coma, learned of the deadlock, and ordered his secretary: "Call up [John T.] King, and tell him to throw it to Harding."

In reality, Penrose had no influence over events. In fact, Daugherty, fearing a backlash, didn't want Penrose's open support. Pennsylvania cast exactly zero votes for Warren Harding on Saturday's ninth ballot.

The convention reconvened at 4:45—forty-five minutes late, as everyone furiously jostled for position. Meanwhile, a troupe of Harding supporters paraded about the hall, carrying banners reading THE REPUBLICANS NEED OHIO and HARDING MEANS OHIO. Their enthusiasm spread throughout the floor and into the galleries. Something was in the air.

But not everyone marched with enthusiasm or sincerity. William Allen White recalled:

In the end I toddled along, followed the Kansas banner in the parade, ashamed, disheveled in body and spirit, making a sad fat figure while the bands played, the trumpets brayed, and the crowd howled for Harding; and in that hour the Republican party bade farewell to the twenty years of liberalism which had grown up under the leadership of Theodore Roosevelt. As I marched, I saw Harding in Chicago back in 1916, in the measly opportunist convention where the whole desire of the party had been to head off Roosevelt. . . . And indeed, . . . my heart was bowed down with a weight of woe. I kept feeling that I should have looked better sulking in my seat, letting the hope of Hoover, with which I licked my spiritual wounds, go glimmering. I kept asking myself, "Is the long chance of Hoover worth this?" . . . A sad spectacle I made, and time has not softened the shabby outlines of the picture in all these long years.

It took fifty minutes for the demonstration to subside and the ninth ballot to begin. Connecticut gave 13 of 14 votes to Harding, but Kansas provided an even bigger breakthrough. When Kentucky, a Lowden stronghold, joined in, the rush was on. Lowden launched a bombshell, releasing his delegates "in favor of no candidate." Most gravitated easily to Harding. Louisiana, Missouri, New York, North Carolina, Jake Hamon's Oklahoma, South Carolina, Tennessee, Texas, and Virginia all swelled the Harding column. Warren Harding had seized 186 votes from Lowden and 50 from Wood and now possessed a virtually insurmountable lead:

Harding 374½
Wood 249
Lowden 121½
Johnson 82
Sproul 78
Coolidge 28

La Follette 24
Poindexter 14
Hoover 6
Butler 2
Lenroot 1
Knox 1
Absent 21$\frac{1}{2}$

As the Harding steamroller began moving, not everyone was pleased—particularly the female Wood supporters. Parmalee Herrick, wife of former Ohio governor Myron T. Herrick, bolted from her seat, fuming, "I cannot stay here and see him nominated." Corinne Roosevelt Robinson stalked out too, muttering some insult at Florence Harding. Ruth Hanna McCormick, wife of Illinois Senator Medill McCormick, shot a look at the Duchess, sitting nearby in the gallery. Someone offered Ruth a fan, but she turned it down. "It would do no good," she sputtered; "the heat is all inside me. Think of that woman going into the White House!"

Harry Daugherty joined the Duchess. While her husband moved toward the presidency, she sat nervously clutching two huge hat pins. "It's terrible, isn't it?" she asked Harry.

"What?"

"All this wild excitement. This yelling and bawling and cat-calling. I can't follow it—"

"I didn't think you would," Daugherty responded, "but something's going to happen down there in a few minutes that may shock you if you don't look out—"

"What do you mean?"

"I've come up here to ask you to keep cool."

"That's a good joke," Florence spat back. "I must say, it's a hundred and ten in this place and you advise me to keep cool!"

"You know what I mean. Something's going to happen on the next ballot and I want you to be prepared for it—"

"What?"

Daugherty leaned forward in conspiratorial fashion, whispering, "We have the votes. Your husband will be nominated on the next ballot—"

She jumped. Her two hatpins plunged deep into Harry Daugherty's side. Not daring to scream, he felt blood trickling down his body. "I had come to save a woman's life," he thought, "and she had unwittingly murdered me! . . . The thing must have pierced a lung!"

Acting as if nothing had happened, he cautioned the Duchess: "Remember now, no excitement. Keep your head and laugh at the antics below—"

"I will," Florence grimly vowed.

Like everyone else, the convention's fifty-five black delegates now viewed Harding as unstoppable. Ohio's Charles A. Cottrill led a delegation to Harding, sounding him out on issues affecting their people and returning satisfied. All fifty-five would now back Harding.

On the tenth ballot, the Harding boom picked up speed—and votes—with nearly every state polled. Louder and louder cheers greeted each tally. Bowing to the inevitable (and counting carefully), Governor Sproul released his votes, and Pennsylvania shoved Harding over the top. The final tally:

Harding 692$^{1}/_{5}$
Wood 156
Johnson 80$^{4}/_{5}$
La Follette 24
Lowden 11
Hoover 9$^{1}/_{2}$
Coolidge 5 (four from New York; only one from Massachusetts)
Butler 2
Lenroot 1
Knox 1
Hays 1
Absent, $^{1}/_{2}$

Nan saw it all, cheering with the rest, but, of course, with her own reasons. "My eyes swam," she would later write, "and I recalled my Freshman school year at Marion, when, in the margins of all my books, I, then but thirteen years old, had written the prophecy of my heart-longing, 'Warren Gamaliel Harding—he's a darling—Warren Gamaliel Harding—President of the United States!'"

H. L. Mencken wasn't pleased at all. "It was a poor show," he wrote. "Harding is of the intellectual grade of an aging cockroach."

Edna Ferber wasn't pleased either. She thought of Wood, Lowden, Hoover, Hiram Johnson, Nicholas Murray Butler—the lot of them—as honest, capable men. But not Harding. She had met him once, at a speaking engagement in Cleveland, and thought the man "a living cartoon of the American Fourth of July stuffed-shirt orator." Now she saw the stuffed shirt nominated for president.

She could not take it. "I knew that I was going to cry," she would write; "I tried hard not to. Perhaps I was weary, nervous, a little hysterical from the noise and the heat and the excitement. But I knew deep down that it was the horrible pain of disillusionment in my country and my people that was making me weep." Tears slipped down her cheeks, past her five-dollar pearls, and onto her blue dress.

Fellow United Press Association correspondent William Slavens McNutt sat next to her and put his big hand upon hers. "Don't bother," McNutt comforted her. "Doesn't matter . . . hundred years from now."

Now came a motion to make the nomination unanimous. Lowden delegate Harold Ickes argued loudly against the move. His Illinois delegation wouldn't listen to him, but the sullen Wisconsin delegation ("a recalcitrant little minority, holier-than-thou," thought Frank Sullivan) didn't need any encouragement. They wouldn't vote for Harding, wouldn't make it unanimous.

Harding and the Duchess sat backstage with Lowden and Nicholas Murray Butler. Michigan's Charles B. Warren bounded in, shouting: "Pennsylvania has voted for you, Harding, and you are nominated!" Harding stood up and took Lowden by one hand and Butler by the other. Choking with emotion, he told them: "If the great honor of the Presidency is to come to me, I shall need all the help that you two friends can give me."

Cabot Lodge was feeling a little guilty about his recent machinations—not regarding Harding or Coolidge, but about knifing old friend TR's anointed heir, Wood. "No matter what anybody tells you," he pled with Teddy's sister, Corinne, "don't believe that I did not stay faithful to you and Wood to the very end. I went down with the ship with my colors flying. Don't let anybody persuade you that I did not."

As they spoke, Warren Harding came near, creating quite a stir. He stopped to speak with her: "Mrs. Robinson, I heard that you made the best speech of the Convention! The only mistake was that it was not for me."

Mrs. Robinson promised Harding her support. When he had departed, Lodge begged again: "Good-bye, my dear; believe me always!"

Reporters surrounded the newly-minted nominee, demanding to know: "How do you feel, Senator?"

"Well, you know how a fellow feels that holds a pair of eights and has to stay in and draws full. You understand the language?"

"What are you going to do now?"

"Well, even a candidate must feed. Haven't had anything to eat since morning."

In Boston, Calvin Coolidge got a call about 7:30. Harding was in. Coolidge's puny little campaign had never really gotten off the ground. He took the news with little emotion (even by his standards)—after all, he was a realistic fellow—and went out for a walk across the Boston Common.

Leonard Wood took it like a soldier. "Of all the candidates," Mark Sullivan wrote, "Wood was the most gallant figure in defeat. He met defeat standing squarely in his solid military boots in the middle of the entrance to his headquarters, giving to every comer smiles of almost jovial composure in return for condolences. That is what duty and taste call for at such a time, and that is what Wood would always do."

Hiram Johnson took it less well; but then again, Hiram Johnson probably would have taken victory with ill grace. With his wife and son and secretary, he sat sulking in his Hotel Blackstone rooms. Popular poet James J. "Jimmy" Montague, a close Johnson friend, phoned Irvin Cobb and Ring Lardner: "Come along down to the Blackstone, we're going to sit shivah with the Johnsons. They need company."

The gloom was intense, and someone opened a bottle of scotch. The phone rang. Johnson's secretary answered. It was Teddy Roosevelt Jr. Johnson knew he was calling to persuade Johnson about the vice-presidency. Everyone in Johnson's suite knew that that would be the only reason Roosevelt would call.

"Tell him I'm not swapping idle conversation with anybody this evening," Johnson fumed. "Tell him I've gone to bed—tell him anything."

"Hiram," Johnson's wife urged, "for his father's sake if for no other reason, you must listen to him. And he's a fine boy and I'm fond of him. So are you."

"This is no time for sentiment," Johnson spat out. "I'm more in a mood for murdering a few people."

He took the call. "Hello, hello. . . . Johnson speaking. . . . No . . . no, not in a million years. . . . No, I tell you, no. . . . Oh, yes. . . . No, sirree. . . . For the last time, damn it to hell, NO!" Then, face reddened by rage more than Scotch, he hung up—hard.

Montague had a question. "Senator, there wasn't any doubt as to what you meant by all those 'noes,'" he asked, "But that solitary 'yes' in the middle of 'em—just here in the bosom of the family, would you mind telling us why you stuck in that lone 'yes'?"

"Oh, that?" Johnson responded, his mood finally lightening. "That was when the young man asked me if I was sure I heard what he was saying."

If Johnson seemed ill prepared for defeat, Harding seemed ill pre-pared for victory. Soon afterward, he received reporters. "Tall, hand-some, commanding of figure, he seemed the very model of a statesman," thought Edna Ferber, "—until you looked into his eyes. Lambent, deep-set, meaningless, there was nothing behind them. They were just eyes; features with which he saw objects and people. They were not windows of the soul[,] because the façade on which they were fastened was nothing but a false front. I never have seen a less happy man."

The Duchess, for all her previous doubts, all the prophecies of "tragedy," beamed—or, at least, beamed in a wizened-dowager sort of way. Adorned in her out-of-fashion, high-collared dress and surrounded by a coterie of starched-muslin Marion belles, Florence seemed less like a candidate's wife than a museum piece. "I discredited the whole scene," said Ferber, "as an optical illusion or an anachronism cleverly faked. But it wasn't."

Florence let joy envelop her. "Oh, girls," she exclaimed, "if only Pa was here! If only Pa could have lived to see this day!" It was a cry not just of delight, but of triumph and of the hurt she had known for decades. She turned to the press. "Pa didn't want me to marry Warren," the Duchess explained. "Pa was a banker, you know, and Warren just ran the paper in Marion. Well, I guess he knows now he was wrong, only I wish he could have lived to see it! . . . President! . . . Oh, girls, think!"

Meanwhile, Harry Daugherty staggered back to his room, dying (perhaps literally) to find out how much blood he had lost to the Duchess's hat pins. He felt the blood running down his leg, to his shoe, squishing about inside. He removed his shoe. The "blood" was mere perspiration, the product of intense heat and more-intense nervous exhaustion.

Now came time to choose a vice president.

Discussion centered on Henry Allen, but Allen had recently enacted legislation calling for mandatory arbitration in labor disputes. The unions hated him, and, even in 1920, the Republican Party feared alienating organized labor. Senator Watson told Allen he was out.

Only then did Watson ask Harding whom he wanted. Harding just shrugged and said: "Search me!"

Actually, Harding did have a plan. But it hadn't worked. Theodore Roosevelt Jr. wasn't the only one approaching Hiram Johnson. Following his nomination, Harding had conferred with William Randolph Hearst (attending the convention with his ace editorialist, Arthur Brisbane). Harding asked Hearst, one newspaper publisher to another, to again speak with Johnson regarding a Harding–Johnson ticket. Hearst did. Johnson again refused.

The party hierarchy turned to Irvine L. Lenroot. Lenroot was progressive but not radical. Once closely allied with Bob La Follette, Lenroot broke with his fellow Wisconsin senator when he voted for war, and Fighting Bob turned on Lenroot with an intense hatred. Lenroot now battled for renomination to the Senate against a La Follette-backed challenger. Despite this, when no other names materialized for the vice-presidency, Lenroot's anointing seemed foreordained.

"We're going to put Lenroot on with Harding," Senator McCormick shouted to Henry L. Stoddard. A reporter overhead McCormick and shouted back: "The hell you are!"

Henry Cabot Lodge recognized McCormick for the purpose of placing Lenroot in nomination. A quartet of respected names, all designed to give the stamp of approval to the move—Tobe Hert, New York's Senator Calder, Arkansas state chairman Harmon L. Remmel, and former Ohio governor Herrick—seconded the motion. The situation seemed so well in hand that Lodge, his voice worn to a frazzle, left the platform, surrendering his gavel to Frank Willis.

All was not in hand. The delegates were restive. One interrupted a Lenroot seconding speech with the cry "Not on your life."

As Oregon delegate Wallace McCamant had entered the hall, Coolidge campaign manager James Reynolds approached him: "Now, remember."

Judge McCamant did. Climbing a chair and furiously waving his hands, he secured Willis's attention. Willis, thinking that McCamant also wanted to second Lenroot, recognized him. McCamant had another agenda:

> When the Oregon delegation came here instructed by the people of our State to present to this Convention as its candidate for the office of Vice President a distinguished son of Massachusetts [Lodge], he requested that we refrain from mentioning his name. But there is another son of Massachusetts who has been much in the public eye during the past year, a man who is sterling in his Americanism and stands for all that the Republican Party holds dear; and on behalf of the Oregon delegation I name for the exalted office of Vice President Governor Calvin Coolidge, of Massachusetts.

McCamant's unexpected words triggered an uproar. Delegations cheered and applauded with a genuine enthusiasm that the convention had not yet witnessed—in fact, that *no* GOP convention had *ever* witnessed. "I have been present at every Republican convention beginning with 1856," Chauncey M. Depew (who had been born in 1834) later telegraphed Coolidge, "and I have never seen such a spontaneous and enthusiastic tribute."

"Coolidge is going to be nominated," Joe Martin predicted to a woman seated next to him, "The cheering for the other fellows was in the galleries. It's the delegates who are cheering now." Delegates stood on their seats to gain the chair's attention, wildly vying to second Silent Cal, with delegates from North Dakota and Michigan finally winning the honors. Arkansas's Harmon Remmel abruptly switched to

Coolidge. The crowd enthusiastically cheered his treason. A handful of other names drew votes: Hiram Johnson, Governor Allen, Colonel Henry W. Anderson of Richmond. Coolidge swamped them all. The count went:

Coolidge 674½
Lenroot 146½
Allen 68½
Anderson 28
Johnson 22½

The "bossed" convention had proven supremely un-bossed. It had stampeded, done its own will, shaped the ticket to its own image. Now came a motion to make the vote unanimous. Not even Wisconsin voted no. *Everyone* was for Silent Cal.

In the press gallery, William Slavens McNutt slammed his fist on the writing counter, startling not just Edna Ferber but everyone nearby. "There goes Harding!" he yelled.

"What do you mean?" Ferber asked archly.

"Harding'll never serve his term out," McNutt explained, "He'll die and Coolidge will be President."

"Don't be silly. What makes you say a thing like that?"

"Wait," McNutt concluded, "you'll see. Coolidge luck. He's shot with it."

Frank Stearns and another Coolidge partisan, forty-four-year-old Louis K. Liggett, founder of the Rexall Drug Store chain, had dispiritedly departed before any of this had transpired. Liggett had returned to his Hotel Blackstone room, when another delegate fairly burst in. "Isn't it great?" the gentleman shouted.

"Great what?" Liggett warily responded.

"The nomination of Coolidge!"

"Nominated for what?"

"Vice President!"

"Great!" Liggett exploded. "I've just sent him a telegram expressing my regrets."

On the fourth floor of Boston's Adams House, Calvin Coolidge picked up the ringing phone. It was Vermont Governor Percival W. Clement, calling from Chicago. Finally, Coolidge said to Grace: "Nominated for Vice President!"

Thinking he was joking, she matter-of-factly replied: "You don't mean it!"

"Indeed I do."

"You are not going to accept it, are you?" she demanded.

"I suppose I shall have to," he replied, even grimmer than usual.

Grimmer still was Florence Harding. The thrill had quickly passed. Her usual forebodings returned. "Warren," she confided, almost choking with emotion, "will be a great President. But I see only tragedy ahead."

## Chapter 15

⁓

# "THE GREATEST LIVING CHAMPION OF WATER"

Now, it was the Democrats' turn.

The Democratic national convention opened on Monday, June 28 at San Francisco's 144,000-square foot Civic Auditorium, the first national convention to be held on the West Coast. William Allen White's syndicate sent him to cover the event. Recuperating from his disappointment in Chicago, he proclaimed the San Francisco affair to be just about the best—or, at least, the most pleasant—convention he had yet attended:

> Of course, the weather was irreproachable. The San Francisco restaurants are the best on the continent. The San Francisco people are most hospitable. They chinked in the spare time of the newspaper correspondents and the visiting delegates and statesmen with parties and excursions all over the Bay region. . . . Among the other newspaper reporters . . . was Edna Ferber, who was always a delight. Together we went to the long string of parties that the townspeople were giving to their visitors. And we knocked around town together. I remember one afternoon . . . , walking two or three miles from the hall to the hotel, down the broad gay streets, each of us holding a sack of ripe juicy cherries, eating the fruit and snapping the seeds into the air while we discoursed of the many strange things in the heart of nature and of man. . . . The convention also was a delight.

Yes, particularly if you were a Republican.

Or, if you were H. L. Mencken. Mencken, so revolted by Chicago's Coliseum, lavished praise upon the Civic Auditorium, pronouncing it "so spacious, so clean, so luxurious in its comforts and so beautiful in its decorations, that the assembled politicos felt like sailors turned loose in the most gorgeous bordellos of Paris."

Mencken savored virtually all that he surveyed. To hear the invariably cynical Sage of Baltimore describe it, the convention was a virtual idyll. "Women dressed in white," he noted, "moved prettily through the delegates, armed only with little white wands, and every wand was tied with a blue ribbon, signifying law and order. When one of these babies glided into a jam of delegates with her wand upraised[,] they melted as if she had been a man-eating tiger, but with this difference: that instead of making off with screams of terror[,] they yielded as if to soft music, their eyes rolling ecstatically and their hearts going pitterpat."

Edna Ferber saw something else. "It was, in its way, almost as saddening a sight as the Republican Convention had been," she recalled. "Usually, once the opening prayer had piously died on the air, there broke out from two to a half-dozen actual fist fights on the floor of the assemblage—battles that raged up and down the aisles until guards separated the contestants. The meeting droned on. Nothing seemed to be accomplished."

Now that the bloom had faded on the Hoover candidacy, Franklin Roosevelt was there—as a McAdoo delegate. Claiming that he couldn't secure a hotel room, FDR cajoled the commander of the Pacific Fleet, Admiral Hugh Rodman, into boarding him on the battleship *New Mexico*. When Josephus Daniels requested the same accommodations, Rodman cabled that he had just given FDR the last suite. Daniels ordered Roosevelt out. Moving to the *New York*, Franklin employed that battleship to host an alcohol-enhanced, Prohibition-violating reception for the rest of the New York delegation. There, FDR met Al Smith's family and charmed Smith's daughter Emily. "I was impressed only as any young girl would have been," she recalled, "at meeting an Assistant Secretary of the Navy, and one so handsome, so debonair, and with a family name so distinguished." Smith requested FDR to second his nomination. FDR, his newfound loyalty to McAdoo overwhelmed by the lure of the spotlight, agreed.

Mencken, meanwhile, continued to enjoy the city. Admirers honored him with a party at the St. Francis Hotel, at which he drank so much wine it "damn near killed me." Keeping him from flaming out entirely was an agreeable local stock company actress named Jane O'Rourke. "I think," he confided to friends, "I am in love."

The booze flowed freely for everyone. San Francisco was a wide-open town, and longtime mayor James Rolph Jr., making sure the delegates felt welcome, dispatched pretty girls to welcome each one on arrival with a hearty hello—and a bottle of illegal hootch.

Only a few contenders and possible contenders were in town—Smith and Palmer and Bryan among them. McAdoo, New Jersey's drippingly wet Governor Edward I. Edwards, Governor Cox ("a candidate for the presidency had no business participating in the rush and turbulence of the convention"), and, of course, Wilson were absent. Cox, nonetheless, had been kind enough to dispatch the Piqua, Ohio, Silver Cornet Band to serenade delegates with such ditties as

> Ohio, Ohio, the hills gave back reply
> We're here to do or die
> Ohio, Ohio, we'll elect Jim Cox
> Or know the reason why.

Cox received a jolt the day before the convention opened, Sunday, June 27, when the *San Francisco Chronicle* reported on activities at Cox headquarters. Cox supporters Senator Atlee Pomerene and seventy-seven-year-old former Ohio governor James E. Campbell were being driven to distraction answering awkward questions regarding their candidate's 1911 divorce. Had Cox been charged with cruelty? Yes. Had he been charged with infidelity? No. Had Mrs. Cox then married her attorney? Yes. The story went nationwide. "We can weather it," explained Cox campaign staffer Judge Timothy Ansberry, "because the publication was not unexpected," but headlines such as

### Divorce Issue Eliminates Cox, Leaders Admit; Discussion Already Shows Nomination Would Be Inadvisable

ran nationwide, and clearly stung.

The Convention opened on June 28 with proper ceremonies—but ill omens. "A huge American flag fluttered from the ceiling," noted Heywood Broun. "The flag was cheered. By and by the flag was raised and there nestling behind it was a large picture of President Wilson. It was not a very good picture, rather red faced and staring and frightened, but it served as a symbol of the man in the White House, and the cheering burst out, or if it didn't burst at any rate, it began."

Broun found the resulting twenty-one-minute pro-Wilson ovation ("of several hundred postmasters, United States marshals, officeholders, and aspirants for political honors at the hands of the people," as the *New York Tribune* noted) to be "the least animated by sincerity" he had yet witnessed at any convention.

New York's delegation abstained from this listless tribute. "The demonstration for President Wilson," said state chairman William Farley, "looked to some of us like a waste of time. . . ."

Their inaction outraged FDR. "Somebody must make a move," he told Al Smith, "or the country will think that New York is the only state to refuse to pay decent respect to the chief executive." Along with Schenectady Mayor George R. Lunn (a former Dutch Reformed minister originally elected as a Socialist), he wrestled the state standard away from delegate Judge Jeremiah T. Mahoney. A dozen Tammanyites tried grabbing it back, until a police officer intervened. Only four other New York delegates joined Roosevelt and Lunn in marching it around the hall. The crowd cheered their efforts. Smith and Tammany Boss Murphy sat on their hands.

National chairman Homer Cummings ("tall, rotund, but not grossly rotund," noted the *Chicago Tribune*, "bald, but not grotesquely bald, sleekly black coated, but not oppressively sartorial") delivered the keynote address, eulogizing Wilson and likening his sufferings to the Crucifixion. Delegates gasped, then applauded. Some thought the address thrust Cummings into contender status.

"It did not seem a great speech to us," Heywood Broun dissented, "although there were elements of excellence in the first hour and a half."

As the convention opened, Wall Street betting was light, favoring Cox at 2–1, with McAdoo and Ambassador to the Court of St. James and former Solicitor General John W. Davis at 2½–1; Edwards at 3–1; Smith and Clark 3½–1; and Palmer, dead last, at 4–1.

Few still took A. Mitchell Palmer seriously. Broun sauntered into Palmer headquarters and departed, mocking Palmer's claims of red-blooded Americanism:

> We assumed, of course, from the tone of Mr. Palmer's manifesto that his opponents for the nomination were Rumanians, Greeks and Icelanders, and weak-kneed ones at that. He also seemed fair to believe they were men who denied the duty of taking an active part in public affairs. Such being the case, it seemed hardly worthwhile to visit the headquarters of such impossible candidates. We happened into Cox's headquarters wholly by accident and were astounded to discover that he, too, is an American and, more than that, "was born an American on a farm of poor but honest parents." Thus encouraged[,] we went to all camps and found that the candidates are all Americans.

While Palmer propagandized and Broun jibed, the convention organized itself. At 1 A.M., Tuesday, June 29, FDR, Mayor Lunn, and reform judge Samuel Seabury lobbed a grenade into the process, proposing to end the unit rule, which binds all the members of a state delegation to cast their ballots as a unit, and hopefully gain McAdoo votes in New York. The next morning, the Rules Committee (despite Al Smith's opposition) voted 24–11 in favor of Roosevelt and his allies, a decision later ratified by the convention as a whole.

At noon, William Jennings Bryan addressed the local Commercial Club, speaking for an hour. Much to his audience's amazement, he downed three full carafes of water. "I am the greatest living champion of water in the world," the arch-prohibitionist explained, "and I have a right to drink all I want."

On Wednesday, June 30, betting money suddenly rushed to Woodrow Wilson, making him the 9–5 favorite, with McAdoo second. National chairman Cummings thought the idea of Wilson's nomination "impossible and unthinkable," but that same day he cabled Wilson that the convention was in a confused state. Reporting that no mention had yet been made of placing the president's name in nomination, he hedged his words to play into the invalid president's third-term ambitions. "Situation as to candidates confused," wired Cummings, "Palmer . . . cannot be nominated. Cox campaign has been badly managed. . . . Chances of McAdoo appear best. . . . Everything thus far has moved off beautifully. . . . It is a Wilson convention in spirit and purpose."

On June 30, Democrats took eight hours to nominate ten largely unknown and uninspiring candidates: Oklahoma Senator Robert L. Owen, former Ambassador to Berlin James W. Gerard of New York; national chairman Cummings; Nebraska Senator Hitchcock; Palmer; Secretary of Agriculture Edwin T. Meredith of Iowa; Cox; Al Smith; McAdoo; and New Jersey Governor Edwards.

The three front-runners were nominated first. Palmer's ovation lasted thirty-six minutes. Cox's elicited a "half-hearted" thirty-two-minute cheer. McAdoo's forty-minute demonstration was the only one of the three generating real enthusiasm.

The great Irish-born Tammany orator Bourke Cockran nominated Al Smith. "We offer [Smith] to you as President of the United States," boomed Cockran. "We will accept no compromise in the convention. If you take him we will give you the state of New York, and if you reject him we will take him back and run him again for Governor."

Smith's time had not yet come. It was, nonetheless, a remarkable moment. Other candidates might rise from humble beginnings—rough farmsteads and primitive log cabins—but they had sprung from humble Protestant, Anglo-Saxon beginnings. Smith had emerged from the sidewalks and tenements of New York's Lower East Side, from mixed Irish–Italian–German heritage, and, above all, a *Catholic* heritage. It had been remarkable enough that Wilson had a Catholic adviser in Joseph Tumulty; that caused enough controversy. But to have a Papist even mentioned for the White House was a startling breakthrough for America's immigrant classes.

But not startling enough for Smith—or any Catholic—to win. Mark Sullivan wrote bluntly:

> The present Democratic Governor of New York is a Catholic and
> there is not a politician here or anywhere but readily realizes the

position of the popular and successful Governor of New York would make that Governor not only an available but extremely desirable candidate for the presidency. The fact that Governor Smith is barely mentioned is due chiefly to the fact that he is a Catholic. That this constitutes a handicap is so widely known that it is taken for granted. All know that the people ought not to have that kind of prejudice but we all know that some people do have it.

Mark Sullivan may have been a Republican, but Mark Sullivan was also a Catholic.

Beyond that, Smith was Wet (in the year Prohibition took effect, this proved detrimental even among Democrats), lacked formal education (quitting school at fourteen), was barely presentable above Fourteenth Street in terms of wardrobe (he looked, thought William Allen White from sophisticated Emporia, Kansas, like an "exalted bouncer of a boxing pavilion"), and almost uncouth in manner, diction, and speech.

Smith, though, was smart and honest and a marvelously efficient governor of the nation's most populous state. Democrats unabashedly loved him. Republicans grudgingly—and sometimes not so grudgingly— respected him.

"Al Smith is in no way different from the rest of us," praised Cockran, "and that is why we love him." FDR bounded over rows of folding chairs to second the nomination. Smith's fish-peddler background might, indeed, be *somewhat* different from FDR's, but he nonetheless displayed proper Rooseveltian enthusiasm. "I love him as a friend," orated FDR; "I look up to him as a man; I am with him as a Democrat."

FDR also delivered a negative message. "The nominee of this convention," he jibed, "will not be selected at 2 A.M. in a hotel room." Franklin had helped sell Al Smith, but more importantly he had helped sell himself. He had, noted Frances Perkins, emerged as "one of the stars of the show."

Of course, not everyone agreed. H. L. Mencken finally awoke from his San Francisco (and Jane O'Rourke)-induced bliss to rumble back into his usual cynical mode and to realize he *hated* FDR's address—"a line of puerile and ineffectual bosh about the navy. As the delegates listened[,] all of their enthusiasm oozed out of them." Smith might well have been nominated, Mencken mused, if Franklin "had not been such an ass." His opinion seemed to be, well, contrarian.

The band struck up "Oh, You Beautiful Doll" when Lillian R. Sire, founder of the Women's National Democratic Club, delivered Smith's other seconding address. Even more raucous cheering followed. The New York delegation band generated moderate enthusiasm, blaring out "Tammany" and "The Bowery," but when it played "The Sidewalks of New York," the place erupted. The song, observed the *Times*, triggered "a demonstration that will stand out in the history of such events." Or, as the *Chicago Tribune* noted, in a world of painfully faked convention enthusiasm, this demonstration "was the real thing."

Mencken stood on a chair, keeping time. "By the end of the first half hour," he noted, "the only persons who were not dancing were a few anti-social Hardshell Baptists from Mississippi and a one-legged war veteran from Ohio."

The remaining speeches elicited scant interest, save for Illinois Congressman Henry T. Rainey's comments regarding A. Mitchell Palmer. "Our candidate's private life is pure and clean," Rainey intoned. "Our candidate in this particular cannot be assailed from any direction." Delegates whispered: Which candidates *weren't* pure and clean?

Ten candidates should have proven sufficient. They weren't. The next day, Thursday, July 1, the convention suffered through four more: arch-segregationist North Carolina Senator Furnifold M. Simmons, Virginia Senator Carter Glass (who for some reason generated excited cheering from a handkerchief-waving "negro woman in the gallery"), John W. Davis (seconded by stage actress Izetta Jewel Brown—and, yes, once again the band blared "Oh, You Beautiful Doll"), and Governor General of the Philippines Francis B. Harrison.

Attending the convention were an array of state and city bosses, the most powerful being Tammany's Charles Francis Murphy, Chicago's George E. Brennan, and former Indiana United States Senator Thomas Taggart. Murphy we have already met. He had been indicted, barely a month previously, on charges of attempting to defraud the federal government. Brennan had lost a leg as a boy in a mining accident. He took up teaching, and then received a position as a state government clerk.

Moving to Chicago in 1897, with relatively little effort he took over the Cook County Democratic Party.

The glad-handing Taggart came to America from Ireland as a small child. He worked at a rail-station lunch counter, then bought a small hotel before gaining entry to Indianapolis politics. In 1886, after all other Democrats declined the nomination, Taggart won the position of county auditor—and the $50,000 in fees it annually provided. Three times he became Indianapolis mayor. In 1912, Taggart proved crucial in securing Woodrow Wilson's presidential nomination. In 1915, then the owner of French Lick, Indiana's nationally famous gambling resort, Taggart was indicted for election fraud. After he beat the charges, Governor Samuel M. Ralston appointed him to the United States Senate.

These three bosses shared a common antipathy to reform, to Prohibition, and to William Gibbs McAdoo—though, on any given day, not in that particular order.

Thursday, July 1 opened with Wall Street odds-makers tabbing McAdoo, Wilson, and, surprisingly, Smith (bettors may have been more sentimental than they let on) as 9–5 favorites, with Marshall and Davis at 2–1, and Cox, Palmer, and Edwards at 3–1.

Far more favorable odds were available for any Democrat advancing to the White House. That same day, a group of Democrats assembled at the Palace Hotel, Governor Cox's headquarters. "And now I ask you," a pro-Cox orator thundered, "who will be the next President of the United States?"

The crowd contained a large man who might have been a Republican—or perhaps just a realistic Democrat. In any case, he was very drunk—or, as the *New York Times* put it, he had "found a means of violating the Volstead Law and had violated it violently."

"Warren G. Harding!" he roared back, and a near riot ensued.

William Jennings Bryan was not drinking. The Anti-Saloon League's Wayne Wheeler had found Bryan in the back of the auditorium, lying on an improvised cot fashioned from a discarded door wobbling atop two primitive supports. Bryan informed Wheeler that he planned to fight for a solid prohibition plank in the platform. Wheeler knew Bryan would lose, but didn't feel like disagreeing with Bryan, who was clearly ill, unhealthy, and worn-out.

Bryan not only addressed the convention—he made it cheer. He demanded a strong Dry plank ("If you can't get enough alcohol to make you drunk, why do you want alcohol at all?"). He advocated Constitutional amendments allowing for a simple-majority Senate ratification of treaties and against universal peacetime military training. His white-hot hatred of Woodrow Wilson gave him strength. "When the United States aided in attacking the arbitrary idea of government in Germany," he thundered, "it was with the hope of banishing it from the world, not for the purpose of transplanting it on American soil."

He grew stronger and stronger: "I believe in God. Some day I shall stand before His Judgment bar, and when I appear there, there shall not be upon my head the blood of people slaughtered while I talked politics." Delegates cheered the Great Commoner for twenty-three straight minutes. Tears streamed down his cheeks. Perhaps he might be nominated yet again. Reality soon set in. Administration forces, led by Secretary of State Colby and Senator Carter Glass, outmaneuvered and outreasoned the Great Commoner. His motions expired in flames. Regarding Bryan's Dry plank, Bourke Cockran jibed that Bryan "presents his case so clearly, that no doubter can fail to see its demerits." It failed, 929$\frac{1}{2}$ to 185$\frac{1}{2}$.

On Friday, July 2, delegates were mystified by the presence of an expensive casket on the third floor of the Auditorium. It was, noted one newspaperman, "large enough to have held any deserving Democrat."

Tammany's skeptical and disaffected delegates merely walked by, shook their heads and muttered: "Told you so."

On Friday, Democrats finally adopted their platform, eight thousand words and thirty-eight planks that, in the end, wasn't any clearer than the much-derided Republican effort. Regarding the hallowed League of Nations, Democrats issued no clarion call, only tortured prose and watery positions: "We do not oppose the acceptance of any reservations, making clearer or more specific the obligations of the United States to the League associates."

The *New York Tribune* found the document to be "colorless and unexplicit." Heywood Broun agreed:

In the platform contest it seems to us that the decision should go to the Republicans. They were able at Chicago to say nothing in just about one-tenth the number of words which the Democrats needed to say the same thing. [Vice President] Marshall announced a few days ago that the platform of a political party ought to be written on a postal card. So it should, and then the card might be dropped into the oblivion of [Postmaster General] Burleson's mail boxes.

Most platforms are forgotten before the last train leaves town from the station. Parties have to live with candidates, and Democrats had yet to ballot for anyone, yet alone nominate anyone—which meant that the real game was just beginning. Some of the jostling occurred a continent away, as witnessed by this letter from the Friday, July 2, *New York Times*:

### Franklin Roosevelt.
#### *To the Editor of the New York Times:*
Your editorial article of June 13, as well as subsequent ones on the same subject, have been too good to need a word in comment.

In the present discussion of the pending convention at San Francisco and the possible candidates, why is it that no one has ever suggested Franklin Roosevelt, a man of certainly as notable achievement as most of those under discussion and of fine personality.

R.H.B.

Cleveland, June 23, 1920.

In San Francisco, FDR appeared closer to another nomination. As the convention began, the *New York Tribune* reported that Tammany favored FDR over the even more obstreperous Lunn for the Empire State's senatorial nomination. The *Times* concurred, observing: "There is some talk even among the Tammany leaders of nominating Mr. Roosevelt for Senator. The latter has fought Tammany here, but his tactics have caused no bitterness. There is a belief in Tammany circles that Roosevelt might make a strong stand and help the Democratic ticket in New York State. There are twelve judgeships at stake this Fall in New York County [Manhattan], and if it should seem likely that the nomination of Mr. Roosevelt would save them, it might be made."

On Friday, July 2, some sources quoted even money on both Wilson and McAdoo. But Washington newsmen were betting differently: McAdoo 1.9–1, Davis 4.7–1, Marshall 9–1, Colby 10–1, Wilson 17.3–1, Cox and Homer Cummings 26.5–1, Champ Clark 36.5–1, Carter Glass 55–1. No one appeared interested in taking Palmer.

That evening, Secretary of State Colby plotted a Wilson nomination. Originally a Republican, Colby was a successful New York attorney who had once represented Mark Twain. Following TR into the Progressive Party, he had run as a Progressive for the United States Senate in 1914, placed TR in nomination at 1916's abortive Progressive convention, then quickly shifted to Wilson and, by dint of shameless flattery, worked his way into the administration.

Colby's crack-brained idea horrified Joe Tumulty. He begged Edith Wilson to restrain Colby until an actual deadlock developed. Colby, sensing that one had already taken shape, telegraphed Wilson (now weakened even further by asthma): "The outstanding characteristic of the convention is the unanimity and fervor of feeling for you. Convention seizes every opportunity for demonstration which is most impressive . . . I propose, unless otherwise definitely instructed, to take advantage of first moment to move suspension of rules and place your name in nomination."

Tumulty, not realizing the message's contents, blindly passed it on to Wilson. Only later did Tumulty receive a call from a California friend, warning how far Colby had gone—and planned to go. "As his devoted friend," Tumulty begged Edith, "I am still of the same view, for I firmly believe it would mar his place in history."

Meanwhile, Postmaster General Burleson had wired Wilson, pleading with Wilson to finally endorse McAdoo. An enraged Wilson nearly fired him and ordered Cummings to blackball Burleson from any important workings of the convention.

In San Francisco, word spread of Colby's machinations. Cummings summoned him to meet with Burleson, Daniels, Senators Joseph T. Robinson and Carter Glass, Tennessee Congressman Cordell Hull, War Trade Board chairman Vance McCormick, and Secretary of War Baker. All agreed that Colby was mad. "You had no right," Daniels snapped, "to send such a message."

"I never saw more indignation and resentment in any small gathering," recalled Daniels. "I felt," Colby later admitted, "like a criminal."

Colby now backtracked, wiring Wilson excuses for inaction. "When he was told of it [Colby's failure]," Secret Service man Edmund Starling remembered, "the president unleashed a tornado of masterful profanity."

The convention began balloting on late Friday night, July 2. With 729½ votes needed to nominate, nobody came close. By comparison, the recent Republican effort seemed marvelously structured. It was the sort of scenario in which anyone—a lackluster governor from Ohio or a hopelessly incapacitated president—might emerge a victor. The first ballot went:

William Gibbs McAdoo 266
Attorney General A. Mitchell Palmer 256
Governor James M. Cox 134
Governor Alfred E. Smith 109
Governor Edward I. Edwards 42
Vice President Thomas R. Marshall 37
Senator Robert L. Owen 33
Ambassador John W. Davis 32
Secretary of Agriculture Edwin T. Meredith 27
Senator Carter Glass 26½
National Chairman Homer S. Cummings 25
Senator Furnifold M. Simmons 24
Ambassador James W. Gerard 21
Senator John Sharp Williams 20
Senator Gilbert Hitchcock 18
House Minority Leader Champ Clark 9
Governor General Francis B. Harrison 6
President of Boston's Metropolitan
    Trust Company Chandler M. Wood 4
William Jennings Bryan 1
William Randolph Hearst 1
Bainbridge Colby 1
Josephus Daniels 1
Senator Oscar W. Underwood ½

Things got a little more serious on the second ballot, with five "candidates" dropping from view: Williams (his votes going to Cox), Wood,

Hearst, Colby, and Underwood. McAdoo, Palmer, and Cox edged up very slightly. Smith slipped from 109 to 101 votes, a sign that his candidacy remained dangerously mired in favorite-son territory. Even Governor General Harrison and Senator Furnifold Simmons had managed to increase their second-ballot support.

After six ballots, Smith's candidacy disintegrated. "The independents in the delegation have stood loyally by Governor Smith," George Lunn informed Tammany's Charles F. Murphy. "It looks now as if he cannot win. We are going to swing a bunch of votes to McAdoo." The news didn't faze Murphy. He was ready to swing a bigger bunch of votes to Cox.

On the seventh ballot, Cox took second place, trailing McAdoo 384–295$\frac{1}{2}$. Palmer clung to 267$\frac{1}{2}$ delegates. Smith collapsed from 98 votes to 4. New Jersey Governor Edwards plummeted from 30 votes to 2.

Home on Long Island, McAdoo attended the nearby Rosemary Open Air Theater, enjoying scenes from *Twelfth Night, Julius Caesar*, and *As You Like It*. Returning to his Huntington estate, he learned that the convention had adjourned until midnight—and went to bed.

The twelfth ballot, on Saturday, July 3, finally witnessed actual movement, with Cox overtaking McAdoo, 404 to 375$\frac{1}{2}$, and Palmer sinking to 201.

Anti-McAdoo feeling was rising. Cox's people distributed little cards spelling their rival's name "McAdieu." McAdoo delegates casting their votes were greeted by loud jeers of "Every Vote is On the Payroll," sung to the tune of "The Battle Hymn of the Republic." If you didn't like McAdoo, you *really* didn't like McAdoo.

Roosevelt was poised to jump ship: "If the three leaders are blocked," he queried his fellow New Yorkers, "why not Davis? Within an hour we ought to know definitely whether the three leaders are blocked."

On the twenty-second ballot (Cox 430, McAdoo 372$\frac{1}{2}$, Palmer 166$\frac{1}{2}$, Davis 52), Wilson received his first and only votes of the convention, two unsolicited votes from Missouri. The exhausted convention adjourned at 10:43, Saturday night, not resuming until 10 A.M., Monday, July 5. Franklin Roosevelt was now being discussed among the New York delegation as vice-presidential timber.

On Sunday, delegates frolicked, savoring San Francisco's sights and sounds and sampling the plentiful local illegal beverages. They also

255

reflected on what had, or had not, thus far transpired. The longer a front-runner delays closing the deal, the smaller his chances become. As Wilson's 1912 campaign manager, William F. McCombs (now openly defiant of Wilson), artfully put it, "McAdoo is dead as a pickerel."

Exactly. That same day, McAdoo's people desperately approached the Murphy–Brennan–Taggart triumvirate for support. The bosses countered that McAdoo should consider a Cox–McAdoo ticket—if he didn't, they'd offer the vice-presidential slot to Franklin Roosevelt. FDR, back supporting McAdoo, claimed little interest in the proposition. If delegates had had their preference, they might have chosen Smith for vice president, but Smith had no interest. What Smith and FDR had in common—besides a professed lack of interest in the vice-presidency— was an interest in the governorship. Smith wanted to keep it. Roosevelt wanted to take it—and if FDR couldn't get the governorship, the Senate might prove a decent consolation prize.

Another significant discussion involved Governor Cox. That Sunday, William Randolph Hearst invited former Ohio congressman George White, a key Cox supporter, to his nearby ranch at Pleasanton in the East Bay and offered to support Cox in exchange for Hearst's appointment as Secretary of the Navy. White never got back to him.

Work resumed at 10:12 A.M., Monday, July 5, with the recitation of the Lord's Prayer and the singing of the Star-Spangled Banner. Delegates should have sung less and prayed more. Fourteen ballots followed in a day best described as pointless, listless trench warfare. Irvin Cobb got 1½ votes on the twenty-third ballot. Missouri cast a half vote for humorist Ring Lardner.

Nothing noteworthy transpired until the thirtieth ballot. Then McAdoo regained the lead, 403½ to Cox's 400½, with Palmer at 165. By now everyone verged on insanity. The next ballot, another pointless affair, saw a mischievous and bored Franklin Roosevelt casting his ballot not for McAdoo or Davis, but for his boss, Josephus Daniels.

Cox was slipping. With 376½ votes on the thirty-fifth ballot, he'd declined on every ballot since the twenty-seventh. Having dropped sharply from his peak of 468½ on the fifteenth ballot, he hovered dangerously close to free-fall.

He stabilized on the thirty-sixth ballot, but now some Davis support had switched to the sagging Palmer, giving him 222 votes—his highest total since the eleventh ballot. The specter of Palmer awakened the dozing McAdoo and Cox forces, and they forced through a 3½-hour recess. Party leaders warned Palmer to quit. Otherwise, his support would melt away, and he would be humiliated. The Fighting Quaker kept fighting.

Voting resumed after dinner. On the thirty-seventh ballot, all seemed normal, with McAdoo 405–386 over Cox, Palmer still reasonably strong at 202½, and Davis regaining ground to post 50½ votes. On the thirty-ninth ballot, Palmer collapsed to 74 votes, with most of his support galloping toward Cox, who now led McAdoo 468½–440. Cox (490) and McAdoo (467) moved up together on the fortieth ballot, as Palmer (19) deflated to virtual invisibility. Cox, however, remained woefully short of the necessary 729½ votes, and the threat of endless balloting and a true dark-horse nominee haunted the convention.

So it went on the forty-first ballot: McAdoo 460, Cox 497½, Palmer 12. But the forty-second recorded a milestone. For the first time, someone garnered a majority: Cox 540½, McAdoo 427, Davis 49½, Glass 24, and Palmer 8. Schenectady's George Lunn demanded that the New York delegation be polled. Though several members had departed for the evening, by gentleman's agreement their votes were still being counted for Cox. "You withdraw that motion now," burly New York delegate Thomas D. McCarthy calmly threatened Lunn. "If you don't, when you wake up in a hospital you will hear that Cox has been nominated." Lunn did (withdraw, not wake up in the hospital), but then moved to adjourn. The convention ignored him and kept voting.

The forty-third ballot saw Cox's lead widen to 567–412, with Davis and Palmer switching positions. Davis fell to 7 votes; Palmer rose to 57½.

The forty-fourth ballot concluded with Cox at 699½ votes—just 26½ votes from victory. McAdoo's floor leaders knew the game was up and moved to make their rival's nomination unanimous. At 1:43 A.M., Tuesday, July 6, the convention—by weary acclamation—nominated James Middleton Cox.

"My heart is in the grave with our cause," wailed William Jennings Bryan, "and I must pause until it comes back to me."

Cox, at his *Dayton News* office, received the news via Associated Press telegraph wire at 4:50 A.M. Eastern time. He sat stunned, still for nearly a minute, then arose to kiss his wife. In the *News*'s plant, he shook hands with printers, then walked a few blocks to the home of his closest friend, the godfather of one of his children, eighty-seven-year-old former congressman John A. McMahon, son-in-law of notorious Civil War Copperhead congressman Clement L. Vallandigham. Finally home, Cox breakfasted and took questions over the phone from his convention manager Edmond H. Moore about a possible running mate.

Unlike Harding, Cox displayed active interest in the topic. "Naturally, I've been thinking about this a good deal," Cox replied, "and my choice is young Roosevelt. His name is good, he's right geographically, and he's anti-Tammany. But since we need a united front, go see Charlie Murphy and say we won't nominate Roosevelt if he objects."

"Do you know him?" Moore asked. Cox didn't.

There was logic to Cox's choice. First, Franklin was a Roosevelt. No harm in that. The ticket needed whatever help it could get. Second, FDR hailed from a big, battleground state. New York's 45 electoral votes had gone Republican in 1916. They had to be won back. Cox was an administration outsider. FDR was an administration insider, who had—mostly—backed McAdoo. Cox was as Wet as one could realistically be in July 1920. Roosevelt was properly vague. Cox was the machine candidate, backed by Taggart and Brennan and Murphy. FDR had mended some fences with Tammany but had made his political reputation, what little he actually had, challenging Tammany in the state senate and in his ill-fated United States Senate primary.

And Cox was lumpy as a Midwest potato—and FDR was an Ivy League Adonis.

Women, after all, were probably going to vote this year.

But how would Charlie Murphy decide? Tammany had stood with Cox from the beginning. Even if FDR weren't such a nettle under Murphy's saddle, courtesy demanded such a gesture. And since Franklin was such a vexation to the Hall, it was simply imperative.

Murphy preferred Bainbridge Colby for vice president, but he was smart, and he was flexible—and, besides, he was *already* considering FDR for veep—to rid New York of him. Murphy, Smith, Taggart, George Brennan, and New York national committeeman Norman E. Mack had indeed conferred on the subject. Mack sputtered, "No sooner does he get to Albany and he just thumbs his nose at us. . . . We've got to get rid of him once and for all, I tell you. He's a troublemaker." They could rid themselves of FDR by dumping him on a doomed national ticket. Even then, Murphy so disliked FDR that it took all of Brennan and Taggart's persuasive powers to persuade him to support Mack's scheme.

So, when Ed Moore approached Murphy, Murphy first feigned hostility. "I don't like Roosevelt," Silent Charlie told Moore. "He is not well known in the country. But Ed, this is the first time a Democratic nominee for the Presidency has shown me courtesy. That's why I would vote for the devil himself if Cox wanted me to. Tell him we will nominate Roosevelt on the first ballot as soon as we assemble."

That was Murphy's way. In 1917 he had decided to run Brooklyn Judge John F. ("Red Mike") Hylan for mayor, but didn't want Hylan tagged as a Tammany candidate. The wily Murphy approached Brooklyn Democratic boss John H. McCooey and said, "I want you to ram [Hylan] down my throat."

Politics could be such a great charade.

Now, Murphy would have FDR rammed down his throat—and *rammed out* of any run for the Senate from New York state in the bargain.

Meanwhile, FDR perambulated about the hall, joking, "I can't afford the honor: I have five children." If things somehow fell through, as they had for Irvine Lenroot, Franklin would be able to say he had not really wanted the job anyway.

But Franklin now did want the nomination and wanted it bad. FDR's allies—attorney John E. Mack (who had cajoled FDR into running for the Senate in 1910), former congressman Lathrop Brown (FDR's best man and Harvard roommate), and Poughkeepsie florist Tom Lynch—worked the crowd, informing all who would listen that Franklin Delano Roosevelt was the man to balance the ticket.

Bainbridge Colby had already removed himself from consideration. So had Illinois Senator Hamilton Lewis and former Missouri governor and ambassador to Russia David R. Francis. Five other names, lackluster even by vice-presidential standards, were placed in nomination: General Lawrence D. Tyson of Tennessee, Montana Governor Samuel D. Stewart, California oilman Edward L. Doheny, former

Idaho governor James H. Hawley, and an unknown Oregonian by the name of W. T. Vaughan.

Cox's man, Judge Timothy Ansberry, approached FDR. "How old are you?" he asked.

"Thirty-eight," Franklin responded. "Why do you want to know?"

"I'm going to nominate you," Ansberry answered. His reason for asking: to ensure that FDR met the Constitutional age threshold of thirty-five.

"Do you think I ought to be around when you do?" FDR wanted to know.

"No," advised Ansberry, "I'd leave the hall."

Even against so gossamer a field, FDR's nomination was by no means guaranteed—just ask Lenroot. But after the first round of seconding speeches, Al Smith stepped to the podium:

> When the Republican Convention was over, I met a Republican friend of mine who said to me, "Al, it makes me think of picking up a fish in cold weather."
>
> I am instructed by the New York delegation to join heartily in seconding the nomination of one of the best-known Democrats in New York, a leader in local legislative reform that comprises a great part of the record of the Democratic Party in our State, and a man who, during the present Administration, has held a position of great power and importance in a Government department. I cheerfully arise here today to second the nomination of Franklin D. Roosevelt for Vice President.

Smith's speech may not have brimmed with enthusiasm (whose would, after forty-four ballots?), but it provided Tammany's imprimatur of its one-time nemesis. The convention nominated FDR by acclamation.

The crowd wanted a speech from Franklin; but for once, he had followed orders and couldn't be found. Josephus Daniels did speak, taking pains to explain why FDR hadn't actually served in the war. Roosevelt and Daniels then went to the *New Mexico*—to dine.

It was Daniels, not FDR, who telegraphed Eleanor:

IT WOULD HAVE DONE YOUR HEART GOOD TO HAVE SEEN THE SPON-
TANEOUS AND ENTHUSIASTIC TRIBUTE PAID WHEN FRANKLIN WAS

NOMINATED UNANIMOUSLY FOR VICE-PRESIDENT STOP ACCEPT MY
CONGRATULATIONS AND GREETINGS STOP WILL YOU BE GOOD ENOUGH
TO SEND MY CONGRATULATIONS AND GREETINGS ALSO TO HIS MOTHER
AS I DO NOT KNOW HER ADDRESS
JOSEPHUS DANIELS

"I was glad for my husband," Eleanor later wrote, "but it never occurred
to me to be much excited."

Nobody else was much excited either; and in that lack of excitement,
many missed an important point: The bosses at San Francisco had had
their way far more than the bosses at Chicago. The candidate of Murphy
and Brennan and Taggart and all the little bosses had won the great
prize. They had been for Cox at the beginning, and they were for him at
the end. They even had reason to be pleased with their vice-presidential
candidate.

"San Francisco represents the greatest triumph in the history of Tammany Hall," noted the magazine *World's Work*. "A Presidential candidate
whom it favored has never been received with anything except contempt
in a national convention."

The bosses had won without threats, promises, or machinations. They
simply held their ground, waiting—like Harry Daugherty—for their
opposition to collapse. Politics, after all, was their business, and in very
businesslike fashion they waited for the sale to be closed.

"While it is true that Cox was named by the bosses," Mark Sullivan
wrote, "they did it in the open. There were no conferences in closed
rooms."

# Chapter 16

## "CONVICT NO. 9653"

McAdoo out. Palmer out. Wilson out.

Wood out. Lowden out. Hoover out.

Now, it was just Harding vs. Cox.

Except it wasn't. A third major candidate remained, one who would not leave home to shake one voter's hand, travel to deliver a single speech, kiss any babies, or thrill to a thundering, booming round of applause.

Meet Atlanta Penitentiary Prisoner No. 9653—Eugene Victor Debs, Socialist Party candidate for president. When party spokesmen claimed that their candidate was unavailable for comment, they meant it.

Gene Debs, son of an Alsatian-immigrant grocer, was born in Terre Haute, Indiana, on November 5, 1855. At fourteen, he took a job scraping paint off railroad cars. "I worked there for a year," he recalled, "and it nearly killed me." Briefly, he next toiled as a grocery clerk, then obtained a position as a railroad fireman, a decision that unalterably changed his life. Joining the Brotherhood of Railroad Firemen, he became editor of its *Locomotive Firemen's Magazine*, and, by 1880, its Grand Secretary.

Personable, smart, and articulate, in 1879 Debs, then a Democrat, won the first of two terms as Terre Haute city clerk. In 1884, voters sent him to the state legislature, where he compiled a moderately progressive record, voting with Republicans to ban discrimination against blacks.

In June 1885, the twenty-nine-year-old Debs married twenty-seven-year-old Kate Metzel, the daughter of middle-class German immigrants.

As aloof as Debs was outgoing, she nonetheless willingly accepted his frequent absences for the union cause. "His wife did not need to be a constantly charming companion," observed biographer Ray Ginger; "she did need to be stable, secure, self-reliant. Kate Metzel certainly had these characteristics. Debs was seeking a typical wife but an unusual marriage."

Debs remained fervently devoted to railway unionism, eventually concluding that more aggressive representation was required. In June 1893, he organized the American Railway Union (ARU), the country's first industrial union. Allowing only "employees born of white parents," it represented 150,000 of the nation's 850,000 rail workers.

Debs was not yet a socialist. That year, he wrote:

> We indulge in none of the current vagaries about a conflict between capital and labor. There are capitalists who fight labor; we do not anticipate any diminution of their numbers, but, we do expect to see them checkmated in their schemes of piracy.

In April 1894, the ARU scored a major triumph, successfully mounting an eighteen-day strike against the Great Northern Railroad. The following month, however, workers at the Chicago-based Pullman Palace Car Company struck to protest company-imposed wage cuts averaging 25 percent. Debs hesitated to join their cause (Pullman employees did not actually work for, or on, the railroads; they merely manufactured sleeper cars); but on inspecting their conditions, their company-owned homes and company-owned stores, he relented. "The paternalism of Pullman is the same as the interest of a slave holder in his human chattels," he admitted. "You are striking to avert slavery and degradation."

On June 21, 1894, the ARU voted to boycott all Pullman cars. Rail traffic around Chicago ground to a halt. After strikers wrecked a Blue Island, Illinois rail yard, United States Attorney General Richard Olney obtained an injunction against the strike. On July 4, President Grover Cleveland dispatched twenty thousand federal troops to Chicago to maintain order. Outraged strikers destroyed seven hundred railcars in the South Chicago Panhandle yards and torched seven buildings at the city's World's Columbian Exposition. On July 17, federal agents arrested Debs and seven other ARU officials, charging them with violating Olney's injunction. Refusing to post bail, Debs found himself in the vermin- and rat-infested Cook County jail.

Press opinion uniformly opposed the strikers—and Debs. "Debs demands," contended the *Brooklyn Union*, "not the mere surrender of the Pullman company, or of the railroads in general, but of the country at large."

He stood trial in January 1895. Charges of conspiracy to obstruct the mails fell by the wayside; but, despite a defense headed by Clarence Darrow, ARU leaders were found guilty of contempt of court and sentenced to six months at Woodstock, Illinois's McHenry County Prison. "Six months in jail," the *Washington Post* wrote approvingly, "is mighty little to pay for such glory and notoriety as [Debs] enjoyed some months ago. It is not often that an insignificant mountebank is snatched from obscurity and made, even for a brief moment, the most conspicuous member of his generation."

The United States Supreme Court rejected his appeal, and he entered Woodstock jail in June 1895.

He entered it a day late, explaining his tardiness and intoxicated appearance by claiming to have been "made sick by eating too many cucumbers" in Chicago. Nobody believed him.

The *Mansfield* (Ohio) *News* headlined:

### Was He on a Toot?
### The Deceptive Cucumber Doubles Up Eugene Debs.
### At Least Debs Says It's So.

Before long, the anti-Debs press was mocking him as "Cucumber" Debs.

It was in prison that Debs first read *Das Kapital*. "Books and pamphlets and letters from Socialists came by every mail," he recalled, "and I began to read and think and dissect the anatomy of the system in which workingmen, however organized, could be shattered and battered and splintered at a single stroke."

Six months at Woodstock had not merely transformed Gene Debs ideologically; it made him a hero. Mail inundated the jail—1,500 letters in just a single week. Celebrities visited. Huge, enthusiastic throngs cheered his November 1895 release. Read one account:

More than 100,000 people blocked the [Chicago] streets and bridges in the vicinity of the depot. The streets were filled with mud and slush and a heavy rain was falling, but the crowd did not seem to pay any attention. Mr. Debs himself refused to enter the carriage hauled by six white horses and as he took his place in the parade he said: "If the rest walk, I shall walk. What is good enough for them is good enough for me."

Debs had been a Democrat and a union leader, but industry blacklisting made the ARU vulnerable. It dissolved in early 1897. In 1896, still coy about his new leanings, Debs had dissolved his ties to the Democratic Party: "I am a Populist, and I favor wiping out both old parties so they will never come into power again. I have been a Democrat all my life and I am ashamed to admit it." He supported William Jennings Bryan for president, but Bryan's issues were not Debs's issues. He cared only fleetingly for the farmer. Free Silver left him cold.

In January 1897, Debs declared himself a Socialist. "The issue is Socialism versus Capitalism," he proclaimed that year. "I am for Socialism because I am for humanity. We have been cursed with the reign of gold long enough. Money constitutes no proper basis of civilization. The time has come to regenerate society—we are on the eve of universal change."

Dissatisfied with the existing Socialist Labor Party, Debs, with Milwaukee newspaper editor Victor Luitpold Berger (who had introduced him to *Das Kapital*), helped found the Social Democracy in America. In 1900, the Social Democracy's political arm, the Social Democratic Party, secured the reluctant Debs (even then nervous about his health) as its presidential candidate. His showing (96,878 votes) was not particularly impressive, but it easily eclipsed the Socialist Labor total (39,739 votes).

In 1901, Social Democrats merged with Socialist Labor Party dissidents to create the new Socialist Party. Three years later, it nominated Debs for the presidency. This time, he garnered 402,283 votes. In 1908, despite acute rheumatism, he ran yet again. Campaigning for sixty-five straight days on the party's "Red Special" train, he addressed an estimated eight hundred thousand people, most of whom had paid between fifteen cents and a half dollar for the privilege. He didn't win (he drew

420,793 votes); but, as he told supporters, "I'd rather vote for what I want and not get it, than for what I don't want and get it."

Between elections, Debs wrote and edited (serving as associate editor of the party organ *Appeal to Reason*), and dabbled in unionism. In June 1905, he helped found the radical International Workers of the World—the IWW or "Wobblies"—remaining allied with it until its "direct action" approach (i.e., industrial sabotage) proved too active for his tastes.

Debs's socialism possessed American—not European—roots. Born, raised, and living his whole life (save for when imprisoned) in small-town Terre Haute, Debs never escaped his origins. Rather than harkening to Marx, he favored allusions to Lincoln—or, even, Christ, who he described in March 1914 as "the master proletarian revolutionist and sower of the social whirlwind," the descendant of "poor working people" rather than the "money-changers, usurers, merchants, lawyers, scribes, priests, or other parasites."

The year 1912 witnessed Debs's fourth—and best—presidential run. He garnered 900,369 votes—6 percent of the popular total, including 16.5 percent in Nevada, 13.4 percent in Arizona, 12.4 percent in Idaho, and 9.5 percent in Florida. He outpaced Teddy Roosevelt in Florida and Taft in Florida, Mississippi, and Arizona. It was high tide. Party membership rolls peaked at 118,045 that year. Over a thousand Socialists held public office, including Schenectady's George Lunn and Milwaukee mayor Daniel Webster Hoan.

In 1916, Debs, now sixty-one but feeling seventy, declined another national nomination. Running instead for Congress from his Terre Haute district, he lost badly to Republican Everett Sanders (future secretary to President Coolidge). "Blessed are they who expect nothing," Debs quipped, "for they shall not be disappointed." But Debs, in fact, had harbored hopes of victory, and the loss hurt.

It wasn't very pleasant nationally, either. Socialists, by mail ballot, had nominated for president the colorless party author and pamphleteer Allen L. Benson. The party expected to win eight congressional seats, increase its presidential vote by 50 to 100 percent, and even capture Oklahoma's electoral votes. Instead, its presidential tally plummeted to 585,113, just 3.2 percent of the vote.

The old issues were falling away. The progressive income tax, popular election of United States senators, a federal reserve system, the Clayton Anti-trust Act, and an eight-hour day for railroad workers were all law. A federal Department of Labor was in place. The country's workmen and farmers were fairly prosperous. Even prominent party journalists Carl Sandburg and John Reed voted Democratic. Party membership dropped to 83,284.

One great issue remained: the war.

Socialists didn't want war. A fair number were of German ancestry and didn't relish fighting the Fatherland. The great majority simply didn't relish dying for their capitalist masters. On April 7, 1917—one day after America's declaration of war—Socialists met in a party convention in St. Louis and formally branded the war "as a crime against the people of the United States" (a decision later officially ratified by party referendum, 21,000 to 350).

The Wilson administration had a different idea of what constituted a crime. In July 1917, Kate Richards O'Hare, editor of the socialist magazine *The Rip-Saw*, delivered a speech in tiny Bowman, North Dakota, attacking conscription and deriding the mothers of soldiers as "mere brood sows." Convicted of an Espionage Act violation, O'Hare received five years at the Missouri State Prison at Jefferson City, Missouri.

On September 5, 1917, federal agents, authorized by Attorney General Thomas W. Gregory, raided the Socialist Party's national headquarters in Chicago, looking for anti-war, anti-draft materials. Not surprisingly, they found plenty.

With Democrats and Republicans out-flagwaving each other, the substantial anti-war vote gravitated to Socialist candidates. In November 1917, Socialist Morris Hillquit, running for mayor of New York, received 22 percent of the vote—besting the party's previous mayoral total by 450 percent. New York Socialists elected eight city councilmen, seven state assemblymen (up from two in the previous election), and a Manhattan municipal judge. Chicago gave Socialists 34 percent of the vote (up from 4 percent in 1916); Dayton, 44 percent.

Still, the government maintained its pressure, jailing numerous prominent Socialists. It would have been remarkable if federal authorities had not targeted Debs, he being as anti-war as any Socialist already arrested. "I have no country to fight for," he proclaimed; "my country is the earth, and I am a citizen of the world."

But he was no pacifist. He just didn't want to fight, or have *any* work-ingman, fight for capitalism. But he would fight if he had to. Once, a German immigrant informed Debs that self-proclaimed patriots had invaded his home. "Tell those cowards to keep well away from the home of Eugene Victor Debs," he exclaimed. "By God! If any of them so much as puts a foot on my property, I will shoot him dead."

On June 16, 1918, Debs traveled to Dayton to address the Ohio state party convention. En route, he visited incarcerated Socialist leaders Charles E. Ruthenberg, Alfred Wagenknecht, and Charles Baker, held in the nearby Stark County Jail for obstructing the draft.

Energized by the visit—and by the enthusiastic 1,200-person crowd that greeted him (Ohio was the center of the party's radical left wing)—Debs lashed into the war effort:

> I realize that, in speaking to you this afternoon, there are certain limitations placed on the rights of free [men]. . . . I may not be able to say all I think[,] but I am not going to say anything that I do not think. I would a thousand times rather be a free soul in jail than a sycophant and coward in the streets. They may put those boys in jail—and some of the rest of us in jail—but they cannot put the Socialist movement in jail.
>
> The master class has always declared the war; the subject class has always fought the battles. The master class has had all to gain and nothing to lose, while the subject class has had nothing to gain and all to lose—especially their lives. . . .
>
> Yes, in good time we are going to sweep into power in this nation and throughout the world. . . . The world is changing daily before our eyes. The sun of capitalism is setting; the sun of Socialism is rising. . . . In due time[,] the hour will strike and this great cause triumphant—the greatest in history—will proclaim the emanci-pation of the working class and the brotherhood of all mankind.

In the audience, federal agents checked draft cards—and took notes. Four days later, a federal grand jury indicted Debs on ten counts of sedi-tion, with penalties of up to twenty years' imprisonment and a $10,000 fine for each count.

At 3:20 P.M. on Sunday, June 30, federal marshals arrested Debs as he stepped out of an automobile to speak to three thousand people at Cleveland's Bohemian Garden. It being a Sunday, Debs couldn't post bail and spent the night in the Cuyahoga County jail. Emerging the next morning, he found himself nominated once more for Congress. He decided not to run.

Debs's trial began on September 9, 1918, at the oak and marble chambers of Cleveland's federal courthouse. For three days, prosecutors presented their case. Debs's counsel, Seymour Stedman (counsel for Victor Berger and company in their trial before Judge Landis), countered by not countering. Calling no witnesses, he jibed, "Let's see, you rest, we rest."

Instead, Stedman requested that Debs be allowed to address the court directly. It was unusual, but Judge David C. Westerhaven agreed. Debs spoke for two hours. Westerhaven then instructed jurors to return a not-guilty verdict on the dubious charges involving ridiculing the federal government, but to consider the draft-obstruction charge. On Thursday, September 12, after deliberating for six hours, the jury returned a guilty verdict.

Stedman asked Debs to speak again in the trial's sentencing phase. Discouraged, Debs said no. But Stedman persisted. Debs relented—but first he would get good and drunk before he wrote out his address.

Fortified with a pint of bourbon, on Saturday, September 14, Debs addressed Judge Westerhaven, with an eloquence that would ensure his place in American history. Heywood Broun, never much of a Debs fan, found his talk "one of the most beautiful and moving passages in the English language. He was for that one afternoon touched with inspiration. If anyone told me that tongues of fire danced upon his shoulders as he spoke, I would believe it."

And, so, Debs spoke:

Your honor, years ago I recognized my kinship with all living beings, and I made up my mind that I was not one bit better than the meanest on earth. I said then, I say now, that while there is a lower class I am in it; while there is a criminal element, I am of it; while there is a soul in prison, I am not free. . . .

Your honor, I have stated in this court that I am opposed to the form of our present government; that I am opposed to the social

269

system in which we live; that I believed in the change of both but by perfectly peaceable and orderly means.

In the struggle—the unceasing struggle—between the toilers and producers and their exploiters, I have tried, as best I might, to serve those among whom I was born, and with whom I expect to share my lot until the end of my days.

I am thinking this morning of the men in the mills and factories; I am thinking of the women who, for a paltry wage, are compelled to work out their lives; of the little children who, in this system, are robbed of their childhood, and in their early, tender years, are seized in the remorseless grasp of Mammon, and forced into the industrial dungeons, there to feed the machines while they themselves are being starved body and soul. . . .

Your honor, I ask no mercy, I plead for no immunity. I realize that finally the right must prevail. I never more fully comprehended than now the great struggle between the powers of greed on one hand and upon the other the rising hosts of freedom. I can see the dawn of a better day of humanity. The people are awakening. In due course of time[,] they will come into their own.

When the mariner, sailing over tropic seas, looks for relief from his weary watch, he turns his eyes toward the Southern Cross, burning luridly above the tempest-vexed ocean. As the midnight approaches[,] the Southern Cross begins to bend, and the whirling worlds change their places, and with starry finger-points the Almighty marks the passage of Time upon the dial of the universe; and though no bell may beat the glad tidings, the look-out knows that the midnight is passing—that relief and rest are close at hand.

Let the people take heart and hope everywhere, for the cross is bending, midnight is passing, and joy cometh with the morning.

He received ten years.

Debs's rhetoric thrilled Heywood Broun. It didn't do much for the *Cleveland Plain Dealer*. Speaking for much of America, it wrote:

Debs's voice is now stilled as it should have been stilled long ago. Doctrines such as he has been pleased to preach are not to be

270

tolerated. The question of free speech is in no wise involved. It is a question of national safety.

Debs appealed his conviction, continuing to speak in the interim. With revolution flowering in Russia, American radicals wanted very much to believe that what was transpiring in Moscow and St. Petersburg foretold worldwide change. Eventually, word would seep out about the Bolsheviks' repression of old comrades and of massacres that would dwarf the blood-stained record of the tsars and Cossacks, but at first the only massacres were of officers and priests and the children of the royal family, and Debs did not seem to mind that very much. In November 1918, he saluted his Red heroes:

> Comrades of the Russian Soviet and the Bolshevik Republic, we salute and honor you on this first anniversary of your great revolutionary triumph, the greatest in point of historic significance and far-reaching influence in the annals of the race.
>
> The chief glory of your revolutionary triumph is that you have preserved inviolate the fundamental principles of international Socialism and refused to compromise. . . . You . . . are resolved that . . . the working-class shall not allow itself to be used . . . to install some interim class into power and perpetuate its own slavery and degradation. . . .
>
> We pledge you . . . to strive with all our energy to emulate your inspiring example by abolishing our imperialistic capitalism, driving our plutocratic exploiters and oppressors from power and establishing the working class republic, the Commonwealth of Comrades.

Such rhetoric did little to convince the nervous American bourgeoisie that Eugene Debs was merely a liberal who meant it.

On March 10, 1919—four months after the Armistice—the Supreme Court ruled on Debs's trial and sentence. Debs, it unanimously ruled in a decision written by Oliver Wendell Holmes, had indeed meant to obstruct the war effort. Debs, now sixty-three, would be in jail for a lot longer than the six months he had spent in Woodstock.

In April 1919, he surrendered to federal authorities to begin serving his sentence in the Moundsville, West Virginia state prison. "I enter the prison doors a flaming revolutionist," said Debs, now "Prisoner 2253," with "my head erect, my spirit untamed, my soul unconquerable."

"From the crown of my head to the soles of my feet," he proclaimed, "I am a Bolshevik, and proud of it. 'The day of the People has arrived!'"

Debs, assigned light clerical duties in the prison hospital, proved popular with fellow prisoners. In June 1919, authorities transferred him to Atlanta's federal penitentiary. "I never in my life met a kinder man," Moundsville Warden Joseph Z. Terrell wrote his Atlanta counterpart Fred Zerbst. "He is forever thinking of others, trying to serve them, and never thinking of himself."

Debs, now "Prisoner No. 9653," shared a cell with five other prisoners and worked in the prison clothes room. Prison regulations limited his outgoing correspondence; but, otherwise, Warden Zerbst proved flexible. When Debs protested compulsory chapel attendance, Zerbst dropped it for everyone. Debs could read the radical press and received virtually as many visitors as he desired. When he took sick—severely sick—Zerbst provided him with a private hospital room and transferred him to light hospital duties. He even provided Debs with regular rations of alcohol—for medicinal purposes, of course.

Meanwhile, agitation mounted for Debs's release, as did a push for another presidential nomination. In early February 1920, Oklahoma Socialists unanimously endorsed a Debs–O'Hare ticket. The boom proved unstoppable. By mid-March, Debs had declared his candidacy.

One early endorsement did not help his cause: that of best-selling poet and notorious German propagandist George Sylvester Viereck. Viereck, whose father was reputedly Kaiser Wilhelm I's illegitimate son, announced that Debs—along with such anti-war luminaries as Bob La Follette, James A. Reed, William Randolph Hearst, and Hiram Johnson—had his *American Monthly*'s support for president.

In May 1920, Socialists met in national convention at Harlem's Finnish Socialist Hall at 127th Street and Fifth Avenue to endorse a national ticket and draft a platform. In the wake of the deep divisions within party ranks, the latter task proved difficult. The Illinois delegation moved to insert support for a dictatorship of the proletariat into the platform. They lost, 74–57.

Religion also divided the convention. A proposed plank declared that "a privileged few in America own the people's churches and regulate their souls." Victor Berger and two of the five expelled New York State assemblymen, Brooklyn's Charles Solomon and East Harlem's August Claessens, opposed it. District of Columbia delegate John H. McIntyre agreed. "I am the father of six children and none of them go to the church," he thundered. "Socialist literature has opened my eyes. If we get religion into our platform, we will get into a religious discussion and forget all about Socialism. Get the votes first and talk religion out of them afterward."

The plank lost.

The final platform called for:

1. All businesses vitally essential to the existence and welfare of the people to be taken over by the nation.
2. Publicly owned interests to be administered by the government and representatives of the workers for service and not for profit.
3. Banks to be acquired by the nation and unified.
4. All insurance to be taken over by the nation.
5. Full civil, political, industrial, and educational rights to be secured to Negroes.
6. Abolition of child labor.
7. A national minimum wage law.
8. Protection of migratory and unemployed workers from oppression.
9. Abolition of detective and strikebreaking agencies.
10. A shorter workday in keeping with increased production.
11. Freedom of speech, press, and assembly.
12. Repeal of the Espionage law.
13. Discontinuance of Espionage law prosecutions.
14. Repeal of arbitrary power of deportation of aliens.
15. Abrogation of injunctions in strikes.
16. Universal suffrage in fact as well as in law.
17. Power of recall of Federal executives and judges.

Indiana delegate Edward Henry, a longtime Debs friend, placed "the Lincoln of the Wabash" in nomination. "A deep-toned bell rang out once," gushed the Socialist *New York Call*, "once, twice, and the national Socialist convention laid aside its deliberations . . . to take up a matter of love, the nomination of Eugene Victor Debs, the nation's most noted citizen. . . ."

Henry spoke of visiting Debs. The year might have been 1920, but Henry's account began like an old-fashioned melodrama:

> When I entered the great prison in Atlanta, Georgia, walking through a hallway with a guard, I saw a tall form and when I looked I saw a man I knew, the same old Comrade of mine and yours. The guard immediately said, "There is the man you want to see," and I said, "Yes, I love him, and I know him as far as I can see him.
>
> "That is the Lincoln of the Wabash from Indiana way."
>
> When I got near this Comrade, he stretched out his hands as he has to me and you many times. He grasped me in my arms while the tears rolled down his cheeks and he said, "Oh, Comrade, I am glad to see you. How are the Comrades back home? How do the Comrades feel over the situation at the present time?"
>
> And the next question he asked was, "Are all my Comrades active on the job wherever they may be?"
>
> And I said, "Yes, they are all doing their part, Comrade. They are all doing what they can."
>
> And Debs's message to the Socialists was, "Go out to the Comrades and urge them to give all their time, all their energy to this greatest of all movements, the Socialist movement of the working class."

It started out melodrama. It ended as Soviet realism.

New York's Metal Workers Union organizer Joseph D. Cannon seconded the nomination, comparing Debs's imprisonment to Christ's crucifixion and asking: "The question is not why is Debs in jail, but why are so many of us not in jail?"

Delegates sobbed. They cheered and paraded in prison lockstep for twenty-one minutes. A band played "The International," and when they stopped, in the brief silence that followed, someone yelled out, "Three cheers for Soviet Russia."

He got them.

The convention nominated the Lincoln of the Wabash by acclamation. Earlier, thirty prominent party leaders, including Berger, Hillquit, and Henry, had wired Pennsylvania State Federation of Labor president James H. Maurer, urging him to accept the vice-presidential nomination. Maurer, who boasted only ten days of formal education, had learned to read only at sixteen. Thrice elected to the state assembly, he now eyed a congressional seat and declined the honor.

Socialists chose between Seymour Stedman and Kate Richards O'Hare (who had unsuccessfully sought the 1916 vice-presidential nomination). Stedman prevailed, 102–26. Though delegates may have sympathized with women's suffrage, they recognized the impracticality of having *both* candidates behind bars. Delegates then made Seymour's nomination unanimous.

Optimism ran high, since Debs would receive support not only from Socialists but also from hundreds of thousands protesting his arrest—and the arrest of others caught up in Mitchell Palmer's dragnet. Morris Hillquit predicted that the ticket would attract between two and three million votes.

Following the convention, Stedman and Hillquit led a 160-person delegation to Washington to petition Palmer for Debs's release. Palmer listened and, inexplicably, didn't notice as one man affixed a small white button to his lapel. Later, at lunch, Joe Tumulty looked puzzled, then asked, "Who are you for, anyhow?" Only then did Palmer realize that he was sporting an I AM FOR DEBS button.

The Socialist Party followed the major parties' tradition of sending a delegation to formally notify its presidential candidate. Its nine members included Stedman, *New York Call* associate editor James Oneal, and party executive secretary Julius Gerber. En route to Atlanta, Stedman quipped, the group hoped to "take up the matter of cabinet appointments."

"I think, from the standpoint of public interest," Stedman added, "that if the matter has been fully presented to the president and if the Department of Justice realizes what it means, they will release Mr. Debs before his notification and acceptance. It might not be a good example to have a prisoner in a penitentiary accept the nomination for the presidency of the United States. It might have a tendency to take away the sting of imprisonment in the eyes of the public."

At 9 A.M., Saturday, May 29, a caravan of Socialists, reporters, and photographers arrived at the Atlanta penitentiary. Gerber was the first to approach Debs. The two embraced. Debs, garbed in sneakers and plain prison blue denim jacket and pants, kissed Gerber on both cheeks. Then Stedman kissed Debs on the cheek, as did Terre Haute's Dr. Madge Patton Stephens, who presented Prisoner No. 9653 with a bouquet of crimson carnations. Also present was inmate Joe Caldwell, a Rhode Islander serving five years on Espionage Act charges, who Warden Zerbst had allowed to attend.

Debs, in good health, was much tanner than his visitors. "Well, Gene, how goes it?" Oneal asked. "You certainly look fine."

One visitor pointed to the Debs button on his suit jacket lapel. "Better take that off," Debs joked. "They'll put you in the penitentiary for wearing that."

The newsreel men realized that they had missed some good shots—it isn't every day one sees running mates actually kissing—and wanted the event re-created. Warden Zerbst allowed Debs to venture outdoors, so cameras might take advantage of natural light. It took a full half hour to re-shoot the events.

This was a very civilized sort of repression.

Oneal read Debs's official notification. Debs was an odd sort of man. Graceful and humorous and forbearing, he could also be nasty and churlish. Accepting his nomination, he lashed into the platform his party had just adopted, snapping that it "could have been made much more effective if it had stressed the class struggle more prominently and if more emphasis had been placed on industrial organization. . . . There is a tendency in the party to become a party of politicians instead of a party of workers. That policy must be checked, not encouraged. We are in politics not to get votes, but to develop the power to emancipate the working class."

Debs continued in that vein, expressing support for the many former Socialists who had defected to the new Communist parties. "I was sorry to read a speech by Berger the other day attacking the Communists," he told the committee. "I have known many comrades in all those parties, I have high regard for them. They are as honest as we are."

He remarked that he was a Bolshevik and intended to remain one. Fellow inmate Caldwell burst into applause, and Debs hastened to clarify himself: "Not a Russian Bolshevik in America but an American Bolshevik—fighting here for what they were fighting for in Russia."

Finally, Debs accepted his nomination. "I have always been a radical," he proclaimed, "never more so than now. I have never been afraid of being too radical, but I have feared to become conservative. . . . I am heartily in favor of the Russian revolution and think we should support it with all our power."

That same day, Woodrow Wilson pardoned Kate Richards O'Hare. Joe Tumulty carefully explained that Mrs. O'Hare's case had nothing to do with Mr. Debs's. Eugene Debs could rot in Atlanta forever, as far as Wilson was concerned.

"I will never consent to the pardon of this man," Wilson had told Tumulty:

> While the flower of American youth was pouring out its blood to vindicate the cause of civilization, this man, Debs, stood behind the lines, sniping, attacking, and denouncing them. Before the war[,] he had a perfect right to exercise his freedom of speech and to express his own opinion, but once the Congress . . . declared war, silence on his part would have been the proper course to pursue. I know there will be a great deal of denunciation of me for refusing this pardon. They will say I am cold-blooded and indifferent, but it will make no impression on me. This man was a traitor to his country and he will never be pardoned during my administration.

Eventually, Debs realized that Wilson would never grant him freedom, no matter how many petitions circulated or how many delegations visited Washington:

> I understand perfectly the feelings of Wilson. When he reviews what he has done, when he realizes the suffering he has brought

about, then he is being punished. It is he, not I, who needs a pardon. If I had it in my power[,] I would give him the pardon which would set him free.

Woodrow Wilson is an exile from the hearts of his people. The betrayal of his ideals makes him the most pathetic figure in the world. No man in public life in American history ever retired so thoroughly discredited, so scathingly rebuked, so overwhelmingly impeached and repudiated as Woodrow Wilson.

Debs free or jailed, Socialists had a campaign to run. This was their great opportunity. The imprisonment of party members and the expulsion of its legislators had generated widespread sympathy. In the post-war period, unemployment and inflation soared. Strikes had rocked one segment of the national economy after another. Socialists opened their campaign on June 13 to the jeers of the capitalist press. "Seymour Stedman . . . spoke, undaunted by the rain," noted the *Chicago Tribune*. "The audience waved high[-]priced straw hats in approval, unmindful of the pattering drops which soaked their silk shirts and ruined the creases in their trousers."

At Atlanta, as at Moundsville, Debs established a rapport with both prison staff and fellow inmates. *New York World* reporter Charles Wood visited Atlanta to learn more about Debs's incarceration. "When he was first brought into this room," sixty-four-year-old prison chaplain Father Michael J. Byrne marveled to Wood, "there was something in his very presence which made you feel that there wasn't any element of viciousness in him. One of the first things a prisoner has to do is to make out a printed form telling of his religious leanings, his church preference and other things for the guidance of the spiritual advisers.

"'No preference,' he wrote. 'Haven't you any religion?' I asked him. 'Yes,' he said. 'I have one of my own.' He spoke very reverently when he said it, and I have learned since that he not only has a religion but he has a religion which he lives in every act. I don't know anything about his political theories, but I do know that he believes in God and that Jesus is his personal inspiration."

Wood asked, "Is it what Debs has said to you, which makes you put confidence in him?"

"No," Father Byrne replied, "and it is not only what he does. It is what he is. Atlanta Prison is a different place since he came here. He is an influence for good. He works in the hospital and manages somehow to cheer the patients up."

Wood asked Debs himself: "What has been your greatest experience since you were sent to prison?"

"I have discovered that love is omnipotent," Prisoner No. 9653 responded:

All the forces of earth cannot prevail against it. Hatred, war, cruelty, greed and lust must all give away before it. It will overthrow all tyrannies. It will empty all prisons. It will not only emancipate the human race eventually but to a great extent it lifts us individually above the struggle while we are in the thick of the fight for human brotherhood.

I know now (it is no credit to me, but it is an experience worth while) that I do not hate a single person. I would not punish a single person. I would not kill another man—even in self defense.

Asked about his nomination, he responded: "Personally, I am a radical. My only fear has always been that I might not be radical enough. In my own party I always led a minority, but I hope to lead a united Socialist Party to the polls this year."

In some ways, this campaign—his "front cell" campaign—was Debs's least burdensome—no trains to catch, no speeches to deliver, no hands to shake. "I will be a candidate at home in seclusion," he joked. "It will be much less tiresome and my managers and opponents can always locate me."

Authorities allowed him to periodically issue statements, though nothing very long or involved, and he could still harpoon opponents as easily as if aboard the "Red Special." "Senator Harding and Governor Cox remind me of two humpty dumpties," he jibed in August. "They are stuffed people, not real. They have not a single idea for a man who is alive. They get their inspiration from the tombs. The whole performance is artificial."

In September, federal authorities announced that Debs could send out five hundred words per week. That same month, supporters circulated a petition for his release. Helen Keller, scientist Charles Steinmetz, financier Jacob H. Schiff, journalist (and former U.S. Minister to Denmark) Norman Hapgood, former South Carolina Governor Coleman Blease, and Farmer-Labor Party presidential candidate Parley Christensen all signed. It did no good.

On September 16, anarchist Michael Buda bombed Wall Street. Debs quipped: "Being in prison is not without its advantages. Had I made a speech in New York the night before the Wall Street explosion[,] there would have been a clear case against me. As it is, I have the perfect alibi."

Despite the threat of government harassment, Socialists issued five million pieces of literature. Sixty thousand individuals donated to the campaign, but the party was in trouble. It wasn't just the arrests and the harassment.

"In the first place," the *New York Call* later explained, "the party organization was all but wrecked by internal dissensions in 1919, and it had by no means recovered from them when the national convention met. . . ." In other words, the defection of the two extreme radical factions that formed the Communist Labor Party and the Communist Party of America torpedoed the party worse than anything A. Mitchell Palmer had done.

During the campaign, Communists, realizing Debs's power and influence not just among radicals but with the general public, tried luring him into their orbit. Debs, however, had quickly developed second thoughts about Leninism (now refusing to endorse joining the Communist International without substantial reservations), and when a Communist delegation quietly visited, he rebuffed their efforts. It wasn't just ideology. Debs sensed that they cared little for his personal plight.

"Gene wishes me to say to you that personally he owes nothing to the Communists," his brother Theodore would write in 1922 to J. Louis Engdahl, by then a Red. "When he was in that hell-hole at Atlanta[,] the Communists with but few exceptions ignored him and the rest of the political prisoners, and their papers, including the one you now edit, were cold-bloodedly silent, not raising a voice nor lifting a finger to secure their release, and so far as they were concerned, Gene would still be rotting in his dungeon in Atlanta."

As the campaign drew to a close, Socialists retained high hopes. Executive Secretary Gerber reiterated Morris Hillquit's earlier prediction of three million votes and predicted that New York State alone would elect at least five Socialist congressmen and thirteen assemblymen.

Debs knew better. His "Last Call to the Voters in 1920" betrayed pessimism—indeed, bitterness. "There is one thing I know on the eve of this election," he wrote: "I shall not be disappointed. The result will be as it should be. The people will vote for what they think they want, to the extent that they think at all, and they, too, will not be disappointed."

"In my maturer years, I no longer permit myself to be either disappointed or discouraged. I hope for everything and expect nothing. The people can have anything they want. The trouble is [that] they do not want anything. At least they vote that way on election day."

*Chapter 17*

≈

# "A Gathering of Asteroids"

Republicans faced a specter.

The specter of 1912—the specter of third parties.

In 1912, William Howard Taft won the Republican nomination. Teddy Roosevelt bolted. Would his former running mate, the ill-tempered Hiram Johnson, do likewise in 1920? In late June, Wall Street sharpies laid 1–3 odds that he would.

He didn't. Elihu Root's platform foggery had worked its magic. So had Harry Daugherty's strategy of not angering anyone—even Johnson. Hiram stayed put.

But would Robert La Follette?

Ballot after ballot at Chicago's Republican convention, Wisconsin faithfully cast its 24 votes for Fighting Bob. He was as stubborn as Johnson. He seemed ready to bolt—and, as if for his convenience, a coalition of radicals had formed and hung out the "help wanted" sign for a nominee.

Progressive opinion admired neither party. "The only difference between the two parties at this moment," the *New Republic* wrote in June 1920, "is that the Republicans promise to be reactionary and Democrats have been reactionary."

Chicago Federation of Labor President John Fitzpatrick, a vitriolic opponent of the American Federation of Labor's Samuel Gompers, worked to fashion a new party, a coalition of non-Socialist Party left-wing organizations. His plan called for each group to simultaneously convene in Chicago in July 1920 and then reconvene together at that city's Hotel Morrison to select a presidential ticket.

Nine groups—a radical ragbag—responded. Best known was the Committee of Forty-Eight, a collection of fairly respectable, conventional progressives. Its most prominent members included Dudley Field Malone, friend to suffragettes in general and to one in particular, and Gifford Pinchot's brother Amos, a noted progressive and civil libertarian in his own right—both previously endorsed by George Sylvester Viereck for vice president. A rising 48er star was former Salt Lake County Attorney and former Utah Republican chairman Parley Parker Christensen. The genial, 6'4" Christensen, a forty-nine-year-old bachelor, won election to the Utah legislature as a Progressive, endorsed Woodrow Wilson in 1916, and had gained credence with radicals by his defense of local IWW members.

Next came the fledgling Labor Party, formed as a federation of nine existing state labor parties in August 1919. It had a following. Over a thousand delegates attended its November 1919 convention. It was radical. Senator La Follette's son Philip later described it as "a 'left' to 'close to Communist' group . . . the men at the core of the Labor party were skilled in Marxian tactics. . . ."

William Randolph Hearst flirted with the new party. In 1920, he owned twelve dailies in eight key cities (including New York, San Francisco, Boston, Chicago, Atlanta, and Los Angeles), magazines (*Cosmopolitan*, *Hearst's*, *Harper's Bazaar*, *Good Housekeeping*, *Motor*, and *Motor Boating*), and even a film studio, Cosmopolitan Film Studios (distributed through Paramount, which wisely gauged the value of publicity in the Hearst press). Long before AOL TimeWarner or Rupert Murdoch, Hearst had created a multi-media empire, and he intended to use it to fulfill his own political—and personal—ambitions. He remained a Democrat, but a radical one, alienated from his party's mainstream not only by economics but by his opposition to the war, the League, and nonrecognition of Russia's Bolshevik government. As 1920 began, some thought he himself would seek the presidential nomination (he had, after all, received 263 votes at the 1904 convention). But as the year progressed, he drew back, indicating that he would support either Borah or Johnson among the Republicans and Champ Clark, Senator James

Reed, or Secretary of State Colby among the Democrats. Beyond that, he dabbled with a third party, the American Constitutional Party, formed in cooperation with former Texas governor James E. ("Pa") Ferguson (impeached for financial improprieties in 1917). The American Constitutional Party would be among those convening in Chicago.

On June 19, William Randolph Hearst issued a signed editorial in his various papers, calling for a new party to assemble "in a new Independence hall." He condemned the Republican Party for lauding the dead TR while rejecting Hiram Johnson, charging that "it considers a dead progressive an asset and a live progressive a liability."

"The Democrat party," Hearst continued, "offers no refuge for independent, upstanding Americans. It has traded its few progressive policies for the promise of a Baruch campaign fund raised from the same predatory interests that control and corrupt the Republican Party. It has abandoned its Americanism and sacrificed its very democracy to become the agent of an autocrat more concerned with magnifying his importance abroad than he is in protecting the welfare of his own people at home."

Hearst's American Party was hardly the last of the radical groups interested in the new radical coalition party. The Nonpartisan League enjoyed substantial support in North and South Dakota, Minnesota, Montana, and Idaho. The World War Veterans, a short-lived left-wing rival to the American Legion, claimed a peak membership of 700,000. Otherwise, pickings were slim, featuring such nondescript entities as the late Henry George's old Single Tax Party, a relic of nineteenth-century fringe politics, and the Private Soldiers and Sailors League.

Some folks drifted in on their own: the People's Money Party, the Farmers Equity Society, the League for the Independence of India—all threatening to bolt if their pet projects were not included in the coalition platform—and Mr. David S. Beach of Bridgeport, Connecticut. Mr. Beach's entourage claimed that he had the support of the Committee of 48 for the presidential nomination. The Committee claimed it had "never heard of him."

Before the new party formally convened on Monday, July 12, Hearst's American Constitutional Party convened at Chicago's Auditorium Hall on Friday night, July 9. It instantly collapsed. Hearst's papers billed the Constitution party confab as a mass meeting, but only sixty-eight persons showed up. After an hour of speechifying, "Pa" Ferguson finally got around to suggesting that Hearst would make a fine candidate (and that legalizing the beer and light wine sales could pay off the war debt), but the next speaker, the Reverend George Chalmers Richmond of the Central Church of St. Louis, contradicted him, plugging Gene Debs for the job and pointing out for some reason that Boies Penrose was opposed to prohibition and "unfit to enter hell." After that, the gathering pretty much fell apart.

Henry Ford was also thinking third party. In the July 10 *Dearborn Independent*, Ford declared: "There is now no choice between Republican and Democratic candidates, between Republican and Democratic platforms; for that matter, between Republican and Democratic Parties . . . a movement of the American people, in rebuke of both the subservient Democratic and Republican Parties, would not be the usual 'third party'—it would be the nation seizing again its own control out of unworthy hands."

Not only were Hearst and Ford courting the new party; so were La Follette and North Dakota Governor Lynn J. Frazier, a member of the Nonpartisan League and another George Sylvester Viereck favorite. But as events unfolded, Hearst telegraphed convention organizers to decline any nomination and to strongly endorse La Follette. Governor Frazier declared himself "not available." Henry Ford, disgusted by the party's public-ownership plank, also barred a candidacy. Finally, so did La Follette.

The new group still didn't have a name when it opened for business on July 11. But it did have a prayer, albeit an unorthodox one. Dr. George Chalmers Richmond provided the opening convocation, but confessed that the gathering was "not concerned about heaven or hell." Richmond accused the GOP of "tak[ing] orders, not from Jesus, but from Wall Street," and blamed Democrats for having "sold out to those forces which face moral ruin and spiritual dissolution." He gave thanks for "the revolution in Russia" and "the new spirit of self-assertiveness among negroes."

Convention radicals (largely the Labor Party) outnumbered convention moderates (largely the Committee of 48) and adopted a platform including universal suffrage, an end to Department of Justice repression, recognition of Russia, Irish independence, the popular election of federal judges, a prohibition on judges declaring laws unconstitutional, and the nationalization of railroads, telegraph lines, water power, and a bewildering variety of other industries—including, for some reason, "large abattoirs." Wars could be declared only by referendum—unless, of course, the country was actually invaded.

Another plank called for full rights for blacks. A rumor swept the convention that a La Follette emissary, New York attorney Gilbert Roe, had demanded that the plank be pulled for "political expediency," contending that it would alienate white Southerners. Roe denounced the allegation as an outright lie, but the incident poisoned already deteriorating relations between the new party and La Follette.

Dudley Field Malone helped set the party's tone. "Let no one fear the term radical," Malone thundered. "We are all radical."

It appeared that many were also prohibitionists, even Malone, who was known to tilt a few. "I hope," he piously pronounced, "labor does not see its destiny through a glass of light wine."

Parley Christensen agreed: "I am in favor of prohibition. I think it is the greatest thing for the workingman that has ever happened."

On Wednesday, July 14, delegates placed Ford, La Follette, and Frazier in nomination anyway. Ford's name elicited boos and laughter. Other nominees included Malone and Christensen, along with Gene Debs, Assistant Secretary of Labor Louis F. Post, Cincinnati Congregationalist clergyman and former state senator Herbert S. Bigelow (kidnapped and horsewhipped in October 1917 after publicly praying for the "moral improvement" of Kaiser Wilhelm), and social worker Jane Addams (who also withdrew).

The first ballot deadlocked:

Dudley Field Malone 166$^{8}$/$_{10}$
Parley Parker Christensen 121$^{1}$/$_{10}$
Eugene V. Debs 68
Henry Ford 12$^{3}$/$_{10}$
Lynn Frazier 12$^{3}$/$_{10}$
Louis F. Post 1$^{2}$/$_{10}$
Herbert S. Bigelow $^{1}$/$_{2}$

On the second ballot, everyone but Malone and Christensen was eliminated. At 2:26 A.M., July 15, 1920, the convention nominated Christensen, 192½ to 174⅗.

Christensen got the news from a United Press International correspondent—several minutes before the convention secretary had tabulated the results. "I wish you had chosen Malone," Christensen informed delegates. "But I am not going to hesitate in accepting a call from a bunch like you."

They offered Malone the vice-presidential nomination. He refused it. So did Labor Party president Max S. Hayes, editor of the *Cleveland Citizen* and a former Socialist. Delegates proposed more than a score of names, including Henry Ford and Carrie Chapman Catt (Christensen said he wanted a female running mate, but without much conviction). Faced with the possibility of Henry Ford on their ticket, delegates begged Hayes to reconsider. He did, and the Farmer-Labor Party, which just days before had dreamt of a La Follette candidacy, was reduced to a slate of complete unknowns.

The actions of adopting a platform and nominating candidates couldn't paper over the ideological and temperamental differences between the warring factions of the coalition. Radicals had carried the day, but they couldn't compel moderates to follow their line. The party barely agreed on its own name. In the end, the Veterans couldn't stand for the pacifistic La Follette. Neither could the Single Taxers, dismissing him as a demagogue. Former Texas governor Ferguson wanted to allow the sale of light wines and beer. Dudley Field Malone and Parley Parker Christensen favored strict prohibition. Some demanded freedom for Ireland; some didn't. Some wanted to nationalize industry; some didn't.

Governor Ferguson bolted. The Single Taxers bolted. The World War Veterans bolted. Christensen and Malone aside, most 48ers had bolted when their faction lost on the platform. The Labor Party-48ers alliance had lasted exactly 29 hours.

Single Taxers returned to their own convention to nominate *Philadelphia Inquirer* reporter Robert Colvin MacAuley for president and 6'8" Cleveland publisher Richard G. Barnum for vice-president. MacAuley fumed about the labor union men—the "board of soviets"—that were really running the show and "rejoice[d] that we are away from the contaminating influence of that bunch."

The 48ers, joining together with the World War veterans and the mysterious Peoples Party, promised to nominate their own ticket—or, at least, their own state tickets. They didn't.

"Individuals who walk out are not worth considering," hissed platform committee chairman Robert M. Buck, a Chicago unionist, "This is no time for anything that is a compromise. The minute has struck for a radical party[,] and a liberal party is not worth a damn."

It was more radical than most realized. Aligned with the Chicago Federation of Labor's John Fitzpatrick was union leader William Z. Foster. Foster, noted the *New York Times*, "stood, but ill-concealed, behind the scenes throughout the labor deliberations. He had exerted a guiding influence in their every movement. He had hoped to see created a machine big enough to smash Gompers, and is intelligent enough to realize that he failed, if only through the fanaticism of the [radical] faction. . . ." Foster would soon emerge as a major operative in the Moscow-directed Communist Party.

Parley Parker Christenson tried playing conciliator. "We have all made mistakes," he begged, "but we must not go away from here and fight each other."

Christensen still offered to step aside for La Follette: "If in any way you can get Senator La Follette as your candidate I will not stand in your way . . . if you can get harmony with other groups, I am not in your way."

La Follette had better things to do.

Christensen returned home to Salt Lake City, his little white wooden home, and his aged, blind mother; had a parade in his honor; and pledged "to move the national capital from Wall Street to Washington."

His mother may have been impressed. Not all his neighbors were. "The news of the nomination of Mr. Christensen for president," noted Utah's *Grand Valley Times*, "will be received with considerable mirth throughout Utah."

Once it was over, one bemused observer concluded, "It was not a convention. It was a gathering of asteroids, where each little planet swung in its own circle; and, for all the group name, each kept its own orbit. There could be no agreement in such an assemblage, since there were no similarities of principles and no qualities of coherence, and after this fortuitous period of conjunction, each little star had swung along on its course again."

World War Veterans chairman Lester Barlow put it less poetically. "I have never seen," Barlow mused, "as many nuts collected in Chicago as in the last three days."

# Chapter 18

◦

# "A Mother's Advice Is Always Safest"

Women wanted to vote.

In some states, they could; in some, they couldn't; and, as of 1919, no federal measure guaranteed them that right. For decades, they had struggled for suffrage. In 1920, that struggle raced to conclusion.

In Colonial times and in the early days of independence, women *had* voted—in New Jersey, New York, Massachusetts, and New Hampshire. But by 1807, all four of those states had rescinded that right. The issue lay dormant until a women's suffrage movement emerged from the anti-slavery movement, most notably in July 1848, when abolitionist Elizabeth Cady Stanton proposed equal suffrage at the first Women's Rights Convention.

In March 1870, the Fifteenth Amendment theoretically granted male ex-slaves the vote. Women of any color remained disenfranchised. In 1878, Stanton's protégé, temperance advocate Susan B. Anthony, accordingly composed her own amendment: "The right of citizens of the United States to vote shall not be denied or abridged by the United States or any State on account of sex."

Nothing happened in Congress for decades, but some movement occurred in the Far West. The Wyoming (1869), Utah (1870; rescinded in 1887; restored in 1895), and Washington (1883) territories each extended the vote. When Wyoming was admitted to the Union in July 1890, it became the first state since New Jersey to permit equal suffrage. Colorado (1893), Utah (1896), and Idaho (1896) soon followed.

290

In 1887, Stanton formed the whites-only National American Woman Suffrage Association (NAWSA). Susan B. Anthony, the NAWSA's original vice president, succeeded her in 1892. In 1901, fifty-two-year-old Mrs. Carrie Chapman Catt, a former Iowa school superintendent and San Francisco newspaper reporter, replaced the now-octogenarian Anthony. In 1904, however, Catt resigned to care for her ailing second husband, George Catt, who passed away in October 1905. When Anthony died the following February, the grief-stricken Catt went abroad to mourn. State-side again in 1915, she resumed leadership of the now-disorganized NAWSA and proposed her "Winning Plan" the next year—an aggressive two-pronged attack on both the state and federal levels, designed to lead to final victory.

To many observers, Mrs. Catt appeared radical, upsetting the proper balance of domestic life. Nonetheless, she represented the traditional suffrage forces—and her forces were not negligible, two million paid adherents—but younger, less patient suffragettes wanted more and wanted it sooner.

Alice Stokes Paul represented the new generation. Raised in comfortable Quaker circumstances, Swarthmore-educated Miss Paul learned how the other half lived through service at the New York School of Social Work. Like Catt, she went abroad, to England in 1906, observing its settlement-house movement, continuing her university studies, and absorbing a more boisterous, aggressive style of protest, one willing to agitate in the streets and suffer for the cause. English authorities arrested Paul seven times, jailing her three times. During one four-week hunger strike, police force-fed her through a nasal tube twice daily.

Returning home in 1909, Miss Paul initially worked within the NAWSA, chairing its key Congressional Committee, but Paul wanted to run her own show. In 1913, she bolted the NAWSA to help found the Congressional Union for Woman Suffrage, which by 1917 had evolved into the National Women's Party. When the popular imagination envisions the typical suffragette, it conjures up Alice Paul's brand of militant activist: the feisty demonstrator, the vocal agitator, and, above all, the picket of the White House. In reality, such activists were atypical. Mrs. Catt outgunned Miss Paul, two million members to 25,000, but it was Paul's aggressive tactics that generated headlines and hastened victory.

Paul first picketed the White House on Monday, March 3, 1913—the day before Woodrow Wilson took office. In 1876, Wilson had thundered: "Universal suffrage is at the foundation of every evil in this country." Just after Election Day 1912, he patronizingly observed:

> The principal objection to giving women the ballot is that they are too logical. A woman's mind leaps instantly from cause to effect, without any consideration whatever for what lies between. She thinks too directly to be enfranchised *en bloc*. She would run into all sorts of trouble.
>
> For instance a woman's mind works like this: If she were voting and taking an active part in politics as men do, and if she was desperately anxious to accomplish a particular thing[,] she would ignore every obstacle that lay in her path and try to get it by instant, direct action. Now, in politics or in life, you must take cognizance of obstacles, if there are any. Logically they ought not to be there. You cannot always proceed in a direct line. You must meet obstacles as they arise, and deal with them the best way you can, and get around them toward your goal. A woman will not do that. If she can not do directly and immediately what seems to her logical, she won't play. That is the reason I think it inadvisable to give the women the ballot now.

Ten thousand suffragettes and their male sympathizers, in seven divisions, all legally assembled, gathered in Washington that March Monday to greet the new administration, but proper permits couldn't protect them from mob violence. "Hoodlums were allowed by the police to break through the procession," wrote one suffrage historian, "slap, trip up, spit upon and insult the marching women. Some on floats were pulled off, others were knocked down, and one of the most disgraceful scenes ever enacted on the streets of the capital shocked those who watched while the police stood idly by." An unnerved Helen Keller canceled her talk at Continental Hall.

Washington Police Superintendent Richard Sylvester soon "retired," and Wilson (who had detoured through city side streets to avoid the ruckus) reluctantly became the first president to receive a delegation of suffragettes in the White House—led not by Carrie Chapman Catt but by Alice Paul. Wilson admitted not having given much thought to suffrage, but said he would in the future. When Congress convened on April 7, 1913, Alice Paul had delegations from all 435 congressional districts present to greet it. The fight was on.

And so was the sarcasm. Writer, poet, and suffragette Alice Duer Miller wrote in 1915:

### Why We Don't Want Men to Vote

- Because man's place is in the army.
- Because no really manly man wants to settle any question otherwise than by fighting about it.
- Because if men should adopt peaceable methods women will no longer look up to them.
- Because men will lose their charm if they step out of their natural sphere and interest themselves in other matters than feats of arms, uniforms, and drums.
- Because men are too emotional to vote. Their conduct at baseball games and political conventions shows this, while their innate tendency to appeal to force renders them unfit for government.

The Republican and Democrat parties endorsed women's suffrage in 1916. Republican Charles Evans Hughes advocated a constitutional amendment. Wilson, still equivocating, merely urged the "action of the individual states."

Alice Paul persevered. Continuous picketing of the White House began on January 10, 1917, with just a dozen women. It wasn't their pitiful numbers that drew attention, but the sheer thought of the weaker sex, out day and night, in sun and rain, silently—and sometimes not so silently—challenging the formidable power, and the still more intractable will, of the most powerful man in America.

When America entered the war, Wilson regarded the armed conflict as another excuse for inaction. "I candidly do not think," Wilson wrote Mrs. Catt on May 8, 1917, "that this is the opportune time to press the claims of our women upon the Congress."

Alice Paul disagreed. On June 20, 1917, representatives of the

Russian revolutionary provisional government visited the White House, entering through the west front gate. Two Women's Party members hoisted a ten-foot-wide banner reading:

> To the Russian Mission: President Wilson and Envoy [Elihu] Root are deceiving Russia. They say: "We are a democracy. Help us win a world war, so democracies may survive."
>
> We women of America tell you that America is not a democracy. Twenty million women are denied the right to vote. President Wilson is the chief opponent of their national enfranchisement.
>
> Help us make this nation really free. Tell our government that it must liberate its people before it can claim free Russia as an ally.

Passersby shouted "Treason!" Men—and women, too—tore the offending banner apart. Woodrow and Edith Wilson (who termed these women "detestable" and "disgusting creatures") surely *wanted to*. Alice Paul vowed to order a new one to display on the same spot.

On Bastille Day, July 14, 1917, police arrested sixteen pickets for obstructing traffic, an offense punishable either by a $25 fine or sixty days in the squalid District of Columbia workhouse at Occoquan, Virginia. The pickets chose the workhouse.

Their plight outraged the public. Ellen Maury Slayden, wife of Texas Congressman James Luther Slayden, wrote:

> For months past[,] women have stood like wooden Indians, one on either side of the two White House gates. . . . The public never complained, but somehow they got on the President's nerves, and he ordered their arrest for obstructing traffic and [they] were hustled off to the workhouse. . . . They were denied the simplest toilet articles of their own, dressed in filthy prison clothes, given beds that were unspeakable, and seated at the table with the lowest drunkards and prostitutes, black and white, arrested on the streets of Washington. The conditions . . . are so outrageous that the publicity this affair gave it may save many a poor wretch in the future. . . . I was at headquarters when our culprits came in[,] and [I] could hardly believe my eyes. They looked ten years older,

unkempt, dirty and ill for want of the commonest conveniences and decencies of life.

One suffrage prisoner of conscience, however, Detroit's Mrs. Paul Reyneau, portrayed their experience in terms far less sympathetic to modern ears:

> Eighteen colored women, the overflow from the colored dormitories, it was claimed, were assigned to sleep in our dormitory. I bathed my face today alongside of a colored woman sent down for drunkenness. We were forced to eat in the same dining room as petty thieves and habitual drunkards, white and colored. Our rest rooms were the same. The prison clothing was coarse and the toilet facilities were poor. Altogether, it was a terrible experience, and we were willing to undergo it.

To their rescue galloped an unlikely knight, but one we have met previously: Dudley Field Malone. Malone, son-in-law of former United States Senator James O'Gorman (beneficiary of 1911's FDR–Tammany election tussle), was a long-time Wilson ally. He stood with him in 1912. He served as Collector of the Port of New York, supervising the customs service, collecting a lucrative $12,000 salary, dispensing patronage, and maintaining a wary eye on Wilson's Tammany adversaries. He helped salvage Wilson's California campaign—and thus his re-election—in 1916.

Malone hurried down from New York, waxed indignant, protested to Wilson (who ordered the women freed), threatened to resign as Collector, and, then, on September 7, 1917, amazingly did just that.

Malone was a knight errant. During the 1916 election, he had met a twenty-four-year-old suffragette from Omaha named Doris Stevens. Stevens was among those in the District of Columbia workhouse. When Malone and Stevens became romantically intertwined is unknown, but at some point it became known to *Mrs.* Malone. The couple divorced in the summer of 1921. Doris and Dudley wed that December.

None of which, however, was general knowledge in September 1917. Malone's ostensibly selfless act further galvanized sympathy for the movement. On September 24, the House voted 180–107 (3 answering "present" and 142 not voting) to establish a suffrage committee.

Suffrage's success paralleled Prohibition's. As the teens began, neither issue seemed poised for national victory. In 1915, for example, suffragettes secured referenda in four key Eastern states: New York, Pennsylvania, Massachusetts, and New Jersey. Their support was negligible: 42 percent in New Jersey, 42.5 percent in New York, 46 percent in Pennsylvania, and just 35.5 percent in Massachusetts.

Though prospects seemed bleak, New York suffragettes kept working, forcing another state referendum in 1917. Enjoying some upstate support, they nonetheless faced hostility from tradition-minded New York City immigrants and from Tammany Hall. "Was it not a well established fact," Mrs. Catt later wrote, "that reforms might sweep the State from Buffalo to Harlem Bridge and inevitably be vanquished by the reactionaries and the vicious of the great city?"

Tammany, however, faced increased opposition not only from Upper East Side reformers but from Lower East Side socialists. Pragmatically, it had already embraced an increasing number of reforms. In 1917, it endorsed suffrage.

Which was more than the *New York Times* did. "The amendment," it editorialized, "should be rejected this year by a majority sufficiently emphatic to put an end to the agitation at least during the period in which the minds of the people are preoccupied with the grave concerns of war."

New York's referendum boasted big-name supporters. William Gibbs McAdoo had long supported suffrage. His New York and Jersey Railroad had allowed women equal pay, and he had fought for equal pay for New York's female teachers. Theodore Roosevelt also now stood foursquare for the vote, his position evolving from studied indifference ("Personally," he wrote while president, "I believe in woman suffrage, but . . . I do not regard it as a very important matter") to support for individual state action in 1912 to, by September 1917, inviting suffragettes to Oyster Bay to plot strategy.

Observers expected a close vote. It wasn't. Surprisingly, outside New York City the amendment *lost* by 1,510 votes, but it swept the five boroughs by an astounding 103,863 votes for an impressive statewide majority of 102,353. The nation took notice.

In October 1917, Alice Paul had been arrested and dispatched to solitary confinement in the District of Columbia jail. Soon afterward, the facility's 22 suffragette inmates went on a hunger strike. Frustrated authorities released them that November. "Jail is Calm and Peaceful Again," headlined the unsympathetic *Washington Post*. Two weeks later, at Washington's Belasco Theater, socialite suffragette Mrs. O. H. P. Belmont bestowed "Prison Pins" fashioned in the shape of cell doors upon each of the 97 suffragettes who had served time. A band played "The Marseillaise." Dudley Field Malone spoke in their honor.

In January 1918, TR himself called for a federal constitutional amendment and demanded "an immediate addition to the Republican National Committee of one woman member for every suffrage state." Wilson, too, was coming around, partly from political calculation, partly from family pressure. Though Edith Wilson remained opposed, two of his three daughters firmly supported suffrage. "When I find two of my daughters such ardent suffragists," Wilson mused, "passionately devoted to the cause, and when I find also such refined cultured ladies as Mrs. Catt . . . equally devoted and conscientious, I must concede that some of my prejudices were unreasonable, and that the desire for the ballot cannot be limited to the relatively few agitators. A cause which could enlist the enthusiastic, devoted idealistic support of such ladies must be wholesome."

Where TR and Wilson led, smart politicians followed. In January 1915, the House had defeated the suffrage amendment, 204–174. On January 10, 1918, it passed, 274–136. Despite Woodrow Wilson's sudden support, Democrats backed suffrage only by a razor-thin 104–102 margin. Republicans voted for it, 165–33.

Suffrage—and its unequal application among the states—recalled a long-standing question concerning racial voting issues. The Constitution apportioned members of the House of Representatives according to population: men, women, children, blacks, whites, Indians, Chinese, natural-born citizens, naturalized citizens, aliens. It didn't matter what you were.

And so the Jim Crow South had it both ways. Blacks counted in terms of congressional and Electoral College power, even in states where they were illegally barred from the polls. If, for example, in 1916, Southern states had had their Electoral College votes determined only by their number of voters (i.e., whites), Charles Evans Hughes would have easily defeated Wilson.

The same principle held for women. In some states, women could vote for president. In some states, they couldn't. Yet, nowhere was this reflected in the states' congressional or Electoral College voting strength. Some advocated the logical change: penalize the non-suffrage states. The situation was growing more interesting by the day.

On October 1, 1918, the Senate rejected a suffrage amendment by just two votes, 54–30. Outraged suffragettes targeted four opponents for defeat: one Democrat (Delaware's Willard Saulsbury Jr., a close Wilson ally in the 1912 campaign) and three Republicans (Massachusetts's John W. Weeks, New Hampshire's George H. Moses, and New Jersey's David Baird). Saulsbury and Weeks fell; Moses and Baird barely survived. On February 10, 1919, the Senate re-voted. Suffrage now failed by a single vote (55–29), with 24 Democrats and 31 Republicans—including Warren Harding and Hiram Johnson—voting aye, and 18 Democrats and 11 Republicans—including Henry Cabot Lodge (whose daughter dared to smoke in public), Boies Penrose, and Frank Brandegee—voting no.

When the new Congress finally convened, however, it was far more amenable to women's rights. On May 21, 1919, the House again passed the amendment, this time 304–89, the GOP voting 200–19, Democrats voting 104–70.

The new Senate voted on June 4, 1919, approving the amendment 66–25 (the GOP voting 36–8, Democrats 20–17). The Amendment was going to the states. The struggle had taken so long that Mrs. Harriet Taylor Upton, who had first watched the debate as an eighteen-year-old on Susan B. Anthony's arm, now attended the 1919 vote as the sixty-five-year-old last remaining member of Anthony's board of directors.

Woodrow Wilson, who had campaigned for re-election as anti-war in November and led the nation into war in April 1917, now utilized the same acrobatic skills for suffrage. In July 1919 he *demanded* that Georgia ratify. Georgia State Senator J. J. Flynt shot back:

We are not willing to have rammed down our throat this amendment . . . which violates that sacred principle of states' rights and the spirit of which is in direct opposition to every principle for which the Democratic Party stands.

If the life of the Democratic Party depends on the passage of this bill[,] it is time for the party to die because this bill works in fundamental opposition to the fundamental principles of our party.

. . . the amendment was mothered by Susan B. Anthony and her kind of northern woman who were close associates of Thad Stevens and Stephen Douglas and who sought to put the black heel on the white neck and place the southern Negro in power.

Georgia couldn't act quickly enough to *reject* the amendment, overwhelmingly rebuffing it on July 24, 1919—the first state to reject federal action on the matter.

It was now, however, *de rigueur* for presidential candidates to endorse suffrage. If women could not vote in *all* states, they could vote in *enough* states to derail any national candidacy. Calvin Coolidge had voted for suffrage as a state legislator and more recently urged ratification as Massachusetts governor—as had Frank Lowden in Illinois. Palmer had voted for it in the House in 1915. In March 1920, Hoover claimed (quite possibly accurately) that he "had always been in favor of woman's suffrage." In April 1920, Wood endorsed suffrage, saying it would create "an amazingly better world."

The battle shifted to the national conventions. At 1912's Progressive Party Convention, Jane Addams had been the first woman to give a seconding address at a major party convention. Now, eight years later, hundreds of women served as delegates and alternates, and the fairer sex delivered seconding addresses for virtually every candidate.

Corinne Roosevelt Robinson and Alexandra Carlisle Pfeiffer did their cause proud in Chicago, but not every woman performed as magnificently. Illinois society woman Mrs. Fletcher Dobyns seconded Lowden's nomination, and, while a suffragette, she was also, as one observer noted, "a quaverer and it sounded as though at any moment she was liable to cry all over the speaker's seat."

Seconding speeches didn't satisfy Alice Paul. Outside the Coliseum, her forces displayed a huge banner reading: VOTE AGAINST THE REPUBLICAN

PARTY AS LONG AS IT BLOCKS SUFFRAGE. Delegates shook their fists at her pickets, shouting, "You won't get anywhere with that stuff."

Inside, as delegates stampeded to nominate Silent Cal for vice president, in the gallery, suffragettes unfurled a yellow banner, this one reading WHY DOES THE REPUBLICAN PARTY BLOCK SUFFRAGE?

Suffragettes bore down on newly minted nominee Harding—more so than against his Democrat counterpart. "Out of a world of sinners[,] we chose the most guilty," spake Miss Paul, probably not realizing the full import of her words. "We intend to campaign against the Republican nominee. We will make it impossible for him to leave his home, or speak at any meeting, without being asked why the Republican Party blocks ratification by the thirty-sixth state."

The Democratic Convention also featured distaff seconding speeches, but included a little something extra: rumors, however faint, but circulating nonetheless, of a female vice-presidential candidacy.

Mrs. May Jester Allen of the Republican national headquarters claimed to have been told by "a prominent Southern Democrat" that Minnesota's thirty-five-year-old Democratic national committeewoman Mrs. Anna Dickie Olesen, a fervently dry McAdoo supporter, was being seriously considered for vice-president. Mrs. Allen informed the *Chicago Tribune*:

> She can make speeches as no woman I ever heard can speak, but she comes from a small community and is not a woman of any vast political experience. She was a Republican two years ago, but she announced that she wanted to work, but wanted to work at a substantial salary. We had no such salary to offer her. She became a Democrat and is drawing a fat salary now in that party.
>
> I know the Democrats are planning to give the women all they possibly can, to lure their vote, and it would be like them to put this woman on their ticket. She is quick as lightning and a diplomat, but so far as I have been able to figure out, without qualifications for such an office.

Rumors also swirled around other women: forty-three-year-old Mrs. Annette A. Adams, the first female Assistant United States Attorney

General; Chicago's fifty-nine-year-old Elizabeth Merrill Bass ("a woman of culture and accomplishments"), chair of the party's women's bureau organization; and Tammany Hall's sixty-three-year-old Miss Elizabeth Marbury, a theatrical producer and one-time publicity agent for dancers Vernon and Irene Castle, a woman as Wet as Mrs. Olesen was Dry. Speculation, however, still festered that the word "he" in the Constitution barred women from the presidency or the vice-presidency.

Mrs. Bass became the first woman to preside over a session of a major party convention, and Democrats promised to dispatch five thousand female speakers to support the ticket. But opposition to suffrage remained, and not just from men. Mrs. Alice Hay Wadsworth, wife of Senator James W. Wadsworth Jr., chaired the National Association Opposed to Woman Suffrage. At one point, Mrs. Wadsworth lunched with Eleanor Roosevelt, attempting to enlist her in the cause. "I was very noncommittal," the once strongly anti-suffrage Eleanor wrote to her mother-in-law.

Mrs. Wadsworth warned states contemplating ratification:

> In behalf of this organization of women determined to uphold the constitution of the United States and the federal principle embodied in State's Rights doctrines upon which our government rests, I express profound respect to you for withstanding the pressure to which suffrage leaders boldly proclaim they are subjecting you and to which they boast you must eventually accede. We infer, you understand, that ratification cannot stand the legal tests bound to ensue in the courts, and that these cases, should ratification be obtained in time for women to vote this year, would hold up the election result and throw the country into political chaos, possibly necessitating a second election.

Twenty-two states ratified the suffrage amendment in 1919. January 1920 saw five more: Rhode Island, Kentucky, Oregon, Indiana, and Wyoming. In February, Nevada, New Jersey, Idaho, Arizona, and New Mexico joined them. It was steady but unexciting progress, but events in Oklahoma and West Virginia soon provided real drama.

In January 1920, Miss Aloysius Larch-Miller, secretary of the Oklahoma

Ratification Committee, though critically ill with influenza, left her sickbed to debate the issue against one of the state's most eloquent "Antis." Larch-Miller won the debate, but lost her life, dying two days later. Oklahoma ratified on February 27.

In March 1920, Democratic Governor John J. Cornwall summoned the West Virginia legislature back into session. The House ratified by a 46–41 margin. The Senate deadlocked 14–14, with pro-ratification Senator Jesse A. Bloch away in San Francisco. Bloch had requested that his vote be paired with a senator of opposing views (i.e., to cancel out each other's votes), but that request also deadlocked 14–14. As pro-suffrage senators stalled for time, knowing they lacked the votes for passage, the forty-year-old Bloch rushed back by train. In Chicago, Republican Party representatives offered to fly him the rest of the way. Bloch agreed, his wife refused. The GOP chartered a train for them, at a cost of $5,000. Complicating matters, one vacancy existed in the state senate. Back in June 1919, Democratic Senator A. R. Montgomery had resigned and moved to Illinois. Montgomery now demanded his seat back—to vote *against* the amendment. His bizarre request triggered days of wrangling in the state capitol. Bloch finally arrived on March 10, and the Senate ratified 16–13. (One opponent, having seen that the game was up, had switched his vote.)

On March 22, Washington State ratified unanimously, leaving one state to go. As Washington acted, Delaware's pro-suffrage Republican governor, John Gillis Townsend Jr., had summoned a special legislative session. Delaware's Senate voted 11–6 in favor. Three days later, its House rejected the amendment 24–10.

That was bad enough, but "Antis" worked not only to hold the line, but circulated petitions in a dozen states that had already ratified, asking them to now submit the matter to referendum. On June 2, 1920, the United States Supreme Court wrecked their strategy, unanimously ruling that no state referendum possessed precedence on federal constitutional matters.

By June 15, 1920, eight states—Georgia, Alabama, Mississippi, South Carolina, Virginia, Maryland, Delaware, and Louisiana—had formally voted no, leaving only five states in play: Connecticut, Vermont, North Carolina, Florida, and Tennessee. Suffrage stood little chance in either

Florida or North Carolina, but Democratic Tennessee and Republican Vermont and Connecticut held possibilities. If just one of them voted aye, the Nineteenth Amendment was law.

But their legislatures were not in session, and neither Vermont Governor Percival W. Clement nor Connecticut's Marcus A. Holcomb displayed any enthusiasm for calling a special session.

All of which increased the level of anti-Republican suffragette ire. At Chicago in July, suffragettes had demanded a platform plank calling on Vermont and Connecticut's governors to summon special sessions. Now they increased their volume. "For the Republicans to bring the Federal suffrage amendment within one state of ratification and leave it there," fumed Carrie Chapman Catt, "is nothing short of betraying the women of the country."

The Democrat platform did request Tennessee, North Carolina, and Florida to ratify, but everyone knew the game was in the Republican states, and Alice Paul and Carrie Chapman Catt kept their pressure on Warren Harding and the GOP. Miss Paul confronted Harding in Marion. He called on Vermont and Connecticut to act. They ignored him.

Few seemed to care what Calvin Coolidge thought, and Calvin Coolidge didn't particularly care what anybody thought. Pro-suffrage though he was, he refused to "interfere in other states," rebuffing any entreaties to sway his fellow New England governors. It just wasn't his style.

Yet Republicans could hardly be blamed for lack of action. They had clearly led the way. As Will Hays later tabulated:

> Of the 36 states which ratified, 28 called special sessions for that purpose. Of these special sessions, 18 were called by Republican governors and 10 by Democratic governors. Of the legislatures ratifying, 27 were Republican, 7 Democratic, and 2 non-partisan. The total legislative vote for ratification in 36 states was 2,545 Republican, 1,211 Democratic, 323 non-partisan, and 47 Socialist and Independent.

While Republicans and suffragettes feuded, opportunity arose in the Democratic South. Tennessee Governor Albert H. Roberts had wobbled

all over the lot, but he had promised to call a special legislative session—
*after* his August 5 primary. He won his primary and kept his promise. On
August 9, Tennessee's legislature convened. Both houses seemed
amenable, but the state constitution mandated that legislators ratifying a
constitutional amendment be voted into office only *after* any amendment
came before it (i.e., that voters know where legislators stand on such vital
issues before they take office and actually act on them). Thus, the present
legislature, elected in 1918, couldn't vote on the matter. National suffrage
would have to wait until 1921—after the presidential election.

The national parties were eyeing Tennessee with grave interest. If
Democratic Tennessee pushed suffrage over the top, while Republican
Connecticut and Vermont dithered, Democrats could undercut much
of the credit the GOP had earned. Some alleged that Tennessee Republicans would thus vote en bloc against ratification, just to deny Democrats bragging rights. Accordingly, Warren Harding wrote Carrie
Chapman Catt:

> I am exceedingly glad to learn that you are in Tennessee seeking
> to consummate the ratification of the equal suffrage amendment.
> If any . . . Republican members of the Tennessee Assembly should
> ask my opinion as to their course, I would cordially recommend an
> immediate favorable action.

But then Harding backtracked, writing to one Tennessee legislator,
regarding the state's constitutional issue:

> I have heard something about a constitutional inhibition against
> your Legislature acting upon the Federal Amendment, but I did
> not know of the explicit provision to which your letter makes ref-
> erence. I quite agree with you that members of the General
> Assembly cannot ignore the State constitution.
>
> Without having seen the document myself I should be reluc-
> tant to undertake to construe it.
>
> I have felt for some time that it would be very fortunate if we
> could dispose of the Suffrage Amendment, and I have done what
> I could in a consistent way to bring about the consummation of

ratification. I have tried throughout it all to avoid trespassing upon the rights of State officials.

It has not seemed to me a proper thing for a candidate on the federal ticket to assume an undue authority in directing State officials as to the performance of their constitutional duties.

I did say and I still believe it would be a fortunate thing for Republicans to play their full part in bringing about ratification. I should be very unfair to you and should very much misrepresent my own convictions if I urged you to vote for ratification when you hold to a very conscientious belief that there is a constitutional inhibition which prevents your doing so until after an election has been held.

I hope I make myself reasonably clear on this subject, I do not want you to have any doubt about my belief in the desirability of completing the ratification but I am just as earnest about expressing myself in favor of fidelity to conscience in the performance of a public service.

No, that wasn't *exactly* "reasonably clear." Harding's letter plunged suffragettes into a panic, an unease compounded when Cox penned a similar murky epistle.

Meanwhile, Farmer-Labor candidate Parley Parker Christensen had arrived in Nashville to show support, issue statements tweaking both Harding and Cox and their respective parties—and gloomily predict rejection in both houses.

Nonetheless, on August 13—Friday the Thirteenth—Tennessee's Senate, despite its state constitution, surprised everyone by ratifying with a comfortable 25–4 margin.

"Antis" prepared for a last stand in the House. Sixty-two of the ninety-nine representatives had pledged support for the amendment, including Governor Roberts's staunch ally, House Speaker Seth M. Walker. But just before the legislature convened, Walker switched sides, warning Roberts that suffrage was political suicide and employing a series of delays and procedural moves designed to thwart passage. As Walker maneuvered and cajoled, suffrage support melted away in the House.

Carrie Chapman Catt, in Nashville since mid-July, had cautioned supporters that the battle would not be as easy as it appeared on paper. With the outcome now in doubt, Alice Paul arrived from Washington with reinforcements—whether Mrs. Catt wanted them or not. Parley Christensen swung by again. William Gibbs McAdoo reappeared in the public eye to telegraph his support.

Forty-five-year-old Miss Josephine A. Pearson led opponents. Five years earlier, Pearson, a former girls' school headmistress, had promised her dying mother that she would fight women's suffrage if the battle ever reached Tennessee. Pearson had powerful allies. Liquor interests didn't want the largely dry suffragette movement to get the vote. Tennessee's railroad and manufacturing magnates feared increased pressure for women and child-labor laws. Cash poured into Pearson's coffers. Trainloads of Southern belles—not all from Tennessee—arrived to lend support.

Pearson, a jaunty leader of a lost cause, sported three red roses—as though they were the emblems of a three-star general. Other women—wearing red roses if opposed to suffrage, yellow if for—jammed the lobby of the city's Hermitage Hotel and the galleries of Tennessee House.

Not all was jauntiness. Pearson's message contained a strong dose of Southern racism, as she defined the three "deadly principles" of the national amendment: "1st. Surrender of state sovereignty. 2nd. Negro woman suffrage. 3rd. Race equality."

But "Antis" possessed no monopoly on prejudice. The Equal Suffrage League of Virginia had declared that claims "that the negro woman's vote will constitute a menace to white supremacy" were "altogether unfounded." The Equal Suffrage League of North Carolina theorized that "If white domination is threatened in the South, it is, therefore, *doubly expedient to enfranchise the women quickly in order that it be preserved.*"

Meanwhile, a breakthrough seemed possible in hitherto unfriendly territory. On Friday, August 13, a North Carolina State Senate committee—thanks in part to some urging by Josephus Daniels—recommended passage by a comfortable 7–1 margin. Tarheel State Governor Thomas W. Bickett also urged passage, arguing that America was no longer an association of states, but a nation, and whatever a majority of the people of the nation wanted was going to be the supreme law of the land. On

Tuesday, August 17, however, the full North Carolina Senate voted 25–23 to delay action until 1921.

In Tennessee, lobbying, horse-trading, and wheeling-and-dealing continued. "Hour after hour," recalled Carrie Chapman Catt, "men and women who went to the different hotels of the city to talk with the legislators, came back to the Hermitage [Hotel] headquarters to report, and every report told the same story—the legislature was drunk!"

From Washington, Woodrow Wilson wired Nashville a tepid message ("in the interest of national harmony and vigor") urging passage and infuriating Speaker Walker. Tennessee, Walker fumed, would never "surrender honest convictions for political expediency or harmony."

From the campaign trail, Franklin Roosevelt chided Warren Harding for his often-confusing statements on the issue. FDR, whose early career had seen similar waffling, dismissed the GOP position on suffrage as being "as clear as mud."

Leading ratification forces was the House's second-youngest member, thirty-year-old Memphis Representative Joe Hanover, one of only two Jews in the Tennessee legislature, who ran for office for the sole purpose of securing suffrage. He faced a barrage of insults, bribe attempts, and physical threats. Governor Roberts finally assigned him a bodyguard.

On Wednesday, August 18, Speaker Walker calculated that he had the votes and brought the matter to the floor. On the first procedural vote, Gibson County's Banks Turner, a supposed "Anti," cast a wavering vote for suffrage. Walker couldn't believe Turner had switched, but the House still deadlocked 48–48, an omen that the body would ultimately kill ratification. A vote to table also ended 48–48. Then came the crucial vote, formal concurrence with the Senate action. If the House again deadlocked, the amendment officially died. Walker called the roll. Called sixth was twenty-four-year-old Republican Harry T. Burn from McMinn County, in southeast Tennessee. Walker regarded Burn, the legislature's youngest member, as a solid "Anti." Burn, voting "Anti" in the first two roll calls, even sported an "Anti" red rose.

Burn muttered a quick, low "Aye." No one reacted. But suddenly it flashed on the assemblage—*the Nineteenth Amendment was going to pass*. A nervous Burn explained that although all might see the red rose in his lapel, they could not see the letter he had received just that morning

307

from his widowed mother, Mrs. Febb Ensminger Burn, writing from the family's 400-acre farm. Removing it from his inside pocket, he read:

> Dear Son: Hurrah and vote for suffrage! I notice some of the speeches against. I have been watching to see how you stood but have not noticed anything. Don't forget to be a good boy and help Mrs. Catt put the "rat" in ratification.
>
> Your Mother.

Burn explained that he realized that if his vote made a difference, he would have to cast it as his mother wished. His switch theoretically made the outcome 49–47, but what if Banks Turner wavered yet again? Turner fairly shouted his "Aye!" The Nineteenth Amendment passed. Yellow roses rained down from the gallery. Outraged "Antis" chased Burn from the house chamber. He made his exit via a third-floor ledge, hiding in the capitol attic.

Speaker Walker tried one last maneuver: "I change my vote from 'Nay' to 'Aye,' and move to reconsider." Walker now had forty-eight hours to twist arms and bring the matter back to the floor for another try. Twist as he might, Walker not only couldn't persuade anyone; in the bargain, he had outsmarted himself. Had his switch not made the final vote 50–46, the amendment would have passed with only a majority of the House's quorum, not of its full membership, and passage could have been challenged on those grounds. Walker's tactical switch removed that basis for challenge.

The next day, Harry Burn emerged from hiding. "I want to take this opportunity," he told the House, "to state that I changed my vote in favor of ratification because: 1) I believe in full suffrage as a right, 2) I believe we had a moral and legal right to ratify, 3) I know that a mother's advice is always safest for her boy to follow, and my mother wanted me to vote for ratification. . . . I desired that my party in both State and nation might say that it was a Republican from the East mountains of Tennessee, the purest Anglo-Saxon section in the world, who made the national woman suffrage possible at this date, not for personal glory but for the glory of his party."

His mother was also heard from later that day, telegraphing the League of Women Voters:

Woman was here to-day, claims to be wife of Governor of Louisiana [most likely it was; Ann Pleasant, Governor Ruffin Pleasant's wife, was in Tennessee campaigning against suffrage], and secured an interview with me and tried by every means to get me to refute and say that the letter I sent to my son was false. The letter is authentic and was written by me and you can refute any statement that any party claims to have received from me. Any statement claiming to be from me is false. I stand squarely behind suffrage and request my son to stick to suffrage until the end. This woman was very insulting to me in my home, and I had a hard time to get her out of my home.

Forty-five-year-old Febb Burn had become a minor celebrity—she had, after all, changed history by changing her son's vote. "Perhaps I shouldn't have used slang in my letter," she apologized to reporters. "But it struck me that . . . suffragettes had struggled so long to get their 'Rat' into ratification that someone ought to lend a hand when they needed it most, and I'm proud to say my boys and I are pals. And I felt that Harry would see me smiling at him when he read that—and know his mother was with him in what we both knew was right."

"The civilization of the world is saved," Governor Cox gushed from the campaign trail. "The mothers of America will stay the hand of war and repudiate those who traffic with a great principle."

"I look upon the enfranchisement of women," bloviated Warren Harding, "as an accomplishment to be rated along with our achievement of independence, our preservation of the nation, our emancipation of the slaves, and our contribution in the world war to the rescue of civilization itself."

In Boston, Calvin Coolidge was, as usual, far terser: "I can only repeat that I am pleased." He expressed hope that Tennessee's action would hold.

There was some doubt. "Antis" accused Joe Hanover of bribing Burn. Both denied the charges. "I preferred to disappoint some of my constituents," Burn contended, "than be false to what I know is right."

At 10:17 A.M. on Tuesday, August 24, Governor Roberts signed the official certificate of ratification. Safeguarding it to the U.S. mails, he dispatched it to U.S. Secretary of State Bainbridge Colby, who held the final legal obligation of certifying additions to the federal constitution.

The opposition still maneuvered. Charles S. Fairchild, Grover Cleveland's Secretary of the Treasury, representing the American Constitutional League (formerly the Men's Anti-Suffrage League), filed a ten-page motion with the District of Columbia's federal district court, alleging that Tennessee's actions had been illegal, alleging that only states had the power to control suffrage. His plea failed.

In Washington, suffragettes stood watch at Colby's 1507 K Street N.W. home, hoping to be present when he signed the proclamation of ratification, hoping newsreels might film the event, and quarreling over whether Alice Paul's radicals or Mrs. Catt's moderates should be present. Colby wanted no part of their factionalism. At 3:45 A.M. on Thursday, August 26, the State Department's legal office phoned Colby to inform him that Governor Roberts's certification had arrived. Colby said to bring it to his house at 8 A.M. "One and a half cups of coffee" later, Colby, employing an ordinary steel pen, signed the document. Not a solitary representative of the suffrage movement saw him do it.

Later that morning, at the State Department, Colby arranged to meet with both suffrage factions—separately. First came Mrs. Catt's group. All went well. Then came time for Miss Paul's entourage. Suddenly, and conveniently, the Spanish Minister arrived, and his visit took precedence. The Women's Party waited patiently. And waited. And waited.

One by one, they drifted away, until all had departed.

That afternoon, President and Mrs. Wilson received Mrs. Catt at the White House. Alice Stokes Paul was not welcome.

That night, Colby addressed suffragettes at Washington's Poli Theatre: "There never was a man," Colby proudly announced, "more deeply or profoundly convinced of the suffrage cause than Woodrow Wilson."

# Chapter 19

⁓

# "BACK TO NORMAL"

Now it was time for Republicans to assemble a campaign.

Normally, nominees replaced national chairmen, installing their own campaign managers at the party helm. In Will Hays, the Republicans possessed the country's finest political technician and tactician. Harding hadn't liked Hays at first; he was just a little too aggressive for the laid-back Harding's tastes. But eventually Harding came to respect Hays's talents and style and kept him on. Harry Daugherty would remain Harding's campaign manager, but he would have to work in tandem with Hays. The combination proved surprisingly harmonious. It is easier, after all, to get along on a winning team than on a losing one.

Just under Hays and Daugherty was forty-year-old Albert Lasker, Republican national committee vice chairman for publicity. Lasker embodied the American success story, rising from immigrant office boy to owner of the prestigious Chicago advertising firm of Lord & Taylor. There, he had created successful ad campaigns for such products as canned milk, Van Camp's Pork and Beans, Puffed Wheat ("Puffed Wheat and Puffed Rice, the Food Shot from Guns"), and Lucky Strike Cigarettes ("Reach For a Lucky Instead of a Sweet"). He specialized in "reason why" advertising, giving the consumer not just slogans ("Shot from Guns"), but also lengthy rationales *why* the slogans were true. Lasker, who had helped mastermind the Republican congressional victory of 1918, would now do the same for Warren Harding—but only reluctantly. Intensely isolationist, in 1920 he had donated $40,000 to Hiram Johnson's cause.

311

Depressed by Harding's nomination, Lasker threatened to quit the RNC. Hays and Harding had to beg him to remain.

Fifty thousand persons greeted the nominee's Marion homecoming, forcing his entourage to elbow its way through enthusiastic crowds. Once they were settled, Warren's boyhood friend Daniel R. ("Dick") Crissinger, a prominent Marion Democrat, praised him as "a real red-blooded American, neither too proud to fight, or too proud to work." Harding spoke of "normalcy" and shook thousands of hands. A front-porch campaign was being born.

To some, Harding represented politics of the lowest denominator. The *New Republic* dismissed him as a "reactionary . . . a party hack, without independence of judgment, without knowledge of international politics, without any of those moral or intellectual qualities which would qualify him even under ordinary conditions for statesmanlike leadership."

To popular novelist Owen Wister, however, Harding was cognizant not merely of his own limits but of those of office and government. "[Harding] will not try to be an autocrat," Wister wrote, "but will do his best to carry on the Government in the old and accepted Constitutional ways. For this I suppose he may be called a reactionary, but as I think that is the right way to carry on the Government it appeals to me favorably."

Calvin Coolidge was not happy. He wanted to be president or governor or senator or small-town lawyer or just about anything except vice president. But he was a party man, and if the party wanted him to be vice president, so be it. On Sunday, June 13, he wrote his father from Boston:

MY DEAR FATHER:—I did not call you last night because it is so hard to talk from here to Plymouth. I knew you would have the news about as soon as I did anyway.

Governor Clement called me right away. I hope you will not be disappointed. The enthusiasm of the convention is said to have been tremendous for me. The leaders had planned to name someone else but the convention ran away from them when an Oregon man nominated me, many other states followed and when Penn. was reached it gave me a majority. The cheering was very great and spontaneous.

Men who were there say the convention wanted me for President. That was prevented by some of the Federal office holders who were bent on having one of their own and controlled enough votes to accomplish it.

I am sure Senator Harding is a good man, and [he is] an old friend of mine. I hope you will not mind.

Your Son, CALVIN COOLIDGE

In Northampton, Dwight Morrow proved more enthusiastic "All the country is talking about you today, Calvin," Morrow said cheerfully. "Are they?" Coolidge responded, displaying more sangfroid than usual. "Well, by tomorrow they'll have found something else to talk about."

They did. Few people cared who Harding's running mate was. *Many* cared who Harding would align himself with: progressives or regulars, internationalists or irreconcilables. On June 18, Harding and Hoover breakfasted in Washington. Previously, Hoover had written to friends about being "greatly disappointed over some tendencies that were apparent at Chicago." Afterward, he told reporters that "Progressives can accomplish more within the Republican party than outside" and expressed faith that Harding would not "submit the administrative side of the government to the domination of any group or coterie."

Not all progressives bought that. In June, Kansas Governor Henry Allen wrote to Harold Ickes, pleading for Ickes to support the ticket. Ickes petulantly dismissed Harding as a "complascent [*sic*] instrument ready for manipulation by the big special interests. He is a platitudinous jellyfish whose election I would regard as distinctly detrimental to the best interests of the country. I can't let you tell me I ought to be a good boy and support for president a man upon whom the Lord conferred a bunch of wet spaghetti instead of a backbone without my letting out some sort of yell of anguish."

Meanwhile, Hays, Lasker, and Daugherty crafted the Harding campaign. It would be well funded, not so much because the Republicans had all the money, but because money goes to winners, and even now, with the public barely knowing him, Warren Harding looked like a winner. Orders went out for pamphlets and posters and 15 million celluloid campaign buttons, for the training of speakers, the renting of

313

headquarters, the purchase of well-placed column inches of newspaper and magazine ads.

The theme: normalcy, a return, as best as possible, to the established order of things, away from frenzied never-ending reform and expensive, pointless, bloody foreign crusades. On June 22, Harding campaign aide Ed Scobey announced: "One of his slogans is 'Back to normal' and another is 'America First.' In connection with the former, I think I can say there is no man better fitted to bring this country back to normal more efficiently than Warren G. Harding."

The Republican national committee issued a series of cheaply printed pamphlets for speakers, pamphlets that skewered the administration. "Speakers Series No. 11," entitled *A BILLION A MONTH: $20,000,000,000 IN ALL: What the Democrats Did With the Stupendous Mass of Wealth Taken From the People to Fight the War*, catalogued such examples of wartime waste as:

We had 617 contracts for 155-millimeter shells, on which we expended $264,955,367. None of these ever reached the firing line.

We ordered 41,000,152 pairs of shoes and received deliveries of 32,227,450 for 3,513,837 men.

We bought our Ordnance Officers 712,510 complete sets of spur straps or about 36 sets per officer.

We ordered $21,000,000 worth of ambulance harness and then found our ambulances were motorized.

Candidates are always their own best—or worst—advertisements. In Warren Harding, Republicans possessed a salable product, handsome, friendly, and kind, and people seemed to sense this. He may not have been profound, but his well-rounded tones sounded credible and reassuring from a platform. The question was: *Where* would he speak? Crisscrossing the country and haranguing the public at every hall and railroad siding might work for Bryan or Debs (or even for TR), but it was generally unseemly for anyone with a real shot at the presidency, particularly in these times. Selling calm and "normalcy," Warren Harding would have to *be* calm and normal.

Hence, the "front-porch" campaign: Have the public come to the candidate, by the thousands and tens of thousands, by car and bus and trolley and specially hired trains, to hear him from the confines of his own front porch. It *had* worked for the Ohio-born William McKinley and James A. Garfield. It *might* work for the Ohio-born Harding.

Another image compelled a front-porch approach: Woodrow Wilson. Wilson had flung himself cross-country, pushing his message, his League, and himself, destroying all three in the bargain. Harding's chances were good. His health wasn't. Best to stay home.

On June 30, over a waffle-and-chipped-beef breakfast at Harding's neo-Georgian Washington home, Harding, Coolidge, and Hays conferred. Harding told reporters that he envisioned a role for Coolidge beyond "mere substitute in waiting," an exceptional statement. Afterward, the two candidates stepped out onto the lawn. A newsreel photographer asked Harding to pretend to search for a four-leaf clover. Remarkably, he found one—and handed it to his shy running mate. Hays thought it a good omen.

Harding and Coolidge talked not only with each other; they also talked into a machine, recording stump speeches to be released on phonograph records on the Fourth of July. The idea wasn't new: Lodge had asked TR to make one in 1904. Teddy sarcastically asked if he should also make a Kinescope of himself dancing. TR finally did make such a recording—in 1912.

Harding's homily was entitled "Americanism." Coolidge's was "Law and Order." Harding's rhetoric was as up-to-date as a Grand Army of the Republic convention: "Let the internationalist dream, and the Bolshevist destroy. God pity him 'for whom no minstrel raptures swell.' In the spirit of the republic we proclaim Americanism and acclaim America."

On one occasion, the new technology failed Harding. August 31 was "Presidential Day" at the Ohio State Fair in Columbus. Republicans planned to crank up the Victrola and play Harding's addresses to the crowds. Fair manager E. V. Walbron (quite possibly a Cox appointee) banned the recordings. "Senator Harding lives within forty miles of Columbus and if he wants his speeches delivered at the State fair[,] he ought to come and deliver them himself."

Calvin Coolidge returned home barely long enough to pack for his annual vacation at his Vermont birthplace. Arriving at his father's white-framed farmhouse on July 4, his forty-eighth birthday, he donned his grandfather's old boots and denim smock, helped hay the 200-acre farm's meadows, cut firewood, milked cows—and worked on his acceptance speech. Thousands of well-wishers and curiosity seekers descended on the tiny hamlet. Photographers snapped his folksy activities. When the Democrats nominated Cox and Roosevelt, the news came via the horse-drawn Ludlow-to-Woodstock stagecoach—a day late. Coolidge had no comment.

Coolidge made hay; so did the campaign. On July 10, Harding followed up on his vague earlier statement promising Coolidge a significant role in the new administration, announcing that Coolidge would attend cabinet meetings. No vice president had ever done so. No president had ever seriously contemplated it.

The following day witnessed ominous developments. The *Ohio State Journal* warned that "already mean, low stories about the personal life of each [candidate] are being whispered about by their partisan opponents." Harding and Cox, it reported mysteriously, are "targets of the low-minded and the loose-tongued."

July 16 witnessed some rare bipartisan humor, when Vice President Marshall telegraphed Coolidge: "Please accept my sincere sympathy." That he wired Coolidge rather than Franklin Roosevelt may have given some hint of what he thought FDR's actual chances were.

The presidential nomination process of the era possessed a choreography as ornate as that of a minuet. Serious candidates rarely attended the national convention. If nominated, they did not address it. Instead, delegations would be dispatched to nominees' homes for formal "notification" ceremonies, usually occurring weeks afterward.

Thus, Harding's campaign officially commenced only on Thursday, July 22, with ninety thousand enthused citizens thronging flag-bedecked Marion. The ubiquitous Columbus Republican Glee Club was on hand. So were over a dozen bands and the silk-hatted Hamilton Club of Chicago, marching four abreast from the train station.

Harding's Mt. Vernon Avenue home had changed. Gravel replaced grass to keep the front lawn from turning into a quagmire. The flagpole from McKinley's front-porch campaign had been relocated from Canton, Ohio, its flag ceremonially raised and lowered each morn and dusk—often by the candidate himself.

The ceremony itself, however, occurred at nearby Garfield Park and its 2,000-seat Chautauqua Auditorium. Senator Lodge delivered the actual notification, a talk even Republican Mark Sullivan found to be filled with "waspy malice" toward the stricken Wilson.

Harding himself covered the usual issues: the tariff, labor relations, farm policy, government ownership of the railways, immigration, the high cost of living (it was always "the high cost of living" in 1920, never "inflation"), war profiteering, prohibition. He hinted at abandoning a League even with reservations. Two intertwined themes came from his heart. The first: his administration would restore party government and end "dictatorial and autocratic personal rule."

"No man is big enough to run this Republic," said Harding. "There never has been one."

The second theme might charitably be called humility or, uncharitably, a deserved sense of inadequacy. Harding pronounced himself "utterly conscious" of his limits. Perhaps reflecting on worse vices than cigarettes or chewing tobacco, he praised the Duchess as "a good scout who knows all my faults and yet has stuck with me all the way."

Genuine solemnity and a reverence for the gravity of events permeated the affair. Will Hays wept. Mark Sullivan marveled that it was "an atmosphere usually associated with churches."

There was, however, an atmosphere *not* usually associated with the sacred.

Olive Clapper, twenty-three-year-old wife of United Press correspondent Raymond Clapper, heard rumors that:

> . . . three newsmen, invited to dine at the home of one of Harding's widow neighbors, were, during the evening, taken upstairs by an innocent eight-year-old member of the woman's family and proudly shown Harding's toothbrush. Said the child, "He always stays here when Mrs. Harding goes away."

The woman in question was *not* Carrie Phillips; but Carrie Phillips remained in Marion, and Carrie's presence created a chilling fear for Warren Harding and those in the know in his campaign.

For whatever reasons, the question of Carrie's blackmailing of her

317

lover remained unresolved. In the wild enthusiasm, all the civic pride surrounding Harding's notification, a sour note revealed itself. Newspapermen noticed something odd that they talked about among themselves: There was one downtown structure bereft of red-white-and-blue, of any sense of joy: the Uhler-Phillips Department Store, owned and operated by Jim Phillips.

In Northampton, for Coolidge's July 27 notification, a solitary building also remained unadorned: Coolidge's own rented duplex reflected its occupant's own understatement and frugality. The nearby Edwards Congregational Church, however, wasn't shy. It hoisted a red-white-and-blue sign reading GOVERNOR COOLIDGE ATTENDS THIS CHURCH. Three bands played constantly from Main Street's specially constructed bandstand. Grace Coolidge served home-made fry cakes to guests.

Republicans asked William Allen White to give the notification speech. Petulant as ever, he begged off: "When they told me . . . I said no, and someone else did the job. I lost no caste with Coolidge, who knew about it. Maybe he respected me, who knows? For he was always more than kind to me."

A huge crowd gathered at Smith College's Allen Field, just blocks from Massasoit Street. Kentucky Governor Edward Morrow stood in for White. Harry Daugherty delivered a message from Harding. Coolidge's address was low-key—even by his standards. Coolidge wanted it that way. In his *Autobiography*, he wrote: "Not being the head of the ticket, of course, it was not my place to raise issues or create policies, but I had the privilege of discussing those already declared. . . ." The *Syracuse Herald* summed it up as "restrained . . . not political. It is indeed thoroughly characteristic of the man. There is nothing remarkable in it."

Bay State political rivalries simmered. Peering about the podium, Coolidge's mentor and friend Senator Murray Crane didn't like what—or, rather, *who*—he saw. "Who invited Senator Lodge to come on this occasion?" he snapped at Frank Stearns.

"I do not know, sir," Stearns responded.

"Did you do it?"

"Certainly I did not."

"Well, I would like to know who did it," Crane concluded. "He has no business here—he is not wanted."

Later that afternoon, Crane collapsed into the arms of Congressman Allen T. Treadway. Former Senator Weeks carried him into the Coolidge home. Doctors pronounced it sunstroke. It was a gross misunderestimation.

Carrie Phillips remained in Marion, too close for comfort. Reporters started hearing things. Even the *Literary Digest*, no purveyor of low gossip, reported: "one hears now and then [in Marion] that Harding 'is not an angel'—as the Senator himself would be the first to admit."

There were disquieting incidents. Professor Arthur Hirsch, head of the History department at Ohio Wesleyan, remembered:

I stood some distance back one forenoon when Mrs. Phillips was standing only a few feet away, on the Harding front lawn, talking to Mr. Harding who sat on the porch corner that he used as a campaign headquarters. With one eye on him and the other on the front door of the residence, she would take one cautious step, then another, toward the porch. Suddenly, Mrs. Harding appeared. A feather duster came sailing out at Mrs. Phillips, then a wastebasket. Mrs. Phillips did not retreat. Next came a piano stool, one of those old, four-legged things with a swivel seat by which it could be lowered or raised. Not until then was there a retreat. She tossed him a kiss and left quietly. Mrs. Phillips was then an attractive woman, with a neat, conservative hair-do, a housedress, and attractive shoes. Her face was especially attractive in contrast with that of Mrs. Harding. And she was well mannered and, in a neighborly way, congenial. I saw her several other times at rallies. At one, in the Marion fairgrounds amphitheater, she sat quietly in the crowd, while Mrs. Harding was on the platform with her husband. The latter had on a big hat with long feathers that kept bobbing this way and that, for Mrs. H. was a nervous creature, excitable and restless. While he was speaking, she would get up and shake her fist at, I suppose, Mrs. Phillips, get all excited, and sit down again. He seemed not to notice her.

The Phillips concern had to be settled. On June 27, Will Hays met with Carrie Phillips. On July 1, Jim Phillips and Harding conferred in

Washington. Finally, Albert Lasker got Phillips to agree to leave Marion for the duration of the campaign, traveling to Japan, Korea, and China, ostensibly to learn the "raw silk trade." The Phillipses hastily packed, not to return until 1921. They got $25,000 up front and $2,000 a month for as long as silence was necessary. How the money was raised, who provided it, and how it was actually dispensed remain unknown.

All this happened backstage. Front-and-center, party progressives struggled to make sense of their new small-town, stand-pat candidate. "He is a better man than Cox," William Allen White mused in July, "and his election will mean more to the Republic than will the election of Cox, dominated by Tammany. . . . Also, doubtless Senator Harding is a man of many varied qualities of mind and heart. But his fool friends are doing him more harm than good by exploiting him as a man of the McKinley type."

Meanwhile, prophets kept prophesizing. In early July, Orono, Maine astrologer George H. Bean wrote to Harding advising that he needn't worry about the campaign. On "August 4, 1920," Bean predicted, "the sun and moon, Venus, Mercury, Mars, Jupiter, Saturn, and Neptune will be on one side of the world, with Uranus in a continuation of the line on the other side.

"Isaiah xiii, 13, will be fulfilled and the nations who participated in the World War will be submerged in the Atlantic Ocean."

The campaign deigned to comment: "Notwithstanding Bean's prophecy, the Harding headquarters intends to keep open day and night until Nov. 2."

That statement's probable author was a forty-nine-year-old former *Washington Times* and *New York Sun* correspondent, Judson Churchill Welliver, now the Harding campaign's director of national publicity and "entertainment creation." Welliver was not impressed by his employer. "Harding," he wrote to Senator Borah on July 1, "is pathetically without color, atmosphere, ideas, or knowledge about affairs generally . . . an ignoramus, a sonorous fraud, a sounding brass. . . . He's awful." Welliver begged Borah to prod Harding on a raft of progressive issues. Borah promised he would, but remained fixated on the League of Nations.

On August 6, Murray Crane fell into a coma. Suffering through the summer and into the fall, he died on Saturday, October 2. The Coolidges' fifteenth wedding anniversary was Monday, October 4. They celebrated a day early so that Calvin might be driven to Dalton, Massachusetts, for the funeral.

All the Commonwealth's dignitaries were present, including Senator Lodge. *Boston Globe* reporter Robert Brady asked Coolidge about Lodge. "I don't think Lodge has many friends," Coolidge responded off the record. "He has a host of admirers. But there is a big difference between admirers and friends. Crane had friends[,] and those friends will stick to Crane dead in state politics. Lodge's admirers will stick to him until he gets his first setback. When that comes, you won't see many people sitting on the mourner's bench."

There *was* one comment on the record. Photographers wanted Coolidge to pose with Lodge. "I came to bury my friend," he snapped. "It is no time for photographs!"

Meanwhile, Judson Welliver's "entertainment creation" was proceeding apace. On August 20, Harding headquarters announced that buxom Gay '90s actress Lillian Russell (a former Progressive and Hiram Johnson supporter) would be campaigning for the candidate, but that announcement was soon overshadowed by a far larger event.

On Tuesday, August 24, Harding's front-porch campaign unveiled a dimension McKinley's had never dreamed of—four dozen stage and film stars, members of "The Harding and Coolidge Theatrical League of America." At dawn, a special train bearing Al Jolson and actors Lew Cody, Leo Carrillo, Eugene O'Brien, and Henry E. Dixie, actresses Blanche Ring, Texas Guinan, Wanda Lyon, and Alice Lloyd, and stunt girl Zena Keefe, chugged into the local station. Babe Ruth, a Democrat, was expected but did not appear.

The biggest crowd yet assembled in Marion awaited them. A fifty-piece band from Chicago escorted them to the front porch. For two hours, politicians talked and entertainers entertained. Blanche Ring fell into uncharacteristic stage fright on being introduced to the candidate. She recovered sufficiently to sing her hit "Rings on Her Fingers, Bells on Her Toes" with Florence Harding. Jolson puckishly whispered in Harding's ear that he wanted the ambassadorship to China, then provided the day's highlight, warbling a ditty he had written for the occasion:

We think the country's ready for a man like Teddy.
One who is a fighter through and through;
We need another Lincoln to do the nation's thinking—
And, Mr. Harding, we've selected you!
CHORUS
Harding and the G. O. P.
Harding on to victory
We're here to make a fuss
Mr. Harding, you're the man for us.

Harding spoke gingerly, first attempting to keep in tune with the festive air of the event, then growing more serious:

> The world cannot be established on dreams, but it can be established on evident truths. It is a perfectly normal humanity which delights in a new sensation. One can only pity a people which becomes blasé. It is better to be simple than surfeited. The new thrill is sought on the stage, and is sought everywhere in human life. Some of our people lately have been wishing to become citizens of the world. Not so long since, I met a fine, elderly daughter of Virginia who would have been justified in boasting her origin in the Old Dominion, and uttering her American pride, but was shocked to hear her say, "I am no longer an American. I am a citizen of the world." Frankly, I am not so universal. I rejoice to be an American and love the name, the land, the people and the flag.

The Chicago Federation of Musicians announced its support. So did the 43,000-member Theatrical Stage Employees and Motion Picture Operators unions. Lurking in the background—until Harding called him to the platform—was the party's 1916 presidential candidate, Charles Evans Hughes. Hughes proclaimed unconditional support.

At White Oak Farm, on the edge of town, the candidate and his Marion cronies mixed with Jolson's Hollywood and Broadway pals. Mixing it up meant violating the Volstead Act. "[Jolson] got drunk as a skunk," one witness recalled, "and sang 'Avalon' from the train depot platform. He just gave it all it was worth. They had to pour him into the train when he left."

The League of Nations simply wouldn't go away. Harding preferred to campaign on domestic issues, excoriating the dislocations in the post-war economy and the hardships of the high cost of living. Republicans pretty much agreed that the Wilson administration had mishandled just about everything since the Armistice. But they were not united on the League. If anything, they were far more disunited on the issue than were the Democrats.

In his formal acceptance, Harding dismissed the League as "con-ceived for world super-government." He planned to "approach the nations of Europe and of the earth, proposing that understanding which makes us a willing participant in the consecration of the nations to a new leadership."

His comments reassured Hiram Johnson and alarmed such pro-League Republicans as Root, Taft, and Hoover. Hoover wrote Harding, warning him not to "surrender to the worst forces in American public life," cautioning that he might lose California as a result.

For the next month, Harding continued drifting. His indecision, as much as the League itself, threatened to become a campaign issue as Cox and Roosevelt hammered away at Harding's "wiggling and wobbling." Harding needed a clear (but not too clear), bold (but not too bold) position—a moderately pro-League position. In Marion on August 28, he delivered a very carefully and tortuously worded major address (written in part by George Harvey), endorsing an "association of nations, cooperating in sublime accord, [to] attain and preserve peace through justice rather than force."

"I would take all that is good," Harding promised, "and excise all that is bad from both organizations."

The pro-League *New York Evening Post* translated Harding's remarks into "the language of every-day":

The paramount issue in this campaign being Republican-victory; such victory being threatened in the first place by Hiram Johnson's club; . . . such victory being threatened from an opposite quarter by discontent among Republicans who are convinced that national honor and duty call for the League; now, therefore, I, Warren G. Harding, feel it necessary to declare that provided I am allowed to keep Hiram Johnson quiet till election day, and provided that I am allowed to reject the League of Nations formulated under a Democratic Administration, I will, when elected President, be perfectly open to reason on this subject of the League.

Taft announced he would now campaign for Harding. Hoover said Harding's "association of nations" expressed "our views." Even William Allen White seemed pleased.

Borah and Johnson were not. Johnson remained aloof. Borah cancelled plans to campaign for the ticket and returned his expense money. Taft and Hoover might grouse, but they were adults. Borah and Johnson were wild men and, even at this late date, might bolt the party.

Facing such pressure—and sensing a growing shift in public opinion—on Thursday, October 7, Harding shifted gears. In Des Moines and in other Iowa stops, he now slammed the League, informing audiences that he desired not "interpretation but rejection." Wilson, he said, abandoning nuance, "favors going into the Paris League and I favor staying out."

He added that he was "in perfect accord" with Borah. In return, Borah pronounced himself pleased with Harding's "forthright stand."

The news shook Hoover, but he remained on board. Two days later, he spoke for Harding at the Columbus Club of Indianapolis. He continued stumping for the League, reminding the GOP (and its nominee) of its votes—albeit with reservations—for it. To demonstrate party loyalty, he blasted Wilson's post-war policy as "a failure by all the tests we can apply . . . with victory accomplished, the leaders of the Democratic Party . . . decided to ignore one half of the people and make peace alone."

Other pro-League Republicans felt betrayed. Yale economist Irving Fisher organized the "League Independents," ultimately numbering sixty-two thousand members in twenty-nine state chapters—eventually leading the organization into the Cox camp. Scores of prominent pro-league clergymen and college presidents (from Oberlin, Vassar, Smith, Bryn Mawr, and Mount Holyoke) ended up endorsing the Democratic ticket.

Prominent pro-League Republicans counterattacked. On October 14, Harvard President Lawrence Lowell announced a "Statement of the 31" (eventually 56) prominent pro-League Republicans still supporting Harding. They included Hoover, Root, Hughes, William Allen White, Nicholas Murray Butler, former Attorney General George W. Wickersham, Henry L. Stimson, Oscar S. Strauss, and the presidents of Columbia, Brown, Dartmouth, Cornell, Stanford, Johns Hopkins, Washington University, Union College, the University of Cincinnati, and the Stephens Institute of Technology.

Democrats and League advocates scoffed. "They would sell their souls for success," jeered the *Atlanta Constitution*.

Seven members of the Hoover League of Harvard, led by its twenty-eight-year-old president, Archibald McLeish, publicly chided their former hero, challenging him: "In 1860, if you had believed in the restriction of slavery, would you have supported Bell or Lincoln? Today, if you believe in the League, will you support the part anti-League Republican Party and its vague nominee rather than Cox? Is it you or the irreconcilables that Harding is double-crossing?"

Hoover didn't really know—or, at least, hoped he didn't know. In late October, he tried to reach Harding for assurance, but couldn't.

As the campaign drew to a close, the *San Francisco Call* quoted Hoover as saying that Harding still supported a League and that he (Hoover) had reached an agreement with California Republican Senatorial candidate Samuel M. Shortridge on the issue. Hiram Johnson snapped:

> Mr. Harding says he has turned his back upon the League; that he desires neither reservations but rejection of it and that if elected he will not go into the League.
>
> Mr. Hoover says Mr. Harding is going into the League.
>
> I believe Mr. Harding.
>
> It is stated in tonight's *Call* that Mr. Hoover has some understanding with Mr. Shortridge about the League.
>
> I believe Mr. Shortridge.

Yet both Johnson and Hoover remained for Harding. The incident revealed the awkward, stumbling, yet very real, success of Harding's low-key strategy. He might not particularly impress anyone, but he had performed the hardest trick in politics, holding a fractious coalition together. Save for Leonard Wood, virtually every prominent Republican—Taft, TR Jr., Corinne Roosevelt Robinson, Johnson, Borah, Hughes, Hoover, Lodge, Lowden—all campaigned for the ticket. "Privately," said one historian, "he gave satisfactory assurances to both factions, and publicly welcomed support by both. That he succeeded in keeping such diametrically opposed groups campaigning together is no mean tribute to his special talents."

The Republican campaign skillfully courted immigrant groups, most actively the nationalities most disgruntled about the peace—the Germans, the Italians, the Hungarians, and the Greeks. The Germans, of course, had to be wooed most gingerly—no use being seen as too pro-German (Franklin Roosevelt had fun when George Sylvester Viereck ultimately endorsed Harding—and Viereck had even more fun twitting FDR). Others could be embraced more directly. Fiorello LaGuardia helped stage a big Italian American Republican National League Rally in New York. Though he never quite got there, Enrico Caruso was to have made the pilgrimage to Marion. The ethnic politicking culminated with "Foreign Voters Day" in Marion on September 18, when foreign-born and first-generation American supporters proclaimed "Thirty races, but one country, one flag." It was two days after Michael Buda blew up Wall Street.

Republicans could also remind new Americans not only of Woodrow Wilson's actions at Versailles, but of his long-standing attitudes toward non–Anglo-Saxons. They happily resurrected Wilson's thoughts from *History of the American People*, regarding the nation's "wretched refuse":

> Now there came multitudes of men of the lowest class from the south of Italy and men of the meaner sort out of Hungary and Poland, men out of the ranks where there was neither skill nor energy nor any initiative of quick intelligence; and they came in numbers which increased from year to year, as if the countries of the south of Europe were disburdening themselves of the more sordid and hapless elements of their population, the men whose

standards of life and of work were such as American workmen had never dreamed of hitherto.

Ethnic groups would remember those words for decades.

Harding's team skillfully employed the newer advertising media of the day—phonograph recordings and newsreels—but one aspect of the GOP's newsreel campaign backfired, the ones showing him golfing. Harding *did* golf. Wilson had golfed. Taft had golfed. But Harding's golfing provoked unusual negativity among moviegoers. "It [the golf clip] has drawn a perfectly surprising amount of unfavorable reaction around the country," Will Hays wrote in a letter. "We get hundreds of letters saying it's a rich man's sport."

The campaign realized its standard-bearer needed to be portrayed not as a patrician on the links but as an American everyman, with a healthy interest in the National Pastime. Lasker, part owner of the Chicago Cubs, arranged with his partner, chewing gum magnate William Wrigley, for the Cubs to visit Marion for an exhibition game and a pilgrimage to the front porch.

Lasker tried getting the New York Giants to attend. The Giants, too connected to Tammany, begged off. So did the Cleveland Indians and world champion Cincinnati Reds, Ohio's two major league teams. So, on September 2, Lasker's Cubs competed against some local semi-pros, the Kerrigan Tailors, a homey, small-town touch that actually worked just as well. Completing the picture, Harding suited up and threw the first three pitches for the Tailors.

"You can't win a ballgame with a one-man team," Harding told the Cubs. "I am opposing one-man play for the nation. The national team now playing for the United States played loosely, and muffed disappointingly, the more domestic affairs, and then struck out at Paris. The contending team tried a squeeze play, and expected to secure six to one against the United States. But the American Senate was ready with the ball at the plate, and we are still flying our pennant which we won at home and held respected against the world. Hail to the team play of America!"

Harding might pose as a pitcher. He would not pose as a saint. Harding biographer Samuel Hopkins Adams would write:

Politics might force [Harding] to shiftiness, but in matters of his own personality there was an impatient honesty about him. With an eye to the church vote, his managers invited a writer of some note to accompany the candidate to the Baptist Church, of which he was a trustee, and write an article exploiting him as a pious worshipper. It chanced to be Communion Sunday and he was not a communicant. He flatly refused to go. Not for the committee nor anyone else would he parade a religiosity which would have been a pose.

Harding's front-porch campaign ultimately enticed 600,000 visitors to his crushed-gravel lawn. They came by car or chartered trains, representing Republican state delegations or farmers or veterans or businessmen or blacks or women or first voters, or, even, traveling salesmen. Each contingent, properly escorted by a brass band, would march up "Victory Way," festooned every twenty feet by white columns surmounted by gilt eagles.

In early September, with the heat of the summer behind him, Harding abandoned the front porch for the campaign hustings, a brief midwestern tour culminating in a detailed, and not particularly exciting, address on farm policy to forty thousand listeners at the Minnesota State Fair, with Harding's voice augmented by a forty-speaker system.

To some extent, Cox and Roosevelt had smoked Harding out, but he was also reacting to positive pressure. Republicans nationwide saw him as a winner. They wanted him at their side. And beyond that, the front porch had long since lost its novelty. It was time to give the public something new.

Harding proved a surprisingly good campaigner. Not nearly as energetic or frenzied as Jim Cox, he didn't need to be. Delivering 112 formal speeches outside Marion—in Indiana (20), West Virginia (16), Kentucky (8), Illinois (7), Oklahoma (6), New York (5), Tennessee (5), Minnesota (4), Pennsylvania (3), and Nebraska (2)—he also proved particularly adept at numerous informal talks.

In the first weeks—indeed, the first months—of the campaign, Calvin Coolidge did virtually nothing. He gave a few speeches in New England, but that was it. He barely ventured beyond Massachusetts. He barely ventured beyond his home or office. In September, he delivered a grand total of four speeches—all in the Bay State.

In October, the campaign dispatched Coolidge, Lowden, and Governor Morrow on an eight-day swing through the upper South—Kentucky, Tennessee, Virginia, West Virginia, and North and South Carolina. Coolidge thought it wouldn't do any good: Dixie was solidly Democratic and would remain so. The RNC thought otherwise, hoping for governorships in Tennessee and North Carolina. The whole idea irked the intensely practical (and often intensely irritated) Coolidge, who wrote Harding and Hays that he should not go "because I ought not to be away so long from Massachusetts and because my abilities do not lie in that direction."

He wrote his father:

I did not want to go on a trip. I do not think it will do any good. I am sure I shall not enjoy it. A candidate should never be sent on a trip of that kind.

To a reporter, he was even more blunt: "I don't like it. I don't like to speak. It's all nonsense. I'd much better be at home doing my work."

Nonetheless, the dreaded expedition went well. Crowds were more-than-decent (even an overflow crowd at the 6,000-seat Richmond Auditorium), the response as good as Republicans had ever received south of the Mason-Dixon Line.

On Thursday, October 28, provincial little Calvin Coolidge invaded Manhattan's exotic canyons for a nighttime march from Wall Street to Carnegie Hall. The *Times* predicted little enthusiasm for the event. They were wrong. Gotham's usually embattled and outgunned Republicans welcomed Silent Cal with open arms, triumphantly accompanying him from Lower Manhattan to Greenwich Village's Washington Square (where white flares erupted as Coolidge's touring car passed underneath its famous arch), to Fifth Avenue's Union League Club, to Carnegie Hall itself, where the candidate addressed an enthusiastic overflow crowd. With each block, the throng grew, until a full 75,000 Harding-Coolidge partisans joined in—lawyers; men from the dry goods and shoe trades; insurance brokers; railroad workers; college boys from Harvard, Yale, and Princeton; citizens from every conceivable occupation and nationality. A huge illuminated red-and-white HARDING AND COOLIDGE sign led the way. Marchers carried long electrified strings of red, white, and blue lights, transforming Broadway into a living, moving, pulsating American flag. Pipers piped. Choruses sang. Men donned silk top hats; women wore white paper pom-poms in their chapeaus; Coolidge retained his ordinary soft brown-felt fedora. Occasionally he rose to wave to the crowd. Even then, thought a reporter for the *Los Angeles Times*, he looked like "the least conspicuous figure in the entire procession." It was all beginning to look like a tide that would drown the Democratic Party and keep it drowned for the foreseeable future.

Oddsmakers certainly thought so. By October, odds on Harding climbed to 7–1—the highest on record. If it were a prize fight, Hiram Johnson jibed, "the police would interfere on the grounds of cruelty."

# *Chapter 20*

# "A PRETTY GOOD CONSTITUTION"

Franklin Roosevelt was a hit.

Most observers greeted his nomination with unalloyed glee. The *New York Times* praised his "fine record . . . unusual intelligence with sterling character. . . . The convention could not have made a better choice." *The Nation*, though faulting him as a big-navy "imperialist," nonetheless declared that "a finer type is not to be found in our public life."

"When parties can pick a man like Frank Roosevelt," journalist Walter Lippmann telegraphed FDR, "there is a decent future in politics."

And Herbert Hoover was not far behind Lippmann, writing:

> Mr. Franklin D. Roosevelt
> 2131 R Street N.W.
> Washington, D. C.

My dear Roosevelt:

The fact that I do not belong to your political tribe does not deter me from offering my personal congratulations to an old friend. I am glad to see you in the game in such a prominent place, and, although I will not be charged with traitorship by wishing you success, I nevertheless consider it a contribution to the good of the country that you have been nominated and it will bring the merit of a great public servant to the front. If you are elected you will do the job properly.

> Yours faithfully,
> /s/ Herbert Hoover

Others dissented. Henry Cabot Lodge wrote to a friend on July 26, 1920: FDR was "a well-meaning, nice young fellow [but] light. . . . His head is evidently turned and the effect upon a not very strong man is obvious."

On the other hand, nobody seemed overly enthusiastic about James Middleton Cox.

The firmly Democratic *New York Globe* called Cox a "man of mediocre ability and unimpeachable party regularity." William Jennings Bryan was less impressed. "Cox's nomination," warned the Great Commoner, "signalizes the surrender of the Democratic party into the hands of the reactionaries." Secretary of War Baker privately considered Cox a "doubtful candidate," acceptable only because Harding was "a zero."

Woodrow Wilson simply jeered, "They've picked the weakest one."

The big questions, however, facing Governor Cox were these: How closely to align himself with Wilson? With the administration? The League?

He had run as the outsider, a man apart from Wilson's battered team. That made sense prior to the convention, with McAdoo and Palmer and Davis splitting the administration vote. But now was time to mend fences, time to deal with the specter in the White House.

Cox—ignoring his campaign manager, Edmond H. Moore—decided to visit Washington to pay homage to the first party leader to lead the party to national victory since Grover Cleveland, but who had also created its current morass—and, to be sure, displayed little or no respect for Cox.

Wilson remained testy. He had wanted the nomination. He had thought that his friends, his cabinet, would help him. They hadn't. Ike Hoover recalled:

> On their return to Washington, the cabinet members met with a cold reception from the President. It was days before any of them got even the slightest notice and yet they were anxious to explain

their positions at once. He had not much patience with them and it was rumored that one would be asked to resign. Daniels was the first to make headway, for he had Doctor Grayson's help. Colby gradually got back in some degree through the influence of Mrs. Wilson; but one of them never did get back. He had no friend at Court or perhaps he did most of the talking and promising before the Convention met. He became a sort of outcast around the White House; the only one who even in a small measure helped to keep him afloat to the end was Tumulty.

On Sunday morning, July 18, Cox (in a conservative grey suit) and Roosevelt (quite jaunty in a striking dark-blue double-breasted jacket and blazingly white trousers and shoes) arrived at the South Portico of the White House. Fifteen minutes later, an attendant wheeled Wilson in. Despite the July heat, a shawl was draped over his shoulders. His once-confident voice was weak. He could not move his left arm. Roosevelt, who had not seen Wilson in ten months, barely heard him whisper, "Thank you for coming. I am very glad you came." They made small talk. Wilson remarked that Cox would enjoy living in the White House.

Emotion washed over Cox. He had never been particularly enthusiastic over the League, and, certainly, never supportive of Wilson's anti-reservationist intransigence; but now, eyes glistening with tears, he exclaimed, "Mr. President, we are going to be million per cent with you and your administration."

"I am very grateful," Wilson said, fainter than ever, "I am very grateful."

The interview ended. Cox confided to Joe Tumulty that he had never been so greatly touched. Facing reporters an hour and a half later, Roosevelt had little more to say than that Cox would be Wilson's "wholly worthy successor." Cox reported that the President was "in splendid shape," alluding to several amusing anecdotes Wilson had related. When reporters asked what they were, he refused to recount any of them. Like Cox's chances in November, they didn't exist.

Roosevelt somehow convinced himself that those chances were real. "Reports are distinctly encouraging about the sentiment throughout the nation," FDR wrote to Eleanor; but before Franklin could verify that sentiment firsthand, he needed a brief getaway. To reach his family at Campobello, he did what any enterprising Assistant Secretary of the Navy might do. At Boston, he hailed a destroyer. The *U.S.S. Hatfield* whisked him to Maine and thence to his Canadian island retreat (he worked on drafting his acceptance speech en route). Hearst's *New York Journal* questioned the use of "a warship for commuting purposes."

Roosevelt returned to New York on Monday, August 2, to open the Democrats' national campaign office. Present were George White, the Democrat national committee's new chairman, and Mississippi Senator Pat Harrison, chairman of the committee's speakers bureau, as well as fifteen members of the "Negro Democratic National Committee." FDR recorded some short stump speeches to be released as phonograph records, then posed with White for the newsreels: FDR on the balcony overlooking Lexington Avenue, White, inside, pretending to sign checks. "I guess I can do this in the movies," said White, "even if we haven't received any money yet."

He wasn't joking.

Wilson still didn't trust FDR, complaining to Daniels after the next day's cabinet meeting that he was "deeply resentful" of Roosevelt's shameless ambition and doubtful loyalty.

Franklin retired from the Navy Department on Friday, August 6, addressing two thousand department employees, receiving a replica of a Paul Revere bowl, and wiring his farewell to all naval personnel on land and at sea. He wrote Daniels that their relationship had never been marred by "a real dispute or antagonism or distrust." Though tempted to finally blast FDR, Daniels responded that he thought of himself as FDR's "older brother," adding a knowingly ironic reference to his subordinate's "beautiful home life."

The new Democratic national chairman, forty-eight-year-old former Marietta, Ohio, congressman and former gold miner George "Klondike Pete" White, was a personal friend of Governor Cox, but he did him no favors. In his first press conference, White painted the Wilson–Cox–Roosevelt meeting as an expression of Cox's support for "*the spirit* of the League" [emphasis added], and announced that "Progressivism [i.e., domestic policy] was the principal issue of the campaign." White's words alarmed sensitive Wilsonians. They—and Wilson—pressured White and

Cox to support the League. Cox panicked, vowing to make support for the League—the now-hated League—his campaign centerpiece.

Saturday, August 7, saw Cox and Roosevelt in Dayton, formally launching their campaign. Neither rain nor oppressive heat and humidity deterred the huge crowd of somewhere between fifty and a hundred thousand well-wishers. They carried thousands of placards, were serenaded by numerous bands, and lustily sang the Cox theme— "We'll elect Jim Cox or know the reason why."

Cox and Roosevelt projected confidence and harmony, marching, straw hats in hand, for over a mile through Dayton streets. Privately, FDR asked if he could attend cabinet meetings. Louis Wehle had come up with that idea months ago when he had first devised the abortive Hoover–Roosevelt ticket. Cox refused.

White-clad Arkansas Senator Joseph T. Robinson gave the actual notification. Missouri's irreconcilable Jim Reed was there with a "cynical smile" and a Panama hat, laboring to return to party graces. Joe Tumulty rode two days by automobile to attend. "The President is feeling fine," Tumulty dissembled; "I never saw him better." McAdoo and Palmer and Smith and Bryan were absent. It was a sorry show of unity.

The *New York Times* called Cox's two-hour, 10,000-word acceptance speech "straightforward, explicit, bold and clear." The *Marion Star* called it undignified. It may or may not have been undignified. It certainly was bold. It was also a gigantic mistake. "The first duty of the new administration will be the ratification of the treaty . . . ," Cox proclaimed. "The League of Nations is in operation. The question is whether we shall or shall not join. As the Democratic candidate[,] I favor going in."

A year before, going in was smart politics. Now it was questionable at best—by November, disastrous.

Two days later, at 3 P.M. on Monday, August 9, FDR's notification occurred, with Franklin delivering a pleasantly brief (3,114 words) formal acceptance speech at his Springwood estate. "I sympathized with my mother-in-law," Eleanor Roosevelt wrote, "when I saw her lawn being trampled by hordes of people." She might have sympathized with her husband more. Democrats sent out fifteen thousand invitations; only five thousand persons showed up. Al Smith, Josephus Daniels, and William Gibbs McAdoo attended, and Franklin also took time to invite many of

Hyde Park's humbler citizens, including the local tenant farmers, into his library for a reception.

Roosevelt spoke forcefully and with great skill. "We oppose money in politics," he vowed. "We oppose the private control of national finances. We oppose the treatment of human beings as commodities, we oppose the saloon-bossed city, we oppose starvation wages, we oppose rule by groups or cliques. . . . We oppose a mere period of coma in our national life."

Newspaper reaction was mixed. Democratic papers responded with appropriate praise. "A noble speech," lauded the *Louisville Courier-Journal*. Vance McCormick's *Harrisburg Patriot* hailed Roosevelt's message as "clean-minded, progressive, well-poised," while the independent *St. Louis Star* mused that it was, indeed, "spiritual."

Republican papers hated it. John Rathom's *Providence Journal* damned the talk as "a sophomoric, superficial composition in which the reader will vainly search not merely for statesmanlike breadth, but more any statesmanlike word." The *Manchester Union* termed it "demagogic." The *Harrisburg Telegraph* conversely dismissed it as "colorless."

The pro-League, nominally Republican *New York Post* loved him, though. FDR, it wrote, "gets . . . the last ounce of appeal power out of each sentence. The physical impression leaves nothing to be asked—the figure of an idealized college football player, almost the poster type in public life—making clean, direct and few gestures; always with a smile ready to share. . . . He speaks with a strong clear voice, with a tenor note in it which rings—sings, one is tempted to say—in key with . . . [an] intangible, utterly charming and surely vote-winning quality."

Mysteriously, James Cox's *Dayton News* response was tepid in the extreme. Wisconsin's *Janesville Gazette*, a Republican journal, took the prize for most enigmatic observation: "There isn't a single unladylike sentence in Mr. Roosevelt's speech."

Administration insiders heard what FDR *didn't* say. "Came back with McAdoo's," Josephus Daniels jotted in his diaries, "& we had jolly time. McAdoo was disappointed that F. D. R. made no reference to W. W."

Former Interior Secretary Franklin K. Lane couldn't make it. Instead, he wrote FDR:

DEAR OLD MAN, — This is hard work—to say that I can't be with you on this great day in your life. You know that only the mandate of the medical autocrats would keep me away, not that I could do you any good by being there, but that you might know that many men like myself take pride in you, rejoice in your opportunity, and keep our faith in Democracy because out of it can come men of ideals like yourself. I know that you will not allow yourself to become cheap, undignified, or demagogical. Remember, that East and West alike, we want gentlemen to represent us, and we ask no man to be a panderer or a hypocrite to get our votes. Frankness, and largeness, and simplicity, and a fine fervor for the right, are virtues that some must preserve, and where can we look for them if not from the Roosevelts and the Delanos?

It is a great day for you and for all of us. Be wise! Don't be brilliant. Get plenty of sleep.

Do not give yourself to the handshakers. For now your word carries far, and it must be a word worthy of all you stand for.

I honestly, earnestly ask God's blessing on you. As always,

FRANKLIN K. LANE

Cox didn't want FDR in the cabinet, but he did want him on the campaign trail. Roosevelt was handsome, articulate, charismatic, and energetic. Beyond that, Democrats had no margin for error. They had to get moving—and fast.

Franklin and Eleanor departed from Hyde Park the next evening, bound for Chicago. The following night, FDR spoke at the Coliseum, then boarded a special campaign train, the *Westboro*, for a swing through several key Western states.

A small staff accompanied him: the ever-faithful Louis McHenry Howe; Tom Lynch, serving as campaign financial manager; advance man Stephen T. Early, a former *Stars and Stripes* staffer; and wiry former Navy public relations man Marvin McIntyre—the latter two beginning long careers with FDR. Former Navy Department functionary Charles H. McCarthy ran FDR's Washington office, hiring a tall, blue-eyed twenty-two-year-old $35-a-week temporary secretary named Marguerite Alice (soon known as "Missy") LeHand. The National Committee possessed nowhere near enough resources to fund FDR's 8,000-mile jaunt, so Franklin kicked in $5,000 of his own. Mother Sara wrote checks totaling $3,000.

Aboard the *Westboro*, Franklin whiled away his time. Stephen Early grew frustrated at Franklin's "playboy" approach to the campaign. "He couldn't be made to prepare speeches in advance," Early would recall, "preferring to play cards instead."

Eleanor skipped FDR's first campaign swing but made his second, finally learning the nuts and bolts of campaigning. While FDR and the boys busied themselves at cards, Louie Howe—whom Eleanor still only barely tolerated—took an interest in her and, in what nobody had ever cared about previously, her opinions. "I was flattered," she remembered, "and before long I found myself discussing a wide range of subjects."

She still avoided the press, however, providing scant insight to reporters. "I gave as little information as possible," she would write, "feeling that was the only right attitude toward any newspaper people when a woman and her home were concerned."

She, nonetheless, became a valued campaigner in her own right, though generally restricted to addressing women's groups. Loosening her up on those occasions was Howe—by making faces at her from the back of the hall.

Franklin milked the Roosevelt name for all it was worth, mightily vexing Republicans. "If he is Theodore Roosevelt," the *Chicago Tribune* fumed, "Elihu Root is Gene Debs, and Bryan is a brewer." The Republican National Committee dispatched Corinne Roosevelt Robinson (to the Midwest) and Lieutenant Col. Theodore Roosevelt Jr. (to the Far West) to counteract Franklin. At Sheridan, Wyoming, TR Jr. told a group of former Rough Riders: "He [FDR] is a maverick. He does not have the brand of our family."

League advocates, like Roosevelt, faced the charge that Britain would control six votes (itself and its commonwealth—Australia, Canada, New Zealand, South Africa, and India) in the League Assembly, against just one for the United States. Reaching Butte, Montana, on Wednesday, August 18, FDR had been struggling with the issue for days. He now argued:

The United States has a lot more than six votes, which will stick with us through thick and thin through any controversy. For instance, does anybody suppose that the votes of Cuba, Haiti, San Domingo, Panama, Nicaragua and of the other Central American states would be cast differently from the vote of the United States? We are in a very true sense the big brother of these little republics.

Then FDR's muscular ego completely bested him, and he smugly intoned: "You know I have had something to do with running a couple of little Republics. The facts are that I wrote Haiti's Constitution myself and, if I do say so, I think it a pretty good Constitution."

In reality, FDR hadn't written Haiti's constitution; but if he had, he should have kept his mouth shut about it. Still, the worst was yet to come. "Why," he exclaimed, "I have been running Haiti or San Domingo for the past seven years."

Chaotic Haiti had been an American protectorate since July 1915 and the Dominican Republic since May 1916, so FDR wasn't breaching any great state secrets, but his timing was incredibly bizarre: news had just broken of a series of Marine massacres in Haiti.

He repeated similar boastings in Helena, Spokane, Deer Lodge (Montana), and Billings, and even in San Francisco five days later. When his remarks began generating national press, however, FDR resorted to his usual defense mechanisms of cravenness, noblesse oblige ("I feel certain that the misquotation was entirely unintentional"), and bravado. In Maine on September 2, he lectured:

> I should think that it would be obvious that one who has been so largely in touch with foreign relations through the Navy Department during the last seven years could not have made a deliberate false statement of this kind.

Republicans thanked FDR very much: They now had another campaign issue. In September, Warren Harding, already working with the NAACP regarding Haiti, vowed that he would not "empower an Assistant Secretary of the Navy to draft a constitution for a helpless neighbor in the West Indies and jam it down their throats at the point of bayonets borne by

United States Marines. . . . Practically all we know is that thousands of native Haitians have been killed by American Marines, and that many of our own gallant men have sacrificed their lives at the behest of an Executive department in order to establish laws drafted by the Assistant Secretary of the Navy, to secure a vote in the League."

FDR feigned outrage, dismissing Harding's charges as "merest dribble," sniffily wiring him:

> Regret to see in today's speech you have put into my mouth an alleged statement about the votes in the League of Nations of Haiti and San Domingo which I had already publicly denied making and which denial was printed in all the leading newspapers. I cannot believe you did this intentionally.
>
> F. D. ROOSEVELT

Harding, thinking his adversary a gentleman, wired an apology. "Because I am devoted to truth and courtesy," he added, "I am asking the newspaper correspondents to carry this telegram as conspicuously as they did the quotation."

A few days later, however, at Waterbury, Connecticut, Senator Borah issued a remarkable personal contradiction: "Franklin Roosevelt said at Butte the other day that he thought Wilson really put it over on the other diplomats on the matter of voting because when it came to voting we had Nicaragua and Haiti and other smaller American countries under our thumb. They immediately asked who put them there. Of course, then he had to deny that he said it. I am willing to admit that he didn't say it, though I was there and heard him say it at the time."

A month later, it got worse still, as thirty-one witnesses signed this affidavit:

> I heard Franklin D. Roosevelt's speech delivered in Butte on August 18, 1920. I heard Mr. Roosevelt discuss the League of Nations. I heard him say he had the votes of Haiti and San Domingo in his pocket and that he turned them over to Secretary Daniels, and I heard him say that he wrote the constitution of Haiti and heard him add "and if I do say it myself it was a pretty good

little constitution." I have read the Associated Press dispatch in which the speech was reported, and in my opinion, it is in all essential particulars fair and correct.

But the campaign had moved on, and Franklin Roosevelt had gotten away with it.

August 21 saw FDR in Centralia, Washington, site of 1919's Armistice Day massacre and the subsequent lynching of IWW member Wesley Everest. "I particularly wanted to make this visit . . . ," Franklin expounded;

> I regard it as a pilgrimage to the very graves of the martyred members of the American Legion who here gave their lives in the sacred cause of Americanism. Their sacrifice challenged the attention of the Nation to the insidious danger to American institutions in our very midst. Their death was not in vain for it aroused the patriotic people of the Great Nation to the task of ridding this land of the alien anarchist, the criminal syndicalist and all similar un-Americans.

Given the atmosphere of the times, it was safe, even a savvy, move, but it may have cost the ticket votes in radical Washington State.

He moved south. In California, during a violent thunderstorm in Fresno, FDR proclaimed James M. Cox to be "the Hiram Johnson of the East"—an ironic comparison on any number of levels, but most uproarious considering Cox's newly found passion for the League.

FDR often went on the attack, accusing Harding of "seeking the support of un-American elements in the electorate." He charged:

> Republican leaders are making open solicitation for the Italian American vote—doing deliberately the things which Theodore Roosevelt gave the last years of his life to stamp out. When the solid American people of the Republic see the hyphen brought back into national affairs and witness the attempt to divide our people in the interest of foreign aspiration and allegiance, they may well beware.

FDR was tireless. He traveled eighteen thousand miles, averaging seven speeches (some said ten) a day. On October 9, he took to the air, flying from Sedalia, Missouri to Kansas City—aloft for one hour and twenty minutes.

"Do you know that lad's got a 'million votes,'" marveled the engineer on his campaign train, "and mine's going to be one of them."

Such talk got to Franklin—Cabot Lodge was indeed right about his vanity. Halfway through the campaign, he asked financial manager Tom Lynch to consider a position with the new administration. "Listen, Frank," Lynch dared to respond, "you're not going to Washington."

"Why not?" FDR asked.

"While you've been speaking," Lynch told him, "I've been getting around in the crowds. They'll vote for you, but they won't vote for Cox and the League."

Others grasped the hopeless futility of it all. "The bitterness toward Wilson is evident everywhere and deeply rooted," Stephen Early wrote from Sioux Falls. "He hasn't a friend."

Sometimes the crowds were small—situations FDR quickly rationalized. "At Binghamton," he wrote, "the local people had difficulty in filling the comparatively small hall. That difficulty may have been due to the fact, however, that Babe Ruth and Madame Galli-Curci were in town at the same time!"

As his campaign ended, FDR arrived in Buffalo. Eleanor had wearied of four weeks on the road, tired of the travel, the hours, the inconvenience, and of her husband's often (necessarily) repetitious—and long—speeches. "It is becoming almost impossible to stop F. now when he begins to speak," she complained to her mother-in-law; "ten minutes is always twenty, thirty is always forty-five, and the evening speeches are now about two hours. . . , when nothing succeeds, I yank at his coat-tails."

Desiring a day at Niagara Falls, she obtained it only in Louis Howe's company. Franklin campaigned to the south, at Jamestown, New York, where, as she remembered it all too well, he was photographed with a gaggle of "lovely ladies who served lunch to my husband and worshipped at his shrine."

Meanwhile, Jim Cox's campaign had gotten off to a rough start. People worried about having a divorced man in the White House. Retired Harvard president Charles W. Eliot, a League supporter, pondered endorsing Cox, but Cox's divorce bothered him. FDR (narrowly having escaped divorce himself) provided advice on how to handle the concern, writing on July 31:

> [T]here has been divorce trouble in the Harding family. Also, Mrs. Harding was divorced by her first husband, and almost immediately afterwards married Mr. Harding. I hate, of course, to have this sort of thing enter into the campaign at all, but if the Cox divorce is made a factor by the opposition, you may be sure that the Harding divorce will be brought out also.
>
> He need not be in the least worried about the family record of Governor Cox. I hate, of course, to have this kind of thing enter into the campaign one way or the other, and I would not want to have my name used in any way. . . . His first wife was a really impossible sort of person, and everyone, including her own family, knows conclusively that the divorce was in no way his fault. As a matter of fact, the custody of the children was given to him.

Eliot endorsed Cox.

In mid-August, the *Los Angeles Times* interviewed Judge Willis Vickery, who had granted Cox's 1911 divorce. "The strong sentiment against divorce crystallizing everywhere, and particularly among women," noted Vickery, "will be one of the important factors which will contribute to the defeat of Governor Cox. A million voters who do not believe in severing the marriage relation will vote against Cox because he is a divorced man."

Anti-divorce elements might question Cox. Progressives eyed him with interest. Harold Ickes conferred with him in Dayton in August: "Cox didn't measure up to my conception of a Presidential candidate," Ickes remembered, "but he greatly outpointed Harding. Besides, he shot straight. He did not regard public office as a private bust. Moreover, he seemed to be sound on Progressive issues, and he assured me that while he believed in Wilson's League of Nations, it was not his intention to make an issue of it during the campaign, or to push it if he should be elected." Ickes enlisted in the Cox–Roosevelt Progressive Republican League.

Cox swung through eighteen states (each state west of the Mississippi, save for the safe ones of Louisiana, Arkansas, and Texas) in twenty-nine days, the longest campaign trip then on record. In California, supporters made him a "Knight of the Raisin."

Cox began 1920 as the staunchest major Wet candidate in either party; but as the campaign progressed, the Drier he got, frittering away whatever advantage he might have enjoyed. "My dear lady," he commented to a woman at Devil's Lake, North Dakota, "I have always voted Dry and I do not intend to interfere with the Seventeenth [*sic*] Amendment."

In Washington State, after meeting with Dry leaders on his campaign train, he proclaimed the prohibition issue settled—"I know when an event has passed and become part of history."

In Oregon, he dismissed the issue as "a bugaboo . . . as dead as slavery." He continued:

So far as the Presidency is concerned, the issue under the Eighteenth Amendment is one of law enforcement. We must judge men by performance rather than promise, and by comparison. As Governor of Ohio I enforced the laws. For the first time in the history of the State I closed not only the front door but the back door of the saloons on the Sabbath. I enforced all the laws. As President of the United States I shall continue to enforce all the laws, regardless of what interests may be affected.

By the time he had reached the epicenter of dry America—Kansas—Cox had almost totally reversed his earlier Wet position. In Hutchinson, Kansas, on September 30, Cox admitted that he would have *voted for* Prohibition:

COX: There were thirty-four votes direct or indirect on the prohibition enforcement measure in the Senate. Senator Harding voted thirty-two times Wet and two times Dry.
VOTER: Under the same circumstances, would you vote Dry?
COX: Under what circumstances?
VOTER: The same circumstances.
COX: I would.

An ill portent arrived with the September 8 Georgia senatorial primary. Mild reservationist incumbent Hoke Smith faced two challengers: staunchly pro-League, pro-administration Governor Hugh M. Dorsey (running with vociferous *Atlanta Constitution* backing), and anti-Wilson, anti-League, racist, anti-Catholic populist Thomas E. Watson (supported by Hearst's *Atlanta American*). The *Constitution* predicted an easy Dorsey win. Watson not only captured 102 of 155 counties, but he also carried his ally, former United States senator Thomas Hardwick, into the governor's mansion. Democratic National Chairman White gingerly termed the disaster "something of a blow."

Meanwhile, Wilson reigned but did not rule. At times he could be lucid, quickly grasping an issue and easily drafting a coherent response. But those occasions remained exceptions. Other incidents revealed how painfully sick he was. Once he complained that letters were not fitting in envelopes. An aide advised folding the paper in thirds. Wilson could not grasp the concept.

"I would read to him," his brother-in-law Stockton Axton revealed,

> . . . a great deal, back there in the autumn of 1920. I would read to him every morning and every afternoon. I would be reading to him, and he would be in a rather abject state, and occasionally would be seized with what, to a normal person, would seem to be inexplicable outbursts of emotion (he would begin sobbing, when there didn't seem to be anything particular in the text to call for it).

Soon after launching their campaign, Cox and Roosevelt had lobbed a bombshell, charging that a "gigantic Republican slush fund" had raised millions from corporations and special interests, spending the cash on buying the election.

On August 21, Will Hays responded:

> Mr. Roosevelt gave as the authority for his accusation "an item" he had "read in a newspaper." Mr. Cox submitted no evidence whatever. Both these men knew that the Republican National Committee had adopted a plan . . . for financing our campaign by a method of decentralized giving, securing small contributions from

345

a great many, with a limit of one thousand dollars as a maximum for any contribution. . . .

Knowing all this, Mr. Roosevelt asserted that our campaign fund would reach the colossal sum of $30,000,000 and Mr. Cox declared, apparently of his own knowledge, that millions have already "gone into the Republican treasury" from "certain interests banded together to buy the presidency". . . .

By reason of the enlarged electorate and the greatly increased cost of all things, we figure that there will be required a total of about $3,000,000, an average of about ten cents per voter. . . . The larger part of the total amount we hope and have reason to believe we shall be able to raise under the plan of limited subscriptions, which thus far has proved successful. . . .

Roosevelt dropped the issue. Cox didn't. Addressing two thousand supporters at Pittsburgh's Syria Mosque, he not only alleged that the GOP possessed a $15 million slush fund, but also produced a document purportedly issued by Republican national treasurer Fred W. Upham mandating an $8,145,000 quota to be collected from Republican organizations in fifty-one cities in twenty-seven states. "The hosts are marshaled," Cox warned; "the money ammunition is on hand, but it will not succeed."

Finally, he called out: "Is there anyone within the sound of my voice who is now unconvinced?"

A lone "yes" came from the gallery.

"What's that?" Cox asked—receiving no answer. "Stand up," he ordered. Finally, a man stood, braving audience catcalls. "You have not," he confronted Cox, "given the name of a single corporation or individual who contributed to the Republican fund."

"No," Cox admitted, "I have not named anyone, but I am turning all my evidence over to the Senate committee."

The controversy briefly jump-started Cox's drifting campaign, but the entire effort soon collapsed. Reporters grilling Hays and Upham observed neither nervousness or evasiveness, but an "attitude of elation." The Republicans were acting like they were *innocent*—and that the charges would soon backfire on Cox.

Hays and Upham reiterated their denials under oath before a Senate committee. Cox refused to appear. Chairman White did, but should have stayed home:

SENATOR KENYON: Have you any evidence, one particle of evidence, to present to this committee to sustain the charges that Governor Cox has made in his speeches?
WHITE: None whatever.

Democrats had trouble keeping what few Indians they had on the reservation. Their campaign was a mess, faction-ridden, divided on strategy, and beset with finger-pointing. Josephus Daniels confided to his diaries on Sunday, September 12, 1920:

Reached New York coming from Maine with the McAdoos. He . . . had urged Cox to declare he was opposed to the repeal of the Volstead act for wine and beer, for authorizing the sale of wine and beer would restore the saloon. That was Cox's mistake, he thought.

Saw George White and Pat Harrison at Democratic headquarters. White thought Irish were offish and Harrison said he could not get them out to speak. They do not feel hopeful about New York, but trust the good reports from the West. Very little money coming in and organization lags. I promised to give dates when I could speak.

In September, the campaign announced that Attorney General Palmer would stump for the ticket, outraging progressives. On September 17, a furious Harold Ickes wrote Chairman White:

I hope these reports are inaccurate[,] because I cannot think of anything that would make it more difficult for voters like myself to support the Democratic national ticket. . . . The Wilson administration reached its lowest ebb when Mr. Palmer was appointed Attorney General. I regard him as the greatest menace to our American Institutions and political system who has occupied prominent political office within my recollection. A few more A. Mitchell Palmers, or a little more of the one A. Mitchell Palmer, and we would have open rebellion in this country. He is a greater menace than "Big Bill" Haywood. He is a true anarchist. Instead of performing his sworn duty to uphold the constitution and laws of the United States[,] he has cynically ignored our constitution and violated our laws. He has denied to citizens their constitutional right and has outraged the sense of justice of the American people. He should have been impeached and driven from office long since.

Palmer stayed home, but McAdoo did campaign, undertaking a three-week West Coast tour to rally progressive support. Cox made a clear bid for Progressive Republican support, promising in San Francisco on September 18 to name Herbert Hoover ("if I can induce him, one of the best engineers in the country") to his cabinet.

Josephus Daniels wrote to his diaries on October 7:

> Spent the morning at Headquarters. . . . Mark Sullivan said Dems. had no organization in most Western states & that Progressives had all gone back. Progressive sentiment was dormant and Wilson had lost out. He said it was incongruous for Cox to talk like a preacher for the League & wear loud checked overcoat & sporting hat, & Reps. were circulating a cartoon showing the incongruity of it.
>
> Reps depend on Irish, Italians, Germans & Negroes & had them all docketed.

Hope glimmered in the border states. In October, columnists Mark Sullivan and David Lawrence wrote that Democratic chances had improved substantially in Kentucky, Tennessee, and Maryland, based largely on a backlash to "overaggressive" Republican efforts "in stimulating the registration of negro women."

"In Kentucky[,] the negro question is uppermost," the *Charlotte Observer* concurred. "The demands of the colored politicians are very embarrassing to the republicans [*sic*], who[,] unlike [Republican]

Chairman [Frank A.] Linney of North Carolina, are afraid to sit down on them. This has helped the democrats [*sic*]. Today, Kentucky looks fine for the Democrats."

To have been encouraged by news that Democrats might carry Kentucky and Tennessee, indicated just how desperate their situation was.

As Cox's frustrations grew, he attacked the press, particularly the California papers ("imbued with a narrow partisan spirit"), the *Saturday Evening Post* ("it resorts to devices of partisan editorial and insidious cartoon"), and the Associated Press. He ended up denying he had criticized the AP.

In California, Cox sought to counteract the publicity Harding had generated when he met with show-business folk in Marion. On September 21, "Jimmie Cox, Skipper" visited Hollywood's relatively new but already substantial First National Studios, where he "acted" in a little film, *Aboard the Ship of State*, and "disported a number of girls in bathing suits." The film was later to be shown at all First National theaters; but where Harding had attracted big-name stars like Jolson and Ethel Barrymore, Cox attracted none.

To a sizable Long Beach Auditorium assemblage that same day, he addressed "the Japanese question." In California, that translated into a general hostility to just about anyone Japanese—immigrant or native-born—within the state's borders. In 1920, the phrase referred to a November ballot proposition severely limiting the rights of Japanese aliens to own real property. Cox told listeners what they wanted to hear—he "would be bound by the constitution to respect the rights of states to settle their own internal problems." Even back in Ohio, he reiterated that opinion. "This," he proclaimed in Elyria, "is a white man's country, not a yellow man's country."

Such matters were mere sidelights. Cox hammered away at the League issue—or, more specifically, hammered away at Harding, deriding him as a "wiggler" and a "wobbler" and painting the issue as one of moral necessity. The League was "inspired by god," he informed upstate New York audiences. To be pro-League was to stand "for the creed of Christ and not the creed of Cain." But Cox wiggled nearly as much as his opponent. Beginning the campaign by supporting reservations (included reservations regarding Article X) and America's right to withdraw from the League "at the first evidence of bad faith," Cox ended it by pledging cooperation with the Congress to secure ratification—and to accept any reasonable reservation offered. It was a distinctly non-Wilsonian position.

FDR simultaneously postured and wobbled, advocating "reasonable reservations" and contending that no provisions in the treaty were "in any way superior to our Constitution or in any way interfere with the rights of Congress to declare war or send our soldiers overseas." The *New York Times* pondered aloud why Woodrow Wilson might take comfort in such support.

In mid-October, Cox, through Speakers Bureau chairman Senator Pat Harrison, challenged Harding to a face-to-face debate on the League. "I would not for a moment," Harrison's Republican counterpart, Indiana Senator Harry New, sniffed, "consider a proposition so utterly absurd." In 1920, nobody seriously disagreed with New.

Cox had nonetheless undertaken the most ambitious presidential campaign to date, visiting 36 states (skipping only Maine, Vermont, and ten Solid South states), and delivering 394 formal speeches (26 on a single day) and scores more of informal talks (in Portland, Oregon, Cox's voice gave out, and a masseur massaged his throat). He traveled twenty-two thousand miles and addressed two million persons.

"I think the picture the public has of [Cox]," wrote Mark Sullivan, "is that of a game young lightweight prize fighter, dancing about and delivering the best punches he knows how against an opponent who is more heavy and solid, but less active."

That was in part the problem. Cox landed a few punches, but most missed their mark. "Cox," concluded Sullivan, "practiced an aggressiveness, which did not move the country[,] merely jarred it, made it lean farther toward Harding."

If it *seemed* that Cox campaigned at breakneck pace, he literally *was* doing so. At Jacksontown, Ohio, a notorious speed trap, four motorcycle policemen pulled over Cox's car as it returned from West Virginia, ordering his chauffeur to appear in court. Cox commanded him to drive on. Later that day, a group of reporters covering his campaign crashed and totaled their car.

On September 22, the Cox campaign train derailed north of Peoria,

Arizona, badly jarring passengers. Unhurt, Cox aided the injured. Awaiting a new train, he sat calmly smoking his pipe.

On August 28, Cox addressed a huge throng gathered at Brooklyn's Gravesend Race Track for the city's annual police department games. Officials installed a "Magnavox" device, "a combination of telemega-phones," to amplify his message. Three hundred thousand persons attended, though many still could not hear his words.

Woodrow Wilson remained silent—locked away in the White House, invisible and glowering, hopeful of a Cox victory, contemptuous of both Cox and Roosevelt, sullenly contemptuous really of everyone. "When the Convention was over and Cox had been nominated," Ike Hoover observed, "there was no interest left in the campaign, so far as the White House occupants were concerned."

Yet there remained a vague, weird optimism. Josephus Daniels and Stockton Axton, Wilson's brother-in-law, tried warning him, but he refused to listen. "You pessimist!" he snapped at Axton. "You don't know the American people. They always rise to a moral occasion. Harding will be deluged."

Joe Tumulty advised Wilson to take action, to outline his message to the American public. He hadn't, and people noticed. In September, Franklin K. Lane wrote to a friend:

> Things look dark to me politically. The little Wilson (as distin-guished from the Great Wilson) is now having his day. Cox is making a manly fight on behalf of the President's League, but the administration is sullen, is doing nothing. Cox will be defeated not by those who dislike him but by those who dislike Wilson and his group. This seems mighty unjust.

On September 16, Tumulty wrote Wilson, again begging him to take action. He got no response. In October, Tumulty reported "a slight drift towards Cox" but warned, "unless you take advantage of it and speed it up, there is very little hope."

"Of course, I will help," Wilson snapped, "I was under the impression I was helping. But I will do it at my own time and in my own way."

But it was *October*. "At my own time" needed to be *soon*.

On Thursday, October 21, thirteen days before the election, Cox desperately begged Edith Wilson to bring her husband to meet him in New York City. Why Cox believed Wilson could travel is unknown. Perhaps he inhabited the same dreamland Wilson lived in. Perhaps he didn't want to risk again playing supplicant to the White House. Edith Wilson responded the next day. Her husband would attend only "if it were physically possible."

On Wednesday, October 28, six days before the election, Wilson issued his first campaign statement, addressing fifteen pro-League Republicans in the White House Green Room. Confined to his "rolling chair," he seemed not to recognize any of them—though he knew some personally. Failing to mention Cox, he fixated on Article X. They strained forward to hear the pale, weak, "nearly inaudible" man before them—and still could not. His voice was unnatural, without force, without power—though not without emotion. Only fifteen persons stood before him, but his prepared statement began "My fellow countrymen," as though he were addressing some great throng in New York, or Chicago, or . . . Pueblo. They left describing his appearance as "nothing less than tragic."

It was.

## Chapter 21

~

# "Wake up, Ethiopia!"

Downhill.

It had been downhill for black Americans for a long time—since, in fact, the passage of the Fifteenth Amendment in February 1870. The poll tax, the white primary (only whites could belong to the Democratic Party in many Southern states), and literacy tests had systematically eviscerated their voting rights. In 1892, the Supreme Court's *Plessy v. Ferguson* decision merely affirmed an existing pattern of separate but "equal" public accommodations. They rarely were.

Black Americans were second-class citizens with third-class options. The white South was arrayed solidly against them. The white North remained solidly apathetic. No, the attitude was worse than apathy. The North had switched sides. White Northern sympathies now resided with their white Southern brothers. "The plain fact is," wrote progressive Ray Stannard Baker in 1909, "most of us in the north do not believe in any real democracy as between white and colored men."

Freed blacks existed in a nether world. No one argued to return blacks to slavery, but few whites thought them capable of self-government or self-reliance—or much of anything else, for that matter.

In such a dismal atmosphere, educator Booker T. Washington had emerged as black America's spokesman. In September 1895, Washington, addressing the Atlanta Cotton Exposition, delivered the most famous elucidation of his philosophy, assuring white Southerners:

As we have proved our loyalty to you in the past . . . we shall stand by you with a devotion that no foreigner can approach, ready to lay down our lives, if need be, in defense of yours, interlacing our industrial, commercial, civil, and religious life with yours in a way that shall make the interests of both races one. In all things that are purely social we can be as separate as the fingers, yet one as the hand in all things essential to mutual progress.

Whites applauded. Jim Crow worsened. Among the first to question Booker Washington's tactics were two college-educated black men, Harvard's first black Phi Beta Kappa, William Monroe Trotter, and Amherst's George Forbes. Founding the acerbic *Boston Guardian* in 1901, they accommodated themselves neither to Jim Crow nor to Booker Washington. "It would be," fumed Forbes, "a blessing for the race if [Washington's] Tuskegee school should burn down."

In October 1901, Theodore Roosevelt invited Washington to dine privately at the White House. A reporter read the White House guest book and printed a brief report of the meeting. The white South erupted in rage. TR, shouted the *Memphis Scimitar*, had committed "the most damnable outrage ever perpetrated by any citizen of the United States when he invited a nigger to dine with him in the White House."

In such an atmosphere operated American race relations.

The few blacks who dared vote tended to vote Republican. The Republican Party in the South possessed large African American contingents, but they accomplished little beyond providing delegates to national conventions, securing small amounts of federal patronage, and reminding Southern Democrats why they were Democrats.

TR's progressivism failed to strengthen the bonds between blacks and the GOP. Roosevelt never again invited Washington to the White House. In August 1906, after being refused service at local saloons, several unidentified black infantrymen shot up the town of Brownsville, Texas. Fearful of losing black votes, TR waited until after that November's congressional elections before acquiescing in the dishonorable discharge of 167 black servicemen. Blacks felt abandoned.

It got worse under Taft. In his March 1909 inaugural address, Taft promised to not appoint blacks to Southern patronage positions if whites objected ("in recognizing the negro race by appointments, one must exercise a careful discretion not thereby to do it more harm than good"). Trotter and fellow black activist and Harvard graduate W. E. B. Du Bois took a chance and supported Woodrow Wilson in 1912.

Wilson repaid them by segregating federal offices to an unprecedented extent. "We were cruelly disappointed when the Democratic party won and the next Congress met," Du Bois wrote. "There was the greatest flood of discriminatory bills both in Congress and among the States that has probably ever been introduced since the Civil War."

On November 12, 1914, Trotter led a delegation to the White House. "Segregation is not humiliating," Wilson lectured them, "but a benefit and ought to so be regarded by you gentlemen." Trotter reminded Wilson of his 1912 campaign promises, and Wilson accused him of political blackmail, sniping that if black Americans felt betrayed after voting for him in 1912, they need not do so again. Trotter persisted, and the outraged Wilson ("You have spoiled the whole cause for which you came") showed him the door, advising the others to obtain a new leader if they wanted to return.

Du Bois now ruefully admitted, "We do not believe Woodrow Wilson admires Negroes."

Third parties weren't much friendlier. Frustrated by the failure of Southern Republican efforts involving blacks—and angered by machine manipulation of black convention delegates—TR's Progressive Party angrily spurned Southern blacks. "The Progressive party in the South," Roosevelt announced, "should be a white party with such colored members as the whites found acceptable."

Nor could blacks count on the even farther-left. In March 1912, Socialist leader Kate Richards O'Hare published a particularly virulent pro-segregation article in an official party publication. It asked:

What is the solution of the race question?

There can be but one. Segregation. If you ask me what I am going to work and speak and write and vote for on the race question, when it is to be settled under a Socialist form of government, I can tell you very quickly. Let us give the blacks one section in the country where every condition is best fitted for them.

Socialists printed 30,000 copies.

Blacks suffered from official Jim Crow segregation, widespread unofficial discrimination, and, in the South, a general abrogation of voting rights—and, most ominously, lynching.

Between 1882 and 1968, 3,446 blacks (of 4,743 total lynching victims) were lynched nationwide. In 1920, 61 persons were lynched—down from 83 in 1919 and further down from 1892's peak of 230 (161 blacks and 69 whites).

Fifty-two of 1920's 61 lynchings occurred in the South, mostly in a handful of states—10 in Texas, 9 in Georgia, 7 in Alabama, and 7 in Florida. Eight victims were white. One was a woman, a black woman. Mobs seized 42 victims from jails or law enforcement custody. In only 14 instances did authorities resist, but in those cases seven attackers died. Fifty-six times, authorities successfully prevented lynchings. One victim was lynched for insisting on the right to vote. Three were burned to death.

From 1882 to 1951, 25.3 percent of lynchings involved accusations of rape or attempted rape. In 1920, 15 victims were accused of rape, 3 of attempted rape, 9 of insulting women, and 1 of peeping through a window.

In July 1920, a Senate committee heard testimony regarding voting rights—or their absence—in Georgia. Henry Lincoln Johnson testified that black Republicans often simply "disappeared" and that "brutal force or suppression" prevented an estimated 85 percent of Georgia's black citizens from voting. "They don't lynch men for belonging to the Republican party, do they?" inquired Iowa's Senator William S. Kenyon.

"Many a negro voting the Republican ticket has disappeared and no tidings have ever been heard of him."

The *Atlanta Constitution* headlined: NEGRO GOP CHIEF USES IMAGINATION.

World War I may not have changed everything for blacks, but it changed a great deal. Prior to 1914, the South took the African American for granted. He was subservient and would stay subservient. The North and West pretty much ignored him. Most whites outside the South rarely saw a black person. When they did, he might be a railway porter or a janitor, the porter or janitor's wife or mother, a domestic. In an age of cheap labor, black labor was the cheapest.

The war offered blacks a chance. Factories needing willing hands, couldn't be choosy about whom they employed, particularly with their normal pool of cheap labor—immigration from Europe—cut off (falling from 1.2 million in 1914 to 100,000 in 1918). Desperate and disgusted, blacks by the tens of thousands migrated from rural Dixie backwaters to the industrialized north. Chicago's black population surged from 44,103 in 1910 to 109,594 in 1920. New York now had 152,467 blacks, Philadelphia 134,229—7.4 percent of its population; blacks comprised 7.5 percent of Cincinnati, 9.4 percent of Columbus, Ohio, 11 percent of Indianapolis, and 6.4 percent of Pittsburgh.

A far touchier situation existed in the armed services. In enacting the Selective Service Act, Congress may not have given much thought that the government would be drafting—and training and arming—black men. But it would. Few white communities wanted large camps of Negro men, armed or unarmed, in their midst. No Southern state wanted *Northern* blacks training anywhere near them. In September 1917, black infantrymen and white civilians tangled in Houston. Seventeen whites were killed. Thirteen black soldiers were later hanged. Franklin Roosevelt's Navy allowed blacks, but only for the dirtiest, most menial of tasks. Not a single black man served in his Marine Corps.

Nonetheless, blacks responded admirably. They did not protest the war. They registered for the draft. They invested heavily in war bonds. They fought bravely.

And they were rewarded with unprecedented violence. The employment of black strikebreakers in East St. Louis in 1917 triggered riots, costing more than forty lives. A riot ravaged Longview, Texas, in July 1919. Another erupted in Washington, D.C., on July 20, 1919, after a report that blacks had raped a white sailor's wife. "The riots seem to be about over today," Franklin Roosevelt wrote three days later; "only one man was killed last night. Luckily the trouble hasn't spread to R Street and though I have troubled to keep out of harm's way, I have heard occasional shots during the evening and night. It has been a nasty episode and I only wish quicker action had been taken to stop it."

Later that month, an incident at a Lake Michigan beach ignited thirteen days of violence in Chicago. A total of 15 whites and 23 blacks died; 178 whites and 342 blacks were injured. Rioters burned a thousand black homes. More violence followed in Knoxville; Omaha; and Elaine, Arkansas.

Blacks needed a forceful advocate, and one had already materialized.

In March 1916, Marcus Mosiah Garvey arrived from Jamaica. Two years earlier, he had founded a black self-help group, the Universal Negro Improvement Association. Inspired by Booker T. Washington, the thickset Garvey nonetheless differed markedly from him in ideology and in style. Washington's earlier black critics pushed for social equality and integration, but the flamboyant Garvey said: Turn your back on the white community, build up your own businesses, keep to yourself, return to your African roots, return to Africa if necessary, and free your homeland. "Wake up, Ethiopia! Wake up, Africa! . . . Let us work toward the one glorious end of a free, redeemed and mighty nation," Garvey harangued cheering crowds. "Let Africa be a bright star among the constellation of nations."

That bright star had its ugly side. "When those crackers lynch a Negro below the Mason-Dixon line," Garvey informed a Carnegie Hall audience, "since it is not safe to lynch a white man in any part of America, we shall press the button and lynch him in Africa."

Garvey had competition—and it wasn't just Washington or Du Bois or Trotter. Former circus magician Timothy Drew (aka Noble Drew Ali) operated the "Moorish American Science Temple," with fez-clad disciples in Newark, Pittsburgh, Detroit, and Chicago. Drew, who taught that black Americans were actually Moors from Morocco, foresaw "the inevitable destruction of the white or European rule, of which the sign from heaven would be a star with a crescent moon." His movement would become the Nation of Islam.

In Chicago, Grover Cleveland Redding's Star Order of Ethiopia and his Ethiopian Missionaries to Abyssinia preached a similar creed. At a Sunday afternoon, June 20, 1920 South Side rally, Redding (fresh from lobbying the Republican national convention regarding an Abyssinian treaty plank) drenched an American flag with gasoline, set it afire, then fired his pistol into it. When he attempted to destroy another flag, white sailor Robert Rose ("My God, you can't burn my flag!") interfered. Rose was shot and killed. A white bystander, cigar-store clerk Joel A. Hoyt, was also killed, and black police officer Joseph Powers was wounded before

Redding was captured. Redding ("Hang me now so I can join my mother, the Queen of Sheba") was executed in June 1921.

Garvey kept his oratory hot but his powder dry. Outfitting followers in splendiferous uniforms, festooned with brass buttons, gleaming swords, and ostrich-plumed hats, he marched them—by the thousands—through Harlem's boulevards. UNIA chapters opened across the country. In August 1918, he established his own newspaper, the *Negro World*, with a circulation that fluctuated between 50,000 and 200,000. Wherever the UNIA boasted 10,000 members—in Harlem, Chicago, Detroit, Philadelphia, Pittsburgh, Cleveland, and Cincinnati—Garvey opened Liberty Halls. In 1919, he founded the Negro Factories Corporation, with 200,000 shares of common stock, par value $5.00, all to be sold to blacks to finance black-owned and -operated enterprises.

Garvey's business empire included grocery stores, a steam laundry, a restaurant, a tailor shop, a millinery, a dressmaking shop, and even a publishing house. Pride of place belonged to his Black Star Steamship Company. Steamships were big, expensive, powerful. They united continents. They symbolized the awakening might of Garvey's idea, of the race itself.

On the line's maiden voyage, the 1,300-ton *Yarmouth* (renamed the *Frederick Douglass*) embarked from Brooklyn to Cuba. It carried $4.8 million worth of booze. The crew got drunk, landed at Norfolk, and had its cargo seized. The *Kanawha*, carrying $2 million worth of whiskey, fared worse, ramming a pier at Norfolk and exploding its boiler.

Garvey's Black Star Line soon attracted the attention of the New York District Attorney's office. Garvey accused Assistant District Attorney Edwin T. Kilroe of conspiring with Garvey's business rivals to frame him. In August 1920, Garvey publicly retracted the charge.

The year 1920 was, as already noted, a year of conventions. Garvey's was a thirty-day affair at Madison Square Garden, jammed nightly with upward of 20,000 supporters. Garvey alarmed whites by trumpeting a world revolution, an alliance of the oppressed and discontented, more than willing to work with the Bolsheviki, the Hindus, the Japanese, and the Chinese: "Why should we not seek an alliance with Trotsky and Lenin?" he asked. "Why should we not ally ourselves with 300,000,000 Hindus who are seeking to free themselves from the British yoke?"

The convention authorized a Washington embassy, the "Black House," to represent the Nation of Africa's interests to the United States government. Said Garvey:

> For fifty years[,] the leaders of the negro race have been cringing men. This is ended. We are unable to elect a leader to the White House, but we intend to have a Black House in Washington where one of our race will serve us for four years.

Clearly, no mere ambassadorship was suitable for a leader of Garvey's skills. An underling took that job. Garvey eyed greater glory: the provisional presidency of Africa. And so the Universal Negro Improvement Association elected Marcus Garvey, clad in cap and flowing gown of purple, green, and gold, to rule an entire continent that neither he nor virtually anyone in the hall had ever visited.

"Wherever I go," Garvey (now addressed as "Your Majesty") told his audience, "whether it be to France, Germany, England or Spain, I find that I am told that this is white man's country and that there is no room for a nigger. The other races have countries of their own and it is time for the 400,000,000 negroes to claim Africa for themselves."

Not every African welcomed their new president. Nigerian Prince Madarikan Deniyi, a member of the Yoruba tribe, explained to reporters:

> As it is impossible for the Governor of New York state to control the Governor of Missouri . . . so it is impossible for the King of Abyssinia to control the native kings and chiefs in West Africa. Therefore, Marcus Garvey . . . of the British West Indies, cannot elect himself as the new leader of the world or president of Africa to rule the Africa people and control 300,000,000 black people. . . .
>
> He can only have himself elected as president of the Universal Negro Improvement Association in New York. The black republic of Liberia has elected her own President and Marcus Garvey must respect him. . . . The native chiefs and kings will not allow any new Negro leader to bring his schemes and tricks into these states. The trouble with Garvey and his followers is that they talk too much.

Garvey was also talking against W. E. B. Du Bois.

Du Bois had first called Garvey "an extraordinary leader of men," but by mid-1920 he began questioning Garvey's vaunted operation. At his Madison Square Garden convention, Garvey launched into a class- and race-based tirade against the extremely light-skinned, half-white Du Bois's "aristocratic" ideas and manners:

> Where did he [Du Bois] get this aristocracy from? He picked it up on the streets of Great Barrington, Mass. He just got it into his head that he should be an aristocrat and ever since that time has been keeping his very beard as an aristocrat; he has been trying to be everything else but a Negro. Sometimes we hear he is a Frenchman and another time he is Dutch and when it is conven-ient he is a Negro [laughter and cheers]. Now I have no Dutch, I have no French, I have no Anglo-Saxon to imitate; I have but the ancient glories of Ethiopia to imitate. [Applause.] The men who built the Pyramids looked like me, and I think the best thing I can do is to keep looking like them. Anyone you hear always talking about the kind of blood he has in him other than the blood you can see, he is dissatisfied with something, and I feel sure that many of the Negroes of the United States of America know that if there is a man who is most dissatisfied with himself, it is Dr. Du Bois.

In truth, not only had Du Bois remained staunchly anti-accommodationist, he was growing more radical. In January 1920, Congress considered leg-islation banning from the mails any materials causing race rioting. Logi-cally, that might have meant publications contributing to recent widespread white rioting. It was instead aimed at such publications as Du Bois's *Crisis*. The *Macon Telegraph* spoke for many Southern whites when it wrote: "Du Boise [*sic*] hates white men because they are white and he is black. . . . There can be no harmony where [*Crisis* and the *Chicago Defender*] are read either by the whites or the blacks. They must be changed or they must be stopped altogether."

In 1920, Du Bois published *Darkwater: Voices from Within the Veil*, a series of essays on the racial problem. "There is no way out unless the white world opens the door," wrote Du Bois:

Either the white world gives up such insult as its modern use of the adjective "yellow" indicates, or its connotation of "chink" and "nigger" implies; either it gives up the plan of color serfdom which its use of the other adjective "white" implies, as indicating everything decent and every part of the world worth living in—or trouble is written in the stars!

*Darkwater* disturbed even white liberals. *The Nation*'s Oswald Garrison Villard complained of Du Bois's "note of bitterness, tinctured with hate, and the teaching of violence which often defeats his own purpose." *The Bookman* found him motivated "by resentment and by hate." The *Chicago Tribune* praised *Darkwater* as "a volume of almost super-intellectual caliber" but thought it "bitter in tone." Some blamed Du Bois's writings for inspiring Grover Cleveland Redding's deadly Star Order of Ethiopia.

"Du Bois," wrote one observer, "is the Karl Marx of the colored race."

Though blacks possessed little hope of obtaining anything from Democrats, they lobbied for strong anti-lynching, pro-voting-rights, and anti-discrimination planks in the GOP platform. They received only the vaguest of promises—that Congress should "consider the most effective means to end lynching."

After Warren Harding obtained the nomination, former Chicago First Ward alderman Oscar S. De Priest and former collector of Internal Revenue at Honolulu Charles A. Cottrill led a representation of black delegates to him before he departed Chicago. "We want a few words with you, Senator," said Cottrill, now a Toledo real estate broker, "as to how you stand on the Colored question, and particularly if you favor segregation."

"You know me, Cottrill. You and I have stumped Ohio. You know I am a Republican, and that ought to be enough."

The black *Cleveland Advocate* dismissed Harding's answer as "inconclusive." "'Republican,'" it contended, "is not always a synonym for justice and equality before the law."

National Chairman Hays initiated a colored voting bureau under Georgia's Henry Lincoln Johnson and authorized Johnson to tour Illinois, Indiana, and Ohio on Harding's behalf. The appointment outraged the by-now invariably outraged *Cleveland Advocate*, which fumed about having "a Colored man from Georgia who has never exercised his right to vote, and who hailed from a state that has not, and WILL NOT, contribute a single electoral vote to the Republican ticket, to 'direct' the Colored voters."

A glimmer of hope appeared, however, from a most unlikely quarter. Normally, Calvin Coolidge avoided specifics. But regarding black rights, he now spoke with unusual force:

> There is especially due to the colored race a more general recognition of their constitutional rights. Tempted with disloyalty they remained loyal, serving in the military forces with distinction, obedient to the draft to the extent of hundreds of thousands, investing $1 out of every five they possessed in Liberty Bonds, surely they hold the double title of citizenship, by birth and by conquest, to be relieved from all imposition, to be defended from lynching and to be freely granted equal opportunities.

Coolidge's words heartened blacks. Very few politicians had so forcefully condemned lynching. The *Advocate* noted with eerie prescience, "If he is elected vice-president, and should Warren Harding—much against our wishes—be called to pick up the harp and become a wandering minstrel where the streets are paved with gold, we still would have a friend on the throne who would go a little better than fifty-fifty. Whoopee for Calvin!"

On September 10, 1920, two significant delegations of black voters arrived on Warren Harding's front lawn: in the morning, the Baptists (led by Henry Lincoln Johnson); in the afternoon, the Methodists (who introduced Harding as "William G. Harding"). Interspersed among them was William Monroe Trotter's less tractable American Equal Rights League. Inside Harding's home, blacks quizzed the candidate. Trotter (whom Henry Lincoln Johnson disliked) asked Harding about ending federal workforce segregation. Harding promised firm consideration ("If the United States cannot prevent segregation in its own service, we are not in any sense a democracy"). Trotter surprisingly departed mollified.

Harding, accompanied by General Pershing, delivered identical speeches to the morning Baptists and the afternoon Methodists. Harding concluded each speech:

If I have anything to do with it, there shall be good American obedience to the law. Brutal, unlawful violence, whether it proceeds from those that break the law or from those that take the law into their own hands, can only be dealt with in one way by true Americans. Fear not. Here upon this beloved soil you shall have that justice that every man and woman of us knows would have been prayed for by Abraham Lincoln. Your people, by their restraint, their patience, their wisdom, integrity, labor and belief in God have earned it, and America will bestow it.

The *Cleveland Advocate* considered these to be Harding's "most direct words" on race issues, helpful in dispelling "some misgivings on the part of some of us."

On Saturday, October 9, Harding was off the front porch and in Oklahoma City. The *Daily Oklahoman* inquired if he would revive Henry Cabot Lodge's long-dead "Force Bill" to guarantee black rights in the South. "I have not come from old Ohio to tell you how to solve your peculiar problems of the south," Harding responded.

Somebody asked me what I would do about the racial question. I cannot come and answer that for you. That is too serious a problem for some of us to solve who do not know it as you do in your daily lives.

But I would not be fit to be President of the United States if I did not tell you in the south precisely the same I would say in the north. I want you to know that I believe in equality before the law. [Applause] That is one of the guarantees of the American constitution.

You cannot give one right to a white man and deny the same right to a black man, but, while I stand for that particular principle, I want you in Oklahoma to know that does not mean the white man and the black man must be made to experience the enjoyment of their rights in each other's company.

Someone asked me, if I am to revive the Force Bill when I am elected President of the United States. I do not know that they said it that-a-way, but let me tell you. The Force Bill had been dead for a quarter of a century. I am a normal American citizen and a normal man could not resurrect the dead.

His equivocation alarmed William Monroe Trotter. Harding seemed to be endorsing segregation. Trotter telegraphed Harding, inquiring if he had "altered [his] statements in Marion to the Equal Rights League." It was not a performance designed to reassure black voters.

Democrats had problems of their own. Some were old, such as the case of two female normal-school women answering a Washington newspaper ad in 1918 and being curtly informed that no "coloreds" were being hired in Josephus Daniels's and Franklin Roosevelt's Department of the Navy.

Or the charge that James M. Cox had taken $40,000 from the company controlling distribution of D. W. Griffith's *Birth of a Nation* to allow Griffith's controversial film to be shown in Ohio (Cox's predecessor, Frank Willis, had banned Griffith's masterpiece). Cox had also supported plans to create a black industrial school at Wilberforce, Ohio (along the lines of the Tuskegee Institute), a move that blacks feared might prove a "wedge" for segregated schooling throughout Ohio. Taking office, Cox had sharply reduced black patronage. In February 1919, he had pointedly ignored the homecoming of Ohio's black Ninth Regiment.

But the real problem the Democrats had in securing black votes in 1920 was what they did in 1920.

Democrats, heavily beholden to the party's Southern wing, avoided saying *anything* favoring equal rights. Henry Lincoln Johnson created a flier, headed: "Everyone admits that lynching and mob-violence are the chief aggravations of the colored man in the United States." Under a column marked "What the Republican Party Says," Johnson cited appropriate quotes from the GOP platform and from recent Harding and Coolidge speeches. Under "What the Democratic Party Says," a heading entitled "Democratic Platform" read "Nothing." Under "Governor Cox," it read "Absolutely nothing." Beneath "Franklin Delano Roosevelt," it read "Not one word."

Democratic inaction, however, was nothing compared to the party's new outpourings of racial venom. On September 16, Arkansas Governor Charles H. Brough dispatched a missive from Ohio Democratic state committee headquarters in Columbus warning fellow Anglo-Saxon Democrats of the perils of a Harding victory. "I was astonished to learn from my friend, Hon. W. W. Durbin . . . chairman of the Ohio democratic executive committee," Governor Brough explained, "that a negro journal, *The Toledo Pioneer* . . . is urging race equality and urging the negroes to unite at the polls. This, of course, strikes at the very heart of white supremacy. . . . The presidential election means everything in the south and I urge you . . . to [explain] to your people just what Senator Harding's triumph would mean in robbing the south of her most cherished birth-right, Anglo-Saxon supremacy."

Cox was on the same page, perhaps the same paragraph. "There is behind Senator Harding the Afro-American party," he charged in an intemperate October 14 speech at the Columbus Coliseum, "whose hyphenated activity has attempted to stir up troubles among the Colored people upon the false claims that it can bring social equality, thereby subjecting the unsuspecting Colored people to the counterattacks of those fomenting racial prejudice, and endangering them to the bloody race riots which distinguished cities like Chicago—citadel of [Mayor] William Hale Thompson, one of the supporters of Senator Harding."

Also in October, Cox wrote to Frank L. Stanton Jr., son of the Georgia poet and humorist:

> An attempt has been made by our opponents to . . . [set] up racial groups each with a selfish purpose. To each . . . something has been promised. . . .
>
> Promises have been made to the Afro-American Party which I do not believe the promisers have any intention of carrying out. There are some classes of social equality which cannot be. To quote the words of the immortal Lincoln, "We do not want the negroes to be slaves, but that does not mean that we want negro women for our wives." I know no better way to express the wiles in the attempt to carry class against class in America.

Cincinnati voters received similar appeals. "For a week or more," the *Cincinnati Times-Star* noted just before Election Day, "local Democrats have been circulating a card on which are portraits of the Republican candidates for president, governor and senator. Grouped around them are pictures of six negro Republican candidates for the legislature. The intimation is that Republican success in Ohio this year will mean negro domination in the state and particularly the general assembly."

How dangerous and ugly the race issue had become was revealed in an October 22 *New York Times* article analyzing Ohio's "new problem"— that thanks to the wartime black migration to the state and the just-passed Nineteenth Amendment, Ohio blacks would cast over 150,000 votes, becoming the state's balance of power. "These black immigrants from [the] South . . . ," the *Times* pointed out, "do not begin to compare in intelligence to the Northern Negroes."

The situation, the *Times* reported, had drawn notice from W. W. Durbin's Democratic State Committee, which no longer hid behind an Arkansas governor but now openly issued "A timely warning to the white men and white women of Ohio," revealing that Republican gubernatorial candidate Harry L. Davis, as mayor of Cleveland, had dared to appoint twenty-seven blacks to the city police force.

The Ohio Democratic state committee concluded:

An ominous cloud has risen on the political horizon which should have the attention of all men and women before casting their ballots. That cloud is the threat of Negro domination in Ohio.

We see negro newspapers in the State boasting loudly of the increased balance of power held by their race through the enfranchisement of their women. We find them openly predicting that full social equality will be ensured them by the election of the Republican candidates.

It is a well-known fact that the influx of negros from the South into the industrial centers of Ohio during the past years has been of such proportions as to give rise to a real race problem. Herded together like cattle and brought here by selfish employers to work in our industrial establishments, their presence has brought about serious consequences in many of our cities.

White workingmen in many communities owning or paying for homes in factory districts can testify to the effect which the importation of these negroes into the community has had upon the value of their properties. In many of our cities it is well known that the best residential districts have not been free from invasion of negroes. It naturally follows that the effects upon the part of Republican candidates and leaders to further intensify Negro ambitions can only result in greatly magnifying the evils we are already facing.

Ohioans should remember that the time has come when we must handle this problem in the same way as the South is handling it, and in such a way bring greater contentment to both whites and negroes. We should remember what history tells us of the dark days when negroes controlled the governments in the South, the enormous expenditures and debts incurred, the indignities heaped upon the white women and children, the vicious attempt of the South Carolina Negro Legislature to give every Negro forty acres and a mule.

Men and women of Ohio, rally to the ballot box and give such a verdict as will forever rid Ohio of this menace to yourselves and your children.

The only thing that could be worse was if the next President of the United States was black.

## Chapter 22

⌒

# "WARREN GAMALIEL HARDING IS NOT A WHITE MAN"

Most people liked Warren Harding.

Not everybody, but most people. Alice Roosevelt Longworth didn't like him; but then again, she didn't like a lot of people.

Professor William Estabrook Chancellor, a professor of political science at Ohio's Wooster College, *specialized* in disliking Warren Harding, *really* disliking Warren Harding—and also specialized in a broader, longer-held dislike of blacks.

There was a connection. Chancellor had convinced himself that Harding's family possessed Negro blood. The specter of a mulatto in the White House disgusted Chancellor.

The fifty-two-year-old Chancellor was a crackpot. Yes, he had graduated Phi Beta Kappa from Amherst, attended Harvard Law, and taught at Johns Hopkins. Yes, he ultimately authored thirty-eight books—many quite sane and issued by respectable publishers—Harper's, G. P. Putnam's Sons, the Century Company, Houghton Mifflin. Yes, he was popular at Wooster College and had served as superintendent of schools in Paterson, New Jersey, and the District of Columbia. Yes, he even had some success in politics. Originally a Republican, he joined 1912's Progressive crusade. By 1916, he was a Democratic presidential elector; two years later, he was a Democratic nominee for Congress. In 1919, voters of the city of Wooster elected him to their city council.

But Chancellor went off on "queer spells" and had once been arrested in Ohio. In 1908, the D.C. school system fired him for "antagonizing its

Board of Education and conduct unbecoming a Superintendent," insubordination, "lying," and fomenting "racial dissension." He was, observed a former Board president, "erratic, eccentric and a man of wild ideas. He couldn't be trusted."

Chancellor wasn't just an ordinary racist, either. There were plenty of those in 1920. He was extraordinary, obsessed with race, jealously protective of all Caucasian prerogatives, and fearful of—no, paranoid about—the smallest steps of black progress.

Initially, Chancellor paid little attention to Harding—or to rumors about Harding. In June 1920, he lunched at a Lima, Ohio hotel. Present was Professor John Wesley Hill, a Methodist minister, Chancellor of Lincoln Memorial University, and an ardent, conservative Republican. Not only was the Reverend Hill one of the very few people who thought Harding had a chance, he was absolutely convinced that Harding was the next president. After Hill departed, someone commented "I heard that Harding had Negro blood in his ancestry. This came out in the spring primaries."

"Yes, I have heard stories to that effect, but I know very little about this man," Chancellor responded. "During the spring primaries, General Wood and his people tried to make race an issue, but it did not work."

"Professor, could a Negro be elected president [of] the United States?"

"Yes, as God has made all the nations of men," Chancellor responded, "the mixing and compounding of the bloodlines are forever going on. Sometimes there comes a man from a particular stock of whom the world is in need. He may have the one trait, which made him great, that came from his race. We can never tell where the needed man will come from."

Professor Chancellor might very well have pontificated so sanguinely. Warren Harding was such a long shot, Chancellor could afford equanimity.

Chancellor also attended the 1920 Chicago convention—hardly an unusual occurrence. Democrats William Gibbs McAdoo and William Jennings Bryan sat in at the Republican convention. Hiram Johnson attended the Democratic. Chancellor arrived on the Convention's last day—in time to see Reverend Hill's unlikely prediction fulfilled and to record his observations regarding the party's black delegates: "None came away empty-handed . . . handled by [Taft's former Postmaster General] Frank H.

Hitchcock who makes a specialty every four years of fixing the Southern delegates in the Republican Convention. . . . He trades in negroes for political slaves to use in Republican Conventions. It was with very great pleasure that the negroes did vote for Harding, because they were told, first, that he had negro blood and, second, that he would appoint negroes to many more offices than any other President has ever done."

Such vaporings inflamed Chancellor's already delicate racial sensibilities. He began investigating Harding. In August, he visited Marion and Columbus. From Columbus, on August 21, he reported his findings: Florence was divorced (hardly news and hardly usable, considering Cox's marital status), Harding had had multiple affairs (Chancellor seemed only moderately interested in them), and—pay lode!—Harding was one eighth black, an octoroon.

Chancellor's Wooster friends prodded him to continue. Now focusing almost exclusively on the racial issue, he returned to Marion and to such Harding family haunts as Blooming Grove, Iberia, Caledonia, Galion, and Steam Corners, Ohio, grilling whomever he could about the candidate's ancestry.

Chancellor secured a copy of Joe Mitchell Chapple's newly issued *Warren G. Harding—The Man*. This brief campaign biography referenced Warren's youngest sister, Carolyn, now Mrs. Heber Votaw, and her career in "the Police Court in Washington." Chancellor scribbled a note in the margins: "I appointed a Mrs. Votaw as a colored woman to the colored schools. Suppose to be a colored woman in Washington? Was she a Teacher there? Truant officer?"

Chancellor was mistaken. He had served as superintendent only from August 1906 through January 1908, and Carolyn and Heber Votaw served as Seventh Day Adventist missionaries in India from 1904 through 1914. His theory's accuracy didn't matter; what mattered was that it caused his suspicions to enter overdrive.

Chancellor claimed to have interviewed "hundreds of persons" who knew the Hardings. Remarkably, all of them, said Chancellor, informed him that the Hardings were part black. In early October, Chancellor finally began to document his evidence. From these "hundreds" of supposed witnesses, Chancellor could collect just four affidavits accusing the Hardings of being, in his terminology, "niggers."

The first, dated Saturday, October 9, was from fifty-eight-year-old Calvin G. Keifer of 315 West Railroad Street, Galion, Ohio. Keifer provided vague reports of the Harding ancestry, including the story of a man named Butler (Keifer claimed to be his relative) who, decades before, had married a Harding and killed a man named "Starnes because he had called Butler's wife a 'nigger.'"

On Sunday, October 10, Chancellor traveled to Akron to interrogate seventy-three-year-old retired carpenter Elias Shaffer. Shaffer, a Blooming Grove native, swore that Warren's uncles were "of Negro blood. They have dark skin, and features and hair of that race that looked like Negroes." His aunts, said Shaffer, were of a similar hue.

In Marion on Wednesday, October 13, Chancellor secured his last two affidavits. Ninety-three-year-old retired farmer Montgomery Lindsay, another Blooming Grove native, corroborated Shaffer's descriptions of the Harding family and also claimed to have heard Amos Kling's declaration that his daughter was marrying a "nigger."

Sixty-two-year-old "Wagon Factory" proprietor George W. Cook related a similar tale: he had "personally heard Mr. Kling make the statement addressed to Bartholomeo Tristam, that he, Kling, wanted nothing further to do with Tristam after Tristam witnessed the marriage of his daughter to a negro."

All of which certainly proved that there were rumors abroad in the land—rumors of very long standing. What they signified remains conjecture. What appears black to some may merely be dark or swarthy to others. For example: Along the way, Chancellor wrote to Democratic Party headquarters in Columbus, saying Harding's father was "obviously a mulatto. He had thick lips, rolling eyes, chocolate skin." But Dr. George Harding was *not* "obviously a mulatto" (see photo).

In October, Chancellor struck, publishing two nefarious handbills, "The Harding Family Tree" and "To the Men and Women of America: An Open Letter."

"The Harding Family Tree" went like this:

### The Right of the American People to Know

| Amos Harding | Wife—Huldah Harding |
|---|---|
| (Black) West Indian Negro | (colored) |

Issue

    George Tryon Harding               1st Wife—Ann Roberts

    (colored)                              (colored)

Issue

    Charles A. Harding              Wife—Mary Ann Crawford

    (colored)                        (pass-for-White)

Issue

    George Tryon Harding          2nd Wife—Phoebe Dickerson

                                     (White)

This marriage was objected to by the brother of [Warren's mother] Phoebe Dickerson for the reason that George Tryon Harding, the second (the father of Warren G. Harding), had Negro blood.

The above is verified by Elias Shaffer, 804 Holloway St., Akron, Ohio, who has known Mr. Harding for fifty years. He went to school with Dr. Geo. Tryon Harding, the second (father of Warren G. Harding), knew his father Charles Harding and Charles Harding's two brothers who were uncles of George T. Harding, the second, and says that they had the color, features, and hair of negroes and were so considered and accepted in the community. Mr. Shaffer is seventy-three years of age, a member of the Grand Army Post at Marion, and a Republican in politics.

Issue

    Warren Gamaliel Harding          Wife—Florence Kling

    (colored)                              (White)

This marriage was objected to by the father-in-law, Mr. Amos H. Kling, a prominent Republican and one of the wealthiest men in Marion, who spoke out publicly and openly denouncing this marriage and said his daughter had disgraced herself and family by marrying a man who had negro blood in his veins. This statement can be verified by a hundred people in Marion, Ohio.

Senator has not publicly or privately denied this statement. All denials have been made by unofficial announcements.

Authority: Professor William E. Chancellor, Wooster University, Wooster, Ohio.

Tens of thousands of handbills were slipped under doorways in the dead of the night—some by paid workers. Rock Island Line rail passengers found copies in southwestern Kansas. Their distribution triggered fist-fights on trains outside Chicago. They appeared throughout Ohio and Indiana, in the battleground border states, in Southern states—Georgia, Virginia, North Carolina, Alabama—where Harding stood no chance in the first place. A quarter million copies were seized and destroyed at the San Francisco Post Office.

Such events generated press notice, though often of a very circum-spect nature. Certain papers—the *New York Times*, the *Atlanta Constitution*, the *Los Angeles Times*, and the *Cincinnati Times-Star*—spoke vaguely of "mud" and "whispering campaigns," hesitating to reveal what all the shouting (or, rather, whispering) was about.

But any number of other papers bluntly informed readers of the sub-stance of the charges. The *Chicago Tribune* (allegation: "some of his ances-tors were colored") went public on October 30; the *Washington Post* and the *Indianapolis Star* on November 1. The Socialist Party's *New York Call* not only revealed the actual story but used it to twit its capitalist rivals, the Republican *Herald* and the Democratic *Times*. "Both [political] par-ties," editorialized the *Call* on November 1, "do regard the possession of Negro blood by any man seeking office to be as unfitting him for public office[,] but they dare not say this openly. There are millions of Negro votes to be cast. So they keep the real story from the voting masses and give the impression that the charges against Harding reflect upon his pri-vate life and character."

Most aggressive was Jimmie Cox's hometown Republican rival, former governor Myron T. Herrick's *Dayton Journal*. The Friday, October 29 *Journal* front-paged this story:

The time has come for plain language. These vile circulars declare that Warren G. Harding has Negro blood in his veins. The ugly details you have no doubt read. This is the vilest plot and conspiracy in the history of the worst epochs of American politics.

Unless there is no such thing as truth in the world, unless there is no such thing as honesty in the world, unless there is no such thing as decency in the world, if our moral standards are not a sham, then the perpetrators of this outrage will suffer the everlasting condemnation of public opinion within the sacred precincts of every home in America. The answer to this conspiracy, this plot, is that its base allegations ARE A LIE.

Warren G. Harding has the blood of but one race in his veins—that of the white race—the pure inheritance of a fine line of ancestors, of good men and women.

That is sufficient!

Meanwhile, people naturally wondered about the single source referenced upon the fliers: "Professor William E. Chancellor, Wooster University, Wooster, Ohio." Dayton grocer Sherwood P. Snyder wrote to Chancellor for verification. Momentarily losing his nerve, on Friday, October 22, Chancellor responded:

Dear Sir:—I know nothing of the question you ask and think what you have heard is quite false.

There is another family of the name "Hardin" at Marion, which is of mixed blood. There is no connection between the families of HARDIN and HARDING.

The situation quickly alarmed Wooster College authorities. Republican or Democrat, they wanted no part of such indecorous controversy. Wooster Dean Elias Compton mailed a copy of the handbill to Chancellor's friend, forty-seven-year-old Bucyrus, Ohio, public school teacher Robert L. Todd (a Wooster graduate). Todd wrote Chancellor. Chancellor again denied involvement. When, on October 25, a *Bucyrus News-Forum* reporter (Todd coincidentally lived next door to its publisher) interviewed Chancellor, he continued denying culpability.

On October 28, another leaflet appeared—*To the Men and Women of America—An Open Letter*:

When one citizen knows beyond the peradventure of doubt what concerns all other citizens but is not generally known[,] duty compels publication.

Warren Gamaliel Harding is not a white man; he is not a creole; he is not a mulatto; he is a mestizo, as his physical features show. Anyone who hears or reads his public utterances is free to pass upon his intellectual and moral traits. Anyone who knows the quality of his public record in various offices is free to pass upon his mind and character as indicating his several race origins.

Are we ready to make the experiment of entrusting the Presidency of this Republic to this hybrid man? To be silent now might be to permit the extending of the interesting local race evolution of the Galion–Blooming Grove–Bucyrus–Marion countryside throughout this land. Shall America be a white man's land? For one, I believe that red man, yellow man, black man, colored man, one and all, are better off under the social control of the white man.

I might cite the names of scores of persons who have always considered Warren Gamaliel Harding a colored man and who resent his present masquerade as a white candidate upon the ticket of a hitherto honorable and dignified party.

Of hundreds of persons interviewed of those who knew him as a rural school boy and as college student, everyone without exception says that Warren Gamaliel Harding was always considered a colored boy and nicknamed accordingly.

It is for us to decide what the Capitals of Europe and Asia and all the rest of the world shall think of us as represented in the person of our President on and after March 4, 1921. Let us have neither Hayti nor Russia here! May God save America from international shame and from domestic ruin!

Now came Chancellor's turn to sign affidavits. On Thursday, October 28, Dean Compton requested him to swear that the Hardings were white. Chancellor refused, but attested:

As to the Harding ancestry, I hereby certify [that] I am in no way responsible for, never wrote, never authorized to write[,] and

A Republican ad in a black newspaper.

TR's old ally, Massachusetts Senator
Henry Cabot Lodge—he derails
Wilson's League of Nations and nearly
derails Warren Harding's nomination.

TR's feisty daughter—Alice Roosevelt Longworth,
pro-Wood and viciously anti-Harding.

Governor Frank O. Lowden of Illinois—
an unexciting but sound politician and
one of the GOP front-runners.

Woodrow Wilson and William Howard Taft at Wilson's March 1913 Inaugural.
(*Library of Congress*)

Socialist presidential candidate Eugene V. Debs.
The antiwar Debs will poll nearly a million
votes while incarcerated in Atlanta Penitentiary.
(*Library of Congress*)

The 1920 Republican National Convention in session in Chicago's overheated Coliseum.

FDR's Vice Presidential Notification at Hyde Park. From left to right: unidentified; Democratic National Chairman Frank White, Mrs. Alfred E. Smith; Governor Smith; Former Democratic National Chairman Homer Cummings; William Gibbs McAdoo, Mrs. McAdoo; Josephus Daniels, Eleanor Roosevelt, Franklin Roosevelt.

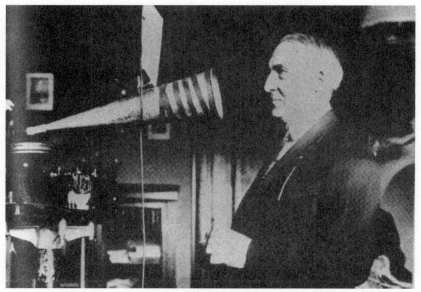

Senator Warren Harding recording a campaign speech. (*Library of Congress*)

The Coolidge family—John, Grace, Calvin, Calvin Jr., and Colonel John Coolidge.

Italian anarchists Bartolomeo Vanzetti
and Nicola Sacco. Their guilt or innocence on murder charges generated
national controversy.

The Wall Street Bombing of September 1920. Political terror visited lower Manhattan long before 9-11.

Suffragettes protesting at the 1920 Democratic Convention. Will all women win the vote in time to cast their ballot in 1920?

A very sick Woodrow Wilson and a not-all-that-healthy Warren Harding at
Harding's March 1921 Inaugural.

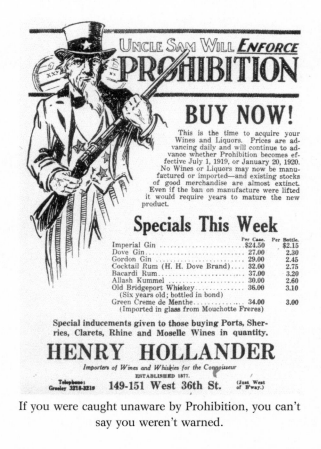

If you were caught unaware by Prohibition, you can't
say you weren't warned.

KNOW NOTHING whatever about the circulars bearing my name or any other paper.

On October 28, a *New York Times* reporter interviewed Chancellor at his modest yellow frame home. Readily admitting authorship of the pamphlets' controversial research, Chancellor still disavowed responsibility for their publication. It all remained a mystery to him.

On Friday afternoon, October 29, the Wooster board of trustees grilled Chancellor and debated what action to take. At 4 P.M., Lawrence V. West, thirty-five-year-old sales manager of the Dayton Steel Foundry, phoned Chancellor, who still claimed to know "nothing whatever about the circulars entitled 'the Harding Family Tree'" or about Harding's "pedigree." Shortly after 10 P.M., Wooster trustees announced their decision: William Estabrook Chancellor was fired.

Professor Chancellor had researched Harding's genealogy. He readily admitted that. Not long afterward, from Pennsylvania to California, hundreds of thousands of handbills detailing his fixations magically appeared. What had happened between those two events? Chancellor possessed neither the cash nor connections necessary to print and distribute documents in such numbers. What had transformed one man's vendetta into a major, black-bag political operation?

Let's start at the top: the White House. What did the Wilson administration know? What did it do? Two accounts exist.

The first became public knowledge even before Election Day, reported, in fact, by the *Chicago Tribune*. Joe Tumulty claimed that "a stranger (some said Chancellor, himself) with an introduction from a Democratic committeeman" visited the White House, with "evidence" of Harding's racial ancestry.

"What's this for?" asked Tumulty.

"Campaign material," came the response. "I thought the national committee might be interested."

Tumulty was firm: "The National Committee wouldn't touch it."

"Why not?"

"Suppose Senator Harding is elected," Tumulty responded. "What a terrible thing it would be for the country if it came out that we had a President alleged to be part negro! I'll have nothing to do with it."

Tumulty claimed it unlikely that Wilson ever knew of the situation.

Edith Wilson later narrated a different tale. As usual, her husband was the hero. In Edith's account, Tumulty *favored* using the documents. "Governor," Tumulty excitedly informed Wilson, "we've got 'em beat! Here is a paper which has been searched out and is absolutely true, showing that Harding has Negro blood in him. This country will never stand for that!"

"Even if that is so," Wilson responded, "it will never be used with my consent. We cannot go into a man's genealogy; we must base our campaigns on principles, not on backstairs gossip. That is not only right but good politics. So I insist you kill any such proposal."

Either story could be true. Both could be false. Both could contain elements of truth. It mattered little. Woodrow Wilson and Joe Tumulty weren't running the campaign. The campaign lay in the hands of Cox and his functionaries.

Both Cox and the Ohio Democratic state committee were unusually and nastily preoccupied with stirring up the racial pot. Considering the nature of the Chancellor operation and the decades that have passed, it's unlikely that mounds of new evidence regarding their direct involvement will ever appear. Yet significant evidence *does* exist.

On Saturday, August 21, Chancellor excitedly wrote forty-year-old Wayne County Democratic chairman W. Howard Ross regarding his potentially explosive research, predicting that it could swing the upcoming election ("Leave it to Marion to work the landslide to Cox!"). At the top of the letter, Chancellor penciled in "or Judge Weygandt." Sixty-two-year-old Wayne County Judge William E. Weygandt was Ross's law partner. Both had Wooster College connections. They encouraged Chancellor to continue.

Ross and Weygandt, however, were small fish, barely bigger minnows than Chancellor himself. There was, however, higher-up party involvement. The October 29 *Dayton Journal* revealed:

Thousands upon thousands of typewritten, mimeographed and even printed statements usually under the heading of "Harding's Family Tree," have been distributed in Dayton and Montgomery County, at first in cowardly secrecy and in the last few days openly

378

and boldly by men low down in the Democratic party, unprincipled heelers and men high up in the Democratic party who have sunk their standards to the very sewers of depravity.

In Reading, Pennsylvania, the Democrat Clerk of the Quarter Sessions of Berks County, forty-eight-year-old Harvey L. Bausher, was actually arrested for handing out the circulars.

Thus, Chancellor was in contact with his local party apparatus, hardly a surprising revelation. And, further, persons distributing the material tended to be Democrats—again, hardly surprising. But how high did the plot reach?

Actually, quite close to Governor Cox. Ohio Republicans had apprehended his adjutant, Roy E. Layton, in the act. On November 1, the Allen County Republican Committee ran advertising revealing:

THIS CIRCULAR [the Chancellor circular] COMES DIRECT FROM THE COX GANG AT COLUMBUS.

IT WAS BROUGHT TO WAPAKONETA [OHIO] BY ADJUTANT GENERAL ROY E. LAYTON, A MEMBER OF COX'S STAFF, who expected to profit by this vile slander by being continued in some position which he has neither the ability nor the character to fill. Like other contemptible curs, Layton was too cowardly to print it and sign his name as this is being signed, but like a sneaking character assassin, he had copies taken on a mimeograph and they were handed out by some "sewer rats" in the pay of the Democratic party.

THIS IS NOT A MERE CHARGE. WE HAVE THE PROOF AT HAND.

Connections to Cox beyond Layton, however, remain murky at best. True, Cox ran a thoroughly racist campaign. And, true, he personally circulated the Harding rumors. On August 20, West Virginia Senator Howard Sutherland revealed to Will Hays that Cox had confided to a game warden that a "great-grandmother of Senator Harding was a negress."

Chancellor, however, claimed that Cox rebuffed his efforts. "Professor Chancellor," the New York Times noted, "said that Governor Cox and Chairman White of the Democratic National Committee had urged him not to make the result of the investigation known before the election."

If Cox and the national Democrats were not involved, who was? It's clear that Chancellor had closely coordinated his activities with the racist Ohio State Democratic committee. After Wooster College fired Chancellor, he regained his nerve, went on the offensive, reiterated his racial charges, and vowed to sue the *Dayton News* for $100,000 for printing his various statements to Sherwood Snyder, Lawrence V. West, and Dean Compton, which he now claimed had never been made.

. . . *and* he wired the Ohio Democratic state committee:

PLEASE TRANSMIT FOLLOWING MESSAGE TO COUNTY CHAIRMEN AND NEWSPAPERS: "HAVE FILED LIBEL SUIT BY ATTORNEY SNELL [*sic*—Hugh A. Snepp], DAYTON AGAINST DAYTON JOURNAL FOR ASSERTING FALSELY THAT I RETRACTED STATEMENT, HARDING IS 'MULATTO.' HAVE NOTIFIED HAYES [perhaps a reference to Will Hays] HE WILL BE SUED PERSONALLY UNLESS HE RETRACTS FALSE STATEMENT SENT TO ALL REPUBLICAN STATE AND COUNTY CHAIRMEN, THAT I RETRACTED. WILL NEVER QUIT THIS FIGHT OF TRUTH."
(*SIGNED*)
WILLIAM ESTABROOK CHANCELLOR,
WOOSTER UNIVERSITY
6:45 A.M.

The state committee reacted not like an embarrassed bystander suddenly thrust into an imbroglio not of its own making, but like a partner in crime, forwarding Chancellor's wire to all county committees, at least one of which, in Allen County, published Chancellor's telegram in the local press.

The state executive committee also issued pamphlets detailing Chancellor's retraction of his retraction—signed by Chairman Ira Andrews and Secretary Frank Lowther.

So once again the finger points to the Ohio Democratic state committee. But why would Cox not be involved?

Perhaps he possessed just plain good sense, or decency. Perhaps his reasoning involved a quite different rumor. It might not have been true. It probably wasn't true. But often people act on what they merely believe to be true.

The rumor: Harding and Cox had once been in-laws.

Jimmie Cox's first wife was a Harding—Mayme Simpson Harding; and during the San Francisco convention, Cox's daughter, Helen Cox Mahoney, was widely quoted as saying the two families were related: "I have always thought of Senator Harding as an uncle. And I shall have to break the established precedent of running down an opponent of my father's. We are all fond of Senator Harding. He is quiet and reserved and conservative, and he used to come to our home in Dayton when I was a little girl."

When Cox received the nomination, reporters tried verifying the story. Helen's husband, Dan Mahoney, a professional public relations man and a key Cox adviser, interrupted before she answered. "No, that's another Harding family," said Mahoney. "If there is any relationship, there isn't any use tracing it. The Harding family that the first Mrs. Cox was related to lived in Kentucky, but it is not the family of the Republican nominee."

The bottom line: If the Hardings had black blood and "if there [was] any relationship," *Cox's own children would be related to a family with black blood*. Given the Governor's statements on racial issues, it was best not to go there.

At the Chicago offices of the Republican national committee, located at the Hotel Auditorium, a caller relayed a disturbing story circulating in his locality—Warren Harding was part black. The office manager informed his staff. "Tell them it's a damned lie," said one forcefully. "Yes," replied Nan Britton, with even greater feeling, "tell them it's a damned lie!"

"I was," she would later write, "defending my own baby."

Will Hays had heard the rumors as early as August, maybe earlier. Anticipating trouble, he commissioned genealogists to compile lily-white Harding family trees, demonstrating their descent from pure pre-Revolutionary War western European stock. Such genealogies would soon be circulating in such papers as the *Washington Post* and the *New York Times*.

When the whispering campaign fully hit, more active measures proved necessary. GOP officials and ordinary citizens alike demanded a forceful denial. Denials, however, would only further fuel the rumors, lending them greater credence, perhaps blowing the entire campaign

381

straight to hell. In mid-October, Ohio Republican state committee chairman George H. Clark wrote to the committee's assistant secretary, Charles Hard:

> You have no conception of how the thing is flying over the state. It is everywhere. It is affecting the woman vote. . . . We have fought this thing through before, and we must fight it out again.

Harding was angry, but deep down he was also unsure of the truth, unsure of his very identity. When *Cincinnati Enquirer* reporter James Miller Faulkner asked Harding about the rumors, he mournfully replied, "How do I know, Jim? One of my ancestors may have jumped the fence." Henry Cabot Lodge was outraged. "Three words—'It's a lie'—will stop this," he wired Florence Harding. "Why does not Harding speak them?"

On October 27, Harding embarked on a brief, frantic whistle-stop tour of Ohio—basically to convince nervous white voters that he wasn't black. He remained incensed. "One morning Harding wanted to go over to Wooster and beat Chancellor up," Hard recalled. "It took some little time to get him to cool off."

"If you just let me see this fellow Chancellor," the usually pacifistic Harding bellowed, "I'll make him a subject for 'niggers' to look at."

On the campaign train, rumors flew of an imminent Harding denial—Hard even so informed reporters. "He told us," recalled the *New York World*'s Charles Michelson, "that the candidate was writing a statement on the tale that he had colored blood in his veins. We were discussing where the train should stop long enough for us to file the matter, etc. when the door was suddenly flung open and Mrs. Harding strode in. She glared at Daugherty and exclaimed, 'I'm telling all you people that Warren Harding is not going to make any statement.' Then she went out. If Pullman doors were slammable, that one would have closed it with a crash. Daugherty rubbed his chin and followed her into the candidate's car. Of course, no statement was forthcoming."

In Marion, Florence had received a call from her friend, Evalyn McLean, wife of *Washington Post* publisher Ned McLean. Carolyn Votaw was scheduled to address a group of District of Columbia blacks. The news enraged Florence. "Get that sister of Warren Harding to come out to Friendship [the McLeans' estate] if you love us," Florence shouted. "Keep her there! Do not let her make that speech if you have to lock her in your cellar!" Carolyn Votaw didn't speak.

One voice urged caution. Senator Penrose had sufficiently recuperated to offer some advice: Keep quiet. "From what I hear," Penrose supposedly said, "we've been having a lot of trouble holding the nigger vote lately."

On October 29, Democrat national chairman White took the offensive, accusing Republicans of circulating an alleged anti-Catholic forgery and protesting the innocence of his own party. "I give my word," said White, "that neither the Democratic national committee nor any agents under its control has resorted to a single mischievous device in this campaign. We have not tried to breed class or religious war." He did not mention race or color.

The next day, Jim Cox's *Dayton News* spoke out—not to condemn the whispering campaign, but to blame Republicans for its origins. That was too much for the rival *Journal*. "Has the *Dayton News* shown either the courage or the decency or the honesty to denounce this guttersnipe campaign?" it asked on October 31. "Never!"

"But on the other hand, by insinuation, innuendo, suggestive reference to this slander has been made in Democratic meetings and parades, with no protest from those in charge of the Democratic party."

That same day, Republican national committee publicity director Scott C. Bone jumped into the fray, charging that:

The Washington correspondent of a large Democratic newspaper here in the East today volunteered the information that to his personal knowledge the lying stuff, in printed, mimeographed or typewritten form, was in evidence on Governor Cox's special train and disseminated by a young man closely connected with the Ohio Democratic State Committee.

White and Durbin denied everything, echoing Cox's *Dayton News* by blaming the tales on gossip originating in several previous Ohio Republican primaries and even at the Chicago convention.

On November 1, Chancellor had announced his suit against the

*Dayton Journal*, charging that it had manufactured his denials. Cox's *Dayton News* backed him up, charging: "The statement *The Journal* published was deliberately made up in the office of that newspaper." For good measure, Cox's paper jibed, "The *Dayton Journal* is recognized as the guttersnipe of American journalism."

The *Journal* meanwhile responded in a front-page editorial:

### The Slanderers Will Confess Their Guilt
### Today In A Suit Against the Journal
### —If They Have The Courage!

The political gutter-snipers, who have used every criminal method their vile minds could conjure in their campaign against the family of Warren G. Harding, plan to play their much boasted eleventh hour sensation today with a suit against *The Journal*, supposed to be filed by Prof. Chancellor, over whose name the campaign has been made.

We hope the cowardly conspirators will get Chancellor to file the suit. The sooner the better! Chancellor is the bird we want in court[,] and the easiest and quickest process to get him there is with his suit. We challenge the shameless, cowardly and low-minded men hiding behind Chancellor to bring additional suits on their own account.

We reiterate that the Democratic party tools have wallowed in the slime of wicked assault on a fine American. We reiterate that they have spread in every possible manner this indefensible conspiracy, struck at the fireside of Warren G. Harding and made war on innocent, cultured and charming women for the low down and despicable purpose of getting votes for their candidate for president.

Bring on your Professor Chancellor. He is just the man we want to meet face to face in the court of justice!

And more, the men who distributed this criminal libel may find themselves in the penitentiary, where they belong.

Chancellor signed his denial of making these vile charges. He denied them by word of voice. If a suit is filed against *The Dayton Journal* today, it will be a petition not for justice but as an agency to further spread and reiterate the most foul campaign that ever disgraced American politics.

The suit will prove to the nation that the Democratic party has been befouled by gangsters that have brought it shame and dishonor.

Go on, use Chancellor again and get what you WILL get, the overwhelming condemnation of an outraged public opinion. Now play your eleventh hour "bombshell" which you have advertised and bragged you would do. Play it! Confess your degradation!

If anyone thought it was bluffing, the *Journal* printed a facsimile of Chancellor's notarized affidavit denying responsibility.

In Marion, on Monday morning, November 1—the day before Election Day—controversy boiled over into violence. Outside a local cigar store, Dr. George Harding accosted Democratic Probate Judge William S. Spencer, an active Cox supporter.

"Judge Spencer," Dr. Harding sputtered, "I am informed on what I believe to be reliable information that you have been exhibiting a picture of me and asserting I have negro blood in my veins."

"Doctor," Spencer tried mollifying him, "I assure you on my honor that never at any time have I done anything of the sort."

"If I believed that you had done so, I would smash your face."

A crowd gathered. Spencer continued to deny all, promising to swear to that in writing. Twenty-nine-year-old Herman B. Irey, accompanied by an unidentified woman, jostled his way through the throng. Irey said he had personally heard Spencer spread the rumors. "You're a liar," Spencer spat back. Irey, one of Dick Crissinger's farmhands, slapped Spencer square in the face. Irey's woman friend egged him on, and he pushed the aged, one-legged Spencer with such force that Spencer fell to the pavement. "Hit him again," cried the crowd. Dr. Harding helped Spencer to his feet, now accepted his denials, and assisted him to the District Attorney's office, where he did indeed swear out an affidavit denying all.

The Hardings never could hold a grudge.

# Chapter 23

≈

# "PERVERTS BY SPECIFIC ORDERS"

Thomas Mott Osborne and the Portsmouth Naval Prison were only a fraction of FDR's problems regarding certain delicate sex-related issues.

War had overcrowded Newport, Rhode Island. The peacetime Navy had stationed two thousand sailors in the lavish resort town; now there were twenty-five thousand. Many lived off base, boarded in private homes ("cheap lodging houses") that were removed in off-hours from normal naval discipline. Alcohol, despite wartime restrictions, was readily available. So were drugs, most prominently cocaine, and, of course, prostitutes.

In July 1917, Rhode Island Governor Livingston Beekman provided Josephus Daniels with a letter from *Providence Journal* publisher John R. Rathom, alleging serious problems. "The situation in Newport is about as bad as can be," the rotund, Australian-born Rathom wrote. "These places have been recognized by the police for years; they have been allowed to operate without any hindrance whatever, and orgies of the most disgraceful character have been carried on for the benefit of sailors, and frequently witnessed by police officers themselves as spectators."

Not all the prostitutes were women. And not all the homosexual sex was paid for. In early 1919, Lieutenant Erastus Mead Hudson of the Medical Corps, a Harvard graduate, was assigned to look into not only homosexual prostitution at Newport but also ordinary consensual homosexual liaisons.

On March 19, 1919, a formal court of naval inquiry convened to investigate these "Ladies of Newport." Though finding the evidence "meager in quantity," the court nonetheless recommended a "most thorough and searching investigation . . . by a corps of highly experienced investigators."

Ordinarily, Josephus Daniels would be the one to authorize such action. But Daniels, who found the situation "serious," was en route to Europe. Before departing, he had instructed Franklin Roosevelt to "keep in touch with the situation."

Because civilians were involved, local naval authorities thought the Department of Justice should investigate. Accordingly, on March 22, 1919, FDR wrote to Attorney General Palmer:

> The Navy Department has become convinced that such conditions of vice and depravity exist . . . as to require a most searching and rigid investigation with a view to finally prosecuting and clearing out those people responsible for it. . . . [Newport locals were] "fostering dens where perverted practices are carried on." . . . This department, eager for the protection of its young men from such contaminating influences, desires to have the horrible practices stopped.

Palmer, busy investigating domestic radicals, had neither the resources nor the inclination for this assignment. The lone investigator he dispatched to Newport quickly dismissed existing evidence as "insufficient" and "considerably exaggerated." The Justice Department then passed the matter back to the Navy.

While Roosevelt, Palmer, and the court of inquiry dithered, Newport's naval personnel took action—ill-advised, stupid action, true, but action nonetheless. In February 1919, forty-four-year-old Chief Seaman's Mate Ervin Arnold arrived from San Francisco. The rough-hewn, poorly educated former Connecticut detective possessed a keen interest, verging on obsession, in investigating homosexuals, boasting that he could "tell them a mile off." At Newport, Arnold would investigate both homosexual prostitution and purely consensual sex.

On March 15, 1919, Arnold, with Lieutenant Hudson's backing, recruited thirteen newly enlisted sailors to entrap homosexuals. "You people will be on the field of operation," Arnold instructed them. "You will have to use your judgment whether or not a full act is completed. If that being the fact, it might lead into something greater. You have got to form that judgment at the time you are on that field with that party."

That meant just what it sounded like.

In April 1919, the Hudson–Arnold operation arrested eighteen offending sailors. Two later deserted, fourteen were convicted, and two were dishonorably discharged. That didn't end matters. Governor Beekman arranged for Newport Red Cross Field Director Charles P. Hall to meet with FDR on April 25. Reverend Hall, contending that the situation remained out of control, urged Roosevelt to consult with Lieutenant Hudson—and to establish a special unit to deal with Newport's homosexual problem.

On May 1, Hudson, Arnold, and FDR conferred. Hudson and Arnold later claimed that they discussed the situation at length; FDR claimed that they spoke for five minutes, without discussing how to proceed. Whatever transpired, four days later Roosevelt assigned Hudson and Arnold to Naval Intelligence to investigate "moral perversion and drugs" at Newport. "It is requested," FDR wrote to Chief of Naval Intelligence Rear Admiral Albert P. Niblack, "that this be the only written communication in regard to this affair, as it is thought wise to keep this matter wholly secret."

To Hudson, FDR also provided a letter addressed "To whom it may concern," stating that the lieutenant was "engaged on important work in which I am interested and any assistance you can render him will be appreciated."

Admiral Niblack wanted no part of this Harvard-boys-playing-house-detectives melodrama. Accordingly, on June 1, FDR was reduced to assigning Hudson and Arnold to his own office, under the mysterious grouping "Section A—Office of Assistant Secretary." Roosevelt further designated Hudson as "Commanding Officer of a group of enlisted . . . men who have been assigned . . . certain confidential special duties as agents of the Assistant Secretary of the Navy."

Hudson returned to Washington on June 6–7, 1919, clearly to discuss his questionable means of operations with FDR, for FDR recommended that he confer with Assistant U.S. Attorney General in Charge of All

Prosecutions Claude R. Porter regarding the legality of Section A methods and whether they placed Hudson's "operatives" under risk of arrest. Hudson met with Porter on June 10 and then on June 25 with Providence's Assistant U.S. District Attorney Harvey D. Baker. Both advised Hudson that there were no legal barriers to his methods, though Porter, not surprisingly, raised some moral questions regarding the operation.

Hudson and Arnold recruited forty-one sailors—ten of whom were mere boys between sixteen and nineteen—and ordered them to entrap homosexuals by whatever means necessary. In July 1919, they netted sixteen Newport civilians, including the forty-six-year-old Episcopal chaplain of the Naval Hospital, Samuel Neal Kent, arrested as "a lewd and wanton person."

Reverend Kent boasted excellent education (Boston Latin School) and reputation. His arrest outraged his fellow Episcopal clergy. At Kent's August 23 trial—and acquittal—two sailors testified that they had been authorized to go "to the limit" to obtain arrests. The notion outraged just about everyone who heard of it.

On September 3, Hamilton Fish Webster, millionaire grandson of former New York governor Hamilton Fish, and the Reverend Dr. Stanley C. Hughes, rector of Providence's Trinity Episcopal Church, met with FDR, complaining bitterly over the Navy's treatment of Kent. Roosevelt defended Kent's prosecution and further slammed the judge who had dismissed the charges against Kent as a political hack. But he also vowed, "If anyone has given orders to commit immoral acts, someone will swing for it."

Roosevelt advised Webster and Hughes to inform Acting Chief of the Bureau of Navigation Captain Richard Leigh of their concerns. Leigh, who had taken an active role in early discussions of the case with FDR, Hudson, and Arnold, advised Roosevelt to mothball Section A until a proper investigation could be conducted. On September 4, FDR did just that.

On September 22, outraged Episcopal Bishop of Rhode Island James DeWolf Perry called on Daniels, now back from Europe, who ordered still another investigation, this time by Admiral Niblack. Niblack concluded that Kent was indeed guilty and instructed naval authorities to seek a second trial. Furthermore, Lieutenant Hudson was informed that

Daniels and FDR were "very much pleased" with his unit's work. Kent, meanwhile, had suffered a nervous breakdown, taking treatment at Battle Creek Sanitarium. Arnold's investigators trailed Kent from Rhode Island to Pennsylvania to Michigan, stormed into the sanitarium, and arrested him.

Kent's second trial began on January 5, 1920. Fourteen character witnesses appeared for Kent. Four of Arnold's "operatives" testified, often in lurid detail. Again, their testimony created revulsion, not at Kent, but at Navy methods. It took just three hours for the jury to acquit Kent of all charges. John Rathom, appalled by Navy tactics, demanded that heads roll.

On January 10, Bishop Perry and twelve clergy from five different Protestant denominations wrote President Wilson. "It must be evident to every thoughtful mind," they protested, "that the use of such vile methods cannot fail to undermine the character and ruin the morals of the unfortunate youths detailed for this duty, render no citizen of the community safe from suspicion and calumny, bring the city into unwarranted reproach, and shake the faith of the people in the wisdom and integrity of the naval administration." They "solemnly request[ed]" that Wilson "at the earliest moment . . . eliminate from the navy all officials, however highly placed, who are responsible for the employment of such execrable methods—contrary alike to the dictates of morality, patriotism, and religion."

All this meant trouble. On January 17, Daniels, hoping to short-circuit a congressional investigation, designated Admiral Herbert O. Dunn, Commander of the First Naval District, to oversee a Court of Naval Inquiry on the worsening controversy. Dunn, a close friend to Daniels, was even closer to FDR, with whom he had vacationed in the Azores in 1918. More recently, FDR had helped obtain an Annapolis appointment for Dunn's wife's nephew.

Daniels's strategy proved futile. The next day, Rathom telegraphed Henry Cabot Lodge and the Senate Committee on Naval Affairs, complaining that "many seamen in the navy have been used for the most vile and nameless practices in order to entrap innocent men." The following day, the Senate Committee on Naval Affairs created a special subcommittee, consisting of Lewis H. Ball (R-Delaware), Henry Wilder Keyes (R-New Hampshire), and William H. King (D-Utah), to investigate.

Roosevelt may have hoped to cow the subcommittee into retreating. On January 22, he attacked Rathom, accusing the editor of a "maliciously vicious, dishonest attack on the United States Navy."

The move didn't work, at least not with the press. The *Boston Herald* termed FDR's move "the most serious mistake of his official life." The *Journal*, responding to what it termed FDR's "wild and clumsy attack," professed puzzlement:

> Mr. Roosevelt's political loyalty to his pussy-footing chief has led him into a bog of falsehood and unfairness, where he does not belong, either by training or inclination. Why this outburst on the eve of a senatorial investigation? Would it not have been more politic, and certainly more just, to have waited in an orderly fashion for the evidence, without this preliminary shriek of alarm? Or is it because Administration officials have come to consider themselves so immune from criticism that they think all they have to do in their own defense is to shout "Liar."

On January 22, Rathom telegraphed FDR, alluding to FDR's personal involvement:

> Many boys wearing the uniform of the United States Navy have been forced into the position of moral perverts by specific orders of officers in the Navy Department, and these conditions were known to the Secretary of the Navy and yourself months ago.

On January 25, however, FDR caught a break, when the skittish Ball Subcommittee voted to conduct hearings in secret. The Dunn Inquiry, meanwhile, opened proceedings in late January. It was a classic case of military cover-up. Wrote historian Lawrence R. Murphy:

> Almost from the moment the court opened, the proceedings intensified rather than reduced concerns over U.S. government behavior. Members of the court were friends, colleagues, or subordinates of those implicated in the scandal; throughout the hearings they demonstrated undeniable partiality. The system of

military justice was skillfully manipulated to protect military officers and enlisted men while placing civilians who questioned the government's conduct [Rathom and the clergy] in awkward, defensive positions, made worse by the aggressiveness of the judge advocate and their attorney's ignorance of naval procedures.

On April 25, 1920, Franklin Roosevelt took the stand and blandly ducked responsibility:

[Rathom's Attorney CLAUDE] BRANCH: "Mr. Roosevelt, would you sanction the method of having enlisted men in the Navy submit their bodies to unnatural vices to obtain evidence [?]"

ROOSEVELT: "As a matter of information, of course, no."

BRANCH: "If you knew it was being done, what would your attitude be in regard to it?"

ROOSEVELT: "Stop it."

BRANCH: "You would consider it extremely improper."

ROOSEVELT: "As stated by me, yes."

BRANCH: "As a lawyer, how do you suppose that evidence of a claim could be obtained[?]"

ROOSEVELT: "As a lawyer, I had no idea. That is not within the average lawyer's education."

BRANCH: "Did you give that matter any thought whatsoever?"

ROOSEVELT: "Of course not[,] any more than how they were going to close whorehouses or [stop] the sale of drugs."

BRANCH: "Did you realize as a lawyer or as a man of intelligence that the investigation of such matters, very often had led to improper actions on the part of the investigator?"

ROOSEVELT: "I never had such an idea. Never entered my head. No, sir."

Navy investigators reserved their wrath for the whistleblowers in the case: Kent's fellow clergymen, and particularly John Rathom. Rathom was no angel. Much of his résumé was manufactured. Many of his wartime stories were inventions of the British Secret Service. The Dunn inquiry quickly became an investigation of Rathom, as Navy attorney

Ensign Henry I. Hyneman peppered him with questions designed to destroy his credibility. Claude Branch openly voiced suspicions that the court was gathering evidence for a lawsuit against his client.

Some witnesses weren't called at all. "The Dunn court was a white-wash," concluded FDR biographer Ted Morgan. "The one man who could have testified that he had kept Franklin informed about the methods of Section A, Lieutenant Hudson, was excused from appearing on account of illness."

Nonetheless, the Dunn Court could hardly avoid certain conclusions, censuring Ervin Arnold for using "enlisted men . . . to obtain evidence in the investigation of perversion . . . which [is] contrary and repugnant to the traditions of the service," and finding FDR's actions "unfortunate and ill-advised" in "either [having] directed or permitted the use of enlisted personnel to investigate perversion."

The Dunn Inquiry and the Senate Navy Subcommittee investigations, nonetheless, created little impact on the national consciousness. The topic may have been *too* salacious, *too* hot for the press to even hint at. There had never quite been a case like it. How was one to write about it? What details to report? Who to blame? Whose morality made any sense at all?

Following FDR's nomination for the vice-presidency, Senator Ball proved even warier of investigating him, fearing that whatever he, Ball, did might seem political. He asked Cabot Lodge if he might better drop the matter. Lodge said no. Still, Ball kept things under wraps.

As the presidential campaign lurched to its conclusion, John Rathom shattered the silence, bringing FDR's Navy Department to the fore—not, however, by highlighting the Newport incident but rather by resuscitating the controversy regarding Thomas Mott Osborne's ill-fated stewardship of Portsmouth Naval Prison. Rathom charged that FDR had "destroyed or sequestered Navy records" during the resulting set-to with Captain Joseph K. Taussig. In Portland, Oregon, Roosevelt denied the accusation.

Later, Roosevelt was campaigning in Newburgh, New York's Hotel Palatine on Saturday evening, October 23. *Journal* editor Arthur L. Fairbrother presented him with a sealed envelope, then walked away. Inside was a lengthy letter from Rathom, repeating the accusation, and rehashing the entire Portsmouth imbroglio. The letter was simultaneously being sent to Republican editors nationwide, as FDR put it, "from the same address and in the same type of envelope as used in sending out propaganda by the Republican National Committee."

Rathom's missive included these choice words:

> What interest you may have in this particular man [Clarence A. Parker, a homosexual sailor returned to duty by Thomas Mott Osborne] must ever remain a mystery unless you care to explain. A charitable construction of your act might be that you wished to please the influential Mr. Osborne . . . as at that time you were contemplating a seat in the United States Senate from New York. . . . Yet even under the stress of campaign eagerness[,] how decent men with the moral welfare of the Navy at heart could directly order the return to honorable service of a man convicted of unnatural offenses to mingle with and contaminate the good men of the service, and this at a time when the country was at war, is beyond all comprehension. . . .
>
> You, even more than Josephus Daniels, have been the evil genius of that department and you have earned the detestation and contempt of every patriotic and skilled naval officer with whom you came in contact.

In his editorial pages, Rathom continued the assault. "If there are two characteristics in which Mr. Roosevelt is utterly lacking," he charged, "they are the qualities of frankness and manliness."

"The inescapable implication," wrote historian Geoff Ward, "was that Roosevelt was himself politically unprincipled, homosexual, or both. . . . Franklin was stunned by Rathom's letter because of the public doubts it raised about his masculinity, but also possibly because it stirred within him echoes of old private doubts about himself."

Roosevelt reacted furiously. He phoned the *Journal*'s Washington correspondent, Sevellon Brown, demanding that Rathom retract his letter. If not, he vowed retaliation: Information about Rathom would soon make the papers. Rathom stood his ground.

On Sunday, October 24, FDR publicly demanded that United States

Attorney for the Southern District of New York Francis G. Caffey prosecute Rathom for criminal libel. "In view of the fact that the circulation of
charges of this character would obviously blacken my character as a candidate for the office of Vice President of the United States," FDR wrote
Caffey, a law partner of Secretary of State Colby, "I believe that they are
not merely libelous but criminally so. It is almost needless to assure you
that they are wholly untrue."

On Wednesday, October 27, Caffey responded, explaining that
Rathom could not have violated federal postal regulations, as his letter
had been hand-carried to FDR, and also announcing his uncertainty
regarding whether federal or state jurisdictions were involved beyond
that. Nothing Caffey said made any sense. Electoral campaigns (and,
often, a free press) were *all about* "blackening" candidates' reputations.
And, as the *Attleboro Sun* pointed out regarding Caffey's hiding behind
the issue of postal regulations, Rathom had reproduced his offending
letter in the *Journal*, which was then *mailed out* to subscribers.

Caffey, however, had no uncertainties about foraging for damaging
material (along with Assistant Attorney General Thomas J. Spellacy,
Franklin's former legal adviser at Navy) in Rathom's Justice Department
files; both acted with Attorney General Palmer's authorization. On
October 27, 1920, Caffey released to the press an embarrassing February
12, 1918, statement given by Rathom to Assistant Attorney General A.
Bruce Bielaski, clarifying, correcting, and, in some cases, contradicting
information found in the *Journal*'s wartime news stories. Beyond that,
Caffey and Spellacy found documentation that Rathom had lied about
virtually every aspect in his official biography, enjoyed a rather sordid
marital history, and had even fabricated his grand middle name "Revel-
stoke." Caffey blandly admitted that his release of this information was
related to the Roosevelt matter.

Rathom fired back:

> I am at a loss to understand why the controversy between Mr. Roo-
> sevelt and myself should so far interest Mr. Caffey, an employ[ee]
> in the pay of the Federal Government, as to induce him to make a
> gratuitous and vicious attack upon my reputation.
>
> His charges, with the inferences he seeks to have drawn from

the publication of the letter referred to, are false, malicious and clearly put forward for political purposes. . . .

Mr. Caffey's attack on me is an attempt to turn public attention from the charges brought by me against Franklin D. Roosevelt in connection with his record as Assistant Secretary of the Navy, which charges stand as I made them. The only conceivable motive for this extraordinary and unparalleled attack at this time by one of the most powerful departments of the Government of the United States is the desire to get in some petty political advantage on the eve of a Presidential election.

The characterization of this letter as a confession is entirely unfounded, and is proved by the language of the letter itself, to a careful reading of which I invite public attention.

Roosevelt wasn't through, however. On Thursday, October 28, 1920, he sued Rathom and two functionaries of the RNC publicity bureau, Scott C. Bone and Edward B. Clark, its manager and assistant manager respectively, for $500,000 for criminal libel.

The *Journal* countered that FDR was "the possessor of an immature mind, a shallow thinker on subjects too deep for him, an amateur statesman—and a professional politician."

The time for words and threats and lawsuits, though, was fast coming to a close.

It was time to vote.

*Chapter 24*

# "IT WAS AN EARTHQUAKE"

And, now, it ended.

Maine traditionally voted early, holding its state and local elections in mid-September until 1960—hence the adage "As Maine goes, so goes the nation." Democrats, desperate for portents of hope, shipped speakers into the state—FDR, Josephus Daniels, Bainbridge Colby, and Homer Cummings. Republicans countered with Calvin Coolidge, Cabot Lodge, and Teddy Roosevelt Jr. On September 13, Republicans carried every county for governor, elected all 31 state senators, all four congressmen, and 140 of 151 state representatives—their strongest showing since 1896. In far-north Aroostook County, Castle Hill Township voted 100-to-1 Republican. "The postmaster stood firm," jibed one wag. Governor Cox downplayed the results, ascribing them to artificial infusions of Will Hays's "pyrotechnics" and money. But he knew better.

The infant polling industry continued its efforts. *The Literary Digest* mailed ballots to voters in six key states: New York, New Jersey, Ohio, Indiana, Illinois, and California. The projection: Harding.

The *New York World* polled 300 newspaper editors. Their projection: Harding.

The *Boston Globe* polled 20,610 women in the five New England States, tracking them down in mills and churches and stores. Cox and Roosevelt carried the Ladies Catholic Benevolent Association in Chelsea and R. P. McLean's Jewelry Store in Marblehead, but that was virtually it. Harding and Coolidge won in a walk, 14,398–5,738.

Customers at Louis K. Liggett's 8,000-store Rexall Drug chain deposited ballots in in-store ballot boxes overseen by specially hired clerks. In 1916, Rexall's poll had not only forecast Wilson's close win; it had predicted his razor-thin victories in New Hampshire and California. In 1920, 1,239,689 customers voted, projecting Harding over Cox 379–152 in the Electoral College. Democratic national chairman White blasted Rexall as pro-Republican.

In San Francisco, Democrats surrendered early, vacating their western headquarters on Saturday, October 30. It wasn't much better back in Manhattan. At 11 A.M. on Election Day, Tuesday, November 2, landlord Coleman du Pont padlocked the national Democratic committee office. Its doors stayed shut until Democrats produced a $2,900 check for their November rent. They shouldn't have been surprised: du Pont was a member of the Republican national committee.

On October 30, a frantic James M. Cox delivered five speeches, culminating in an address to three thousand Democrats in the 14,000-seat Chicago Coliseum. Cox flayed what he called the "basest conspiracy of the ages" responsible for torpedoing the League. He vowed defeat for every anti-League senator running for re-election. He derided "cheap and spurious patriotism" and the "selfishness" that led America away from involvement in the wider world. He ridiculed "George Burchard Harvey" (really George Brinton McClellan Harvey) and Room 404 of the Blackstone. He read his audience each and every word of Christ's parable of the Good Samaritan—and women wept.

James Middleton Cox had pulled out all the stops, and it wasn't going to do any good.

The next morning, his train pulled into Dayton. As bells tolled mournfully from nearby Emmanuel Church, campaign aide James W. Faulkner emerged from his berth. Stifling tears, Faulkner informed Cox: "Those bells tell me that at this very moment my mother at early mass in Cincinnati is praying confidently for your election, and you haven't a chance. It's a damn shame."

Franklin Roosevelt hammered away to the end. In Poughkeepsie on the day before Election Day, he reiterated his basic message: The election boiled down to "whether the U.S. is to finish the end of the war or quit cold, whether we are to join the other forty odd nations in the great working League of Nations that will serve to end war for all time or whether we will turn our back on them. . . ." He bashed Republicans as the "executors and legatees of the political will of Mark Hanna." If he believed he had a chance, he was the only one aboard his campaign train who did.

In Chicago, on Election Eve, five thousand Socialist Party supporters sang "The Marseillaise" and carried banners reading "FREE ALL POLITICAL AND INDUSTRIAL PRISONERS," "COX SAYS THE LEAGUE OF NATIONS IS THE WORK OF GOD; WE WANT A MAN ON THE JOB; ELECT DEBS; ELECT DEBS," and "LONG LIVE THE RUSSIAN SOVIET."

In Toledo, Socialist leaflets fluttered down from the skies—and from four aeroplanes. Somewhere in the litter, four lucky leaflets entitled finders to unspecified "cash prizes." It all sounded very capitalistic to the uninitiated.

Their candidate remained at Atlanta Prison. That day, Gene Debs issued his final campaign statement:

> I have followed the battle closely as circumstances would allow, and I feel confident the result will mark a distinct advance in the socialist movement. . . .
>
> The election is on the second. On the third our campaign reopens. There is no interval between. Not an hour is lost. It will end only when capitalism is dead and labor is free.
>
> Let us open our next campaign with all the enthusiasm that revolutionary idealism inspires. Let us strike hands tight together like comrades for the cause. We have had factional strife enough. Let us unite, close up the ranks, settle differences among ourselves, in a decent spirit, and put all our united effort and energy into the task of organizing the workers industrially and politically for their emancipation.
>
> To each and all of you, my comrades and friends who have stood by us so loyally since we began to serve our time, I send thanks and love in behalf of us all. You have been the best of friends and the most devoted of comrades. And our hearts go out to you all. . . . I love you all, and as I think of all you have been to me only my silence and my tears can tell you what is in my heart.

I thank the capitalist masters for putting me here. They know where I belong under their criminal and corrupt system. It is the only compliment they could pay me.

But there was a bitterness in Debs—and a nagging contempt for the masses he claimed to love. "I shall not be disappointed as the people will get what they think they want," he sneered, "in so far as they think at all."

From Northampton that day, Calvin Coolidge wrote his father at Plymouth Notch:

The campaign is over. Some mistakes were made, always are I suppose, but the ones this year were so foolish [that] I do not see how they could have been made by men really trying to elect the ticket.

I am at home today. Came home yesterday. Boys are well. Your dog is growing well. She has bitten the ice man, the milkman, and the grocerman. It is good to have some way to get even with them for the high prices they charge for everything.

In the morning Mr. Stearns will try to find out how to telephone returns to you. I shall be passing the evening at my [Boston] headquarters in the [Hotel] Touraine.

Tell Aurora [the housekeeper] I hope she is well.

Jim Cox remained imprisoned in frenzied activity. Back and forth, back and forth, Cox traveled, hoping against hope that one more stop, one more speech, might catch lightning in a bottle, might make *the* difference. Superstitiously, he ended his campaign in Toledo, since the one time he hadn't, he had lost to Frank Willis. Addressing an overflow crowd at the Toledo Coliseum on Election Eve, he spoke of his upcoming victory as a "victory for humanity"; but as he rambled on, his message became increasingly less humane and less rational.

The Republicans, he charged, spewing his usual racial animus, "said at the outset of this campaign, 'We can count on the Negro vote: that will come to us in solid mass.' I say to you there has been entirely too much said in secret places about social equality for the future good and serenity of our people. That is a dangerous thing."

Finally, he exploded: "Every traitor in America will vote tomorrow for Warren G. Harding."

People walked out of the hall.

And William Randolph Hearst walked out on the Democratic Party. He had warned Cox that he would only support him if jettisoned the Wilson "millstone." "Be a Democrat, Be an American, And be President," Hearst warned in his *New York American*. Cox wouldn't listen, and the still-radical Hearst endorsed the conservative Harding, the overriding issue being, as Hearst put it in front-page editorials, "the defeat of the Wilson foreign league."

Cox's train reached Dayton at dawn on Election Day. He slept till 9:00, casting his vote at 10:19 A.M. at a combination confectionery store/barbershop/print shop in Carrmonte, a half mile from his lavish Trail's End mansion. Cox, with his wife and his daughter and son-in-law, waited in line for fifteen minutes, making small talk about going bear-hunting in Mississippi after the election. "There's a lot of excitement in Carrmonte today," Cox told an elderly woman. "Yep," she snapped back, "this town needs to be waked up."

Republican national chairman Will Hays oozed confidence. On Election Eve, he took in the play *The Half-Moon*, at Forty-second Street's Liberty Theater, basking in the presence of fellow first-nighters Charlie Chaplin and Flo Ziegfeld. Warren Harding had been home for days, having made his last appearance outside Marion on Saturday night, October 30, speaking to ten thousand at Columbus's jam-packed Memorial Hall. He'd spent Election Eve at his office, chatting with visitors and newsmen, reading both Suetonius and Edgar Saltus's popular history of ancient Rome, *Imperial Purple*, and, by all accounts, sleeping soundly that night.

In Harlem, the United Communist Party circulated placards urging a voter boycott. THE WHOLE ELECTION BUSINESS IS A FAKE TO FOOL YOU, its signs read. OVERTHROW THE CAPITALIST GOVERNMENT, ESTABLISH THE SOVIET GOVERNMENT. Police arrested three men for their distribution. They protested that they were not communists, only $20-a-day hired hands.

In Marion, it rained on election morning, but turnout was heavy. Warren and the Duchess motored to the Precinct C voting booth of

Marion's Fourth Ward, at a small red brick garage on South Greenwood Street, three blocks from home. A bad cold had dogged Florence for days. Alongside was George Christian, the senator's secretary, and Frank Blacksten, the family chauffeur. Eleven people were ahead of them in line. Warren was number thirteen. Wilson would have liked that. Like the Coxes, they waited fifteen minutes. America was nothing if not democratic. When the Duchess, adorned in white kid gloves, black satin hat, black shoes, blue dress, and pleated black cape, received her paper ballots, she exclaimed, "Goodness! Do I have to fill out all these?" She did.

The precinct election clerk called out: "Warren G. Harding."

"More or less notorious," the candidate responded, taking time to pose for newspaper and newsreel cameras. Bundled in his dark brown soft felt hat and heavy winter overcoat, he crowded into the little voting booth. Emerging in a flash, he handed his marked ballot to election official Patrick Kelly. "Hold the ballot once more, Senator," a reporter yelled. "All right," Harding called back, "make an honest scenario. But I can't vote for myself more than once."

"Twice," a woman shouted, and everybody laughed.

It rained in Hyde Park, but locals jammed District 3's polling station to cheer the Roosevelt family—Franklin and Eleanor and mother Sara and brother Rosie and his wife Betty—when they arrived at 10:45 A.M. Eleanor, Sara, and Betty all cast their first presidential votes. Franklin was number 207 to vote, Eleanor 208.

In Northampton, neighbors and local schoolchildren cheered as the Coolidges' two sons—exuberant twelve-year-old Calvin Jr. and the very reserved fourteen-year-old John—began Election Day by raising the American flag on the modest flagpole dominating their minuscule front lawn. Just before 9 A.M., Calvin, Grace, and their housekeeper, Mrs. Bertha Reckhan, rode to City Hall, where four wards, including the Coolidges' Second, voted. Hand in hand, the governor and his bride strolled to the polling place. At precisely 9:19, Calvin voted for himself for vice president. Only then did Grace, always deferential in public, vote. They mingled for a while, then rode to Boston and the State Suite at the Hotel Touraine, where waves of supporters would come to call.

No crowds watched Woodrow Wilson. He and Joe Tumulty had voted by absentee ballot—on October 30—mailing their ballots back to New

Jersey. Their wives cast their ballots for the first time, thanks, as the *Washington Post* inexplicably explained it, to the new "Tenth amendment."

Farmer-Laborite Parley Parker Christensen balloted in Salt Lake City, then returned home to mind his blind, aged mother. In Germantown, Ohio, Dr. & Mrs. Aaron S. Watkins wrote in Dr. Watkins—the Prohibitionist Party wasn't on the Ohio ballot. Eugene V. Debs couldn't vote at all.

William Allen White wrestled with his conscience and his ego. "Every time I considered voting for either of them I decided to vote for the other," he would write. "I ended by thinking hard about Cox as I went into the election booth and so managed for a moment to justify a vote for Harding. I could have done it the other way quite as easily."

In Augusta, Georgia, black women attempting to vote were refused on the grounds that state law required registration six months before voting. "No white women presented themselves at the polls," a wire service reported.

In Boston, letters signed by "Mrs. Malcolm A. Webster," secretary of the "Massachusetts Election Commission," warned recipients that state law provided fines of up to $500 and up to a year in jail for those providing "false statements" while registering to vote. Neither "Mrs. Malcolm A. Webster" nor the "Massachusetts Election Commission" actually existed. State Attorney General J. Weston Allen noted that the letters only went to "colored voters," particularly first-time black women voters.

Twelve miles from Orlando, Florida, in tiny Ocoee, two well-to-do local black men, orange grove owner Mose Norman and orange grove foreman July Perry, approached the local polling place, attempting to vote. The Klan had warned that such moves would meet retribution. Officials lied that Norman had not paid his poll tax and therefore couldn't vote. He returned, armed with a shotgun. They seized his gun and beat him up. Later, a white mob surged into Ocoee. July Perry shot and killed two of its members. Somewhere between five and fifty blacks died in the ensuing melee. The mob dragged Perry from the local jail, lynched him, and riddled his body with bullets. For good measure, they destroyed Ocoee, burning to the ground twenty-five homes, two churches, and a Masonic lodge.

After voting, Harding golfed with Harry Daugherty at Columbus's

Scioto Golf Club, forty miles from Marion. The Duchess, though, wanted Warren home for supper. It was his fifty-fifth birthday. His father and sister would be there, and she had prepared a special white cake, frosted in pink, with fifty-five candles. Chauffeur Frank Blacksten sped home along rain-slicked roads. Ten miles from Marion, he careened off the road, just missing a telephone pool and nearly killing the nominee.

After dinner, a delegation of about twenty *Marion Star* employees arrived on their boss's front porch to present him with a birthday present—a gold printer's make-up rule. "Fellow members of *The Star*," Harding started up, pausing as emotion flooded over him, "you and I have been associated together for many years. I know you, and you know I wouldn't cheat you. I am coming into a position of very great responsibilities if the present returns are interpreted correctly. I don't know whether I can meet them adequately. I know one thing, I can meet them with the same justice and fairness as in the dealings which I have had with you."

He spied white-bearded seventy-six-year-old Lewis Miller. "There is my old friend Miller," he continued, "the oldest employee on *The Star*. Thirty years we've been together. Sometimes the road was thorny. Sometimes I have known him to draw his pay when I had to borrow it from my mother. There were other times when I had to borrow Miller's pay back from him in the morning."

By now, the crowd was in tears, and Harding's voice shook with emotion and with the awesome responsibility he felt. "I am just a plain fellow," he continued, "but if I've been on the square with you, I wouldn't cheat you now. I am going to be on the square with everybody. Somehow this has touched me."

Around the country, the polls closed. People didn't receive results from the Internet or from television or, mostly, even radio back then. By and large, if they wanted to know what happened before reading their newspapers, they had to leave home and *go somewhere*. Party faithful traveled to party headquarters or clubhouses or to rallies; but if you weren't part of the local courthouse or customhouse crowd, didn't have a job as postmaster or postmistress, didn't know or like the precinct committee, there were plenty of other places to learn the score of the biggest ball game in town.

In Chicago, the *Tribune* provided fourteen sites (most complete with bands) where, starting at 6:30 P.M., the public watched returns being posted. The *Tribune* also arranged for Chicago Telephone Company operators to provide callers with sketchy results.

The paper also flashed returns to gala parties in London, Paris, Berlin, Coblenz, Prague, Vienna, and Warsaw—the information reaching Europe "in exactly seven minutes after being dispatched from the *The Chicago Tribune* offices in New York."

District of Columbia police roped off Pennsylvania Avenue for crowds viewing returns flashed on two large double screens affixed to the *Washington Post*'s offices. Three blocks away, the upstart National Radio School vowed to scoop the mighty *Post*. "Outstripping the fastest wires . . . collaborating with the Powerful Set at Arlington," it promised to "flash the count while the ballots are warm in the handling." At the Shoreham Hotel, starting at 10 P.M., more sedate citizens could listen to "special music" while receiving returns. Republicans gathered at the city's Masonic Temple, Democrats at their own headquarters, to receive results by radio.

In Atlanta, over ten thousand people poured into Five Points, not only watching returns projected onto a huge screen by "more than a score" of *Atlanta Constitution* staffers, but being entertained by "the occasional insertion on the screen from the facile pen of Lewis Gregg, the *Constitution*'s staff artist."

Atlanta's black population kept to themselves and got returns over a leased wire at the First Congregational Church over on Courtland Street.

In Jim Cox's Dayton, voters received returns at the local Y.W.C.A., where tea was served and a school orchestra provided proper accompaniment, or at the Montgomery County Women's Republican Club, the Dayton Teachers Club, or the Elks.

In rain-swept New York, the Republican *Tribune* called it for Harding and Coolidge at 8 P.M. Downtown, just across from City Hall, the Democratic *World* held out a mere quarter-hour longer, when flashing lights atop its domed twenty-six-story Park Row tower turned red, signaling a GOP victory. On Forty-second Street, the Times Tower's signals for a Harding victory were a white searchlight to the south and red lights on the building's flagpole. If Cox won, white lights would flood the flagpole

405

and the searchlight would point north. Not until 9:30 did the bitter-end *Times* flash the Harding signal.

New York City's Socialists pretty much knew how the story would turn out—but they watched anyway. Downtown, at Twelfth Street and Fourth Avenue, they saw returns projected on the side of the *New York Call* building. At Harlem's New Star Casino, at 117th Street and Park Avenue—from 8 P.M. to 4 A.M.—Socialists danced the night away.

It rained in Boston too, but the biggest crowd in forty years, ten thousand strong, watched the results flashed by the *Globe* on a huge sheet festooned across the Liggett Building at Adams Square. In Los Angeles, at First and Broadway, the staunchly Republican *Times* displayed returns via their own "stereopticon" slides, as well as providing returns to telephone callers. "In these bulletins," the *Times* noted, "special attention will be given to the Presidential contest, the California Senate fight, Congress in the Ninth District, the judgeships and important local contests; also the anti-Jap law, the prohibition amendment and the single tax."

Back in Manhattan, 1,500 socialite (not socialist) alumnae of exclusive St. Timothy's School danced at the Hotel Commodore's ballroom as election returns flashed on a huge screen. "The idea of reading the returns on the screen while dancing appealed to many women voters," noted the *Times*, "who came from their country homes to cast their ballot. . . ."

The city's Ohio Society, savoring a victory either way, hosted a gala for eight hundred at the Waldorf. "A program will begin at 8 o'clock," noted the *Times*, "interspersed with motion pictures and vaudeville." Everybody who was anybody in Manhattan hosted election-returns festivities—everybody, including even tenor Enrico Caruso.

Politics fascinated city slickers and small-town bumpkins alike. In Indianapolis, voters watched tallies flashed on the local Merchants Heat & Light Company, which promised viewers "No Street Cars—No Traffic."

In Dayton, film-goers could receive returns at Loew's Dayton ("with vaudeville for just 15¢ 25¢ 35¢ every evening"), the Columbia ("prices 28¢ until 6 P.M., 39¢ thereafter"), or at Ascher's New Auditoreum ("special election returns announced by the Magnavox, the new telemegraphone"), while live theater devotees could take in returns along with *The Master of Ballantrae* at the Victory or the less highbrow *Liberty Girls* at the Lyric.

Warren Harding's neighbors could obtain returns at all three of
Marion's theaters, the Marion, the Grand, and the Orpheum, the local
outpost of the Keith vaudeville chain. Patrons at the Grand's regular 7:15
and 9:00 shows obtained returns while watching William Farnum in *Drag
Harlan*, "An Exhilarating Romance of the Speediest Two-Gun Wizard the
West Ever Knew," and live acts Shean and Ruth ("Comedy, Singing,
Dancing") and The Brandas ("Comedy, Juggling and Dancing"). And if
moviegoers missed those shows they could catch:

### ALSO — SPECIAL SHOW
Starting at 10:45 and continuing until midnight, will be given for
the benefit of ladies and others who may desire a congenial and
comfortable place in which to receive the news.
Usual Prices.

At the Orpheum, returns came alongside Harry Carey ("The
Humanest Actor On the Screen") in another Western, *Bullet Proof*, plus
live "vodvil" acts such as the stage comedy *Bohemia*, acrobats Prosper
and Market, and "youthful violinist" Jenny Middleton. All for just 25
cents (for cheap seats) or 40 cents (for something decent).

By and large, if they wanted to know what happened before reading
their newspapers, they had to leave home and go somewhere.

By and large.

A few—but growing number of—Americans had discovered radio—
or "wireless," as they called it. America's first commercial radio station,
Pittsburgh's KDKA, was licensed by the Department of Commerce on
October 27, 1920, to debut at 360 meters (833.3 kHz) on November 1. It
didn't sign on, however, until the following night. Owned by Westinghouse, which hoped to sell a lot more radio receivers if people could
enjoy steady programming, KDKA's very first broadcast proved to be the
election returns.

It wasn't much of an operation. Within a shack atop Westinghouse's
East Pittsburgh plant roof, technicians fiddled with a microphone, two
fifty-watt oscillators, and four fifty-watt modulators. The transmitter consisted of a strand of wire strung to "a nearby smokestack." Only a thousand listeners, mostly Pittsburghers, heard KDKA's pioneer broadcast.

The Atlanta station of the Georgia Railway and Power Company, however, picked up KDKA's signals and relayed them to wireless operators within another 600-mile radius. So did the Georgia School of Technology's Macon station, which relayed returns to another ten thousand operators in the South.

The *Detroit News*'s amateur station 8MK (later WWJ), on the air regularly since August 20, also broadcast returns. Returns reached their announcer by being run up the stairs, rather than by phone or telegraph. At street level, a *News* employee shouted results through a megaphone—and probably reached more listeners than the station itself.

Democrats feigned optimism. At 8 P.M., National Chairman George White announced that his party had dodged the bullet: Al Smith had been re-elected in New York, and "direct returns from Kentucky, Idaho and West Virginia [indicate] we shall carry those three States by safe majorities. Thus the first of the Republican pre-election claims are demolished." Actually, the GOP claims were accurate: Democrats lost in all four states.

In Wooster, while William E. Chancellor and his three children prudently remained home, a small crowd of drunks received results at the local Western Union office and resolved to teach the teacher a lesson. Four of Chancellor's students heard rumors of their plans. Armed with shotguns and rifles, they evacuated Chancellor and his family, then faced off equally armed hooligans until two cars of police arrived. Chancellor's students remained through the night to guard his house.

In Marion, after the gang from the *Star* had departed, Harding elbowed his way through thousands of well-wishers to reach the house next door, now his campaign office, to receive returns from a leased Associated Press wire and from Will Hays in New York. At 10:30 P.M., Daugherty turned to Harding, saying "There is no doubt about the result. I am going over to Dr. Sawyer's to get some sleep." The Hardings wanted Harry to stay—or, at least, to spend the night with them, but the exhausted Daugherty wanted to escape the crowd. "This will be the most exciting night Marion has ever experienced," he told Harding. "You should be very happy. You are elected by the biggest majority any President has ever received. Nothing can change the result. Cox has been overwhelmingly defeated. It is certain, and I congratulate you. But before I go[,] I want to say something you ought to know. Unless you have made promises, you will enter the White House one of the freest men ever elected President of the United States. I have not made a single promise to any man or interests for any position or favor."

Harding, again moved by events, replied, "I have made no promises except those contained in public speeches. You have conducted an unusual campaign, with hardships and abuse, and you will never know how much I appreciate it. Next to Mrs. Harding[,] you are the best friend I have in the world."

"Don't count me," Florence protested. "You two old cronies take all the credit for everything done in this household."

"You are all happy over the result now," Harry said as he left, "but considering the great responsibilities, I don't feel so gay. But it's over, and God bless you."

Warren stayed up until 2:00 A.M. and shook five thousand hands. The crowd lifted Florence on its shoulders and joyously passed her around the yard. She didn't mind.

Woodrow Wilson initially planned on receiving bulletins as late as 11 P.M.—well past his regular bedtime. Rumors swirled that he would resign if Republicans won. "So obsessed is Mr. Wilson," wrote the *Chicago Tribune*, "with the anticipation of popular vindication at the polls . . . that some of his associates profess to entertain fears that the election of Harding would not only shock him severely but produce disastrous effect upon his mental and physical condition." Early returns were so bad that he retired at 9:00.

Governor Cox's superstitions continued. He would obtain returns in his *Dayton News* office from a gold telegraph key used by both Grover Cleveland and Woodrow Wilson to receive their victorious returns. Specially installed phone lines connected him with FDR and the White House.

Cox reached his office at 7:30 P.M. Outside, his own newsboys shouted the dismal early totals. A great crowd waiting outside heard precious little good news. Cox barely carried his home county. Ohio—and just about everywhere else—was lost. A whoop went up when Cox won Abraham Lincoln's birthplace, Kentucky's Larue County, by five hundred votes, but precious else justified even mild cheers. At 10:15 P.M., National

Chairman White surrendered. At 11 P.M., the *Dayton News* issued a special edition. Its headline read: REPUBLICAN LANDSLIDE; HARDING WINS.

"I will make no statement tonight," Cox coldly informed reporters, "and whatever my paper says is purely impersonal."

Franklin Roosevelt's family, along with Louis Howe and his wife, received returns in a forlorn little smoking room at Hyde Park. Eleanor took it worse than he did.

An *Atlanta Constitution* reporter brought results to Gene Debs in Warden Fred Zerbst's office. Zerbst handed out what he called "campaign cigars." Debs predicted he'd get two million votes. "This is the first campaign in which I participated and not felt all used up on election night," he reflected. "In 1912, I toured the country on a special train for sixty-eight days in which time I made 535 speeches. Election night, my throat was raw: I was so tired I couldn't rest. Three weeks were required for me to recuperate. It is much easier this time. And if the popular vote increases, I doubt if they will ever let me make another speech."

When he heard of Harding's win, Debs smiled and trotted out his tried-and-true concession speech: "Blessed are those that expect nothing, for. . . ." With no rallies to attend or speeches to give, he went to bed: "In the next hour, I was in dreamland sailing the seven seas in quest of new worlds to conquer."

Some Socialists had predicted three million votes for Debs. In New York, they forecast between 175,000 and 200,000 votes for their candidates—plus the election of five congressmen, two state senators, and at least thirteen assemblymen. They fell far short of their hopes. Nationally, Debs secured just 919,799 votes—the party's highest raw vote total, but, at 3.4 percent, a sharp decline from 1912's 6 percent. Even with women now voting, Debs barely topped his 1912 vote total of 900,369 and barely exceeded lackluster 1916 party candidate Allan Benson's 3.2 percent. Most support came from the East, with 204,146 votes in New York alone. The old far Western strongholds were fading fast.

"The vote . . . was particularly disappointing," noted Debs biographer Ray Ginger, "since it did not represent votes for socialism. Thousands upon thousands had cast their votes for the prisoner in order to protest the infringements of civil liberties. The election finally established what

410

everybody had known: the Socialist Party had almost disappeared as an organized movement."

Debs still spoke bravely of Wilson and Palmer's rebuke and how "Socialism will flourish like a green tree under the Harding administration. We know its nature and hail its advent." But once again, he betrayed contempt for the masses he professed to love so much: "The great body of people do not progress of their own volition. They do not think for themselves, but follow their so-called leaders. They do not move until they are moved by the very conditions created by their own ignorance and stupidity."

Other minor candidates trailed even Debs. Farmer-Labor Party spokesmen predicted enough electoral votes to throw the election into the House of Representatives. Despite strong showings in Washington and South Dakota, the Christensen–Hays ticket garnered just 265,411 votes and not a single electoral vote. Prohibitionists Aaron Watkins and D. Leigh Colvin recorded 189,408 votes, the party's lowest total since 1884. In Texas, American Party candidates former Governor J. E. "Pa" Ferguson of Texas and William J. Hough of New York, received 47,968 votes—9.86 percent of the state total. Socialist-Labor standard-bearers, St. Louis interior decorator William Wesley Cox and New York attorney August Gillhaus (31,715 votes—plus 1,515 votes obtained in Oregon on the "Industrial Labor" ticket), and Single-Taxers Robert C. Macauley and Richard G. Barnum (5,837 votes) brought up the rear.

The biggest minor party of the night was the Democratic—or at least it felt like a minor party, as Republicans swept almost all quarters. Harding received 60.2 percent of the popular vote—the biggest popular percentage in history to that date, easily exceeding Teddy Roosevelt's 56.4 percent in 1904, Andrew Jackson's 56 percent in 1828, and U. S. Grant's 55.6 percent in 1872. He crushed Cox—16,152,200 votes to 9,147,353. His 7,004,847-vote plurality was the biggest to date.

In the Electoral College, he steamrollered Cox 404–127, an even greater majority than predicted by the Rexall poll. He was the first Republican to carry recently admitted Oklahoma, Arizona, and New Mexico and the first to carry Tennessee since Grant in 1868. Calvin Coolidge's reluctant campaigning seemed to have paid off—or, as William Allen White grudgingly admitted, "The back woods of the Green

Mountains could speak the language of the back woods of the Appalachians."

Harding carried New York City, the first Republican since William McKinley in 1896, taking all five boroughs and every Assembly district in the entire state, save for Al Smith's Lower East Side home district. He carried Tammany boss Charlie Murphy's district, two to one. He carried his own normally Democratic Marion precinct, 373 to 76. He carried Cox's home district by 12 votes. He carried Northampton (which had a Democratic mayor), two to one. He carried Plymouth Notch, 158–15 (it had been 91–89 for Hughes four years before). He carried Hyde Park by 86 votes (in tiny Hyde Park, that was a comfortable margin), and he captured Woodrow Wilson's Princeton, five to one, and Wilson's own normally Democratic district, 318–145.

Harding piled up huge margins in small states—77.8 percent of the vote in North Dakota and 75.8 percent in Vermont, and, better yet, amazing margins in key big states. Pundits predicted that he'd take New York (the biggest prize with 45 electoral votes) by between 300,000 and 350,000 votes and Illinois by 380,000. He ended up capturing New York by a record 1,089,929 votes and Illinois by 886,085 (Cox received just 25.5 percent of the state total).

In Massachusetts, Harding and Coolidge won, 681,153 to 276,691. Cox took just 28.9 percent of the two-party vote (Wilson had received 48 percent in 1916). Boston went Republican for the first time in twenty-four years, and it wasn't close—95,034 to 62,513. Only two Bay State towns—Blackstone and Milford, both in Worcester County—remained in the Cox column.

In some states, Cox was lucky to finish second. With just 21 percent of the vote in Washington, he barely edged out Farmer-Labor candidate Parley Christensen (19 percent). In South Dakota, it was even closer: Cox squeaked by the Utah radical by a mere 331 votes—35,938 to 35,607.

Harding didn't just have coattails, he had a wedding train. Except for the solid South, Republicans won virtually everywhere and won crushingly. Thirty-four governorships were up for grabs. Republicans captured twenty-five.

House Republicans gained 61 seats, giving them 301, ten more than the Democrats had won in 1912. Democrats lost a full 32 percent of their seats. Minority Leader Champ Clark lost, ending his twenty-six-year House career. Future Secretary of State Cordell Hull forfeited his Tennessee seat. Democrats survived in the Deep South, but not always easily. Eighteen-year-old Tallulah Bankhead's father (and future Speaker of the House), William B. Bankhead, came perilously close to losing his normally sacrosanct Huntsville, Alabama seat. Harry McLeary Wurzbach defeated Postmaster General Burleson's brother-in-law to become Texas's first native Republican congressman.

Republicans captured every House seat in Connecticut (5), Delaware (1), Idaho (2), Indiana (13), Iowa (11), Kansas (8), Maine (4), Minnesota (10), Montana (2), Nebraska (6), New Hampshire (2), New Jersey (12), New Mexico (1), North Dakota (3), Ohio (22), Oregon (3), Rhode Island (3), South Dakota (3), Utah (2), Vermont (2), Washington (5), West Virginia (6), Wisconsin (11), and Wyoming (1). They took 15 of 16 Massachusetts seats (giving the GOP all but one of New England's 32 House seats), 12 of 13 Michigan seats, and 35 of 36 in Pennsylvania.

Farmer-Labor candidates for senator and governor in Washington ran ahead of the Democrats—and ran ahead in Washington's 1st and 3rd Congressional districts. They barely finished behind the Democrat standard-bearer in the 4th. In the 2nd, Democrats didn't bother running.

Republicans gained ten United States Senators, giving them 59 of the 96 seats in the upper house. The took open races in Colorado, Oklahoma, and South Dakota (all pick-ups) and defeated Democratic incumbents in Arizona, California, Idaho, Kentucky, Maryland, Nevada, and Oregon.

"It wasn't a landslide," muttered a stunned Joe Tumulty, "it was an earthquake."

The *Literary Digest* had erred by 9 percent in California, 18 percent in Indiana, 19 percent in Illinois, 23 percent in New York, 24 percent in New Jersey, and 27 percent in Ohio—on a nationwide average by 21 percent.

The 300 editors reporting back to the *New York World* had similarly miscued. Their statewide pluralities missed by an average of 22 percent. The *World* underestimated Harding's margin in all but two states. It awarded six Harding states to Cox.

Of the pre-election polls, the humble Rexall Drug survey had done best—missing by only 9 percent—and calling every state right but two: normally Democratic Tennessee and Oklahoma.

In Woodrow Wilson's New Jersey, only a single Democrat, Warren County's Harry Runyon, won election to the State House of Representatives (the party's smallest previous total was 14 in 1914). Runyon automatically became minority leader—and the Democratic representation on every House committee.

In New York, Dudley Field Malone, having failed to secure the Farmer-Labor presidential nomination, ran for governor on the F-L ticket. William Randolph Hearst endorsed—and then un-endorsed—him, before finally reluctantly backing Al Smith. Malone received 69,098 votes—not enough to make up the difference, as Smith fell to former Judge Nathan L. Miller—who, not long before, had nominated Herbert Hoover for president.

In Tennessee, Governor Albert H. Roberts fell to Republican Alf Taylor, brother of popular former three-term Democratic governor "Fiddling Bob" Taylor. In Niota, State Representative Harry Burn awaited returns with his mother and twenty-two-year-old brother. Burn feared defeat after making women's suffrage a reality. Now engaged to Miss Myra Reagan of nearby Reagan, Tennessee, he needed the salary. Much to his, and *everyone's*, surprise, he won—by less than 200 votes, but he won.

Socialist expectations were uniformly dashed. Wisconsin party officials forecast three Socialist congressmen, eight state senators, and "at least" twenty-five assemblymen. They elected one state senator, nine assemblymen, and no congressmen. Victor Berger lost his House seat by 6,773 votes.

New York Socialists predicted 300,000 votes for gubernatorial candidate Joseph D. Cannon. He received 159,804. A bright spot was the election of former Congressman Meyer London to his old Lower East Side seat.

And, of course, women voted and, like their male counterparts, voted by and large for Harding. Cynics might observe that Harding was handsomer than Cox, but then Franklin Roosevelt was handsomer, younger, and far taller than Calvin Coolidge. In any case, looks were hardly the compelling point. Republicans simply contained a built-in edge on the female vote. Southerners and newly arrived immigrants, the core of the Democratic constituency, exhibited comparatively little interest in—and not a little hostility to—women's suffrage, and that went for their womenfolk as well. Compared to Republican-leaning women, relatively fewer Southern and immigrant females bothered registering or voting. In Boston's staunchest Republican wards, total registration increased by 102.3 percent, 118 percent, and 125.7 percent respectively. The three heaviest Democratic wards increased registration by just 16 percent, 51.9 percent, and 50 percent. In largely Democratic Boston, the two-party presidential vote increased by 68.5 percent from 1916. In Massachusetts's rural, heavily Republican towns, it increased 92.1 percent.

"In Illinois," historian Andrew Sinclair noted, "the only state where the votes of men and women were counted separately, 74.1 per cent of the men voted and only 46.5 per cent of the women. But the total vote in Illinois was 10.7 per cent above the national average. In the South, where woman suffrage was unpopular, women ignored the election almost completely. A careful analysis of the vote showed that men probably voted in much the same numbers as they had since 1904, while the women's vote represented about 35 percent of eligible women voters."

Observers expressed amazement that women could comprehend the cumbersome and lengthy paper ballots of the time. At Manhattan's St. Nicholas Avenue and West 114th Street, a poll-watcher timed voters. Women averaged three minutes in the polling booth, men six.

On the other hand, there was this report:

Newport, Ky., Nov. 2—A Newport woman, voting for the first time, marked her ballots in a voting precinct this morning, carefully folded the papers and started for home. Judges stopped her at the door, explaining the ballots would be counted better if left at the polling place.

Oklahoma's second district provided the new Congress with its only female member, Muskogee Republican Alice M. Robertson, dairy farmer, cafeteria proprietor, and former town postmistress. The sixty-five-year-old "Miss Alice," as the daughter of missionaries, possessed a keen interest in "laws helping Indians," but not in women's suffrage, having served as president of Oklahoma's Anti-Suffrage Association. Robertson wouldn't campaign outside her cafeteria, but inside its tiny confines she was a demon, sitting and talking and eating a bowl of soup alongside prospective voters—one dinner hour, consuming seventeen bowls. Robertson celebrated her narrow victory "by preparing some extra fruit salad and fried chicken."

In sparsely populated Nevada, suffragette Anne Martin, having failed to secure the Republican U.S. Senate nomination, ran on the Farmer-Labor ticket. She received 4,981 votes—18.2 percent of the total—and cost incumbent Democrat Charles B. Henderson his job.

Back East, three female Prohibition Party senate nominees rolled up smaller percentages—but substantially larger totals: New York's Ella A. Boole (159,623 votes), Pennsylvania's Leah Cobb Marion (132,610), and Indiana's Culla J. Bayhinger (13,323). Mrs. Boole did it the hard way, competing with another distaff candidate, the Farmer-Labor Party's Miss Rose Schneiderman, who herself garnered 27,934 votes.

Fireworks, bands, and parades enlivened Northampton, but Calvin and Grace Coolidge did not see them in Boston. When everything seemed settled, the vice president–elect issued a statement. The election, he twanged, marked "the end of the period which has seemed to substitute words for things."

"We have won the fight," crowed Henry Cabot Lodge. "We have destroyed Mr. Wilson's League of Nations and . . . we have torn up Wilsonism by the roots. It was a marvelous result."

In the heartland, there was pandemonium. There was joy. "State Street is blocked at Madison—," the *Chicago Tribune* reported:

automobiles can't get through. Another job for the mounted police. A band swings down State Street. A crowd falls in behind it. A white bearded old gentleman wearing a big colored paper hat is leading a snake dance at the end of the column. A pretty girl snatches his kettle drum. A short chase. He recovers the music— and steals a kiss. Applause from the bystanders.

At midnight in the Windy City, Nan Britton boarded a train for Marion, leaving her daughter Elizabeth Ann behind to be cared for by her sister.

The train was due in town at 7 A.M. At 6:30 she asked a porter, "Well, . . . who is our new President?"

"Harding's the man, Miss."

She met her lover just a block from his home, at a "little house" used by campaign clerical workers. A Secret Service man had arranged it. The shades were drawn. They moved deeper into the shadows, from the dining room into the kitchen. She sat on his lap.

Nan Britton recorded this sordid little moment in her sordid little memoirs:

> After affectionate greetings, I exclaimed softly, "Oh, sweetheart, isn't it wonderful that you are President!" He held me close, kissing me over and over again. Our eyes were now becoming accustomed to the darkness and I could see his face dimly outlined. Oh, how dear he was! I repeated my exclamation. "Isn't it wonderful that you are President!" He looked at me some time before he answered. Then his "Um . . . say, dearie, do you love me!" showed me that the glories of a victorious hero were submerged in the grander glories of a lover's delight in being with his woman. "*This* is the best thing that's happened to me lately, dearie!" he whispered.

He asked about "our little girl." He slipped Nan "two (or maybe three—I cannot remember) five-hundred dollar bills." They went their separate ways.

"Harding's the man, Miss."

# Chapter 25

❧

# "POWER MUST FAIL"

William Jennings Bryan kicked Woodrow Wilson when he was down.

The Great Commoner urged Wilson to resign immediately, with Vice President Marshall becoming president, appointing Senator Harding Secretary of State, and then himself resigning to make way for the new president-elect. Wilson, fumed Bryan, had "laid the foundations for the disaster. . . . The President attempted to drive out of public life every Democrat who dared to differ from him even in minute details, while he made no effort to strengthen the Democrats who made him the keeper of their conscience." Many accused Bryan of going too far, of pummeling a defeated, sick old man. "If the President is too sick to be criticized," Bryan countered, "he is too sick to hold office."

Roosevelt, agile at rationalizing setbacks, quickly rebounded, resuming private practice, entering the bond business, and engaging Missy LeHand (from his Washington campaign office) as his personal secretary. Sara Roosevelt confided to her diary that her son seemed "rather relieved not to be elected Vice-President." Franklin, writing to a friend, referred to himself as "Franklin D. Roosevelt, Ex. V.P., Canned. (Erroneously reported dead.)"

Warren Harding vacationed. At Oklahoma City, the Hardings visited with oilman Jake Hamon, now in line for Secretary of the Interior. Hamon's private life, as lively as Harding's, was far less private. Jake had taken up with redheaded Clara Barton Smith. He appointed Clara his secretary, married her off to his nephew, Frank Hamon, and then

418

dispatched Frank to the West Coast, leaving Jake and Clara to live bliss-fully as man and niece. Harding ordered Hamon to dump Clara if he wanted a role in Washington.

The Hardings departed; a Harding transition official arrived. Hamon hosted a dinner for him, and Clara—angry at the thought of being jettisoned—threw a duck in Hamon's face. They argued in their rooms. If Hamon abandoned her, Clara wanted cash. Hamon struck her with a chair. Clara shot him, and four days later he died. The news reached the Hardings at Balboa, Panama. "Too bad he had that one fault," Warren mused, "that admiration for women."

Albert Fall became Secretary of the Interior. Personally popular with his colleagues, the Senate approved him in minutes, the fastest confirma-tion in history. Harry Daugherty got Attorney General, though virtually everyone—friend and foe—cringed.

Some appointments were remarkably good ("the best minds," as Harding called them) and even bold: Charles Evans Hughes at State, fin-ancier Andrew Mellon at Treasury, Henry C. Wallace at Agriculture, Will Hays as Postmaster General, Chicago banker Charles G. Dawes as Director of the Budget, Herbert Hoover at Commerce, and William Howard Taft eventually to the Supreme Court. Leonard Wood wanted Secretary of War. John W. Weeks got the position. Wood found himself shunted back to the Philippines.

Hoover's appointment took courage. Republican regulars didn't want The Great Engineer in the party, let alone the cabinet. Daugherty relayed their displeasure to his chief, but Harding stood his ground:

I am sorry, that so many people impress you as hostile to Mr. Hoover to a place in the cabinet. Of course, I do not want the administration to start out with a quarrel with the Senate or any considerable faction in the Republican Party. I do hold him in very high esteem and think his *appointment would appeal to the cordial approval of the country*. The more I consider him[,] the more do I come to think well of him. Of course, I have no quarrel with those who do not think as I do, but *inasmuch as I have the responsibility to assume[,] I think my judgment must be trusted in the matter*.

"Mellon and Hoover," he had Daugherty inform Republican regulars Senators Penrose and Knox, "or no Mellon." Hoover went in.

Besides best minds, there were best friends. Fall and Daugherty fell into that category, but many others also received appointments. Some were tolerable. Others were not. Brother-in-law Herber H. Votaw turned out to be a surprisingly good Superintendent of Federal Prisons. Others fared poorly. "Dick" Crissinger, with slim qualifications save loyalty, became Comptroller of the Currency and later a governor of the Federal Reserve System. Colonel George Harvey's debut as ambassador to the Court of St. James, clad in knee breeches, silk stockings, and silver-buckled shoes, provoked much mirth. At Florence's urging, the oily Colonel Charles R. Forbes assumed control of the newly formed Veterans Administration. Early Harding booster Mont Reily became governor of Puerto Rico and nearly touched off a nationalist rebellion.

The country finally changed hands on Inauguration Day, March 4, 1921.

No one knew if Woodrow Wilson would participate. He finally did, struggling painfully to ride alongside Warren Harding to the Capitol. Aides had to help him up two steps to a side entrance. At their top, he rested. Ignoring a nearby "rolling chair," he shuffled gamely down a corridor to sign his last few official papers.

Senator Knox asked if Wilson would remain for Vice President Coolidge's inaugural. He had only to traverse a few more steps, but the challenge scared him. "The Senate has thrown me down," he bitterly replied, "but I am not going to fall down." Cabot Lodge informed Wilson that the Senate was adjourning and asked if he had any further communications for it. "Senator Lodge," Wilson snapped, with a loathing that all who saw it never forgot, "I have no further communication to make. I thank you. Good morning." With that, Woodrow Wilson departed for his new home on 2340 S Street N.W., just above Dupont Circle.

Republicans thought Harding's forty-minute inaugural address to be just fine. Democrats hated it. H. L. Mencken was predictably outraged. "He writes the worst English that I have ever encountered," the Sage of Baltimore sputtered. "It reminds me of a string of wet sponges; it reminds me of tattered washing on the line; it reminds me of stale bean soup, of college yells, of dogs barking idiotically through endless nights. It is so bad that a sort of grandeur creeps into it."

Calvin Coolidge delivered a ten-minute address, the shortest vice-presidential inaugural ever.

It was a day of firsts. The new chief executive had been first to ride to his inaugural in an automobile. He had employed an artificial sound system for his speech. "The amplifier is all very well," observed one wag, "but what Harding needs is a condenser."

There was no inaugural ball, but Harding attended a private gala at Ned and Evalyn McLean's estate. Calvin Coolidge dined with old acquaintances from the Massachusetts Senate. By 10, he was in bed. He told reporters that it was good once more to have "a regular job," though, on his $12,000 salary, he could not afford a home in Washington. Nor would he accept the gift of one from Frank Stearns. "More hotel life, I guess," said Grace, and the Coolidges settled into residence at the New Willard.

For a while, Congress debated a bill to purchase a Sixteenth Street mansion for use as a vice-presidential home. Not everyone approved. One day, Mr. and Mrs. Nicholas Murray Butler visited the White House. President Harding was called to other business, and Professor Butler mentioned the measure to Mrs. Harding. "Not a bit of it, not a bit of it," she exploded. "I am going to have that bill defeated. Do you think I am going to have those Coolidges living in a house like that? An hotel apartment is plenty good enough for them."

The bill was defeated.

The Wilsons settled into their new residence. Wilson's sister-in-law, Margaret Axson Elliott, found it to be "a quiet, dignified, spacious home. But I never liked it. To me it always seemed a dead house. Here he had never laughed and joked and played the fool with his daughters; here he had never planned for the future. For he knew, as did everyone else, that for him there would be no future."

Tumulty had been dismissed. Admiral Grayson remained. Harding had assigned him to duty in Washington, specifically to care for Wilson. Wilson never learned of Harding's generosity.

The former president whiled away his time, sometimes at the ballpark, sometimes at the theater. At one vaudeville show, he sat quietly toward the rear, his presence creating no great stir. But then an old actor addressed the audience, and this is what he said:

My only boy was killed in the war, and not in words can I express how much I miss him. Today I visited the Walter Reed Army Hospital, and I saw there what were literally pieces of still[-]living men. And when I looked upon this horrible result of war[,] I was glad my boy was not among these poor victims but was sleeping peacefully in France. But one of the greatest casualties this war has produced is the distinguished man who is in this audience tonight.

The audience knew of whom he spoke. They turned toward their former president, jumping from their seats, applauding and cheering wildly, waving handkerchiefs. An actress left the stage and presented Wilson with a bouquet.

The Klan came and went in the 1920s, expiring of its own stupidity. Prohibition ended not much later. But the '20s saw a more durable victory for the old America. The 1921 National Origins Act created an annual 3 percent quota of the foreign-born members of nationality groups listed in the 1910 census. Anti-immigration feeling persisted, however, resulting in 1924's Johnson–Reed Act, allowing only 150,000 immigrants annually, and slashing quotas to just 2 percent of a nationality's 1890 census representation, a sampling favoring northwestern Europeans. It completely excluded Orientals.

William Estabrook Chancellor continued peering into Warren Harding's peccadilloes and ancestry. In the waning days of the Wilson administration, postal authorities threatened Chancellor with arrest for inciting hatred against Harding and burned his papers. Chancellor fled to Quebec. Returning in early 1922, he self-published *Warren Gamaliel Harding, President of the United States. A Review of Facts Collected from Anthropological, Historical, and Political Researches*. Federal agents suppressed the book. Chancellor fled again to Canada, eking out a living peddling government bonds.

In March 1921, Franklin Roosevelt assumed chairmanship of the new Woodrow Wilson Memorial Foundation, designed to bestow humanitarian awards in the former president's honor. Wilson, unimpressed, testily questioned the use of the word "Memorial" ("I am not dead") and even refused Franklin's simple request for an autograph.

Roosevelt received even less respect from the Senate Naval Affairs

Subcommittee investigating the Newport naval base scandal. On July 19, 1921, it found him "morally responsible" for the "indefensible" assignment of enlisted men ("some of them mere boys") to investigate the area's "immoral conditions" and allowing them "their 'own discretion and judgment' whether they should or should not actually permit to be performed on them immoral acts."

Roosevelt scurried to devise a defense, spiritedly based on the time-honored stratagems of changing-the-subject and taking-the-offense, and accused the subcommittee of double-crossing him regarding a chance to testify and issuing its report before he could fully exculpate himself. "Throughout their report," he wrote, "I accuse them of deliberate falsification of facts, of misstatements of the record, and a deliberate attempt to deceive."

Chairman Lewis Ball denied tendering any such invitation and reminded FDR that not only had he already testified before both the subcommittee and the Dunn court of inquiry (there for nine and a half hours), but that each time, he had indicated that he had nothing more to add. "The character of the statement given to the papers by Mr. Roosevelt," Ball concluded, "is characteristic of the man."

It was a public-relations nightmare for the former Assistant Secretary of the Navy. LAY SCANDAL TO F.D. ROOSEVELT, headlined the *New York Times*. DETAILS ARE UNPRINTABLE.

Just days later, on July 28, Franklin journeyed up the Hudson to a Boy Scout outing at Bear Mountain. A snapshot showed him in shirt-sleeves, with arms folded across his chest. It was the last photo taken of him standing unaided.

Franklin traveled once more, to Campobello. Exhausted on arrival, on Wednesday, August 10 he swam the unusually frigid waters of the Bay of Fundy. Returning home, he felt chilled and awoke the next day with a 102° fever and severe back and leg pain. By Friday, he was paralyzed.

It was polio, and this "twentieth-century Apollo" was now a helpless cripple, unable to stand, to move about, to rejoice in the present, or, at just thirty-nine, to hope in the future.

Meanwhile, Warren Harding's presidency was proceeding apace: disarmament treaties signed, taxes lowered, the national debt reduced by $26 billion, unemployment reduced from 12 percent to 3 percent, the steel industry's twelve-hour day abolished, the Bureau of the Budget implemented, the first federal conference on unemployment, the first federal social welfare law, and the first federal highway program.

In December 1921, Harding did what Wilson never would, commuting Gene Debs's sentence, effective that Christmas Day. "I want him to eat his Christmas dinner with his wife," he ordered Daugherty. The government gave Debs $5.00, transportation home, and a new suit—choice of dark blue or brown. Harding insisted that Debs visit him at the White House on the way home to Terre Haute. "Well," boomed Harding, "I have heard so damned much about you, Mr. Debs, that I am now glad to meet you personally." Freeing Debs gained Harding little credibility with liberals. Overall, it cost him popularity. He didn't much mind.

The League of Nations? America wasn't in it, wasn't going in it, and people cared less and less.

There were disappointments. The House passed an anti-lynching bill, but Southern Democrats blocked Senate passage. When Republicans pulled the measure, blacks blamed them for its defeat. Harry Daugherty's handling of a rail strike alienated labor. The Republican congressional majority proved to be fragile, fractious, and altogether too large. In 1922, the GOP lost 6 Senate and 77 House seats. A 1923 *Collier's Magazine* poll placed Henry Ford ahead of Harding, 88,865 votes to 51,755 (with William Gibbs McAdoo at 19,407). Ford even beat Harding in Ohio.

Harding turned out to be more independent in thought and action than people had predicted or than history has generally recorded, though he never paraded his independence. Biographer Andrew Sinclair noted of Harding's low-key style:

> The subtlety of Harding's method of procedure was not to be used again until Eisenhower. . . . By pretending to be casual and lazy, a golfer and a sport, Harding allowed others to take the burden of pushing through measures. If they succeeded, he would take the credit. If they failed, the fault was theirs. He stood above the ploys of the mere politicians. For he was President. He did not want to be the fount of authority, but the forum before which special interests pleaded their cases. He wished to appear

relaxed and confident in order that everybody should believe that he had things under control. If his friends then thought that *they* had things under control, so much the better for their deluded vanity.

When Harding wanted something for himself, he certainly tried to get it. He allowed others to go their own way over matters that did not interest him in order to gain their support for what he wanted. It was this stubbornness about his own ambitions that had put him in the White House. Perhaps one of Harding's greatest gifts was to make other people feel superior to him. . . .

The problem, however, was that in the process, Harding often felt inferior to the task at hand, particularly when that task was the presidency. "I am not fit for this office," he morosely confessed to Nicholas Murray Butler, "and should never have been here."

Storm clouds of scandal appeared on the horizon—nothing relating to Carrie Philips or Nan Britton, nothing to Harding personally—but to his less distinguished appointments, to his "best friends." Charles R. Forbes and Veterans Administration attorney Charles F. Cramer (who blew his brains out with a .45 in March 1923 after Forbes's February "resignation") looted their agency of over $200 million. Alien Property Custodian Thomas W. Miller was eventually convicted of taking bribes. Secretary of the Interior Fall accepted a $100,000 "loan" from oilman Edward Doheny while approving Doheny's leasing of naval oil reserves at Teapot Dome, Wyoming and Elk Hills, California. Harry Daugherty and his unofficial assistant at the Justice Department Jesse Smith (who blew his own brains out in Daugherty's Wardham Park Hotel apartment) were suspected of illegally selling government alcohol supplies, taking bribes not to enforce prohibition, and selling pardons.

What Harding knew about it all remains debatable. He certainly knew about Forbes's thefts. At one private meeting, he grabbed Forbes and shouted that he was a "yellow rat" and a "double-crossing bastard." He eased Forbes out of the Veterans Administration, but did not prosecute him. "My God, this is a hell of a job," he exclaimed. "I have no trouble with my enemies. But my damn friends . . . my goddamn friends. . . . They're the ones that keep me walking the floor nights!"

In the summer of 1923, Harding embarked upon an ambitious cross-country tour to present his agenda to the American people in "a voyage of understanding." An oddly Wilsonian ploy for the master of the front-porch strategy, his junket covered not only the American West but also made him the first president to visit Alaska. Herbert Hoover came along, and to him Harding confided his fears. Recalled Hoover:

> One day after lunch when we were a few days out, Harding asked me to come to his cabin. He plumped at me the question: "If you knew of a great scandal in our administration, would you for the good of the country and the party expose it publicly or would you bury it?" My natural reply was "Publish it, and at least get credit for integrity on your side." He remarked that this method might be politically dangerous. I asked for more particulars. He said that he had received some rumors of irregularities, centering around Smith, in connection with cases in the Department of Justice. . . . I asked what Daugherty's relations to the affair were. He abruptly dried up and never raised the question again.

The trip—and the truth—proved too much for Harding. In Seattle, buffeted by intense heat, he took sick. Doctors diagnosed it as food poisoning, but it was a heart attack. By the time his special train reached San Francisco, he had to be put to bed at the Palace Hotel. On Thursday evening, August 2, 1923, he felt better, and the Duchess read to him from a *Saturday Evening Post* article, "A Calm Review of a Calm Man." It was about him, and he liked it. "That's good," Harding said. "Go on."

And he died.

People had almost forgotten about Calvin Coolidge. True, Harding allowed him at cabinet meetings, but Coolidge said little or nothing at the sessions, and had even less influence presiding over the Senate. "I soon found that the Senate had but one fixed rule, subject to exceptions of course," he wrote, "which was to the effect that the Senate would do anything it wanted to do whenever it wanted to do it. When I had learned that, I did not waste much time with the other rules, because they were so seldom applied."

Colonel House dismissed him as "a timid man." Senators ignored

him. At the Senate restaurant, he dined alone. Warren Harding supposedly said that he would be dropped from the ticket in 1924.

Now he would be president. While Harding had traveled west,
Coolidge went north. On the night of August 2, at his father's Plymouth
Notch home, Calvin retired, thinking that Harding had passed out of
danger. Now Harding was dead, and Colonel John Coolidge's home possessed no telephone. No one answered the one across the road at the
general store. Officials in Washington had to telegraph Bridgewater,
eight miles to the north. The telegraph operator notified a visiting
reporter, who raced to the Notch. By the light of a kerosene lamp, John
Coolidge answered the door—and learned his son would now be president of the United States.

"I was awakened," wrote Coolidge, "by my father coming up the stairs
calling my name. I noticed that his voice trembled. As the only times I
had ever observed that before were when death had visited our family, I
knew that something of the gravest nature had occurred."

Coolidge dressed, then knelt in prayer, before maneuvering down the
creaky narrow wooden stairs. By now, a carload of reporters had arrived
from Ludlow, to the south. As always, Calvin was practical. Some might
have worried about world peace or the economy or who would remain
in the cabinet. Coolidge thought mechanics. He needed to be sworn in:
What were the words? Who could do it? He found the words, then
thought a notary public could do it. John Coolidge was a notary. Calvin
Coolidge would be sworn in by his seventy-eight-year-old father. At 1:10
A.M., in the downstairs, low-ceilinged parlor room where both his mother
and his sister had died, in the lonely Vermont morning, he took the oath
by the flickering, sooty light of a kerosene lamp. Then he walked alone
through the darkness—to their graves.

And what really went through Coolidge's mind? "I thought," he
would recall, "I could swing it."

They kept the news of Harding's death from Woodrow Wilson, but
when he heard it, it troubled him. Wilson still cherished his hatreds,
but even though Wilson considered Harding a fool, he now had difficulty hating the man. He sent a message to Florence Harding, made a
painful journey back to the White House to show his respect. He felt
too ill to attend the funeral, but reconsidered, enduring two hours in

Washington's sultry August sun. Viewing Harding's flag-draped casket, he looked shaken. Who could have predicted, as the two men had last ridden together, that Woodrow Wilson would now be alive and Warren Harding dead? A cavalry officer inquired as to Senator Lodge's whereabouts. "I am not Senator Lodge's keeper," Wilson snapped. As the embarrassed officer rode off, Wilson muttered, "What asylum did that Colonel escape from?"

It was a day of ghosts. A car passed the former president's Pierce-Arrow. Inside was Colonel George Harvey. Wilson saw him. He leaned out of the car, and then as quickly as this specter of Wilson's early career had appeared, he vanished.

Sunday, November 11, 1923, was the fifth anniversary of the Armistice. The night before, sound trucks rolled up to Wilson's S Street home, and he struggled bravely to deliver a radio address, to what was then the largest audience in the infant industry's history. On Armistice Day itself, he addressed a crowd from his porch. Throughout the day, a multitude gathered. They came on foot and they came by trolley, twenty thousand of them. They came with a sense of reverence. Many spoke of themselves as pilgrims. Joe Tumulty was there, although Wilson didn't want him. He had broken with Tumulty in April 1922—as he had broken with so many—after Tumulty publicly hinted that Wilson still supported Governor Cox's ambitions. Tumulty came anyway, even hiring a band for the occasion. It was the least he could do.

Wilson's voice was weak. The crowd barely understood him. He finished, then started again: "Just one word more, I cannot refrain from saying it." And here he gained strength. "His final words," noted the *New York World*, "more vibrant and intense, reached far down the street."

This was the old Wilson, sure of himself, sure that his enemies were dolts and knaves. "I am not one of those who have the least anxiety about the triumph of the principles I have stood for," he informed the crowd. "I have seen fools resist Providence before, and I have seen their destruction, as will come upon them again, utter destruction and contempt. That we shall prevail is as sure as that God reigns."

They were indeed his final words—at least as far as public utterances went. Edith Wilson helped him back into the house, and the crowd went away.

Wilson's dreams did not. On January 21, 1924, he outlined his upcoming campaign for a return to the presidency, even planning his acceptance and inaugural speeches, still excoriating the "heinous . . . treason" that had betrayed his League of Nations, equating it to betrayal "on the field of battle."

By month's end, his health had suddenly and irrevocably deteriorated. On Friday, February 2, he murmured to Edith, "I am ready." At 11:15 the next morning, he breathed his last. The next day, Edith wrote to Henry Cabot Lodge that he would not be welcome at her husband's funeral. Joe Tumulty attended. Colonel House stayed away.

Mary Hulbert Peck heard the news in Manhattan. She went to church that day—a Christian Science service—and returned home to her minuscule apartment. She picked up a book he had given her, *The Oxford Book of Verse*, and read:

> For power must fail
> And pride must fall,
> And the love of the dearest friends grow small—
> But the glory of the Lord is in all.

Sometime in 1923 or 1924, prep school student Ray Baker Harris visited Florence Harding. "I suppose you have very many friends at school?" she asked.

He nodded in agreement.

"I have only a year or two at the most," she matter-of-factly informed the young man. "But you are young—young enough to see how many of my husband's friends will be loyal to him."

She knew what lay ahead, both for herself—she died in Marion on November 21, 1924—and for her husband's doomed reputation.

Washington observers did not expect Calvin Coolidge to be nominated in 1924. Observers never expected Calvin Coolidge to achieve anything. Yet Coolidge won his party's nomination after facing the weakest of opposition. The convention then nominated Frank Lowden for vice president. He turned them down. They nominated him again. He turned them down again. They got the message.

At the Democratic convention, Al Smith battled William Gibbs McAdoo (tarred by the brush of having been on Edward Doheny's payroll). Against the Catholic and wet Smith, McAdoo now enjoyed Ku Klux Klan backing. Smith enjoyed the backing of Franklin D. Roosevelt. Roosevelt, through hours of painful rehabilitation, had learned to maneuver on crutches and had put his life back together. Eleanor and Louis Howe remained alongside, but his greatest assistance came from Missy LeHand, who accompanied him everywhere, on long voyages aboard the 71-foot houseboat *Larooca* and at Warm Springs, Georgia, where the spa waters played a pivotal role in his rehabilitation. "The water," he would say, "put me where I am, and the water has to bring me back."

Al Smith wanted the great Tammany orator Bourke Cockran to again nominate him, but Cockran had died the previous year. Roosevelt pinch-hit, attempting to resurrect his political career. Twenty thousand Democrats raptly watched as Franklin hobbled alone the fifteen feet to the Madison Square Garden platform to nominate "the Happy Warrior of the political battlefield, Alfred E. Smith." His speech thrilled them.

Franklin D. Roosevelt was back. Within a year, Louis Wehle was plotting to make him not *Vice* President, but *President*—and FDR wasn't saying no to that either.

One hundred and three ballots followed Roosevelt's speech, ballots seeing neither Smith nor McAdoo emerge as the exhausted convention's nominee. The honor instead went to conservative John W. Davis. In November, Coolidge (running with Charles Dawes, Frank Lowden having successfully refused the nomination) triumphed—382 electoral votes to 136, 15,725,016 popular votes to 8,386,503. Robert La Follette finally ran third-party, receiving 4,822,856 votes, carrying Wisconsin (13 electoral votes) and outpolling Davis in 12 other states.

The Socialists? Debs was too sick to attempt another run. The party supported La Follette—a strategy wrecking its wreckage. At the party's February 1925 convention, just 45 delegates attended.

In New York, Al Smith ran for re-election as governor, handily defeating Theodore Roosevelt Jr., who had replaced Franklin as Assistant Secretary of the Navy. Eleanor Roosevelt (her anti-TR Jr. feelings overriding her anti-Catholic prejudices) installed a giant teapot (for Teapot Dome) atop her car and campaigned for Smith. Alice Roosevelt

Longworth—sweet Alice—retorted that she wanted to do the same with Lucy Mercer affixed to her vehicle.

Coolidge had not won public confidence by dint of conversational skills. He dumped Harry Daugherty, cleaned up the scandals, and quickly restored public confidence in government. The national debt, $22.3 billion in 1923, dropped to $16.9 billion by 1929. He cut taxes in four of the six years of his tenure. By 1927, 98 percent of the population paid no income tax at all. The tax burden on those making under $10,000 fell from $130 million in 1923 to under $20 million in 1929. Unemployment averaged 3.3 percent. From 1924 through 1929, the Gross National Product increased annually by 7 percent.

The country enjoyed the Coolidge years. He did not. In July 1924, Calvin Coolidge Jr. died after developing blood poisoning from a blister on his foot. He was sixteen. Coolidge never recovered emotionally. Compounding his loss, Colonel John Coolidge died at Plymouth Notch in March 1926. "It costs," he wrote in his *Autobiography*, "a great deal to be President."

And so on August 2, 1927—the fourth anniversary of his becoming president—Calvin Coolidge handed out little strips of paper to reporters at a Rapid City, South Dakota schoolhouse. Each contained the identical typewritten message: "I do not choose to run for president in 1928."

He had not informed Grace of his intentions.

In 1921, the case of Nicola Sacco and Bartolomeo Vanzetti began percolating, with defense attorney Fred Moore, anarchist leader Carlo Tresca, and the Sacco–Vanzetti Defense Committee achieving remarkable results in drawing the nation's liberal community to their cause. On February 19, 1921—months before the case went to trial—the New England Civil Liberties Union wrote to supporters, soliciting funds for a defense and characterizing it as a travesty of justice. They charged that "the real reason for the prosecution seems to be that Sacco and Vanzetti are 'foreigners' and are influential radicals. The same conclusion has been reached by the American Civil Liberties Union, the *New Republic*, the *Nation* and other organizations. . . ."

Their trial opened on May 31, 1921, and lasted six weeks. Prosecutor Frederick Katzmann presented forensic evidence, Sacco and Vanzetti's evasive and untruthful answers to arresting officers, and eyewitnesses tying the defendants to the crime. The defense countered with witnesses placing them elsewhere, including one locating Sacco at the Italian Consulate in Boston that day. The trial closed on July 14, 1921. After deliberating for just five hours, jurymen found the defendants guilty. Sacco rose from his seat, pointed an accusing finger at them, and repeated over and over again, in English and Italian, "You kill two innocent men."

Abroad, the case triggered waves of anti-Americanism. Crowds marched and mobs rioted in Paris, London, Mexico City, Buenos Aires, and Berlin. Workers in Uruguay struck. A crowd of ten thousand stormed the United States' London embassy. Bombs exploded at Ambassador Myron Herrick's Paris home and the American consulate at Nice.

Nicola Sacco and Bartolomeo Vanzetti were executed in the electric chair at Charlestown, Massachusetts, on August 23, 1927. Their funeral march measured eight miles. Their deaths ignited new protests.

"The men in Charleston prison are shining spirits," wrote Heywood Broun. "They are too bright, we shield our eyes and kill them. We are the dead, and in us there is not feeling or imagination nor the terrible torment of lust for justice. And in the city where we sleep, smug gardeners walk to keep the grass above our little houses sleek and cut whatever blade thrusts up a head above its fellows."

Al Smith finally got his presidential nomination. It wasn't worth much, because 1928 was a Republican year. The country was prosperous, largely contented and hopeful, and not ready to junk Prohibition, elect a Catholic, or vote against Herbert Clark Hoover, who spent the 1920s transforming the once-sleepy Commerce Department into a dynamo of activity and progressivism—and influencing virtually every other facet of the federal government. "That man," Coolidge fussed in May 1928, "has offered me unsolicited advice for six years, all of it bad."

Hoover captured the Republican nomination on the first ballot, defeating Frank Lowden 837 to 74. In November, he crushed Smith, 21,391,381 votes to 15,016,443 and 444 electoral votes to 87. North Carolina, Virginia, Florida, and Texas all voted Republican, but Calvin Coolidge's heavily Catholic Massachusetts went for Smith. New York didn't, but narrowly elected a Democratic governor—Franklin D. Roosevelt. FDR was now no longer the future of Democratic politics; he was the present.

Missy LeHand was part of FDR's present—and Eleanor, increasingly on her own, accepted that. According to FDR's son Elliott, a physical relationship now existed between Missy and his father. Of life in the governor's mansion, he wrote:

> Mother allocated a back bedroom as her own. Around the corner and down the hall on the second floor, Father had the imposing master bedroom with big windows on two sides, next to Missy's. These two rooms were joined by a little door with clear glass panels, curtained on her side. Mother thought that this was a perfectly suitable arrangement in view of the role Missy played in Father's life.
>
> It was not unusual to enter his sunny corner room and find Missy with him in her nightgown. There was no attempt to conceal their relationship. . . .
>
> I would go in at the start of the day, and the three of us would talk with no embarrassment between us. It was no mystery. Mother had not shared life with Father for more than twenty years. . . .
>
> I am certain that she had no fear of sin in their relationship, in spite of her Catholic background.

Herbert Hoover's triumph proved to be very short. Inaugurated in the first week of March 1929, everything collapsed for him in the last week of October, when Wall Street crashed and took the economy, the country, and Herbert Hoover with it.

"My period of popularity lasted nearly fourteen years," he later mused, "which seems about the average . . . democracy is a harsh employer."

But at least he had a job.

Thanks to William Randolph Hearst's help, FDR rolled over Al Smith for the Democratic nomination in 1932. Then FDR flattened Herbert Hoover that November, 22,821,277 votes to 15,761,254 and 472 electoral votes to 59—a landslide not at big as Warren Harding's, but a landslide nonetheless.

Just after that, Louis Wehle visited Franklin at Albany. FDR was upstairs, on his newspaper-strewn bed. He reached into the pile of papers to pull out some pasteboard boxes, boxes jammed with index cards, some yellow and some white. "I've been wanting to show you these," he informed Wehle. "You remember in January 1920, you said that if I built up on the acquaintances I'd make on my campaign for Vice President, it might lead me to the Presidency. Well, Louis Howe and I took that seriously. See these yellow cards: Louis and I put down on these the names, connections, and addresses of the men I met all over the country on our 1920 swings. Ever since, we have followed them up and kept in touch with them. They are the nucleus of my personal organization today."

Calvin Coolidge moved back to Northampton, returning to his little rented apartment at 21 Massasoit Street. He could not remain there. A steady parade of automobiles, filled with the adoring and the merely curious, constantly motored past. Passersby trampled his front yard, peered through his windows, and generally made life miserable. He finally took a home of his own, a rather grand estate named "The Beeches." It had land around it, and a fence.

But Coolidge could not put a fence around the economy. He had little love for Hoover, but that did little to ease the pain he felt as businesses shuttered, farms were foreclosed, and millions went jobless and hungry. The sixty-year-old former president went downtown to his law office on the morning of January 5, 1933, did what he had to do, and rode home. Getting ready to shave, he dropped dead of a heart attack.

Now there were two.

## Chapter 26

⁓

# "Fear Itself"

Theodore Roosevelt. Harding. Wilson. Coolidge. All dead.

Now only two remained. But survival had been purchased at great price. Herbert Hoover's reputation lay in tatters. "Great" no longer referred to "Great Humanitarian" or "Great Engineer," it referred to "The Great Depression," a cataclysm beyond his powers to defeat. Bold, jaunty Franklin Roosevelt now stood at his moment of triumph—figuratively. He could not stand at all without crutches or canes or helping hands. Little more than twelve years had passed since 1920, but the world had changed so much.

Now Franklin Roosevelt would replace Herbert Hoover as president.

It seemed incomprehensible that the economy could worsen after November 1932. But it did, horribly; and, as it did, the nation's banking system verged on collapse. Its crash would yank what remained of the country down with it.

By February 1933, Hoover had determined a course of action. A bank holiday was imperative. But its legality was dubious. On February 18, with just two weeks to run in his term, he had a letter hand-delivered to FDR, asking for his public support to close the banks until their solvency could be determined.

Roosevelt ignored it: The greater the crash on Hoover's watch, the greater the recovery and the acclaim on his. On Tuesday, February 28, Hoover wrote again. The next day, twelve days after Hoover's first plea, Roosevelt responded, blandly alibiing that a secretary had lost Hoover's original missive and protesting that nothing could be done anyway ("frankly I doubt if anything short of a fairly general withdrawal of deposits can be prevented now").

Roosevelt arrived by train in rain-swept Washington at 9:35 P.M., Thursday, March 2. Businesses no longer accepted out-of-state bank checks, and Eleanor worried about how they would pay for their suite at the Mayflower Hotel. That next evening, Hoover and Roosevelt conferred at the White House. Their meeting was tense, edgy. Hoover begged for FDR's backing to close the banks. Again Franklin refused.

Meanwhile, Roosevelt had assembled an administration. Harold Ickes would be at Interior (after Hiram Johnson declined the job); Cordell Hull at State; Henry C. Wallace's son, Henry A. Wallace, at Agriculture; Frances Perkins (the first woman cabinet member) at Labor; and Homer Cummings as Attorney General. William Gibbs McAdoo wouldn't be in the cabinet, having won election to the United States Senate from California. Neither would Carter Glass, who turned down Treasury. J. Edgar Hoover remained at the FBI, though many Democrats wanted him replaced with a properly Democratic big-city police chief. Louis Howe, an inveterate reader of mysteries and crime dramas, argued that J. Edgar's retention was necessary to preserve the Bureau's professionalism. Cummings agreed.

On Inauguration morning, FDR summoned his cabinet to St. John's Protestant Episcopal Church. "You know," he informed Postmaster General-designate James A. Farley, "I think a thought to God is the right way to start off my administration. A proper attitude toward religion, and belief in God, will in the end be the salvation of all peoples. For ourselves it will be the means of bringing us out of the depths of despair into which so many have apparently fallen."

FDR's old Groton headmaster, Dr. Endicott Peabody, presided. Peabody had voted for Hoover as the "more capable man," but wasn't displeased to see his old student assume the nation's highest office.

It was cold and dreary as Roosevelt's seven-car motorcade arrived at the north portico of the White House for the Hoovers. Franklin was his usual cheerful self, the weight of his new obligations unable to faze him. In fact, the challenge energized him. Hoover was Hoover, glum and foreboding. Roosevelt vainly attempted conversation. Hoover sat silent. His stillness unnerved Roosevelt. Desperate to draw Hoover out, FDR nervously prattled about the "lovely steel" of a recently constructed federal building. "It must have seemed insane," Eleanor remembered, "but it indicates how desperate [Franklin] was in search of small talk."

The crowd cheered as Roosevelt and Hoover's Pierce-Arrow rolled down Pennsylvania Avenue. Hoover tipped his silk hat. Then he remembered. He was so stupid: These were not cheers for him, but for the man who had defeated him. His hat went back down. There it stayed.

At the Capitol, black-silk-robed, white-bearded Charles Evans Hughes, now Chief Justice, administered the oath. Roosevelt had never been a great extemporaneous speaker, but he was brilliant delivering prepared remarks, adding tone and substance by inflection and emphasis. Today he was at his peak.

"This is preeminently the time to speak the truth," he intoned, "the whole truth, frankly and boldly. Nor need we shrink from honestly facing conditions in our country today. This great Nation will endure as it has endured, will revive and will prosper. So, first of all, let me assert my firm belief that the only thing we have to fear is fear itself—nameless, unreasoning, unjustified terror which paralyzes needed efforts to convert retreat into advance."

His words galvanized a wounded nation. Hoover, sitting in a leather armchair at FDR's left, listened impassively.

The night before, FDR had hung back from helping Hoover. Now he sounded a clarion call:

> In the event that the national emergency is still critical, I shall not evade the clear course of duty that will then confront me. I shall ask the Congress for the one remaining instrument to meet the crisis—broad Executive power to wage a war against the emergency, as great as the power that would be given to me if we were in fact invaded by a foreign foe.

FDR was threatening an economic dictatorship.

The parades and balls began. A peculiar mix of nervousness and gaiety filled Washington. Marines ringed the Capitol. A hundred Philadelphia police and fifty more of New York's finest augmented eight hundred Metropolitan police. Revolution—and violence—was in the air. In Miami, barely more than two weeks previously, a class-obsessed Italian immigrant had nearly killed Roosevelt, instead fatally wounding Chicago Mayor Anton J. Cermak.

Nonetheless, Democrats were in a buoyant mood as they resumed power after a twelve-year exile, and a half-million onlookers, better than half the population of the Washington area, cheered the three-mile-long parade that included twenty-six governors, eighteen thousand troops, a band from all-black Howard University, six carloads of Confederate veterans—and General Douglas MacArthur. The remarkably robust FDR propped himself up for three and a half hours while the parade tramped past. At his left stood Edith Wilson, escorted by Bernard Baruch. This was her day too—and Admiral Grayson's. He chaired the Inaugural Committee. Fifty thousand New York Democrats attended, and when the Tammany delegation proudly marched through the icy wind past their new president, a smiling Al Smith led the way.

Unprecedented pomp greeted revelers at the various inaugural balls. The nation's foremost bandleaders—Guy Lombardo, Rudy Vallee, Eddie Duchin, and Eli Dantzig—provided the music, along with lesser-known ensembles such as the Indian Reservation Band of Oklahoma, a holdover from the 1929 affair, and the Philadelphia Harmonica Symphony.

Herbert Hoover slunk out of town. A convoy of Army trucks hauled his belongings out of the White House. After the inaugural, he left for Union Station to board a special train to New York and temporary quarters at the Waldorf-Astoria. At Union Station, a strange thing happened. People began cheering and crowding around him. Women pressed flowers into Lou Hoover's hands. One gave Herbert a box of candy. Children lined up to meet him. The crowd's enthusiasm, and actual love, temporarily lifted the downcast ex-president's gloom.

He got on the train.

Franklin Roosevelt and Herbert Hoover never saw each other again.

# Epilogue

~

# "Malevolent Detachment"

Tidying up the messy loose ends of our 1920s drama, we present the fate of our often ill-starred cast.

**Senator Frank B. Brandegee** of Connecticut, in ill health and having suffered severe financial reversals in real estate, killed himself by inhaling "illuminating gas" at his Washington mansion on October 14, 1924. He was sixty.

**Nan P. Britton** wrote a bestseller, *The President's Daughter*, based on her relationship with Warren Harding. She relocated to Chicago in 1933, operating an employment office under an assumed name and residing with her companion and business partner, Miss Gertrude Davis, in "a comfortable apartment" near Lake Michigan. She died in Sandy, Oregon, on March 21, 1991. She was ninety-four.

**Elizabeth Ann Britton**, President Harding's illegitimate daughter, married in September 1938, maintaining her anonymity until 1964, when she revealed that she was Mrs. Henry E. Blaesing, a Glendale, California, housewife and mother of three sons—the first of whom she named Warren. She died in Oregon on November 17, 2005, at the age of eighty-six.

**Heywood Broun** ran for Congress as a Socialist in 1930. In April 1933, facing expulsion after addressing a Communist Party rally, he resigned his Socialist Party membership. That same year, he helped found the American Newspaper Guild and was elected its first president. In 1939, haunted by premonitions of impending death, Broun, assisted by Msgr. (later Archbishop) Fulton J. Sheen, converted to Catholicism. He died of pneumonia at New York's Columbia Presbyterian Hospital on December 18, 1939. Broun was fifty-one. "He was a hard fighter," wrote Franklin Roosevelt, "but always a fair fighter. . . . "

**William Jennings Bryan** battled Clarence Darrow in 1925's "Monkey Trial" of evolutionist John T. Scopes. Bryan proclaimed Scopes's guilty verdict a triumph over "the forces of darkness." He departed Dayton, Tennessee, addressing huge crowds from his locomotive platform—an estimated fifty thousand persons in two hundred miles—before apoplexy claimed him two days later on July 26, 1925. The Great Commoner was sixty-five.

**Carrie Chapman Catt** opposed the Equal Rights Amendment that Alice Paul proposed in 1923. She also opposed repealing Prohibition but, nevertheless, soon warmed to Franklin Roosevelt's administration. Mrs. Catt, eighty-eight, died at her New Rochelle home on March 9, 1947.

**Professor William Estabrook Chancellor** returned to the United States after Harding's death, teaching at Cincinnati's Xavier University from 1927 through 1940 and serving on the Norwood, Ohio city council from 1933 through 1940. Chancellor, ninety-six, died on May 4, 1963.

**The Chicago Coliseum**, home of the 1920 Republican National Convention, eventually housed roller derby, the Chicago Blackhawks, and the Chicago Bulls. The venue's unlikely last hurrah was Abbie Hoffman's August 1968 Yippie "LBJ's un-birthday" party. Demolished in 1982, it survives as "Coliseum Park," a children's playground and dog run.

**Parley Parker Christensen**, the 1920 Farmer-Labor candidate for president, spent two years in Moscow in the early 1920s, twice meeting Lenin. In 1926, he unsuccessfully ran for the U.S. Senate from Illinois before moving to California and serving ten years on the Los Angeles city council. Christensen, eighty-four, died in Los Angeles on February 10, 1954.

**Edward Young Clarke**, the KKK's publicity man, was convicted in 1924 for violating the Mann Act, i.e., transporting women across state lines for immoral purposes. In 1932, Clarke devised a prosperity scheme called Esskaye, based upon the magical properties of the numeral seven. Locked up as insane, Clarke convinced doctors that he wasn't. In 1934, however, authorities convicted Clarke of mail fraud regarding Esskaye.

In March 1949, en route to Atlanta Penitentiary, the seventy-three-year-old Clarke escaped from his federal parole supervisor.

**Bainbridge Colby**, Robert Lansing's successor as Secretary of State, returned to New York and to private practice with Woodrow Wilson as his official partner. The firm soon dissolved. An ardent Wet, Colby campaigned for FDR in 1932, but quickly accused FDR of having fallen "hook, line, and sinker to the Communists and Socialists by whom he is surrounded." He opposed FDR in both 1936 and 1940. Colby, eighty, died at Bemus Point, New York, on April 11, 1950.

**Grace Goodhue Coolidge** remained in Northampton, did defense work in World War II, and distinguished herself as one of New England's premier Red Sox fans. She died in her sleep at Northampton on July 8, 1957. She was seventy-eight.

**James Middleton Cox** made even more money in the newspaper business. In 1933, Franklin D. Roosevelt appointed Cox vice chairman of the U.S. delegation to the World Economic Conference (after Cox refused the post of ambassador to Berlin). In 1946, he declined appointment to the U.S. Senate. Cox, eighty-seven, died in Dayton, Ohio, on July 15, 1957. In 2003, the company he founded, Cox Enterprises, employed seventy-seven thousand persons, operated three hundred separate businesses, and reported revenues of $10.7 billion.

**Margaretta Blair Cox**, Cox's second wife, died of asphyxiation at her Dayton home after smoking in bed. Firemen could not understand why she remained in a smoke-filled bathroom when both stairwells remained clear. She was seventy.

**Josephus Daniels** served for eight years as ambassador to Mexico under FDR, who still called him "Chief." Mexicans recalled Daniels's shelling of Vera Cruz while he was Navy Secretary, but he soon won them over despite a frugality that enabled him to annually bank $10,000 of his $17,500 salary. In early January 1948, Daniels, suffering from bronchitis, insisted on attending Methodist Sunday services. He contracted pneumonia and died in Raleigh that January 15. Daniels, the last surviving member of Woodrow Wilson's cabinet, was eighty-five.

**Harry Micajah Daugherty** beat the rap. Indicted for conspiracy to defraud the government, he went free after two juries deadlocked. Daugherty pled the Fifth Amendment, some said, to protect Warren Harding more than himself. "I never talk about dead men or living women," he later said. In 1932, with Thomas Dixon (of *The Birth of a Nation* fame), he wrote a defense of his—and Harding's—career, *The Inside Story of the Harding Tragedy*. Daugherty, eighty-one, died of congestive heart failure in his Columbus apartment on October 12, 1941.

**Eugene Victor Debs** suffered a nervous breakdown in October 1926 and entered Elmhurst, Illinois's Lindlahr Sanitarium. A kidney ailment weakened him further. Unable to speak, he motioned for paper and pencil, scrawling these words from the poem *Invictus*: "It matters not how strait the gate, How charged with punishments the scroll, I am the master of my fate: I am the captain of my soul." Gene Debs died that October 20. He was seventy.

**W. E. B. Du Bois**, though named by Warren Harding as a special envoy to Liberia in 1923, did indeed become "the Karl Marx of the colored race," and, moving steadily leftward, he was indicted for failure to register as a foreign agent in 1951, won the Lenin Peace Prize in 1959, and formally joined the Communist Party in 1961. The CPUSA eventually named its youth arm the W. E. B. Du Bois Clubs in his honor. Du Bois, ninety-five, died in Accra, Ghana, on August 27, 1963.

**W. W. Durbin** was ousted as Ohio Democratic state chairman after failing to support the anti-Klan plank at the 1924 national convention. In May 1932, authorities indicted him for "circulating unsigned election literature, attempted bribery and attempted blackmail." Later that year, he broke ranks with the Ohio delegation to support FDR at the party's Chicago convention. Roosevelt returned the favor by appointing him Register of the U.S. Treasury. Durbin, seventy-one, died of a cerebral hemorrhage at his Kenton, Ohio home on February 4, 1937.

**Albert Bacon Fall**, Harding's corrupt Secretary of the Interior, served ten months in the New Mexico State Prison—the first Cabinet officer to do time. He died on November 30, 1944, at El Paso's Hotel Dieu Hospital, where he had been a patient since 1942. Fall was eighty-three.

**Edna Ferber** won the 1925 Pulitzer Prize for her novel *So Big* and eventually produced such bestsellers as *Showboat, Cimarron,* and *Giant*. She died of cancer on April 16, 1968 at her Park Avenue penthouse. She was eighty-two.

**James E. ("Pa") Ferguson**, 1920 American Party presidential candidate, was barred in 1924 from holding Texas public office, which didn't prevent his wife, Miriam A. ("Ma") Ferguson, from being elected governor that year and again in 1932. (She did, however, lose three other times.) Pa Ferguson, seventy-three, died on September 21, 1944.

**Colonel Charles R. Forbes**, Harding's crooked Veterans Administration chief, was released from prison in November 1927 and made his living selling restaurant kitchenware. He died at Walter Reed Army Hospital on April 11, 1952. He was seventy-four.

**Henry Ford**, facing a $1 million libel suit, closed the *Dearborn Independent* in July 1927 and retracted his previous anti-Semitic statements. Many questioned his sincerity, particularly after he accepted the Grand Cross of the Order of the German Eagle from Hitler's government in December 1938. Ford died at his Dearborn estate on April 7, 1945. He was eighty-three.

**Marcus Garvey**'s popularity quickly faded. The NAACP denounced him as a "robber of innocent Negroes," ridiculed his back-to-Africa plan, and, not surprisingly, found itself outraged when Garvey cordially conferred with Klan leader Edward Y. Clarke. In 1922, federal authorities indicted Garvey on rather flimsy evidence for mail fraud regarding his Black Star Steamship Company. He conducted a spirited, though unsuccessful, defense and entered Atlanta Penitentiary in February 1925. Calvin Coolidge commuted his sentence in November 1927. Deported to Jamaica, Garvey died there on June 10, 1940. "Fortunately for himself and for others," editorialized the *New York Times,* "he was not able to translate his dream into widespread slaughter. It came down at last to some fairly successful retail stealing, for which he did penance. Now he is dead." He was sixty.

**Rear Admiral Cary T. Grayson** assumed leadership of the American Red Cross in 1935. He died of anemia in Washington on February 15, 1938. He was fifty-nine.

**Jake L. Hamon, Jr.** (Jake Hamon's son) continued in the family business, making a fortune in the Texas oil fields. When the eighty-two-year-old Jake Jr. died in Amsterdam in 1985, he left an estate valued at $200 million.

**Will H. Hays** left the Harding cabinet in March 1922 to assume the new position of President of the Motion Picture Producers and Distributors of America—in effect, he was the "czar" of the film industry (other candidates were Herbert Hoover and Hiram Johnson). Serving until 1945, he established Hollywood's code of morals for film content. Hays, seventy-four, died of heart disease at his Indiana home on March 7, 1954.

**William Randolph Hearst** metamorphosed from feared radical to despised conservative, constructing spectacular mansions such as San Simeon, promoting the motion picture career of his mistress Marion Davies, and becoming the target of Orson Welles's *Citizen Kane*. Hearst, eighty-eight, died at Miss Davies's Beverly Hills home on August 14, 1951. The family did not allow her to attend his funeral.

**Herbert C. Hoover**, no longer a progressive, spent the 1930s vainly arguing against Franklin Roosevelt's New Deal. In 1946, President Truman appointed him head of the Famine Emergency Commission, formed to alleviate hunger in a war-torn world, and later to reorganize the federal executive branch—a mission popularly known as the Hoover Commission. His reputation seemed, at last, partially restored. His energy belied his years (in 1960, when he was eighty-six, he wrote 55,952 letters). "He had the last laugh," wrote James Reston: "He convinced most of his critics in the end and outlived the rest of them." Hoover died in his thirty-first-floor Waldorf-Astoria apartment on October 20, 1964. He was ninety.

**J. Edgar Hoover** not only survived the passing of Franklin Roosevelt in 1945, he survived *everybody*, remaining as FBI chief until his death on May 2, 1972. He was seventy-seven.

**Colonel Edward Mandell House** served as a confidential adviser to Franklin Roosevelt in his 1932 presidential campaign and was later occasionally called upon by FDR for advice. In January 1933, he wrote a magazine article musing that the country might be ready for dictatorship. In June 1937, he retracted that view and predicted that "my friend" FDR would not seek a third term. He also predicted world peace. House, seventy-nine, died at his Manhattan townhouse on March 28, 1938.

**Dr. Erastus Mead Hudson**, Franklin Roosevelt's homosexual-hunting navy lieutenant, became an internationally recognized expert on fingerprinting and testified for defendant Bruno Richard Hauptmann in the

Lindbergh kidnapping case. Appointed to the Medical Advisory Board of the U.S. Trade Commission in 1942, Hudson died in Washington, D.C. on September 12, 1943. He was fifty-five.

**The International Workers of the World** (IWW) quickly faded from view but seemed to have finally revived as the twenty-first century unveiled itself. No longer organizing miners or lumbermen, Wobblies were spotted in New York City in January 2006 organizing Starbucks employees.

**Hiram W. Johnson** helped lead resistance to FDR's 1937 court-packing scheme. Johnson, still in the Senate, died at Bethesda Naval Hospital on August 6, 1945. One of his last votes was against the United Nations Charter—one of only two votes in opposition. He was seventy-eight.

**Reverend Samuel Neal Kent** of Newport left the active ministry, working instead for the Chautauqua Association of Philadelphia and the English Speaking Union of the United States, although occasionally he served as a cruise-ship chaplain. He died on November 1, 1943, in Daytona Beach, Florida. Kent was seventy.

**John T. King**, Theodore Roosevelt and Leonard Wood's key political adviser, found himself indicted (along with Harry Daugherty) in early 1926 on charges of defrauding the government and later on income tax charges. He died of pneumonia in Bridgeport, Connecticut, that May 14. He was fifty-one.

**Robert Lansing,** Wilson's Secretary of State, returned to private practice, specializing in international law. A diabetic for thirty years, Lansing, sixty-four, died of myocarditis at his Washington home on October 30, 1928. In 1953, his nephew, John Foster Dulles, became Dwight Eisenhower's Secretary of State. Foster Dulles's son, Avery, converted to Catholicism and became a cardinal.

**Albert D. Lasker**, Harding's campaign advertising guru, served as chairman of the War Shipping Board. He supported Charles Dawes in 1924 and Wendell Willkie in 1940. In 1942, Lasker sold his advertising agency, Lord & Taylor, and devoted his life to philanthropy. He died of cancer in New York City on May 30, 1952. He was seventy-two.

**The League of Nations** failed to prevent World War II and transferred all its assets to the United Nations on April 18, 1946. It was twenty-six.

**Missy LeHand** became, in Elliott Roosevelt's words, "the true hostess of the White House"—not too surprising, considering that she lived on the third floor. She suffered a stroke in 1941 and retired as FDR's secretary. Missy, only forty-six, died of a cerebral thrombosis in Boston's Chelsea Naval Hospital on July 31, 1944. FDR's will earmarked up to half of his estate for her medical care.

The *Literary Digest* continued presidential polling, picking winners in 1924, 1928, and 1932 (coming within 0.71 percent of 1932's actual result). But then in 1936, based on 2.3 million ballots returned, it forecast that Kansas Governor Alf Landon would defeat FDR 57 to 43 percent and garner 370 electoral votes. In the real election, Landon received 38 percent and 8 electoral votes. The fiasco shattered the *Digest*'s credibility. In June 1937, it merged with *The Review of Reviews*, finally folding the following spring. It was forty-seven.

**Henry Cabot Lodge**'s influence faded quickly after Calvin Coolidge assumed the presidency. "Coolidge's secret thoughts of Lodge are not fit to print," William Howard Taft wrote his wife. Lodge, seventy-four, died in Cambridge, Massachusetts, following a stroke, on November 9, 1924. His grandson, Henry Cabot Lodge, Jr., followed him into the Senate, losing his seat in 1952 to John F. Kennedy; he also ran for vice president on Richard Nixon's ticket in 1960, losing again to the Kennedy ticket. In February 1953, Dwight Eisenhower appointed Lodge Jr. as U.S. Ambassador to the United Nations, successor organization to the League of Nations.

**Alice Roosevelt Longworth**, Theodore Roosevelt's sharp-tongued daughter, remained in Washington after her husband Nick's death in 1931 and continued her acerbic ways, viewing the world, as she put it, with "malevolent detachment." "I'm the old fire horse," she explained toward the end: "I just perform. I give a good show—just one of the Roosevelt show-offs." She died at her Dupont Circle mansion on February 20, 1980. She was ninety-six.

**Frank Orren Lowden**'s wife, Florence Pullman Lowden, died in 1937, leaving her husband $4.5 million. Frank Lowden died of cancer in Tucson on March 20, 1943. He was eighty-two.

**Helen Harding Cox Mahoney**, daughter of James M. Cox, died after a fall at her suburban Dayton home on May 16, 1921. She was only twenty-five.

**Dudley Field Malone** divorced suffragette Doris Stevens in 1929. He assisted Clarence Darrow in the 1925 Scopes evolution trial and, despite his earlier views on the subject, spent much of the 1920s protesting Prohibition—often by drinking heavily. In 1932, he helped secure Franklin Roosevelt's nomination—but then endorsed Herbert Hoover. Moving to California, Malone became counsel to Twentieth Century-Fox and portrayed Winston Churchill in Warner Brothers's 1943 paean to Stalin, *Mission to Moscow*. Malone, sixty-eight, died of a heart attack in Culver City on October 5, 1950.

**William Gibbs McAdoo** divorced Eleanor Wilson in July 1934. In September 1935, McAdoo, seventy-one, married twenty-six-year-old San Diego public health nurse Doris Cross. Despite FDR's support, McAdoo, a senator from California, was denied renomination in 1938. McAdoo, seventy-seven, died of a heart attack while visiting Washington on February 1, 1941.

**H. L. Mencken** initially liked fellow Wet FDR, but soon turned on "Roosevelt Minor" with a fury that made his criticism of Harding seem like a Valentine. Incapacitated by a 1948 stroke, Mencken died on January 29, 1956, at the red-brick Baltimore house that had served as his home virtually uninterrupted since age three. He was seventy-five.

**Kate Richards O'Hare**, former Socialist Party activist who was jailed for antiwar activities, became California's Assistant State Director of Penology in 1939. She died in January 1948, aged seventy-one.

**Thomas Mott Osborne**, warden at Monmouth Naval Prison, never held another responsible government position. Complicating his life was a $25,000 alienation-of-affection suit launched against him by a young woman aggrieved in the matter of her ex-convict fiancé, Osborne's aide and occasional bodyguard. On Wednesday evening, October 20, 1926, a body was found outside a theater in Auburn, New York. It was Osborne, who had suffered a heart attack at age sixty-seven. Newspapers refrained from revealing that the deceased carried no identification, save for his old "Tom Brown" prison badge, wore a false beard and teeth, and had disguised his nostrils, in the manner of movie master of disguise Lon Cheney. It is best not to consider what he was up to.

**A. Mitchell Palmer** was found by the Senate Judiciary Committee in April 1922 to have been not guilty of "usurpation of authority" during the Palmer Raids, and that although there was some rough treatment of the accused, they had generally suffered from no "great hardship or deprivation." That same year, Palmer suffered a heart attack and abandoned his political ambitions. He did, however, maintain close relations with former neighbor Franklin Roosevelt, and FDR entrusted Palmer to write the 1932 Democratic platform—a document that Roosevelt took care to keep under glass on his Oval Office desk but never to implement. Palmer, sixty-four, died in Washington on May 11, 1936, of heart disease following an appendicitis operation.

**Alice Stokes Paul** earned three law degrees in the 1920s, drafted the ill-fated federal Equal Rights Amendment in 1923, and, in 1938, helped organize the World Woman's Party. Paul, ninety-two, died in Moorestown, New Jersey, on July 9, 1977.

**Mary Allen Hulbert Peck**, Woodrow Wilson's mysterious correspondent and friend, died in Norwalk, Connecticut, on December 17, 1939. She was seventy-six.

**Andrew J. Peters**, mayor during Boston's police strike, returned to the private practice of law and to other sundry private matters, most notably those concerning a beautiful young girl with a beautiful name, Starr Faithfull. The affair—actually, a series of rapes—started in 1917 when she was twelve. Peters paid somewhere between twenty and eighty thousand dollars to silence her outraged—but unusually practical—family. Starr moved to New York, became a showgirl, and was found drowned—but fully dressed—on a Long Island beach on June 8, 1931. Some suspected Peters, but as he still retained some influence (he seconded Al Smith at the 1928 Democratic convention), nothing was done to him. Peters, sixty-six, died of pneumonia on June 26, 1938. The Starr Faithfull case has never been solved.

**Alexandra Carlisle Pfeiffer** continued her stage career against her second husband's wishes. In 1923, Dr. Albert Pfeiffer sued for divorce, charging desertion. In 1934, while she was in her Chicago apartment, eleven floors above, her estranged third husband, J. Elliot Jenkins, shot and killed himself. Jenkins left two suicide notes. One read: "To the hotel bellboys: I'm sorry I wasn't able to tip you while I was here. Thank you for your good service." Atop the note, he left seventeen dollars. Alexandra Pfeiffer died alone at her room in Times Square's Hotel Astor on April 22, 1936. She was fifty.

**Carrie Fulton Phillips** died on February 3, 1960, in Marion in what the *New York Times* described as "an institution for the aged maintained by public welfare." She left behind a cardboard box containing ninety-eight letters from Harding that confirmed their relationship, often in graphic detail. She was eighty-seven.

**Corinne Roosevelt Robinson's** son Theodore became an assistant secretary of the Navy under Calvin Coolidge. Nonetheless, she refused to serve as a Republican elector in the 1932 presidential contest out of consideration for her "beloved niece" Eleanor ("For her I have the deepest affection and respect"). Corinne Robinson died of pleural pneumonia at her Upper East Side home on February 17, 1933. President-elect, Mrs. Roosevelt, and Alice Roosevelt Longworth attended her Park Avenue funeral. Among the pallbearers were her grandsons, the future syndicated columnists, Joseph and Stewart Alsop. She was seventy-one.

**Eleanor Roosevelt** served as an American delegate to the United Nations under Presidents Truman and Kennedy, wrote a newspaper column, "My Day," and actively encouraged the liberal wing of the Democratic Party. She died of tuberculosis in New York City on November 7, 1962. She was seventy-eight.

**Franklin D. Roosevelt** never seemed to lack for confidence as he won four terms as president, defeated the Axis powers, and created the United Nations, the successor to Woodrow Wilson's League of Nations. But he had second thoughts about his 1920 performance. "I, too," he confided in 1939 to Colonel Frank Knox (the 1936 Republican vice-presidential candidate who would become Roosevelt's wartime Secretary of the Navy), "was inexperienced in national campaigns in 1920 and later regretted many of the things I said at that time!" He died at Warm Springs, Georgia, on April 12, 1945, aged sixty-three.

**Theodore Roosevelt, Jr.** served as governor of Puerto Rico, Governor-General of the Philippines, and editor of Doubleday, Doran & Co. He landed with Allied amphibious forces in Algeria, in Sicily, and at Utah Beach on D-Day. Brigadier General Roosevelt died of a heart attack in

Normandy on July 12, 1944, just thirty-six days after the invasion. He was fifty-six.

**Lucy Mercer Rutherford**, Franklin Roosevelt's wartime mistress, married wealthy New Yorker Winthrop Rutherford in February 1920. Lucy was twenty-eight, her groom fifty-eight. Married or not, she maintained contact with FDR and was at his side in April 1945 when he expired at Warm Springs. Lucy Mercer Rutherford died in New York City on July 31, 1948—four years to the day after Missy LeHand, FDR's secretary, died. She was fifty-seven.

**Nicola Sacco and Bartolomeo Vanzetti** remained cultural icons, symbols of American injustice. On August 23, 1977, Massachusetts Governor Michael Dukakis officially pardoned the two men. Yet doubts have steadily mounted against presuming their innocence. In 1943, anarchist leader and key Sacco and Vanzetti supporter Carlo Tresca, who had first begun hearing rumors of their guilt as early as 1922, admitted to leftist intellectual Max Eastman, "Sacco was guilty but Vanzetti was innocent." He had earlier made the same admission to socialists Norman Thomas and John P. Roche.

In October 1961, ballistics tests revealed that some of the bullets found in factory guard Alessandro Berardelli's body came from Sacco's Colt automatic pistol. In 1982, Ideale Gambera, son of one of Sacco and Vanzetti's four-man defense committee, wrote author Francis Russell: "Everyone [among the anarchist leadership] knew that Sacco was guilty and that Vanzetti was innocent as far as the actual participation in killing." In December 2005, further confirmation of their guilt emerged when a September 1929 letter that Pultizer Prize–winning novelist Upton Sinclair had written to a friend, an attorney in Los Angeles, was made public. "Alone in a hotel room with [Sacco and Vanzetti defense counsel] Fred [Moore], I begged him to tell me the full truth," Sinclair, a political radical, wrote. "He then told me that the men were guilty, and he told me in every detail how he had framed a set of alibis for them."

"This letter is for yourself alone," Sinclair concluded. "Stick it away in your safe, and some time in the far distant future the world may know the real truth about the matter. I am here trying to make plain my own part in the story."

**The San Francisco Civic Auditorium**, site of the 1920 Democratic

National Convention, functions to this day. However, being that it functions in San Francisco, and San Francisco being what it is, it is now the Bill Graham Civic Auditorium, in honor of the famed concert promoter of the city's Haight-Ashbury era.

**Thomas D. Schall**, Hiram Johnson's seconder at the 1920 convention, evolved from progressive Congressman to the Senate's most vitriolic opponent of Franklin Roosevelt's New Deal. On the morning of December 22, 1935, the blind Schall was run over in Washington traffic. His death coincided with a national conference of traffic safety experts. Schall was fifty-eight.

**Colonel William J. Simmons**, founder of the modern Ku Klux Klan, after a series of legal battles, surrendered Klan leadership in 1924, having been bought off for somewhere between $90,000 and $145,500. He pondered founding a rival Klan—the Hidden Hosts, Knights of the Flaming Sword—but nothing came of the idea. In 1936, the Klan's former national headquarters in Atlanta became a Catholic school. In April 1944, the Invisible Empire, facing a $685,000 IRS tax lien, formally dissolved. Simmons, sixty-four, died in Atlanta on May 18, 1945.

**Al Smith** broke with Franklin Roosevelt, declaring the New Deal anathema. "Don't let anyone tell you that President Roosevelt is a Communist," said Al Smith in his last speech of the 1936 campaign against FDR. "That is not so. Or don't let anyone tell you he is a Socialist. That is not so. He is neither a Communist nor a Socialist—any more than I am—but something has taken place in this country—there is a certain kind of foreign 'ism' crawling over this country. What it is I don't know. What its first name will be when it's christened I haven't the slightest idea. But I know it is here, and the sin about it is that [Roosevelt] doesn't seem to know it." The Happy Warrior died of lung and heart disease on October 4, 1944. He was seventy.

**Frank W. Stearns**, Calvin Coolidge's most ardent backer, converted to Catholicism in 1935. He died of pneumonia at his Boston home on March 6, 1939. He was eighty-two.

**Seymour Stedman**, Eugene Debs's 1920 running mate, became vice president of the City State Bank of Chicago. It failed in 1929. Four years later, authorities indicted him for receiving deposits during its insolvency, but they dropped the charges two years later. Stedman, seventy-eight, died at his Chicago home on July 9, 1948.

**Lothrop Stoddard**, author of *The Rising Tide of Color*, continued writing racist books, including 1922's proto-Nazi *The Revolt against Civilization: The Menace of the Underman*. In 1921, with Margaret Sanger, he helped found the American Birth Control League and served on its board of directors. In 1940, Stoddard interviewed Hitler, Himmler, and Goebbels for the North American Newspaper Alliance and conferred with prominent German eugenicists. He died in Washington, D.C. on May 1, 1950. He was sixty-six.

**Mark Sullivan** composed the six-volume *Our Times: 1900–1925*, a multidiscipline popular history of American politics and culture that should have won him the Pulitzer Prize. It didn't. A syndicated columnist to the end, he died of a heart attack at his Avondale, Pennsylvania home on August 13, 1952. He was seventy-seven.

**William Howard Taft** resigned as Chief Justice of the Supreme Court in February 1930 and died that March 8. "To me he was a friend," said Calvin Coolidge, "kindly, genial, and helpful. He often came to my office when I was in Washington and always brought mature thought and good cheer." Taft was seventy-two.

**Captain Joseph K. Taussig**, critic of FDR's naval prison policies, rose to the rank of admiral, retiring just prior to Pearl Harbor. Recalled to active duty in 1943, he served as senior member on the Navy's clemency and prison inspection board, receiving the Legion of Merit. Taussig, seventy, died of a heart attack at Bethesda Naval Hospital on October 29, 1947.

**Judge Webster Thayer**, presiding judge in the Sacco and Vanzetti case, lost his Worcester, Massachusetts home to a bomb on the night of September 27, 1932. He remained under police guard until his death in Boston the following April 18, of a stroke. He was seventy-five.

**Carlo Tresca**, early organizer of Sacco and Vanzetti's defense, was convicted of sending obscene material (an ad for a book on birth control) through the mails in 1924, but after serving four months was freed by President Coolidge. On the evening of January 11, 1943, Tresca and an associate strolled through Greenwich Village. At 9:40 p.m., they were at Fifth Avenue and 15th Street when a dark sedan pulled alongside. A man jumped out and fired three shots, one hitting Tresca in the temple. He died instantly. Fascists, Communists, and mobsters were suspected. No one was ever convicted. Tresca was sixty-three.

**William Monroe Trotter**, the fiery civil rights leader, despondent over the loss of his *Boston Guardian,* jumped from a Roxbury roof to his death on his sixty-fifth birthday, April 7, 1934.

**Joseph P. Tumulty**, Woodrow Wilson's private secretary, entered Washington private practice, refusing to engage in lobbying. Tumulty, seventy-four, died at his Maryland home on April 8, 1954.

**George Sylvester Viereck**, despite personal friendships with Freud and Einstein, continued his pro-German activities even after Hitler came to power, served as a ghostwriter for Colonel House (House autographed a copy of *Philip Dru: Administrator* to Viereck), and was packed off to prison during World War II for violating the Foreign Agents Registration Act. He died of a massive cerebral hemorrhage in Holyoke, Massachusetts, on March 19, 1962. He was seventy-seven.

**Wayne Bidwell Wheeler**, boss of the Anti-Saloon League, suffered horrendous personal tragedy. In August 1927, a gasoline stove exploded at Wheeler's Little Point Sable, his Michigan summer cottage. His wife's apron caught fire, enveloping her entire body, even the inside of her mouth, in flames. Her eighty-one-year-old father, recuperating from a heart attack, witnessed the scene, suffered another heart attack, and died on the spot. Wrapping his wife in a carpet and treating her with baking soda, Wheeler rushed her to a hospital. She died the next morning. Wheeler very soon followed. Beset by kidney disease, he died at the Battle Creek Sanitarium on September 5, 1927. When Wheeler died, Will Rogers remarked: "The best fight a man can put up is to have his enemies say, if he passes out in the middle of the fight, is: 'Well, I am glad he is out of the way.'" Wayne B. Wheeler was fifty-seven.

**William Allen White** remained an "unreconstructed liberal," ran for governor of Kansas as an anti-Klan independent in 1924, and vigorously urged support for Britain prior to Pearl Harbor. Less notably, in 1928, he attacked Al Smith for allegedly supporting gambling and prostitution while in the state legislature. He later withdrew those charges. White, eighty-five, died at Emporia, Kansas, on January 29, 1944. His *Autobiography*, published posthumously in 1946, won the Pulitzer Prize for biography.

**Edith Bolling Galt Wilson** personally answered each piece of mail she received—but only if it contained a stamped, self-addressed envelope. In 1939, she published her autobiography, *My Memoir*. Mrs. Wilson died at her Washington home on December 29, 1961. She was eighty-nine.

**General Leonard Wood** returned from the Philippines in 1927 to be operated on for a brain tumor. "I'm much like a banged-up freight car," he said to those shocked by his appearance, "that is still running on its wheels." Wood died after nearly seventeen hours on the operating table at Boston's Peter Bent Brigham Hospital on August 7, 1927. He was sixty-six.

# Notes

**CHAPTER 1**

9. Woodrow Wilson thought thirteen: *Fort Wayne News*, 1 January 1913, p. 1; *Coshocton Tribune*, 3 January 1913, p. 1; *Oakland Tribune*, 3 March 1913, p. 3; Bell, p. 303; Walworth, p. 144; Lawrence, p. 183; Dos Passos (*Mr. Wilson's War*), pp. 446, 474.

10. "canny, tenacious . . . a little exclusive": Tumulty, p. 457.

11. "He is a good hater": MacMillan, p. 5.

11. "a foe of Bryanism . . . practices of labor unions": Link (*Progressive Era*), pp. 8–9.

12. "And he calls that a conference": Axson, p. 234.

12. At Princeton . . . master: *Boston Globe*, 30 January 1910, p. 14; Russell (*President Makers*), pp. 150–151.

13. "Will America tolerate . . . apart?": *Current Literature*, February 1912, p. 2; Cooper (*Warrior and the Priest*), pp. 102–103; Daniels (*Wilson*), p. 82.

13. "We have beaten . . . The game is up": *Boston Globe*, 11 February 1911, p. 2; White (*Wilson*), pp. 189–190; Russell (*President Makers*), p. 156.

14. ". . . measures of men": *Boston Globe*, 16 September 1910, p. 5; *Outlook*, 24 September 1910, p. 140; Russell (*President Makers*), p. 158; Cooper (*Warrior and the Priest*), p. 121.

14. " . . . parties of the State": *Trenton Evening Times*, 16 January 1911, pp. 1–2; *Trenton Evening Times*, 18 January 1911, pp. 1, 3; Cooper (*Warrior and the Priest*), pp. 175–176; Russell (*President Makers*), p. 165; George and George, p. 62.

15. "To the Governor . . . he's an ingrate and a liar": *Boston Globe*, 1 January 1911, p. 47; *Trenton Evening Times*, 4 June 1911, p. 9; *Chicago Tribune*, 11 August 1911, p. 5; M. Lyons, pp. 16–17; Walworth, p. 189; George and George, p. 72.

15. Moving leftward, Wilson . . . "Marse Henry" Watterson: *Boston Globe*, 18 January 1912, p. 8; *Boston Globe*, 31 January 1912, p. 9; *Outlook*, 27 January 1912, p. 149; M. Lyons, pp. 21–22; Walworth, pp. 214–216.

15. Those who have loved . . . neither anger nor remorse: Axson, p. 204.

15. "My ambition . . . strive to satisfy it": Levin, p. 92; Dos Passos (*Mr. Wilson's War*), p. 61.

15. "the strangest and . . . human history": Seymour, pp. 1, 40; Levin, p. 92.

16. "Never begin by arguing . . . start your business": Perrett, p. 22.

17. Clark/Harmon/Marshall: M. Lyons, p. 23; Eaton, pp. 228–229.

17. Marshall 30: Walworth, p. 219; Eaton, p. 228; Swanberg, pp. 276–277; Nasaw, pp. 227–228.

17. "... heard of again": *Boston Globe*, 29 June 1912, p. 1; *Boston Globe*, 3 July 1912, pp. 1, 4; Fleming, p. 16. Marshall's best-remembered remark was the more mundane "What this country needs is a good five-cent cigar."

17. "I wish it to be ... could have prevented that": Spragens, p. 247; Olasky, p. 197.

17. "... human traits and red corpuscles": Walworth, p. 241; Manners, p. 160.

18. "... a nervous breakdown": *Atlanta Constitution*, 7 August 1915, pp. 1, 5; *Trenton Evening Times*, 7 August 1915, p. 1; Ross (*Power with Grace*), pp. 31–32; Levin, p. 48; Anthony (*First Ladies*), p. 349.

18. "Oh my God ... What am I going to do?": G. Smith, p. 9.

18. "... may have taken ten minutes": Wilson, p. 56; Walworth, p. 427; G. Smith, p. 14; Ross (*Power with Grace*), pp. 34–35; Dos Passos (*Mr. Wilson's War*), pp. 132–133.

19. "Oh, you can't love me" ... "I want you to be my wife": Wilson, pp. 60–61; G. Smith, p. 16; Anthony (*First Ladies*), p. 351.

19. "The President was simply obsessed ... people would not approve": I. Hoover, p. 67.

19. "She fell out of bed with surprise": MacMillan, p. 8; Anthony (*First Ladies*), p. 355.

20. "How do you expect me ... possibly *want* to be loved": Levin, p. 27.

20. "... intelligence and humor": Hulbert, pp. 158–179; E. W. McAdoo and Gaffey, p. 131; Weinstein, p. 189; Olasky, p. 192. Ellen's depression lasted until 1910.

20. "... one unhappiness in her marriage: Weinstein, p. 189.

21. "... like the apothecary's clerk": *NY Times*, 8 April 1912, p. 1; Walworth, pp. 247–248; White (*Woodrow Wilson*) pp. 266–267, 269; Levin, p. 131; Caroli, p. 355; Olasky, p. 196. In 1912, Champ Clark's campaign circulated "scurrilous literature" in the Western states, presumably regarding the Peck affair. The rumors resurfaced in 1916 and generated additional rumors that Bernard Baruch had paid Mrs. Peck $75,000 for her silence. Mrs. Peck claimed that in 1916 she was shadowed by the President's opponents and offered up to $300,000 for Wilson's letters. (M. Lyons, p. 44; Hulbert, pp. 260–264; Anthony [*First Ladies*], p. 359.)

21. Wilson's September 18, 1915 letter: Wilson, p. 78; Walworth, pp. 230-31; Ross (*Power with Grace*), pp. 43-44; Levin, p. 113.

21. "... Your own, Woodrow": http://www.theromantic.com/LoveLetters/woodrowwilson.htm. Corresponding with Edith Wilson, Wilson wrote of his regret over breaching the "standards of honourable behavior"—a "folly long ago loathed and repented of" that made him "stained and unworthy" of her love—"the contemptible error and madness of a few months." (Chace, p. 46.)

22. Admission ... happiness to be married: Levin, pp. 114–115; Olasky, p. 201.

22. ... Saturday, December 18, 1915: *NY Times*, 7 October 1915, pp. 1, 4; *LA Times*, 18 December 1915, p. 1; Ross (*Power with Grace*), pp. 52–57. When Wilson proposed, he sent a letter to Mrs. Peck, letting her know. She never replied. (Ross [*Power with Grace*], p. 45.)

22. "It would be an irony ... chiefly with foreign affairs": Johnson, p. 648.

23. "I agree with the American people ... *kept—who will keep—us* out of war": Boller, p. 203.

23. The Republican candidate in 1916 ... "Charles Evasive Hughes": *Lima Times-Democrat*, 14 October 1916, p. 4; *Sandusky Star Journal*, 28 October 1916, p. 10; Stone, pp.

97–115; Link (*Woodrow Wilson and the Progressive Era*), pp. 244–247. In 1916, an estimated 20 percent of TR's 1912 supporters voted for Wilson.

23. . . . picking up his marbles and going home: Link (*Woodrow Wilson and the Progressive Era*), pp. 319–320; Ross (*Power with Grace*), pp. 80–82; Cooper (*Breaking the Heart of the World*), pp. 30–31; Kane, p. 192; Levin, p. 164.

23. . . . lost the Golden State by 3,800 votes: *NY Times*, 8 November 1916, p. 1; *Washington Post*, 8 November 1916, p. 9; Daniels (*Wilson*), pp. 275–276; Boller, p. 206; Stone, p. 115.

23. "'Tis not so deep . . . 'Twill serve": Dos Passos (*Mr. Wilson's War*), p. 184.

24. ". . . end should be like this": *NY Times*, 14 November 1916, p. 4; Levin, pp. 169–175; I. Hoover, p. 112; Anthony (*First Ladies*), pp. 359–360.

24. "No one can see him . . . Cabinet or those around him": George and George, p. 188.

25. . . . "threatened his own prestige": White (*Masks*), p. 357.

25. "Wilson trusted only errand boys": White (*Masks*), p. 383.

25. "to make the world safe for democracy": *Messages and Papers of the President*, pp. 8226–8233; Daniels (*Wilson*), p. 279.

## CHAPTER 2

26. . . . Food Administrator Herbert Hoover: Starling, p. 118; Dos Passos (*Mr. Wilson's War*), pp. 441–442.

27. . . . "far as the eye can see": I. Hoover, p. 76; Dos Passos (*Mr. Wilson's War*), pp. 446, 474; Ferrell (*Woodrow Wilson and World War I*), p. 138; Watt, p. 87; Fleming, p. 318.

27. "It was the natural one": Lansing, pp. 39–40.

27. At Buckingham Palace . . . "an odious man": Fleming, p. 324.

27. "I never knew . . . like Lloyd George": R. Smith, p. 91.

27. The United States' peace commission . . . conscience of the world: Lansing, p. 45; Bailey (*The Lost Peace*), p. 87; Cooper (*Breaking the Heart of the World*), pp. 33–36.

28. "Colonel House would seek . . . more loyal than he": I. Hoover, p. 93.

28. ". . . What misery it will cause!": Sullivan (V), p. 536; Dos Passos (*Mr. Wilson's War*), p. 443.

29. "Please do not misunderstand . . . we are a tough bunch": MacMillan, p. 23.

29. "until the pips squeak": Watt, p. 90; Leuchtenburg, p. 53.

29. "Logic! Logic! . . . going to include pensions": Ferrell (*Woodrow Wilson and World War I*), p. 143; Fleming, pp. 364–365.

29. "much easier to make war than peace": MacMillan, p. xxx.

29. "a general association . . . great and small states alike": Filler, pp. 126–130.

29. "I am disgusted . . . he threatens to leave": Bailey (*Lost Peace*), p. 223; MacMillan, p. 200.

30. "If this . . . throughout the world": MacMillan, pp. 317–321; Fleming, pp. 339–340.

30. . . . It was a dangerous game: Wilson, pp. 245–246; Bailey (*Lost Peace*), p. 209; Dos Passos (*Mr. Wilson's War*), pp. 474–475; Coit, p. 251; Watt, p. 87; George and George, p. 240; MacMillan, p. 175. Some historians contend that this incident did not occur until later in Wilson's return.

31. . . . Bullitt resigned in May: Watt, pp. 98–99; Schlesinger, pp. 12–13; Morgan (*Reds*), pp. 133–134.

31. Wilson, alone of the Four . . . openly arrived at": Lansing, pp. 61, 65–66; George and George, pp. 248–249; Sullivan (V), pp. 544–545.

31. . . . Rumors flew of poison: H. Hoover (*Ordeal of Woodrow Wilson*), pp. 198–200; Coit, p. 254; G. Smith, pp. 48–49; Fleming, pp. 365–366; Levin, pp. 290–297; Weinstein, pp. 336–337.

32. . . . after this little spell of sickness: I. Hoover, pp. 98–99.

32. . . . rested completely on the Sabbath: Ferrell (*Woodrow Wilson and World War I*), pp. 159–161: Bailey (*Lost Peace*), pp. 221–223; Levin, pp. 30–31, 33–34.

33. I don't like the way the colors . . . called in before the Big Three: Weinstein, p. 342.

34. . . . resort was to find a "precedent": H. Hoover (*Years of Adventure*), p. 468.

34. Wilson even went over Orlando's head . . . he slunk back): Lansing, pp. 115–116; Macmillan, pp. 279–305; George and George, pp. 258–262; Asinof, p. 107.

34. accused him of planting such stories through his son-in-law and secretary, Gordon Auchincloss: George and George, pp. 261, 266.

34. . . . thus, of no consequence: George and George, pp. 264–265; Dos Passos (*Mr. Wilson's War*), pp. 481–482.

35. "House," Wilson lectured . . . without fighting for it": George and George, pp. 266–267.

### CHAPTER 3

36. . . . Wilson's shocked expression: Ward, pp. 431–432; C. Black, pp. 105–106; Morgan (*F.D.R.*), p. 213; Anthony (*First Ladies*), p. 368.

37. . . . steamed south to Boston: *NY Times*, 24 February 1919, pp. 1–2; *Chicago Tribune*, 24 February 1919, pp. 1–2; Freidel (*The Ordeal*), pp. 14–15; C. Black, p. 106. Years later, Josephus Daniels and Wilson press secretary Ray Stannard Baker puffed up the event further to depict FDR as having guided the ship to safety.

37. . . . promptly arrested him: *Boston Globe*, 24 February 1919, p. 1; *Chicago Tribune*, 24 February 1919, p. 2; *NY Times*, 25 February 1919, p. 2; *Chicago Tribune*, 25 February 1919, p. 1; *Boston Globe*, 25 February 1919, p. 8; Wilson, pp. 240–241.

37. ". . . supported him in the past": *Boston Globe*, 24 February 1919, pp. 7, 9; *Atlanta Constitution*, 25 February 1919, p. 1; Wilson, p. 241; Fuess, p. 184; Ward, p. 453; Perrett, p. 21.

38. ". . . his human kind forever": *Boston Globe*, 24 February 1919, pp. 1, 9; *Chicago Tribune*, 25 February 1919, pp. 1–2; George and George, pp. 235, 243; Watt, p. 85; Perrett, p. 21.

38. ". . . hatred I feel toward Wilson": Garraty, p. 312; Leuchtenburg, p. 59.

38. ". . . approved by Theodore Roosevelt": *Providence Journal*, 29 October 1920, p. 4; *Dayton Journal*, 30 October 1920, p. 2; Widenor, p. 311 *fn*.

38. ". . . White Rabbit to go to breakfast with me": *Chicago Tribune*, 27 February 1919, pp. 1–2; *NY Times*, 1 March 1919, pp. 1–2; Watt, pp. 85–86; Fleming, pp. 345–346; George and George, pp. 232, 236, 243.

39. . . . already raging animosity: *NY Times*, 1 March 1919, pp. 1, 3; *Atlanta Constitution*, 4 March 1919, p. 1; Ferrell (*Woodrow Wilson*), p. 166. Just a week previously, the *Chicago Tribune* had headlined a brief story: THINKS WILSON WILL BE NAMED FOR THIRD TERM. (*Chicago Tribune*, 23 February 1919, p. 1.)

39. . . . and Wilson did not: *Boston Globe*, 4 March 1919, pp. 1, 6; Sullivan (V), p. 548 *fn*.; Cooper (*Breaking the Heart of the World*), pp. 56–57, 67–68; George and George, p. 238.

39. ". . . strands wired and twisted together": Watson, p. 190; Ferrell (*Woodrow Wilson*), p. 166; George and George, pp. 277, 279–280.

39. This business of the President . . . thing could be secured": Miller, p. 161.
40. ". . . murrain on him!": Wilson, pp. 241–243; Sullivan (V), p. 549; Fleming, pp. 349–351; Longworth, pp. 285–286; Leuchtenburg, p. 59.
40. . . . dismissed his words as mere "blah": *Chicago Tribune*, 10 July 1919, p. 8; Lodge, pp. 152–155; Cooper (*Breaking the Heart of the World*), pp. 118–120; Watt, p. 510.
40. . . . conversing, swaying no one: *NY Times*, 20 August 1919, pp. 1–2; Ferrell (*Woodrow Wilson*), p. 167; Dos Passos (*Mr. Wilson's War*), pp. 483–485; Cooper (*Warrior and the Priest*), pp. 340–341.
40. . . . independence of all Members of the League: Ferrell (*Woodrow Wilson*), p. 166; George and George, pp. 281–282.
40. . . . oversimplification of events: *Outlook*, 20 June 1920, pp. 372–373; Lodge, pp. 311–312, 321–323; Sinclair (*Available Man*), pp. 93–95.
41. ". . . must not include rest of any kind": H. Hoover (*Ordeal of Woodrow Wilson*), p. 272; Bailey (*Great Betrayal*), p. 99; Ward, p. 461; Tumulty, p. 438; Sullivan (V), p. 553.
41. He hated the experience: Ferrell (*Woodrow Wilson*), p. 169; Cooper (*Breaking the Heart of the World*), p. 180; http://history.acusd.edu/gen/recording/wilson.html.
42. . . . rest from the campaign trail: Hulbert, pp. 257, 267–277; Wilson, p. 281; Starling, p. 150; Ross (*Power with Grace*), pp. 189–190; Levin, pp. 328–330; Anthony (*First Ladies*), p. 370.
43. ". . . Secretary of State of the United States. My God!": *Boston Globe*, 17 September 1919, pp. 1–2; Tumulty, pp. 441–442: Levin, pp. 324–327; Lawrence, p. 285; Bailey (*Great Betrayal*), pp. 124–127; Cooper (*Breaking the Heart of the World*), pp. 168–172; MacMillan, pp. 490–491.
43. ". . . to stop and rest": Link (*Papers of Woodrow Wilson*), pp. 64: 619-20. FDR appointed Bullitt as the United States' first Ambassador to the Soviet Union and later Ambassador to France. Bullitt's first wife was the sister of prominent biographer Catherine Drinker Bowen; his second was Louise Bryant, widow of radical journalist John Reed. Later, he was engaged to Franklin Roosevelt's secretary, Missy LeHand. (James Roosevelt [*My Parents*], p. 107.)
44. . . . requests of Dr. Grayson to stop and rest: *LA Times*, 18 September 1919, p. 1; *Atlanta Constitution*, 18 September 1919, pp. 1, 17; *Boston Globe*, 22 September 1919, p. 16.
44. ". . . character of a party issue": Link (*Papers of Woodrow Wilson*), pp. 64: 54–57; Annin, pp. 314–316; Creel, p. 340; MacMillan, p. 490. See Thomas A. Bailey's *Woodrow Wilson and the Great Betrayal*, pp. 117–122, for a detailed analysis of the failure of Wilson's Western tour. "It would be difficult," noted Bailey, "to prove that a single vote was changed by Wilson's western appeal."
44. . . . the tide was finally turning: *NY Times*, 26 September 1919, p. 1; Lawrence, p. 280.
44. . . . "heathen idols of ancient Rome": *NY Times*, 26 September 1919, pp. 1, 3; *Washington Post*, 26 September 1919, pp. 1–2; *Chicago Tribune*, 26 September 1919, p. 7.
45. . . . world never dreamed of before: Filler, pp. 133–138; Stevenson, pp. 66–67.
46. "Germany must never again he allowed . . . lesson must be taught to Germany": Perrett, p. 25.
46. I stood close behind him . . . faithful valet said gloomily: Starling, p. 152.
46. "I seem to have gone to pieces": *Chicago Tribune*, 27 September 1919, pp. 1, 10; *LA Times*, 27 September 1919, pp. 1–2; Sullivan (V), p. 556; Weinstein, p. 355; Ferrell (*Woodrow Wilson*), p. 169.

47.  ". . . found him on the bathroom floor unconscious": Wilson, p. 287; Stevenson, p. 67.

47.  ". . . the president is paralyzed!": I. Hoover, p. 101; Ferrell (*Woodrow Wilson*), p. 169; Bailey (*Great Betrayal*), p. 132; Weinstein, p. 356; Levin, p. 337; Ross (*Power with Grace*), pp. 197–199; Anthony (*First Ladies*), p. 370.

47.  his patient was a "very sick man": *Chicago Tribune*, 3 October 1919, p. 1; *LA Times*, 3 October 1919, pp. 1, 3.

47.  . . . do nothing during the entire crisis: Tumulty, pp. 443–444; Lawrence, pp. 284–285; Dos Passos (*Mr. Wilson's War*), pp. 492–493; Ferrell (*Woodrow Wilson*), p. 171; Ross (*Power with Grace*), pp. 200–202; Bailey (*Great Betrayal*), p. 140; Levin, pp. 339–340; Weinstein, p. 360; Anthony (*First Ladies*), p. 374.

48.  . . . Lodge dug in his heels: Cooper (*Breaking the Heart of the World*), pp. 252–257; Coit, p. 297; Levin, pp. 372–373. In May 1917, Congressman Gardner, among the earliest advocates for preparedness, resigned from Congress to enlist in the infantry. He died in January 1918 of pneumonia while at Camp Wheeler, Georgia. (*Washington Post*, 15 January 1918, p. 1; *Chicago Tribune*, 15 January 1918, p. 1.)

48.  ". . . seemed to exhaust him: I. Hoover, pp. 103–104.

48.  ". . . for months to come": Link (*Papers of Woodrow Wilson*), pp. 64: 618–619.

48.  ". . . perfectly helpless imbecile": Anthony (*Florence Harding*), pp. 160–161.

49.  . . . not to be received by a U.S. president: Ross (*Power with Grace*), pp. 227–229; Levin, pp. 399–410; Anthony (*First Ladies*), pp. 377–378; Dos Passos (*Mr. Wilson's War*), p. 493. Crauford-Stuart also incurred Bernard Baruch's hostility. Baruch, it seemed, had carried on a dalliance with a German agent, May Ladenburg. Crauford-Stuart had been part of a British intelligence sting operation—which remarkably involved both Franklin Roosevelt and Alice Longworth Roosevelt—that recorded Baruch revealing false classified information to Ladenburg.

49.  . . . act or joint resolution so provide": Creel, p. 339; Watt, p. 511.

49.  "knife thrust at the heart of the treaty": Bailey (*Great Betrayal*), p. 157; Leuchtenburg, p. 62.

50.  ". . . had been permitted to grow": Cooper (*Breaking the Heart of the World*), p. 258; MacMillan, p. 491.

50.  ". . . but an utter contempt": Link (*Papers of Woodrow Wilson*), pp. 64: 43–45; Weinstein, pp. 361–362; Anthony (*First Ladies*), p. 377.

50.  . . . absorbing the afternoon sun: *Atlanta Constitution*, 19 November 1919, p. 2; H. Hoover (*Ordeal of Woodrow Wilson*), pp. 281–282; Link (*Wilson the Diplomatist*), p. 151; George and George, p. 302.

50.  . . . also defeated his own treaty: *NY Times*, 20 November 1919, pp. 1–2; *Chicago Tribune*, 20 November 1919, pp. 1–2; Lodge, pp. 190–192; Link (*Wilson the Diplomatist*), p. 151; George and George, p. 303.

51.  "We were jubilant . . . quite as happy as we were": Longworth, p. 292; Anthony (*First Ladies*), p. 377; Anthony (*Florence Harding*), p. 161. Democrat Thomas P. Gore was legally blind. An opponent of the New Deal, he was defeated for renomination in 1936. His grandsons included author Gore Vidal and Senator Albert Gore, father of Vice President Albert Gore.

51.  . . . never again offered him advice: George and George, pp. 305–306; Dos Passos (*Mr. Wilson's War*), pp. 493–494; Watt, p. 511.

51.  ". . . Mrs. Wilson is President!": Anthony (*First Ladies*), p. 375; Perrett, p. 26.

51. ". . . was good physically": *Washington Post*, 6 December 1919, pp. 1–2; *NY Times*, 6 December 1919, p. 1; *Atlanta Constitution*, 6 December 1919, pp. 1, 6; Wilson, pp. 298–299; Cooper (*Breaking the Heart of the World*), pp. 285–288.

51. . . . Wilson retorted acerbically: Wilson, p. 299; G. Smith, pp. 132–135; Coit, p. 295; Levin, pp. 389–392; Weinstein, p. 363; Perrett, p. 27. No contemporary account records this repartee. Some historians contend that it was an invention of Mrs. Wilson's imagination.

52. . . . astonishment when it had passed: *NY Call*, 19 March 1920, p. 3.

52. . . . wrote Attorney General Palmer requesting an opinion: Starling, pp. 156–157; G. Smith, pp. 146–147; C. Black, p. 120.

52. ". . . I [and Vice-President Marshall] will resign": G. Smith, p. 142; Cooper (*Breaking the Heart of the World*), p. 318; Levin, p. 419; Weinstein, p. 364; Coletta, p. 97.

52. ". . . great and solemn referendum": Dunn and Kuehl, p. 1; Farrell (*Woodrow Wilson*), p. 221; Coletta, pp. 96–97.

53. ". . . prove the control of his party": *Providence Journal*, 9 January 1920, p. 2; Hibben, pp. 364–365; Farrell (*Woodrow Wilson*), pp. 221–222; Coletta, p. 98.

53. ". . . for the purpose of resigning": Cooper (*Breaking the Heart of the World*), pp. 319–320; Farrell (*Woodrow Wilson*), p. 222.

53. . . . Republicans rejected it: *Providence Journal*, 27 January 1920, p. 2; *Atlanta Constitution*, 28 January 1920, p. 1; *NY Times*, 31 January 1920, p. 1.

53. "No, Ambassador . . . The Senate must take its medicine": Watt, p. 511.

54. On Thursday, February 12, Lansing . . . resigned: *Chicago Tribune*, 14 February 1920, pp. 1, 2; Bailey (*Great Betrayal*), pp. 245–246; Wilson, pp. 300–301; Weinstein, p. 365; Levin, pp. 421–423; Cooper (*Breaking the Heart of the World*), p. 336; Noggle, p. 203; Lawrence, pp. 284–285, 287–288. Between December 1919 and March 1920, half the Cabinet departed: Carter Glass at Treasury, William Redfield at Commerce, David Houston at Agriculture, Lansing at State, and Franklin K. Lane at Interior. (Kane, p. 189.)

54. . . . better shape than before the illness came: Creel, p. 340 *fn.*; Weinstein, pp. 366–367.

54. ". . . He never has failed us": George and George, p. 313; Leuchtenburg, p. 63; Cooper (*Breaking the Heart of the World*), pp. 362–373.

**CHAPTER 4**

55. ". . . the president is about six": Pringle (*Roosevelt*), p. 4; Wagenknecht (*American Profile*), p. 27. The author of the remark, Sir Cecil Spring-Rice, was best man at Roosevelt's second wedding. (Brands, p. 108.)

56. "The light . . . has gone out of my life": Brands, p. 162.

57. "Hasten forward quickly there": Wagenknecht (*American Profile*), p. 28.

57. ". . . madman and the White House?": Russell (*President Makers*), p. 85.

57. "Now . . . that damn cowboy is president": Pringle (*Roosevelt*), p. 229.

57. Teddy Roosevelt would soon overturn . . . debt by over $90 million: Johnson, p. 620.

57. "They'll take Taft or they'll get me": Wagenknecht (*American Profile*), p. 343; Sullivan (III), p. 289; Sinclair (*Available Man*), p. 45.

58. . . . "How is the horse?": Pringle (*Taft*), pp. 235–336; Sullivan (III), pp. 14–15; Chace, p. 24.

58. ". . . will make out?" . . . "But he's weak": Sullivan (IV), pp. 331–332.

58.  . . . La Follette was out: Pringle (*Roosevelt*), pp. 553–554; Sullivan (IV), pp. 472–474; Chace, pp. 104–105.

58.  "Even a rat in a corner . . . will fight": Pringle (*Roosevelt*), p. 561; Chace, p. 111.

59.  "To anyone who had ever seen . . . was a perfect description": Butler (*Vol. 1*), p. 242.

59.  . . . promote their Progressive doctrines: Thayer, pp. 370–371.

60.  The final vote was . . . 348 present and not voting: *Chicago Tribune*, 23 June 1912, p. 1.

60.  "I'm feeling like a bull moose!": Nye, p. 287; Boller, p. 196; Stein, p. 196.

60.  ". . . done over into political terms": *NY Times*, 6 August 1912, pp. 1–2; Gable, p. 75.

60.  . . . aberrations of THEODORE ROOSEVELT: *NY Times*, 8 August 1912, p. 8.

61.  ". . . I'm not hurt badly": *LA Times*, 15 October 1912, p. 12; *Washington Post*, 15 October 1912, pp. 1–2; *Chicago Tribune*, 15 October 1912, p. 1; Brands, p. 721; Manners, pp. 279–287; O'Toole, pp. 217–222; Chace, pp. 231–232; Daniels (*Wilson*), p. 125. Schrank, eventually found insane, died in a Wisconsin mental institution in September 1943, receiving no visitors in 31 years of incarceration.

61.  "Vote for Taft, pray for Roosevelt, and bet on Wilson": Manners, p. 268.

61.  "The only question now is which corpse gets the most flowers": Eaton, p. 224.

61.  . . . and a "Byzantine logothete": *Washington Post*, 8 December 1915, p. 1.

61.  ". . . unless it is in an heroic mood": *Boston Globe*, 11 March 1916, p. 12; Fuess, p. 356.

62.  . . . difference between Wilson and Hughes was "a shave": Boller, p. 203; Wagenknecht (*American Profile*), p. 342.

62.  ". . . proud enough to be kicked": T. Roosevelt (*Fear God and Take Your Own Part*), pp. 124, 193, 386; Thayer, pp. 408, 416, 420, 429; Tumulty, pp. 236–237.

62.  ". . . of the tortured dead": *Boston Globe*, 4 November 1916, p. 16; Widenor, pp. 246–247.

62.  ". . . that is very compelling": *Atlanta Constitution*, 13 May 1917, p. 1; Pringle (*Roosevelt*), pp. 416–417; Sullivan (V), pp. 496–497; C. Black, p. 82; Cooper (*Warrior and the Priest*), pp. 324–325.

63.  . . . Dr. Jekyll in their souls: White (*Autobiography*), pp. 544–545.

63.  ". . . and would not hesitate to act": Daniels (*Cabinet Diaries*), p. 216.

64.  . . . in perfect harmony on everything: Duffy, pp. 308–309; Manners, p. 305; O'Toole, pp. 366–367.

64.  . . . next President of the United States: *Washington Post*, 29 March 1918, p. 3.

64. "the Republican candidate for President in 1920": Hagedorn, p. 397.

65.  ". . . the Presidency to me?": Hagedorn, p. 397; White (*Masks*), p. 403; Cooper (*Warrior and the Priest*), p. 328.

65.  . . . The young lion was gone: *Washington Post*, 18 July 1918, p. 9; *NY Times*, 20 July 1918, p. 6; *Washington Post*, 21 July 1918, p. 1; Sullivan (V), pp. 498–499; Fleming, pp. 232–235; Manners, pp. 306–307; Renahan, pp. 192–200; Brands, pp. 797–801; O'Toole, p. 390.

65.  . . . the Great Adventure: *NY Times*, 17 September 1918, p. 13; Pringle (*Roosevelt*), p. 421.

65.  "There was only one way to give . . . must be—and would be—destroyed": Fleming, p. 235.

66.  "I shall never make another . . . anyone who wants the nomination": Stein, p. 220.

66.  . . . I don't see how I could refuse to run: Sullivan (V), p. 502; Stein, pp. 220–221; Manners, p. 308; Russell (*Shadow of Blooming Grove*), p. 311.

67.  . . . set forth questions which are non-justiciable: *Outlook*, 22 January 1919, p. 134; Pringle (*Roosevelt*), p. 423. This was TR's last written utterance, dictated on January 3, 1919.

67. . . . equally good man of another color: *NY Times*, 3 November 1918, p. 12; Renahan, p. 216; Du Bois, p. 269. This was TR's last public address.

67. ". . . the will of the American people": Creel, p. 160; Chace, pp. 2–3; Ward, p. 421; C. Black, p. 103.

67. . . . termed "an attack of lumbago": *NY Times*, 7 November 1918, p. 1; *NY Times*, 7 November 1918, p. 1; *NY Times*, 12 November 1918, p. 15.

68. ". . . cataclysm might have been avoided": White (*Autobiography*), pp. 548–549.

68. ". . . like Quentin, have died for my country": Robinson, pp. 362–363; Hays, p. 239.

69. "No, I don't like him . . . will surely receive the nomination": Harris, p. 9.

69. . . . promise to support him will prove of no avail: Watson, pp. 167–169.

70. . . . was having trouble breathing. Alarmed, Otis rushed in: *Chicago Tribune*, 25 December 1918, p. 3; *Washington Post*, 25 December 1918, p. 5; *Atlanta Constitution*, 7 January 1919, p. 8; *LA Times*, 7 January 1919, p. 12; *Cleveland Advocate*, 11 January 1919, p. 1; Sullivan (V), p. 503; Hays, p. 238; O'Toole, pp. 402–404; Thayer, p. 449; Manners, p. 308.

70. ". . . detestation which flowed from Wilson's lips": Pringle (*Roosevelt*), p. 422; Fleming, p. 330; Watt, p. 57.

70. ". . . there would have been a fight": Thayer, p. 450; Manners, p. 310; Renahan, p. 222; Ward, p. 422; Morgan (*F.D.R.*), p. 212.

70. ". . . illness of perhaps years": Freidel (*The Ordeal*), p. 4; Miller, p. 156; Morgan (*F.D.R.*), p. 212; Ward, p. 423.

70. ". . . his influence and example": Freidel (*The Ordeal*), p. 4; Miller, p. 156.

70. ". . . Theodore is looking on": Garraty, p. 349; Morgan (*F.D.R.*), p. 212.

71. . . . joining in the Lord's Prayer: *Atlanta Constitution*, 9 January 1919, pp. 1–2; *Outlook*, 22 January 1919, p. 133; Manners, pp. 311–312; Chace, p. 5.

71. No one there, not widow . . . TR's friend, William Howard Taft: Duffy, p. 309.

**CHAPTER 5**

72. . . . life in the newspaper business: *McClure's Magazine*, March 1921, pp. 22–24.

73. . . . she was just shy of thirty-one: *Current Opinion*, August 1920, p. 189; *Outlook*, 22 September 1920, p. 140; *World's Work*, September 1920, pp. 444–445; Anthony (*Florence Harding*), p. 43. DeWolfe died in 1894.

73. In response, Dr. Harding . . . on the streets: Anthony (*Florence Harding*), p. 57.

73. ". . . innocence of any child": *Outlook*, 10 November 1920, p. 454; *Literary Digest*, 27 November 1920, p. 57; Sullivan (VI), p. 94.

74. . . . their child in Nebraska: Anthony (*Florence Harding*), pp. 61–62. In the 1890s, Harding suffered three nervous breakdowns, recuperating each time at Battle Creek, Michigan.

74. . . . eyed Joseph B. Foraker's United States Senate seat: Sinclair (*Available Man*), p. 192.

75. . . . Ohio Democratic governor: *Outlook*, 6 August 1910, p. 753; Blackwell, p. 205.

75. Daugherty: *Washington Post*, 30 December 1911, p. 1; *LA Times*, 13 January 1933, p. 4; *NY Times*, 13 January 1933, p. 15; *LA Times*, 21 January 1933, p. 4.

75. . . . odd way, they drew closer: Anthony (*Florence Harding*), pp. 95–96.

75. ". . . greatest fakir of all times": Sinclair (*Available Man*), p. 50; Bagby, p. 37.

75. ". . . to bully and browbeat": *NY Times*, 29 February 1920, p. 7; Sinclair (*Available Man*), p. 50.

76.  . . . not his strong points": Longworth, pp. 202–203; Teichmann, p. 111. The Long-worths' marriage wasn't much better than the Hardings'. Actually, it was worse. Long-worth enjoyed a long dalliance with *Washington Times-Herald* editor and publisher Eleanor Medill ("Cissy") Patterson. Alice replied in kind, taking up with Idaho's Senator Borah. It was generally believed that Borah had fathered her child Paulina, origi-nally to be named *Deborah* (emphasis added). (Caroli, pp. 412–415.)

76.  Well, the mad Roosevelt . . . specialty, along other lines: Russell (*Blooming Grove*), p. 236.

76.  I love your mouth . . . beauty to thus adore: Anthony (*Florence Harding*), pp. 105–106.

77.  ". . . pushed him into the water": Adams (*Incredible Era*), p. 76; Sinclair (*Available Man*), p. 52; Eaton, p. 264.

77.  . . . know of to political happiness: Sinclair (*Available Man*), p. 110; Downes, p. 292; Murray (*Harding Era*), p. 20.

78.  ". . . continue with the old party": Sinclair (*Available Man*), p. 54; Dean, p. 35.

78.  He won the primary comfortably . . . less than a majority of votes cast: *Chillicothe Con-stitution*, 13 August 1914, p. 1; Adams (*Incredible Era*), p. 78; Dean p. 35.

78.  ". . . Go to the polls and beat the Pope": J. M. Cox, p. 178; Sinclair (*Available Man*), p. 55; Downes, pp. 212–215; Anthony (*Florence Harding*), pp. 110–111.

78.  "My daughter married a nigger . . . but he's a smart nigger": Dean, p. 27.

78.  "That's presidential timber": Fausold, p. 128.

78.  "utterly unacceptable": *NY Times*, 4 June 1916, p. 1; *Washington Post*, 5 June 1916, pp. 1–2; *Washington Post*, 6 June 1916, p. 1.

78.  ". . . persons likely to be president": *NY Times*, 8 June 1916, p. 1; Eaton, p. 253.

78.  "keyed nothing and was without note": Cobb, p. 272.

79.  ". . . get out of that under a thousand dollars": Britton, pp. 47–50; Ferrell (*Strange Deaths of President Harding*), pp. 72–74. Ferrell, a careful scholar, contends that there is insufficient proof of this incident (and of the whole affair), but the hotel register he reproduces makes the opposite case. The locations of the hotels Nan mentions are convenient to trains arriving at Pennsylvania Station from Washington.

81.  ". . . if we could have our child—together!": Britton, pp. 78–81.

81.  . . . They named the baby Elizabeth Ann Christian: Britton, pp. 83–86. Harding's next-door neighbor and personal secretary was George Christian.

81.  ". . . too big for the job if he can get it": Robinson, p. 328; Russell (*Blooming Grove*), p. 300.

82.  . . . "should be, 'Harding and Back to Normal'": Downes, p. 301; Murray (*Harding Era*), p. 22.

82.  ". . . make a front-porch campaign like McKinley's and we'll do the rest": White (*Puritan in Babylon*), p. 204.

83.  ". . . largely an illusion of the people": Daugherty, p. 18; Anthony (*Florence Harding*), p. 167.

83.  . . . garnered a single vote: *Chicago Tribune*, 9 November 1919, pp. 1, 10.

83.  "doubtful to begin with": Anthony (*Florence Harding*), p. 218.

83.  . . . want to end up like Wilson: Anthony (*Florence Harding*), p. 218; Russell (*Blooming Grove*), p. 301.

83.  . . . personal life was a mess: Anthony (*Florence Harding*), pp. 61, 62, 149–150, 194, 204, 302.

83.  ". . . died of servitude and overwork": W. G. McAdoo (*Crowded Years*), pp. 388–389.

84. . . . of the *Indianapolis Star: NY Times*, 17 December 1919, p. 4; *LA Times*, 17 December 1919, p. 1; *Washington Post*, 17 December 1919, p. 1; *Indianapolis Star*, 22 December 1919, p. 7.

84. ". . . thing to contemplate": Murray (*Harding Era*), p. 25; Dean, p. 51.

84. . . . back at Daugherty in stunned disbelief: Fausold, p. 128.

84. ". . . that made McKinley successful": *Washington Post*, 1 January 1920, pp. 1, 5; Bagby, p. 41.

84. "Kindliness and kindness . . . in his voice, in his manners": Lowry, p. 18.

85. "Following his election . . . gracious opinions of his fellow men": Cobb, p. 276.

85. "The truest greatness lies in being kind": Daugherty, p. 19; Russell (*Blooming Grove*), pp. 272–273; Spragens, p. 280.

85. In Montana on April 23 . . . Lowden, but also Hoover: *Washington Post*, 25 April 1920, p. 1; *NY Times*, 9 May 1920, p. 3; Adams, p. 126; Bagby, p. 51.

85. . . . headlined: HARDING FLASH IN PAN: *Chicago Tribune*, 29 April 1920, p. 4; *Ohio State Monitor*, 1 May 1920, p. 1; J. Lane, p. 243; Russell (*Blooming Grove*), p. 346.

86. . . . Harding was still in the race: *LA Times*, 6 May 1920. p. 1; *NY Times*, 6 May 1920, p. 2; *Chicago Tribune*, 6 May 1920. p. 5; Adams, pp. 126–127; J. Lane, p. 243; Spragens, p. 281; Russell (*Blooming Grove*), pp. 346–347; Bagby, pp. 39, 40, 52.

86. ". . . sustainment in triumphant nationality": *Boston Globe*, 15 May 1920, pp. 1, 5; *Boston Globe*, 13 June 1920, p. 13; Cooper (*Pivotal Decades*), p. 365; Downes, p. 411; Sinclair (*Available Man*), p. 84; Leuchtenburg, p. 89; Spragens, p. 281.

86. "Harding," biographer John Dean . . . the nation's pulse correctly": Dean, p. 57.

86. The June 6 *Literary Digest* poll . . . Harding 42,212: *NY Times*, 6 June 1920, p. 30.

87. ". . . in the Marion brass band": White (*Puritan in Babylon*), p. 204.

87. "bungalow mind": R. Smith, p. 97.

87. . . . Harding will be nominated: Murray (*Politics of Normalcy*), p. 8.

87. ". . . The stars, Jupiter, never lie": Anthony (*Florence Harding*), pp. 172–175.

89. ". . . and still believe in your deliberate good sense: *NY Times*, 10 July 1964, pp. 1, 27; Anthony (*Florence Harding*), pp. 179–184; Russell (*Blooming Grove*), pp. 344–345.

**CHAPTER 6**

91. . . . struck with crimson and gold: Coolidge (*Autobiography*), p. 13.

91. . . . all he had loved and lost: Lathem (*Your Son Calvin Coolidge*), p. vii.

91. "The lines he laid out. . . . The work he did endured": Coolidge (*Autobiography*), p. 12.

92. . . . it was fresh and clean: Coolidge (*Autobiography*), pp. 29–30.

92. . . . and it's not easy: Washburn, p. 64; McCoy, p. 8; Sobel, p. 25.

92. "A drabber, more colorless boy . . . enigma to us all": Sobel, p. 32.

92. ". . . should get a few dollars together": Fuess, p. 67.

93. . . . heads of the rest of us: Lathem (*Meet Calvin Coolidge*), p. 19.

93. His proposal consisted . . . be married to you": Ross (*Grace Coolidge*), p. 16.

94. "We thought we were made . . . rejoiced in her graces": Coolidge (*Autobiography*), p. 93.

94. ". . . when earnings may be small": Coolidge (*Autobiography*), p. 94.

94. ". . . better serve the people": Coolidge (*Autobiography*), pp. 95–96.

94. . . . better than he looks: Washburn, p. 56; Whiting, p. 74; White (*A Puritan in Babylon*), p. 68; Fuess, p. 97.

95. ". . . bless their honest Irish hearts": Lathem (*Your Son Calvin Coolidge*), p. 111; Russell (*President Makers*), p. 242.

96. . . . silent, [and] abiding convictions: *Boston Globe*, 8 January 1914, p. 4; *Outlook*, 20 June 1920, p. 373; Coolidge (*Have Faith in Massachusetts*), pp. 3–9; Coolidge (*Autobiography*), pp. 106–107; Whiting, pp. 96–98; McCoy, pp. 54–55; Fuess, p. 118.

96. ". . . willing to be lieutenant-governor": *Boston Globe*, 22 September 1915, pp. 1, 7; Coolidge (*Autobiography*), p. 121; McCoy, p. 73.

97. ". . . that I began to look him up": *The Outlook*, 8 September 1920, p. 60; Fuess, pp. 129–130; McCoy, pp. 63–64.

97. "Our party will have no part . . . than not see them remedied": Sobel, pp. 106–107.

97. "In all my years of work . . . courage I had more trust": *Outlook*, 28 April 1920, p. 766.

97. . . . but just making war speeches: Fuess, p. 156; Ross (*Grace Coolidge*), p. 51; Sobel, p. 111.

98. . . . guarantee the welfare of all: *Boston Globe*, 28 October 1916, p. 5; Fuess, p. 168.

98. Once, three fairly prominent . . . Coolidge twanged. "Good-bye": Fuess, pp. 181–182.

98. . . . to the newly consolidated positions: Whiting, pp. 125–130; Fuess, pp. 190–191; White (*A Puritan in Babylon*), p. 172; Sobel, pp. 118–119.

98. ". . . Now there is Coolidge'": *Outlook*, 8 September 1920, pp. 60–61; Fuess, p. 179. In 1927, Coolidge appointed Morrow ambassador to Mexico. He was elected to the United States Senate from New Jersey in 1931. Morrow's daughter, Anne, married aviator Charles Lindbergh in May 1929.

99. . . . overcrowded, dirty, vermin-infested: White (*A Puritan in Babylon*), p. 151; Russell (*A City in Terror*), pp. 48–52; Russell (*The Great Interlude*), p. 39; McCoy, p. 84; Asinof, p. 160; Sobel, p. 127. A recent government study had set $1,575 as the minimum needed to raise a family of five. Prior to the strike, the Boston Social Club had requested a $200 raise. The city offered $140.

99. ". . . community is in his hands": *Chicago Tribune*, 12 September 1919, pp. 1–2; *LA Times*, 12 September 1919, p. 1. FDR was much less agitated by the strike than Wilson. Coolidge had wired FDR, asking him to prepare to dispatch naval personnel to Boston if necessary. "The Navy will, of course," FDR wired back noncommittally, "keep with the Army in carrying out such orders as may be given by the president." (Freidel [*The Ordeal*], p. 31.)

99. . . . powerful message in support of Curtis: *Boston Globe*, 12 September 1919, p. 11; Coolidge (*Have Faith in Massachusetts*), pp. 219–220; Fuess, p. 222.

100. On Friday, September 12 . . . hold another office," he snapped: Sobol, p. 142.

100. ". . . anybody, any time, anywhere": *Boston Globe*, 15 September 1919, p. 1; *NY Times*, 15 September 1919, p. 1; Coolidge (*Have Faith in Massachusetts*), pp. 222–223; Whiting, pp. 139–140; White (*A Puritan in Babylon*), p. 166; Fuess, pp. 223, 225–226; Murray (*Red Scare*), pp. 122–134; Russell (*A City in Terror*), pp. 191–192; McCoy, pp. 93–94; Sobel, p. 144.

100. ". . . Americans must stand together" : *Boston Globe*, 6 November 1919, p. 12; Fuess, pp. 238–239. Wilson, of course, remained quite ill at this time. "It has been suggested," Claude Fuess writes, "by a person in the White House at the time that it was drafted and sent by Secretary Tumulty. The words, however, were those which the President might have used if he had been well."

101. ". . . Modification of injunction processes: *Chicago Tribune*, 9 November 1919, p. 11.

101. . . . never consulted Frank Stearns about it: *Boston Globe*, 5 January 1920, pp. 1, 7;

*Chicago Tribune*, 5 January 1920, p. 21; *LA Times*, 5 January 1920, p. 2; *LA Times*, 8 January 1920, p. 1; *Washington Post*, 17 January 1920, p. 1; *Providence Journal*, 17 January 1920, p. 2; Whiting, p. 162; Fuess, p. 244; McCoy, p. 110; Russell (*President Makers*), pp. 260–261.

101. . . . Coolidge had possibilities: *Boston Globe*, 8 October 1919, p. 12; *Outlook*, 28 April 1920, pp. 756–757.

102. ". . . the day's work as such": *Boston Globe*, 26 January 1920, pp. 1–2; *NY Times*, 26 January 1920, p. 1; *LA Times*, 26 January 1920, p. 1; *Atlanta Constitution*, 26 January 1920, p. 8; *Providence Journal*, 26 January 1920, p. 1; Washburn, pp. 96, 149; Whiting, pp. 163–166; Bagby, p. 46; McCoy, pp. 110–111.

102. ". . . that of public servant": *NY Times*, 27 January 1920, p. 14.

103. . . . expression of the life of the commonwealth: *Boston Globe*, 9 January 1915, pp. 1, 9; *Chicago Tribune*, 9 January 1920, p. 3; *NY Times*, 9 January 1920, p. 16.

103. . . . shuttered his Washington headquarters: *NY Times*, 30 January 1920, p. 19; *Atlanta Constitution*, 30 January 1920, p. 16; Bagby, pp. 46, 51; McCoy, p. 111.

103. . . . for anybody at all, really: *NY Times*, 28 April 1920, p. 1; *LA Times*, 28 April 1920, p. 2; Fuess, p. 247; Bagby, p. 51; McCoy, pp. 111–112.

103. . . . practice of a legislative deception: *NY Times*, 7 May 1920, p. 1; *Atlanta Constitution*, 7 May 1920, p. 9; *Boston Globe*, 10 May 1920, pp. 7, 16; Whiting, pp. 130–131; Fuess, pp. 187–188; Hamm, p. 252.

103. . . . rare and refreshing statesmanship: *NY Times*, 8 May 1920, p. 14.

104. . . . had a habit of being nice: Russell (*President Makers*), p. 261; Downes, pp. 369, 375.

104. . . . Frank Stearns knew how to sell: *Chicago Tribune*, 6 May 1920, p. 30; Russell (*President Makers*), p. 261.

**CHAPTER 7**

105. ". . . will end it in Heaven": R. N. Smith (*Uncommon Man*), p. 87.

106. . . . moral and political example: H. Hoover (*Years of Adventure*), p. 9.

106. ". . . I'd ask him how he had done it": E. Lyons (*Herbert Hoover*), p. 92; Irwin, pp. 45–46.

106. . . . merely ahead of their time: Irwin, p. 58; Comfort, pp. 38–39, 125.

106. "because I had to eat": Irwin, p. 69.

107. . . . the bride and groom wore brown: Irwin, p. 84; E. Lyons (*Herbert Hoover*), p. 110. Lou was Episcopal. They were married by a Roman Catholic priest, Father Ramon Mestres, at the Monterey Mission. The original clergyman scheduled to perform the ceremony had died unexpectedly six weeks earlier. It was not uncommon for Catholic clergy in the still-largely Mexican Monterey area to marry Protestants.

108. To lower . . . women and children: H. Hoover (*Years of Adventure*), p. 259.

109. ". . . as well as to do our job": Nash (*The Humanitarian*), p. 376.

109. . . . he assured the Great Humanitarian: Burner, p. 82; R. Smith, pp. 85, 90; Nash (*The Humanitarian*), pp. 143, 151; Best, p. 6.

109. "He is a real man . . . make me in love with duty!": Nash (*The Humanitarian*), p. 150.

109. ". . . when it comes to loving you": Sullivan (V), pp. 413–422; R. Smith, p. 90; McGerr, pp. 293–294.

110. "Be nice to Hoover . . . with Congress or politicians": R. Smith, p. 89.

110. "I haven't come to get anything . . . I am here to serve and to help": Perrett, p. 112.

110. . . . across Europe and the Middle East: Humanitarianism certainly motivated American post-war relief efforts, but there were also more prosaic domestic political concerns. The Armistice triggered a huge agricultural surplus. Hoover's relief efforts alleviated a suddenly uncomfortable situation for America's farmers. (Noggle, p. 60.)

110. ". . . for myself to that which you received today": *NY Times*, 17 August 1919, p. 4; *Chicago Tribune*, 17 August 1919, p. 115; Irwin, pp. 247–248; H. Hoover (*Years of Adventure*), p. 360; E. Lyons (*Herbert Hoover*), p. 129; Comfort, pp. 128–129. Some estimates placed the number of children at only 5,000. (Comfort, p. 128; E. Lyons [*Herbert Hoover*], p. 129.)

110. "[T]hey were," Hoover biographer . . . him cry": E. Lyons (*Herbert Hoover*), p. 129.

111. . . . Wilson wouldn't budge: *Atlanta Constitution*, 17 March 1920, p. 13; E. Lyons (*Herbert Hoover*), pp. 132–134; Watt, p. 450; Fleming, pp. 375–376, 381.

111. "It all flashed into our minds . . . would ultimately bring destruction": H. Hoover (*Years of Adventure*), pp. 461–462; Watt, p. 407; Perrett, pp. 23–24.

111. "With all my . . . lesser evil": H. Hoover (*Years of Adventure*), p. 468; Perrett, p. 23.

111. "Mr. Hoover," Keynes wrote . . . have given us the Good Peace": Keynes, p. 257.

111. ". . . dubbed me, falsely, a 'leading American'": H. Hoover (*Cabinet & The Presidency*), p. 4.

111. . . . publicity machine for just that purpose: Nash (*The Humanitarian*), p. 376.

112. . . . had not lived long enough anywhere to vote at all: *NY Times*, 9 January 1920, p. 3.

112. . . . Theodore Roosevelt's third-party crusade: E. Lyons (*Herbert Hoover*), p. 139.

112. . . . had become "good friends": Nash (*Master of Emergencies*), p. 428; Best, p. 60.

112. . . . succeed in these great issues: *NY Times*, 2 April 1920, p. 17; Best, p. 11.

112. "I am not a party man. . . each party stands on those issues": R. Smith, p. 96.

112. ". . . There could not be a better one": E. Lyons (*Herbert Hoover*), p. 143; Freidel (*The Ordeal*), p. 57; Miller, p. 167; Ward, p. 471; Bagby, p. 43; Best p. 61; Morgan (*F.D.R.*), p. 219.

113. . . . vote for him now as against anybody else: F. Lane, p. 334.

113. . . . remained as to his Democrat credentials: *NY Times*, 8 January 1920, pp. 2, 11.

113. The "best people" all seemed to favor Hoover: *NY Times*, 30 April 1920, p. 2; *NY Times*, 5 May 1920, p. 2; *Current Opinion*, May 1920, pp. 589–590; Bagby, pp. 42–43.

114. If Lodge and Johnson et al. . . . lose his truculent attitude: Best, p. 64.

114. . . . in his syndicated newspaper column: *Current Opinion*, March 1920, p. 291.

114. . . . "neither a real Republican nor a real American": Best, p. 109.

114. . . . been with the Progressive-Republicans: *NY Times*, 15 January 1920, p. 17; *Chicago Tribune*, 15 January 1920, p. 10; *LA Times*, 15 January 1920, p. 14; *Atlanta Constitution*, 15 January 1920, p. 16; Best, p. 56.

114. ". . . wouldn't vote for any Englishman": *NY Times*, 22 January 1920, p. 21; *Providence Journal*, 22 January 1920, p. 3.

115. ". . . sovereignty of the world to the British Empire": *LA Times*, 25 January 1920, p. 17; Freidel (*The Ordeal*), p. 57.

115. . . . remake the GOP into a true progressive force: *NY Times*, 22 January 1920, p. 21; *LA Times*, 24 January 1920, p. 12; R. N. Smith (*Uncommon Man*), p. 97.

115. . . . Democratic party was a bankrupt: Daniels (*Cabinet Diaries*), p. 487.

115. And former Treasury Secretary McAdoo . . . but a "sexless one" besides: Bagby, p. 67.

115. . . . 74 percent of women) supported his candidacy: *LA Times*, 1 February 1920, p. 11.

115. ". . . decline to pledge my vote blindfolded": *Chicago Tribune*, 9 February 1920, p. 1; *Atlanta Constitution*, 9 February 1920, p. 1; Best, p. 58.

116. "I did not gather," Cummings recorded . . . which was distasteful to him": Bagby, p. 44.

116. . . . say so without contest: Daniels (*Cabinet Diaries*), p. 502.

117. ". . . whose American aspirations I greatly preferred": H. Hoover (*Cabinet and Presidency*), pp. 33–34.

117. ". . . see myself as a sacrifice": Burner, p. 152; Smith (*Hoover*), pp. 96–97.

117. ". . . no doubt about his ability": Sinclair (*Available Man*), p. 125.

118. . . . few facts, and is once more silent: http://ibiblio.org/gutenberg/etext03/tmrow10.txt.

118. . . . Hoover's candidacy in the solid South: Morgan (*F.D.R.*), p. 221.

118. . . . scotching rumors of any third-party effort: *NY Times*, 19 March 1920, p. 13; *Atlanta Constitution*, 17 March 1920, p. 13; *NY Times*, 5 April 1920, p. 17; *Atlanta Constitution*, 4 April 1920, p. 1.

118. . . . from winning March's New Hampshire *Democratic* primary: *NY Times*, 10 March 1920, p. 1; *NY Times*, 2 January 1921, p. E16.

118. ". . . approve of my husband running for the Presidency": *NY Times*, 11 April 1920, p. 17.

119. . . . behind Wood and Harding: *Atlanta Constitution*, 17 March 1920, p. 1.

119. ". . . Republican Presidential nomination": *NY Times*, 7 April 1920, p. 2; *LA Times*, 7 April 1920, p. 114; Bagby, pp. 44, 72.

119. . . . barely apace with McAdoo: *Washington Post*, 25 April 1920, p. 1; *NY Times*, 9 May 1920, p. 3.

119. . . . referendum on the League: *NY Times*, 7 March 1920, p. 1; *LA Times*, 7 March 1920, p. 1; *Washington Post*, 7 April 1920, p. 1; *The Outlook*, 14 April 1920, pp. 637–638; *Atlanta Constitution*, 5 May 1920, p. 1; *NY Times*, 6 May 1920, p. 1; Bagby, pp. 44–45, 51–52. Hoover also removed his name from Georgia's April 20 primary ballot. (*Atlanta Constitution*, 21 February 1920, p. 1; *Chicago Tribune*, 26 February 1920, p. 5.)

120. When Hoover ceased to be an . . . too formidable to be ignored or flouted: Best, p. 116.

121. In May 1920 . . . "Yes, if we have to": *NY Times*, 26 May 1920, pp. 1, 4.

**CHAPTER 8**

122. "a twentieth-century Apollo": Kane, p. 292. Only one previous president was taller, Lincoln at 6'4". Washington and Arthur also measured 6'2".

122. ". . . as well as a definite objective": *NY Tribune*, 7 July 1920, p. 3; *Current Opinion*, September 1920, p. 321.

123. . . . FDR's half-brother, was 25: Kane, pp. 339–340. Rosy, a Republican who married an Astor, was a firm anti-Semite. In 1926, he wrote FDR from Bermuda: "The place is packed. Mostly an awful class of Jews, objectionable when sober, and worse when drunk." FDR's parents, on the other hand, were snobbishly anti-German. (Morgan [*F.D.R.*], pp. 32, 44, 47.)

123. "The Roosevelts," observed one biographer . . . Vanderbilts, but they were snootier": Morgan (*F.D.R.*), p. 37.

123. ". . . Franklin had to be slapped—hard": Freidel (*A Rendezvous with Destiny*), p. 34; http://www.enterstageright.com/archive/articles/0799fdrcharity.htm. At Harvard, Franklin had also dated Dorothy Quincy and Dorothy Dana, the Catholic granddaughter of author Charles Henry Dana and Henry Wadsworth Longfellow. Mother did not approve of his dating a Papist.

123. ". . . on the *Commonwealth* for Europe": *Boston Globe*, 9 October 1902, p. 11; Morgan (*F.D.R.*), pp. 82–83; C. Black, pp. 32–33; Ward, p. 551; Lash, p. 105; Olasky, p. 212. Miss Sohier did not return from Europe until the following July. Marrying insurance executive Herbert B. Shaw in 1910 in a "brilliant" Boston society wedding, she had two children, divorced in 1925, and, for the rest of her long life, thoroughly disliked Franklin Roosevelt. (*Boston Globe*, 25 July 1903, p. 7; *NY Times*, 1 May 1910, p. C5; C. Black, p. 33.)

124. . . . late younger brother Elliott: Ward, p. 551; Beasley, Beasley, and Shulman, p. 452; Eleanor Roosevelt, p. 40. Woodrow Wilson had also proposed to a cousin, his first cousin Harriet "Hattie" Woodrow. Following her refusal, he transformed himself from "Tommy Wilson" to "Woodrow Wilson." (Walworth, pp. 29–31; Freud and Bullitt, p. 23; Olasky, p. 189.)

124. By November 1903, Franklin had . . . to her son marrying a Roosevelt: C. Black, p. 33.

124. . . . received three hundred wedding gifts: *Washington Post*, 17 March 1905, p. 4; *NY Times*, 18 March 1905, p. 2; *LA Times*, 18 March 1905, p. 2; B. Cook, pp. 165–167; Eleanor Roosevelt, pp. 49–50; Caroli, pp. 233–235; C. Black, p. 43. TR capped the day by dancing an Irish jig on the balcony of Delmonico's for 600 members of the Sons of St. Patrick. (*Chicago Tribune*, 18 March 1905, pp. 1, 7.)

124. . . . Sara now lived at No. 47: *NY Times*, 18 March 1905, p. 2.

124. . . . March 1907, died that November: C. Black, pp. 43, 47, 72; Beasley, Beasley, and Shulman, p. xxiii; Kane, pp. 340–341.

125. ". . . he would never go on": *World's Work*, October 1920, p. 449; Eleanor Roosevelt, p. 63.

125. . . . uniform apple barrels: *NY Tribune*, 7 July 1920, p. 2.

125. . . . state senate seat, 15,798 to 14,568: Malcolm (1911), p. 568; Elliott Roosevelt and Brough (*Hyde Park*), p. 50; Morgan (*F.D.R.*), pp. 114–116; C. Black, pp. 52–53.

125. ". . . looking down his nose at most people": Perkins, pp. 10–13; Finan, p. 78; C. Black, p. 58. Perkins observed that state senator Roosevelt "really didn't like people very much . . . had a youthful lack of humility, a streak of self-righteousness, and a deafness to the hopes, fears and aspirations which are the common lot." She later marveled at his "capacity to grow."

125. . . . dog-like loyalty, an invaluable asset: Stiles, p. 25; Morgan (*F.D.R.*), pp. 132–135. FDR economic adviser James P. Warburg considered Howe "evil personified." FDR's son James found him "an egotist [who] never let Father forget he'd put him where he was." (J. Roosevelt, pp. 238–239.)

125. . . . something more sinister: anti-Catholicism: C. Black, p. 56. "Roosevelt," wrote biographer Black, "seemed to outgrow his anti-papist tendencies, especially when he began to correspond with popes. However, Catholicism always rankled with Eleanor as authoritarian, if not saturnine." Elliott Roosevelt also saw his mother as anti-Catholic. (Elliott Roosevelt and Brough [*Rendezvous with Destiny*], p. 96; Elliott Roosevelt and Brough [*Mother R.*], pp. 159–166.)

126. . . . a reformer to be reckoned with: *NY Times*, 22 January 1911, p. SM11; *Washington Post*, 28 January 1911, p. 4; *NY Times*, 30 January 1911, p. 3; *Chicago Tribune*, 1 April 1911, p. 1; *LA Times*, 1 April 1911, p. 11; *NY Times*, 15 March 1917, p. 11; *NY Times*, 18 May 1943, p. 23; C. Black, p. 57; Stiles, pp. 26–36; Tully, pp. 42–43; Finan, pp. 80–84; Connable and Silberberg, pp. 249–250; Flynn, pp. 261–262; Weiss, pp. 48–49; Handlin, pp. 42–44; LaCerra, pp. 44–46; Roseberry, pp. 83–89, 119–122.

126. ". . . President of the United States": Stiles, pp. 32, 34; Morgan (*F.D.R.*), p. 134. As early as June 1912, Howe was writing to FDR as "Beloved and Revered Future President."

127. . . . Triangle Shirtwaist Fire tragedy: Perkins, pp. 13–14; C. Black, p. 59.

127. . . . managing a narrow victory: Malcolm (1913), p. 677; Morgan (*F.D.R.*), p. 136.

127. . . . Assistant Secretary of the Navy: *Washington Post*, 16 March 1913, p. 12; Perkins, p. 15; Stiles, p. 34; Lash, pp. 176–177; Morgan (*F.D.R.*), pp. 137–141.

127. He would serve under an unlikely . . . abolished officers' wine messes: Daniels (*Editor in Politics*), *passim*; Sullivan (V), pp. 577–580; C. Black, p. 68; *NY Times*, 16 January 1948, p. 17; *Chicago Tribune*, 16 January 1948, p. 1; *LA Times*, 16 January 1948, p. 1; *Washington Post*, 16 January 1948, pp. 1, B2.

127. ". . . sleeps well at night": *Chicago Tribune*, 2 February 1919, p. E3; McGerr, p. 298.

127. In the 604 densely printed . . . when he was making trouble": Ward, p. 433.

127. "Whenever a Roosevelt rides, he rides in front": Ferrell (*Woodrow Wilson*), p. 32; Morgan (*F.D.R.*), p. 143; Daniels (*Cabinet Diaries*), p. 4 *fn*.

128. Mr. R told me on the night. . . . May history repeat itself?: Daniels (*Cabinet Diaries*), p. 10.

128. Roosevelt brought with him Louis . . . back home in New York: C. Black, p. 69.

128. . . . Gerard humiliated Roosevelt, 210,765 to 85,203: Elliott Roosevelt and Brough (*Hyde Park*), pp. 76–77; Morgan (*F.D.R.*), pp. 160–162; Ward, p. 250 *fn*.; C. Black, pp. 70–71.

129. ". . . very precise idea of what constituted loyalty": Morgan (*F.D.R.*), pp. 163–170, 192; C. Black, pp. 72–73, 79, 87; LaCerra, pp. 48–51; Fleming, pp. 148–149; Ferrell (*Woodrow Wilson*), p. 49; Daniels (*Cabinet Diaries*), pp. 212, 490.

129. . . . detailed instructions on what to do: C. Black, pp. 80–81, 87–88; Cooper (*Warrior and the Priest*), p. 348; Ward, pp. 433, 436; Morgan (*F.D.R.*), pp. 186–190.

129. . . . Smith became governor: Daniels (*Cabinet Diaries*), p. 313; Morgan (*F.D.R.*), pp. 193–194; LaCerra, p. 56; C. Black, pp. 87–88.

129. ". . . possible but highly profitable": *New York Times*, 17 July 1917, p. 3.

130. . . . the Roosevelt plan: Elliott Roosevelt and Brough (*Hyde Park*), p. 87; Miller, pp. 152–153; Morgan (*F.D.R.*), p. 204; Lash, p. 210; C. Black, p. 97; Anthony (*First Ladies*), p. 361.

130. "It was impossible not to . . . seemed mired in falsehood": B. Cook, p. 218.

131. . . . love letters with her: Elliott Roosevelt and Brough (*Hyde Park*), pp. 83–89; Elliott Roosevelt and Brough (*Mother R.*), p. 29; B. Cook, pp. 217–220; Fleming, pp. 149–150; Miller, p. 154; Morgan (*F.D.R.*), pp. 201–207; J. Roosevelt, pp. 99–101; C. Black, pp. 96–98; Anthony (*First Ladies*), p. 364. Mercer may not have been FDR's only dalliance. In 1921, Livingston "Livy" Davis, an old Harvard chum, Navy Department employee, and drinking buddy, playfully wrote FDR, suggesting two topics for books he might now write: "The Ladies of Washington: or Thirty Days and Evenings as a Bachelor" and "Frivolities of a Capital: On the Trail of Roosevelt, or 29 Concussive Nights in a Different Place and Bed." When Davis, a Boston banker, blew his brains out in January 1932, he left FDR $1,000 "in grateful remembrance of joyful comradeship." (*NY Times*, 12 January 1932, p. 18; *NY Times*, 27 February 1932, p. 33.)

131. . . . he stayed with Eleanor: Elliott Roosevelt and Brough (*Hyde Park*), pp. 94–96; Caroli, pp. 259–260; B. Cook, pp. 227–232; Morgan (*F.D.R.*), pp. 207–212; Miller, p. 152; Freidel (*Rendezvous with Destiny*), p. 33; J. Roosevelt, p. 101.

132. . . . been somewhat veiled in mystery: Elliott Roosevelt and Brough (*Mother R.*), pp. 29–30; B. Cook, p. 230.

132. . . . never saw him again: *NY Times*, 13 September 1918, p. 11; Renehan, p. 215; C. Black, p. 83.

132. ". . . missed by torpedoes and shells": Morgan (*F.D.R.*), p. 201.

133. ". . . accomplish this work": H. Schmidt, p. 100. In the summer of 1933, Butler claimed that he was approached by wealthy conservatives with a scheme to seize power from newly elected FDR.

133. ". . . New Orleans in 1860 for stud purposes": H. Schmidt, pp. 100–101.

133. ". . . investigate how many were killed or wounded": *The Nation*, 10 July 1920, p. 111; http://www.thirdworldtraveler.com/Independent_Media/Conquest_Haiti_SNM.html.

133. ". . . war that was waged in Haiti": http://www.boondocksnet.com//ai/ail/haiti_sd_soc.html.

134. . . . him the commandant of the prison: *NY Times*, 24 May 1914, p. 47; *NY Times*, 20 November 1914, p. 1; Daniels (*Cabinet Diaries*), pp. 116, 177, 203; Rollins, pp. 9–16, 49–56; Ward, pp. 444–446; Morgan (*F.D.R.*), p. 219; Davis, pp. 586–597; Freidel (*A Rendezvous with Destiny*), pp. 36–37; Rollins, p. 153.

134. . . . "unlawful and unnatural acts": *NY Times*, 29 December 1915, pp. 1, 5; *Chicago Tribune*, 29 December 1915, p. 13; *LA Times*, 29 December 1915, p. 1.

134. . . . ex-reform school inmate as his handyman: Ward, p. 444.

134. . . . with former Portsmouth inmates: Daniels (*Cabinet Diaries*), p. 373.

134. ". . . blamed Franklin D. for that": *Atlanta Constitution*, 13 February 1920, p. 15; Ward, p. 446 *fn*.

134. ". . . permit the degradation of the Navy": Freidel (*The Ordeal*), p. 43; Ward, p. 472; Morgan (*F.D.R.*), p. 220.

134. ". . . can only harm the service itself": Ward, p. 472; Morgan (*F.D.R.*), p. 220.

135. Taussig, backed by Rear Admiral . . . demanded that Daniels conduct a formal inquiry: *Atlanta Constitution*, 13 February 1920, p. 15; Freidel (*The Ordeal*), p. 44.

135. . . . returning ten in a single instance: Freidel (*The Ordeal*), p. 44; Ward, p. 472; Morgan (*F.D.R.*), p. 220. Taussig privately contended that most of the offenders were upper class and received a benefit of the doubt not afforded to sailors of lower social strata.

135. ". . . think is the best thing to do?": Freidel (*The Ordeal*), pp. 44–45; Ward, pp. 474–475.

135. ". . . shake the Admiral warmly by the hand": *Chicago Tribune*, 23 December 1919, p. 1; *Providence Journal*, 5 January 1920, pp. 1, 8; Daniels (*Cabinet Diaries*), p. 484; Miller, p. 168; Davis, p. 591; Morgan (*F.D.R.*), p. 202; Ward, p. 468.

136. . . . very institution of the Navy itself: *Washington Post*, 18 January 1920, pp. 1–2; Sullivan (VI), pp. 535–536. Sims's account of the United States Navy in the war, *The Victory at Sea*, won the 1920 Pulitzer Prize for history.

136. ". . . or anyone any permission to spend any money": *NY Times*, 2 February 1920, p. 7; Daniels (*Cabinet Diaries*), p. 490; Freidel (*The Ordeal*), pp. 48–49; Morgan (*F.D.R.*), p. 217; Ward, p. 477.

136. . . . then issued a "clarification": Daniels (*Cabinet Diaries*), p. 490; Morgan (*F.D.R.*), p. 217; C. Black, p. 111.

136. . . . They withdrew their request: Daniels (*Cabinet Diaries*), p. 521; Morgan (*F.D.R.*), p. 216; Ward, p. 486.

137. ". . . let [Brooklyn] speech pass": Daniels (*Cabinet Diaries*), pp. 497, 542; Morgan (*F.D.R.*), p. 217; C. Black, p. 112.

137. ". . . the great prize next summer": Freidel (*The Ordeal*), pp. 51, 55; Morgan (*F.D.R.*), pp. 215–216.

137. ". . . bad luck of the early worm": Freidel (*The Ordeal*), pp. 51, 55; Rollins, p. 153; Davis, p. 608; Miller, p. 167; Ward, pp. 454–455.

138. . . . approach Hoover and Hoover to approach *him*: Morgan (*F.D.R.*), p. 218; Ward, pp. 470–471; Davis, p. 609; C. Black, p. 118. The same day that Wehle visited House, Eleanor Roosevelt wrote to a friend: "What do the people in your part of the country think of Mr. Hoover? He's the only man I know who has first hand knowledge of European questions & great responsibility & understands business, not only from the capitalistic point of view, but also from the worker's standpoint." (Ward, p. 470.)

139. . . . convince Hoover to cast his lot with a sinking ship: Wehle, pp. 81–84; Morgan (*F.D.R.*), p. 218; Ward, p. 471.

**CHAPTER 9**

140. . . . our industries and our commerce: *Messages and Papers of the President*, p. 8231; Cooper (*Warrior and the Priest*), p. 320.

140. ". . . 'Made in Germany' stamped on the bottom": Behr, p. 68; Anthony (*First Ladies*), p. 364; Pfannestiel, p. 4; Ferrell (*Woodrow Wilson*), p. 205; McGerr, pp. 290, 292.

141. . . . Wisconsin Socialist Congressman Victor Berger: Ferrell (*Woodrow Wilson*), p. 208; Pfannestiel, p. 4; Goldstein, p. 108; F. Cook, p. 77.

141. . . . projectile force of a French .75: Ramsaye, pp. 781–786; Sullivan (V), pp. 423–440; Pfannestiel, p. 4; McGerr, pp. 288–292; http://historymatters.gmu.edu/d/4970.

141. ". . . officers cannot conduct newspapers": Mock, p. 45.

142. "People generally, and the press . . . campaign of 'hate' at home": Gossett, p. 341.

142. . . . from $3.10 to $8.00 a pair: *Atlanta Constitution*, 11 April 1920, p. 9B; *Bridgeport Telegram*, 15 April 1920, p. 4; *New York Times*, 15 April 1920, p. 15; *New York Times*, 21 April 1920, p. 18; *Boston Globe*, 19 April 1920, pp, 1, 8; *Atlanta Constitution*, 19 April 1920, pp. 1, 31; *Coshocton Tribune*, 30 April 1920, p. 10.

142. "Please hurry home. Let someone else do it": Hicks, p. 3.

142. ". . . *far more important than the League of Nations*": NY Times, 24 May 1919, p. 4; *Boston Globe*, 24 June 1919, p. 14; Bailey (*Great Betrayal*), p. 17; Leuchtenburg, p. 58.

143. "YOU CANNOT UNDERSTAND . . . NECESSITY OF LIFE": Fleming, p. 395.

143. . . . shuttering theaters in New York and Chicago: Perrett, pp. 29–38, 41–50; Pfannestiel, pp. 5–7; Leuchtenburg, pp. 74–75; Hicks, pp. 40–41, 46–48; McGerr, p. 304.

143. "I have seen the future, and it works": Draper (*Roots of American Communism*), p. 115.

144. . . . set back the labor movement by ten years: *Current Opinion*, April 1919, p. 225; Hanson, pp. 24–96; Murray (*Red Scare*), pp. 58–66; Leuchtenburg, p. 71; Goldstein, pp. 144–145; Asinof, pp. 132–138; http://historylink.org/essays/output.cfm?file_id=861. Anna Louise Strong moved to Russia in 1920, working as a correspondent and even teaching English to Trotsky. She relocated to the People's Republic of China in 1958, remaining there until her death in 1970.

145. . . . did not open their own mail: Murray (*Red Scare*), pp. 68–73; F. L. Allen (*Only Yesterday*), pp. 49–50; Avrich (*Sacco and Vanzetti*), pp. 140–147; Noggle, p. 103; Coben, pp. 203–204; Goldstein, p. 145; Pietrusza (*Judge and Jury*), pp. 147–148; Morgan (*Reds*), p. 70.

145. . . . past the rubble and the scattered blood and flesh: *Washington Post*, 3 June 1920, pp.

1–2; *Chicago Tribune*, 3 June 1920, pp. 1, 2; *NY Times*, 3 June 1920, pp. 1–2; Avrich (*Sacco and Vanzetti*), pp. 149–156; Murray (*Red Scare*), pp. 78–80; Perrett, pp. 54–55; Whitehead, pp. 39–40.

145. "... Get yourself straight to bed!": *Atlanta Constitution*, 3 June 1920, p. 2; J. Roosevelt, p. 44; Freidel (*The Ordeal*), p. 29; Miller, pp. 161–162; Ward, pp. 455–456.

146. ... "'thank thee, Franklin!' and all that": *Washington Post*, 3 June 1920, p. 1; Avrich (*Sacco and Vanzetti*), p. 153; Coben, pp. 205–206; Ward, p. 456; Morgan (*F.D.R.*), p. 214; J. S. Cox and Theoharis, pp. 55–56.

146. "... no more than so much carrion": Longworth, pp. 282–283; Ward, p. 455.

146. "... passerby instead of the anarchist!": Ward, p. 456; Lash, pp. 239–240; B. Cook, pp. 244–245.

146. "We could not take a step ... grinding of a piece of flesh": Ward, p. 456.

146. ... the morning after ... who were behind that kind of outrage: Coben, p. 206.

146. ... nation's 200,000 radicals: J. S. Cox and Theoharis, pp. 56–57; Murray (*Red Scare*), p. 193; Gitlow, p. 61; Whitehead, p. 41.

147. ... threw Palmer's case out of court: Avrich (*Sacco & Vanzetti*), p. 174; J. S. Cox and Theoharis, pp. 56–57; Whitehead, p. 47.

147. ... nicknamed the "Soviet Ark": *NY Times*, 21 December 1919, pp. 1, 3; R. Schmidt, pp. 246–248, 257–262; F. Cook, pp. 96–98; Madison, pp. 214–237; Whitehead, pp. 47–49. Goldman and Berkman soon saw through the Bolshevik experiment and fled the workers' paradise for Weimar, Germany.

147. "... methods and torture known to the police": *Providence Journal*, 3 January 1920, pp. 1–2; *Providence Journal*, 4 January 1920, pp. 1–4; *Providence Journal*, 5 January 1920, pp. 1–2; Murray (*Red Scare*), pp. 212–217; Preston, pp. 218–219; Gitlow, pp. 61–62; Goldstein, pp. 156–157; Perrett, pp. 61–62.

147. ... issued a report blasting Palmer: *NY Times*, 28 May 1920, p. 6; Coleman, pp. 313–314; Pfannestiel, pp. 124–125; Preston, pp. 221–222.

148. ... the "faking fighter": *Atlanta Constitution*, 1 May 1920, pp. 1, 3; F. L. Allen (*Only Yesterday*), p. 70; Leuchtenburg, p. 80.

148. ... The audience cheered: *Chicago Tribune*, 7 May 1919, pp. 1–2; *Washington Post*, 7 May 1919, p. 2; *Chicago Tribune*, 8 May 1919, p. 17; *Atlanta Constitution*, 8 May 1919, p. 17. The story is more complex than is usually told. Challenged by Hagerman, Goddard drew a pistol and fired two shots. Hagerman fired one or two warning shots. Goddard didn't respond. Only then did Hagerman shoot Goddard. Goddard had been arrested for, but subsequently acquitted of, murder in 1893. On the other hand, the next day at Victory Forum, R. B. Wilder was arrested for failing to stand when a soldier carrying a flag passed in review.

148. ... seemed to care much that they weren't: *Chicago Tribune*, 12 November 1919, pp. 1–2; *LA Times*, 12 November 1919, p. 1; *NY Times*, 12 November 1919, pp. 1–2; *Providence Journal*, 27 January 1920, p. 15; *Chicago Tribune*, 14 March 1920, p. 5; *LA Times*, 28 March 1920, p. 3; Murray (*Red Scare*), pp. 181–189; R. Schmidt, pp. 105–109; Goldstein, pp. 155–156; Haywood, pp. 352–358; Noggle, p. 112; Asinof, pp. 198–203; Cooper (*Pivotal Decades*), pp. 328–329; Rumer, pp. 93–94; Perrett, pp. 95–97. The coroner's report read that "no scars that could be located on the body outside where the rope cut neck," casting doubt on the castration story, though several witnesses indicated that that is what happened.

Seven Wobblies were convicted of second-degree murder, receiving sentences of from 25 to 40 years. Two were acquitted. One went insane and was committed to a state institution. (http://www.historylink.org/essays/output.cfm?file_id=5605).

149. . . . wanted a Soviet-style government here: *The Nation*, 17 April 1920, pp. 510–511.

149. ". . . and save space on our ships": Bruns, p. 266; Leuchtenburg, p. 66.

149. . . . two minutes before setting Petroni free: *Chicago Tribune*, 20 February 1919, p. 3; *NY Times*, 21 February 1919, p. 24; *Atlanta Constitution*, 21 February 1919, p. 1; Sullivan (VI), p. 169; Leuchtenburg, p. 66; Perrett, p. 53.

149. . . . signed them the following year: Joint Legislative Committee Investigating Seditious Activities, *passim*; Hapgood, pp. 107–112; Murray (*Red Scare*), pp. 98–102, 238; R. Schmidt, pp. 123–125; Sullivan (VI), p. 172; Pfannestiel, *passim*; Draper, pp. 146, 203; Finan, pp. 144–145; Morgan (*Reds*), pp. 71–72, 77–78.

149. ". . . sanction the Assembly's action": *NY Times*, 2 April 1920, p. 14; Allen, pp. 69–70.

150. ". . . nothing short of a calamity": *Providence Journal*, 10 January 1920, pp. 1–2; *Providence Journal*, 22 January 1922, p. 10; *NY Times*, 2 April 1920, p. 15; F. L. Allen (*Only Yesterday*), p. 70; Bagby, p. 37; Leuchtenburg, p. 79.

150. . . . refused to take their seats: *Providence Journal*, 8 January 1920, p. 1; *NY Times*, 31 March 1920, pp. 1, 2; *Washington Post*, 1 April 1920, p. 1; *Outlook*, 6 October 1920, pp. 222–223; Warner and Daniel, pp. 118–119; Murray (*Red Scare*), pp. 235–238. The expulsion was largely a Republican operation. In the 116–28 vote, Democrats voted only 18–17 for the ouster, while Republicans voted 98–11. In the 104–40 vote, Democrats voted 15-20 to expel, while Republicans voted 89–20. Al Smith denounced the whole thing.

150. . . . and the seat remained vacant: Pietrusza (*Judge and Jury*), pp. 139–149. *Chicago Tribune*, 10 March 1918, p. 1; *Chicago Tribune*, 3 April 1918, p. 1; *Providence Journal*, 11 January 1920, p. 4; Murray (*Red Scare*), pp. 226–229. Davis later served as FDR's ambassador to the Soviet Union. His memoir, *Mission to Moscow*, became the 1943 Warner Brothers film of the same name.

150. ". . . on that basis he was re-elected": Pietrusza (*Judge and Jury*), pp. 139–146, 148–149.

151. ". . . discharging them on that ground": Freidel (*The Ordeal*), pp. 30–31; Morgan (*F.D.R.*), p. 214; Perrett, p. 58; Ward, p. 458 *fn*.

151. ". . . soviet government were all elected": *NY Times*, 15 May 1920, p. 3; Pfannestiel, p. 10; Whitehead, p. 44.

151. . . . establish a government on soviet principles: *NY Times*, 3 September 1919, p. 8; *Atlanta Constitution*, 3 September 1919, p. 9; *NY Times*, 26 June 1920, p. 8; Draper (*Roots of American Communism*), pp. 173–186; Coleman, pp. 314–315; Gitlow, pp. 6, 28–29; Wayne, pp. 166–167; Pfannestiel, p. 11; Madison, pp. 524–525; Leuchtenburg, p. 68; E. Lyons (*Red Decade*), pp. 33–34; Whitehead, p. 45. Moscow later pressured the two parties to merge and become the United Communist Party (later the Communist Party USA).

152. . . . Take the ladies with you: Russell (*Tragedy in Dedham*), p. 64; Eastman, pp. 174–178; Montgomery, pp. 6, 10; Gallagher, p. 79; Avrich (*Sacco and Vanzetti*), p. 199.

153. . . . the slug that murdered Berardelli: *Boston Globe*, 6 May 1920, p. 1; Frankfurter, p. 38; MacLeish and Prichard, p. 156; Weeks, p. 18; Busch, p. 59; Gallagher, p. 85; Montgomery, pp. 4–5. Unlike Sacco, Vanzetti carried with him no extra shells for his weapon, thus providing further credence to the theory that it had been taken from

Berardelli during the South Braintree robbery. One of the South Braintree robbers had grappled with Berardelli before shooting him four times. (Busch, p. 58; Montgomery, p. 105.)

The following day was payday at the mills, and author Robert Montgomery theorized that Sacco and Vanzetti had armed themselves and were picking up Buda's car anticipating another robbery. (Russell [*Tragedy in Dedham*], p. 12.)

Both defense attorney Fred Moore and their fellow Italian anarchists informed radical novelist Upton Sinclair that the accused lied to police because they were about to secure dynamite. (Avrich [*Sacco and Vanzetti*], p. 204.)

Buda fled to Italy and never returned, claiming that doing so would jeopardize his life.

153. . . . South Braintree robbery and murders: *Boston Globe*, 2 July 1920, p. 5.

153. . . . anarchist community connections: Avrich (*Sacco and Vanzetti*), pp. 58–66.

153. . . . blast would eventually claim thirty-three lives: *NY Times*, 17 September 1920, pp. 1–3, 6; *Boston Globe*, 17 September 1920, pp. 1, 10; *Chicago Tribune*, 17 September 1920, pp. 1–2; Avrich (*Sacco and Vanzetti*), pp. 205–207; F. L. Allen (*Only Yesterday*), pp. 72–75; Murray (*Red Scare*), pp. 257–258. The horse that pulled the wagon died too.

154. ". . . probably *was* the result of a bomb plot": Boylan, p. 15.

154. ". . . indeed, a virtual certainty": Avrich (*Sacco and Vanzetti*), p. 162; Morgan (*Reds*), pp. 70–71.

154. . . . fourteenth-story bedroom to the pavement below: *NY Times*, 30 May 1921, p. 22; Avrich (*Sacco and Vanzetti*), pp. 181–195; Post, pp. 178–182; Russell (*Tragedy in Dedham*), pp. 87–91; Montgomery, pp. 162–163, 169–178; Perrett, pp. 62–63; F. Cook, pp. 109–115; Whitehead, pp. 46–47.

## CHAPTER 10

155. The automobile had replaced . . . had previously required hotel rooms: Kyvig, pp. 21–24.

156. . . . column in *The Vaudeville News*: Gabler (*Winchell*), pp. 43–44, 73–77.

156. . . . "but you discovered money!": Perrett, pp. 356–357; Morris, pp. 171–172.

157. . . . officially qualified as Jazz Age sophisticates: U.S. Bureau of the Census, p. 75.

157. . . . low percentages of that category: U.S. Bureau of the Census, p. 103. America was also a young nation. The median age was just 25; 31.6 percent of the population was under 15. Just 7.4 percent was over 60. (Kyvig, p. 7.)

157. . . . amount of Protestants among them: U.S. Bureau of the Census, p. 103.

158. ". . . It will send you to hell": Bruns, p. 167.

159. . . . after the war was over, in July 1919: Merz, pp. 26–27, 40–41; Asbury, pp. 129–130.

159. ". . . to see it as a great moral question": *World's Work*, October 1920, p. 624; Johnson, pp. 69–70; Sinclair (*Available Man*), p. 64; Sinclair (*Era of Excess*), pp. 159, 252.

159. . . . went into effect. It refused: Merz, p. 49; Sinclair (*Era of Excess*), pp. 146–149, 168; Asbury, p. 134; Clark, pp. 128–130; Behr, p. 78.

159. . . . seemingly irresistible dry cause: Sinclair (*Era of Excess*), pp. 135–140; Pringle (*TR*), pp. 140–144.

159. . . . more efficient prohibition enforcement: Clark, pp. 203–204; Freidel, pp. 20, 171; Miller, p. 171; Ward, p. 420 *fn*. Until receiving the Democratic nomination in 1932, FDR was never much of a "Wet," being pretty much a "Damp" or "Moist." That year, he was the Driest candidate the Democrats had to choose from.

160. . . . Palmer wobbled all over the place: *Chicago Tribune*, 2 August 1917, p. 1; Sinclair (*Era of Excess*), p. 159; Craig, p. 17; Coben, p. 252.

160. . . . It was now or never: *NY Times*, 2 August 1917, p. 3; Merz, p. 31; Asbury, pp. 131–132; Kobler, pp. 209–210; Hamm, p. 242.

160. . . . beverage purposes is hereby prohibited: *Chicago Tribune*, 2 August 1917, p. 1; *LA Times*, 2 August 1917, pp. 1, 3; *NY Times*, 18 December, 1917, p. 13; Sinclair (*Era of Excess*), pp. 158–162; Asbury, pp. 131–132; Kobler, p. 211.

160. . . . commence on January 17, 1920: Merz, pp. 49, 317–328; Sinclair (*Era of Excess*), pp. 146–149, 168; Asbury, p. 134; Clark, pp. 128–130; Behr, p. 78.

161. ". . . They are dead!": *Chicago Tribune*, 17 January 1920, p. 2; *NY Times*, 17 January 1920, p. 3; Asbury, pp. 143–144; Coffey, pp. 7–11; Coletta, pp. 78–79.

161. ". . . surface of the earth, or in the air": F. L. Allen, p. 248; Asbury, pp. 142–143; Sinclair (*Era of Excess*), p. 185; Clark, p. 162; Kobler, p. 122.

161. . . . worth of high-quality liquor: *NY Times*, 7 January, 1921, p. 1; *Atlanta Constitution*, 7 June 1924, p. 4.

161. . . . liked Harding more, and that was that: *LA Times*, 20 July 1920, p. 14; *LA Times*, 21 July 1920, pp. 1, 4; *Chicago Tribune*, 21 January 1920, p. 5; *Atlanta Constitution*, 21 January 1920, p. 1.

161. . . . nomination on the second ballot: http://www.prohibitionists.org/History/aaron_watkins_bio.htm.

161. . . . and New York mayoral candidate: *LA Times*, 23 July 1920, pp. 1, 9; *NY Times*, 8 September 1959, p. 35.

162. ". . . And my only regret is that it is terribly true": Ramsaye, pp. 641–644; Schickel, p. 270; Chalmers, pp. 26–27; Brownlow and Kobal, pp. 40–44, 62–67. Wilson later had the comment disavowed. Interesting enough, he lavished similar praise on 1914's "viciously anti-Indian" *Adventures of Buffalo Bill*, which starred Buffalo Bill Cody himself. (Spears, p. 392.)

163. "I didn't dare allow the president . . . doing just that thing": Schickel, p. 269.

163. ". . . practical fraternity among men": Sullivan (VI), pp. 545–547; Chalmers, p. 30; Rice, pp. 1–2; Mecklin, pp. 4–5; Feldman, pp. 12–13.

163. . . . Simmons was "King Kleagle": Rice, pp. 4–5; Chalmers, p. 117.

163. "[I]t is well to remember. . . have escaped the law": Lipset and Raab, pp. 116–119.

164. . . . gins in Georgia and Alabama: *NY Times*, 11 October 1920, p. 1.

164. ". . . will brook no interference": *Chicago Tribune*, 31 October 1920, p. 1; Boylan, pp. 63–65.

164. ". . . such offenses against the law": *Washington Post*, 29 November 1920, p. 10. From 1882 to 1937, 5,112 American lynchings occurred: 3,657 blacks (71.6 percent) and 1,455 whites (28.4 percent). Between 1919 and 1929, 416 blacks were lynched; 15 percent of these victims were also burned. Though many people assumed that most lynchings of blacks were motivated by sexual incidents, this was not the case. The National Association for the Advancement of Colored People (NAACP) estimated that of black lynchings from 1889 to 1919, only 19 percent involved accusations of rape; 35.8 percent involved charges of murder. (Gilje, pp. 101–103.)

164. "Now," Simmons roared . . . my imperial wizardry, come on": Chalmers, pp. 32–33.

164. "the best weekly ever turned out by a tractor plant": Lee, p. 16.

165. ". . . be glad to discuss them with you": B'nai B'rith, *passim*; Baldwin, pp. 120, 123; Watts, pp. 377–384.

165. "Has anything come between us?": Lee, p. 34; Baldwin, p. 133.

165. ". . . infamous pasquinade of the guttersnipe variety": *NY Times*, 7 March 1920, p. X3; *NY Times*, 18 May 1922, p. 11; Baldwin, p. 143; Lee, pp. 22, 28. In 1934, FDR appointed Charles C. Daniels, an expert on Indian affairs, to serve as a Special Assistant to the Attorney General to oversee the Iroquois Indian Confederacy. (*NY Times*, 21 March 1951, p. 33.)

166. . . . "The International Jew: The World's Problem": Dearborn Independent, *passim*.

166. ". . . may be swamped by Asiatic blood": *The Bookman*, January 1921, pp. 301–302; L. Stoddard, p. 301; Gossett, pp. 390–397; Higham, p. 272.

166. Author F. Scott Fitzgerald provided . . . *The Great Gatsby*: Fitzgerald, pp. 17–18.

166. ". . . of what is precious in the Nordic inheritance": *NY Times*, 11 July 1920, p. 82.

**CHAPTER 11**

167. ". . . wildest flights are but too true": J. Lane, p. 2; Hagedorn (Vol. 1), p. 39.

168. ". . . what I shall do without him": Hagedorn (Vol. 1), p. 80.

168. . . . niece and ward of Supreme Court Justice Stephen J. Field: *Chicago Tribune*, 19 November 1890, p. 1.

168. "You will be pleased to hear . . . an army surgeon named Wood": J. Lane, p. 26.

168. ". . . negative virtue can ever atone": Holme, pp. 227–228.

169. . . . killed in action near Manila in December 1899: J. Lane, p. 26. Laughing off warnings of danger, Lawton took a fatal bullet in the chest. (*Chicago Tribune*, 20 December 1899, p. 1.)

169. . . . Roosevelt to create a naval version: *New York Archives*, Fall 2005, pp. 10–15.

169. . . . rebuked him. Wood ignored him: *NY Times*, 16 December 1914, p. 5; *Washington Post*, 20 December 1914, p. ES2; Sullivan (V), pp. 212–213; J. Lane, p. 188; Hagedorn (Vol. 2), pp. 151–152.

170. . . . just as it is at the present day: *Chicago Tribune*, 26 August 1915, pp. 1, 4; *NY Times*, 28 August 1915, p. 6; Holme, p. 190; Sullivan (V), pp. 216–218.

170. . . . Harding received a single vote each: *Washington Post*, 6 May 1916, p. 2; *LA Times*, 7 June 1916, p. 4; J. Lane, pp. 206–207; Hagedorn (Vol. 2), pp. 188–189; Eaton, pp. 252, 255. Sculptor Gutzon Borglum, long an ardent Roosevelt partisan, was to be at the convention to push Wood's nomination. Borglum, creator of Mount Rushmore, went on to become an influential Klan leader. (Chalmers, pp. 31, 106, 169, 200, 282.)

171. . . . of the man on my left: *Chicago Tribune*, 28 January 1918, p. 1; *NY Times*, 28 January 1918, p. 1; *Current Opinion*, July 1918, pp. 3–4; J. Lane, pp. 220–221; Hagedorn (Vol. 2), pp. 259–260; Holme, p. 5.

171. . . . "It was quite natural we should be": Longworth, p. 304.

171. "It would seem," sighed . . . the feast for the heir": Russell (*Blooming Grove*), p. 327.

171. ". . . he won't give us the nigger!": *Chicago Tribune*, 29 September 1919, pp. 1–2.

171. . . . been fired or a life lost: *NY Times*, 7 October 1919, pp. 1, 3; Hagedorn (Vol. 2), pp. 335–336; J. Lane, p. 235.

171. ". . . law and order": *Atlanta Constitution*, 6 October 1919, p. 12; *Atlanta Constitution*, 8 October 1919, pp. 1, 4; *Outlook*, 25 February 1920, p. 326; J. Lane, p. 239; R. Schmidt, pp. 221–222.

172. ". . . if not the courage[,] of a coup d'état": Lippmann, p. 165; Eaton, p. 261.

172. We made presidents out of . . . an end to his candidacy: Sinclair (*Available Man*), p. 125.

172. . . . Such men cannot be trusted: *Washington Post*, 20 April 1919, p. 2.

173. ". . . was certain that he could keep King in leash": Hagedorn (Vol. 2), pp. 331–332; Russell (*Blooming Grove*), p. 327.

173. . . . William Cooper Procter: *NY Times*, 8 December 1919, p. 2; J. Lane, pp. 241–242; Russell (*Blooming Grove*), p. 335.

174. I cannot help but feel that you . . . kind of speeches you are making: J. Lane, p. 236.

175. . . . must have broken my skull: Hagedorn (Vol. 1), p. 210.

175. . . . "is not affected": *NY Times*, 26 March 1920, p. 17; Hagedorn (Vol. 2), pp. 60–63, 89–90.

176. . . . he'd prefer Frank Lowden. He probably meant it: Hutchinson, p. 423.

176. ". . . been accustomed to choose its Presidents": Sullivan (VI), p. 42.

176. ". . . see the possibility of good": *The Outlook*, May–August 1920, p. 17; Hutchinson, p. 431.

176. . . . fit well on a Lowden ticket: *Chicago Tribune*, 8 November 1919, p. 4; *NY Times*, 8 November 1919, p. 7.

176. "In no sense of the word," . . . Governor of Massachusetts": Hutchinson, pp. 411–412.

176. "Why not the other way around?". . . Presidency than a Pullman": Hutchinson, p. 412.

177. "I like to think that the Presidency . . . plane of a patent medicine": Hutchinson, p. 414.

177. "most demoralizing departure . . . representative government": Hutchinson, p. 439.

177. . . . South Dakota primary: Russell (*Blooming Grove*), p. 335.

177. . . . "would have enjoyed the French Revolution": Perrett, p. 106; Gilbert, p. 183.

177. "The difference between . . . policy that separates them": Gilbert, p. 191.

178. . . . and Johnson ran for governor in 1910: *LA Times*, 14 November 1908, p. 1; *LA Times*, 10 December 1908, pp. 1, 5; *Current Literature*, August 1912, p. 156; Bean, pp. 282–286; Sullivan (III), p. 458.

178. . . . father renomination to the Assembly: *LA Times*, 17 August 1910, pp. 1–2; *NY Times*, 18 August 1910, p. 3; Olin, p. 29.

178. . . . railroad and utility regulation: Greenbaum, pp. 98–99; http://www.governor.ca.gov/govsite/govsgallery/h/documents/inaugural_23.html.

178. . . . party was disintegrating: Starr, p. 270. That same year, Heney, running as a Progressive, lost for U. S. Senate.

179. . . . enjoyed from regular Republicans: *LA Times*, 10 November 1916, p. 1; Olin, pp. 157, 187, 222 *fn.*; Sullivan (V), pp. 239–243.

179. "There is no contact between . . . faces in front of him": *NY Tribune*, 9 July 1920, p. 1.

179. "do not unite a people . . . people timid and fearful": Greenbaum, p. 102.

179. "Socialists," said Johnson, ". . . they must be protected": Greenbaum, p. 105.

179. ". . . unjust and wicked annexations": *Atlanta Constitution*, 3 June 1919, p. 7; Greenbaum, p. 104.

180. "Much to my surprise, Lowden had made . . . So I went along": Watkins, pp. 179–180.

180. . . . Dakota Republican convention: *Chicago Tribune*, 3 December 1919, p. 12; Hutchinson, p. 427.

180. . . . March 9's New Hampshire contest: *NY Times*, 10 March 1920, p. 1; Bagby, p. 50.

180. . . . and Lowden 3,510: *NY Times*, 16 March 1920, p. 1; Hutchinson, p. 440.

181. . . . Johnson ran unopposed: *Washington Post*, 16 March 1920, p. 1; Bagby, p. 50.

181. . . . Virginia's Republican convention: *NY Times*, 18 March 1920, p. 3.

181. . . . a junior-grade Hiram Johnson, 850: *NY Times*, 24 March 1920, p. 1; *NY Times*, 25 March 1920, p. 17; *Atlanta Constitution*, 25 March 1920, p. 4; Bagby, p. 50; Hutchinson, pp. 439–440; Russell (*Blooming Grove*), p. 345; H. Allen (*Poindexter of Washington*), p. 221.

181. . . . particular, he won five of them: *Decatur Daily Review*, 5 April 1920, p. 6; *NY Times*, 6 April 1920, p. 1; *Atlanta Constitution*, 6 April 1920, p. 1; Bagby, p. 50; Hutchinson, p. 440; Allen, p. 221.

181. . . . Governor Emanuel Philipp: *Lincoln Evening State Journal*, 7 April 1920, p. 1; *Chicago Tribune*, 8 April 1920, p. 13; *NY Times*, 8 April 1920, p. 1; *Washington Post*, 8 April 1920, p. 1.

181. . . . personally favored Frank Lowden: *NY Times*, 7 April 1920, p. 1; *Chicago Tribune*, 7 April 1920, p. 1; *Washington Post*, 8 April 1920, p. 1.

182. . . . quelled the resultant "riot": *Atlanta Constitution*, 7 April 1920, p. 2; *Chicago Tribune*, 8 April 1920, p. 13. Johnson's wife, Georgia Douglas Johnson (1880–1966), eventually established herself as one of the nation's leading black poets.

182. . . . went for Herbert Hoover: *Chicago Tribune*, 14 April 1920, p. 1; Bagby, pp. 50–51; Hutchinson, pp. 443–444; Russell (*Blooming Grove*), pp. 345–346; Michigan Bureau of Elections to Author, 20 May 2005.

182. . . . collected just 27,699 votes: *Atlanta Constitution*, 14 March 1920, p. 6A; *Atlanta Constitution*, 21 March 1920, p. 1; *Lima News & Times-Democrat*, 22 May 1920, p. 4; Russell (*Blooming Grove*), p. 345; Bagby, p. 51. Pershing also entered the Michigan primary. He finished fifth.

182. . . . Harding received only 722 votes: *Washington Post*, 25 April 1920, p. 1; *NY Times*, 9 May 1920, p. 3; *NY Times*, 4 May 1920, p. 2; Adams (*Incredible Era*), p. 126; Bagby, p. 51.

182. . . . by fraud. Perhaps he had: *NY Times*, 3 April 1920, p. 15; *LA Times*, 1 May 1920, p. 3; Dullard, p. 510; Bagby, p. 51; Russell (*Blooming Grove*), p. 346. The totals: Wood 52,908, Johnson 51,685, Hoover 959.

182. . . . finished ahead of Johnson: *Chicago Tribune*, 29 April 1920, p. 4; *Ohio State Monitor*, 1 May 1920, p. 1; J. Lane, p. 243; Russell (*Blooming Grove*), p. 346; Bagby, p. 51.

182. . . . leaning to Wood and/or Hoover: *LA Times*, 28 April 1920, p. 2; Fuess, p. 247; Bagby, p. 51.

182. . . . vote for somebody else: *Washington Post*, 29 April 1920, p. 1; Allen, p. 221.

182. . . . Johnson 2–1 (14,663–7,113): *LA Times*, 4 May 1920, pp. 1–2; Bagby, p. 51.

183. . . . He enjoyed doing it: *Atlanta Constitution*, 5 May 1920, p. 1; *NY Times*, 6 May 1920, p. 1; Bagby, pp. 44–45, 51–52.

183. . . . verified his front-runner status: *Indianapolis Star*, 5 May 1920, p. 1; Adams (*Incredible Era*), pp. 126–127; J. Lane, p. 243; Spragens, p. 281; Russell (*Blooming Grove*), pp. 346–347; Bagby, pp. 39, 40, 52; Dean, p. 56.

183. . . . been decent presidential timber: *Chicago Tribune*, 19 May 1920, p. 1.

183. . . . registered voters participated: *Sandusky Star-Journal*, 28 February 1920, p. 1; *Reno Evening Gazette*, 18 May 1920, p. 1; *Chicago Tribune*, 19 May 1920, p. 1; *Oshkosh Daily Northwestern*, 19 May 1920, p. 7; *NY Times*, 20 May 1920, p. 7; *Washington Post*, 27 April 1920, p. 5; Vermont Board of Elections E-mail to Author, 17 May 2005.

183. . . . still received 14,557 votes: *Atlanta Constitution*, 19 May 1920, p. 9; *Atlanta Constitution*, 24 May 1920, p. 3; *Washington Post*, 24 May 1920, p. 1; *Oshkosh Daily Northwestern*, 24 May 1920, p. 1; Best, p. 110; Oregon Department of State to Author, 17 May 2005.

183. . . . the mysterious William Grant Webster: *Oshkosh Daily Northwestern*, 24 May 1920, p. 1; *Reno Evening Gazette*, 27 May 1920, p. 1.

183. . . . at the earliest legal moment: *Decatur Review*, 30 May 1920, p. 6.

184. . . . inquiry was really aimed at Wood: J. Lane, p. 243; Bagby, pp. 52–53.

184. . . . Rockefeller Jr. to pony up $25,000: *Mansfield News*, 30 May 1920, p. 1; Downes, pp. 406–408.

184. . . . Butler $40,550: *NY Times*, 28 May 1920, p. 1; *Washington Post*, 28 May 1920, p. 1; *Atlanta Constitution*, 28 May 1920, p. 1; Harris, p. 10; Russell (*Blooming Grove*), p. 352; Bagby, p. 53; J. Lane, p. 244; Sinclair (*Available Man*), p. 134.

185. . . . had bought their votes: *Chicago Tribune*, 2 June 1920, p. 1; *NY Times*, 2 June 1920, pp. 1–2; Hutchinson, pp. 452–453; Downes, pp. 408–409.

185. . . . published on June 5, was: *LA Times*, 27 April 1920, p. II4; *NY Times*, 6 June 1920, p. 30.

186. ". . . my name be not even mentioned in the convention": *NY Times*, 19 April 1920, p. 15; Pusey, pp. 402–403. Steinbrink represented gambler Arnold Rothstein in the early public phases of the Black Sox scandal. He later became national chairman of B'nai B'rith. (Pietrusza [*Rothstein*], p. 416.)

## CHAPTER 12

188. . . . female teachers in the New York City school system: Synon, *passim*; W. G. McAdoo, *passim*; Johnson, pp. 639–640.

188. ". . . would catch the rays of the sun": *Boston Globe*, 6 August 1911, p. 36; W. G. McAdoo, p. 109; Synon, pp. 41–42.

188. . . . prize: Secretary of the Treasury: W. G. McAdoo, pp. 178–179; M. Lyons, pp. 8–9, 119, 128; Chace, pp. 191–192.

189. "a blow in the solar plexus of the money monopoly": Johnson, p. 640.

189. When war came, McAdoo shifted . . . Liberty Loan program: Craig, pp. 32–35.

189. "He was a strange paradox . . . anything he undertook": Wehle, p. 60.

189. "Indeed," wrote historian . . . historic accolades he deserved": Johnson, p. 639.

189. . . . "the most selfish man I ever met": Perrett, p. 110; Johnson, p. 640.

189. . . . A single thing he ever did: Craig, p. 33. McAdoo's autobiography runs rife with such insufferable passages as "To be appointed the attorney of a railroad company, at so early an age, was considered a decided recognition of one's ability." (W. G. McAdoo, p. 43.)

190. . . . White House on May 7, 1914: *Atlanta Constitution*, 10 May 1914, p. 3; W. G. McAdoo, pp. 272–277; Synon, p. 126. McAdoo's first wife, Sarah Houston Fleming, died in 1911. She had been an invalid for many years.

190. ". . . anybody but himself": *Chicago Tribune*, 23 November 1920, p. 1; *Atlanta Constitution*, 1 December 1918, p. 6; Kane, p. 189; Craig, p. 39.

190. . . . he had left United Artists: *LA Times*, 2 March 1919, p. 14; *LA Times*, 5 July 1919, p. 13; *LA Times*, 7 January 1920, p. 14; Ramsaye, pp. 794–796; Schickel, pp. 401–403; Eyman, p. 130; Schulberg, pp. 96–98, 100; Gelman, p. 26. Before joining United Artists, McAdoo had been offered a $50,000 salary to head Universal Studios. He refused, writing Universal president Carl Laemmle in November 1918: "I doubt my qualifications for the position you offer," saying that he intended to practice law in New York.

McAdoo claimed that his press secretary, Oscar A. Price, had sparked the idea for United Artists by suggesting to Fairbanks during the Liberty Loan drive of 1918 that he distribute his own films. B. P. Schulberg, later head of Paramount, claimed that McAdoo stole the idea from him. In July 1919, McAdoo-led United Artists toyed with the idea of a Wilson biopic.

190. "I never saw a man before take . . . any politics I have ever seen": Bagby, p. 63.

191. . . . and McAdoo withdrew: Bagby, pp. 65–66. McAdoo wrote disingenuously: "Of course, the President's silence makes it very awkward for me, even if I had an inclination to stand for the Presidency—which, as you know, I have not. . . ."

191. ". . . *thought of* in her presence: Anthony (*First Ladies*), p. 360.

191. ". . . thought it would cost me my life": *Providence Journal*, 11 January 1920, p. 2; Coben, p. 253.

192. . . . Pulitzer Prize for this total fabrication: *NY Times*, 18 June 1920, p. 1; *Chicago Tribune*, 18 June 1920, p. 1; Tumulty, pp. 492–493; Levin, pp. 448–453; Stein, pp. 243–245; Fleming, pp. 455–457; G. Smith, p. 160; Weinstein, p. 367; Bagby, pp. 68–69.

192. . . . replacement as Treasury Secretary, Carter Glass: *Atlanta Constitution*, 19 June 1920, p. 7; *Dayton Journal*, 19 June 1920, p. 1; *NY Times*, 20 June 1920, p. 1; *Chicago Tribune*, 19 June 1920, pp. 1–2; *NY Times*, 19 June 1920, pp. 1–2; *Atlanta Constitution*, 19 June 1920, pp. 1–2; Beasley and Smith, pp. 206–207; Annin, pp. 328–329.

192. ". . . his nomination as a possibility": *Chicago Tribune*, 22 June 1920, p. 3; *NY Times*, 22 June 1920, p. 1; *Atlanta Constitution*, 22 June 1920, p. 1.

192. . . . "No, he does not, as I read it!": *Chicago Tribune*, 24 June 1920, p. 1; Beasley and Smith, p. 208; Bagby, pp. 69–70.

192. . . . McAdoo quickly denied all: *Washington Post*, 24 June 1920, p. 3; *Atlanta Constitution*, 24 June 1920, p. 3; *NY Tribune*, 24 June 1920, p. 4.

192. . . . "better than I expected": *NY Tribune*, 23 June 1920, p. 2; Weinstein, p. 367.

192. . . . it were forced upon him: *NY Times*, 28 June 1920, p. 1; *Chicago Tribune* 28 June 1920, p. 1; *Atlanta Constitution*, 28 June 1920, p. 1; *LA Times*, 28 June 1920, p. 2; *Washington Post*, 28 June 1920, p. 1.

193. . . . delayed his confirmation until that August: *NY Times*, 4 November 1914, p. 1; *Chicago Tribune*, 4 November 1914, p. 4; *NY Times*, 14 November 1916, pp. 1, 4; *Washington Post*, 30 August 1919, p. 1; Morgan (*Reds*), pp. 72–73.

193. ". . . America be swayed by such doctrines?": Coben, p. 197.

193. ". . . individuals who were probably innocent": Coben, p. 201.

194. . . . deporting as many as possible: *Atlanta Constitution*, 6 November 1919, p. 6; *Washington Post*, 12 May 1936, p. 9.

194. Like a prairie fire, . . . foundations of society: *The Forum*, February 1920, p. 173.

194. . . . many a conservative) in the country: *Atlanta Constitution*, 2 March 1920, pp. 1A, 5.

194. . . . "but to Palmer that was a compliment": Morgan (*Reds*), p. 72.

194. . . . Governor Edwards all easily outpacing him: Bagby, p. 72; Michigan Bureau of Elections E-mail to Author, 20 May 2005.

194. . . . campaign was basically finished: *NY Times*, 22 April 1920, pp. 1, 2; Bagby, p. 72.

195. "mildly liberal, mildly wet, mildly able": Perrett, p. 111; Craig, p. 18.

195. . . . later for the *Cincinnati Enquirer*: *NY Tribune*, 6 July 1920, p. 3; *Sandusky Star-Journal*, 15 July 1920, p. 10; *NY Times*, 16 July 1941, p. 24; *Review of Reviews*, August 1920, pp.

149–150; Bagby, p. 73; Kane, p. 195. Cox was originally named James Monroe Cox. "Middleton" may have derived from Cox's early stomping ground of Middletown, Ohio.

195. Jimmy Cox . . . usually had to be done over in the office: Stone, p. 22.

196. . . . Mary Cox married her divorce lawyer: *Sandusky Star Journal*, 20 June 1920, p. 6; *Mansfield News*, 21 June 1911, p. 2; *Coshocton Daily Tribune*, 21 June 1911, p. 2; *Sandusky Star-Journal*, 22 June 1911, p. 2; *Indiana Gazette*, 23 June 1911, p. 3; *NY Times*, 23 June 1911, p. 1; *NY Tribune*, 6 July 1920, p. 3; *NY Tribune*, 7 July 1920, p. 3; *LA Times*, 14 August 1920, p. 1; *NY Times*, 16 July 1941, p. 24; Cebula, p. 67; Bagby, p. 73; Stone, pp. 25–27. Mary Cox married her Cleveland attorney, Richard Henry Lee (two years her junior), in January 1914. Mr. & Mrs. Lee had a son, Richard H. Lee Jr., in 1915. They (and her twelve-year-old son John W. Cox) resided in Pelham Manor, New York. As far as the press was concerned in 1920, they did not exist. (*NY Times*, 22 February 1914, p. B5; *Chicago Tribune*, 16 September 1917, p. 3.)

196. ". . . 'safe' kind of liberal": *Review of Reviews*, August 1920, pp. 152–154; J. M. Cox, p. 117; Craig, p. 18.

196. . . . three-term governor besides Rutherford B. Hayes: *NY Times*, 16 July 1941, p. 24; J. M. Cox, pp. 188, 211; Bagby, p. 73; Stone, p. 26; Blackwell, p. 206.

197. . . . early morning of December 1, 1919: *Elyria Chronicle-Telegram*, 1 December 1920, p. 10; *Sandusky Star-Journal*, 1 December 1919, p. 15; *NY Tribune*, 7 July 1920, p. 3; Cebula, p. 67.

197. . . . suggested his own reservations: Bagby, p. 75.

197. ". . . bluffing and advertising can do much good": *Current Opinion*, August 1920, p. 187; Bagby, pp. 74–75.

198. . . . Cox won delegates in next-door Kentucky: *Atlanta Constitution*, 13 May 1920, p. 8; Dullard, p. 515; Eaton, pp. 281–282; Bagby, pp. 72, 78; Craig, p. 52.

198. . . . only then, James Middleton Cox: *NY Times*, 13 June 1920, p. 30; Bagby, pp. 59, 64, 77.

199. With spring came the prospect . . . if they had just kept silent: I. Hoover, p. 107.

199. On May 31, 1920 . . . Wilson jibed, "would be a fake": Levin, pp. 446–447.

200. "We must not take any chances": G. Smith, pp. 161–162; Ferrell (*Woodrow Wilson*), pp. 224, 297. Woolley is credited with the slogan "He kept us out of war," although his original version was "With honor, he has kept us out of war," and he resented the change. (*Washington Post*, 16 December 1958, p. B2.)

200. "seriously contemplates permitting himself . . . said it would kill him": Stein, p. 246.

200. ". . . you know Cox's nomination would be a joke": Bagby, p. 62; Craig, p. 19; G. Smith, p. 161; Beasley and Smith, p. 208.

200. "If anything comes up . . . juggling of false friends": G. Smith, p. 162.

**CHAPTER 13**

202. ". . . mayor, and military hero": *Chicago Tribune*, 8 June 1920, p. 3.

202. . . . back anyone supporting her program: *Chicago Tribune*, 8 June 1920, p. 2; *LA Times*, 21 August 1924, p. 6; *NY Times* 21 August 1924, p. 11. The often-contentious Miss Gaston died in August 1924 of throat cancer, supposedly triggered by her having been run over earlier that year by a Chicago streetcar.

202. . . . remained unpledged and up for grabs: Russell (*Blooming Grove*), p. 355; Watkins, pp. 184–185.

202. Hiram Johnson . . . Calvin Coolidge: 8–1: *Chicago Tribune*, 8 June 1920, p. 2.

202. Adding to the mess . . . participated in 1912's train wreck: Harris, p. 12.

203. . . . never would see Elizabeth Ann: Britton, pp. 125, 127, 130–131; Russell (*Blooming Grove*), p. 360; Anthony (*Florence Harding*), pp. 189–190.

203. "dehumanize the Republican Party": *Chicago Tribune*, 8 June 1920, pp. 1–2; *NY Tribune*, 8 June 1920, p. 1; *Atlanta Constitution*, 8 June 1920, pp. 1, 4; *Washington Post*, 8 June 1920, pp. 1–2.

203. ". . . Two days later . . . all elements of the party": *LA Times*, 10 June 1920, p. 4.

204. . . . considered hiring him for president: Hays, *passim; NY Times*, 8 March 1954, pp. 1, 27; *Washington Post*, 8 March 1954, p. 14.

204. ". . . and the floor with their simian friends": *Frederick Post*, 18 July 1984, p. 15; Ward, p. 495 *fn*.

204. "The dirtiest man that I have . . . sandwich counter in Chicago": Rodgers, p. 222.

204. "It isn't the humidity . . . it's the heat": *NY Tribune*, 13 July 1920, p. 6.

204. "It distressed us . . . the spats were a mistake": *NY Tribune*, 8 July 1920, p. 1.

205. ". . . most common denominator": Ferber, pp. 250–251; Watkins, p. 184. In April 1920, Ferber, an active Republican, co-hosted (with, among others, George Ade, Ethel Barrymore, Jesse Lasky, Booth Tarkington, and William Allen White) a weekend conference in Atlantic City for "Republican authors, artists, and publicists." (*Chicago Tribune*, 15 April 1920, p. 7.)

205. You know there is no chance . . . No one knows: Lathem, p. 161.

205. . . . no Hoover third party: *NY Tribune*, 8 June 1920, p. 2.

205. ". . . Johnson emblem]": *NY Tribune*, 8 June 1920, p. 2; Best, p. 112.

206. "It was," noted the head of Massachusetts's delegation . . . have ever seen": *The Outlook*, 8 September 1920, p. 60; Fuess, p. 251; McCoy, pp. 114–115.

206. ". . . is not for him!": H. L. Stoddard (*As I Knew Them*), pp. 531–532; McCoy, p. 113; Bagby, p. 46.

206. "The rest of what he said . . . courage to repeat it": Fuess, p. 257.

207. . . . know what to make of it: *NY Tribune*, 4 June 1920, p. 2; *NY Times*, 7 June 1920, p. 3; *NY Tribune*, 8 June 1920, pp. 2–3; *Atlanta Constitution*, 10 June 1920, p. 1; *LA Times*, 11 June 1920, p. 1; Whiting, p. 174; Harris, p. 10; Russell (*Blooming Grove*), pp. 355–356. The Hardings stayed at the LaSalle Hotel.

207. "A big poster," it wrote . . . it is a good picture": *NY Times*, 7 June 1920, p. 3.

207. ". . . can be entirely reactionary": *NY Tribune*, 8 June 1920, p. 2.

208. . . . afford to abide by the result: *NY Times*, 13 June 1920, p. 1; *Chicago Tribune*, 13 June 1920, p. 6; White (*Masks*), p. 405; Werner, p. 6; Kane, p. 199; Russell (*Blooming Grove*), pp. 341–342.

208. "Make it two eleven": Eaton, p. 265; Russell (*Blooming Grove*), p. 342 *fn*.

208. ". . . in the Leonard Wood stampede": *NY Times*, 2 January 1920, p. 2.

209. . . . every move from the reporters: Daugherty, p. 37; Anthony (*Florence Harding*), p. 190.

209. . . . Daugherty gently declined: Russell (*Blooming Grove*), p. 358.

209. . . . Daugherty away with a $25,000 donation: Hutchinson, pp. 441, 456 *fn*.; Sullivan (VI), pp. 23–24; Russell (*Blooming Grove*), pp. 358–359; Sinclair (*Available Man*), p. 142; Hagedorn (Vol. 2), p. 363; Werner, p. 11.

210. ". . . ceases—you understand that?": Daugherty, pp. 29–30; Sullivan (VI), pp. 55–56. Emerson became governor of Illinois in 1929.

210. ". . . was rarely, if ever, ignored": Anthony (*Florence Harding*), p. 188.

210. ". . . word about a human being": Daugherty, p. 37; Anthony (*Florence Harding*), p. 190.

210. ". . . has kept us out of peace": *NY Tribune*, 9 June 1920, pp. 1, 8–9; *Outlook*, 20 June 1920, p. 377; Hendrick, pp. 131–144; Eaton, p. 329; Russell (*Blooming Grove*), p. 367.

210. ". . . and all influence in it": *Chicago Tribune*, 9 June 1920, pp. 5, 6; Ferrell (*Woodrow Wilson*), p. 228.

211. . . . "the tail of Mr. Wilson's kite": *NY Tribune*, 9 June 1920, p. 1.

211. . . . Iowa Senator Albert Cummins: Garraty, p. 393.

212. . . . *Sun* found it "deplorable": *NY Times*, 11 June 1920, p. 4.

212. "as thrashed out in the Senate": *Washington Post*, 11 June 1920, p. 6.

212. . . . what they got from Democrats: *Washington Post*, 11 June 1920, pp. 1, 6; Hendrick, pp. 145–154; Russell (*Blooming Grove*), p. 370; Hutchinson, p. 459; Cebula, p. 105; Dunn and Kuehl, pp. 3–4; http://www.presidency.ucsb.edu/showplatforms.php?platindex=R1920.

212. "words scrawled on a wall by feeble-minded children": Craig, p. 21.

213. ". . . because it is his wish": *NY Times*, 11 June 1920, p. 3; *Boston Globe*, 11 June 1920, p. 2; *NY Times*, 13 June 1920, p. 7; Russell (*Blooming Grove*), p. 371; Sinclair (*Available Man*), p. 151.

213. . . . interminable string of nominating speeches: *Chicago Tribune*, 12 June 1920, p. 4.

214. . . . and I want Leonard Wood: Caroli, pp. 133–136; Hagedorn (Vol. 2), p. 357; Russell (*Blooming Grove*), p. 374.

214. ". . . like the echo of a Gatling gun against a stone wall": *LA Times*, 12 June 1920, p. 1.

214. ". . . oratory since Demosthenes": *LA Times*, 12 July 1920, p. 4.

214. . . . each began with an "L": *NY Tribune*, 12 June 1920, p. 4.

214. . . . knifing of Charles Evans Hughes: *NY Tribune*, 12 June 1920, p. 4; *Atlanta Constitution*, 12 June 1920, p. 12; *Outlook*, 20 June 1920, p. 378.

215. . . . Slighted, Borah refused: Longworth, p. 310.

215. . . . appropriately appreciative hand: *LA Times*, 12 July 1920, p. 4; *NY Tribune*, 12 June 1920, p. 4; Russell (*Blooming Grove*), p. 374. Schall lost his sight in 1908 when an "electric cigar lighter" exploded in his face.

215. . . . waves of genuine enthusiasm: *NY Tribune*, 12 June 1920, p. 3; *Chicago Tribune*, 12 June 1920, p. 4; *Washington Post*, 12 June 1920, p. 4; Hendrick, p. 130; Sullivan (VI), p. 83; Whiting, p. 178; McCoy, pp. 116–117.

216. . . . turgid nominating speeches: *NY Tribune*, 12 June 1920, p. 1; *Outlook*, 20 June 1920, pp. 377–378; Sullivan (VI), p. 83.

216. . . . ("a gent with whiskers . . . was angling for vice president: *NY Tribune*, 7 June 1920, p. 3; *LA Times*, 12 June 1920, p. 3.

216. . . . hammered away at the administration: *Chicago Tribune*, 12, 1920, p. 4; Butler (Vol. 1), p. 277.

216. . . . New York's delegation was an interesting . . . for Irvine Lenroot: Fausold, p. 131.

216. . . . only hostility from the floor: *NY Tribune*, 12 June 1920, p. 3; Daugherty, p. 41; H. L. Stoddard (*It Costs to be President*), p. 87; H. L. Stoddard (*As I Knew Them*), pp. 466–467; Russell (*Blooming Grove*), p. 374.

216. ". . . grand opera, and hog-calling": *Atlanta Constitution*, 12 June 1920, p. 12; Sullivan (VI), pp. 51–52; Downes, p. 417; Sinclair (*Available Man*), p. 139.

217. . . . Senator Warren C. Harding: *NY Tribune*, 12 June 1920, p. 3; *LA Times*, 12 June

1920, p. 2; *Washington Post*, 12 June 1920, p. 4; Hendrick, p. 129; Johnson, pp. 78–79; Daugherty, p. 42; Russell (*Blooming Grove*), p. 375.

217. ". . . votes to nominate Senator Harding": *Chicago Tribune*, 13 June 1920, p. 6.

217. Will Hays found it all "quite spontaneous": Hays, p. 248.

217. . . . "unmistakably spontaneous": *Atlanta Constitution*, 12 June 1920, p. 12.

217. . . . she thought he was just great: Britton, pp. 134–135. "Gus" Kreager seconded Harding. (Russell [*Blooming Grove*], p. 295.)

218. ". . . over the hubbub of protesting delegates": *NY Tribune*, 12 June 1920, p. 3; *Atlanta Constitution*, 12 June 1920, pp. 1, 12; Hays, p. 248; Harris, p. 14.

218. . . . convention's relief—passed: *Chicago Tribune*, 12 June 1920, p. 4.

218. ". . . devote myself to my newspaper": Butler (Vol. 1), p. 279; White (*Puritan in Babylon*), p. 211 *fn.*; Fuess, p. 260.

218. ". . . hisses from other delegations: *Chicago Tribune*, 12 June 1920, p. 4.

218. . . . not from a Lowden supporter: Hutchinson, p. 460; Eaton, p. 270.

218. . . . let McCamant vote for Wood: *Washington Post*, 11 June 1920, p. 1; *Chicago Tribune*, 12 June 1920, pp. 3, 4.

219. Wood 287 . . . Charles B. Warren 1: *NY Tribune*, 13 June 1920, p. 1; *NY Times*, 12 June 1920, p. 1; *Chicago Tribune*, 12 June, 1920, p. 1; Daugherty, p. 43; Coolidge (*Autobiography*), p. 147; Sinclair (*Available Man*), p. 140.

219. Wood 289-1/2 . . . Borah 1: *NY Tribune*, 13 June 1920, p. 1; *NY Times*, 12 June 1920, p. 1.

220. Wood 303 . . . Borah 1: *NY Tribune*, 12 June 1920, p. 3; *NY Tribune*, 13 June 1920, p. 1; *NY Times*, 12 June 1920, p. 1; Sinclair (*Available Man*), p. 140; Eaton, p. 271.

221. Wood 314-1/2 . . . Borah 1: Eaton, p. 271; Sullivan (VI), p. 58 *fn.*

221. ". . . to think it over": *NY Times*, 12 June 1920, p. 1; *Chicago Tribune*, 12 June 1920, p. 1; Sullivan (VI), pp. 57–58; Sinclair (*Available Man*), pp. 140–141.

221. ". . . corruption of the American people": *Atlanta Constitution*, 12 June 1920, p. 1.

221. ". . . likely candidate for President tonight": *NY Times*, 12 June 1920, p. 1; Eaton, p. 90.

222. ". . . unite on except myself": Sinclair (*Available Man*), p. 136.

222. . . . alienate *any* potential supporter: Daugherty, pp. 43–44; Harris, pp. 15–16.

222. ". . . Hesperus. He was discouraged": White (*Autobiography*), p. 584.

222. ". . . whiskey on his unshaven face": Quoted in Anthony (*Florence Harding*), p. 192.

223. . . . re-filed for the United States Senate: *NY Tribune*, 12 June 1920, p. 3; *Washington Post*, 12 June 1920, p. 1; Sullivan (VI), pp. 71–72; Russell (*Blooming Grove*), pp. 371–372, 379.

223. . . . remained largely in his camp: Daugherty, p. 44; Sinclair (*Available Man*), pp. 141–142; Downes, pp. 419–420; Harris, p. 15.

223. . . . so positive, turned him down: Sinclair (*Available Man*), pp. 144–145; Eaton, pp. 271–272; Bagby, p. 90; Sullivan (V), p. 244.

**CHAPTER 14**

225. ". . . Harding is the best of the second[-]raters": *Literary Digest*, 3 July 1920, pp. 555–557; Gilbert, p. 5; Boller, pp. 212–213; Hagedorn (Vol. 2), p. 361; Anthony (*Florence Harding*), p. 193; Gilbert, p. 5; W. G. McAdoo, p. 388; Sullivan (VI), pp. 59–61, 74 *fn.*; Harris, pp. 16–17; Russell (*Blooming Grove*), p. 383.

225. Harding could not sleep . . . Wadsworth coldly responded: Fausold, p. 130.

225. ". . . no reason he couldn't be president: Adams, p. 154; Sullivan (VI), pp. 63–64; Fuess, p. 258; Sinclair (*Available Man*), pp. 144, 311; Russell (*Blooming Grove*), p. 383; Morello, p. 48; Hutchinson, p. 463.

226. ". . . anyone else to propose": Sullivan (VI), p. 60; Fausold, pp. 129–130.

226. ". . . a run for his money": Harris, p. 17; Russell (*Blooming Grove*), p. 383.

226. "Harding of Ohio" . . . large field of dark horses": Bagby, p. 91.

226. ". . . only Republican vote he had ever cast": H. L. Stoddard (*It Costs to be President*), p. 75.

227. . . . presenting Martin with a handful: Martin, pp. 141–142; Russell (*Blooming Grove*), pp. 385–386. Martin became Speaker of the House in 1947 and again in 1953.

227. . . . be here as a presidential candidate": Russell (*Blooming Grove*), p. 386; Harris, pp. 24–25.

228. Lowden 303 . . . Knox 1: *NY Tribune*, 13 June 1920, pp. 1, 4; *LA Times*, 13 June 1920, p. 7; Sinclair (*Available Man*), p. 145; Russell (*President Makers*), p. 219.

228. Wood 311-1/2 . . . Lenroot 1: *NY Tribune*, 13 June 1920, p. 1; *LA Times*, 13 June 1920, p. 7; Daugherty, pp. 45–47; Sinclair (*Available Man*), p. 146; Eaton, p. 275; Russell (*President Makers*), p. 219.

229. Wood 312 . . . Lenroot 1: *NY Tribune*, 13 June 1920, p. 1; *LA Times*, 13 June 1920, p. 7; Sinclair (*Available Man*), p. 146; Eaton, p. 275; Russell (*President Makers*), p. 219.

230. Lowden 307 . . . Lenroot 1: *NY Tribune*, 13 June 1920, p. 1; *LA Times*, 13 June 1920, p. 7; Daugherty, p. 47; Harris, p. 21; Sinclair (*Available Man*), p. 146.

230. ". . . This is an outrage!": *NY Tribune*, 13 July 1920, p. 1; Daugherty, pp. 47–48; Hays, p. 250; Russell (*President Makers*), p. 219.

230. ". . . I concurred in this:" Hutchinson, p. 465; Downes, pp. 422–423.

231. He was wrong. The wheels . . . conclude a deal with Harding: Hutchinson, p. 465.

231. . . . Kansas . . . then for Hoover: White (*Autobiography*), pp. 586–587; Eaton, p. 276.

231. . . . The Hays candidacy was over: Russell (*The President Makers*), p. 220; Hutchinson, pp. 466–467; Eaton, pp. 276–277. Roraback, in poor health, committed suicide in May 1937.

231. . . . on Saturday's ninth ballot: Adams, p. 151; *Washington Post*, 10 January 1922, p. 1; Butler p. 278; Daugherty, p. 49; Watson, pp. 221–222; Harris, pp. 28–29. Despite Penrose's ill health, he easily won re-election in 1920. He died in office at age 61 on December 31, 1921, leaving behind a hoard of $226,000 in cash.

       Pennsylvania's senators were a fragile bunch. Philander C. Knox expired of "apoplexy" on October 12, 1921. Knox's successor, William E. Crow, died in office in August 1922. (Adams, p. 141.)

232. . . . in all these long years: White (*Autobiography*), pp. 586–587.

233. Harding 374-1/2 . . . Absent 1/2: *NY Tribune*, 13 June 1920, p. 1; *LA Times*, 13 June 1920, p. 7; *Atlanta Constitution*, 13 June 1920, p. 6; Hays, p. 250; Daugherty, pp. 51–52; Fuess, p. 260; J. Lane, pp. 246–247; Sinclair (*Available Man*), p. 149.

233. ". . . going into the White House!": Anthony (*Florence Harding*), pp. 195–196. Ruth Hanna McCormick was the daughter of William McKinley's trusted associate Ohio Senator Mark Hanna.

234. . . . "I will," Florence grimly vowed: Daugherty, pp. 53–54; Sullivan (VI), p. 67.

234. . . . would now back Harding: *Atlanta Constitution*, 13 June 1920, p. 6; *Washington Post*, 13 June 1920, p. 3.

234. Harding 692-1/5 . . . Absent, 1/2: *NY Tribune*, 13 June 1920, p. 1; *LA Times*, 13 June 1920, p. 7; Daugherty, pp. 54–55; Sinclair (*Available Man*), p. 149.

234. ". . . Harding—President of the United States!'": Britton, p. 135.

235. ". . . of the intellectual grade of an aging cockroach": Rodgers, p. 222.

235. ". . . hundred years from now": Ferber, pp. 252–253; Watkins, p. 187.

235. . . . wouldn't make it unanimous: Watkins, p. 187; C. Black, p. 120; *Atlanta Constitution*, 13 June 1920, p. 6; Sullivan (VI), p. 80.

235. ". . . that you two friends can give me": *NY Tribune*, 13 June 1920, pp. 2, 4; *Washington Post*, 13 June 1920, p. 3; Butler (Vol. 1), p. 279; White (*Puritan in Babylon*), p. 211 *fn*.; Eaton, pp. 277–278. In 1925, Calvin Coolidge tried to appoint Warren Attorney General. The Senate deadlocked 40–40, and Vice President Charles Dawes, napping at his New Willard Hotel quarters, was unavailable to break the tie. The Senate later rejected Warren, 46–39. (Fuess, pp. 364–365.)

236. . . . "Good-bye, my dear; believe me always!": Hagedorn (Vol. 2), p. 369.

236. ". . . Haven't had anything to eat since morning": *Chicago Tribune*, 13 June 1920, p. 1; *Literary Digest*, 27 November 1920, p. 57; Sinclair (*Available Man*), p. 154; Dean, p. 66.

236. . . . walk across the Boston Common: Fuess, p. 264; McCoy, pp. 118–119; Ross (*Grace Coolidge*), p. 55.

236. ". . . what Wood would always do": Hagedorn (Vol. 2), pp. 368–369.

237. ". . . sure I heard what he was saying": Cobb, pp. 274–276; *Washington Post*, 29 June 1919, p. A9.

237. "Tall, handsome, commanding of figure . . . seen a less happy man": Ferber, p. 253.

238. ". . . President! . . . Oh, girls, think!": Ferber, pp. 253–254.

238. The "blood" was mere perspiration: Daugherty, p. 55.

238. . . . Harding just shrugged and said: "Search me!": Watson, pp. 223–224.

238. . . . Hearst did. Johnson again refused: Older, p. 429; Swanberg, p. 333.

238. . . . "The hell you are!": H. L. Stoddard (*It Costs to be President*), pp. 70–71; H. L. Stoddard (*As I Knew Them*), pp. 466–467; McCoy, p. 120.

239. . . . "Now, remember": *Washington Post*, 8 February 1948, p. M17.

239. . . . Calvin Coolidge, of Massachusetts: *Boston Globe*, 27 June 1920, p. 55; *Washington Post*, 6 January 1933, p. 4; *Chicago Tribune*, 6 January 1933, p. 5; White (*Puritan in Babylon*), p. 213; Fuess, p. 262; Sullivan (VI), p. 79; McCoy, p. 120; Sobel, p. 187. Lodge had won Oregon's vice-presidential primary.

239. ". . . such a spontaneous and enthusiastic tribute": Sullivan (VI), p. 83.

240. . . . *Everyone* was for Silent Cal: *NY Tribune*, 13 June 1920, p. 2; *Atlanta Constitution*, 13 June 1920, pp. 1A-2, 6C; *NY Tribune*, 14 June 1920, p. 1; *Literary Digest*, 10 July 1920, pp. 55–56; Sullivan (VI), pp. 78–81; White (*Puritan in Babylon*), p. 214; Martin, pp. 143–144; Sobel, p. 188.

240. ". . . Coolidge luck. He's shot with it": Ferber, p. 253. Frederick M. Davenport told much the same story in the June 12, 1920 *Outlook*, making the prophet an anonymous close friend of Coolidge and the prophecy precede the nomination. (*Outlook*, 20 June 1920, p. 378; Fuess, p. 264.)

240. ". . . telegram expressing my regrets": *Literary Digest*, 3 July 1920, p. 57.

241. ". . . he replied, even grimmer than usual: *NY Tribune*, 13 June 1920, p. 2; *Boston Globe*, 13 June 1920, p. 10; Sullivan (VI), p. 84; Adams, p. 167; Fuess, pp. 264–265; White (*Puritan in Babylon*), pp. 214–215; Ross (*Grace Coolidge*), pp. 55–56. Coolidge later

perked up, uncharacteristically handing out very expensive cigars to reporters who invaded his quarters. Then he returned to normal, writing out some notes and ignoring them.

241. "Warren," she confided, almost . . . see only tragedy ahead": Harris, p. 26.

**CHAPTER 15**

242. ". . . The convention also was a delight": White (*Autobiography*), p. 590. The cherries *must* have been good: Edna Ferber wrote about them in *her* memoirs. (Ferber, p. 260.)

243. ". . . most gorgeous bordellos of Paris": *Frederick Post*, 18 July 1984, p. 15.

243. ". . . and their hearts going pitterpat": Ward, pp. 495–496.

243. ". . . Nothing seemed to be accomplished": Ferber, p. 259.

243. Franklin Roosevelt was there—as a McAdoo delegate: *NY Times*, 1 July 1920, p. 2.

243. ". . . with a family name so distinguished": *Washington Post*, 29 June 1920, p. 6; Warner and Daniel, pp. 122–123; Ward, p. 497; C. Black, pp. 120–122; Freidel (*The Ordeal*), p. 62.

244. . . . he confided to friends, "I am in love": Rodgers, pp. 222–223, 244. They kept in touch afterward—until she was arrested for credit fraud in 1923; then he wouldn't take her calls.

244. The booze flowed freely . . . bottle of illegal hootch: Rodgers, p. 222.

244. . . . know the reason why: *NY Tribune*, 23 June 1920, p. 2; *Chicago Tribune*, June 28, 1920, p. 3; J. M. Cox, pp. 227–228.

244. Cox received a jolt the day . . . ran nationwide, and clearly stung: *Atlanta Constitution*, 28 June 1920, p. 1; *NY Times*, 28 June 1920, p. 5; *Syracuse Herald*, 28 June 1920, p. 37; *Dayton Journal*, 28 June 1920, p. 1; *NY Tribune*, 29 June 1920, p. 2.

245. ". . . didn't burst at any rate, it began": *NY Tribune*, 29 June 1920, p. 3.

245. Broun: *NY Tribune*, 29 June 1920, pp. 1, 3.

245. "The demonstration for . . . like a waste of time. . . .": *NY Tribune*, 29 June 1920, p. 2.

245. "FDR/Lunn altercation; ": *NY Times*, 29 June 1920, pp. 1–2; *LA Times*, 29 June 1920, p. 4; *Washington Post*, 29 June 1920, p. 3; *Chicago Tribune*, 29 June 1920, p. 1; *NY Tribune*, 29 June 1920, pp. 1–2; *Schenectady Union-Star*, 29 June 1920, p. 5; Beasley and Smith, p. 209; Eaton, pp. 283–284; Freidel (*The Ordeal*), pp. 62–63; G. Smith, pp. 162–163; C. Black, p. 121; Ward, p. 496.

When Eleanor learned of the altercation, she wrote her husband: "You & Tammany don't seem to agree very well. Mama is very proud of your removing the state standard from them. I have a feeling you enjoyed it, but won't they be very much against you in the State Convention?"

Historian Geoff Ward notes that with each telling, FDR's account of the battle grew more harrowing, with fewer partisans on his side and greater hordes swelling the enemy camp.

245. Cummings: *Chicago Tribune*, 29 June 1920, p. 2; *NY Tribune*, 30 June 1920, p. 3; *Boston Globe*, 4 July 1920, p. 33; *The Outlook*, 28 July 1920, pp. 563–564; Fleming, p. 458.

245. "It did not seem . . . the first hour and a half.": *NY Tribune*, 30 June 1920, p. 3.

246. Betting odds: *NY Tribune*, 29 June 1920, p. 1.

246. . . . the candidates are all Americans: *NY Tribune*, 24 June 1920, p. 4.

246. . . . ratified by the convention as a whole: *Schenectady Union-Star*, 28 June 1920, p. 1; *Schenectady Union-Star*, 29 June 1920, p. 1; *Schenectady Union-Star*, 30 June 1920, pp. 1, 2; *Chicago Tribune*, 29 June 1920, p. 1; *NY Times*, 30 June 1920, pp. 1–2; *Washington*

*Post*, 30 June 1920, p. 5; *NY Times*, 2 July 1920, pp. 1–2; Freidel (*The Ordeal*), p. 62. Seabury is best remembered for his role in removing New York Mayor James J. Walker from office.

246. ". . . right to drink all I want": *Washington Post*, 1 July 1920, p. 6.

247. On Wednesday, June 30, betting . . . with McAdoo second: Stein, p. 247.

247. ". . . Wilson convention in spirit and purpose": Stein, p. 247; Levin, p. 451.

247. . . . New Jersey Governor Edwards: *Chicago Tribune*, 1 July 1920, pp. 1–2; *NY Times*, 1 July 1920, pp. 1–2; Eaton, p. 284.

248. . . . some people do have it: *Syracuse Herald*, 28 June 1920, p. 37. Catholics might not yet be nominated, but they could marry into a candidate's family. Cox's son-in-law, Daniel J. Mahoney, was Catholic, as were Florence Harding's brother, Vetallis "Tal" Kling and his wife Nona. (*LA Times*, 7 July 1920, p. 16; Anthony [*Florence Harding*], p. 220.)

248. "exalted bouncer of a boxing pavilion": White (*Masks*), p. 469.

248. ". . . in a hotel room": *LA Times*, 1 July 1920, p. 13; *Chicago Tribune*, 7 July 1920, p. 3; Warner and Daniel, pp. 123–125; Miller, p. 168; Freidel (*The Ordeal*), pp. 63–64; Ward, p. 509.

248. "one of the stars of the show": Perkins, p. 27.

249. Of course, not everyone agreed . . . seemed to be, well, contrarian: Rodgers, p. 233.

249. . . . demonstration "was the real thing": *Chicago Tribune*, 1 July 1920, pp. 1–2; *LA Times*, 1 July 1920, p. 13; *Washington Post*, 1 July 1920, p. 6; *Chicago Tribune*, 2 July 1920, p. 3; *Schenectady Gazette*, 1 July 1920, p. 1; Sullivan (VI), pp. 490–492; Coffey, pp. 38–39; Finan, pp. 152–153; Slayton, pp. 146–148.

249. "By the end of the first half hour . . . war veteran from Ohio": Ward, p. 508.

249. ". . . assailed from any direction": *Chicago Tribune*, 1 July 1920, p. 2. Rainey became Speaker of the House in 1933 but dropped dead the following year.

249. . . . Francis B. Harrison: *NY Times*, 2 July 1920, pp. 1–2; *Washington Post*, 2 July 1920, p. 3. Davis became the 1924 Democratic nomination. He later argued the losing side of *Brown v. Board of Education*. Harrison, a former Tammany congressman, had authored the nation's first narcotics control legislation, the 1914 Harrison Act.

249. . . . defraud the federal government: *Sandusky Star-Journal*, 23 June 1920, p. 10; Weiss, pp. 62–63.

250. . . . Cook County Democratic Party: *Chicago Tribune*, 9 August 1928, pp. 1, 8; *NY Times*, 9 August 1928, p. 19; *Washington Post*, 9 August 1928, p. 4.

250. . . . to the United States Senate: *NY Times*, 7 March 1929, p. 18; *Washington Post*, 7 March 1929, p. 5; *LA Times*, 7 March 1929, p. 3. Taggart was the rarest of Irish-born bosses: he was *not* a Catholic (he was Episcopalian). Ralston is best remembered for being elected to the Senate in 1922—with Klan support. (Chalmers, p. 167.)

250. . . . Cox, Palmer, and Edwards at 3–1: *NY Times*, 2 July 1920, p. 2.

250. . . . roared back, and a near riot ensued: *NY Times*, 2 July 1920, p. 3.

251. . . . It failed, 929-1/2 to 185-1/2: *Chicago Tribune*, 29 June 1920, p. 6; *Atlanta Constitution*, 2 July 1920, p. 1; *NY Tribune*, 3 July 1920, p. 3; *Atlanta Constitution*, 3 July 1920, p. 1; *LA Times*, 3 July 1920, pp. 1–2; Coletta, pp. 128–130; Hibben, pp. 366–367; *Washington Post*, 4 July 1920, p. 6; Coffey, pp. 36–38; Eaton, p. 285.

   An Irish independence plank, sponsored by California oilman Doheny, also met defeat.

251. . . . "Told you so": *NY Tribune*, 3 July 1920, p. 3.

251. ". . . States to the League associates": *NY Tribune*, 3 July 1920, p. 4; Dunn and Kuehl, p. 7; Eaton, p. 284.

251. "colorless and unexplicit": *NY Tribune*, 14 July 1920, Part II, p. 1.

252. ". . . [Postmaster General] Burleson's mail boxes": *NY Tribune*, 3 July 1920, p. 3.

252. ". . . save them, it might be made": *NY Tribune*, 27 July 1920, p. 1; *NY Times*, 2 July 1920, p. 2. Roosevelt candidacies seemed never-ending in New York. The day before, TR's nephew, Theodore Douglas Robinson of Herkimer, declared his bid for an upstate Republican state senate nomination. (*NY Times*, 2 July 1920, p. 5.)

　　　　Lunn lost the September United States Senate primary to Lieutenant Governor Harry C. Walker.

253. . . . interested in taking Palmer: *NY Times*, 3 July 1920, p. 2; Stein, p. 247.

253. . . . worked his way into the administration: *NY Times*, 12 April 1950, p. 27; *Chicago Tribune*, 12 April 1950, p. A6; Greenbaum, pp. 153–154; Eaton, p. 256; Stein, p. 216; Weinstein, p. 366.

253. ". . . place your name in nomination": G. Smith, p. 163; Stein, p. 247; Eaton, p. 286; Weinstein, p. 367; Fleming, p. 459.

253. ". . . would mar his place in history": Fleming, p. 459; Levin, p. 452.

253. . . . important workings of the convention: G. Smith, p. 163; Levin, p. 453; Fleming, pp. 458–459.

253. . . . Colby later admitted, "like a criminal": G. Smith, p. 164; Stein, pp. 248–249; Levin, pp. 451–452; Fleming, p. 459; Eaton, p. 286.

254. ". . . tornado of masterful profanity": G. Smith, p. 164; Starling, p. 157.

254. . . . Senator Oscar W. Underwood 1/2: *Chicago Tribune*, 3 July 1920, pp. 1–2; *Atlanta Constitution*, 3 July 1920, pp. 1, 5; J. M. Cox, p. 230.

255. . . . increase their second-ballot support: *NY Tribune*, 4 July 1920, pp. 1, 3; *NY Tribune*, 7 July 1920, p. 2; *Chicago Tribune*, 3 July 1920, pp. 1–2; *Atlanta Constitution*, 3 July 1920, pp. 1, 5.

255. ". . . swing a bunch of votes to McAdoo": *NY Tribune*, 14 July 1920, p. 1; Freidel (*The Ordeal*), p. 64.

255. . . . plummeted from 30 votes to 2: *NY Tribune*, 4 July 1920, p. 3; *NY Tribune*, 7 July 1920, p. 2; *NY Times*, 6 July 1920, p. 1; Eaton, pp. 286–287.

255. Home on Long Island, McAdoo . . . and went to bed: *NY Tribune*, 4 July 1920, p. 1.

255. ". . . Palmer sinking to 201: *NY Tribune*, 4 July 1920, p. 3; *NY Times*, 6 July 1920, p. 1; Eaton, p. 287; J. M. Cox, p. 230.

255. ". . . *really* didn't like McAdoo: *Washington Post*, 5 July 1920, p. 6; Freidel (*The Ordeal*), p. 62; Morgan (*F.D.R.*), p. 225.

255. ". . . whether the three leaders are blocked": *NY Times*, 4 July 1920, p. 1. During the July 3 balloting, FDR periodically switched from McAdoo to Davis. Angling for senator, he wanted to curry favor with all sides. Rumors circulated of a Davis–Roosevelt ticket. (*NY Times*, 5 July 1920, p. 2; Freidel [*The Ordeal*], p. 61.)

255. . . . New York delegation as vice-presidential timber: *NY Tribune*, 7 July 1920, p. 2; *NY Times*, 4 July 1920, pp. 1, 3; *NY Tribune*, 4 July 1920, pp. 1, 3; *LA Times*, 4 July 1920, p. 2.

256. "McAdoo is dead as a pickerel": *Washington Post*, 4 July 1920, p. 6; *NY Times*, 5 July 1920, p. 1; M. Lyons, pp. 143–144; Chace, pp. 191–192.

256. . . . little interest in the proposition: *Chicago Tribune*, 5 July 1920, p. 1; *NY Times*, 5 July 1920, p. 3.

256. . . . White never got back to him: Butler (Vol. II), p. 327.

256. . . . listless trench warfare: *NY Tribune*, 7 July 1920, p. 2; *NY Times*, 6 July 1920, pp. 1, 3.

256. . . . but for his boss, Josephus Daniels: *NY Tribune*, 7 July 1920, p. 2; *NY Times*, 6 July 1920, p. 3; J. M. Cox, p. 230.

256. . . . hovered dangerously close to free-fall: *NY Times*, 6 July 1920, p. 1.

257. . . . The Fighting Quaker kept fighting: *NY Tribune*, 7 July 1920, p. 2; *NY Times*, 6 July 1920, pp. 1, 3; Coben, p. 261.

257. . . . nominee haunted the convention: *NY Tribune*, 7 July 1920, p. 2; *NY Times*, 6 July 1920, pp. 1, 5; Eaton, pp. 288–289; Coben, p. 261; J. M. Cox, pp. 230–231.

257. . . . ignored him and kept voting: *NY Times*, 6 July 1920, p. 5; *NY Tribune*, 6 July 1920, pp. 3, 5; *NY Tribune*, 7 July 1920, pp. 1, 2, 3; *NY Tribune*, 6 July 1920, p. 3; *NY Tribune*, 7 July 1920, pp. 1, 3; *NY Times*, 7 July 1920, p. 2; *Schenectady Union-Star*, 7 July 1920, p. 1; Eaton, p. 289; Freidel (*The Ordeal*), pp. 64–65; J. M. Cox, pp. 231–232.

257. . . . just 26-1/2 votes from victory: *Chicago Tribune*, 7 July 1920, p. 1.

257. ". . . until it comes back to me": *NY Tribune*, 7 July 1920, p. 1; *Chicago Tribune*, 7 July 1920, p. 4; Sullivan (VI), p. 126; Hibben, p. 366.

258. ". . . we won't nominate Roosevelt if he objects": Morgan (*F.D.R.*), p. 226; Miller, pp. 168–169.

258. "Do you know him?": *NY Times*, 7 July 1920, p. 3; J. M. Cox, p. 32.

259. . . . I tell you. He's a troublemaker": *Chicago Tribune*, 7 July 1920, pp. 1–2; LaCerra, pp. 56–58.

259. ". . . first ballot as soon as we assemble": J. M. Cox, p. 232; Weiss, p. 72; Morgan (*F.D.R.*), p. 226; Lash, p. 251.

259. ". . . down my throat": Walsh, p. 6; Weiss, p. 67; Pietrusza (*Rothstein*), p. 142.

259. ". . . I have five children": *LA Times*, 7 July 1920, p. 3; Freidel (*The Ordeal*), p. 67 *fn.*

259. . . . the man to balance the ticket: Freidel (*The Ordeal*), pp. 61, 66; Elliott Roosevelt and Brough (*Hyde Park*), pp. 36, 67; Ward, p. 510; Fleming, p. 460.

260. . . . by the name of W. T. Vaughan: *NY Tribune*, 7 July 1920, p. 2; *NY Times*, 7 July 1920, pp. 1–2; *Atlanta Constitution*, 7 July 1920, pp. 1–2; Eaton, p. 289.

260. . . . "No," advised Ansberry, "I'd leave the hall": Freidel (*The Ordeal*), pp. 67–68; Miller, p. 169.

260. . . . Roosevelt for Vice President: *NY Times*, 7 July 1920, pp. 1–2; *NY Tribune*, 7 July 1920, p. 1; C. Black, p. 124.

260. . . . the *New Mexico*—to dine: *NY Times*, 7 July 1920, p. 2; *Atlanta Constitution*, 7 July 1920, pp. 1–2; C. Black, p. 124.

261. . . . JOSEPHUS DANIELS: Eleanor Roosevelt, p. 107; Elliott Roosevelt and Brough (*Hyde Park*), p. 115.

261. "I was glad for my husband . . . be much excited": Eleanor Roosevelt, p. 107.

261. ". . . contempt in a national convention": *World's Work*, September 1920, p. 426; Weiss, p. 72.

261. "While it is true that Cox . . . no conferences in closed rooms": Stone, p. 28.

**CHAPTER 16**

262. ". . . nearly killed me.": Debs, p. 43; Young, pp. 263–264; Madison, p. 487.

262. . . . ban discrimination against blacks: Young, pp. 299–308: Ginger, pp. 42–44; Wayne, pp. 3–4; Madison, pp. 488–489.

263. ". . . but an unusual marriage": Young, pp. 315–316; Ginger, pp. 43–44; Chace, pp. 73–74, 88–89.
263. "employees born of white parents,": http://www.museum.state.il.us/exhibits/athome/1850/voices/curtis/aru.htm.
263. We indulge in none of the current . . . in their schemes of piracy: Wayne, p. 5.
263. "The paternalism of Pullman . . . avert slavery and degradation": Wayne, p. 7.
264. ". . . but of the country at large": *Chicago Tribune*, 13 July 1894, pp. 1, 11.
264. ". . . conspicuous member of his generation": *Washington Post*, 19 December 1894, p. 4.
264. . . . Woodstock jail in June 1895: *In Re Debs, Petitioner*, 158 U.S. 564 (1895).
264. . . . "Cucumber" Debs: *Mansfield News*, 12 June 1895, p. 1; *Washington Post*, 14 September 1895, p. 6; *Fort Wayne Weekly Gazette*, 14 May 1896, p. 12; Ginger, pp. 164–177; Coleman, pp. 161–170; Wayne, p. 11; Morais and Cahn, pp. 50–51; Chace, pp. 80–81.
264. ". . . and splintered at a single stroke": Debs, p. 46.
265. More than 100,000 people blocked . . . them is good enough for me: Coleman, p. 170; Chace, pp. 81–82; Madison, p. 493.
265. ". . . and I am ashamed to admit it": Coleman, p. 152.
265. ". . . on the eve of universal change": *Chicago Tribune*, 1 January 1897, p. 5; Madison, p. 495; Morais and Cahn, p. 56; Chace, p. 85.
265. ". . . Socialist Labor total (39,739 votes): *Washington Post*, 10 March 1900, p. 9; Coleman, pp. 200–211; Chace, p. 86; Kane, p. 167.
266. ". . . lawyers, scribes, priests, or other parasites.": http://www.marxists.org/history/usa/parties/spusa/1914/0300-debs-jesussupreme.pdf; Ginger, pp. 372–373.
266. ". . . for they shall not be disappointed": Coleman, p. 273; Wayne, p. 155.
266. . . . plummeted to 585,113, just 3.2 percent of the vote: *NY Times*, 5 November 1916, p. 3.
267. . . . Party membership dropped to 83,284: Niven, p. 285; Pietrusza (*Judge and Jury*), pp. 138–139.
267. . . . ratified by party referendum, 21,000 to 350: Leuchtenburg, p. 43; Pfannestiel, p. 8; Coleman, pp. 275–278.
267. "mere brood sows": *Washington Post*, 15 December 1917, p. 4; *Washington Post*, 3 February 1920, p. 2; *Chicago Tribune*, 14 May 1920, p. 6; *LA Times*, 14 May 1920, p. 15; *NY Times*, 30 May 1920, p. 3; *NY Call*, 1 June 1920, p. 2.
267. . . . Not surprisingly, they found plenty: *LA Times*, 6 September 1917, pp. 1, 5; Wayne, p. 157; Pietrusza (*Judge and Jury*), pp. 138, 141.
267. . . . Dayton, 44 percent: *NY Times*, 7 November 1917, p. 2; *NY Times*, 8 November 1917, p. 5; Jackson, p. 738; Leuchtenburg, pp. 43–44.
267. "I have no country to fight for . . . I am a citizen of the world": Madison, p. 500.
268. "Tell those cowards to keep well away . . . I will shoot him dead": Coleman, p. 280.
268. . . . and the brotherhood of all mankind: Debs, pp. 417–433; Coleman, pp. 284–287; Boyer and Morais, p. 200; Madison, pp. 502–503; Wayne, p. 162.
268. . . . $10,000 fine for each count: *Atlanta Constitution*, 1 July 1918, pp. 1, 6.
269. . . . He decided not to run: *NY Times*, 1 July 1918, pp. 1, 6; *Atlanta Constitution*, 1 July 1918, p. 1; *Washington Post*, 1 July 1918, p. 1; Wayne, pp. 162–163.
269. "Let's see, you rest, we rest": Ginger, p. 368.
269. . . . before he wrote out his address: Ginger, pp. 373–374. Debs's early biographer McAlister Coleman downplayed Debs's drinking but could not ignore it, admitting

that among certain "neurotic professional uplifters" it assumed "legendary proportions." Debs's foremost biographer, Ray Ginger, notes that "Debs's friends had long
noticed that liquor made him even more eloquent, more sensitive, more gentle—and
it was true." (Coleman, p. 174.)

269. ". . . as he spoke, I would believe it": Ginger, p. 377.

270. . . . joy cometh with the morning: Boyer and Morais, p. 201; http://www.edchange.org/
multicultural/speeches/eugene_debs_sedition.html.

271. Debs's voice is now stilled . . . It is a question of national safety: Coleman, p. 298.

271. . . . the Commonwealth of Comrades: Ginger, p. 383.

271. . . . months he had spent in Woodstock: *Debs v. United States*, 249 U.S. 211 (1919);
*Chicago Tribune*, 11 March 1919, p. 7.

272. ". . . spirit untamed, my soul unconquerable": Wayne, p. 164; Madison, p. 504.

272. ". . . day of the People has arrived!'": *Chicago Tribune*, 14 April 1919, p. 1; Coleman, p.
301; Wayne, p. 167; Murray (*Red Scare*), pp. 25–26.

272. ". . . never thinking of himself": Coleman, pp. 304–305; Ginger, p. 389.

272. . . . for medicinal purposes, of course: Socialists repaid Zerbst by flaying him as a
"sneak" and a "liar" at the May 1920 convention. (*NY Call*, 13 May 1920, p. 2.)

272. . . . Debs had declared his candidacy: *Washington Post*, 3 February 1920, p. 2.

272. . . . support for president: *Chicago Tribune*, 14 February 1920, p. 8; *Atlanta Constitution*,
1 April 1920, p. 1; http://www.lib.uiowa.edu/spec-coll/Bai/johnson2.htm.

273. . . . They lost, 74–57: *LA Times*, 13 May, 1920, p. 6; *Frederick Post*, 14 May 1920, p. 1;
*Kennebec Journal*, 14 May 1920, p. 1.

273. . . . The plank lost: *NY Call*, 13 May 1920, p. 2; *LA Times*, 13 May 1920, p. 6; *Oshkosh
Northwestern*, 13 May 1920, p. 1; *Kennebec Journal*, 14 May 1920, p. 1.

273. . . . recall of Federal executives and judges: *NY Call*, 14 May 1920, p. 1.

274. ". . . Debs, the nation's most noted citizen": *NY Call*, 14 May 1920, p. 1.

274. ". . . movement of the working class": *NY Call*, 14 May 1920, pp. 1–2.

274. "so many of us not in jail?": *NY Call*, 14 May 1920, p. 2; *Chicago Tribune*, 14 May 1920,
p. 6; *LA Times*, 14 May 1920, p. 15.

275. "Three cheers for Soviet Russia": *Bridgeport Telegram*, 14 May 1920, p. 11; *Atlanta Constitution*, 14 May 1920, p. 3; Coleman, pp. 316–317; Wayne, pp. 171–174.

275. . . . and declined the honor: *NY Times*, 12 March 1916, p. 14; *NY Call*, 11 May 1920,
p. 1; *LA Times*, 13 May 1920, p. 6; *NY Times*, 17 March 1944, p. 17.

275. . . . Seymour's nomination unanimous: *NY Call*, 14 May 1920, pp. 2, 5; *Syracuse Herald*,
14 May 1920, p. 4; *Chicago Tribune*, 10 July 1948, p. 8.

275. . . . between two and three million votes: *Syracuse Herald*, 14 May 1920, p. 4.

275. . . . an I AM FOR DEBS button: *NY Call*, 16 May 1920, pp. 1–2; *Lincoln Evening State
Journal*, 10 July 1920, p. 3; *Washington Post*, 1 July 1920, p. 6.

276. . . . imprisonment in the eyes of the public: *Atlanta Constitution*, 28 May 1920, p. 1.

276. . . . half hour to re-shoot the events: *NY Call*, 30 May 1920, pp. 1, 3; *NY Times*, 30 May
1920, p. 1; *Atlanta Constitution*, 30 May 1920, pp. 1, 3; Coleman, p. 317; Wayne, pp.
176–177.

276. ". . . power to emancipate the working class": *NY Call*, 30 May 1920, p. 3; *Atlanta Constitution*, 30 May 1920, pp. 1, 3; Ginger, p. 307; Morais and Cahn, pp. 113–114.

277. ". . . They are as honest as we are": *NY Call*, 30 May 1920, p. 3; *NY Times*, 30 May 1920,
p. 3; Morais and Cahn, p. 114.

277. ". . . were fighting for in Russia": *Mansfield News*, 30 May 1920, p. 1.

277. ". . . should support it with all our power": *NY Times*, 30 May 1920, p. 3; *Atlanta Constitution*, 30 May 1920, p. 1; *Washington Post*, 30 May 1920, p. 3; *LA Times*, 30 May 1920, p. 3; *Chicago Tribune*, 30 May 1920, p. 8.

277. ". . . far as Wilson was concerned: *NY Call*, 30 May 1920, p. 1; *NY Times*, 30 May 1920, p. 3; *Atlanta Constitution*, 30 May 1920, p. 1A; *Washington Post*, 30 May 1930, p. 1.

277. ". . . pardoned during my administration: Tumulty, p. 505; Coleman, p. 311; Noggle, p. 113; Davis, pp. 602–603; Ginger, p. 405; Madison, pp. 504–505.

278. . . . repudiated as Woodrow Wilson: Ginger, p. 406.

278. ". . . ruined the creases in their trousers": *Chicago Tribune*, 14 June 1920, p. 10.

279. ". . . manages somehow to cheer the patients up": Boylan, p. 41.

279. . . . another man—even in self defense: Boylan, p. 43.

279. ". . . Socialist Party to the polls this year" : Wayne, p. 174.

279. ". . . can always locate me": Wayne, p. 176.

279. ". . . The whole performance is artificial": Wayne, p. 182.

280. . . . Christensen all signed. It did no good: *Atlanta Constitution*, 25 September 1920, p. 1.

280. ". . . I have the perfect alibi": *Atlanta Constitution*, 25 September 1920, p. 1.

280. . . . the arrests and the government harassment: Wayne, pp. 183–184.

280. ". . . when the national convention met": *NY Call*, 6 November 1920, p. 10.

280. . . . they cared little for his personal plight: Wayne, pp. 186–187; Ginger, p. 406; *NY Times*, 5 October 1920, p. 7.

280. ". . . in his dungeon in Atlanta": Wayne, p. 248 *fn.*; *NY Times*, 23 November 1932, p. 19.

281. . . . Socialist congressmen and thirteen assemblymen: *Winona Republican-Herald*, 26 October 1920, p. 1; *NY Times*, 31 October 1920, p. E3; Wayne, p. 188.

281. "In my maturer years, I no longer . . . vote that way on election day": Ginger, p. 404.

**CHAPTER 17**

282. . . . Wall Street sharpies laid 1–3 odds that he would: *NY Tribune*, 25 June 1920, p. 2.

282. ". . . and Democrats have been reactionary": *New Republic*, 30 June 1920, p. 141.

283. . . . radicals by his defense of local IWW members: *Chicago Tribune*, 15 July 1920, p. 2; *New Republic*, 4 August 1920, p. 273; *Current Opinion*, September 1920, pp. 322–323; http://www.marxists.org/archive/cannon/works/1925/questions.htm.

283. ". . . were skilled in Marxian tactics": Fine, pp. 378–383; La Follette, pp. 67–68.

284. . . . would be among those convening in Chicago: *Atlanta Constitution*, 7 January 1920, p. 13; *Chicago Tribune*, 15 March 1920, p. 17; *Atlanta Constitution*, 6 April 1920, p. 1; *Washington Post*, 14 May 1920, p. 1; Older, p. 429; Swanberg, p. 333.

284. ". . . his own people at home": *Chicago Tribune*, 20 June 1920, p. 5; *LA Times*, 20 June 1920, p. 2; *Atlanta Constitution*, 21 June 1920, p. 1.

284. . . . Private Soldiers and Sailors League: *NY Times*, 4 July 1920, p. 73; *Chicago Tribune*, 10 July 1920, p. 1; *NY Times*, 10 July 1920, pp. 1–2; *NY Tribune*, 12 July 1920, pp. 1, 3; *NY Tribune*, 14 July 1920, p. 1; *Atlanta Constitution*, 14 July 1920, p. 1; R. Schmidt, pp. 109–115.

284. "never heard of him": *Chicago Tribune*, 10 July 1920, pp. 1–2; *Boston Globe*, 12 July 1920, p. 7.

285. . . . gathering pretty much fell apart: *LA Times*, 10 July 1920, p. 1.

285. ". . . own control out of unworthy hands": *NY Times*, 11 July 1920, p. 2.

285. . . . himself "not available": *NY Times*, 10 July 1920, p. 2; *NY Times*, 11 July 1920, p. 1.

285. Finally, so did La Follette: *Atlanta Constitution*, 1 April 1920, p. 1; *NY Tribune*, 14 July 1920, p. 1; *NY Tribune*, 14 July 1920, pp. 1, 3; *NY Tribune*, 15 July 1920, pp. 1, 4; *NY Tribune*, 17 July 1920, pp. 1, 3; *Coshocton Tribune*, 15 July 1920, p. 4; *New Republic*, 28 July 1920, p. 247; Fine, pp. 392–393.

285. ". . . spirit of self-assertiveness among negroes": *Atlanta Constitution*, 14 July 1920, p. 2.

286. . . . the country was actually invaded: *NY Times*, 11 May 1920, p. 1; *The Nation*, 27 October 1920, pp. 476–478; Brooks, pp. 117–119; Fine, p. 391.

286. . . . between the new party and La Follette: *Chicago Tribune*, 15 July 1920, p. 1; *Boston Globe*, 15 July 1920, p. 1; *NY Times*, 15 July 1920, p. 3.

286. ". . . labor does not see its destiny through a glass of light wine.": *NY Tribune*, 14 July 1920, p. 3.

286. ". . . workingman that has ever happened": *NY Tribune*, 16 July 1920, p. 4; *Current Opinion*, September 1920, p. 323.

287. Nominations/First ballot: *Boston Globe*, 15 July 1920, p. 1; *Chicago Tribune*, 15 July 1920, p. 1; *NY Times*, 15 July 1920, pp. 1, 3; *NY Times*, 13 November 1951, p. 29; *Coshocton Tribune*, 15 July 1920, p. 4; *Sandusky Star-Journal*, 15 July 1920, pp. 1–2; Fine, pp. 393–394; Kane, p. 196.

287. . . . Christensen, 192-1/2 to 174-3/5: *Sandusky Star-Journal*, 15 July 1920, pp. 1–2.

287. . . . reduced to a slate of complete unknowns: *Coshocton Tribune*, 15 July 1920, p. 4; *NY Times*, 16 July 1920, p. 14.

288. ". . . contaminating influence of that bunch": *Lima News*, 14 July 1920, p. 1; *Cook County Herald*, 16 July 1920, p. 3; *Oshkosh Daily Northwestern*, 14 July 1920, p. 8; *Kingsport Times*, 6 August 1920, p. 4; Brooks, p. 117.

288. . . . own state tickets. They didn't: *Chicago Tribune*, 15 July 1920, p. 1; *NY Times*, 16 July 1920, p. 14.

288. ". . . a liberal party is not worth a damn": *Chicago Tribune*, 15 July 1920, p. 1; *NY Times*, 15 July 1920, p. 3.

288. ". . . through the fanaticism of the [radical] faction": *NY Times*, 16 July 1920, p. 14; R. Schmidt, pp. 224–227.

288. ". . . I am not in your way": *Coshocton Tribune*, 15 July 1920, p. 1.

288. ". . . Wall Street to Washington": *NY Times*, 24 June 1920, p. 15; *Kennebec Journal*, 3 November 1920, p. 9.

288. ". . . considerable mirth throughout Utah": *Grand Valley Times*, 15 July 1920, p. 1.

289. ". . . had swung along on its course again": *Oneonta Star*, 21 July 1920, p. 4.

289. ". . . as in the last three days": *NY Tribune*, 17 July 1920, p. 3.

**CHAPTER 18**

291. . . . through a nasal tube twice daily: *NY Times*, 10 July 1977, p. 42; Stevens, pp. 13–18.

292. "Universal suffrage is at the foundation of every evil in this country": Levin, p. 181.

292. ". . . give the women the ballot now": Lawrence, pp. 136–137.

293. . . . 435 congressional districts present to greet it: *Chicago Tribune*, 4 March 1913, pp. 1–2; *LA Times*, 4 March 1913, p. 1; *NY Times*, 4 March 1913, pp. 2, 5; *Atlanta Constitution*, 4 March 1913, pp. 1, 7; *Washington Post*, 4 March 1913, pp. 1, 3; American Woman Suffrage Association, pp. 102–103; Stevens, pp. 21–23.

283. . . . renders them unfit for government: http://womenshistory.about.com/library/weekly/aa081700a.htm.

293. "action of the individual states": Levin, p. 182.

293. . . . most powerful man in America: Ross (*Power with Grace*), p. 314; Levin, p. 182; Stevens, p. 63.

293. ". . . of our women upon the Congress": Sinclair (*Emancipation*), p. 332.

294. . . . new one to display on the same spot: *NY Times*, 21 June 1917, pp. 1–2; Ross (*Power with Grace*), p. 313; Anthony (*First Ladies*), p. 359; Levin, p. 183.

294. . . . The pickets chose the workhouse: *Atlanta Constitution*, 15 July 1917, p. 4; *NY Times*, 20 July 1917, p. 1; Stevens, pp. 91–107; Lawrence, pp. 137–138; Clift, pp. 131–132.

295. ". . . conveniences and decencies of life": Slayden, p. 320; Levin, p. 184.

295. . . . were willing to undergo it: *NY Times*, 20 July 1917, p. 1.

295. . . . September 7, 1917, amazingly did just that: *Chicago Tribune*, 8 September 1917, p. 1; *Washington Post*, 8 September 1917, p. 2; Ross (*Power with Grace*), p. 315; Clift, p. 141. Sigmund Freud wrote of Malone in *Woodrow Wilson: A Psychological Study*.

295. . . . Doris and Dudley wed that December: *NY Times*, 10 December 1921, p. 4.

296. . . . establish a suffrage committee: Catt and Shuler, p. 318. Democrats voted 82–74 in favor; Republicans voted 96–32. Fifty-nine Democrats and 81 Republicans did not vote.

296. . . . and just 35.5 percent in Massachusetts: Catt and Shuler, pp. 292–293.

296. . . . the vicious of the great city?": Catt and Shuler, p. 282.

296. . . . the grave concerns of war": *NY Times*, 3 November 1917, p. 14.

296. . . . equal pay for New York's women teachers: Craig, p. 32.

296. . . . suffragettes to Oyster Bay to plot strategy: *Washington Post*, 6 August 1912, p. 2; *NY Times*, 7 September 1917, p. 9; *NY Times*, 9 September 1917, p. 8; Sinclair (*Emancipation*), pp. 324–325.

296. . . . The nation took notice: *NY Times* 7 November 1917, pp. 1, 3; *Chicago Tribune* 7 November 1917, p. 1; Malcolm (1918), p. 470; Catt and Shuler, pp. 297–298.

297. . . . Dudley Field Malone spoke in their honor: *Washington Post*, 28 November 1917, p. 2; *Atlanta Constitution*, 28 November 1917, p. 6; *Washington Post*, 2 December 1917, p. 34; *NY Times*, 10 December 1917, p. 13.

297. ". . . for every suffrage state": *Boston Globe*, 4 January 1918, p. 6; Wagenknecht (*Seven Worlds*), p. 88.

297. ". . . such ladies must be wholesome": Lawrence, p. 136.

297. . . . Republicans voted for it, 165–33: *Atlanta Constitution*, 10 January 1918, p. 1; *Chicago Tribune*, 11 January 1918, p. 1; American Woman Suffrage Association, p. 172.

298. . . . penalize the non-suffrage states: Constitutional precedent existed for reducing a state's representation. The so-called "3/5 rule" provided that for purposes of congressional representation, slaves (euphemistically designated as "all other Persons") counted as only 3/5 of a man. To modern ears, this sounds insulting, if not worse. In practical terms, it served to limit slaveholders' political power, and thus benefited the slave. Thus, paradoxically, slaves would have been far better off if not counted at all. The same would hold for women in non-suffrage states.

298. . . . and Frank Brandegee—voting no: *Atlanta Constitution*, 11 February 1919, p. 3; M. Lyons, p. 24. Previous Senate vote totals: 1887, 16–34; 1914, 35–34. Weeks chaired the intriguingly named Committee on the Disposition of Useless Executive Papers.

298. . . . Democrats voting 104–70: *Atlanta Constitution*, 22 May 1919, p. 1.

298. . . . member of Anthony's board of directors: *Chicago Tribune*, 5 June 1919, pp. 1, 4; *Atlanta Constitution*, 5 June 1919, pp. 1, 2. Again, Harding and Johnson voted for suffrage. Lodge, Penrose, and Brandegee again voted no. In 1920, Mrs. Upton became vice chairman of the Republican national committee.

299. . . . and place the southern Negro in power: *Atlanta Constitution*, 22 July 1919, p. 4.

299. . . . reject federal action on the matter: *Atlanta Constitution*, 25 July 1919, pp. 1–2; *NY Times*, 25 July 1919, p. 15.

299. . . . suffrage as a state legislator: *Fitchburg Daily Sentinel*, 26 June 1919, p. 3; Coolidge (*Autobiography*), p. 97.

299. . . . "an amazingly better world": *NY Times*, 13 January 1915, p. 1; *Washington Post*, 6 January 1920, p. 3; *NY Times*, 9 January 1920, p. 21; *Chicago Tribune* 15 January 1920, p. 10; *NY Times*, 22 March 1920, p. 3; *LA Times*, 22 March 1920, p. 11; *NY Times*, 4 April 1920, p. E6.

299. . . . addresses for virtually every candidate: *Chicago Tribune*, 8 August 1912, p. 2; *NY Times*, 27 June 1920, p. 2; Chace, pp. 167–168. Democrats featured 41 female delegates at large, 63 district delegates, and 204 alternates.

299. ". . . over the speaker's seat": *LA Times*, 12 June 1920, p. 1; Hutchinson, p. 460.

300. ". . . get anywhere with that stuff": *NY Times*, 12 June 1920, p. 3.

300. . . . BLOCK SUFFRAGE?: *Atlanta Constitution*, 13 June 1920, pp. 1A–2A, 6C.

300. ". . . ratification by the thirty-sixth state": *NY Times*, 13 June 1920, p. 3.

300. . . . female vice-presidential candidacy: *LA Times*, 1 July 1920, p. 13.

300. . . . without qualifications for such an office: *Chicago Tribune*, 12 June 1920, p. 2; *Chicago Tribune*, 3 July 1920, p. 3. Mrs. Olesen was the Democratic nominee for U.S. Senator in 1922. She finished third, with only 17.9 percent of the vote.

301. . . . barred women from the presidency or the vice-presidency: *Washington Post*, 20 June 1920, p. 2; *Atlanta Constitution*, 29 June 1920, p. 12; Kane, p. 193.

301. . . . female speakers to support the ticket: *Chicago Tribune*, 10 August 1920, p. 7.

301. "I was very noncommittal": Gustafson, Miller, and Perry, p. 100; Lash, pp. 126–127; B. Cook, p. 240. The NAOWS eventually became the anti-Bolshevik Woman Patriot Corporation. (Hapgood, p. 88.)

301. . . . possibly necessitating a second election: Catt and Shuler, pp. 371–372.

302. . . . Oklahoma ratified on February 27: *LA Times*, 26 February 1920, p. 17; *Atlanta Constitution*, 28 February 1920, p. 1; Catt and Shuler, p. 391; National American Woman Suffrage Association, p. 145; *American Heritage*, December 1978, p. 15.

302. . . . game was up, had switched his vote: *Washington Post*, 5 March 1920, p. 3; *Chicago Tribune*, 9 March 1920, p. 1; *NY Times*, 10 March 1920, p. 1; Catt and Shuler, pp. 393–394; *American Heritage*, December 1978, p. 15; http://www.polsci.wvu.edu/ipa/par/Vol_14_No_3_wom.html.

302. . . . possessed precedence on federal constitutional matters: *Hawke v. Smith*, No. 2, 253 U.S. 231 (1920); *NY Times*, 2 June 1920, p. 1; *Atlanta Constitution*, 2 June 1920, pp. 1, 5; Catt and Shuler, pp. 414–417; Wheeler, p. 247. Anti-Saloon League counsel Wayne B. Wheeler filed an *amici curiae* brief in support of the suffragettes.

303. . . . summon special sessions: *LA Times*, 7 June 1920, p. 17; *NY Times*, 10 June 1920, p. 4.

303. ". . . the women of the country": *NY Tribune*, 17 July 1920, p. 3.

303. . . . and Connecticut to act. They ignored him: *NY Times*, 22 June 1920, p. 2; *NY Times*,

23 June 1920, p. 3; *Chicago Tribune*, 23 June 1920, p. 2; *NY Times*, 2 July 1920, p. 3; *New Republic*, 7 July 1920, p. 165. Harding also received a delegation of Antis.

303. . . . It just wasn't his style: *NY Times*, 26 June 1920, p. 3.

303. . . . and 47 Socialist and Independent: Hays, p. 261.

304. I am exceedingly glad to learn . . . immediate favorable action: Catt and Shuler, p. 439.

305. . . . performance of a public service: Catt and Shuler, pp. 267, 443–444; Wheeler, pp. 260–261. The party vote in Tennessee was Democrats 55–34–1 in the House and 18–3 in the Senate, Republicans 15–12–2 in the House and 7–1 in the Senate. (*Boston Globe*, 19 August 1920, p. 1.)

305. Cox penned a similar murky epistle: *Mansfield News*, 19 August 1920, p. 1; *Gettysburg Times*, 20 August 1920, p. 3.

305. . . . predict rejection in both houses: *Decatur Review*, 8 August 1920, p. 1.

305. . . . comfortable 25–4 margin: *NY Times*, 14 August 1920, p. 1; Clift, p. 195.

306. . . . public eye to telegraph his support: *Kingsport Times*, 6 August 1920, p. 1; *Kingsport Times*, 10 August 1920, p. 1; *NY Times*, 12 August 1920, pp. 1, 3; *Oakland Tribune*, 15 August 1920, p. 15.

306. . . . galleries of Tennessee House: *NY Times*, 18 August 1920, p. 1; Catt and Shuler, p. 441; Wheeler, pp. 111–117, 214–242, 259; Clift, pp. 190–191. Delaware fought a similar "war of the roses," with the same color scheme: reds against, yellows for. (http://www.hsd.org/ Woman_SuffragistBattleinDE.htm)

306. ". . . 3rd. Race equality": *American Heritage*, December 1978, pp. 22–23.

306. . . . IN ORDER THAT IT BE PRESERVED": Wheeler, pp. 290–291.

307. . . . delay action until 1921: *NY Times*, 12 August 1920, p. 1; *Gastonia Daily Gazette*, 13 August 1920, p. 1; *NY Times*, 14 August 1920, p. 7; *Oakland Tribune*, 15 August 1920, p. 15; *NY Times*, 18 August 1920, p. 1; *Atlanta Constitution*, 18 August 1920, p. 1; Catt and Shuler, pp. 479–480.

307. ". . . the legislature was drunk!": Catt and Shuler, p. 442; National American Woman Suffrage Association, p. 151; Wheeler, p. 260.

307. . . . political expediency or harmony: *Chicago Tribune*, 14 August 1920, pp. 1, 5; *Atlanta Constitution*, 15 August 1920, pp. 1A, 5A.

307. "as clear as mud": *NY Times*, 14 August 1920, p. 3; *Atlanta Constitution*, 14 August 1920, p. 3.

307. . . . assigned him a bodyguard: *American Heritage*, December 1978, pp. 31–32; Wheeler, p. 119; Clift, pp. 196–198.

308. "Dear Son . . . Your Mother": *NY Times*, 19 August 1920, p. 1; *Charleston Daily Mail*, 31 August 1920, p. 6; National American Woman Suffrage Association, p. 152; *American Heritage*, December 1978, p. 32; Clift. p. 199.

308. ". . . and move to reconsider": *NY Times*, 19 August 1920, p. 1; Catt and Shuler, pp. 422–461; Wheeler, p. 265.

308. . . . wanted me to vote for ratification: Wheeler, p. 266; Clift. p. 202.

309. Woman was here to-day, claims . . . to get her out of my home: Wheeler, p. 266.

309. . . . what we both knew was right": *Charleston Daily Mail*, 31 August 1920, p. 6; *Frederick News*, 23 August 1995, p. A-18.

309. ". . . with a great principle": *NY Times*, 19 August 1920, p. 1.

309. ". . . rescue of civilization itself": *Mansfield News*, 19 August 1920, p. 1.

309. "I can only repeat that I am pleased": *Mansfield News*, 19 August 1920, p. 1; *Gettysburg Times*, 20 August 1920, p. 3.

309. "... what I know is right": *Mansfield News*, 19 August 1920, p. 1; *Gastonia Daily Gazette*, 20 August 1920, p. 1; *Charleston Daily Mail*, 31 August 1920, p. 6.

310. ... control suffrage. His plea failed: *Fairchild v. Hughes*, 258 U.S. 126; *Washington Post*, 26 August 1920, p. 1; Catt and Shuler, pp. 446, 455, 459; Wheeler, p. 273.

310. ... drifted away, until all had departed: *NY Times*, 27 August 1920, pp. 1, 3; *Chicago Tribune*, 27 August 1920, p. 5; *LA Times*, 27 August 1920, pp. 1–2.

310. "... than Woodrow Wilson": *NY Times*, 27 August 1920, pp. 1, 3.

**CHAPTER 19**

311. ... winning team than on a losing one: Bagby, p. 123; Downs, pp. 453–455.

312. ... had to beg him to remain: Morello, *passim*; Russell (*Blooming Grove*), p. 402; Cooper (*Pivotal Decades*), p. 370.

312. ... campaign was being born: *Chicago Tribune*, 6 July 1920, pp. 1, 6; *Washington Post*, 6 July 1920, p. 4; *Atlanta Constitution*, 6 July 1920, p. 16.

312. "... conditions for statesmanlike leadership": *New Republic*, 30 June 1920, p. 140; Dean, p. 67.

312. "... Government it appeals to me favorably": Garraty, p. 394. Wister (1860–1938),

313. "... Your Son, CALVIN COOLIDGE": Lathem (*Your Son, Calvin Coolidge*), p. 171.

313. In Northampton, Dwight Morrow proved ... something else to talk about: Fuess, p. 268.

313. "... the domination of any group or coterie": *Chicago Tribune*, 19 June 1920, p. 2; Downes, pp. 440–443.

313. "... some sort of yell of anguish": Watkins, p. 188; Downes, pp. 444–445.

314. "... efficiently than Warren G. Harding": *NY Tribune*, 23 June 1920, p. 2.

314. ... ambulances were motorized: Republican National Committee, *passim*.

315. ... Hays thought it a good omen: *LA Times*, 1 July 1920, p. 15; *Washington Post*, 1 July 1920, p. 2; McCoy, p. 123. Such breakfasts no doubt contributed to Harding's ill health. In front view, Harding looked fine. In profile, he looked positively Taftian. It's no wonder he dropped dead.

315. "... Americanism and acclaim America": *NY Times*, 25 February 1919, p. 2; *Chicago Tribune*, 25 February 1919, p. 1; *NY Tribune*, 29 June 1920, p. 3; *Chicago Tribune*, 30 June 1920, p. 5; *NY Times*, 30 June 1920, p. 8; *Schenectady Gazette*, 30 June 1920, p. 1; Wagenknecht (*American Profile*), p. 256.

315. "... come and deliver them himself": *Boston Globe*, 25 August 1920, p. 5.

316. ... day late. Coolidge had no comment: *Boston Globe*, 18 July 1920, p. E2; *LA Times*, 20 July 1920, p. 1; Coolidge (*Autobiography*), p. 151; Fuess, pp. 269–270; McCoy, p. 124.

316. ... ever seriously contemplated it: *NY Tribune*, 11 July 1920, p. 1; *Atlanta Constitution*, 11 July 1920, p. 6A.

316. "... and the loose-tongued": *NY Times*, 12 July 1920, p. 2.

316. "Please accept my sincere sympathy": *The Outlook*, 30 June 1920, p. 407; *Syracuse Herald*, 16 July 1920, p. 1; Fuess, p. 265.

317. "waspy malice": *Chicago Tribune*, 22 June 1920, p. 3; *Lancaster Daily Eagle*, 22 June 1920, p. 1; *NY Times*, 23 July 1920, pp. 1, 4; *LA Times*, 23 July 1920, p. 18; Sullivan (VI), p. 106; Adams, p. 173; Bagby, pp. 123–124.

317. "... associated with churches": *Chicago Tribune*, 22 June 1920, p. 3; *Lancaster Daily Eagle*, 22 June 1920, p. 1; *NY Times*, 23 July 1920, pp. 1, 4; *LA Times*, 23 July 1920, p. 18; *Literary Digest*, 31 July 1920, pp. 7–9; *Outlook*, 4 August 1920, pp. 593–594;

Hendrick, pp. 155–166; Sullivan (VI), p. 106; Dean, p. 70; Anthony (*First Ladies*), p. 382; Bagby, pp. 123–124.

317. ". . . when Mrs. Harding goes away": Russell (*Blooming Grove*), p. 401. Carrie Phillips's daughter Isabelle was 22 in 1920.

318. . . . owned and operated by Jim Phillips: White (*Masks*), p. 409; Russell (*Blooming Grove*), p. 401; Anthony (*Florence Harding*), p. 201.

318. . . . fry cakes to guests: *NY Tribune*, 28 June 1920, p. 4; McCoy, p. 124.

318. ". . . always more than kind to me": White (*Autobiography*), p. 591; White (*Puritan in Babylon*), p. 217 *fn*.

318. . . . Coolidge wanted it that way: *Boston Globe*, 28 July 1920, pp. 1, 9; *Kennebec Journal*, 28 July 1920, pp. 1–2; Hendrick, pp. 167–173; McCoy, pp. 124–126: Sobel, p. 202.

318. ". . . discussing those already declared": Coolidge (*Autobiography*), pp. 151–152.

318. ". . . nothing remarkable in it": *Syracuse Herald*, 28 July 1920, p. 8.

318. ". . . no business here—he is not wanted": Fuess, pp. 272–273.

319. . . . a gross misunderestimation: *Kennebec Journal*, 28 July 1920, p. 2; Lathem (*Your Son, Calvin Coolidge*), p. 170.

319. ". . . would be the first to admit": *Literary Digest*, 10 July 1920, p. 46.

319. I stood some distance back . . . not to notice her: Russell (*Blooming Grove*), pp. 401–402.

320. . . . actually dispensed remain unknown: *NY Times*, 10 July 1964, pp. 1, 27; *Chicago Tribune*, 10 July 1964, pp. 1–2; Russell (*Blooming Grove*), p. 402; Ferrell (*Strange Deaths of President Harding*), pp. 157–158, 185; Anthony (*Florence Harding*), pp. 201, 204, 210, 256; Anthony (*First Ladies*), p. 382. As Lasker was buying off Phillips, his reason-why advertising was trumpeting Harding's "beautiful and simple family life." (*McCall's Magazine*, October 1920, p. 45.)

320. ". . . man of the McKinley type": Hinshaw (*White*), p. 224; Downs, pp. 445–447.

320. ". . . open day and night until Nov. 2": *NY Times*, 12 July 1920, pp. 1–2; *NY Tribune*, 12 July 1920, p. 1.

320. . . . fixated on the League of Nations: Noggle, p. 196; Downs, pp. 468–469.

321. ". . . no time for photographs!": *Boston Globe*, 3 October 1920, pp. 1, 16; *Chicago Tribune*, 3 October 1920, p. 15; *NY Times*, 3 October 1920, p. 18; *Washington Post*, 4 October 1920, p. 4; *Washington Post*, 5 October 1920, p. 7; Fuess, p. 273; White (*Puritan in Babylon*), pp. 218–219; Sobel, pp. 203–204.

321. . . . overshadowed by a far larger event: *Washington Post*, 21 August 1920, p. 1.

322. . . . Mr. Harding, you're the man for us: *Chicago Tribune*, 22 August 1920, p. 4; *Boston Globe*, 25 August 1920, p. 5; *Washington Post*, 25 August 1920, p. 1; *LA Times*, 25 August 1920, p. 13; *Chicago Tribune*, 25 August 1920, p. 9; *Lancaster Eagle*, 25 August 1920, p. 1; *Atlanta Constitution*, 6 September 1920, p. 10; Adams, p. 171; Downes, pp. 470–471; Russell (*Blooming Grove*), pp. 406–407.

322. . . . land, the people and the flag: *Washington Post*, 25 August 1920, p. 1.

323. . . . him into the train when he left": *Atlanta Constitution*, 1 September 1920, p. 17; Anthony (*Florence Harding*), pp. 218–220.

323. ". . . to a new leadership": Dunn and Kuehl, pp. 5–6; Adams, p. 175.

323. ". . . worst forces in American public life": Dunn and Kuehl, p. 6; Spragens, p. 282; Bagby, p. 136.

323. ". . . both organizations": *NY Times*, 15 October 1920, pp. 1–2; Sullivan (VI), pp. 121–122; Adams, p. 176; Downes, pp. 574–578; Dunn and Kuehl, p. 9; Bagby, pp.

136–137, 140; Ferrell (*Woodrow Wilson*), p. 227. The Republican platform had, in fact, supported an "association" of nations.

324. The paramount issue in this . . . subject of the League: Sullivan (VI), pp. 122–123.

324. Taft announced he would now . . . White seemed pleased: Dunn and Kuehl, p. 10.

324. . . . might bolt the party: *NY Times*, 3 September 1920, p. 3; Bagby, p. 137.

324. ". . . and I favor staying out": *NY Times*, 8 October 1920, p. 1; *Atlanta Constitution*, 8 October 1920, pp. 1, 10; *Outlook*, 20 October 1920, p. 310; Bagby, p. 144; Dunn and Kuehl, p. 10; Russell (*Blooming Grove*), p. 411; Cooper (*Breaking the Heart of the World*), p. 392.

324. "in perfect accord" . . . "forthright stand": *Atlanta Constitution*, 17 October 1920, p. A2B; Bagby, p. 138.

324. ". . . and make peace alone": *Atlanta Constitution*, 19 September 1920, p. 1A; *Chicago Tribune*, 10 October 1920, p. 3; *Outlook*, 20 October 1920, p. 310; Best, p. 146.

324. . . . endorsing the Democratic ticket: *NY Times*, 19 September 1920, p. XX2; Dunn and Kuehl, pp. 10–11, 19; Bagby, p. 138.

325. . . . Stephens Institute of Technology: *NY Times*, 15 October 1920, pp. 1–2; *LA Times*, 15 October 1920, p. 1; *NY Times*, 20 October 1920, p. 2; *NY Times*, 27 October 1920, p. 2; Adams, pp. 176–177; Best, pp. 135–136; Dunn and Kuehl, pp. 13–16; Bagby, pp. 139–140; Adams, pp. 176–177; Ferrell (*Woodrow Wilson*), pp. 227–228; Cooper (*Breaking the Heart of the World*), pp. 393–394; Garraty, pp. 398–399; Russell (*Blooming Grove*), p. 411.

325. "They would sell their souls for success": *Atlanta Constitution*, 17 October 1920, p. A2B.

325. ". . . Harding is double-crossing?": *NY Times*, 27 October 1920, p. 2; Best, p. 140. FDR later (1939) appointed McLeish (1892–1982), a noted poet (Pulitzer Prize, 1933), to the positions of Librarian of Congress and then Assistant Director of the Office of War Information, World War II's equivalent of George Creel's Committee on Public Information.

325. . . . Harding for assurance, but couldn't: Dunn and Kuehl, p. 16.

325. . . . I believe Mr. Shortridge: *LA Times*, 2 November 1920, p. 6; *Gastonia Daily Gazette*, 2 November 1920, p. 1; *NY Times*, 3 November 1920, p. 22; *Atlanta Journal*, 3 November 1920, p. 7.

326. . . . campaigned for the ticket: Bagby, p. 125.

326. ". . . tribute to his special talents": Bagby, p. 141; Downes, p. 434.

326. . . . Michael Buda blew up Wall Street: *Decatur Review*, 19 September 1920, p. 1; *NY Times*, 25 September 1920, p. 11; Downes, pp. 477–482.

327. . . . had never dreamed of hitherto: Freidel (*Rendezvous with Destiny*), p. 523; Huthmacher, p. 22.

327. ". . . it's a rich man's sport": Downs, p. 473. FDR and Harding had once been golfing buddies. Roosevelt later wrote that their relationship "was really only a casual one, though it is true that I used to play golf with him on several occasions before he was nominated for the Presidency. After May, 1920, I never saw him again. As a golf companion he was always most agreeable and a good sport whether he won or lost." (Freidel [*The Ordeal*], p. 76 *fn.*)

327. ". . . team play of America!": *Washington Post*, 31 August 1920, p. 1; *Marion Star*, 2 September 1920, pp. 1–2; *Chicago Tribune*, 2 September 1920, p. 13; *The Sporting News*, 2 September 1920, p. 3; *Chicago Tribune*, 3 September 1920, pp. 2, 5; *Atlanta Constitution*,

3 September 1920, p. 11; *NY Times*, 3 September 1920, p. 3; Downs, pp. 473–474; Morello, pp. 56–59. The Cubs had previously been owned by William Howard Taft's older half-brother, Charles P. "Chubby Charlie" Taft.

328. . . . would have been a pose: Adams, pp. 172–173; Sullivan (VI), p. 103.

328. . . . numerous informal talks: *NY Times*, 8 September 1920, pp. 1–2; 9; *Chicago Tribune*, 9 September, p. 4; Sullivan (V), p. 544; Dean, p. 72.

329. ". . . do not lie in that direction": *Boston Globe*, 23 September 1920, p. 7; McCoy, p. 128; Fuess, p. 274; White (*Puritan in Babylon*), p. 218.

329. . . . trip of that kind: *Marion Star*, 9 October 1920, p. 1; Lathem (*Your Son, Calvin Coolidge*), p. 171; Fuess, p. 274; Sobel, p. 205.

329. ". . . better be at home doing my work": Sobel, p. 205.

329. . . . south of the Mason-Dixon Line: *Gastonia Daily Gazette*, 19 October 1920, p. 1; *Gastonia Daily Gazette*, 22 October 1920, p. 1; Fuess, p. 274.

330. . . . drowned for the foreseeable future: *NY Times*, 26 October 1920, p. 3; *NY Times*, 29 October 1920, pp. 1, 3; *LA Times*, 29 October 1920, pp. 1–2; *Providence Journal*, 29 October 1920, p. 2; *Dayton Journal*, 29 October 1920, pp. 1, 16; McCoy, p. 128; Bagby, p. 125. The same night, Grace Coolidge, clad in a "sou'wester and a raincoat" and carrying "the flag of the Commonwealth," led a Boston torchlight parade, the first time women had ever marched in a political parade in that city. (*Boston Globe*, 29 October 1920, pp. 1, 9.)

330. "the police would interfere on the grounds of cruelty": Leuchtenburg, p. 87.

## CHAPTER 20

331. ". . . The convention could not have made a better choice": *NY Times*, 7 July 1920, p. 9.

331. ". . . not to be found in our public life": *The Nation*, 17 July 1920, p. 57.

331. "When parties can pick a man like Frank . . . decent future in politics": C. Black, p. 124.

332. . . . /s/ Herbert Hoover: Carlin, Cole, Miller, and Walch, p. 8; Davis, p. 615; Freidel (*The Ordeal*), p. 69 *fn.*; C. Black, p. 124.

332. ". . . strong man is obvious": Garraty, p. 397; Freidel (*The Ordeal*), p. 71.

332. "man of mediocre ability and unimpeachable party regularity": Stone, p. 29.

332. ". . . the Democratic party into the hands of the reactionaries": Craig, p. 21.

332. . . . Harding was "a zero": Noggle, p. 189. Baker thought both vice-presidential candidates better than their running mates.

332. "They've picked the weakest one": Weinstein, p. 368.

333. On their return to Washington . . . to the end was Tumulty": I. Hoover, p. 107.

333. . . . chances in November, they didn't exist: *Atlanta Constitution*, 14 July 1920, p. 1; *NY Times*, 19 July 1920, p. 1; J. M. Cox, pp. 240–243; Tumulty, pp. 499–500; Freidel (*The Ordeal*), pp. 73–74; G. Smith, pp. 164–165; Ross (*Power with Grace*), p. 231; Cebula, p. 108; Levin, p. 453; C. Black, p. 125; Miller, p. 172; Freidel (*Rendezvous with Destiny*), pp. 38–39; Bagby, p. 127.

334. ". . . warship for commuting purposes": *NY Times*, 8 September 1920, p. 2; *Boston Globe*, 8 September 1920, p. 4; Freidel (*The Ordeal*), pp. 74–75. Roosevelt boasted that this was the fourth time he had steered a destroyer through to Campobello.

334. ". . . received any money yet": *NY Times*, 3 August 1920, p. 3; *Washington Post*, 3 August 1920, p. 1.

334. "deeply resentful": Daniels (*Cabinet Diaries*), p. 542; C. Black, p. 125.

334. . . . "beautiful home life": *NY Times*, 7 August 1920, p. 4; *Washington Post*, 7 August 1920, p. 2; Freidel (*The Ordeal*), pp. 75–76; Miller, p. 172; C. Black, pp. 97, 125–126.

335. . . . League—his campaign centerpiece: *Chicago Tribune*, 21 July 1920, p. 5; *NY Times*, 22 July 1920, p. 4; *Chicago Tribune*, 30 July 1920, p. 4; *Atlanta Constitution*, 31 July 1920, p. 1; Cebula, p. 109; Bagby, pp. 128, 134.

335. ". . . Cox or know the reason why": *NY Times*, 8 August 1920, p. 3; *Decatur Review*, 8 August 1920, p. 1.

335. . . . Cox refused: Wehle, p. 88; Morgan (*F.D.R.*), p. 227; C. Black, p. 126; Miller, pp. 171–172.

335. . . . "I never saw him better": *NY Times*, 8 August 1920, p. 3; Bagby, p. 128.

335. "straightforward, explicit, bold and clear": *NY Times*, 8 August 1920, p. 26.

335. The *Marion Star* called it undignified: *Chicago Tribune*, 8 August 1920, p. 1.

335. ". . . Democratic candidate[,] I favor going in": *NY Times*, 8 August 1920, p. 26; *LA Times*, 8 August 1920, p. 2; *Decatur Review*, 8 August 1920, p. 1; *Outlook*, 18 August 1920, p. 667; Sullivan (VI), p. 93.

336. ". . . mere period of coma in our national life": *NY Times*, 8 August 1920, p. 3; *NY Times*, 9 August 1920, p. 3; *Outlook*, 18 August 1920, p. 660; Eleanor Roosevelt, p. 108; Freidel (*The Ordeal*), pp. 77–78; Miller, p. 172; C. Black, p. 127.

336. ". . . surely vote-winning quality": Miller, p. 174; Elliott Roosevelt and Brough (*Hyde Park*), pp. 115–116.

336. ". . . in Mr. Roosevelt's speech": *Charleston Daily Mail*, 21 August 1920, p. 4.

336. ". . . no reference to W. W.": Daniels (*Cabinet Diaries*), p. 545; C. Black, p. 126.

337. DEAR OLD MAN, — This is . . . FRANKLIN K. LANE": F. Lane, pp. 351–352.

338. . . . Sara wrote checks totaling $3,000: Freidel (*The Ordeal*), pp. 78–79; Elliott Roosevelt and Brough (*Hyde Park*), pp. 119–121; C. Black, p. 127; Davis, p. 627; Miller, p. 174; J. Roosevelt, p. 105; Bagby, p. 129.

338. ". . . play cards instead": C. Black, p. 127.

338. ". . . range of subjects": Elliott Roosevelt and Brough (*Hyde Park*), pp. 122, 124–125; Miller, p. 175.

338. ". . . her home were concerned": Eleanor Roosevelt, p. 108.

338. . . . from the back of the hall: Eleanor Roosevelt, p. 108; Anthony (*First Ladies*), pp. 382–383.

338. ". . . have the brand of our family": *NY Times*, 5 August 1920, p. 3; *Chicago Tribune*, 13 August 1920, p. 6; *Atlanta Constitution*, 18 September 1920, p. 1; *NY Times*, 20 September 1920, p. 16; *Chicago Tribune*, 22 September 1920, p. 11; Elliott Roosevelt and Brough (*Hyde Park*), p. 125; Freidel (*The Ordeal*), pp. 71, 85; Stiles, p. 66; Miller, p. 170.

339. ". . . these little republics": Freidel (*The Ordeal*), p. 81; Morgan (*F.D.R.*), p. 215; Davis, p. 621; Miller, p. 176.

339. ". . . a pretty good Constitution": *NY Times*, 19 August 1920, p. 11; *Kingsport Times*, 20 August 1920, p. 9; *Chicago Tribune*, 26 August 1920, p. 3; *Providence Journal* 19 October 1920, p. 14; Freidel (*The Ordeal*), p. 81; Ward, p. 536; Davis, p. 621; Miller, p. 176.

339. ". . . the past seven years": Ferrell (*Woodrow Wilson*), p. 224; H. Schmidt, p. 111.

340. ". . . to secure a vote in the League": *NY Times*, 18 September 1920, p. 11; Freidel (*The Ordeal*), pp. 81–82; Stiles, p. 69; Ward, p. 536; Miller, p. 176; Freidel (*Rendezvous with Destiny*), p. 39; Davis, p. 621.

340. ". . . as they did the quotation": *NY Times*, 18 September 1920, p. 11; *NY Times*, 22

September 1920, p. 3; *Boston Globe*, 22 September 1920, p. 9; *Washington Post*, 22 September 1920, p. 1; *Providence Journal*, 19 October 1920, p. 14; Downes, p. 549.

340. ". . . heard him say it at the time": *Providence Journal*, 19 October 1920, p. 14.

341 . . . all essential particulars fair and correct: *Providence Journal*, 19 October 1920, p. 14; *Marion Star*, 20 October 1920, pp. 1, 7; *The Nation*, 6 October 1920, p. 364; Morgan (*F.D.R.*), pp. 230–231.

341. ". . . and all similar un-Americans": *Chicago Tribune*, 22 August 1920, p. 5; Freidel (*The Ordeal*), p. 84; Morgan (*F.D.R.*), p. 231; Davis, p. 620; Ward, p. 535.

341. "the Hiram Johnson of the East": *NY Times*, 25 August 1920, p. 4.

341. . . . and allegiance, they may well beware: *NY Times*, 23 September 1920, p. 4; *Atlanta Constitution*, 23 September 1920, p. 13.

342. . . . (some said ten) a day: *NY Times*, 10 October 1920, p. 3; *Providence Journal*, 10 October 1920, p. 2; Bagby, p. 129.

342. . . . "and mine's going to be one of them": Ferrell (*Woodrow Wilson*), p. 224.

342. ". . . vote for Cox and the League": Freidel (*The Ordeal*), p. 89 *fn.*; Morgan (*F.D.R.*), pp. 231–232.

342. . . . "He hasn't a friend": Freidel (*Rendezvous with Destiny*), p. 39; Farrell (*Woodrow Wilson*), p. 228.

342. ". . . were in town at the same time!": Stiles, pp. 69–70.

342. ". . . I yank at his coat-tails": Elliott Roosevelt and Brough (*Hyde Park*), p. 123.

342. ". . . and worshipped at his shrine": Eleanor Roosevelt, p. 108; Elliott Roosevelt and Brough (*Hyde Park*), p. 125.

343. . . . children was given to him: Morgan (*F.D.R.*), p. 228.

343. Eliot endorsed Cox: *NY Times*, 28 August 1920, p. 1; *NY Times*, 19 October 1920, p. 2.

343. " . . . against Cox because he is a divorced man": *LA Times*, 14 August 1920, p. 1.

343. ". . . push it if he should be elected": *Bedford (PA) Gazette*, 20 August 1920, p. 4; Watkins, p. 189.

344. . . . "Knight of the Raisin": *Chicago Tribune*, 3 September 1920, p. 2; *NY Times*, 3 September 1920, pp. 1–2; Sullivan (VI), p. 128; *Atlanta Constitution*, 7 September 1920, p. 3.

344. . . . with the Seventeenth [*sic*] Amendment": *Atlanta Constitution*, 8 September 1920, p. 10.

344. ". . . and become part of history": *NY Times*, 12 September 1920, p. 1.

344. . . . regardless of what interests may be affected: *NY Times*, 14 September 1920, p. 1; *Atlanta Constitution*, 14 September 1920, p. 1; *The Nation*, 6 October 1920, pp. 364–365.

344. . . . admitted that he would have . . .COX: "I would": *Atlanta Constitution*, 1 October 1920, pp. 1–2.

345. . . . "something of a blow": *Washington Post*, 22 August 1920, p. 7; *Atlanta Constitution*, 6 September 1920, p. 6; *NY Times*, 10 September 1920, p. 3; *Washington Post*, 11 September 1920, p. 11.

345. "I would read to him," his brother-in-law . . . in the text to call for it): Weinstein, p. 369.

345. . . . spending the cash on buying the election: *Chicago Tribune*, 21 August 1920, p. 5; *Outlook*, 1 September 1920, p. 5; *Outlook*, 10 November 1920, p. 447.

346. . . . which thus far has proved successful: *Outlook*, 1 September 1920, p. 5; Hays, p. 272.

346. ". . . ammunition is on hand, but it will not succeed": *NY Times*, 20 August 1920, p. 1; *Atlanta Constitution*, 20 August 1920, pp. 1, 14; *Washington Post*, 27 August 1920, p. 1; *Lancaster Daily Eagle*, 27 August 1920, p. 1; *Providence Journal*, 1 November 1920, p. 3; *World's Work*, November 1920, pp. 10–12; Bagby, pp. 132–133.

346. "attitude of elation": *Atlanta Constitution*, 25 August 1920, p. 2; *Atlanta Constitution*, 12 September 1920, p. 3A.

347. Chairman White did, but should . . . WHITE: "None whatever": *Atlanta Constitution*, 25 August 1920, p. 2; *Oshkosh Daily Northwestern*, 1 September 1920, p. 1; *Reno Evening Gazette*, 1 September 1920, pp. 1–2; *Washington Post*, 2 September 1920, p. 6; *The Outlook*, 15 September 1920, p. 85; Hays, p. 275.

347. . . . give dates when I could speak: Daniels (*Cabinet Diaries*), p. 557.

348. I hope these reports are inaccurate . . . driven from office long since: Watkins, p. 191.

348. ". . . best engineers in the country": *Atlanta Constitution*, 19 September 1920, p. 1A; Bagby, p. 129.

348. . . . & had them all docketed: Daniels (*Cabinet Diaries*), pp. 561–562.

348. . . . "in stimulating the registration of negro women": *Atlanta Constitution*, 14 October 1920, pp. 1, 9; *Winona Republican-Herald*, 25 October 1920, pp. 1, 14.

348. ". . . looks fine for the Democrats": *Gastonia Daily Gazette*, 27 October 1920, p. 1.

349. . . . denying he had criticized the AP: *Boston Globe*, 21 September 1920, p. 10; *Atlanta Constitution*, 22 September 1920, p. 10; *Chicago Tribune*, 22 September 1920, p. 7; *LA Times*, 2 October 1920, p. 5; *Atlanta Constitution*, 2 October 1920, p. 11; *Atlanta Constitution*, 3 October 1920, p. 13B; *NY Times*, 25 October 1920, p. 2; *Winona Republican-Herald*, 28 October 1920, p. 1; *Gastonia Daily Gazette*, 28 October 1920, p. 1.

349. . . . Barrymore, Cox attracted none: *LA Times*, 21 September 1920, p. II14; *Atlanta Constitution*, 22 September 1920, p. 1; *Chicago Tribune*, 22 September 1920, p. 7; *Oshkosh Daily Northwestern*, 22 September 1920, p. 9.

349. . . . not a yellow man's country: *Atlanta Constitution*, 22 September 1920, p. 1; *Boston Globe*, 22 September 1920, p. 9; *Washington Post*, 17 October 1920, p. 2.

350. . . . distinctly non-Wilsonian position: *Atlanta Constitution*, 19 October 1920, p. 1; Dunn and Kuehl, p. 8; Bagby, pp. 144–145.

350. . . . might take comfort in such support: *Atlanta Constitution*, 24 October 1920, p. 8A; *NY Times*, 24 October 1920, p. 7; Cooper (*Breaking the Heart of the World*), p. 389.

350. ". . . proposition so utterly absurd": *NY Times*, 15 October 1920, p. 2.

350. . . . addressed two million persons: Bagby, pp. 128–129.

350. ". . . solid, but less active": *Atlanta Constitution*, 12 September 1920, p. 3A.

350. ". . . farther toward Harding": Sullivan (VI), p. 130.

351. ". . . crashed and totaled their car: *NY Times*, 16 August 1920, pp. 1, 3; *Atlanta Constitution*, 16 August 1920, p. 1; *Kingsport Times*, 17 August 1920, p. 1; *Atlanta Constitution*, 13 September 1920, p. 1.

351. . . . calmly smoking his pipe: *Atlanta Constitution*, 23 September 1920, p. 1.

351. . . . could not hear his words: *NY Times*, 27 August 1920, p. 11; *NY Times*, 29 August 1920, p. 2; *LA Times*, 29August 1920, p. 13.

351. ". . . occupants were concerned": I. Hoover, p. 106.

351. ". . . Harding will be deluged": Ferrell (*Woodrow Wilson and World War I*), p. 229; G. Smith, p. 167; Weinstein, p. 193. Daniels wrote in his diary on October 12: "Cabinet. The Presdt thinks Cox will win." (Daniels [*Cabinet Diaries*], p. 563.)

351. ". . . This seems mighty unjust": F. Lane, p. 356; Farrell (*Woodrow Wilson*), pp. 228–229.

352. "if it were physically possible": Levin, pp. 455, 563.

352. . . . "nothing less than tragic": *NY Times*, 28 October 1920, p. 1; *Chicago Tribune*, 28

October 1920, pp. 1, 4; *Providence Journal*, 28 January 1920, p. 1; Wilson (*My Memoir*), p. 306; G. Smith, pp. 167–168; Levin, p. 456.

## CHAPTER 21

353. ". . . between white and colored men": McGerr, p. 191.

354. . . . essential to mutual progress: Washington, pp. 222–223. When Washington spoke in September 1895 at the Atlanta Cotton Exposition, Du Bois supported his ideas. (Du Bois [*Autobiography*], p. 209.)

354. ". . . Tuskegee school should burn down": McCartney, p. 66.

354. ". . . him in the White House": *Cleveland Advocate*, 25 January 1919, p. 1; Sullivan (III), pp. 133–142; McGerr, p. 195.

354. ". . . Blacks felt abandoned: Pringle (*Theodore Roosevelt*), pp. 459–464; Sullivan (III), pp. 453–454; Wagenknecht (*Seven Worlds of Theodore Roosevelt*), pp. 133–134, 233–236; Franklin, pp. 441–442; McGerr, p. 195; Cooper (*Warrior and the Priest*), p. 210.

355. . . . supported Woodrow Wilson in 1912: *Chicago Tribune*, 5 March 1909, p. 4; Weyl and Marina, p. 321; Du Bois (*Autobiography*), p. 264; Downes, p. 538.

355. ". . . since the Civil War": *North American Review*, December 1913, p. 800; Du Bois (*Autobiography*), p. 264.

355. ". . . if they wanted to return: *Chicago Tribune*, 13 November 1914, p. 13; *LA Times*, 13 November 1914, pp. 1, 4; *East North Central Daily Herald*, 15 November 1995, p. 12; Jordan, pp. 10–13; Booker, pp. 132–134; Franklin, p. 454; McGerr, p. 196; Cooper (*Warrior and the Priest*), pp. 273–274.

355. "We do not believe Woodrow Wilson admires Negroes": Weyl and Marina, p. 325.

355. ". . . whites found acceptable": *Washington Post*, 3 August 1912, p. 1; Eaton, p. 226; Franklin, p. 453.

356. . . . condition is best fitted for them: Foley, pp. 81–82, 268; http://www.marxists.org/history/usa/parties/spusa/1912/0325-ohare-niggerequality.pdf.

356. . . . peeping through a window: *Atlanta Constitution*, 1 January 1921, pp. 1, 6; *Washington Post*, 1 January 1921, p. 3; *NY Times*, 2 January 1921, p. E15; http://www.english.uiuc.edu/maps/poets/g_l/lynching/lynching.htm; http://www.yale.edu/ynhti/curriculum/units/1979/2/79.02.04.x.html#b.

356. . . . NEGRO GOP CHIEF USES IMAGINATION: *LA Times*, 9 July 1920, p. 7; *Atlanta Constitution*, 9 July 1920, p. 6; *Frederick Post*, 10 July 1920, p. 8.

357. . . . and 6.4 percent of Pittsburgh: U.S. Census Bureau, pp. 108, 110.

357. . . . served in his Marine Corps: Franklin, pp. 455–476; Du Bois (*Autobiography*), pp. 266–267.

357. . . . They fought bravely: *Dayton Forum*, 23 August 1918, p. 1; *Dayton Forum*, 4 October 1918, p. 1; *Ohio State Monitor*, 27 September 1919, p. 1.

357. ". . . quicker action had been taken to stop it": Freidel (*The Ordeal*), pp. 29–30; Morgan (*F.D.R.*), p. 214; R. Schmidt, pp. 67–68, 216–218. Wilson told Grayson "the American negro returning from abroad would be our greatest medium in conveying Bolshevism in America." (R. Schmidt, p. 180.)

358. ". . . among the constellation of nations": Franklin, p. 490.

358. ". . . and lynch him in Africa": http://www.pbs.org/wgbh/amex/garvey/filmmore/pt.html.

359. . . . was executed in June 1921: *Elyria Chronicle-Telegram*, 21 June 1920, pp. 1, 6; *Syracuse Herald*, 21 June 1920, pp. 1–2; *NY Tribune*, 22 June 1920, p. 4; *Syracuse Herald*, 29

June 1920, p. 19; *Chicago Tribune*, 22 June 1920, pp. 1, 4; *Chicago Tribune*, 14 January 1921, p. 1; *Chicago Tribune*, 22 June 1921, p. 6; *LA Times*, 25 June 1921, p. 6; Perrett, p. 239; Tuttle, pp. 256–257; McCartney, pp. 88–89.

359. . . . Norfolk and exploding its boiler: *Cincinnati Union*, 3 January 1920, p. 1; *NY Times*, 20 January 1920, p. 3; *Atlanta Constitution*, 5 February 1920, p. 13; *Kingston Daily Gleaner*, 13 February 1920, p. 3; *Cleveland Advocate*, 18 September 1920, p. 1; *NY Times*, 12 June 1940, p. 25; Boylan, pp. 140–141.

359. . . . retracted the charge: *Syracuse Herald*, 18 August 1920, p. 4.

359. ". . . themselves from the British yoke?": *Boston Globe*, 3 August 1920, p. 8; *Kingston Daily Gleaner*, 10 September 1920, p. 9.

360. . . . serve us for four years: *Kingston Daily Gleaner*, 16 August 1920, p. 7; *NY Times*, 18 August 1920, p. 2; *Kingston Daily Gleaner*, 10 September 1920, p. 9.

360. ". . . claim Africa for themselves": *NY Times*, 3 August 1920, p. 7; *NY Times*, 18 August 1920, p. 2.

360. . . . is that they talk too much: *Kingston Daily Gleaner*, 9 September 1920, p. 4.

361. "an extraordinary leader of men": Du Bois (*Autobiography*), p. 273; Rudwick, p. 216.

361. Where did he [Du Bois] get this aristocracy . . . it is Dr. Du Bois: Rudwick, pp. 218–219.

361. ". . . must be stopped altogether": Rudwick, p. 240.

362. . . . deadly Star Order of Ethiopia: Du Bois (*Darkwater*), *passim*; *Chicago Tribune*, 22 June 1920, p. 1; *Current Opinion*, July 1920, pp. 82–85; *The Bookman*, January 1921, pp. 303–304; Rudwick, p. 242.

362. . . . "is the Karl Marx of the colored race": *Chicago Tribune*, 22 June 1920, p. 1.

362. "consider the most effective means to end lynching": *Cleveland Advocate*, 19 June 1920, pp. 1, 8; *Cleveland Advocate*, 10 July 1920, p. 8; Downs, p. 537.

362. ". . . if you favor segregation": *Cleveland Advocate*, 3 July 1920, p. 8; Downes, p. 387.

363. ". . . 'direct' the Colored voters": *Cleveland Advocate*, 24 July 1920, pp. 1, 8; *Cleveland Advocate*, 31 July 1920, p. 1; *Cleveland Advocate*, 21 August 1920, p. 1.

363. . . . granted equal opportunities: *NY Times*, 28 July 1920, p. 6; McCoy, p. 125.

363. ". . . Whoopee for Calvin!": *Cleveland Advocate*, 14 August 1920, p. 8.

364. ". . . and America will bestow it": *NY Times*, 11 September 1920, p. 2; *Chicago Tribune*, 11 September 1920, p. 4; *Kennebec Journal*, 11 September 1920, pp. 1, 4; *Cincinnati Union*, 18 September 1920, p. 2; *Cleveland Advocate*, 2 October 1920, p. 8; Downes, pp. 541–545; J. Murphy, pp. 29–32.

364. . . . "some misgivings on the part of some of us": *Cleveland Advocate*, 2 October 1920, p. 8. Harding, however, did nothing (despite entreaties for action) to eliminate, even temporarily, segregation in Marion public facilities during "Colored Voters' Day." (Downes, pp. 542–543.)

365. . . . normal man could not resurrect the dead: *Chicago Tribune*, 11 October 1920, p. 9; Downes, pp. 546–547; J. Murphy, pp. 45–48.

365. ". . . to the Equal Rights League": Downes, p. 547; J. Murphy, p. 48.

365. . . . Roosevelt's Department of the Navy: *Dayton Forum*, 23 August 1918, p. 1.

365. . . . banned Griffith's masterpiece: *Dayton Forum*, 18 October 1918, p. 1; *Cleveland Advocate*, 19 October 1918, p. 8; *Cleveland Advocate*, 18 September 1920, p. 8; *NY Times*, 15 May 1924, p. 21.

365. . . . Ohio's black Ninth Regiment: *Cleveland Advocate*, 28 July 1917, p. 8; *Cleveland*

*Advocate*, 12 January 1918, pp. 1, 8; *Dayton Forum*, 18 October 1918, p. 1; *Cleveland Advocate*, 19 October 1918, p. 8; *Cleveland Advocate*, 26 October 1918, p. 8; *Cleveland Advocate*, 5 June 1920, p. 8; *Cleveland Advocate*, 17 July 1920, p. 1; *Cleveland Advocate*, 2 October 1920, p. 3; *NY Times*, 15 May 1924, p. 21.

365. . . . "NOT ONE WORD": Downes, pp. 539–540.

366. ". . . birth-right, Anglo-Saxon supremacy": *Atlanta Constitution*, 21 September 1920, p. 8; Downes, p. 551. Durbin, William Jennings Bryan's 1896 campaign chairman, not only served as Ohio Democratic chairman, he was perhaps the finest amateur magician in the nation (and would have made an exceptional professional), having founded and led the International Brotherhood of Magicians, and even constructing a sizable museum of the "black arts" in his home town. (*Washington Post*, 5 February 1937, p. 10.)

366. ". . . supporters of Senator Harding": *Boston Globe*, 15 October 1920, p. 9; *Cleveland Advocate*, 23 October 1920, p. 1; Huthmacher, p. 32; J. Murphy, p. 58. Cox's address was a major miscalculation, a virtual declaration of war on immigrant voters—particularly Germans, Italians, and Greeks—a "motley array of questionable groups and influences . . . an array that to survey brings the crimson blush of humiliation to an American."

366. . . . class in America: *NY Times*, 27 October 1920, p. 2; *Gastonia Daily Gazette*, 27 October 1920, p. 1.

367. ". . . particularly the general assembly": *Dayton Journal*, 1 November 1920, p. 6.

368. . . . yourselves and your children: *NY Times*, 22 October 1920, p. 2; *Cleveland Advocate*, 30 October 1920, pp. 1, 8; Downs, pp. 551–552.

**CHAPTER 22**

370. ". . . man of wild ideas. He couldn't be trusted": *NY Times*, 30 June 1904, p. BR523; *Washington Post*, 12 August 1906, pp. 1, 10; *Washington Post*, 5 January 1908, p. 1; *NY Times*, 2 January 1912, p. 10; *NY Times*, 5 January 1912, p. 12; *NY Times*, 23 November 1919, p. BR3; *NY Times*, 30 October 1920, pp. 1–2; *Chicago Tribune*, 1 November 1920, p. 11; *Washington Post*, 1 November 1920, pp. 1, 3; Anthony (*Florence Harding*), p. 124; J. Murphy, pp. 41, 189–191. Chancellor's wife, Louise Beecher, who had died in 1908, was, ironically, the niece of abolitionist Henry Ward Beecher. She requested that their four children be raised by relatives, as she considered her husband unfit for the duty. (Anthony [*Florence Harding*], p. 124; *NY Times*, 30 October 1920, p. 2; *Chicago Tribune*, 1 November 1920, p. 11.)

370. ". . . where the needed man will come from": *NY Times*, 14 October 1936, p. 26; J. Murphy, pp. 3–4.

371. ". . . than any other President has ever done": Anthony (*Florence Harding*), p. 191; J. Murphy, p. 16. Frank Hitchcock actually worked for Wood, not Harding. (*NY Times*, 6 August 1920, p. 17.)

   Joke circulating in 1920: *Sambo*—Did yo' heah de big news, Ephum? Dey done nomernate Mistah Hahding at Chicago.
   *Ephraim*—Sho! Who'd de white folks nomernate? (Adams, p. 179.)

371. . . . one eighth black, an octoroon: J. Murphy, p. 27.

371. ". . . Was she a Teacher there? Truant officer?": Chapple, pp. 51–52; J. Murphy, p. 43.

371. . . . in India from 1904 through 1914: Anthony (*Florence Harding*), p. 124; *Washington*

*Post*, 12 August 1906, p. 1; *Washington Post*, 5 January 1951, p. 1; *Washington Post*, 24 October 1951, p. B2.

371. . . . in his terminology, "niggers": J. Murphy, pp. 46–49.

372. ". . . called Butler's wife a 'nigger'": Adams, pp. 281–282; J. Murphy, pp. 46–47; Anthony (*Florence Harding*), pp. 229–230.

372. On Sunday, October 10 . . . Shaffer, were of a similar hue: J. Murphy, p. 47.

372. . . . daughter was marrying a "nigger": J. Murphy, pp. 48–49; Anthony (*Florence Harding*), p. 229.

372. ". . . marriage of his daughter to a negro": Anthony (*Florence Harding*), p. 230.

372. ". . . obviously a mulatto": J. Murphy, pp. 39–40.

374. ". . . Professor William E. Chancellor, Wooster University, Wooster, Ohio: Russell (*Blooming Grove*), pp. 403–404; J. Murphy, p. 55.

374. . . . destroyed at the San Francisco Post Office: *NY Times*, 29 October 1920, p. 1; Sullivan (VI), p. 132; Sinclair (*Available Man*), pp. 170–171; Russell (*Blooming Grove*), pp. 414–415; Downes, p. 555.

374. "mud," "whispering campaigns": Russell (*Blooming Grove*), p. 415; *Atlanta Constitution*, 30 October 1920, p. 1; *NY Times*, 30 October 1920, pp. 1–2; *LA Times*, 31 October 1920, p. 1; *Dayton Journal*, 1 November 1920, p. 6; *NY Call*, 1 November 1920, p. 10.

374. . . . *Indianapolis Star* on November 1: *Chicago Tribune*, 30 October 1920, p. 1; *Washington Post*, 1 November 1920, pp. 1–2; *Indianapolis Star*, 1 November 1920, p. 6.

374. ". . . private life and character": *NY Call*, 1 November 1920, p. 10. In point of fact, the *Call* had it wrong. The October 31, 1920 *Herald* spoke openly of "an insidious assertion . . . of negro ancestry." (*Dayton Journal*, 2 November 1920, p. 3; Russell [*Blooming Grove*], p. 415.)

375. . . . That is sufficient!: *Dayton Journal*, 29 October 1920, p. 1; Russell (*Blooming Grove*), pp. 412–413; Downes, p. 558.

375. ". . . families of HARDIN and HARDING": *Dayton Journal*, 30 October 1920, p. 1; *Lima News & Times-Democrat*, November 1920, p. 2. The 1920 federal census recorded every "Hardin" in Marion as white.

375. . . . continued denying culpability: J. Murphy, pp. 65–67.

376. . . . and from domestic ruin!: Russell (*Blooming Grove*), p. 414; *NY Times*, 29 October 1920, p. 1. The flier was, however, dated October 18.

377. . . . my name or any other paper: *Dayton Journal*, 30 October 1920, p. 1; *Lima News & Times-Democrat*, 31 October 1920, p. 34; *Lima News & Times-Democrat*, 1 November 1920, p. 5; *Dayton Journal*, 2 November 1920, p. 1; J. Murphy, p. 71.

377. . . . It all remained a mystery to him: *NY Times*, 30 October 1920, pp. 1–2; *Dayton Journal*, 30 October 1920, p. 1; *Lima News & Times-Democrat*, 31 October 1920, p. 34; J. Murphy, pp. 85–86.

377. . . . Chancellor was fired: *NY Times*, 30 October 1920, p. 1; *Chicago Tribune*, 30 October 1920, p. 1; *Atlanta Constitution*, 30 October 1920, p. 1; *LA Times*, 30 October 1920, p. 1; *Providence Journal*, 30 October 1920, p. 14; Adams, pp. 182–183; Sullivan (VI), p. 133 *fn.*; J. Murphy, pp. 75–81.

378. . . . unlikely that Wilson ever knew of the situation: *Chicago Tribune*, 2 November 1920, p. 5; Adams, p. 181; Perrett, p. 115; Anthony (*Florence Harding*), p. 230.

378. ". . . kill any such proposal": Wilson, pp. 305–306; Russell (*Blooming Grove*), p. 405; Felknor, p. 93.

378. . . . encouraged Chancellor to continue: *Zanesville Times-Record*, 12 March 1941, p. 4; *Lima News*, 1 December 1954, p. 12; J. Murphy, pp. 27–28.

379. Thousands upon thousands of typewritten . . . very sewers of depravity": Russell (*Blooming Grove*), pp. 412–413; Downes, p. 558.

379. . . . for handing out the circulars: *NY Times*, 31 October 1920, p. 2; Daugherty, pp. 59–60; J. Murphy, p. 84.

379. . . . WE HAVE THE PROOF AT HAND: *Lima News & Times-Democrat*, 1 November 1920, p. 5.

379. . . . Harding was a negress": *Ohio History*, Vol. 75, p. 101; Anthony (*Florence Harding*), p. 230.

380. . . . claimed had never been made: *NY Times*, 2 November 1920, p. 2; *Sandusky Star-Journal*, 1 November 1920, p. 1; J. Murphy, p. 91.

380. . . . telegram in the local press: *Lima News & Times-Democrat*, 1 November 1920, p. 2. The *New York Times* may have referred to this telegram when it wrote: "According to one person who talked to the Professor recently, he told him that he made a report to the Democratic State Committee." (*NY Times*, 30 October 1920, pp. 1–2.)

380. . . . and Secretary Frank Lowther: *Ohio History*, Vol. 75, p. 105.

381. Jimmie Cox's first wife was a Harding—Mayme Simpson Harding: Cebula, p. 16; http://www.heritagepursuit.com/Hamilton/HamiltonBio571.htm.

381. ". . . in Dayton when I was a little girl": *Trenton Times*, 7 July 1920, p. 11; *Elyria Chronicle-Telegram*, 10 July 1920, p. 2; *NY Tribune*, 11 July 1920, Section VII, p. 2; *Syracuse Herald*, 15 July 1920, p. 13; *Sandusky Star-Journal*, 17 July 1920, p. 1.

381. ". . . family of the Republican nominee": *LA Times*, 7 July 1920, p. 6; *Lima News & Times-Democrat*, 14 July 1920, p. 3.

381. ". . . "defending my own baby": Britton, p. 147.

381. . . . *Washington Post* and the *New York Times*: *NY Times*, 31 October 1920, pp. 1–2; *Washington Post*, 1 November 1920, p. 3.

382. ". . . must fight it out again": Sinclair (*Available Man*), p. 171; Russell (*Blooming Grove*), p. 405; Anthony (*Florence Harding*), p. 231; J. Murphy, p. 61.

382. ". . . jumped the fence": Adams, p. 280; Sinclair (*Available Man*), p. 172; Anthony (*Florence Harding*), p. 232.

382. . . . "Why does not Harding speak them?": Anthony (*Florence Harding*), p. 232.

382. . . . get him to cool off": Sinclair (*Available Man*), p. 171; Anthony (*Florence Harding*), p. 232; J. Murphy, p. 61.

382. . . . subject for 'niggers' to look at": Anthony (*Florence Harding*), p. 232.

382. . . . no statement was forthcoming": Michelson, p. 227; Anthony (*Florence Harding*), p. 233.

383. . . . Carolyn Votaw didn't speak: Anthony (*Florence Harding*), p. 231.

383. ". . . holding the nigger vote lately": Sinclair (*Available Man*), p. 171.

383. ". . . no protest from those in charge of the Democratic party": *Dayton Journal*, 31 October 1920, p. 1.

383. ". . . even at the Chicago convention: *NY Times*, 1 November 1920, pp. 1–2; *Atlanta Constitution*, 1 November 1920, p. 1; *Providence Journal*, 1 November 1920, p. 3; *Dayton Journal*, 1 November 1920, p. 1; *Providence Journal*, 2 November 1920, p. 2. Cox's *Dayton News* also blamed Harding's fellow Republicans. "General Wood," it contended, "originally circulated these charges in the Republican primaries." (J. Murphy, p. 86.)

384. ". . . guttersnipe of American journalism": *Dayton Journal*, 2 November 1920, p. 1.

385. . . . Confess your degradation!: *Dayton Journal*, 1 November 1920, p. 1.

385. . . . swear out an affidavit denying all: *NY Times*, 2 November 1920, p. 2; *Boston Globe*, 2 November 1920, pp. 1–2; *Chicago Tribune*, 2 November 1920, p. 1. Irey then proceeded to the Mayor's office, offering to pay a fine for assaulting Judge Spencer. As Spencer filed no complaint, there was nothing to pay.

**CHAPTER 23**

386. "cheap lodging houses": Committee on Naval Affairs, p. 3.

386. ". . . officers themselves as spectators": Daniels (*Cabinet Diaries*), p. 175; L. Murphy, pp. 10–35; Ward, p. 438.

387. ". . . highly experienced investigators": Committee on Naval Affairs, p. 16; L. Murphy, p. 15; Melosh, p. 100; Ward, p. 439; Morgan (*F.D.R.*), p. 234.

387. "keep in touch with the situation": L. Murphy, pp. 16, 231.

387. . . . the horrible practices stopped: Committee on Naval Affairs, p. 19; L. Murphy, pp. 16, 231; Morgan (*F.D.R.*), p. 235; Ward, p. 440; C. Black, p. 108.

387. "insufficient" and "considerably exaggerated": L. Murphy, p. 17.

387. . . . and purely consensual sex: Committee on Naval Affairs, pp. 4, 8, 15; L. Murphy, p. 10; Loughery, pp. 6–8; Morgan (*F.D.R.*), p. 234.

388. ". . . on that field with that party": Committee on Naval Affairs, pp. 17–18; L. Murphy, pp. 69–70, 242; Ward, p. 440; Morgan (*F.D.R.*), p. 235.

388. . . . Newport's homosexual problem: Committee on Naval Affairs, pp. 9–10, 19, 23; L. Murphy, pp. 69–70, 232; Ward, pp. 440–441.

388. ". . . wise to keep this matter wholly secret": Committee on Naval Affairs, pp. 4–5, 7–8, 10, 20–21, 23–24, 32; L. Murphy, pp. 71–72; Morgan (*F.D.R.*), pp. 236, 243; Ward, p. 441.

388. ". . . render him will be appreciated": Committee on Naval Affairs, p. 25; Morgan (*F.D.R.*), p. 237; Ward, pp. 441–442.

388. ". . . agents of the Assistant Secretary of the Navy": Committee on Naval Affairs, pp. 4, 7; Morgan (*F.D.R.*), p. 237; L. Murphy, pp. 72, 228, 233; Ward, pp. 441–442; Miller, p. 165. FDR later testified that Section A was assigned to his office to ensure secrecy— "to keep the investigation out of the files, the routine files, of the Department, and to prevent publicity."

389. . . . moral questions regarding the operation: Committee on Naval Affairs, pp. 25, 31; Morgan (*F.D.R.*), p. 237. The Ball subcommittee concluded: "This statement of Porter to Hudson apparently was not reported back to Franklin D. Roosevelt by Hudson.

"If this be true that Hudson did not report back to Assistant Secretary Franklin D. Roosevelt, then the Dunn court of inquiry erred when it recommended merely that Hudson be censured for his part in the proceedings. The court should have recommended that Hudson be tried by general court-martial, and if found guilty dismissed from the service. Such an act on Hudson's part appears to the committee to constitute extreme neglect of duty. From later developments the committee is of the opinion that Hudson did make known to Franklin D. Roosevelt . . . in some manner the remarks of Assistant United States Attorney General Porter, for on June 29 Secretary Daniels wrote a letter to the Attorney General . . . requesting the department to furnish at once legal services required to sift evidence collected, prepare cases for trial, and that a representative of the department be assigned to the office of Hudson." (*NY*

*Times*, 1 July 1919, p. 5; *NY Times*, 17 July 1920, p. 4; *Washington Post*, 13 November 1926, p. 3; *NY Times*, 18 August 1928, p. 46.)

389. . . . "a lewd and wanton person": Committee on Naval Affairs, pp. 4, 26; L. Murphy, pp. 97–101; Loughery, p. 10; Melosh, p. 73; Ward, p. 442; Halley, p. 42. The accused were held for months without being apprised of the charges against them. (*Providence Journal*, 23 January 1920, p. 3; Committee on Naval Affairs, pp. 13–14, 35–37.)

389. . . . everyone who heard of it: Committee on Naval Affairs, p. 26; L. Murphy, pp. 101–102; Loughery, p. 10; Morgan (*F.D.R.*), p. 237; C. Black, p. 108.

389. ". . . someone will swing for it": Committee on Naval Affairs, pp. 11, 26; *Washington Post*, 4 February 1920, p. 1; Morgan (*F.D.R.*), p. 238; Ward, p. 443. FDR had already met with Hudson and Arnold, who remained convinced of Kent's guilt.

389. . . . On September 4, FDR did just that: Committee on Naval Affairs, pp. 27–28; Ward, p. 443; L. Murphy, pp. 104–106. Leigh eventually rose to the rank of Rear Admiral and the position of Commander-in-Chief of the Fleet. When FDR assumed the presidency in 1933, he bypassed Leigh for promotion to Chief of Naval Operations. Leigh retired. (*LA Times*, 28 February 1922, p. 2; *LA Times*, 10 June 1922, p. A1.)

390. . . . into the sanitarium, and arrested him: Committee on Naval Affairs, p. 11; *Providence Journal*, 20 January 1920, p. 2; *NY Times*, 25 January 1920, p. 12; *Atlanta Constitution*, 25 January 1920, p. 10A; *Washington Post*, 3 May 1920, p. 11; *Washington Post*, 24 May 1920, p. 6; *Atlanta Constitution*, 24 May 1920, p. 3; Daniels (*Cabinet Diaries*), p. 533 *fn.*; Morgan (*F.D.R.*), pp. 238–239; Davis (*F.D.R.*), p. 597; L. Murphy, pp. 108–117; Ward, p. 443. In early September 1919, Lieutenant Hudson had informed Bishop Perry of FDR's knowledge of the operation. (Committee on Naval Affairs, pp. 27–28.)

390. . . . demanded that heads roll: *Providence Journal*, 6 January 1920, p. 5; *Providence Journal*, 7 January 1920, p. 7; *Providence Journal*, 9 January 1920, pp. 1, 12; Committee on Naval Affairs, p. 28; L. Murphy, pp. 121–151; Halley, pp. 42–44; Melosh, pp. 84–86, 91; Loughery, p. 11. Evidence presented at Kent's second trial strongly suggests his guilt. Why his fellow Episcopal clergy rallied to his defense remains debatable. "Close examination of the navy's allegations and of the ministers' countercharges," notes historian George Chauncey Jr., "suggests that the ministers feared that the navy's charges against the two churchmen threatened to implicate them all."

390. . . . morality, patriotism, and religion: *Providence Journal*, 23 October 1920, p. 3; *Providence Journal*, 25 January 1920, p. 2; L. Murphy, pp. 156–157. It's doubtful if Wilson ever saw this letter. It was forwarded immediately to Daniels.

390. . . . appointment for Dunn's wife's nephew: Committee on Naval Affairs, p. 6; *NY Times*, 18 January 1920, p. 9; *LA Times*, 21 January 1920, pp. 1–2; *Sandusky Register*, 21 January 1920, p. 2; *Providence Journal*, 23 January 1920, p. 1; Daniels (*Cabinet Diaries*), p. 589; L. Murphy, pp. 158, 163; Melosh, p. 100; Morgan (*F.D.R.*), p. 239.

390. . . . King (D-Utah), to investigate: Committee on Naval Affairs, p. 5; *Providence Journal*, 20 January 1920, p. 2; *Providence Journal*, 23 January 1920, p. 1; *Atlanta Constitution*, 20 January 1920, p. 2; *Bridgeport Telegram*, 20 January 1920, p. 1; *Bridgeport Telegram*, 23 January 1920, p. 4; L. Murphy, p. 162.

391. ". . . on the United States Navy": *Providence Journal*, 23 January 1920, pp. 1, 3; *Boston Globe*, 23 January 1920, p. 11; L. Murphy, pp. 162–163.

391. . . . defense is to shout "Liar": *Providence Journal*, 23 January 1920, p. 12; L. Murphy, pp. 164–165.

391. . . . yourself months ago: *Providence Journal*, 23 January 1920, pp. 1, 12; *Boston Globe*, 23 January 1920, p. 11; *Boston Globe*, 27 January 1920, p. 5; *NY Times*, 27 January 1920, p. 6; L. Murphy, pp. 162–164; Freidel (*The Ordeal*), p. 47.

391. . . . conduct hearings in secret: *Providence Journal*, 25 October 1920, p. 1; L. Murphy, p. 251. The subcommittee had met behind closed doors the previous day, but did not establish its policy until January 25.

392. . . . ignorance of naval procedures: *Washington Post*, 2 March 1920, p. 3; L. Murphy, p. 169.

392. ". . . Never entered my head. No, sir": L. Murphy, pp. 234–235; Morgan (*F.D.R.*), pp. 240–242.

393. . . . for a lawsuit against his client: Committee on Naval Affairs, pp. 33–34; *Boston Globe*, 24 May 1920, p. 5; *Kennebec Journal*, 24 May 1920, p. 3; L. Murphy, pp. 240–241.

393. ". . . on account of illness": Morgan (*F.D.R.*), p. 242.

393. ". . . to investigate perversion": L. Murphy, pp. 242–243. No copy of the Dunn Inquiry report now exists. Transcripts of its hearings survive.

393. . . . kept things under wraps: Freidel (*The Ordeal*), p. 71. It's possible that, with Warren Harding's personal life so seamy, Ball feared opening up a can of worms if he injected anything sexual into the campaign.

394. ". . . National Committee": *NY Times*, 26 October 1920, p. 19; *Kennebec Journal*, 26 October 1920, p. 6; *Providence Journal*, 27 October 1920, p. 3; *Portsmouth (NH) Herald*, 17 November 1954, p. 4; L. Murphy, p. 255; Ward, pp. 549–550.

394. . . . with whom you came in contact: *Providence Journal*, 25 October 1920, p. 3; *Kennebec Journal*, 26 October 1920, p. 6; Ward, p. 550.

394. ". . . of frankness and manliness": Rollins, p. 165.

394. ". . . private doubts about himself": Ward, p. 550. Ward, while concluding that FDR was indeed "not homosexual," details Franklin's early pretty-boy, "mama's boy" persona. Correspondingly, Louis Wehle noted that "Despite [FDR's] thorough masculinity, there was underneath a characteristically feminine quality. . . . some traits that we are all prone to regard as primarily feminine were more obvious in Roosevelt's mental make-up than in those of most men. To me there was both a clue to this analysis and a partial confirmation of it in his almost literal resemblance to his mother, and in the extent to which he depended upon her even as he reached middle age." (Wehle, p. 115.)

394. Roosevelt reacted furiously . . . Rathom stood his ground: L. Murphy, p. 255.

395. ". . . that they are wholly untrue": *NY Times*, 26 October 1920, p. 19; *Boston Globe*, 26 October 1920, p. 8; *Providence Journal*, 27 October 1920, p. 3; L. Murphy, p. 256.

395. ". . . related to the Roosevelt matter: *Boston Globe*, 28 October 1920, pp. 1, 6; *Providence Journal*, 31 October 1920, p. 2; *The Nation*, 17 November 1920, pp. 557–559; *NY Times*, 6 December 1957, p. 29; Ward, pp. 553–554; L. Murphy, pp. 256–257; C. Black, p. 131. On November 5, Caffey ruled that "no violation of federal law" existed.

       During the Dunn Inquiry, Ensign Henry I. Hyneman made public a February 6, 1918 Rathom letter to Attorney General Gregory, very similar to his February 12, 1918 letter to Bielaski. (*Boston Globe*, 28 May 1920, p. 5.)

396. . . . of which I invite public attention: *Providence Journal*, 29 October 1920, p. 3; *Boston Globe*, 29 October 1920, p. 13; *NY Times*, 29 October 1920, pp. 10, 16. Following the election, FDR's operatives continued rummaging through Rathom's Justice Department

files to obtain evidence for his libel suit. "What we want are the main facts," he ordered Charles H. McCarthy, "showing Rathom's life has been a thoroughly disreputable one in almost every part of the globe; that he has left a bad reputation behind him in every place, and that he is in no way to be believed. . . ." (L. Murphy, p. 257.)

396. . . . $500,000 for criminal libel: *NY Times*, 26 October 1920, p. 19; *Providence Journal*, 29 October 1920, p. 1; *Atlanta Constitution*, 29 October 1920, p. 4; *Fitchburg Daily Sentinel*, 29 October 1920, p. 11; *Decatur Review*, 29 October 1920, p. 1; Ward, p. 553; Miller, p. 176; L. Murphy, pp. 256, 258. Charges against Bone and Clark were quickly dropped. No one is quite sure what finally happened to the suit against Rathom.

396. ". . . and a professional politician": L. Murphy, p. 257.

## CHAPTER 24

397. . . . But he knew better: *NY Times*, 14 September 1920, pp. 1–2; *LA Times*, 14 September 1920, p. 1; *Atlanta Constitution*, 15 September 1920, pp. 1–2; Hays, p. 265; Downes, pp. 583–584; Chaddock and Robinson, p. 31; Bagby, p. 142.

397. . . . The projection: Harding: Chaddock and Robinson, pp. 49–50.

397. The *New York World* polled 300 newspaper editors. Their projection: Harding: Chaddock and Robinson, p. 15.

397. . . . won in a walk, 14,398–5,738: *Boston Globe*, 24 October 1920, pp. 1, 12.

398. . . . blasted Rexall as pro-Republican: *Gastonia Daily Gazette*, 25 September 1920, p. 6; *NY Times*, 31 October 1920, p. E6; *Wellsboro Agitator*, 10 November 1920, p. 5; Chaddock and Robinson, pp. 31, 70–71.

398. . . . of the Republican national committee: *NY Times*, 3 November 1920, p. 6; Craig, p. 25.

398. . . . Samaritan—and women wept: *Boston Globe*, 31 October 1920, p. 20; *Chicago Tribune*, 31 October 1920, p. 1; *NY Times*, 31 October 1920, pp. 1–2; Bagby, p. 145.

398. ". . . It's a damn shame": J. M. Cox, pp. 279–280.

399. . . . his campaign train who did: *NY Times*, 1 November 1920, p. 2; Lash, p. 257.

399. ". . . LIVE THE RUSSIAN SOVIET": *Chicago Tribune*, 1 November 1920, p. 17.

399. . . . capitalistic to the uninitiated: *NY Times*, 1 November 1920, p. 23.

400. . . . compliment they could pay me: *Atlanta Constitution*, 2 November 1920, p. 9; *Chicago Tribune*, 3 November 1920, p. 15.

400. ". . . they think at all": *Washington Post*, 3 November 1920, p. 3.

400. . . . housekeeper] I hope she is well: Lathem (*Your Son, Calvin Coolidge*), p. 171; Fuess, p. 275.

401. . . . People walked out of the hall: *Chicago Tribune*, 2 November 1920, p. 1; *Providence Journal*, 2 November 1920, p. 2; *Indianapolis News*, 2 November 1920, p. 1; *Oneonta Daily Star*, 2 November 1920, p. 1; Bagby, p. 145. Cox ironically ended his campaign with the words "Peace on earth; good will toward men." (*Decatur Daily Review*, 3 November 1920, p. 1; *Gastonia Daily Gazette*, 2 November 1920, p. 1.)

401. ". . . defeat of the Wilson foreign league": *Chicago Tribune*, 27 October 1920, p. 4; Nasaw, p. 274.

401. ". . . town needs to be waked up": *Washington Post*, 2 November 1920, p. 1; *Atlanta Constitution*, 3 November 1920, p. 7; *Decatur Daily Review*, 3 November 1920, p. 1. This was not Mrs. Cox's first vote; she had voted previously in Illinois.

401. . . . sleeping soundly that night; *NY Times*, 31 October 1920, p. 3; *NY Times*, 1 November 1920, p. 3; *Boston Globe*, 1 November 1920, p. 2; *Chicago Tribune*, 2

November 1920, p. 3; Hays, p. 266; Daugherty, pp. 64–65; Anthony (*Florence Harding*), p. 234.

401. . . . $20-a-day hired hands: *Boston Globe*, 2 November 1920, p. 8; *Washington Post*, 2 November 1920, p. 2.

402. . . . shouted, and everybody laughed: *Marion Star*, 2 November 1920, p. 11; *NY Times*, 2 November 1920, p. 1; *Atlanta Constitution*, 3 November 1920, p. 7; Russell (*Blooming Grove*), p. 416; Anthony (*Florence Harding*), p. 235.

402. . . . to vote, Eleanor 208: *Chicago Tribune*, 3 November 1920, p. 2; *Atlanta Constitution*, 3 November 1920, p. 7; *NY Times*, 3 November 1920, p. 22; *Washington Post*, 3 November 1920, p. 5; Elliott Roosevelt and Brough (*Hyde Park*), p. 127; Lash, p. 257; Wayne, p. 252; Davis, p. 622.

402. . . . supporters would come to call: *Boston Globe*, 3 November 1920, p. 15; *NY Times*, 3 November 1920, p. 4; *Chicago Tribune*, 3 November 1920, p. 2; *Atlanta Constitution*, 3 November 1920, p. 7; *Providence Journal*, 3 November 1920, p. 2; *Decatur Daily* Review, 3 November 1920, p. 1; Fuess, pp. 275–276.

403. . . . the new "Tenth amendment": *NY Times*, 31 October 1920, p. 5; *Washington Post*, 31 October 1920, p. 2; *Chicago Tribune*, 31 October 1920, p. 5; *Providence Journal*, 31 October 1920, p. 3. Three members of Wilson's cabinet—Postmaster General Burleson, Interior Secretary John B. Payne, and Treasury Secretary David F. Houston—did not vote at all. (*Providence Journal*, 3 November 1920, p. 5.)

403. . . . blind, aged mother: *Kennebec Journal*, 3 November 1920, p. 9.

403. . . . wasn't on the Ohio ballot: *Sandusky Star-Journal*, 2 November 1920, p. 4.

403. ". . . other way quite as easily": White (*Autobiography*), p. 591.

403. . . . a wire service reported: *Indianapolis Star*, 3 November 1920, p. 11.

403. . . . first-time black women voters: *Boston Globe*, 2 November 1920, p. 8.

403. . . . two churches, and a Masonic lodge: *NY Times*, 4 November 1920, p. 1; *NY Call*, 4 November 1920, p. 2; *Boston Globe*, 4 November 1920, p. 3; *Providence Journal*, 4 November 1920, p. 13; Green, pp. 204–205; Brown, p. 68; Rice, p. 48.

404. . . . nearly killing the nominee: Oddly enough, just two days before the 1912 election, Wilson had also been involved in an auto accident, hitting the roof of his vehicle and receiving a three-inch scalp wound. (*Boston Globe*, 5 November 1912, p. 4.)

404. ". . . Somehow this has touched me": *Marion Star*, 3 November 1920, p. 11; *Providence Journal*, 3 November 1920, p. 5; *Schenectady Gazette*, 30 June 1920, p. 4; *NY Times*, 3 November 1920, p. 5; *Washington Post*, 3 November 1920, p. 5; *Lancaster (OH) Daily Eagle*, 9 August 1923, p. 1; Sullivan (VI), p. 137; Russell (*Blooming Grove*), pp. 416–417.

405. . . . callers with sketchy results: *Chicago Tribune*, 1 November 1920, p. 3; *Chicago Tribune*, 3 November 1920, p. 5.

405. ". . . from the *The Chicago Tribune* offices in New York": *Chicago Tribune*, 4 November 1920, pp. 1, 10.

405. . . . to receive results by radio: *Washington Post*, 1 November 1920, p. 5; *Washington Post*, 2 November 1920, p. 4.

405. ". . . *Constitution*'s staff artist": *Atlanta Constitution*, 3 November 1920, p. 6.

405. . . . on Courtland Street: *Atlanta Constitution*, 2 November 1920, p. 4.

405. . . . Teachers Club, or the Elks: *Dayton Journal*, 2 November 1920, p. 7.

406. . . . *Times* flash the Harding signal: *NY Times*, 2 November 1920, p. 2; *LA Times*, 3 November 1920, p. 2.

406. . . . danced the night away: *NY Call*, 1 November 1920, p. 5; *NY Call*, 3 November 1920, p. 2.

406. It rained in Boston too, but . . . at Adams Square: *Boston Globe*, 3 November 1920, p. 8.

406. ". . . amendment and the single tax": *LA Times*, 2 November 1920, p. 6.

406. . . . country homes to cast their ballot: *NY Times*, 2 November 1920, p. 17; *NY Times*, 3 November 1920, p. 11.

406. . . . tenor Enrico Caruso: *NY Times*, 2 November 1920, p. 4.

406. . . . "No Street Cars—No Traffic": *Indianapolis Star*, 2 November 1920, p. 16.

406. . . . *Liberty Girls* at the Lyric: *Dayton Journal*, 1 November 1920, p. 11.

407. . . . 40 cents (for something decent): *Marion Star*, 30 October 1920, p. 9; *Marion Star*, 1 November 1920, p. 12.

408. . . . ten thousand operators in the South: *Atlanta Constitution*, 3 November 1920, p. 11; Ostroff, Smith, and Wright, pp. 23–24; Morris, p. 439; Cooper (*Pivotal Decades*), pp. 370–371.

408. . . . listeners than the station itself: http://donmoore.tripod.com/genbroad/elec1924.html; http://earlyradiohistory.us/WWJ.htm.

408. ". . . pre-election claims are demolished": *Washington Post*, 3 November 1920, p. 5.

408. . . . guard his house: Russell (*Blooming Grove*), p. 481; J. Murphy, pp. 92–93.

409. ". . . and God bless you": *NY Times*, 3 November 1920, p. 5; Daugherty, pp. 65–66.

409. . . . She didn't mind: Anthony (*Florence Harding*), p. 236.

409. ". . . mental and physical condition": *NY Times*, 2 November 1920, p. 1; *Chicago Tribune*, 2 November 1920, p. 3; *Providence Journal*, 3 November 1920, p. 5.

409. . . . with FDR and the White House: *Chicago Tribune*, 3 November 1920, p. 12; *NY Times*, 3 November 1920, p. 22; *Washington Post*, 3 November 1920, p. 5.

410. . . . is purely impersonal": *Washington Post*, 2 November 1920, p. 1–2; *NY Times*, 3 November 1920, pp. 4, 5; *LA Times*, 3 November 1920, pp. 2, 3; *Atlanta Constitution*, 3 November 1920, pp. 1, 7; *Washington Post*, 3 November 1920, pp. 1, 5.

410. . . . took it worse than he did: Elliott Roosevelt and Brough (*Hyde Park*), p. 127.

410. "Blessed are those that expect nothing, for. . . .": *Atlanta Constitution*, 1 November 1920, p. 1; *Atlanta Constitution*, 3 November 1920, p. 3.

410. ". . . in quest of new worlds to conquer": Wayne, pp. 188–189.

410. . . . strongholds were fading fast: *NY Times*, 31 October 1920, p. E3; Wayne, p. 189; Kane, p. 314.

411. ". . . as an organized movement": Ginger, p. 404.

411. ". . . their own ignorance and stupidity": *Atlanta Constitution*, 1 November 1920, p. 1.

411. . . . brought up the rear: *Reno Evening Gazette*, 11 August 1920, p. 7; *NY Times*, 18 December 1920, p. 13; *NY Times*, 30 October 1948, p. 15; Kane, pp. 199, 314–315; Brooks, p. 120; http://www.e-paranoids.com/j/ja/james_e__ferguson.html.

412. "The back woods . . . of the Appalachians": White (*Puritan in Babylon*), p. 218.

412. . . . Democratic district, 318–145: *Washington Post*, 3 November 1920, p. 9; *NY Times*, 3 November 1920, pp. 1–3, 5; *NY Times*, 4 November 1920, p. 1; Warner and Daniel, p. 126; Lathem (*Your Son, Calvin Coolidge*), pp. 172–173.

412. . . . just 25.5 percent of the state total: *NY Times*, 1 November 1920, p. 3; *Chicago Tribune*, 1 November 1920, p. 7.

412. . . . remained in the Cox column: *Boston Globe*, 4 November 1920, pp. 1, 5; *Providence Journal*, 3 November 1920, p. 6; Huthmacher, p. 42.

412. . . . 331 votes—35,938 to 35,607: *NY Call*, 5 November 1920, p. 4; H. Allen (*Poindexter*), pp. 224–225; Fine, pp. 376, 394–395; http://www.polidata.us/pub/reports/46000vhb.pdf. Christensen also garnered a respectable 7 percent in Montana.

412. . . . Republicans captured twenty-five: *NY Call*, 4 November 1920, p. 3.

413. . . . first native Republican congressman: *NY Times*, 4 November 1920, p. 3; *Washington Post*, 4 November 1920, p. 4; http://www.tsha.utexas.edu/handbook/online/articles/view/WW/fwu4.html.

413. . . . 37 of 38 in Pennsylvania: http://clerk.house.gov/members/electionInfo/1920election.pdf.

413. . . . Democrats didn't bother running: H. Allen (*Poindexter*), p. 225; *The Nation*, 6 October 1920, p. 365.

413. ". . . it was an earthquake": Cooper (*Pivotal Years*), p. 372; Sinclair (*Available Man*), p. 174; Leuchtenburg, p. 88; Boller, p. 213.

413. . . . on average by 21 percent: Chaddock and Robinson, pp. 68, 73.

413. . . . six Harding states to Cox: Chaddock and Robinson, pp. 15–17.

414. . . . Democratic Tennessee and Oklahoma: *Wellsboro Agitator*, 10 November 1920, p. 5; Chaddock and Robinson, p. 70.

414. . . . on every House committee: *NY Times*, 4 November 1920, p. 1; *Literary Digest*, 27 November 1920, pp. 57, 60–61.

414. . . . Herbert Hoover for president: *NY Times*, 15 July 1920, p. 1; *Washington Post*, 30 July 1920, p. 4; *NY Times*, 26 October 1920, p. 3; *NY Times*, 6 October 1950, p. 25; Pietrusza (*Rothstein*), p. 426; Swanberg, p. 335; Malcolm (1921), p. 534. Miller, like Smith, was also Catholic and had seven daughters to prove it.

414. . . . than 200 votes, but he won: *Charleston Daily Mail*, 31 August 1920, p. 6; *NY Times*, 4 November 1920, pp. 1, 5; *Iowa City Press-Citizen*, 15 November 1920, p. 5; *Atlanta Constitution*, 16 January 1921, p. 4; *NY Times*, 27 June 1946, p. 21; Clift, p. 204. Harry Burn's Niota lies just 32 miles from Dayton, site of 1925's Scopes Evolution Trial.

414. . . . Lower East Side seat: *NY Call*, 1 November 1920, p. 3; Malcolm (1921), pp. 534, 537, 549, 560.

415. . . . Republican towns, it increased 92.1 percent: Huthmacher, p. 44.

415. . . . of eligible women voters": *NY Times*, 18 December 1920, p. 13; Sinclair (*Available Man*), p. 174; Chaddock and Robinson, p. 92. In the Rexall poll, 848,497 men, but only 202,555 women, voted.

415. . . . polling booth, men six: *NY Times*, 3 November 1920, p. 6.

415. . . . at the polling place: *Sandusky Star-Journal*, 2 November 1920, p. 4.

416. ". . . fruit salad and fried chicken": *Washington Post*, 5 November 1920, p. 9; *Atlanta Constitution*, 5 November 1920, p. 1; *Chicago Tribune*, 5 November 1920, p. 1; *NY Times*, 7 November 1920, p. 26; *Atlanta Constitution*, 24 November 1920, p. 16; *Literary Digest*, 4 December 1920, pp. 56, 58; Foerstel, pp. 230–231; Catt, p. 312.

416. . . . Charles B. Henderson his job: R. Elliott and Rowley, p. 266; http://clerk.house.gov/members/electionInfo/1920election.pdf.

416. . . . herself garnered 27,934 votes: *NY Times*, 17 October 1920, p. E1; *NY Times*, 3 November 1920, p. 3; http://clerk.house.gov/members/electionInfo/1920election.pdf.

416. ". . . substitute words for things": *Boston Globe*, 3 November 1920, p. 2; *NY Times*, 3 November 1920, p. 4; Fuess, p. 276; Leuchtenburg, p. 89.

416. ". . . a marvelous result": Dunn and Kuehl, p. 18; Garraty, p. 399; Ferrell (*Woodrow Wilson*), p. 229.

416. . . . Applause from the bystanders: *Chicago Tribune*, 3 November 1920, p. 5.

417. . . . They went their separate ways: Britton, pp. 147–152; Russell (*Blooming Grove*), pp. 419–420; Anthony (*Florence Harding*), pp. 248–249.

## CHAPTER 25

418. ". . . he is too sick to hold office": *NY Call*, 5 November 1920, p. 1; Sullivan (VI), p. 548; Hibben, p. 367; Coletta, pp. 137–138.

418. ". . . (Erroneously reported dead.)": Freidel (*The Ordeal*), pp. 91–93; Elliott Roosevelt and Brough (*Hyde Park*), pp. 127–129, 131; Morgan (*F.D.R.*), p. 233; Miller, p. 176; Davis, pp. 622–623, 627; Ward, p. 556; Lash, p. 258.

419. ". . . that admiration for women": *Washington Post*, 27 November 1920, p. 8; *LA Times*, 27 November 1920, p. 1; *NY Times*, 27 November 1920, p. 6; *Chicago Tribune*, 30 November 1920, p. 10; Sullivan (VI), p. 339; Anthony (*Florence Harding*), pp. 164, 239–240; Russell (*Blooming Grove*), pp. 348, 421–422.

419. . . . *must be trusted in the matter*: Sinclair (*Available Man*), p. 184.

420. ". . . or no Mellon": Daugherty, p. 100; Murray (*Politics of Normalcy*), p. 26; E. Lyons (*Herbert Hoover*), p. 144; R. N. Smith (*Uncommon Man*), p. 97.

420. . . . touched off a nationalist rebellion: *NY Times*, 4 April 1921, p. 12; *Washington, Post*, 14 July 1942, p. 21; *Washington Post*, 21 August 1928, pp. 1–2.

420. . . . just above Dupont Circle: *Chicago Tribune*, 5 March 1921, p. 3; *NY Times*, 5 March 1921, pp. 1, 5; Sullivan (V), p. 567; Sinclair (*Available Man*), p. 198.

420. ". . . It is so bad that a sort of grandeur creeps into it": Mencken, p. 39.

421. ". . . Harding needs is a condenser": *NY Times*, 5 March 1921, pp. 1, 3; Fuess, pp. 282–283; Ross (*Grace Coolidge*), pp. 61–62; Sobel, pp. 211–212.

421. . . . settled into residence at the New Willard: Ross (*Grace Coolidge*), p. 62.

421. ". . . plenty good enough for them": Butler (Vol. I), pp. 355–356.

421. ". . . there would be no future": M. A. Elliott, p. 299.

421. . . . never learned of Harding's generosity: *NY Times*, 4 August 1923, p. 7.

422. . . . man who is in this audience tonight: *NY Times*, 10 June 1923, p. 9; Ross (*Power with Grace*), p. 251.

422. . . . living peddling government bonds: Adams, pp. 273–283; Russell (*Blooming Grove*), pp. 528–531; J. Murphy, pp. 121–129, 140–141, 154–157.

422. . . . simple request for an autograph: *NY Times*, 27 June 1921, p. 10; G. Smith, p. 216; C. Black, p. 144; Ross (*Power with Grace*), p. 238. FDR's later paralysis did soften Wilson's heart and considerably eased the previously awkward relations between the two men.

423. . . . the *New York Times*. DETAILS ARE UNPRINTABLE: Committee on Naval Affairs, *passim;* *Lima News & Times-Democrat*, 19 July 1921, p. 14; *NY Times*, 20 July 1921, p. 4; *Atlanta Constitution*, 20 July 1921, p. 2; *Bridgeport Telegram*, 20 July 1921, p. 1; L. Murphy, pp. 260–273; Morgan, pp. 242–243; Elliott Roosevelt and Brough (*Hyde Park*), pp. 126–127, 133–134. FDR also surreptitiously prepared the subcommittee's minority report.

  In March 1921, Daniels issued mere letters of censure for Hudson and Arnold and two other officers. FDR argued against even that slap of the wrist.

"Daniels," wrote historian Lawrence R. Murphy, "failed to exonerate Roosevelt, although he overruled the condemnatory language recommended by the Dunn court." (L. Murphy, p. 249.)

423. . . . taken of him standing unaided: Freidel (*The Ordeal*), p. 97; Elliott Roosevelt and Brough (*Hyde Park*), p. 134; C. Black, p. 135. It may have been on this trip that FDR contracted the polio virus.

424. . . . cost him popularity. He didn't much mind: *Washington Post*, 25 December 1921, p. 5; *Atlanta Constitution*, 26 December 1921, pp. 1, 7; Daugherty, pp. 115–121; Ginger, pp. 413–415; Coleman, pp. 318–319, 324–326; Wayne, pp. 191–192; Sinclair (*Available Man*), pp. 226–228, 238.

424. . . . Ford even beat Harding in Ohio: *World's Work*, March 1923, pp. 487–494; Schlesinger, p. 51; Sinclair (*Available Man*), p. 280; Russell (*Blooming Grove*), pp. 564, 586; Baldwin, p. 184. Some sources say that Harding had privately called upon Ford to cease his anti-Semitic campaign. (Lee, p. 42.)

425. ". . . other people feel superior to him": Sinclair (*Available Man*), p. 223.

425. ". . . walking the floor nights!": Daugherty, pp. 180–185; Russell (*Blooming Grove*), pp. 522–526, 554–558; Perrett, pp. 134–136; Murray (*Politics of Normalcy*), pp. 102–104; Ferrell (*Strange Deaths of President Harding*), pp. 32, 114–121; Sinclair (*Available Man*), p. 283; Schlesinger, p. 51.

426. ". . . never raised the question again: Sinclair (*Available Man*), pp. 284–285.

426. . . . And he died: *NY Times*, 3 August 1923, pp. 1–2; Ferrell (*Strange Deaths of President Harding*), pp. 12–20; Russell (*Blooming Grove*), pp. 558–592; Sinclair, pp. 285–286; Adams, pp. 373–376.

426. ". . . because they were so seldom applied": Coolidge (*Autobiography*), p. 162.

426. "a timid man": White (*Autobiography*), p. 236.

427. . . . dropped from the ticket in 1924: Sobel, pp. 227–228; Fuess, pp. 293, 300–301.

427. ". . . gravest nature had occurred": Coolidge (*Autobiography*), pp. 173–174; Fuess, p. 308. Plymouth Notch lacked electricity until 1925.

427. . . ."I could swing it": Fuess, p. 311; Ross (*Grace Coolidge*), p. 81; Cashman, p. 94.

428. . . . Wilson's early career had appeared, he vanished: *NY Times*, 4 August 1923, p. 7; *NY Times*, 5 August 1923, p. 1; *NY Times*, 8 August 1923, p. 1; *NY Times*, 9 August 1923, p. 7; *Chicago Tribune*, 9 August 1923, p. 2; G. Smith, pp. 224–225; Ross (*Power with Grace*), pp. 243–244.

428. . . . It was the least he could do: *The Outlook*, 26 April 1922, p. 675.

428. . . . "more vibrant and intense, reached far down the street": Boylan, p. 146.

428. ". . . is as sure as that God reigns": Coit, p. 311; Wilson (*My Memoir*), pp. 355–356; G. Smith, pp. 205–207, 228–232; Ross (*Power with Grace*), p. 243; Levin, p. 489.

429. . . . "on the field of battle": Stein, pp. 252–253; Levin, pp. 488, 490–491.

429. . . . the next morning, he breathed his last: *Chicago Tribune*, 3 February 1924, pp. 1–2; *Atlanta Constitution*, 7 February 1924, p. 7; Ross (*Power with Grace*), pp. 254–259; Coit, p. 312.

429. . . . But the glory of the Lord is in all: Hulbert, pp. 278–279; Levin, pp. 493–494.

429. ". . . husband's friends will be loyal to him": Harris, p. 5; *NY Times*, 21 November 1924, p. 3.

430. ". . . the water has to bring me back": Elliott Roosevelt and Brough (*Hyde Park*), pp. 153–173, 201–202; Morgan, pp. 256–257. Biographer Conrad Black notes: "From

1925 to 1928[,] Roosevelt spent 116 of 208 weeks away from home, trying to regain full use of his limbs. Eleanor was with him for four of those weeks, Sara for two, and Missy LeHand for 110." (C. Black, p. 158; Alter, p. 55.)

430. . . . His speech thrilled them: *LA Times*, 27 June 1924, p. 3; Perkins, p. 37; Elliott Roosevelt and Brough (*Hyde Park*), p. 207; Morgan, pp. 269–272.

430. . . . FDR wasn't saying no to that either: Wehle, pp. 90–92.

431. . . . Franklin as Assistant Secretary of the Navy: Perkins, p. 68; Anthony (*First Ladies*), p. 403; Elliott Roosevelt and Brough (*Mother R.*), pp. 159–161. The Republican *Los Angeles Times* bluntly described him as "hopelessly an invalid."

431. ". . . a great deal to be President": Coolidge (*Autobiography*), p. 192.

431. "I do not choose to run for president in 1928": Sobel, pp. 368–370.

431. ". . . the *Nation* and other organizations. . . .": Montgomery, pp. 73–74.

432. . . . "You kill two innocent men": *Boston Globe*, 1 June 1921, pp. 1, 20; *Boston Globe*, 7 July 1921, pp. 1, 9; *Boston Globe*, 15 July 1921, pp. 1, 3; *NY Times*, 15 July 1921, p. 6; Perrett, pp. 67–70. Moore eventually came to believe that Sacco was most likely guilty and that Vanzetti was possibly guilty. Sacco, for his part, grew to hate Moore. He fired him in 1924 after Moore committed him to the Bridgewater State Hospital for the Criminally Insane after he staged a hunger strike. (Gallagher, p. 82.)

432. . . . the American consulate at Nice: *Boston Globe*, 20 October 1921, pp. 1–2; *NY Times*, 23 October 1921, p. 1; *Washington Post*, 20 July 1927, pp. 1, 11; *NY Times*, 10 August 1927, p. 1; *NY Times*, 11 August 1927, p. 4; *NY Times*, 19 April 1933, p. 17; Russell (*Tragedy in Dedham*), p. 218; F. L. Allen, p. 85; Sann, p. 180.

432. . . . deaths ignited new protests: *Chicago Tribune*, 23 August 1927, pp. 1–2; Perrett, p. 293.

432. ". . . head above its fellows": Boylan, p. 256; Hutchens and Oppenheimer, pp. 382–383; Pietrusza (*Roaring Twenties*), p. 43.

432. ". . . advice for six years, all of it bad": White (*Puritan in Babylon*), p. 400.

433. . . . in spite of her Catholic background: Elliott Roosevelt and Brough (*Hyde Park*), pp. 258–259. Elliott Roosevelt's older brother James dismissed the idea of an FDR–LeHand affair as "utterly ridiculous," as well as the rumors involving Eleanor with Nancy Cook and Marion Dickerman. James does admit that his mother "may have had an affair" with New York State Trooper Earl Miller. (J. Roosevelt, pp. 105–106, 110–112.)

433. ". . . is a harsh employer": H. Hoover (*Cabinet & The Presidency*), p. 4 *fn*.

434. ". . . They are the nucleus of my personal organization today": Wehle, p. 108.

434. . . . he dropped dead of a heart attack: Eleanor Roosevelt and her son James got into a giggling fit at the funeral. (J. Roosevelt, p. 248.)

## CHAPTER 26

436. . . . general withdrawal of deposits can be prevented now": Miller and Walch, pp. 129–136; Moley (*New Deal*), p. 145; Moley (*After Seven Years*), pp. 139–142; C. Black, pp. 264–265; Flynn, p. 20; E. Lyons (*Herbert Hoover*), p. 316; Alter, pp. 179–182.

436. . . . close the banks. Again Franklin refused: *NY Times*, 4 March 1933, p. 3; Moley (*After Seven Years*), pp. 144–146; Flynn, pp. 25–26; C. Black, pp. 268–269. Roosevelt proclaimed his own bank holiday on March 6, 1933, essentially copying Hoover's aborted plan. (Flynn, pp. 27–28; C. Black, p. 274; Hinshaw, p. 285; Cashman, pp. 149–150.)

436. . . . Bureau's professionalism. Cummings agreed: Moley (*After Seven Years*), pp. 111–127; Moley (*New Deal*), pp. 77–81, 92–95; Farley, pp. 33–34; Wehle, pp. 128–133; Morgan (*F.D.R.*), pp. 370–372; C. Black, pp. 260–263; Alter, pp. 158–167.

436. ". . . so many have apparently fallen": Farley, p. 36; Perkins, pp. 139–141.

436. . . . the nation's highest office: *NY Times*, 5 March 1933, p. 3; *Washington Post*, 5 March 1933, p. 2; Farley, p. 37; Lash, p. 360; Morgan (*F.D.R.*), p. 373; C. Black, p. 269.

437. . . . His hat went back down. There it stayed: *NY Times*, 5 March 1933, pp. 1, 4; Eleanor Roosevelt, p. 164; J. Roosevelt, p. 143; Alter, pp. 213–214.

437. ". . . convert retreat into advance": Moley (*New Deal*), p. 97.

437. . . . by a foreign foe: *Chicago Tribune*, 5 March 1933, p. 2; *LA Times*, 5 March 1933, p. 5; *Washington Post*, 5 March 1933, p. 2; *Oakland Tribune*, 5 March 1933, p. 2; Moley (*New Deal*), pp. 121–124; Alter, p. 219. It was Howe who had inserted the words "the only thing we have to fear is fear itself." (Moley [*New Deal*], pp. 115, 127.)

438. . . . fatally wounding Chicago Mayor Anton J. Cermak: *Washington Post*, 4 March 1933, p. 1; Moley (*New Deal*), pp. 65–68; Morgan (*F.D.R.*), pp. 369–370.

438. . . . a smiling Al Smith led the way: *LA Times*, 5 March 1933, pp. 3, 5; *Washington Post*, 5 March 1933, p. 13; *Oakland Tribune*, 5 March 1933, p. 1; *Syracuse Herald*, 5 March 1933, pp. 1, 3; *LA Times*, 15 April 1938, p. 1; J. Roosevelt, p. 143; Anthony (*First Ladies*), p. 474; Alter, pp. 223–224.

438. . . . and the Philadelphia Harmonica Symphony: *Washington Post*, 5 March 1933, pp. 10, 20.

438. Herbert Hoover slunk out of town . . . lifted the downcast ex-President's gloom: *NY Times*, 5 March 1933, pp. 1, 4; *Oakland Tribune*, 5 March 1933, pp. 1, 3.

438. Franklin Roosevelt and Herbert Hoover never saw each other again: C. Black, p. 273.

**EPILOGUE**

439. Senator Frank B. Brandegee: *Chicago Tribune*, 15 October 1924, p. 5; *LA Times*, 15 October 1924, p. 1; *NY Times*, 15 October 1924, p. 1.

439. Nan P. Britton: *NY Times*, 15 July 1964, p. 18; *LA Times*, 18 July 2004, p. B4; Anthony (*Florence Harding*), pp. 531–532; Communication from Carl S. Anthony to Author, 12 August 2005; ssdi.genealogy.rootsweb.com/cgi-bin/ssdi.cgi; *Cleveland Plain Dealer*, 31 May 2006.

439. Elizabeth Ann Britton: *NY Times*, 15 July 1964, p. 18; *Washington Post*, 18 July 1964, p. A2; Ferrell (*Strange Deaths of President Harding*), p. 77; Anthony (*Florence Harding*), p. 532; Communication from Carl S. Anthony to Author, 12 August 2005.

439. Heywood Broun: *NY Times*, 29 April 1933, p. 15; *NY Times*, 19 December 1939, p. 23; Washington Post, 21 December 1939, p. 5; Kramer, pp. 206–308.

440. William Jennings Bryan: *Chicago Tribune*, 27 July 1925, p. 1; *LA Times*, 27 July 1925, pp. 1–2; *NY Times*, 27 July 1925, pp. 1–2; Eaton, p. 299.

440. Carrie Chapman Catt: *NY Times*, 10 March 1947, p. 21.

440. Professor William Estabrook Chancellor: Sullivan (VI), p. 133 *fn.*; J. Murphy, pp. 156–157, 176–181, 189–190; Communication from Audrey Oliker to Author, 13 March 2005.

440. The Chicago Coliseum: *Chicago Tribune*, 16 February 1964, p. C3; *NY Times*, 28 August 1968, p. 31; www.ccchronicle.com/back/2003_fall/2003–09–22/citybeat2.html.

440. Parley Parker Christensen: *LA Times*, 2 December 1921, pp. 1, 3; *NY Times*, 22 January

1922, p. 38; *LA Times*, 11 February 1954, p. 26; *NY Times*, 11 February 1954, p. 29; Draper (*American Communism*), pp. 32, 448.

440. Edward Young Clarke: *NY Times*, 2 March 1923, p. 6; *Washington Post*, 12 January 1932, p. 3; *Chicago Tribune*, 27 June 1932, p. 7; *Washington Post*, 20 July 1934, p. 16; *Gettysburg Times*, 24 March 1949, p. 3; *NY Times*, 29 March 1949, p. 14; Chalmers, pp. 105, 107.

441. Bainbridge Colby: *NY Times*, 12 April 1950, p. 27; *Chicago Tribune*, 12 April 1950, p. A6; Greenbaum, pp. 160–161; Sullivan (V), p. 568; Wolfskill and Hudson, pp. 97, 154, 249.

441. Grace Goodhue Coolidge: *NY Times*, 9 July 1957, pp. 1, 29.

441. James Middleton Cox: *LA Times*, 16 July 1957, pp. 1, 12; Elliott Roosevelt and Brough (*Rendezvous with Destiny*), p. 41; www.coxenterprises.com; www.bioguide.congress.gov/scripts/biodisplay.pl?index=C000835

441. Margaretta Blair Cox: *NY Times*, 7 November 1960, p. 15.

441. Josephus Daniels: *Chicago Tribune*, 16 January 1948, p. 1; *LA Times*, 16 January 1948, p. 1; *NY Times*, 16 January 1948, p. 17; *Washington Post*, 16 January 1948, pp. 1, B2.

441. Harry Micajah Daugherty: *NY Times*, 13 October 1941, p. 17; *Washington Post*, 13 October 1941, p. 1; Sullivan (VI), pp. 353–357.

442. Eugene Victor Debs: *Chicago Tribune*, 21 October 1925, pp. 1, 5; *LA Times*, 21 October 1925, pp. 1, 3; *NY Times*, 21 October 1925, p. 25; Ginger, pp. 438–457; Morais and Cahn, pp. 118–125.

442. W. E. B. Du Bois: *Chicago Tribune*, 28 August 1963, p. 2; *NY Times*, 28 August 1963, p. 27; *Washington Post*, 29 August 1963, p. B3; *LA Times*, 24 November 1964, pp. 2, 17; *Chicago Defender*, 31 August 1963, p. 3.

442. W. W. Durbin: *LA Times*, 26 August 1924, p. 1; Van Wert Daily Bulletin, 1 June 1932, p. 8; Zanesville Times-Recorder, 1 June 1932, p. 1; *Washington Post*, 5 February 1937, p. 10.

442. Albert Bacon Fall: *Chicago Tribune*, 1 December 1944, p. 1; *LA Times*, 1 December 1944, p. 2; *NY Times*, 1 December 1944, p. 23.

442. Edna Ferber: *NY Times*, 17 April 1968, pp. 1, 32. The penthouse's previous occupant was Swedish match king Ivar Krueger.

442. James E. ("Pa") Ferguson: *Chicago Tribune*, 22 September 1944, p. 22; *NY Times*, 22 September 1944, p. 19; *Washington Post*, 22 September 1944, p. 3; Gustafson, Miller, and Perry, pp. 121–130.

443. Colonel Charles R. Forbes: *LA Times*, 27 November 1927, p. 12; *Chicago Tribune*, 12 April 1952, p. B4.

443. Henry Ford: *Chicago Tribune*, 8 July 1927, p. 1; *NY Times*, 8 July 1927, pp. 1, 10; *Chicago Tribune*, 12 January 1942, p. 3; *NY Times*, 12 January 1942, p. 12; *LA Times*, 8 April 1947, pp. 1–2; *NY Times*, 8 April 1947, pp. 1, 32.

443. Marcus Garvey: *NY Times*, 21 August 1922, p. 7; *Atlanta Constitution*, 22 August 1922, p. 14; *Washington Post*, 24 November 1927, p. 3; *Chicago Defender*, 18 May 1940, pp. 1–2; *NY Times*, 12 June 1940, p. 25; *NY Times*, 13 June 1940, p. 22; *Chicago Defender*, 22 June 1940, p. 3; Boylan, p. 141; Perrett, pp. 240–241; Franklin, pp. 491–492; McCartney, pp. 79–80.

443. Rear Admiral Cary T. Grayson: *NY Times*, 16 February 1938, pp. 1, 14.

443. Jake Hamon: www.dallaslibrary.org/HAMON/hamons.htm

443. Will H. Hays: *NY Times*, 8 March 1954, pp. 1, 27; *Washington Post*, 8 March 1954, p. 14; Ramsaye, pp. 803–821.

444. William Randolph Hearst: ª, 15 August 1951, pp. 1, 20–21; Swanberg, passim; Nasaw, passim.

444. Herbert C. Hoover: *NY Times*, 21 October 1964, pp. 1, 41, 46.

444. J. Edgar Hoover: *NY Times*, 3 May 1972, pp. 1, 53.

444. Colonel Edward Mandell House: *LA Times*, 12 June 1937, p. 3; *LA Times*, 29 March 1938, pp. 1, 10; *NY Times*, 29 March 1938, pp. 1, 10; *Washington Post*, 29 March 1938, pp. 1, 4.

444. Dr. Erastus Mead Hudson: *NY Times*, 18 September 1943, p. 55; L. Murphy, p. 290.

445. The International Workers of the World (IWW): *NY Sun*, 4 January 2006, pp. 1, 3.

445. Hiram W. Johnson: *LA Times*, 7 August 1945, pp. 1, 6; *LA Times*, 7 August 1945, pp. 1, 23.

445. Reverend Samuel Neal Kent: L. Murphy, pp. 291–292; Loughery, p. 13.

445. John T. King: *Chicago Tribune*, 14 May 1926, p. 1; *NY Times*, 14 May 1926, p. 23; *Washington Post*, 14 May 1926, p. 1; Sullivan (VI), pp. 351–352; Behr, p. 119.

445. Robert Lansing: *NY Times*, 31 October 1928, pp. 1, 14; *Chicago Tribune*, 31 October 1928, p. 4.

445. Albert D. Lasker: *NY Times*, 31 May 1952, p. 1; *Washington Post*, 31 May 1952, p. 15; Morello, p. 96.

445. The League of Nations: *Chicago Tribune*, 19 April 1946, p. 3; *NY Times*, 19 April 1946, pp. 1, 16, 28.

446. Missy LeHand: *NY Times*, 1 August 1944, p. 15; *Washington Post*, 1 August 1944, p. 2; Elliott Roosevelt and Brough (*Rendezvous with Destiny*), pp. 26, 94, 287, 318; Elliott Roosevelt, p. 51; J. Roosevelt, pp. 107–108; Anthony (*First Ladies*), p. 505.

446. The *Literary Digest*: www.towson.edu/~roberts/475/L01intro.htm.

446. Henry Cabot Lodge: *LA Times*, 10 November 1924, pp. 1–2; Fuess, p. 343.

446. Alice Roosevelt Longworth: Longworth, *passim*; *NY Times*, 21 February 1980, p. 1; *Washington Post*, 21 February 1980, pp. 1, C4.

446. Frank Orren Lowden: *Washington Post*, 23 January 1928, p. 1; *Chicago Tribune*, 21 March 1943, pp. 1, 20; *NY Times*, 21 March 1943, p. 26; *NY Times*, 22 March 1943, p. 18; Eaton, pp. 313, 318.

446. Helen Harding Cox Mahoney: *Lima News*, 16 May 1921, p. 1; *Bridgeport Telegram*, 17 May 1921, p. 5; *Chicago Tribune*, 17 May 1921, p. 7; *Sandusky Star Journal*, 17 May 1921, p. 1.

447. Dudley Field Malone: *NY Times*, 6 October 1950, p. 25; Pietrusza (*Rothstein*), p. 426.

447. William Gibbs McAdoo: *LA Times*, 2 February 1941, pp. 1–2; Levin, p. 514.

447. H. L. Mencken: *NY Times*, 30 January 1956, pp. 1, 20; Mencken, pp. 224–339.

447. Kate Richards O'Hare: Sochen, pp. 111–112.

447. Thomas Mott Osborne: *NY Times*, 21 October 1920, p. 15; *NY Times*, 22 October 1920, p. 21; Ward, p. 474 fn. Osborne, who died the day following Gene Debs's death, was buried in a Portsmouth prisoner's uniform (www.cayuganet.org/forthill/osbornetm/tmo.html).

448. A. Mitchell Palmer: *NY Times*, 11 April 1922, p. 32; *Chicago Tribune*, 12 May 1936, p. 16; *NY Times*, 12 May 1936, p. 26; Coben, pp. 263–265.

448. Alice Stokes Paul: *NY Times*, 10 July 1977, p. 42; *Washington Post*, 10 July 1977, p. 42.

448. Mary Allen Hulbert Peck: *NY Times*, 18 December 1939, p. 23.

448. Andrew J. Peters: *NY Times*, 27 June 1938, p. 17; Russell (*A City in Terror*), pp. 224–227; Russell (*The Great Interlude*), p. 42; Leighton, pp. 258–274; Beatty, pp. 206–207; Pietrusza (*Rothstein*), pp. 362–363.

448. Alexandra Carlisle Pfeiffer: *Chicago Tribune*, 29 May 1923, p. 7; *Chicago Tribune*, 10 June 1934, p. 1; *NY Times*, 10 June 1934, p. 29; *NY Times*, 23 April 1936, p. 23; Chicago Tribune, 3 May 1936, p. D5.

449. Carrie Fulton Phillips: *NY Times*, 26 August 1964, p. 41; *NY Times*, 28 September 1968, p. 31; Ferrell (*Strange Deaths of President Harding*), pp. 154–155; Anthony (*Florence Harding*), p. 530; Ohio Historical Society to Author, 11 August 2005.

449. Corinne Roosevelt Robinson: *NY Times*, 17 February 1933, p. 15; *Washington Post*, 18 February 1933, p. 1; *NY Times*, 21 February 1933, p. 19; *NY Times*, 29 August 1989, p. 1A; Beasley, Beasley & Shulman, pp. 442–443.

449. Eleanor Roosevelt: *LA Times*, 8 November 1962, pp. 1, 6; *NY Times*, 8 November 1962, pp. 1, 34, 35.

449. Franklin D. Roosevelt: Freidel (*The Ordeal*), pp. 81–82 *fn.*; Freidel (*A Rendezvous with Destiny*), p. 40.

449. Theodore Roosevelt, Jr.: *Chicago Tribune*, 14 July 1944, pp. 1–2.

450. Lucy Mercer Rutherford: *NY Times*, 12 February 1920, p. 11; *Washington Post*, 12 February 1920, p. 14; *LA Times*, 12 August 1966, p. 23; *NY Times*, 12 August 1966, p. 1; *NY Times*, 2 May 1982, p. 66; Elliott Roosevelt and Brough (*Rendezvous with Destiny*), pp. 287–289, 408–410; Elliott Roosevelt and Brough (*Mother R.*), pp. 19, 21, 30–31, 37–38; J. Roosevelt, pp. 102–104; C. Black, p. 99. Rutherford's first wife was the daughter of Vice President Levi P. Morton.

450. Nicola Sacco and Bartolomeo Vanzetti: *NY Times*, 30 May 1962, p. 40; *Washington Times*, 21 August 1997, p. 8; *Washington Times*, 23 August 1997, p. 2; *LA Times*, 24 December 2005, p. B3; *LA Times*, 3 January 2006, p. B10; Russell (*Tragedy in Dedham*), pp. 449–450, 463–466; Gallagher, pp. 86–87, 90–91; Russell (*The Great Interlude*), pp. 136–142; www.saccovanzettiproject.org/pages/context/dukakis.htm; edition.cnn.com/2006/SHOWBIZ/books/01/27/books.sinclair.reut/. Earlier evidence of Upton's disquieting conversations with Moore had long circulated, but this was the most direct and damning development (Russell [*Tragedy in Dedham*], pp. 16–17, 256–257; Avrich [*Sacco and Vanzetti*], pp. 160–162; Kaiser and Young, pp. 83, 155, 183; Arthur, pp. 216–221).

450. The San Francisco Civic Auditorium: www.billgrahamcivic.com.

451. Thomas D. Schall: *Chicago Tribune*, 23 December 1935, pp. 1, 6; *LA Times*, 23 December 1935, pp. 1–2.

451. Colonel William J. Simmons: *NY Times*, 13 February 1924, p. 5; *LA Times*, 15 December 1936, p. 8; *NY Times*, 22 June 1944, p. 21; *NY Times*, 22 May 1945, p. 19; Chalmers, pp. 100–108.

451. Al Smith: *LA Times*, 5 October 1944, pp. 1, 4; Wolfskill and Hudson, pp. 162–166, 178–179; Handlin, pp. 170–89; Finan, pp. 301–350; Slayton, pp. 343–402.

451. Frank W. Stearns: *NY Times*, 7 March 1939, p. 23.

451. Seymour Stedman: *Chicago Tribune*, 10 July 1948, p. 8; NY Times, 10 July 1948, p. 15.

452. Lothrop Stoddard: Chicago Tribune, 2 May 1950, p. 18; NY Times, 2 May 1950, p. 17; Gossett, pp. 390–397; E. Black, pp. 133–134, 167, 298, 317–318; www.nyu.edu/projects/sanger/abcl.htm.

452. Mark Sullivan: *NY Times*, 15 August 1952, p. 15.

452. William Howard Taft: *Chicago Tribune*, 9 March 1930, p. 1; *LA Times*, 9 March 1930, p. 12.

452. Captain Joseph K. Taussig: NY Times, 30 October 1947, p. 25; *Chicago Tribune*, 30 October 1947, p. 52.

452. Judge Webster Thayer: *Chicago Tribune*, 28 September 1932, p. 4; *Chicago Tribune*, 19 April 1933, p. 4; *NY Times*, 19 April 1933, p. 17. A juror in the case had his home bombed in August 1927.

452. Carlo Tresca: *Chicago Tribune*, 12 January 1943, p. 9; *NY Times*, 12 January 1943, pp. 1, 14; *Washington Post*, 12 January 1943, p. 14; Dos Passos (*The Theme is Freedom*), pp. 174–178 ; Gallagher, *passim*. H. L. Mencken reprinted the same ad in his *American Mercury*, daring the government to prosecute. They didn't.

453. William Monroe Trotter: *NY Times*, 8 April 1934, p. 30.

453. Joseph P. Tumulty: *LA Times*, 9 April 1954, p. 29.

453. George Sylvester Viereck: *Dixon Evening Telegraph*, 8 September 1954, p. 4; *NY Times*, 20 March 1962, p. 37. Viereck's son was the respected author Peter Viereck.

453. Wayne Bidwell Wheeler: *NY Times*, 14 August 1927, p. 1; *Chicago Tribune*, 6 September 1927, p. 1; *NY Times*, 6 September 1927, pp. 1, 23; *LA Times*, 7 September 1927, p. 1; Coffey, pp. 212–213; Kobler, pp. 339–340; Sinclair (*Era of Excess*), p. 352; Behr, pp. 224–225.

453. William Allen White: *Chicago Tribune*, 30 January 1944, p. 16; *NY Times*, 30 January 1944, p. 38; *Chicago Tribune*, 11 May 1947, p. B4.

454. Edith Bolling Galt Wilson: *Washington Post*, 30 December 1961, p. C2; Ross (*Power with Grace*), pp. 323–345; Levin, pp. 496–518.

454. General Leonard Wood: *Chicago Tribune*, 7 August 1927, pp. 1, 5; Hagedorn (Vol. 2), pp. 477–481.

# Bibliography

## BOOKS

*Messages and Papers of the Presidents*. New York: Bureau of National Literature, 1923.

Adams, Samuel Hopkins. *Incredible Era: The Life and Times of Warren Gamaliel Harding*. Boston: Houghton Mifflin, 1939.

Affron, Charles. *Lillian Gish: Her Legendary Life*. New York: Scribner, 2001.

Alexander, Michael. *Jazz Age Jews*. Princeton: Princeton University Press, 2001.

Allen, Frederick Lewis. *Only Yesterday: An Informal History of the 1920s*. New York: Harper & Brothers, 1931.

Allen, Howard W. *Poindexter of Washington: A Study in Progressive Politics*. Carbondale: Southern Illinois University Press, 1981.

Alter, Jonathon. *The Defining Moment: FDR's Hundred Days and the Triumph of Hope*. New York: Simon & Schuster, 2006.

Anderson, Jervis. *A. Philip Randolph: A Biographical Portrait*. New York: Harcourt, Brace, Jovanovich, 1973.

Annin, Robert Edwards. *Woodrow Wilson: A Character Study*. New York: Dodd, Mead, 1924.

Anthony, Carl Sferrazza. *First Ladies: The Saga of the Presidents' Wives and Their Power, 1789–1961*. New York: Quill, 1990.

———. *Florence Harding: The First Lady, the Jazz Age & the Death of America's Most Scandalous President*. New York: Morrow, 1998.

Arthur, Anthony. *Radical Innocent: Upton Sinclair*. New York: Random House, 2006.

Asbury, Herbert. *The Great Illusion: An Informal History of Prohibition*. Garden City: Doubleday, 1950.

Asinof, Eliot. *1919: America's Loss of Innocence*. New York: Donald J. Fine, 1990.

Avrich, Paul. *Anarchist Voices: An Oral History of Anarchism in America*. Princeton: Princeton University Press, 1995.

———. *Sacco and Vanzetti: The Anarchist Background*. Princeton: Princeton University Press, 1991.

Axson, Stockton. *"Brother Woodrow": A Memoir of Woodrow Wilson*. Princeton: Princeton University Press, 1993.

Bagby, Wesley M. *The Road to Normalcy: The Presidential Campaign and Election of 1920*. Baltimore: Johns Hopkins University Press, 1962.

Bailey, Thomas A. *Woodrow Wilson and the Great Betrayal*. New York: Macmillan, 1947.

———. *Woodrow Wilson and the Lost Peace*. New York: Macmillan, 1947.

Baldwin, Neil. *Henry Ford and the Jews: The Mass Production of Hate*. New York: Public Affairs, 2001.

Bartlett, Ruhl J., ed. *The Record of American Diplomacy* (4th ed.). New York: Alfred A. Knopf, 1964.

Baruch, Bernard. *Baruch: My Own Story*. New York: Henry Holt, 1957.

Bean, Walton. *Boss Ruef's San Francisco: The Story of the Union Labor Party, Big Business, and the Graft Prosecution*. Berkeley: University of California Press, 1967.

Beasley, Henry R., Maurine H. Beasley, and Holly C. Shulman, eds. *The Eleanor Roosevelt Encyclopedia*. Westport, Connecticut: Greenwood Press, 2001.

Beatty, Jack. *The Rascal King: The Life and Times of James Michael Curley, 1874–1958*. Reading, Massachusetts: Perseus, 1992.

Behr, Edward. *Prohibition: Thirteen Years That Changed America*. New York: Arcade, 1996.

Bell, H. C. F. *Woodrow Wilson and the People*. Garden City: Doubleday, Doran, 1945.

Best, Gary Dean. *The Politics of American Individualism: Herbert Hoover in Transition, 1918–1929*. Westport, Connecticut: Greenwood Press, 1975.

Black, Conrad. *Franklin Delano Roosevelt: Champion of Freedom*. New York: Public Affairs, 2003.

Black, Edwin. *War Against the Weak: Eugenics and America's Campaign to Create a Master Race*. New York: Four Walls Eight Windows, 2003.

Blackwell, J. Kenneth. *Ohio Election Statistics, 2001–2002*. Columbus: Ohio Secretary of State's Office, 2003.

Blum, John Morton. *Woodrow Wilson and the Politics of Morality*. Boston: Little, Brown, 1956.

B'nai B'rith of the Anti-Defamation League. *An Exposure of the Hoax Which Is Being Foisted upon the American Public by Henry Ford in His Weekly Newspaper Entitled "The Dearborn Independent" and in the Pamphlet Which He Is Distributing Entitled "The World's Foremost Problem."* Chicago: Anti-Defamation League, 1920.

Boller, Paul F Jr. *Presidential Campaigns*. New York: Oxford University Press, 1984.

Booker, Christopher B. *I Will Wear No Chain!: A Social History of African American Males*. Westport, Connecticut: Praeger, 2000.

Boyer, Richard O., and Herbert M. Morais. *Labor's Untold Story: The Adventure Story of the Battles, Betrayals and Victories of American Working Men and Women*. New York: United Electrical, Radio & Machine Workers of America, 1955.

Boylan, James. *The World and the 20's: The Best from New York's Legendary Newspaper*. New York: Dial Press, 1973.

Brands, H. W. *T.R.: The Last Romantic.* New York: Basic Books, 1997.

Britton, Nan. *The President's Daughter.* New York: Elizabeth Ann Guild, 1927.

Brooks, Robert C. *Political Parties and Electoral Problems.* New York: Harper & Brothers, 1923.

Brown, Canter Jr. *Florida's Black Public Officials, 1867–1924.* Tuscaloosa: University of Alabama Press, 1998.

Brownlow, Kevin. *The Parade's Gone By. . . .* New York: Bonanza Books, 1968.

Brownlow, Kevin, and John Kobal. *Hollywood: The Pioneers.* New York: Knopf, 1979.

Bruns, Roger A. *Preacher: Billy Sunday & Big-Time American Evangelism.* New York: Norton, 1992.

Burgchardt, Carl R. *Robert M. La Follette, Sr.: The Voice of Conscience.* New York: Greenwood Press, 1992.

Burner, David. *Herbert Hoover: A Public Life.* New York: Alfred A. Knopf, 1979.

Busch, Francis X. *Prisoners at the Bar: An Account of the Trials of the William Haywood Case, the Sacco–Vanzetti Case, the Loeb–Leopold Case, the Bruno Hauptmann Case.* Indianapolis: Bobbs-Merrill, 1952.

Butler, Nicholas Murray. *Across the Busy Years.* New York: Charles Scribners' Sons, 1940.

Carlin, John W., Wayne S. Cole, Dwight M. Miller, and Timothy Walch, eds. *Herbert Hoover and Franklin D. Roosevelt: A Documentary History.* Westport, Connecticut: Greenwood Press, 1998.

Caroli, Betty Boyd. *The Roosevelt Women.* New York: Basic Books, 1998.

Cashman, Sean Dennis. *America in the Twenties and Thirties: The Olympian Age of Franklin Delano Roosevelt.* New York: New York University Press, 1989.

Catt, Carrie Chapman, and Nettie Rogers Shuler. *Woman Suffrage and Politics: The Inner Story of the Suffrage Movement.* New York: Charles Scribner's Sons, 1923.

Cebula, James M. *James Cox: Journalist and Politician.* New York: Garland, 1985.

Chace, James. *1912: Wilson, Roosevelt, Taft & Debs—The Election That Changed the Country.* New York: Simon & Schuster, 2004.

Chaddock, Robert E., and Claude E. Robinson. *Straw Votes, a Study of Political Prediction.* New York: Columbia University Press, 1932.

Chalmers, David M. *Hooded Americanism: The History of the Ku Klux Klan.* Chicago: Quadrangle Books, 1965.

Chapple, Joe Mitchell. *Warren G. Harding—The Man.* Boston: Chapple Publishing Co., 1920.

Clark, Norman H. *Deliver Us from Evil: An Interpretation of American Prohibition.* New York: Norton, 1976.

Clift, Eleanor. *Founding Sisters and the Nineteenth Amendment.* Hoboken: Wiley, 2003.

Cobb, Irvin S. *Exit Laughing.* Indianapolis: Bobbs-Merrill, 1941.

Coben, Stanley. *A. Mitchell Palmer: Politician.* New York: Columbia University Press, 1963.

Coffey, Thomas M. *The Long Thirst: Prohibition in America: 1920–1933.* New York: Norton, 1975.

Cohen, Morris R. *The Faith of a Liberal: Selected Essays by Morris R. Cohen*. New York: Henry Holt, 1946.

Coit, Margaret L. *Mr. Baruch: The Man, the Myth, the 80 Years*. Boston: Houghton Mifflin, 1957.

Coleman, McAlister. *Eugene V. Debs: A Man Unafraid*. New York: Greenberg, 1930.

Coletta, Paolo E. *William Jennings Bryan*. Lincoln: University of Nebraska Press, 1964.

Comfort, Mildred Houghton. *Herbert Hoover, Humanitarian*. Minneapolis: T. S. Denison, 1960.

Cook, Blanche Wiesen. *Eleanor Roosevelt, Volume I: 1884–1933*. New York: Penguin, 1992.

Cook, Fred J. *The FBI Nobody Knows*. New York: Macmillan, 1964.

Cooke, Alistair, ed. *The Vintage Mencken*. New York: Vintage Books, 1955.

Coolidge, Calvin. *The Autobiography of Calvin Coolidge*. New York: Cosmopolitan Book Corp., 1929.

———. *Have Faith in Massachusetts: A Collection of Speeches and Messages*. Boston: Houghton Mifflin, 1919.

Cooper, John Milton. *Breaking the Heart of the World: Woodrow Wilson and the Fight for the League of Nations*. New York: Cambridge University Press, 2001.

———. *Pivotal Decades: The United States, 1900–1920*. New York: Norton, 1990.

———. *The Warrior and the Priest: Woodrow Wilson and Theodore Roosevelt*. Cambridge, Massachusetts: Belknap, 1983.

Cox, James M. *Journey Through My Years*. New York: Simon and Schuster, 1946.

Cox, John Stuart, and Athan G. Theoharis. *The Boss: J. Edgar Hoover and the Great American Inquisition*. Philadelphia: Temple University Press, 1988.

Craig, Donald B. *After Wilson: The Struggle for Control of the Democratic Party, 1920–1934*. Chapel Hill: University of North Carolina Press, 1992.

Creel, George. *The War, the World and Wilson*. New York: Harper & Brothers, 1920.

Daniels, Josephus. *The Cabinet Diaries of Josephus Daniels, 1913–1921*. Lincoln: University of Nebraska Press, 1963.

———. *Editor in Politics*. Chapel Hill: University of North Carolina Press, 1941.

———. *The Life of Woodrow Wilson*. Chicago: John C. Winston, 1924.

Daugherty, Harry M. (with Thomas Dixon). *The Inside Story of the Harding Tragedy*. New York: Churchill, 1932.

Davis, Kenneth. *FDR: The Beckoning of Destiny 1882–1928*. New York: Putnam, 1972.

Dean, John W. *Warren G. Harding*. New York: Times Books, 2004.

Dearborn Independent. *The International Jew: The World's Foremost Problem, Being a Reprint of a Series of Articles Appearing in the Dearborn Independent from May 22 to October 2, 1920*. Dearborn, Michigan: Dearborn Publishing Co., 1920.

Debs, Eugene V. *Writings and Speeches of Eugene V. Debs*. New York: Hermitage Press, 1948.

Dorsett, Lyle W. *Billy Sunday and the Redemption of Urban America*. Grand Rapids: William B. Eerdmans, 1991.

Dos Passos, John. *Mr. Wilson's War*. Garden City: Doubleday, 1962.

———. *U.S.A.: The 42nd Parallel, Nineteen-Nineteen. The Big Money*. New York: Modern Library, 1937.

———. *The Theme Is Freedom*. New York: Dodd, Mead, 1956.

Downes, Randolph C. *The Rise of Warren Gamaliel Harding: 1865–1920*. Columbus: Ohio State University Press, 1970.

Draper, Theodore. *American Communism and Soviet Russia: The Formative Period*. New York: Viking Press, 1960.

———. *The Roots of American Communism*. New York: Viking, 1957.

Du Bois, W. E. B. *The Autobiography of W. E. B. Dubois: A Soliloquy on Viewing My Life from the Last Decade of Its First Century*. New York: International Publishers, 1968.

———. *Darkwater: Voices from Within the Veil*. New York: Harcourt Brace & Howe, 1920.

Duffy, Herbert S. *William Howard Taft*. New York: Minton, Balch, 1930.

Dullard, John P., compiler. *Manual of the Legislature of New Jersey* (1921 edition). Trenton: State of New Jersey, 1921.

Dunn, Lynn K., and Warren F. Kuehl. *Keeping the Covenant: American Internationalists and the League of Nations, 1920–1939*. Kent, Ohio: Kent State University Press, 1997.

Eaton, Herbert. *Presidential Timber: A History of Nominating Conventions, 1886–1960*. London: Free Press of Glencoe, 1964.

Elliott, Margaret Axson. *My Aunt Louisa and Woodrow Wilson*. Chapel Hill: University of North Carolina Press, 1944.

Elliott, Russell R., and William D. Rowley. *History of Nevada*. Lincoln: University of Nebraska Press, 1987.

Eyman, Scott. *Mary Pickford: America's Sweetheart*. New York: Donald I. Fine, 1990.

Farley, James A. *Jim Farley's Story: The Roosevelt Years*. New York: Whittlesey House, 1948.

Fausold, Martin L. *James W. Wadsworth Jr.: The Gentleman from New York*. Syracuse: Syracuse University Press, 1975.

Feldman, Glenn. *Politics, Society and the Klan in Alabama, 1915–1949*. Tuscaloosa: University of Alabama Press, 1999.

Felknor, Bruce L. *Smear, Sabotage, and Reform in U.S. Elections*. New York: Praeger, 1992.

Ferber, Edna. *A Peculiar Treasure*. New York: Doubleday, Doran, 1939.

Ferrell, Robert H. *The Strange Deaths of President Harding*. Columbia and London: University of Missouri Press, 1996.

———. *Woodrow Wilson and World War I, 1917–1921*. New York: Harper & Row, 1985.

Filler, Louis, ed. *The President Speaks: From McKinley to Lyndon Johnson*. New York: G. P. Putnam's Sons, 1964.

Finan, Christopher M. *Alfred E. Smith: The Happy Warrior*. New York: Hill and Wang, 2002.

531

Fine, Nathan. *Labor and Farmer Parties in the United States, 1828–1928*. New York: Russell & Russell, 1961.

Fitzgerald, F. Scott. *The Great Gatsby*. New York: Scribner's, 2003.

Fleming, Thomas. *The Illusion of Victory: Americans in World War I*. New York: Basic Books, 2003.

Foerstel, Karen. *Biographical Dictionary of Congressional Women*. Westport, Connecticut: Greenwood Press, 1999.

Foley, Barbara. *Spectres of 1919: Class and Nation in the Making of the New Negro*. Urbana: University of Illinois Press, 2003.

Franklin, John Hope. *From Slavery to Freedom: A History of Negro Americans* (3rd ed.). New York: Vintage Books, 1969.

Freidel, Frank. *Franklin D. Roosevelt: The Ordeal*. Boston: Little Brown, 1954.

———. *Franklin D. Roosevelt: A Rendezvous with Destiny*. Boston: Little Brown, 1989.

Freud, Sigmund, and William C. Bullitt. *Woodrow Wilson: A Psychological Study*. Somerset, New Jersey: Transaction Publishers, 1999.

Fuess, Claude M. *Calvin Coolidge: The Man from Vermont*. Boston: Little Brown, 1940.

Gable, John Allen. *The Bull Moose Years: Theodore Roosevelt and the Progressive Party*. Port Washington, New York: Kennikat Press, 1978.

Gabler, Neal. *An Empire of Their Own: How the Jews Invented Hollywood*. New York: Doubleday, 1988.

———. *Winchell: Gossip, Power and the Power of the Culture of Celebrity*. New York: Alfred A. Knopf, 1994.

Gallagher, Dorothy. *All the Right Enemies: The Life and Murder of Carlo Tresca*. Piscataway, New Jersey: Rutgers University Press, 1988.

Garraty, John A. *Henry Cabot Lodge: A Biography*. New York: Alfred A. Knopf, 1968.

Gelman, Barbara. *Photoplay Treasury: Nostalgic Picture-and-Word Stories from the Most Popular of the Fan Magazines*. New York: Crown, 1972.

George, Alexander L., and Juliette L. George. *Woodrow Wilson and Colonel House: A Personality Study*. New York: John Day, 1956.

Gilbert, Clinton W. *The Mirrors of Washington*. New York: G. P. Putnam's Sons, 1921.

Gilje, Paul A. *Rioting in America*. Bloomington: Indiana University Press, 1996.

Ginger, Ray. *The Bending Cross: Biography of Eugene Victor Debs*. New Brunswick, New Jersey: Rutgers University Press, 1949.

Gish, Lillian, and Ann Pinchot. *Lillian Gish: The Movies, Mr. Griffith and Me*. Englewood Cliffs: Prentice-Hall, 1969.

Gitlow, Benjamin. *The Whole of Their Lives: Communism in America, a Personal History and Intimate Portrayal of Its Leaders*. New York: Charles Scribner's Sons, 1948.

Goldstein, Robert J. *Political Repression in Modern America: From 1870 to 1976*. Champaign: University of Illinois Press, 2001.

Gossett, Thomas F. *Race: The History of an Idea in America*. Dallas: Southern Methodist University Press, 1963.

Green, Robert P. *Equal Protection and the African American Constitutional Experience: A Documentary History.* Westport, Connecticut: Greenwood Press, 2000.

Greenbaum, Fred. *Men Against Myths: The Progressive Response.* Westport, Connecticut: Praeger, 2000.

Gustafson, Melanie, Kristie Miller, and Elisabeth I. Perry, eds. *We Have Come to Stay: American Women and Political Parties, 1880–1960.* Albuquerque: University of New Mexico Press, 1999.

Hagedorn, Hermann. *Leonard Wood: a Biography (Volumes 1 & 2).* New York: Harper & Brothers, 1931.

Halley, Janet E. *Don't: A Reader's Guide to the Military's Anti-Gay Policy.* Durham, North Carolina: Duke University Press, 1999.

Hamm, Richard F. *Shaping the Eighteenth Amendment: Temperance Reform, Legal Culture, and the Polity, 1880–1920.* Chapel Hill: University of North Carolina Press, 1995.

Handlin, Oscar. *Al Smith and His America.* Boston: Little Brown, 1958.

Hanson, Ole. *Americanism versus Bolshevism.* Garden City: Doubleday, Page, 1920.

Hapgood, Norman. *Professional Patriots.* New York: Boni, 1927.

Harris, Ray Baker. *Warren G. Harding: An Account of His Nomination for the Presidency by the Republican Convention of 1920.* Washington: Privately printed, 1957.

Hays, Will H. *The Memoirs of Will H. Hays.* Garden City: Doubleday, 1955.

Haywood, William D. *Bill Haywood's Book: The Autobiography of William D. Haywood.* New York: International Publishers, 1929.

Hendrick, Frank. *Republicanism of Nineteen-Twenty.* Albany, New York: Albany Evening Journal, 1920.

Hibben, Paxton. *The Peerless Leader: William Jennings Bryan.* New York: Farrar and Rinehart, 1929.

Hicks, John D. *Rehearsal for Disaster: The Boom and Collapse of 1919–1920.* Gainesville: University of Florida Press, 1961.

Higham, John. *Strangers in the Land: Patterns of American Nativism 1860–1925.* New Brunswick, New Jersey: Rutgers University Press, 1955.

Hinshaw, David. *Herbert Hoover, American Quaker.* New York: Farrar, Straus, 1950.

———. *A Man from Kansas: The Story of William Allen White.* New York: G. P. Putnam's Sons, 1945.

Hirsch, H. N. *The Enigma of Felix Frankfurter.* New York: Basic Books, 1981.

Hofstadter, Richard. *The Age of Reform.* New York: Vintage Books, 1955.

Holbrook, Stewart H. *Dreamers of the American Dream.* Garden City: Doubleday, 1957.

Holme, John G. *The Life of Leonard Wood.* Garden City: Doubleday, Page, 1920.

Hoover, Herbert. *The Memoirs of Herbert Hoover: The Cabinet & The Presidency 1920–1933.* New York: MacMillan, 1952.

———. *The Memoirs of Herbert Hoover: Years of Adventure 1874–1920.* New York: MacMillan, 1951.

———. *The Ordeal of Woodrow Wilson.* New York: McGraw-Hill, 1958.

Hoover, Irwin Hood ("Ike"). *42 Years in the White House.* Boston: Houghton Mifflin, 1934.

Hulbert, Mary Allen. *The Story of Mrs. Peck: An Autobiography.* New York: Minton, Balch, 1933.

Hutchens, John K., and George Oppenheimer. *The Best in the World: A Selection of News and Feature Stories, Editorials, Humor, Poems and Reviews from 1921 to 1928.* New York: Viking Press, 1973.

Hutchinson, William T. *Lowden of Illinois: The Life of Governor Frank O. Lowden: Vol. 2—Nation and Countryside.* Chicago: University of Chicago Press, 1957.

Huthmacher, J. Joseph. *Massachusetts People and Politics 1919–1933.* New York: Atheneum, 1969.

Irwin, Will. *Herbert Hoover: A Reminiscent Biography.* New York: Century, 1928.

Jackson, Kenneth T., ed. *The Encyclopedia of New York City.* New Haven: Yale University Press, 1995.

Johnson, Paul. *A History of the American People.* New York: HarperCollins, 1997.

Jones, Maldwyn Allen. *American Immigration.* Chicago: University of Chicago Press, 1960.

Jordan, William G. *Black Newspapers and America's War for Democracy, 1914–1920.* Chapel Hill: University of North Carolina Press, 2001.

Kaiser, David E., and William Young. *Postmortem: New Evidence in the Case of Sacco and Vanzetti.* Amherst: University of Massachusetts Press, 1985.

Kane, Joseph Nathan. *Facts About the Presidents.* New York: Pocket Books, 1964.

Keynes, John Maynard. *The Economic Consequences of the Peace.* New York: Charles Scribner's Sons, 1919.

Kobler, John. *Ardent Spirits: The Rise and Fall of Prohibition.* New York: G. P. Putnam's Sons, 1973.

Kramer, Dale. *Heywood Broun: A Biographical Portrait.* New York: Current Books, 1949.

Kyvig, David E. *Daily Life in the United States, 1920–1939: Decades of Promise and Pain.* Westport, Connecticut: Greenwood Press, 2002.

La Follette, Philip (edited by Donald Young). *Adventures in Politics: The Memoirs of Philip La Follette.* New York: Holt, Rinehart and Winston, 1970.

LaCerra, Charles. *Franklin Delano Roosevelt and Tammany Hall of New York.* Lanham, Maryland: University Press of America, 1997.

Lane, Franklin K. *The Letters of Franklin K. Lane, Personal and Political.* Boston: Houghton Mifflin, 1922.

Lane, Jack C. *Armed Progressive: General Leonard Wood.* San Rafael: Presidio Press, 1978.

Lansing, Robert. *The Big Four and Others of the Peace Conference.* Boston: Houghton Mifflin, 1921.

Lash, Joseph P. *Eleanor and Franklin: The Story of Their Relationship Based on Eleanor Roosevelt's Private Papers.* New York: Norton, 1971.

Lathem, Edward Connery, ed. *Your Son, Calvin Coolidge: A Selection of Letters from Calvin Coolidge to His Father.* Montpelier: Vermont Historical Society, 1968.

Lawrence, David. *The True Story of Woodrow Wilson.* New York: George H. Doran, 1924.

Lee, Albert. *Henry Ford and the Jews.* New York: Stein & Day, 1980.

Leighton, Isabel, ed. *The Aspirin Age:1919–1941.* New York: Simon & Schuster, 1949.

Leuchtenburg, William E. *The Perils of Prosperity 1914–32*. Chicago: University of Chicago Press, 1959.

Link, Arthur S. *The Papers of Woodrow Wilson*. Princeton: Princeton University Press, 1991.

———. *Wilson the Diplomatist: A Look at His Major Foreign Policies*. Baltimore: Johns Hopkins Press, 1957.

———. *Woodrow Wilson and the Progressive Era:1910–1917*. New York: Harper Torchbooks, 1963.

Lippmann, Walter. *Force and Ideas: The Early Writings*. New York: Liveright, 1970.

Lipset, Seymour Martin, and Earl Raab. *The Politics of Unreason: Right Wing Extremism in America, 1790–1970*. New York: Harper & Row, 1970.

Lodge, Henry Cabot. *The Senate and the League of Nations*. New York: Charles Scribner's Sons, 1925.

Longworth, Alice Roosevelt. *Crowded Hours: Reminiscences of Alice Roosevelt Longworth*. New York: Charles Scribner's Sons, 1933.

Loughery, John. *The Other Side of Silence: Men's Lives and Gay Identities: A Twentieth-Century History*. New York: Henry Holt, 1999.

Lyons, Eugene. *Herbert Hoover: A Biography*. Garden City: Doubleday, 1964.

———. *The Red Decade*. Indianapolis: Bobbs-Merrill, 1941.

Lyons, Maurice F. *William F. McCombs: The President Maker*. Cincinnati: Bancroft, 1922.

MacLeish, Archibald, and E. F. Pritchard Jr., eds. *Law and Politics: Occasional Papers of Felix Frankfurter, 1913–1938*. New York: Harcourt, Brace, 1939.

Madison, Charles A. *Critics & Crusaders: A Century of American Protest*. New York: Frederick Ungar, 1959.

Malcolm, James. *The New York Red Book: An Illustrated State Manual*. Albany, New York: J. B. Lyon, editions of 1911, 1913, 1918, and 1921.

Manners, William. *TR & Will: A Friendship That Split the Republican Party*. New York: Harcourt, Brace & World, 1969.

Martin, Joe, with Robert J. Donovan. *My First Fifty Years in Politics*. New York: McGraw-Hill, 1960.

McAdoo, Eleanor Wilson, and Margaret Y. Gaffey. *The Woodrow Wilsons*. New York: MacMillan, 1937.

McAdoo, William Gibbs. *Crowded Years: The Reminiscences of William G. McAdoo*. Boston: Houghton Mifflin, 1931.

McCartney, John T. *Black Power Ideologies: An Essay in African American Political Thought*. Philadelphia: Temple University Press, 1992.

McGerr, Michael E. *A Fierce Discontent: The Rise and Fall of the Progressive Movement in America, 1870–1920*. New York: Free Press, 2003.

Mecklin, John Moffatt. *The Ku Klux Klan: A Study of the American Mind*. New York: Russell & Russell, 1963.

Melosh, Barbara, ed. *Gender and American History since 1890*. New York: Routledge, 1993.

Mencken, H. L. *A Carnival of Buncombe*. Baltimore: Johns Hopkins, 1956.

Michelson, Charles. *The Ghost Talks*. New York: G. P. Putnam's Sons, 1944.

Miller, Nathan. *FDR: An Intimate History*. New York: New American Library, 1983.

Moley, Raymond. *After Seven Years*. New York: Harper & Brothers, 1939.
———. *The First New Deal*. New York: Harcourt, Brace & World, 1966.
Montgomery, Robert H. *Sacco–Vanzetti: The Murder and the Myth*. New York: Devin-Adair, 1960.
Morais, Herbert M., and William Cahn. *Gene Debs: The Story of a Fighting American*. New York: International Publishers, 1948.
Morello, John A. *Selling the President, 1920: Albert D. Lasker, Advertising, and the Election of Warren G. Harding*. Westport, Connecticut: Praeger, 2001.
Morgan, Ted. *F.D.R.: A Biography*. New York: Simon & Schuster, 1985.
———. *Reds: McCarthyism in Twentieth-Century America*. New York: Random House, 2003.
Morris, Lloyd. *Not So Long Ago*. New York: Random House, 1949.
Murphy, John A. *The Indictment*. Pataskala, Pennsylvania: Brockston Publishing, 2000.
Murphy, Lawrence R. *Perverts by Official Order: The Campaign Against Homosexuality by the United States Navy*. New York: Harrington Park Press, 1988.
Murray, Robert K. *The Harding Era: Warren G. Harding and His Administration*. Minneapolis: University of Minnesota Press, 1969.
———. *The Politics of Normalcy: Governmental Theory and Practice in the Harding–Coolidge Era*. New York: Norton, 1975.
———. *Red Scare: A Study in National Hysteria, 1919–1920*. New York: McGraw-Hill, 1964.
Nasaw, David. *The Chief: The Life of William Randolph Hearst*. Boston: Houghton Mifflin, 2000.
Nash, George H. *The Life of Herbert Hoover: The Humanitarian, 1914–1917*. New York: Norton, 1988.
———. *The Life of Herbert Hoover: Master of Emergencies, 1917–1918*. New York: Norton, 1996.
National American Woman Suffrage Association. *Victory, How Women Won It: A Centennial Symposium, 1840–1940*. New York: H. W. Wilson, 1940.
Niven, Penelope. *Carl Sandburg*. New York: Scribner's, 1991.
Noggle, Burl. *Into the Twenties: The United States from Armistice to Normalcy*. Urbana: University of Illinois Press, 1974.
Nye, Russell B. *Midwestern Progressive Politics: A Historical Study of Its Origins and Development, 1870–1958*. New York: Harper & Row, 1965.
Olasky, Marvin. *The American Leadership Tradition: The Inevitable Impact of a Leader's Faith on a Nation's Destiny*. New York: Free Press, 1999.
Older, Cora Miranda Baggerly. *William Randolph Hearst: American*. New York: D. Appleton-Century, 1936.
Olin, Spencer C. *California's Prodigal Sons: Hiram Johnson and the Progressives 1911–1917*. Berkeley: University of California Press, 1968.
Ostroff, David H., F. Leslie Smith, and John W. Wright II. *Perspectives on Radio and Television: Telecommunication in the United States*. Mahwah, New Jersey: Lawrence Erlbaum Associates, 1998.
O'Toole, Patricia. *When Trumpets Call: Theodore Roosevelt After the White House*. New York: Simon & Schuster, 2005.

Perkins, Frances. *The Roosevelt I Knew.* New York: Viking, 1946.

Perrett, Geoffrey. *America in the Twenties: A History.* New York: Simon and Schuster, 1982.

Pfannestiel, Todd J. *Rethinking the Red Scare: The Lusk Committee and New York's Crusade Against Radicalism, 1919–1923.* New York: Routledge, 2003.

Pietrusza, David. *Judge and Jury: The Life & Times of Judge Kenesaw Mountain Landis.* South Bend: Diamond Communications, 1998.

———. *The Roaring Twenties.* San Diego: Lucent, 1998.

———. *Rothstein: The Life, Times, and Murder of the Criminal Genius Who Fixed the 1919 World Series.* New York: Carroll & Graf, 2003.

Post, Louis F. *The Deportations Delirium of Nineteen-Twenty: A Personal Narrative of an Historic Official Experience.* Chicago: C. H. Kerr, 1923.

Preston, William Jr. *Aliens and Dissenters: Federal Suppression of Radicals, 1903–1933.* New York: Harper Torchbooks, 1963.

Pringle, Henry F. *The Life and Times of William Howard Taft: A Biography.* New York: Farrar & Rinehart, 1939.

———. *Theodore Roosevelt: A Biography.* New York: Harcourt, Brace Jovanovich, 1956.

Pusey, Merlo J. *Charles Evans Hughes.* New York: Columbia University Press, 1967.

Ramsaye, Terry. *A Million and One Nights: A History of the Motion Picture Through 1925.* New York: Simon & Schuster, 1986.

Renehan, Edward J. Jr. *The Lion's Pride: Theodore Roosevelt and His Family in Peace and War.* New York: Oxford University Press, 1998.

Republican National Committee. *A Billion a Month: $20,000,000,000 in All: What the Democrats Did With the Stupendous Mass of Wealth Taken From the People to Fight the War.* Washington: Republican National Committee, 1920.

Rice, Arnold S. *The Ku Klux Klan in American Politics.* Washington: Public Affairs Press, 1962.

Robinson, Corinne Roosevelt. *My Brother, Theodore Roosevelt.* New York: C. Scribner's Sons, 1921.

Rodgers, Marion Elizabeth. *Mencken: The American Iconoclast.* New York: Oxford University Press, 2005.

Rollins, Alfred B. Jr. *Roosevelt and Howe.* New York: Alfred A. Knopf, 1962.

Roosevelt, Eleanor. *The Autobiography of Eleanor Roosevelt.* New York: DaCapo Press, 1992.

Roosevelt, Elliott. *Eleanor Roosevelt, with Love: A Centenary Remembrance.* New York: E. P. Dutton, 1984.

Roosevelt, Elliott, and James Brough. *Mother R.: Eleanor Roosevelt's Untold Story.* New York: G. P. Putnam's Sons, 1975.

———. *A Rendezvous with Destiny: The Roosevelts of the White House.* New York: G. P. Putnam's Sons, 1977.

———. *An Untold Story: The Roosevelts of Hyde Park.* New York: G. P. Putnam's Sons, 1973.

Roosevelt, James, with Bill Libby. *My Parents: A Differing View.* Chicago: Playboy Press, 1976.

Roosevelt, Theodore. *Fear God and Take Your Own Part*. New York: George H. Doran, 1916.

Ross, Ishbel. *Grace Coolidge and Her Era: The Story of a President's Wife*. New York: Dodd Mead, 1962.

———. *Power with Grace: The Life Story of Mrs. Woodrow Wilson*. New York: G. P. Putnam's Sons, 1975.

Rudwick, Elliott M. *W. E. B. Du Bois: A Study in Minority Group Leadership*. Philadelphia: University of Pennsylvania Press, 1960.

Rumer, Thomas A. *The American Legion: An Official History 1919–1989*. New York: M. Evans, 1990.

Russell, Francis. *A City in Terror: The 1919 Boston Police Strike*. New York: Viking, 1975.

———. *The Great Interlude: Neglected Events & Persons from the First World War to the Depression*. New York: McGraw-Hill, 1964.

———. *The President Makers: From Mark Hanna to Joseph P. Kennedy*. Boston: Little, Brown, 1976.

———. *The Shadow of Blooming Grove: Warren G. Harding in His Times*. New York: McGraw-Hill, 1968.

———. *Tragedy in Dedham: The Story of the Sacco–Vanzetti Case*. New York: McGraw-Hill, 1962.

Schickel, Richard. *D. W. Griffith: An American Life*. New York: Limelight Editions, 1996.

Schlesinger, Arthur M. Jr. *The Crisis of the Old Order*. New York: Houghton Mifflin, 1957.

Schmidt, Hans. *The United States Occupation of Haiti, 1915–1934*. New Brunswick, New Jersey: Rutgers University Press, 1995.

Schmidt, Regin. *Red Scare: FBI and the Origins of Anticommunism in the United States, 1919–1943*. Copenhagen: Museum Tusculanum Press, University of Copenhagen, 2000.

Schulberg, Budd. *Moving Pictures: Memories of a Hollywood Prince*. New York: Stein and Day, 1981.

Seymour, Charles, ed. *The Intimate Papers of Colonel House* (4 vols.). Boston: Houghton Mifflin, 1926.

Sinclair, Andrew. *The Available Man: The Life Behind the Mask of Warren Gamaliel Harding*. New York: Macmillan, 1965.

———. *The Emancipation of the American Woman*. New York: Harper & Row, 1965.

———. *Era of Excess: A Social History of the Prohibition Movement*. New York: Harper & Row, 1964.

Slayden, Ellen Maury. *Washington Wife: Journal of Ellen Maury Slayden from 1897–1919*. New York: Harper & Row, 1963.

Slayton, Robert A. *Empire Statesman: The Rise and Redemption of Al Smith*. New York: Free Press, 2001.

Smith, Gene. *When the Cheering Stopped: The Last Years of Woodrow Wilson*. New York: Morrow, 1964.

Smith, Richard Norton. *An Uncommon Man: The Triumph of Herbert Hoover*. New York: Simon and Schuster, 1984.

Sobel, Robert. *Coolidge: An American Enigma*. Washington, D.C.: Regnery, 1998.

Sochen, June. *Movers and Shakers: American Women Thinkers and Activists, 1900–1970*. New York: Quadrangle, 1973.

Spears, Jack. *Hollywood: The Golden Era*. New York: Castle, 1971.

Spragens, William C. *Popular Images of American Presidents*. New York: Greenwood Press, 1988.

Starling, Edmund W., as told to Thomas Sugrue. *Starling of the White House*. Chicago: Peoples Book Club, 1946.

Starr, Kevin. *Inventing the Dream: California through the Progressive Era*. New York: Oxford University Press, 1985.

Stein, Charles W. *The Third-Term Tradition: Its Rise and Collapse in American Politics*. New York: Columbia University Press, 1943.

Stevens, Doris. *Jailed for Freedom*. New York: Boni and Liveright, 1920.

Stevenson, Elizabeth. *Babbitts and Bohemians: The American 1920s*. New York: Macmillan, 1973.

Stiles, Lela. *The Man Behind Roosevelt: The Story of Louis McHenry Howe*. Cleveland: World Publishing Co., 1954.

Stoddard, Henry Luther. *As I Knew Them: Presidents and Politics from Grant to Coolidge*. New York: Harper & Brothers, 1927.

———. *It Costs to Be President*. New York: Harper & Brothers, 1938.

———. *Presidential Sweepstakes: The Story of Political Conventions and Campaigns*. New York: G. P. Putnam's Sons, 1948.

Stoddard, Lothrop. *The Rising Tide of Color against White World-Supremacy*. New York: Charles Scribner's Sons, 1920.

Stone, Irving. *They Also Ran: The Story of the Men Who Were Defeated for the Presidency*. New York: Doubleday, 1968.

Sullivan, Mark. *Our Times (Volume III: Pre-War America)*. New York: Charles Scribner's Sons, 1939.

———. *Our Times (Volume IV: The War Begins)*. New York: Charles Scribner's Sons, 1939.

———. *Our Times (Volume V: Over Here, 1914–1918)*. New York: Charles Scribner's Sons, 1939.

———. *Our Times (Volume VI: The Twenties)*. New York: Charles Scribner's Sons, 1939.

Swanberg, W. A. *Citizen Hearst*. New York: Scribner's, 1962.

Synon, Mary. *McAdoo: The Man and His Times*. Indianapolis: Bobbs-Merrill, 1924.

Tarr, Joel Arthur. *A Study in Boss Politics: William Lorimer of Chicago*. Urbana: University of Illinois Press, 1971.

Teichmann, Howard. *Alice: The Life and Times of Alice Roosevelt Longworth*. Englewood Cliffs: Prentice-Hall, 1979.

Thayer, William Roscoe. *Theodore Roosevelt: An Intimate Biography*. Boston: Houghton Mifflin, 1919.

Tumulty, Joseph P. *Woodrow Wilson as I Knew Him*. Garden City: Doubleday, Page, 1924.

Tuttle, William M. Jr. *Race Riot: Chicago in the Red Summer of 1919*. New York: Atheneum, 1982.

Wade, Wyn Craig. *The Fiery Cross: The Ku Klux Klan in America.* New York: Touchstone, 1987.

Wagenknecht, Edward. *American Profile, 1900–1909.* Amherst: University of Massachusetts Press, 1982.

———. *The Seven Worlds of Theodore Roosevelt.* New York: Longmans, Green, 1958.

Walsh, George. *Gentleman Jimmy Walker: Mayor of the Jazz Age.* New York: Praeger, 1974.

Walworth, Arthur. *Woodrow Wilson: Volume 1.* New York: Longmans, Green, 1958.

Ward, Geoffrey C. *A First-Class Temperament: The Emergence of Franklin Roosevelt.* New York: Harper & Row, 1989.

Warner, Emily Smith, and Daniel Hawthorne. *The Happy Warrior: A Biography of My Father, Alfred E. Smith.* New York: Doubleday, 1956.

Washburn, R. M. *Calvin Coolidge: His First Biography.* Boston: Small, Maynard, 1923.

Washington, Booker T. *Up from Slavery: An Autobiography.* New York: A. L. Burt, 1901.

Watkins, T. H. *Righteous Pilgrim: The Life and Times of Harold L. Ickes, 1874–1952.* New York: Henry Holt, 1990.

Watson, James E. *As I Knew Them.* Indianapolis: Bobbs-Merrill, 1936.

Watt, Richard M. *The Kings Depart: The Tragedy of Germany: Versailles and the German Revolution.* London: Weidenfeld and Nicolson, 1968.

Watts, Steven. *The People's Tycoon: Henry Ford and the American Century.* New York: Alfred A. Knopf, 2005.

Wayne, H. Morgan. *Eugene V. Debs: Socialist for President.* Syracuse: Syracuse University Press, 1962.

Weeks, Robert P. *Commonwealth vs. Sacco and Vanzetti.* Englewood Cliffs: Prentice-Hall, 1958.

Wehle, Louis B. *Hidden Threads of History: Wilson Through Roosevelt.* New York: Macmillan, 1953.

Weinstein, Edwin A. *Woodrow Wilson: A Medical and Psychological Biography.* Princeton: Princeton University Press, 1981.

Weiss, Nancy Joan. *Charles Francis Murphy, 1858–1924: Respectability and Responsibility in Tammany Politics.* Northampton, Massachusetts: Smith College, 1968.

Werner, M. R. *Privileged Characters.* New York: R. M. McBride, 1935.

Wheeler, Marjorie Spruill, ed. *Votes for Women!: The Woman Suffrage Movement in Tennessee, the South, and the Nation.* Knoxville: University of Tennessee Press, 1995.

White, William Allen. *The Autobiography of William Allen White.* New York: Macmillan, 1946.

———. *Masks in a Pageant.* New York: MacMillan, 1928.

———. *A Puritan in Babylon: The Story of Calvin Coolidge.* New York: Macmillan, 1939.

———. *Woodrow Wilson: The Man, His Times, His Task.* Boston: Houghton Mifflin, 1924.

Whitehead, Don. *The FBI Story: A Report to the People.* New York: Random House, 1956.

Widenor, William C. *Henry Cabot Lodge and the Search for an American Foreign Policy.* Berkeley: University of California Press, 1980.

Wilson, Edith Bolling Galt. *My Memoir.* Indianapolis: Bobbs-Merrill, 1939.

Wolfskill, George, and John A. Hudson. *All But the People: Franklin D. Roosevelt and His Critics, 1933–39.* New York: Macmillan, 1969.

Wooddy, Carroll Hill. *The Case of Frank L. Smith: A Study in Representative Government*. Chicago: University of Chicago Press, 1931.

Young, Marguerite. *Harp Song for a Radical: The Life and Times of Eugene Victor Debs*. New York: Alfred A. Knopf, 1999.

**NEWSPAPERS**

*Albany* (New York) *Times-Union*
*Atlanta Constitution*
*Bedford* (Pennsylvania) *Gazette*
*Boston Globe*
*Boston Herald*
*Boston Post*
*Bridgeport* (Connecticut) *Telegram*
*Charleston* (West Virginia) *Daily Mail*
*Chicago East North Central Daily Herald*
*Chicago Defender*
*Chicago Tribune*
*Cincinnati Union*
*Cleveland Advocate*
*Coshocton* (Ohio) *Tribune*
*Dayton Forum*
*Dayton Journal*
*Decatur* (Illinois) *Daily Review*
*Denton* (Maryland) *Journal*
*Dixon* (Illinois) *Evening Telegraph*
*Elyria* (Ohio) *Chronicle-Telegram*
*Fitchburg* (Massachusetts) *Daily Sentinel*
*Fort Wayne Weekly Gazette*
*Frederick* (Maryland) *Post*
*Gastonia* (North Carolina) *Daily Gazette*
*Gettysburg Times*
*Grand Valley* (Utah) *Times*
*Indianapolis Star*
*Iowa City Press-Citizen*
*Kennebec* (Maine) *Journal*
*Kingsport* (Tennessee) *Times*

*Kingston* (Jamaica) *Daily Gleaner*
*Lancaster* (Ohio) *Daily Eagle*
*Lima* (Ohio) *News & Times-Democrat*
*Lincoln* (Nebraska) *Evening State Journal*
*Los Angeles Times*
*Mansfield* (Ohio) *News*
*Marion* (Ohio) *Daily Star*
*New York Call*
*New York Sun*
*New York Times*
*New York Tribune*
*Ohio State Monitor*
*Oneonta* (New York) *Daily Star*
*Oshkosh* (Wisconsin) *Daily Northwestern*
*Portsmouth* (New Hampshire) *Herald*
*Reno Evening Gazette*
*Sandusky* (Ohio) *Star-Journal*
*Schenectady Gazette*
*Schenectady Union-Star*
*The Sporting News*
*Syracuse Herald*
*Syracuse Herald American*
*Trenton Evening Times*
*Van Wert* (Ohio) *Daily Bulletin*
*Warren* (Pennsylvania) *Evening Mirror*
*Washington Post*
*Washington Times*
*Wellsboro* (Pennsylvania) *Agitator*
*Winona* (Minnesota) *Republican-Herald*
*Zanesville* (Ohio) *Times-Recorder*

**PERIODICALS**

*American Heritage*
*The Bookman*
*Current Literature*
*Current Opinion*
*The Forum*
*The Literary Digest*
*McCall's Magazine*
*McClure's Magazine*

*The Nation*
*The New Republic*
*New York Archives*
*North American Review*
*Ohio History*
*The Outlook*
*The Western Journal of Black Studies*
*World's Work*

## REPORTS

Committee on Naval Affairs. *Report of the Committee on Naval Affairs, United States Senate, Sixty-Seventh Congress, First Session, Relative to the Alleged Immoral Conditions and Practices at the Naval Training Station, Newport, R. I.* Washington: Government Printing Office, 1921.

Joint Legislative Committee Investigating Seditious Activities (Lusk Committee). *Revolutionary Radicalism: Its History, Purpose and Tactics with an Exposition and Discussion of the Steps Being Taken and Required to Curb It, Being the Report of the Joint Legislative Committee Investigating Seditious Activities, Filed April 24, 1920, in the Senate of the State of New York. Volume 3.* Albany: J. B. Lyon, 1920.

U.S. Bureau of the Census. *Abstract of the Fourteenth Census of the United States, 1920.* Washington: Government Printing Office, 1923.

## JUDICIAL DECISIONS

*Debs v. United States*, 249 U.S. 211 (1919)

*In re Debs, Petitioner*, 158 U.S. 564 (1895)

*Fairchild v. Hughes*, 258 U.S. 126 (1922)

*Hawke v. Smith, No. 2*, 253 U.S. 231 (1920)

# Acknowledgments

~

As always, there are many, many thanks to convey.

Thanks to my agent and friend, Robert Wilson of Wilson Media, for his assistance in placing *1920*, and to my friend Cathy Karp who assisted me in review of the manuscript.

Thanks to Alan Schwartz for graciously providing me with a photograph of his great-great uncle, Albert Lasker.

Thanks to my friend Bob Going; author Carl Sferrazza Anthony; Audrey Oliker, widow of Michael A. Oliker, for assistance regarding Professor William Chancellor; Gayle McCotter of Bremerton, Washington, for helping research the Harding and Cox genealogies; to the Ohio Historical Society; to Marian Crounse for assistance in securing microfilms of Ohio newspapers; and to Santa Barbara County Assistant District Attorney Gordon Auchincloss for providing information on the Auchincloss family.

Thanks to Philip Turner and Keith Wallman of Carroll & Graf, who helped transform my earlier effort, *Rothstein: The Life, Times, and Murder of the Criminal Genius Who Fixed the 1919 World Series*, into an Edgar Award nominee and who aided invaluably in the production of this book, and to Carroll & Graf copy editor Phil Gaskill, an invaluable safety net.

Libraries are wonderful things. I happily extend thanks to the New York State Library, the New York State Archives, the University at Albany Library, the Schaffer Library of Union College, the Schenectady (New York) County Public Library, the Schenectady County Community

College Library, the University of Rhode Island Library, Miki Goral of the UCLA Library, and Spencer Howard, Archives Technician at the Herbert Hoover Presidential Library.

Newspapers are not at their best when reporting final primary returns, but state boards of elections proved very responsive. Thanks go to: Vermont State Archivist Greg Sanford; Brenda Bayes of the Elections Division, State of Oregon Secretary of State's Office; Eric Donnewald of the Illinois State Board of Elections; Bradley S. Wittman of the Elections Liaison Division of the Michigan Department of State Bureau of Elections; and Norma Blake of the New Jersey State Library. Thanks also to Tom Chansky of the Office of the Ohio Secretary of State for supplying data on Ohio gubernatorial elections.

And thanks to my wife, Patricia Basford Pietrusza, for her patience in listening to each battle along the way in the development of this latest effort.

To learn more about *1920*, visit www.davidpietrusza.com.

# Index

# About the Author

DAVID PIETRUSZA, CASEY Award winner, has authored or edited more than thirty books. His latest, *Rothstein: The Life, Times, and Murder of the Criminal Genius Who Fixed the 1919 World Series*, was nominated for the Mystery Writers of America Edgar Award® in the Best Fact Crime category. An expert on the 1920s, Pietrusza has served on the Board of Directors of the Calvin Coolidge Memorial Foundation. He lives in upstate New York.